Tracy,

Hope you find some enjoyment in this book. Some of the stories look like they ~~will be pretty~~ good.

Aunt Louise
12/84

Contents

FOREWORD

Mark Twain is not considered an abstruse or difficult writer. Rather, he has always been thought of as an accessible author. When reading Twain one has little need to turn to the dictionary, look through reference works on Greek and Roman mythology, or consult convoluted notes placed inconveniently throughout the work. Twain escapes his own humorous definition of a literary classic: "... a book which people praise and don't read."

Mark Twain is our preeminent American humorist. His grasp of life's absurdities is always firm and incisive; whether he's mocking blue-blood society, the advance of technology, the muddy prose of fellow writers, the romance of western migration, or people's perpetual gullibility, Twain sets a uniquely American tone in his writing.

Almost everyone has read, or seen a dramatization of, *The Adventures of Tom Sawyer, The Adventures of Huckleberry Finn,* or *The Prince and the Pauper,* and has at some time paraphrased Twain's classic comment, "Everyone talks about the weather but nobody does anything about it." Since Twain is so well known, one might well ask why there is a need for a book called *The Hidden Mark Twain.*

Perhaps the only thing that might be considered "hidden" about Twain is the fact that Mark Twain was a pen name—Samuel Clemens was the author's real name. Most people are familiar with the story of the young Clemens hearing the river boat pilots' cry of "Mark twain" when they were testing the river's depth, and his decision to use the term as his own personal pun and pen name.

Mark Twain was a prolific writer. He generally had several projects underway simultaneously as well as a number of ideas for other projects. In the almost three-quarters of a century since his death some of the enormous body of his work has slipped into obscurity. With some authors that might be a blessing, but with Twain it is a loss to the reading public. *The Hidden Mark Twain* brings back these lesser-known works, with their original illustrations. These works are not "hidden" in the sense that they show an unknown side to Twain's work—as had been the case with the Victorian thrillers Louisa May Alcott wrote to keep the family finances afloat. Rather, they are works that have not received the attention they merit.

What happened to Tom Sawyer and Huckleberry Finn after their famous adventures? Twain enjoyed the pair and wrote two subsequent books about them. The first, *Tom Sawyer Abroad,* is a fantastical yarn: Tom Sawyer, Huckleberry Finn, and their loyal friend Jim sail over Europe and northern Africa in a runaway hot air balloon and become embroiled in outlandish escapades. In *Tom Sawyer, Detective,* Tom and Huck take a trip to Tom's Aunt Sally's and Uncle Silas' farm, and

Tom defends his uncle in a tense murder trial. He proves Uncle Silas' innocence with a dazzling display of logic and insight.

The Stolen White Elephant is a collection of humorous stories and essays. The title story pokes fun at the bumbling efforts of the New York City Police Department to find a very large, very rare, and very white elephant. Many may feel that this story still has relevant overtones, the police techniques of today being uncannily similar to the techniques of the late 1800s.

Other stories in this collection show Twain's unique humor. "About Magnanimous-Incident-Literature" is a masterful parody of Victorian morality tales. In the section "The Benevolent Author," Twain tells of an established writer who launches a young writer's career. However, instead of showing gratitude, the young man cruelly exploits his mentor and the "benevolent" author gasps on his deathbed, "Clearly the books have deceived me; they do not tell the whole story. Beware the struggling young author my friends. Whom God sees fit to starve, let not man presumtuously rescue to his own undoing." "The Loves of Alfonso Fritz Clarence and Rosannah Ethelton" reflects Twain's interest in the growing technology of his time and his incorporation of the new technology into his writing. The two young lovers, Alfonso and Rosannah, fall in love over the telephone; their love is almost thwarted by a jealous villian, again over the telephone, and they are married over the telephone, never having seen one another.

The £1,000,000 Bank-Note is another collection of short pieces. In the title story two brothers make a wager: What would happen to an honest, intelligent man, set adrift in London with no money, no friends, and a Bank of England note for one million pounds, with no way to account for his possession of the note? One brother says the man would starve and/or go to jail, the other brother believes that he could live a month on the strength of the note alone. When the brothers decide to test their theory on a passing American, they get more than they bargained for.

Other stories include "A Cure for the Blues," Twain's satiric discussion of G. Ragsdale McClintock's book, *The Enemy Conquered; Or Love Triumphant,* a novel so maudlin, so verbose, so populated with cardboard characters that Twain contends it stands alone in the annals of literature (he hopes), and that its absurdity serves as the preeminent "cure for the blues." No author need ever despair of any work after reading, or rereading, *The Enemy Conquered; or Love Triumphant,* the entire text of which is provided for the reader.

Twain also discusses mental telepathy, modern ships and naval history—a sketch about the German naval authorities not allowing Noah to launch his ark is particularly funny—and how fallacious it is to tax authors.

The American Claimant is a novel that reflects many of Twain's concerns about youthful idealism, democracy, and self-deception. Colonel Mulberry Sellers, the confidence man first introduced in *The Gilded Age,* resurfaces as (he claims) the rightful Earl of Rossmore, unjustly barred from his fortune and lands. The "Pretender," the current Earl of Rossmore, is amused by Sellers' letters requesting his lands and money, but his son Berkeley, insists on leaving England, finding the American claimant, verifying his claim, and handing over the estate to Sellers.

Traveling incognito, Berkeley finds that life as an unemployed, unskilled transient is vastly different from life as a wealthy peer. His view of America as a country of democratic equals is shattered; his romantic views cannot withstand life's reality. In short order Berkeley realizes that living as part of a wealthy, privileged group is much to be envied; life as a poor but honest worker in the company of other poor and honest fellows is not as jolly and ennobling as he had thought.

Twain mocks youthful idealism, American and British aristocracy, the myth that America is a classless society, and the average person's enormous capacity for self-deception in the farcical comedy of *The American Claimant*.

Editorial Wild Oats is a freewheeling account of Twain's escapades with the written word, from his first brush with "creative" journalism on his uncle's newspaper, to his mature and professional stance that anything becomes true once it is in print.

Whether you have read the works of James Fenimore Cooper or not, Twain's "Fenimore Cooper's Literary Offenses" is a delicious piece of criticism. His analysis of the work of Cooper, in particular the "classic" *Deerslayer*, is a goldmine for those who agree with Twain's negative assessment of Cooper's work. Even those who admire Cooper will profit from Twain's eighteen rules governing fiction, rules that are readily applicable to writing of any nature. The rules range from the somewhat tongue-in-cheek—"They require that personages in the tale be alive, except in the case of corpses, and that the reader shall be able to tell the corpses from the others" to standard rules of writing—"Use good grammar; Avoid slovenliness of style; Employ a simple and straightforward style." Cooper's woodsman Natty Bumpo might be king of the wilderness, but he cannot stand up to Twain's acid onslaught.

Extracts From Adam's Diary and *Eve's Diary* together serve as a classic representation of the war between the sexes. Adam finds Eve to be too prissy, too concerned with categorizing the flora and fauna of Eden, too sensitive, too dependent on him for companionship. When they have their first child, he thinks it is a fish. Altogether, Adam feels life was better before Eve came on the scene.

Eve's Diary is written in a more flowing, less self-absorbed style than Adam's. She worries that Adam is so clumsy and introverted; she cries at dawn when the stars disappear, thinking they are gone forever; she is aware of the concept of kindness from the very beginning of her existence. Eve epitomizes Twain's belief in women's generous and nurturing qualities.

Though their early times together are rocky, Adam and Eve survive the Fall and build a rich life together. Adam ultimately comes to appreciate Eve's special qualities and says at her grave, "Wheresoever she was, *there* was Eden."

'1601' A Tudor Fireside Conversation shows Twain's puckish humor. In the piece, he rounds up Queen Elizabeth I, several of her ladies-in-waiting, William Shakespeare, Sir Walter Raleigh, and various other Elizabethan luminaries for an incongruous discussion. The contrast between their exalted positions and the topic of their conversation gives the story its unique humor.

The Hidden Mark Twain is a rich and varied collection that explores his lesser-known—though not lesser—works. Readers will enjoy encountering old friends again and discovering new works that add to their pleasure in Twain's inimitable style.

New York
1984

ANNE FICKLEN

Tom Sawyer Abroad

Chapter 1

TOM SEEKS NEW ADVENTURES

Do YOU reckon Tom Sawyer was satisfied after all them adventures? I mean the adventures we had down the river, and the time we set the darky Jim free and Tom got shot in the leg. No, he wasn't. It only just p'isoned him for more. That was all the effect it had. You see, when we three came back up the river in glory, as you may say, from that long travel, and the village received us with a torchlight procession and speeches, and everybody hurrah'd and shouted, it made us heroes, and that was what Tom Sawyer had always been hankering to be.

For a while he *was* satisfied. Everybody made much of him, and he tilted up his nose and stepped around the town as though he owned it. Some called him Tom Sawyer the Traveller, and that just swelled him up fit to bust. You see he laid over me and Jim considerable, because we only went down the river on a raft and came back by the steamboat, but Tom went by the steamboat both ways. The boys envied me and Jim a good deal, but land! they just knuckled to the dirt before TOM.

Well, I don't know; maybe he might have been satisfied if it hadn't been for old Nat Parsons, which was postmaster, and powerful long and slim, and kind o' good-hearted and silly, and bald-headed, on account of his age, and about the talkiest old cretur I ever see. For as much as thirty years he'd been the only man in the village that had a reputation— I mean a reputation for being a traveller, and of course he was mortal proud of it, and it was reckoned that in the course of that thirty years he had told about that journey over a million times and enjoyed it every time. And now comes along a boy not quite fifteen, and sets everybody admiring and gawking over *his* travels, and it just give the poor old man the high strikes. It made him sick to listen to Tom, and to hear the people say "My land!" "Did you ever!" "My goodness sakes alive!" and all such things; but he couldn't pull away from it, any more than a fly that's got its hind leg fast in the molasses. And always when Tom come to a rest, the poor old cretur would chip in on *his* same old travels and work them for all they were worth, but they were pretty faded, and didn't go for much, and it was pitiful to see. And then Tom would take another innings, and then the old

3

man again—and so on, and so on, for an hour and more, each trying to beat out the other.

You see, Parsons' travels happened like this: When he first got to be postmaster and was green in the business, there come a letter for somebody he didn't know, and there wasn't any such person in the village. Well, he didn't know what to do, nor how to act, and there the letter stayed and stayed, week in and week out, till the bare sight of it gave him a conniption. The postage wasn't paid on it, and that was another thing to worry about. There wasn't any way to collect that ten cents, and he reckon'd the Gov'ment would hold him responsible for it and maybe turn him out besides, when they found he hadn't collected it. Well, at last he couldn't stand it any longer. He couldn't sleep nights, he couldn't eat, he was thinned down to a shadder, yet he da'sn't ask anybody's advice, for the very person he asked for advice might go back on him and let the Gov'ment know about the letter. He had the letter buried under the floor, but that did no good; if he happened to see a person standing over the place it'd give him the cold shivers, and loaded him up with suspicions, and he would sit up that night till the town was still and dark, and then he would sneak there and get it out and bury it in another place. Of course people got to avoiding him and shaking their heads and whispering, because, the way he was looking and acting, they judged he had killed somebody or done something terrible, they didn't know what, and if he had been a stranger they would've lynched him.

Well, as I was saying, it got so he couldn't stand it any longer; so he made up his mind to pull out for Washington, and just go to the President of the United States and make a clean breast of the whole thing, not keeping back an atom, and then fetch the letter out and lay it before the whole Gov'ment, and say, "Now, there she is—do with me what you're a mind to; though as heaven is my judge I am an innocent man and not deserving of the full penalties of the law and leaving behind me a family that must starve and yet hadn't had a thing to do with it, which is the whole truth and I can swear to it."

So he did it. He had a little wee bit of steamboating, and some stage-coaching, but all the rest of the way was horseback, and it took him three weeks to get to Washington. He saw lots of land and lots of villages and four cities. He was gone 'most eight weeks, and there never was such a proud man in the village as when he got back. His travels made him the greatest man in all that region, and the most talked about; and people come from as much as thirty miles back in the country, and from over in the Illinois bottoms, too, just to look at him—and there they'd stand and gawk, and he'd gabble. You never see anything like it.

Well, there wasn't any way, now, to settle which was the greatest traveller; some said it was Nat, some said it was Tom. Everybody allowed that Nat had seen the most longitude, but they had to give in that whatever Tom was short in longitude he had made up in latitude and climate. It was about a stand-off; so both of them had to whoop up their dangerous adventures, and try to get ahead *that* way. That bullet-wound in Tom's leg was a tough thing for Nat Parsons to buck against, but he bucked the best he could; and at a disadvantage, too, for Tom didn't set still as he'd orter done, to be fair, but always got up and sauntered around and worked his limp while Nat was painting up the adventure that *he* had in Washington; for Tom never let go that limp when his leg got well, but practised it nights at home, and kept it good as new right along.

Nat's adventure was like this; I don't know how true it is; maybe he got it out of a paper, or somewhere, but I will say this for him, that he *did* know how to tell it. He could make anybody's flesh crawl, and he'd turn pale and hold his breath when he told it, and sometimes women and girls got so faint they couldn't stick it out. Well, it was this way, as near as I can remember:

He come a-loping into Washington, and put up his horse and shoved out to the President's house with his letter, and they told him the President was up to the Capitol, and just going to start for Philadelphia—not a minute to lose if he wanted to catch him. Nat 'most dropped, it made him so sick. His horse was put up, and he didn't know what *to* do. But just then along comes a darky driving an old ramshackly hack, and he see his chance. He rushes out and shouts: "A half a dollar if you git me to the Capitol in half an hour, and a quarter extra if you do it in twenty minutes!"

"Done!" says the darky.

Nat he jumped in and slammed the door, and away they went a-ripping and a-tearing over the roughest road a body ever see, and the racket of it was something awful. Nat passed his arms through the loops and hung on for life and death, but pretty soon the hack hit a rock and flew up in the air, and the bottom fell out, and when it come down Nat's feet was on the ground, and he see he was in the most desperate danger if he couldn't keep up with the hack. He was horrible scared, but he laid into his work for all he was worth, and hung tight to the arm-loops and made his legs fairly fly. He yelled and shouted to the driver to stop, and so did the crowds along the street, for they could see his legs spinning along under the coach, and his head and shoulders bobbing inside, through the windows, and he was in awful danger; but the more they all shouted the more the nigger whooped and yelled and lashed the horses and shouted, "Don't you fret, I's gwine to git you dah in time, boss; I's gwine to do it, sho'!" for you see he thought they were all hurrying him up, and of course he couldn't hear anything for the racket he was making. And so they went ripping along, and everybody just petrified to see it; and when they got to the Capitol at last it was the quickest trip that ever was made, and everybody said so. The horses laid down, and Nat dropped, all tuckered out, and he was all dust and rags and barefooted; but he was in time and just in time, and caught the President and give him the letter, and everything was all right, and the President give him a free pardon on the spot, and Nat give the nigger two extra quarters instead of one, because he could see that if he hadn't had the hack he wouldn't 'a' got there in time, nor anywhere near it.

It *was* a powerful good adventure, and Tom Sawyer had to work his bullet-wound mighty lively to hold his own against it.

Well, by-and-by Tom's glory got to paling down gradu'ly, on account of other things turning up for the people to talk about—first a horse-race, and on top of that a house afire, and on top of that the circus, and on top of that the eclipse; and that started a revival, same as it always does, and by that time there wasn't any more talk about Tom, so to speak, and you never see a person so sick and disgusted.

Pretty soon he got to worrying and fretting right along day in and day out, and when I asked him what *was* he in such a state about, he said it 'most broke his heart to think how time was slipping away, and him getting older and older, and no wars breaking out and no way of making a name for himself that he could see. Now that is the way boys is always thinking, but he was the first one I ever heard come out and say it.

So then he set to work to get up a plan to make him celebrated; and pretty soon he struck it, and offered to take me and Jim in. Tom Sawyer was always free and generous that way. There's a-plenty of boys that's mighty good and friendly when *you've* got a good thing, but when a good thing happens to come their way they don't say a word to you, and try to hog it all. That warn't ever Tom Sawyer's way, I can say that for him. There's plenty of boys that will come hankering and grovelling around you when you've got an apple, and beg the core off of you; but when they've got one, and you beg for the core and remind them how you give them a core one time, they say thank you 'most to death, but there ain't a-going to be no core. But I notice they always git come up with; all you got to do is to wait.

Well, we went out in the woods on the hill, and Tom told us what it was. It was a crusade.

"What's a crusade?" I says.

He looked scornful the way he's always done when he was ashamed of a person, and says—

"Huck Finn, do you mean to tell me you don't know what a crusade is?"

"No," says I, "I don't. And I don't care to, nuther. I've lived till now and done without it, and had my health, too. But as soon as you tell me, I'll know, and that's soon enough. I don't see any use in finding out things and clogging up my head with them when I mayn't ever have any occasion to use 'em. There was Lance Williams, he learned how to talk Choctaw

WE WENT OUT IN THE WOODS ON THE HILL, AND TOM TOLD US
WHAT IT WAS. IT WAS A CRUSADE.

here till one come and dug his grave for him. Now, then, what's a crusade? But I can tell you one thing before you begin; if it's a patent-right, there's no money in it. Bill Thompson he——"

"Patent-right!" says he. "I never see such an idiot. Why, a crusade is a kind of war."

I thought he must be losing his mind. But no, he was in real earnest, and went right on, perfectly ca'm:

"A crusade is a war to recover the Holy Land from the paynim."

"Which Holy Land?"

"Why, *the* Holy Land—there ain't but one."

"What do *we* want of it?"

"Why, can't you understand? It's in the hands of the paynim, and it's our duty to take it away from them."

"How did we come to let them git hold of it?"

"We didn't come to let them git hold of it. They always had it."

"Why, Tom, then it must belong to them, don't it?"

"Why of course it does. Who said it didn't?"

I studied over it, but couldn't seem to git at the right of it, no way. I says:

"It's too many for me, Tom Sawyer. If I had a farm and it was mine, and another person wanted it, would it be right for him to——"

"Oh, shucks! you don't know enough to come in when it rains, Huck Finn. It ain't a farm, it's entirely different. You see, it's like this. They own the land, just the mere land, and that's all they *do* own; but it was our folks, our Jews and Christians, that made it holy, and so they haven't any business to be there defiling it. It's a shame, and we ought not to stand it a minute. We ought to march against them and take it away from them."

"Why, it does seem to me it's the most mixed-up thing I ever see! Now if I had a farm and another person——"

"Don't I tell you it hasn't got anything to do with farming? Farming is business, just common low-down business; that's all it is, it's all you can say for it; but this is higher, this is religious, and totally different."

"Religious to go and take the land away from people that owns it?"

"Certainly; it's always been considered so."

Jim he shook his head, and says:

"Mars Tom, I reckon dey's a mistake about it somers—dey mos' sholy is. I's religious myself, en I knows plenty religious people, but I hain't run across none dat acts like dat."

It made Tom hot, and he says:

"Well, it's enough to make a body sick, such mullet-headed ignorance! If either of you'd read anything about history, you'd know that Richard Cur de Loon, and the Pope, and Godfrey de Bulleyn, and lots more of the most noble-hearted and pious people in the world, hacked and hammered at the paynims for more than two hundred years trying to take their land away from them, and swum neckdeep in blood the whole time—and yet here's a couple of sap-headed country yahoos out in the backwoods of Missouri, setting themselves up to know more about the rights and wrongs of it than they did! Talk about cheek!"

Well, of course, that put a more different light on it, and me and Jim felt pretty cheap and ignorant, and wished we hadn't been quite so chipper. I couldn't say nothing, and Jim he couldn't for a while; then he says:

"Well, den, I reckon it's all right; beca'se ef dey didn't know, dey ain't no use for po' ignorant folks like us to be trying to know; en so, ef it's our duty, we got to go en tackle it en do de bes' we can. Same time, I feel as sorry for dem paynims as Mars Tom. De hard part gwine to be to kill folks dat a body hain't been 'quainted wid and dat hain't done him no harm. Dat's it, you see. Ef we wuz to go 'mongst 'em, jist we three, en say we's hungry, en ast 'em for a bite to eat, why, maybe dey's jist like yuther people. Don't you reckon dey is? Why, *dey'd* give it, I know dey would, en den—"

"Then what?"

"Well, Mars Tom, my idea is like dis. It ain't no use, we *can't* kill dem po' strangers dat ain't doin' us no harm, till we've had practice—I knows it perfectly well, Mars Tom—'deed I knows it perfectly well. But ef we takes a' ax or two, jist you en me en Huck, en slips acrost de river to-night arter de moon's gone down, en kills dat sick fam'ly dat's over on the Sny, en burns de house down, en—"

"Oh, you make me tired!" says Tom. "I don't want to argue any more with people like you and Huck Finn, that's always wandering from the subject, and ain't got any more sense than to try to reason out a thing that's pure theology by the laws that protect real estate!"

Now that's just where Tom Sawyer warn't fair. Jim didn't mean no harm, and I didn't mean no harm. We knowed well enough that he was right and we was wrong, and all we was after was to get at the *how* of it, and that was all; and the only reason he couldn't explain it so we could understand it was because we was ignorant—yes, and pretty dull, too, I ain't denying that; but, land! that ain't no crime, I should think.

But he wouldn't hear no more about it—just said if we had tackled the thing in the proper spirit, he would 'a' raised a couple of thousand knights and put them in steel armor from head to heel and made me a lieutenant and Jim a sutler, and took the command himself and brushed the whole paynim outfit into the sea like flies and come back across the world in a glory like sunset. But he said we didn't know enough to take the chance when we had it, and he wouldn't ever offer it again. And he didn't. When he once got set, you couldn't budge him.

But I didn't care much. I am peaceable, and don't get up rows with people that ain't doing nothing to me. I allowed if the paynim was satisfied I was, and we would let it stand at that.

Now Tom he got all that notion out of Walter Scott's book, which he was always reading. And it *was* a wild notion, because in my opinion he never could've raised the men, and if he did, as like as not he would've got licked. I took the book and read all about it, and as near as I could make it out, most of the folks that shook farming to go crusading had a mighty rocky time of it.

Chapter 2

THE BALLOON ASCENSION

WELL, TOM got up one thing after another, but they all had tender spots about 'em somewheres, and he had to shove 'em aside. So at last he was about in despair. Then the St. Louis papers begun to talk a good deal about the balloon that was going to sail to Europe, and Tom sort of thought he wanted to go down and see what it looked like, but couldn't make up his mind. But the papers went on talking, and so he allowed that maybe if he didn't go he mightn't ever have another chance to see a balloon; and next he found out that Nat Parsons was going down to see it, and that decided him, of course. He wasn't going to have Nat Parsons coming back bragging about seeing the balloon, and him having to listen to it and keep quiet. So he wanted me and Jim to go too, and we went.

It was a noble big balloon, and had wings and fans and all sorts of things, and wasn't like any balloon you see in pictures. It was away out toward the edge of town, in a vacant lot, corner of Twelfth Street; and there was a big crowd around it, making fun of it, and making fun of the man,—a lean pale feller with that soft kind of moonlight in his eyes, you know,—and they kept saying it wouldn't go. It made him hot to hear them, and he would turn on them and shake his fist and say they was animals and blind, but some day they would find they had stood face to face with one of the men that lifts up nations and makes civilizations, and was too dull to know it; and right here on this spot their own children and grandchildren would build a monument to him that would outlast a thousand years, but his name would outlast the monument. And then the crowd would burst out in a laugh again, and yell at him, and ask him what was his name before he was married, and what he would take to not do it, and what was his sister's cat's grandmother's name, and all the things that a crowd says when they've got hold of a feller that they see they can plague. Well, some things they said *was* funny,—yes, and mighty witty too, I ain't denying that,—but all the same it warn't fair nor brave, all them people pitching on one, and they so glib and sharp, and him without any gift of talk to answer back with. But, good land! what did he want to sass back for? You see, it couldn't do him no good, and it was just nuts for them. They *had* him, you know. But that was his way. I reckon he couldn't help it; he was made so, I judge. He was a good-enough sort of cretur, and hadn't no harm in him, and was just a genius, as the papers said, which wasn't his fault. We can't all be sound: we've got to be the way we're made. As near as I can make out, geniuses think they know it all, and so they won't take people's advice, but always go their own way, which makes everybody forsake them and despise them, and that is perfectly natural. If they was humbler, and listened and tried to learn, it would be better for them.

The part the professor was in was like a boat, and was big and roomy, and had water-tight lockers around the inside to keep all sorts of things in, and a body could sit on them, and make beds on them, too. We went aboard, and there was twenty people there, snooping around and examining, and old Nat Parsons was there too. The professor kept fussing around, getting ready, and the people went ashore, drifting out one at a time, and old Nat he was the last. Of course it wouldn't do to let him go out behind *us*. We mustn't budge till he was gone, so we could be last ourselves.

But he was gone now, so it was time for us to follow. I heard a big shout, and turned around—the city was dropping from under us like a shot! It made me sick all through, I was so scared. Jim turned gray and couldn't say a word, and Tom didn't say nothing, but looked excited. The city went on dropping down, and down, and down; but we didn't seem to be doing nothing but just hang in the air and stand still. The houses got smaller and smaller, and the city pulled itself together, closer and closer, and the men and wagons got to looking like ants and bugs crawling around, and the streets like threads and cracks; and then it all kind of melted together, and there wasn't any city any more: it was only a big scar on the earth, and it seemed to me a body could see up the river and down the river about a thousand miles, though of course it wasn't so much. By-and-by the earth was a ball—just a round ball, of a dull color, with shiny stripes wriggling and winding around over it, which was rivers. The Widder Douglas always told me the earth was round like a ball, but I never took any stock in a lot of them superstitions o' hers, and of course I paid no attention to that one, because I could see myself that the world was the shape of a plate, and flat. I used to go up on the hill, and take a look around and prove it for myself, because I reckon the best way to get a sure thing on a fact is to go and examine for yourself, and not take anybody's say-so. But I had to give in, now, that the widder was right. That is, she was right as to the rest of the world, but she warn't right about the part our village is in; that part is the shape of a plate, and flat, I take my oath!

The professor had been quiet all this time, as if he was asleep; but he broke loose now, and he was mighty bitter. He says something like this:

"Idiots! They said it wouldn't go; and they wanted to examine it, and spy around and get the secret of it out of me. But I beat them. Nobody knows the secret but me. Nobody knows what makes it move but me; and it's a new power—a new power, and a thousand times the strongest in the earth! Steam's foolishness to it! They said I couldn't go to Europe. To Europe! Why, there's power aboard to last five years, and feed for three months. They are fools! What do they know about it? Yes, and they said my air-ship was flimsy. Why, she's good for fifty years! I can sail the skies all my life if I want to, and steer where I please, though they laughed at that, and said I couldn't. Couldn't steer! Come here, boy; we'll see. You press these buttons as I tell you."

He made Tom steer the ship all about and every which way, and learnt him the whole thing in nearly no time; and Tom said it was perfectly easy. He made him fetch the ship down 'most to the earth, and had him spin her along so close to the Illinois prairies that a body could talk to the farmers, and hear everything they said perfectly plain; and he flung out printed bills to them that told about the balloon, and said it was going to Europe. Tom got so he could steer straight for a tree till he got nearly to

HE SAID HE WOULD SAIL HIS BALLOON AROUND THE WORLD.

it, and then dart up and skin right along over the top of it. Yes, and he showed Tom how to land her; and he done it first-rate, too, and set her down in the prairies as soft as wool. But the minute we started to skip out the professor says, "No, you don't!" and shot her up in the air again. It was awful. I begun to beg, and so did Jim; but it only give his temper a rise, and he begun to rage around and look wild out of his eyes, and I was scared of him.

Well, then he got on to his troubles again, and mourned and grumbled about the way he was treated, and couldn't seem to git over it, and especially people's saying his ship was flimsy. He scoffed at that, and at their saying she warn't simple and would be always getting out of order. Get out of order! That gravelled him; he said that she couldn't any more get out of order than the solar sister.

He got worse and worse, and I never see a person take on so. It give me the cold shivers to see him, and so it did Jim. By-and-by he got to yelling and screaming, and then he swore the world shouldn't ever have his secret at all now, it had treated him so mean. He said he would sail his balloon around the globe just to show what he could do, and then he would sink it in the sea, and sink us all along with it, too. Well, it was the awfulest fix to be in, and here was night coming on!

He give us something to eat, and made us go to the other end of the boat, and he laid down on a locker, where he could boss all the works, and put his old pepper-box revolver under his head, and said if anybody come fooling around there trying to land her, he would kill him.

We set scrunched up together, and thought considerable, but didn't say much—only just a word once in a while when a body had to say something or bust, we was *so* scared and worried. The night dragged along slow and lonesome. We was pretty low down, and the moonshine made everything soft and pretty, and the farm-houses looked snug and homeful, and we could hear the farm sounds, and wished we could be down there; but, laws! we just slipped along over them like a ghost, and never left a track.

Away in the night, when all the sounds was late sounds, and the air had

AND HERE WAS NIGHT COMING ON!

a late feel, and a late smell, too,—about a two-o'clock feel, as near as I could make out,—Tom said the professor was so quiet this time he must be asleep, and we'd better—

"Better what?" I says in a whisper, and feeling sick all over, because I knowed what he was thinking about.

"Better slip back there and tie him, and land the ship," he says.

I says: "No, sir! Don't you budge, Tom Sawyer."

And Jim—well, Jim was kind o' gasping he was so scared. He says:

"Oh, Mars Tom, *don't!* Ef you teches him, we's gone—we's gone sho'! I ain't gwine anear him, not for nothin' in dis worl'. Mars Tom, he's plumb crazy."

Tom whispers and says: "That's *why* we've got to do something. If he wasn't crazy I wouldn't give shucks to be anywhere but here; you couldn't hire me to get out,—now that I've got used to this balloon and over the scare of being cut loose from the solid ground,—if he was in his right mind. But it's no good politics, sailing around like this with a person that's out of his head, and says he's going round the world and then drown us all. We've *got* to do something, I tell you, and do it before he wakes up, too, or we mayn't ever get another chance. Come!"

But it made us turn cold and creepy just to think of it, and we said we wouldn't budge. So Tom was for slipping back there by himself to see if he couldn't get at the steering-gear and land the ship. We begged and begged him not to, but it warn't no use; so he got down on his hands and knees, and begun to crawl an inch at a time, we a-holding our breath and watching. After he got to the middle of the boat he crept slower than ever, and it did seem like years to me. But at last we see him get to the professor's head, and sort of raise up soft and look a good spell in his face and listen. Then we see him begin to inch along again toward the professor's feet where the steering-buttons was. Well, he got there all safe, and was reaching slow and steady toward the buttons, but he knocked down something that made a noise, and we see him slump down flat an' soft in the bottom, and lay still. The professor stirred, and says, "What's that?" But everybody kept dead still and quiet, and he begun to mutter and mumble and nestle, like a person that's going to wake up, and I thought I was going to die, I was so worried and scared.

Then a cloud slid over the moon, and I 'most cried, I was so glad. She buried herself deeper and deeper into the cloud, and it got so dark we couldn't see Tom. Then it began to sprinkle rain, and we could hear the professor fussing at his ropes and things and abusing the weather. We was afraid every minute he would touch Tom, and then we would be goners, and no help; but Tom was already on his way back, and when we felt his hands on our knees my breath stopped sudden, and my heart fell down 'mongst my other works, because I couldn't tell in the dark but it might be the professor, which I thought it *was*.

Dear! I was so glad to have him back that I was just as near happy as a person could be that was up in the air that way with a deranged man. You can't land a balloon in the dark, and so I hoped it would keep on raining, for I didn't want Tom to go meddling any more and make us so awful uncomfortable. Well, I got my wish. It drizzled and drizzled along the rest of the night, which wasn't long, though it did seem so; and at daybreak it cleared, and the world looked mighty soft and gray and pretty, and the forests and fields so good to see again, and the horses and cattle standing sober and thinking. Next, the sun come a-blazing up gay and splendid, and then we began to feel rusty and stretchy, and first we knowed we was all asleep.

Chapter 3

TOM EXPLAINS

WE WENT to sleep about four o'clock, and woke up about eight. The professor was setting back there at his end, looking glum. He pitched us some breakfast, but he told us not to come abaft the midship compass. That was about the middle of the boat. Well, when you are sharp-set, and you eat and satisfy yourself, everything looks pretty different from what it done before. It makes a body feel pretty near comfortable, even when he is up in a balloon with a genius. We got to talking together.

There was one thing that kept bothering me, and by-and-by I says:

"Tom, didn't we start east?"

"Yes."

"How fast have we been going?"

"Well, you heard what the professor said when he was raging round. Sometimes, he said, we was making fifty miles an hour, sometimes ninety, sometimes a hundred; said that with a gale to help he could make three hundred any time, and said if he wanted the gale, and wanted it blowing the right direction, he only had to go up higher or down lower to find it."

"Well, then, it's just as I reckoned. The professor lied."

"Why?"

"Because if we was going so fast we ought to be past Illinois, oughtn't we?"

"Certainly."

"Well, we ain't."

"What's the reason we ain't?"

"I know by the color. We're right over Illinois yet. And you can see for yourself that Indiana ain't in sight."

"I wonder what's the matter with you, Huck. You know by the *color?*"

"Yes, of course I do."

"What's the color got to do with it?"

"It's got everything to do with it. Illinois is green, Indiana is pink. You show me any pink down here, if you can. No, sir; it's green."

"Indiana *pink?* Why, what a lie!"

"It ain't no lie; I've seen it on the map, and it's pink."

You never see a person so aggravated and disgusted. He says:

"Well, if I was such a numskull as you, Huck Finn, I would jump over. Seen it on the map! Huck Finn, did you reckon the States was the same color out-of-doors as they are on the map?"

"Tom Sawyer, what's a map for? Ain't it to learn you facts?"

"Of course."

"Well, then, how's it going to do that if it tells lies? That's what I want to know."

"Shucks, you muggins! It don't tell lies."

"It don't, don't it?"

"No, it don't."

"All right, then; if it don't, there ain't no two States the same color. You git around *that*, if you can, Tom Sawyer."

He see I had him, and Jim see it too; and I tell you, I felt pretty good, for Tom Sawyer was always a hard person to git ahead of. Jim slapped his leg and says:

"I tell *you!* dat's smart, dat's right down smart. Ain't no use, Mars Tom; he got you *dis* time, sho!" He slapped his leg again, and says, "My *lan'*, but it was smart one!"

I never felt so good in my life; and yet *I* didn't know I was saying anything much till it was out. I was just mooning along, perfectly careless, and not expecting anything was going to happen, and never *thinking* of such a thing at all, when, all of a sudden, out it come. Why, it was just as much a surprise to me as it was to any of them. It was just the same way it is when a person is munching along on a hunk of corn-pone, and not thinking about anything, and all of a sudden bites into a di'mond. Now all that *he* knows first off is that it's some kind of gravel he's bit into; but he don't find out it's a di'mond till he gits it out and brushes off the sand and crumbs and one thing or another, and has a look at it, and then he's surprised and glad—yes, and proud too; though when you come to look the thing straight in the eye, he ain't entitled to as much credit as he would 'a' been if he'd been *hunting* di'monds. You can see the difference easy if you think it over. You see, an accident, that way, ain't fairly as big a thing as a thing that's done a-purpose. Anybody could find that di'mond in that corn-pone; but mind you, it's got to be somebody that's got *that kind of a corn-pone*. That's where that feller's credit comes in, you see;

and that's where mine comes in. I don't claim no great things,—I don't reckon I could 'a' done it again,—but I done it that time; that's all I claim. And I hadn't no more idea I could do such a thing, and warn't any more thinking about it or trying to, than you be this minute. Why, I was just as ca'm, a body couldn't be any ca'mer, and yet, all of a sudden, out it come. I've often thought of that time, and I can remember just the way everything looked, same as if it was only last week. I can see it all: beautiful rolling country with woods and fields and lakes for hundreds and hundreds of miles all around, and towns and villages scattered everywheres under us, here and there and yonder; and the professor mooning over a chart on his little table, and Tom's cap flopping in the rigging where it was hung up to dry. And one thing in particular was a bird right alongside, not ten foot off, going our way and trying to keep up, but losing ground all the time; and a railroad train doing the same thing down there, sliding among the trees and farms, and pouring out a long cloud of black smoke and now and then a little puff of white; and when the white was gone so long you had almost forgot it, you would hear a little faint toot, and that was the whistle. And we left the bird and the train both behind, *'way* behind, and done it easy too.

But Tom he was huffy, and said me and Jim was a couple of ignorant blatherskites, and then he says:

"Suppose there's a brown calf and a big brown dog, and an artist is making a picture of them. What is the *main* thing that that artist has got to do? He has got to paint them so you can tell them apart the minute you look at them, hain't he? Of course. Well, then, do you want him to go and paint *both* of them brown? Certainly you don't. He paints one of them blue, and then you can't make no mistake. It's just the same with the maps. That's why they make every State a different color; it ain't to deceive you, it's to keep you from deceiving yourself."

But I couldn't see no argument about that, and neither could Jim. Jim shook his head, and says:

"Why, Mars Tom, if you knowed what chuckleheads dem painters is, you'd wait a long time before you'd fetch one er *dem* in to back up a fac'. I's gwine to tell you, den you kin see for you'self. I see one of 'em a-paintin' away, one day, down in ole Hank Wilson's back lot, en I went down to see, en he was paintin' dat old brindle cow wid de near horn gone—you knows de one I means. En I ast him what he's paintin' her for, en he say when he git her painted, de picture's wuth a hundred dollars. Mars Tom, he could a got de cow fer fifteen, en I *tole* him so. Well, sah, if you'll b'lieve me, he jes' shuck his head, dat painter did, en went on a-dobbin'. Bless you, Mars Tom, *dey* don't know nothin'."

Tom he lost his temper. I notice a person 'most always does that's got laid out in an argument. He told us to shut up, and maybe we'd feel better. Then he see a town clock away off down yonder, and he took up the glass and looked at it, and then looked at his silver turnip, and then at the clock, and then at the turnip again, and says:

"That's funny! That clock's near about an hour fast."

So he put up his turnip. Then he see another clock, and took a look, and it was an hour fast too. That puzzled him.

"That's a mighty curious thing," he says. "I don't understand it."

Then he took the glass and hunted up another clock, and sure enough it was an hour fast too. Then his eyes began to spread and his breath to come out kinder gaspy like, and he says:

"Ger-reat Scott, it's the *longitude!*"

I says, considerably scared:

"Well, what's been and gone and happened now?"

"Why, the thing that's happened is that this old bladder has slid over Illinois and Indiana and Ohio like nothing, and this is the east end of Pennsylvania or New York, or somewheres around there."

"Tom Sawyer, you don't mean it!"

"Yes, I do, and it's dead sure. We've covered about fifteen degrees of longitude since we left St. Louis yesterday afternoon, and them clocks are *right*. We've come close on to eight hundred miles."

I didn't believe it, but it made the cold streaks trickle down my back just the same. In my experience I knowed it wouldn't take much short of two weeks to do it down the Mississippi on a raft.

Jim was working his mind and studying. Pretty soon he says:

"Mars Tom, did you say dem clocks uz right?"

"Yes, they're right."

"Ain't yo' watch right, too?"

"She's right for St. Louis, but she's an hour wrong for here."

"Mars Tom, is you tryin' to let on dat de time ain't de *same* everywheres?"

"No, it ain't the same everywheres, by a long shot."

Jim looked distressed, and says:

"It grieves me to hear you talk like dat, Mars Tom; I's right down ashamed to hear you talk like dat, arter de way you's been raised. Yassir, it'd break yo' Aunt Polly's heart to hear you."

Tom was astonished. He looked Jim over, wondering, and didn't say nothing, and Jim went on:

"Mars Tom, who put de people out yonder in St. Louis? De Lord done it. Who put de people here whar we is? De Lord done it. Ain' dey bofe his children? 'Cose dey is. *Well*, den! is he gwine to *scriminate* 'twixt 'em?"

"Scriminate! I never heard such ignorance. There ain't no discriminating about it. When he makes you and some more of his children black, and makes the rest of us white, what do you call that?"

Jim see the p'int. He was stuck. He couldn't answer. Tom says:

"He does discriminate, you see, when he wants to; but this case *here* ain't no discrimination of his, it's man's. The Lord made the day, and he made the night; but he didn't invent the hours, and he didn't distribute them around. Man did that."

"Mars Tom, is dat so? Man done it?"

"Certainly."

"Who tole him he could?"

"Nobody. He never asked."

Jim studied a minute, and says:

"Well, dat do beat me. I wouldn't 'a' tuck no sich resk. But some people ain't scared o' nothin'. Dey bangs right ahead; *dey* don't care what happens. So den dey's allays an hour's diff'unce everywhah, Mars Tom?"

"An hour? No! It's four minutes difference for every degree of longitude, you know. Fifteen of 'em's an hour, thirty of 'em's two hours, and so on. When it's one o'clock Tuesday morning in England, it's eight o'clock the night before in New York.''

Jim moved a little way along the locker, and you could see he was insulted. He kept shaking his head and muttering, and so I slid along to him and patted him on the leg, and petted him up, and got him over the worst of his feelings, and then he says:

"Mars Tom talkin' sich talk as dat! Choosday in one place en Monday in t'other, bofe in the same day! Huck, dis ain't no place to joke—up here whah we is. Two days in one day! How you gwine to got two days inter one day? Can't git two hours inter one hour, kin you? Can't git two niggers inter one nigger skin, kin you? Can't git two gallons of whiskey inter a one-gallon jug, kin you? No, sir, 'twould strain de jug. Yes, en even den you couldn't, *I* don't believe. Why, looky here, Huck, s'posen de Choosday was New Year's—now den! is you gwine to tell me it's dis year in one place en las' year in t'other, bofe in de identical same minute? It's de beatenest rubbage! I can't stan' it—I can't stan' to hear tell 'bout it.''

Then he begun to shiver and turn gray, and Tom says:

"*Now* what's the matter? What's the trouble?''

Jim could hardly speak, but he says:

"Mars Tom, you ain't jokin', en it's *so?*''

"No I'm not, and it *is* so.''

Jim shivered again, and says:

"Den dat Monday could be de las' day, en dey wouldn't be no las' day in England, en de dead wouldn't be called. We mustn't go over dah, Mars Tom. Please git him to turn back; I wants to be whah—''

All of a sudden we see something, and all jumped up, and forgot everything and begun to gaze. Tom says:

"Ain't that the—'' He catched his breath, then says: "It *is*, sure as you live! It's the ocean!''

That made me and Jim catch our breath, too. Then we all stood petrified but happy, for none of us had ever seen an ocean, or ever expected to. Tom kept muttering:

"Atlantic Ocean—Atlantic. Land, don't it sound great! And that's *it*—and *we* are looking at it—we! Why, it's just too splendid to believe!''

Then we see a big bank of black smoke; and when we got nearer, it was a city—and a monster she was, too, with a thick fringe of ships around one edge; and we wondered if it was New York, and begun to jaw and dispute about it, and, first we knowed, it slid from under us and went flying behind, and here we was, out over the very ocean itself, and going like a cyclone. Then we woke up, I tell you!

We made a break aft and raised a wail, and begun to beg the professor to turn back and land us, but he jerked out his pistol and motioned us back, and we went, but nobody will ever know how bad we felt.

The land was gone, all but a little streak, like a snake, away off on the edge of the water, and down under us was just ocean, ocean, ocean—millions of miles of it, heaving and pitching and squirming, and white sprays blowing from the wave-tops, and only a few ships in sight, wallowing around and laying over, first on one side and then on t'other, and sticking their bows under and then their sterns; and before long there warn't no ships at all, and we had the sky and the whole ocean all to ourselves, and the roomiest place I ever see and the lonesomest.

Chapter 4

STORM

AND IT got lonesomer and lonesomer. There was the big sky up there, empty and awful deep; and the ocean down there without a thing on it but just the waves. All around us was a ring, where the sky and the water come together; yes, a monstrous big ring it was, and we right in the dead center of it—plumb in the center. We was racing along like a prairie fire, but it never made any difference, we couldn't seem to git past that center no way. I couldn't see that we ever gained an inch on that ring. It made a body feel creepy, it was so curious and unaccountable.

Well, everything was so awful still that we got to talking in a very low voice, and kept on getting creepier and lonesomer and less and less talky, till at last the talk ran dry altogether, and we just set there and "thunk," as Jim calls it, and never said a word the longest time.

The professor never stirred till the sun was overhead, then he stood up and put a kind of triangle to his eye, and Tom said it was a sextant and he was taking the sun to see whereabouts the balloon was. Then he ciphered a little and looked in a book, and then he begun to carry on again. He said lots of wild things, and amongst others he said he would keep up this hundred-mile gait till the middle of tomorrow afternoon, and then he'd land in London.

We said we would be humbly thankful.

He was turning away, but he whirled around when we said that, and

THE PROFESSOR SAID HE WOULD KEEP UP THIS HUNDRED-MILE
GAIT TILL TOMORROW.

give us a long look of his blackest kind—one of the maliciousest and suspiciousest looks I ever see. Then he says:

"You want to leave me. Don't try to deny it."

We didn't know what to say, so we held in and didn't say nothing at all.

He went aft and set down, but he couldn't seem to git that thing out of his mind. Every now and then he would rip out something about it, and try to make us answer him, but we dasn't.

It got lonesomer and lonesomer right along, and it did seem to me I couldn't stand it. It was still worse when night begun to come on. By-and-by Tom pinched me and whispers:

"Look!"

I took a glance aft, and see the professor taking a whet out of a bottle. I didn't like the looks of that. By-and-by he took another drink, and pretty soon he begun to sing. It was dark now, and getting black and stormy. He went on singing, wilder and wilder, and the thunder begun to mutter, and the wind to wheeze and moan amongst the ropes, and altogether it was awful. It got so black we couldn't see him any more, and wished we couldn't hear him, but we could. Then he got still; but he warn't still ten minutes till we got suspicious, and wished he would start up his noise again, so we could tell where he was. By-and-by there was a flash of lightning, and we see him start to get up, but he staggered and fell down. We heard him scream out in the dark:

"They don't want to go to England. All right, I'll change the course. They want to leave me. I know they do. Well, they shall—and *now!*"

I 'most died when he said that. Then he was still again,—still so long I couldn't bear it, and it did seem to me the lightning wouldn't *ever* come again. But at last there was a blessed flash, and there he was, on his hands and knees, crawling, and not four feet from us. My, but his eyes was terrible! He made a lunge for Tom, and says, "Overboard *you* go!" but it was already pitch-dark again, and I couldn't see whether he got him or not, and Tom didn't make a sound.

There was another long, horrible wait; then there was a flash, and I see

YOU WANT TO LEAVE ME. DON'T TRY TO DENY IT.

Tom's head sink down outside the boat and disappear. He was on the rope-ladder that dangled down in the air from the gunnel. The professor let off a shout and jumped for him, and straight off it was pitch-dark again, and Jim groaned out, "Po' Mars Tom, he's a goner!" and made a jump for the professor, but the professor warn't there.

Then we heard a couple of terrible screams, and then another not so loud, and then another that was 'way below, and you could only *just* hear it; and I heard Jim say, "Po' Mars Tom!"

Then it was awful still, and I reckon a person could 'a' counted four thousand before the next flash come. When it come I see Jim on his knees, with his arms on the locker and his face buried in them, and he was crying. Before I could look over the edge it was all dark again, and I was glad, because I didn't want to see. But when the next flash come, I was watching, and down there I see somebody a-swinging in the wind on the ladder, and it was Tom!

"Come up!" I shouts; "come up, Tom!"

His voice was so weak, and the wind roared so, I couldn't make out what he said, but I thought he asked was the professor up there. I shouts:

"No, he's down in the ocean! Come up! Can we help you?"

Of course, all this in the dark.

"Huck, who is you hollerin' at?"

"I'm hollerin' at Tom."

"Oh, Huck, how kin you act so, when you know po' Mars Tom's—" Then he let off an awful scream, and flung his head and his arms back and let off another one, because there was a white glare just then, and he had raised up his face just in time to see Tom's, as white as snow, rise above the gunnel and look him right in the eye. He thought it was Tom's ghost, you see.

Tom clumb aboard, and when Jim found it *was* him, and not his ghost, he hugged him, and called him all sorts of loving names, and carried on like he was gone crazy, he was so glad. Says I:

"What did you wait for, Tom? Why didn't you come up at first?"

"I dasn't, Huck. I knowed somebody plunged down past me, but I didn't know who it was in the dark. It could 'a' been you, it could 'a' been Jim."

That was the way with Tom Sawyer—always sound. He warn't coming up till he knowed where the professor was.

The storm let go about this time with all its might; and it was dreadful the way the thunder boomed and tore, and the lightning glared out, and the wind sung and screamed in the rigging, and the rain come down. One second you couldn't see your hand before you, and the next you could count the threads in your coat-sleeve, and see a whole wide desert of waves pitching and tossing through a kind of veil of rain. A storm like that is the loveliest thing there is, but it ain't at its best when you are up in the sky and lost, and it's wet and lonesome, and there's just been a death in the family.

We set there huddled up in the bow, and talked low about the poor professor; and everybody was sorry for him, and sorry the world had made fun of him and treated him so harsh, when he was doing the best he could, and hadn't a friend nor nobody to encourage him and keep him

THE THUNDER BOOMED, AND THE LIGHTNING GLARED,
AND THE WIND SCREAMED IN THE RIGGING.

from brooding his mind away and going deranged. There was plenty of
clothes and blankets and everything at the other end, but we thought we'd
ruther take the rain than go meddling back there.

Chapter 5

LAND

WE TRIED to make some plans, but we couldn't come to no agreement.
Me and Jim was for turning around and going back home, but Tom allowed
that by the time daylight come, so we could see our way, we would be so
far toward England that we might as well go there, and come back in a
ship, and have the glory of saying we done it.

About midnight the storm quit and the moon come out and lit up the
ocean, and we begun to feel comfortable and drowsy; so we stretched out
on the lockers and went to sleep, and never woke up again till sun-up.
The sea was sparkling like di'monds, and it was nice weather, and pretty
soon our things was all dry again.

We went aft to find some breakfast, and the first thing we noticed was
that there was a dim light burning in a compass back there under a hood.
Then Tom was disturbed. He says:

"You know what that means, easy enough. It means that somebody has
got to stay on watch and steer this thing the same as he would a ship, or
she'll wander around and go wherever the wind wants her to."

"Well," I says, "what's she been doing since—er—since we had the
accident?"

"Wandering," he says, kinder troubled—"wandering, without any doubt.
She's in a wind, now, that's blowing her south of east. We don't know
how long that's been going on, either."

So then he p'inted her east, and said he would hold her there till we
rousted out the breakfast. The professor had laid in everything a body
could want; he couldn't 'a' been better fixed. There wasn't no milk for
the coffee, but there was water, and everything else you could want, and
a charcoal stove and the fixings for it, and pipes and cigars and matches;
and wine and liquor, which warn't in our line; and books, and maps, and
charts, and an accordion; and furs, and blankets, and no end of rubbish,
like brass beads and brass jewelry, which Tom said was a sure sign that he
had an idea of visiting among savages. There was money, too. Yes, the
professor was well enough fixed.

After breakfast Tom learned me and Jim how to steer, and divided us
all up into four-hour watches, turn and turn about; and when his watch
was out I took his place, and he got out the professor's papers and pens
and wrote a letter home to his aunt Polly, telling her everything that had
happened to us, and dated it "*In the Welkin, approaching England,*" and
folded it together and stuck it fast with a red wafer, and directed it, and
wrote above the direction, in big writing, "*From Tom Sawyer, the Erronort,*" and said it would stump old Nat Parsons, the postmaster, when it
come along in the mail. I says:

"Tom Sawyer, this ain't no welkin; it's a balloon."

"Well, now, who *said* it was a welkin, smarty?"

"You've wrote it on the letter, anyway."

"What of it? That don't mean that the balloon's the welkin."

"Oh, I thought it did. Well, then, what is a welkin?"

I see in a minute he was stuck. He raked and scraped around in his
mind, but he couldn't find nothing, so he had to say:

"*I* don't know, and nobody don't know. It's just a word, and it's a
mighty good word, too. There ain't many that lays over it. I don't believe
there's *any* that does."

"Shucks!" I says. "But what does it *mean?*—that's the p'int."

"*I* don't know what it means, I tell you. It's a word that people uses
for—for—well, it's ornamental. They don't put ruffles on a shirt to keep
a person warm, do they?"

"Course they don't."

"But they put them *on*, don't they?"

"Yes."

"All right, then; that letter I wrote is a shirt, and the welkin's the ruffle
on it."

I judged that that would gravel Jim, and it did.

"Now, Mars Tom, it ain't no use to talk like dat; en, moreover, it's
sinful. You knows a letter ain't no shirt, en dey ain't no ruffles on it,
nuther. Dey ain't no place to put 'em on; you can't put 'em on, and dey
wouldn't stay ef you did."

"Oh, *do* shut up, and wait till something's started that you know
something about."

"Why, Mars Tom, sholy you can't mean to say I don't know about
shirts, when, goodness knows, I's toted home de washin' ever sence—"

"I tell you, this hasn't got anything to *do* with shirts. I only—"

"Why, Mars Tom, you said yo'self dat a letter—"

"Do you want to drive me crazy? Keep still. I only used it as a metaphor."

That word kinder bricked us up for a minute. Then Jim says—rather timid, because he see Tom was getting pretty tetchy:

"Mars Tom, what is a metaphor?"

"A metaphor's a—well, it's a—a—a metaphor's an illustration." He see *that* didn't git home, so he tried again. "When I say birds of a feather flocks together, it's a metaphorical way of saying—"

"But dey *don't*, Mars Tom. No sir, 'deed dey don't. Dey ain't no feathers dat's more alike den a bluebird en a jaybird, but ef you waits till you catches *dem* birds together, you'll—"

"Oh, give us a rest! You can't get the simplest little thing through your thick skull. Now don't bother me any more."

Jim was satisfied to stop. He was dreadful pleased with himself for catching Tom out. The minute Tom begun to talk about birds I judged he was a goner, because Jim knowed more about birds than both of us put together. You see, he had killed hundreds and hundreds of them, and that's the way to find out about birds. That's the way people does that writes books about birds, and loves them so that they'll go hungry and tired and take any amount of trouble to find a new bird and kill it. Their name is ornithologers, and I could have been an ornithologer myself, because I always loved birds and creatures; and I started out to learn how to be one, and I see a bird setting on a limb of a high tree, singing with its head tilted back and its mouth open, and before I thought I fired, and his song stopped and he fell straight down from the limb, all limp like a rag, and I run and picked him up and he was dead, and his body was warm in my hand, and his head rolled about this way and that, like his neck was broke, and there was a little white skin over his eyes, and one little drop of blood on the side of his head; and, laws! I couldn't see nothing more for the tears; and I hain't never murdered no creature since that warn't doing me no harm, and I ain't going to.

But I was aggravated about that welkin. I wanted to know. I got the subject up again, and then Tom explained, the best he could. He said when a person made a big speech the newspapers said the shouts of the people made the welkin ring. He said they always said that, but none of them ever told what it was, so he allowed it just meant outdoors and up high. Well, that seemed sensible enough, so I was satisfied, and said so. That pleased Tom and put him in a good humor again, and he says:

"Well, it's all right, then; and we'll let by-gones be by-gones. I don't know for certain what a welkin is, but when we land in London we'll make it ring, anyway, and don't you forget it."

He said an erronort was a person who sailed around in balloons; and said it was a mighty sight finer to be Tom Sawyer the Erronort than to be Tom Sawyer the Traveller, and we would be heard of all round the world, if we pulled through all right, and so he wouldn't give shucks to be a traveller now.

Toward the middle of the afternoon we got everything ready to land, and we felt pretty good, too, and proud; and we kept watching with the glasses, like Columbus discovering America. But we couldn't see nothing but ocean. The afternoon wasted out and the sun shut down, and still there warn't no land anywheres. We wondered what was the matter, but reckoned it would come out all right, so we went on steering east, but went up on a higher level so we wouldn't hit any steeples or mountains in the dark.

It was my watch till midnight, and then it was Jim's; but Tom stayed up, because he said ship-captains done that when they was making the land, and didn't stand no regular watch.

Well, when daylight come, Jim give a shout, and we jumped up and looked over, and there was the land sure enough,—land all around, as far as you could see, and perfectly level and yaller. We didn't know how long we'd been over it. There warn't no trees, nor hills, nor rocks, nor towns, and Tom and Jim had took it for the sea. They took it for the sea in a dead ca'm; but we was so high up, anyway, that if it had been the sea and rough, it would 'a' looked smooth, all the same, in the night, that way.

We was all in a powerful excitement now, and grabbed the glasses and hunted everywheres for London, but couldn't find hair nor hide of it, nor any other settlement,—nor any sign of a lake or a river, either. Tom was clean beat. He said it warn't his notion of England; he thought England looked like America, and always had that idea. So he said we better have breakfast, and then drop down and inquire the quickest way to London. We cut the breakfast pretty short, we was so impatient. As we slanted along down, the weather began to moderate, and pretty soon we shed our furs. But it kept *on* moderating, and in a precious little while it was 'most too moderate. We was close down, now, and just blistering!

We settled down to within thirty foot of the land,—that is, it was land if sand is land; for this wasn't anything but pure sand. Tom and me clumb down the ladder and took a run to stretch our legs, and it felt amazing good,—that is, the stretching did, but the sand scorched our feet like hot embers. Next, we see somebody coming, and started to meet him; but we heard Jim shout, and looked around and he was fairly dancing, and making signs, and yelling. We couldn't make out what he said, but we was scared anyway, and begun to heel it back to the balloon. When we got close enough, we understood the words, and they made me sick:

"Run! Run fo' yo' life! Hit's a lion; I kin see him thoo de glass! Run, boys; do please heel it de bes' you kin. He's bu'sted outen de menagerie, en dey ain't nobody to stop him!"

It made Tom fly, but it took the stiffening all out of my legs. I could only just gasp along the way you do in a dream when there's a ghost gaining on you.

Tom got to the ladder and shinned up it a piece and waited for me; and as soon as I got a foothold on it he shouted to Jim to soar away. But Jim had clean lost his head, and said he had forgot how. So Tom shinned along up and told me to follow; but the lion was arriving, fetching a most ghastly roar with every lope, and my legs shook so I dasn't try to take one of them out of the rounds for fear the other one would give way under me.

But Tom was aboard by this time, and he started the balloon up a little, and stopped it again as soon as the end of the ladder was ten or twelve feet above ground. And there was the lion, a-ripping around under me, and roaring and springing up in the air at the ladder, and only missing it

RUN! RUN FO' YO' LIFE!

about a quarter of an inch, it seemed to me. It was delicious to be out of his reach, perfectly delicious, and made me feel good and thankful all up one side; but I was hanging there helpless and couldn't climb, and that made me feel perfectly wretched and miserable all down the other. It is most seldom that a person feels so mixed, like that; and it is not to be recommended, either.

Tom asked me what he'd better do, but I didn't know. He asked me if I could hold on whilst he sailed away to a safe place and left the lion behind. I said I could if he didn't go no higher than he was now; but if he went higher I would lose my head and fall, sure. So he said, "Take a good grip," and he started.

"Don't go so fast," I shouted. "It makes my head swim."

He had started like a lightning express. He slowed down, and we glided over the sand slower, but still in a kind of sickening way; for it *is* uncomfortable to see things sliding and gliding under you like that, and not a sound.

But pretty soon there was plenty of sound, for the lion was catching up. His noise fetched others. You could see them coming on the lope from every direction, and pretty soon there was a couple of dozen of them under me, jumping up at the ladder and snarling and snapping at each other; and so we went skimming along over the sand, and these fellers doing what they could to help us to not forgit the occasion; and then some other beasts come, without an invite, and they started a regular riot down there.

We see this plan was a mistake. We couldn't ever git away from them at this gait, and I couldn't hold on forever. So Tom took a think, and struck another idea. That was, to kill a lion with the pepper-box revolver, and then sail away while the others stopped to fight over the carcass. So he stopped the balloon still, and done it, and then we sailed off while the fuss was going on, and come down a quarter of a mile off, and they helped me aboard; but by the time we was out of reach again, that gang was on hand once more. And when they see we was really gone and they couldn't get us, they sat down on their hams and looked up at us so kind of

AND THERE WAS THE LION, A-RIPPING AROUND UNDER ME.

disappointed that it was as much as a person could do not to see *their* side of the matter.

Chapter 6

IT'S A CARAVAN

I WAS so weak that the only thing I wanted was a chance to lay down, so I made straight for my locker-bunk, and stretched myself out there. But a body couldn't get back his strength in no such oven as that, so Tom give the command to soar, and Jim started her aloft.

We had to go up a mile before we struck comfortable weather where it was breezy and pleasant and just right, and pretty soon I was all straight again. Tom had been setting quiet and thinking; but now he jumps up and says:

"I bet you a thousand to one *I* know where we are. We're in the Great Sahara, as sure as guns!"

He was so excited he couldn't hold still; but I wasn't. I says:

"Well then, where's the Great Sahara? In England or in Scotland?"

"'Tain't in either; it's in Africa."

Jim's eyes bugged out, and he begun to stare down with no end of interest, because that was where his originals come from; but I didn't more than half believe it. I couldn't, you know; it seemed too awful far away for us to have travelled.

But Tom was full of his discovery, as he called it, and said the lions and the sand meant the Great Desert, sure. He said he could 'a' found out, before we sighted land, that we was crowding the land somewheres, if he had thought of one thing; and when we asked him what, he said:

"These clocks. They're chronometers. You always read about them in sea voyages. One of them is keeping Grinnage time, and the other is keeping St. Louis time, like my watch. When we left St. Louis it was four in the afternoon by my watch and this clock, and it was ten at night by this Grinnage clock. Well, at this time of the year the sun sets at about seven o'clock. Now I noticed the time yesterday evening when the sun went down, and it was half-past five o'clock by the Grinnage clock, and half-past eleven A.M. by my watch and the other clock. You see, the sun rose and set by my watch in St. Louis, and the Grinnage clock was six hours fast; but we've come so far east that it comes within less than half an hour of setting by the Grinnage clock, now, and I'm away out—more than four hours and a half out. You see, that meant that we was closing up on the longitude of Ireland, and would strike it before long if we was p'inted right—which we wasn't. No, sir, we've been a-wandering—wandering 'way down south of east, and it's my opinion we are in Africa. Look at this map. You see how the shoulder of Africa sticks out to the west. Think how fast we've travelled; if we had gone straight east we would be long past England by this time. You watch for noon, all of you, and we'll stand up, and when we can't cast a shadow we'll find that this Grinnage clock is coming mighty close to marking twelve. Yes, sir, *I* think we're in Africa; and it's just bully.''

Jim was gazing down with the glass. He shook his head and says:

"Mars Tom, I reckon dey's a mistake som'er's. I hain't seen no niggers yit.''

"That's nothing; they don't live in the desert. What is that, 'way off yonder? Gimme a glass.''

He took a long look, and said it was like a black string stretched across the sand, but he couldn't guess what it was.

"Well,'' I says, "I reckon maybe you've got a chance, now, to find out whereabouts this balloon is, because as like as not that is one of these lines here, that's on the map, that you call meridians of longitude, and we can drop down and look at its number, and—''

"Oh, shucks, Huck Finn, I never see such a lunkhead as you. Did you s'pose there's meridians of longitude on the *earth?*''

"Tom Sawyer, they're set down on the map, and you know it perfectly well, and here they are, and you can see for yourself.''

"Of course they're on the map, but that's nothing; there ain't any on the *ground.*''

"Tom, do you know that to be so?''

"Certainly I do.''

"Well, then, that map's a liar again. I never see such a liar as that map.''

He fired up at that, and I was ready for him, and Jim was warming his opinion, too, and next minute we'd 'a' broke loose on another argument, if Tom hadn't dropped the glass and begun to clap his hands like a maniac and sing out—

"Camels!—Camels!''

So I grabbed a glass, and Jim, too, and took a look, but I was disappointed, and says—

"Camels your granny; ther're spiders.''

"Spiders in the desert, you shad? Spiders walking in a procession? You don't ever reflect, Huck Finn, and I reckon you really haven't got anything to reflect *with*. Don't you know we're as much as a mile up in the air, and that that string of crawlers is two or three miles away? Spiders, good land! Spiders as big as a cow? Perhaps you'd like to go down and milk one of 'em. But they're camels, just the same. It's a caravan, that's what it is, and it's a mile long.''

"Well, then, 'e's go down and look at it. I don't believe in it, and ain't going to till I see it and know it.''

"All right," he says, and give the command: "Lower away.''

As we come slanting down into the hot weather, we could see that it was camels, sure enough, plodding along, an everlasting string of them, with bales strapped to them, and several hundred men in long white robes, and a thing like a shawl bound over their heads and hanging down with tassels and fringes; and some of the men had long guns and some hadn't, and some was riding and some was walking. And the weather—well, it was just roasting. And how slow they did creep along! We swooped down, now, all of a sudden, and stopped about a hundred yards over their heads.

The men all set up a yell, and some of them fell flat on their stomachs, some begun to fire their guns at us, and the rest broke and scampered every which way, and so did the camels.

We see that we was making trouble, so we went up again about a mile, to the cool weather, and watched them from there. It took them an hour to get together and form the procession again; then they started along, but we could see by the glasses that they wasn't paying much attention to anything but us. We poked along, looking down at them with the glasses, and by-and-by we see a big sand mound, and something like people the other side of it, and there was something like a man laying on top of the mound that raised his head up every now and then, and seemed to be watching the caravan or us, we didn't know which. As the caravan got nearer, he sneaked down on the other side and rushed to the other men and horses—for that is what they was—and we see them mount in a hurry; and next, here they come, like a house afire, some with lances and some with long guns, and all of them yelling the best they could.

WE SWOOPED DOWN, NOW, ALL OF A SUDDEN.

They come a-tearing down onto the caravan, and the next minute both sides crashed together and was all mixed up, and there was such another popping of guns as you never heard, and the air got so full of smoke you could only catch glimpses of them struggling together. There must 'a' been six hundred men in that battle, and it was terrible to see. Then they broke up into gangs and groups, fighting tooth and nail, and scurrying and scampering around, and laying into each other like everything; and whenever the smoke cleared a little you could see dead and wounded people and camels scattered far and wide and all about, and camels racing off in every direction.

At last the robbers see they couldn't win, so their chief sounded a signal, and all that was left of them broke away and went scampering across the plain. The last man to go snatched up a child and carried it off in front of him on his horse, and a woman run screaming and begging after him, and followed him away off across the plain till she was separated a long ways from her people; but it warn't no use, and she had to give it up, and we see her sink down on the sand and cover her face with her hands. Then Tom took the hellum, and started for that yahoo, and we come a-whizzing down and made a swoop, and knocked him out of the saddle, child and all; and he was jarred considerable, but the child wasn't hurt, but laid there working its hands and legs in the air like a tumble-bug that's on its back and can't turn over. The man went staggering off to overtake his horse, and didn't know what had hit him, for we was three or four hundred yards up in the air by this time.

We judged the woman would go and get the child, now; but she didn't. We could see her, through the glass, still setting there, with her head bowed down on her knees; so of course she hadn't seen the performance, and thought her child was clean gone with the man. She was nearly a half a mile from her people, so we thought we might go down to the child, which was about a quarter of a mile beyond her, and snake it to her before the caravan people could git to us to do us any harm; and besides, we reckoned they had enough business on their hands for one while, anyway, with the wounded. We thought we'd chance it, and we did. We swooped

THE LAST MAN TO GO SNATCHED UP A CHILD, AND CARRIED IT OFF
IN FRONT OF HIM ON HIS HORSE.

WE COME A-WHIZZING DOWN, MADE A SWOOP, AND KNOCKED HIM OUT
OF THE SADDLE, CHILD AND ALL.

down and stopped, and Jim shinned down the ladder and fetched up the
kid, which was a nice fat little thing, and in a noble good humor, too,
considering it was just out of a battle and been tumbled off a horse; and
then we started for the mother, and stopped back of her and tolerable near
by, and Jim slipped down and crept up easy, and when he was close back
of her the child goo-goo'd, the way a child does, and she heard it, and
whirled and fetched a shriek of joy, and made a jump for the kid and
snatched it and hugged it, and dropped it and hugged Jim, and then
snatched off a gold chain and hung it around Jim's neck, and hugged him
again, and jerked up the child again, a-sobbing and glorifying all the time;
and Jim he shoved for the ladder and up it, and in a minute we was back
up in the sky and the woman was staring up, with the back of her head
between her shoulders and the child with its arms locked around her neck.
And there she stood, as long as we was in sight a-sailing away in the sky.

Chapter 7

TOM RESPECTS THE FLEA

"NOON!" SAYS Tom, and so it was. His shadder was just a blot around
his feet. We looked, and the Grinnage clock was so close to twelve the
difference didn't amount to nothing. So Tom said London was right north
of us or right south of us, one or t'other, and he reckoned by the weather
and the sand and the camels it was north; and a good many miles north,
too; as many as from New York to the city of Mexico, he guessed.

Jim said he reckoned a balloon was a good deal the fastest thing in the
world, unless it might be some kinds of birds—a wild pigeon, maybe, or
a railroad.

But Tom said he had read about railroads in England going nearly a hundred miles an hour for a little ways, and there never was a bird in the world that could do that—except one, and that was a flea.

"A flea? Why, Mars Tom, in de fust place he ain't a bird, strickly speakin'—"

"He ain't a bird, eh? Well, then, what is he?"

"I don't rightly know, Mars Tom, but I speck he's only jist a' animal. No, I reckon dat won't do, nuther, he ain't big enough for a' animal. He mus' be a bug. Yassir, dat's what he is, he's a bug."

"I bet he ain't, but let it go. What's your second place?"

"Well, in de second place, birds is creturs dat goes a long ways, but a flea don't."

"He don't, don't he? Come, now, what *is* a long distance, if you know?"

"Why, it's miles, and lots of 'em—anybody knows dat."

"Can't a man walk miles?"

"Yassir, he kin."

"As many as a railroad?"

"Yassir, if you give him time."

"Can't a flea?"

"Well,—I s'pose so—ef you gives him heaps of time."

"Now you begin to see, don't you, that *distance* ain't the thing to judge by, at all; it's the time it takes to go the distance *in* that *counts,* ain't it?"

"Well, hit do look sorter so, but I wouldn't 'a' b'lieved it, Mars Tom."

"It's a matter of *proportion,* that's what it is; and when you come to gauge a thing's speed by its size, where's your bird and your man and your railroad, alongside of a flea? The fastest man can't run more than about ten miles in an hour—not much over ten thousand times his own length. But all the books says any common ordinary third-class flea can jump a hundred and fifty times his own length; yes, and he can make five jumps a second too,—seven hundred and fifty times his own length, in one little second—for he don't fool away any time stopping and starting— he does them both at the same time; you'll see, if you try to put your finger on him. Now that's a common, ordinary, third-class flea's gait; but

AND WHERE'S YOUR RAILROAD, ALONGSIDE OF A FLEA?

you take an Eyetalian *first*-class, that's been the pet of the nobility all his life, and hasn't ever knowed what want or sickness or exposure was, and he can jump more than three hundred times his own length, and keep it up all day, five such jumps every second, which is fifteen hundred times his own length. Well, suppose a man could go fifteen hundred times his own length in a second—say, a mile and a half. It's ninety miles a minute; it's considerable more than five thousand miles an hour. Where's your man *now?*—yes, and your bird, and your railroad, and your balloon? Laws, they don't amount to shucks 'longside of a flea. A flea is just a comet b'iled down small.''

Jim was a good deal astonished, and so was I. Jim said—

"Is dem figgers jist edjackly true, en no jokin' en no lies, Mars Tom?"

"Yes, they are; they're perfectly true."

"Well, den, honey, a body's got to respec' a flea. I ain't had no respec' for um befo', sca'sely, but dey ain't no gittin' roun' it, dey do deserve it, dat's certain."

"Well, I bet they do. They've got ever so much more sense, and brains, and brightness, in proportion to their size, than any other cretur in the world. A person can learn them 'most anything; and they learn it quicker than any other cretur, too. They've been learnt to haul little carriages in harness, and go this way and that way and t'other way according to their orders; yes, and to march and drill like soldiers, doing it as exact, according to orders, as soldiers does it. They've been learnt to do all sorts of hard and troublesome things. S'pose you could cultivate a flea up to the size of a man, and keep his natural smartness a-growing and a-growing right along up, bigger and bigger, and keener and keener, in the same proportion—where'd the human race be, do you reckon? That flea would be President of the United States, and you couldn't any more prevent it than you can prevent lightning."

"My lan', Mars Tom, I never knowed dey was so much *to* de beas'. No, sir, I never had no idea of it, and dat's de fac'."

"There's more to him, by a long sight, than there is to any other cretur, man or beast, in proportion to size. He's the interestingest of them all.

WHERE'S YOUR MAN NOW?

THAT FLEA WOULD BE PRESIDENT OF THE UNITED STATES,
AND YOU COULD NOT PREVENT IT.

People have so much to say about an ant's strength, and an elephant's, and a locomotive's. Shucks, they don't begin with a flea. He can lift two or three hundred times his own weight. And none of them can come anywhere near it. And, moreover, he has got notions of his own, and is very particular, and you can't fool him; his instinct, or his judgment, or whatever it is, is perfectly sound and clear, and don't ever make a mistake. People think all humans are alike to a flea. It ain't so. There's folks that he won't go near, hungry or not hungry, and I'm one of them. I've never had one of them on me in my life.''

"Mars Tom!"

"It's so; I ain't joking."

"Well, sah, I hain't ever heard de likes o' dat befo'."

Jim couldn't believe it, and I couldn't; so we had to drop down to the sand and git a supply and see. Tom was right. They went for me and Jim by the thousand, but not a one of them lit on Tom. There warn't no explaining it, but there it was and there warn't no getting around it. He said it had always been just so, and he'd just as soon be where there was a million of them as not; they'd never touch him nor bother him.

We went up to the cold weather to freeze 'em out, and stayed a little spell, and then come back to the comfortable weather and went lazying along twenty or twenty-five miles an hour, the way we'd been doing for the last few hours. The reason was, that the longer we was in that solemn, peaceful desert, the more the hurry and fuss got kind of soothed down in us, and the more happier and contented and satisfied we got to feeling, and the more we got to liking the desert, and then loving it. So we had cramped the speed down, as I was saying, and was having a most noble good lazy time, sometimes watching through the glasses, sometimes stretched out on the lockers reading, sometimes taking a nap.

It didn't seem like we was the same lot that was in such a state to find land and git ashore, but it was. But we had got over that—clean over it. We was used to the balloon, now, and not afraid any more, and didn't want to be anywheres else. Why, it seemed just like home; it 'most seemed as if I had been born and raised in it, and Jim and Tom said the same.

And always I had had hateful people around me, a'nagging at me, and pestering of me, and scolding, and finding fault, and fussing and bothering, and sticking to me, and keeping after me, and making me do this, and making me do that and t'other, and always selecting out the things I didn't want to do, and then giving me Sam Hill because I shirked and done something else, and just aggravating the life out of a body all the time; but up here in the sky it was so still and sunshiny and lovely, and plenty to eat, and plenty of sleep, and strange things to see, and no nagging and no pestering, and no good people, and just holiday all the time. Land, I warn't in no hurry to git out and buck at civilization again. Now, one of the worst things about civilization is, that anybody that gits a letter with trouble in it comes and tells you all about it and makes you feel bad, and the newspapers fetches you the troubles of everybody all over the world, and keeps you down-hearted and dismal 'most all the time, and it's such a heavy load for a person. I hate them newspapers; and I hate letters; and if I had my way I wouldn't allow nobody to load his troubles onto other folks he ain't acquainted with, on t'other side of the world, that way. Well, up in a balloon there ain't any of that, and it's the darlingest place there is.

We had supper, and that night was one of the prettiest nights I ever see. The moon made it just like daylight, only a heap softer; and once we see a lion standing all alone by himself, just all alone on the earth, it seemed like, and his shadder laid on the sand by him like a puddle of ink. That's the kind of moonlight to have.

Mainly we laid on our backs and talked; we didn't want to go to sleep. Tom said we was right in the midst of the Arabian Nights, now. He said it was right along here that one of the cutest things in that book happened; so we looked down and watched while he told about it, because there ain't anything that is so interesting to look at as a place that a book has talked about. It was a tale about a camel-driver that had lost his camel, and he come along in the desert and met a man, and says—

"Have you run across a stray camel to-day?"

And the man says—

"Was he blind in his left eye?"

"Yes."

"Had he lost an upper front tooth?"

"Yes."

"Was his off hind leg lame?"

"Yes."

"Was he loaded with millet-seed on one side and honey on the other?"

"Yes, but you needn't go into no more details—that's the one, and I'm in a hurry. Where did you see him?"

"I hain't seen him at all," the man says.

"Hain't seen him at all? How can you describe him so close, then?"

"Because when a person knows how to use his eyes, everything has got a meaning to it; but most people's eyes ain't any good to them. I knowed a camel had been along, because I seen his track. I knowed he was lame in his off hind leg because he had favored that foot and trod light on it, and his track showed it. I knowed he was blind on his left side because he only nibbled the grass on the right side of the trail. I knowed he had lost an upper front tooth because where he bit into the sod his teeth-print showed it. The millet-seed sifted out on one side—the ants told me that; the honey leaked out on the other—the flies told me that. I know all about your camel, but I hain't seen him.''

Jim says—

"Go on, Mars Tom, hit's a mighty good tale, and powerful interestin'.''

"That's all,'' Tom says.

"*All?*'' says Jim, astonished. "What 'come o' de camel?''

"I don't know.''

"Mars Tom, don't de tale say?''

"No.''

Jim puzzled a minute, then he says—

"Well! Ef dat ain't de beatenes' tale ever *I* struck. Jist gits to de place whah de intrust is gittin' red-hot, en down she breaks. Why, Mars Tom, dey ain't no *sense* in a tale dat acts like dat. Hain't you got no *idea* whether de man got de camel back er not?''

"No, I haven't.''

I see, myself, there warn't no sense in the tale, to chop square off, that way, before it come to anything, but I warn't going to say so, because I could see Tom was souring up pretty fast over the way it flatted out and the way Jim had popped onto the weak place in it, and I don't think it's fair for everybody to pile onto a feller when he's down. But Tom he whirls on me and says—

"What do *you* think of the tale?''

Of course, then, I had to come out and make a clean breast and say it did seem to me, too, same as it did to Jim, that as long as the tale stopped square in the middle and never got to no place, it really warn't worth the trouble of telling.

Tom's chin dropped on his breast, and 'stead of being mad, as I reckoned he'd be, to hear me scoff at his tale that way, he seemed to be only sad; and he says—

"Some people can see, and some can't—just as that man said. Let alone a camel, if a cyclone had gone by, *you* duffers wouldn't 'a' noticed the track.''

I don't know what he meant by that, and he didn't say; it was just one of his irrulevances, I reckon—he was full of them, sometimes, when he was in a close place and couldn't see no other way out—but I didn't mind. We'd spotted the soft place in that tale sharp enough, he couldn't git away from that litttle fact. It gravelled him like the nation, too, I reckon, much as he tried not to let on.

Chapter 8

THE DISAPPEARING LAKE

WE HAD an early breakfast in the morning, and set looking down on the desert, and the weather was ever so bammy and lovely, although we warn't

high up. You have to come down lower and lower after sundown, in the
desert, because it cools off so fast; and so, by the time it is getting towards
dawn you are skimming along only a little ways above the sand.

We was watching the shadder of the balloon slide along the ground, and
now and then gazing off across the desert to see if anything was stirring,
and then down on the shadder again, when all of a sudden almost right
under us we see a lot of men and camels laying scattered about, perfectly
quiet, like they was asleep.

We shut off the power, and backed up and stood over them, and then
we see that they was all dead. It give us the cold shivers. And it made us
hush down, too, and talk low, like people at a funeral. We dropped down
slow, and stopped, and me and Tom clumb down and went amongst them.
There was men, and women, and children. They was dried by the sun and
dark and shrivelled and leathery, like the pictures of mummies you see in
books. And yet they looked just as human, you wouldn't 'a' believed it;
just like they was asleep.

Some of the people and animals was partly covered with sand, but most
of them not, for the sand was thin there, and the bed was gravel, and
hard. Most of the clothes had rotted away; and when you took hold of a
rag, it tore with a touch, like spider-web. Tom reckoned they had been
laying there for years.

Some of the men had rusty guns by them, some had swords on and had
shawl belts with long, silver-mounted pistols stuck in them. All the camels
had their loads on, yet, but the packs had busted or rotted and spilt the
freight out on the ground. We didn't reckon the swords was any good to
the dead people any more, so we took one apiece, and some pistols. We
took a small box, too, because it was so handsome and inlaid so fine; and
then we wanted to bury the people; but there warn't no way to do it that
we could think of, and nothing to do it with but sand, and that would
blow away again, of course.

Then we mounted high and sailed away, and pretty soon that black spot
on the sand was out of sight and we wouldn't ever see them poor people
again in this world. We wondered, and reasoned, and tried to guess how
they come to be there, and how it all happened to them, but we couldn't
make it out. First we thought maybe they got lost, and wandered around
and about till their food and water give out and they starved to death; but
Tom said no wild animals nor vultures hadn't meddled with them, and so
that guess wouldn't do. So at last we give it up, and judged we wouldn't
think about it no more, because it made us low-spirited.

Then we opened the box, and it had gems and jewels in it, quite a pile,
and some little veils of the kind the dead women had on, with fringes
made out of curious gold money that we warn't acquainted with. We
wondered if we better go and try to find them again and give it back; but
Tom thought it over and said no, it was a country that was full of robbers,
and they would come and steal it, and then the sin would be on us for
putting the temptation in their way. So we went on; but I wished we had
took all they had, so there wouldn't 'a' been no temptation at all left.

We had had two hours of that blazing weather down there, and was
dreadful thirsty when we got aboard again. We went straight for the water,
but it was spoiled and bitter, besides being pretty near hot enough to scald

WE OPENED THE BOX, AND IT HAD GEMS AND JEWELS IN IT.

your mouth. We couldn't drink it. It was Mississippi River water, the best in the world, and we stirred up the mud in it to see if that would help, but no, the mud wasn't any better than the water.

Well, we hadn't been so very, very thirsty before, whilst we was interested in the lost people, but we was, now, and as soon as we found we couldn't have a drink, we was more than thirty-five times as thirsty as we was a quarter of a minute before. Why, in a little while we wanted to hold our mouths open and pant like a dog.

Tom said to keep a sharp lookout, all around, everywheres, because we'd got to find an oasis or there warn't no telling what would happen. So we done it. We kept the glasses gliding around all the time, till our arms got so tired we couldn't hold them any more. Two hours—three hours—just gazing and gazing, and nothing but sand, sand, *sand,* and you could see the quivering heat-shimmer playing over it. Dear, dear, a body don't know what real misery is till he is thirsty all the way through and is certain he ain't ever going to come to any water any more. At last I couldn't stand it to look around on them baking plains; I laid down on the locker, and give it up.

But by-and-by Tom raised a whoop, and there she was! A lake, wide and shiny, with pa'm-trees leaning over it asleep, and their shadders in the water just as soft and delicate as ever you see. I never see anything look so good. It was a long ways off, but that warn't anything to us; we just slapped on a hundred-mile gait, and calculated to be there in seven minutes; but she stayed the same old distance away, all the time; we couldn't seem to gain on her; yes, sir, just as far, and shiny, and like a dream; but we couldn't get no nearer; and at last, all of a sudden, she was gone!

Tom's eyes took a spread, and he says—

"Boys, it was a *my*ridge!" Said it like he was glad. I didn't see nothing to be glad about. I says—

"Maybe. I don't care nothing about its name, the thing I want to know is, what's become of it?"

Jim was trembling all over, and so scared he couldn't speak, but he wanted to ask that question himself if he could 'a' done it. Tom says—

"What's *become* of it? Why, you see, yourself, it's gone."

"Yes, I know; but where's it gone *to?*"

He looked me over and says—

"Well, now, Huck Finn, where *would* it go to! Don't you know what a myridge is?"

"No, I don't. What is it?"

"It ain't anything but imagination. There ain't anything *to* it."

It warmed me up a little to hear him talk like that, and I says—

"What's the use you talking that kind of stuff, Tom Sawyer? Didn't I see the lake?"

"Yes—you think you did."

"I don't think nothing about it, I *did* see it."

"I tell you you *didn't* see it either—because it warn't there to see."

It astonished Jim to hear him talk so, and he broke in and says, kind of pleading and distressed—

"Mars Tom, *please* don't say sich things in sich an awful time as dis. You ain't only reskin' yo' own self, but you's reskin' us—same way like Anna Nias en Siffira. De lake *wuz* dah—I seen it jis' as plain as I sees you en Huck dis minute."

I says—

"Why, he seen it himself! He was the very one that seen it first. *Now,* then!"

"Yes, Mars Tom, hit's so—you can't deny it. We all seen it, en dat *prove* it was dah."

"Proves it! *How* does it prove it?"

"Same way it does in de courts en everywheres, Mars Tom. One pusson might be drunk, or dreamy or suthin', en he could be mistaken; en two might, maybe; but I tell you, sah, when three sees a thing, drunk er sober, it's *so*. Dey ain't no gittin' aroun' dat, en you knows it, Mars Tom."

"I don't know nothing of the kind. There used to be forty thousand million people that seen the sun move from one side of the sky to the other every day. Did that prove that the sun *done* it?"

"Course it did. En besides, dey warn't no 'casion to prove it. A body 'at's got any sense ain't gwine to doubt it. Dah she is, now—a sailin' thoo de sky, like she allays done."

Tom turned on me, then, and says—

"What do *you* say—is the sun standing still?"

"Tom Sawyer, what's the use to ask such a jackass question? Anybody that ain't blind can see it don't stand still."

"Well," he says, "I'm lost in the sky with no company but a passel of low-down animals that don't know no more than the head boss of a university did three or four hundred years ago."

It warn't fair play, and I let him know it. I says—

"Throwin' mud ain't arguin', Tom Sawyer."

"Oh, my goodness, oh, my goodness gracious, dah's de lake ag'in!" yelled Jim, just then. "*Now,* Mars Tom, what you gwine to say?"

Yes, sir, there was the lake again, away yonder across the desert, perfectly plain, trees and all, just the same as it was before. I says—

"I reckon you're satisfied now, Tom Sawyer."

But he says, perfectly ca'm—

"Yes, satisfied there ain't no lake there."

Jim says—

"*Don't* talk so, Mars Tom—it sk'yers me to hear you. It's so hot, en you's so thirsty, dat you ain't in yo' right mine, Mars Tom. Oh, but don't she look good! 'clah I doan' know how I's gwine to wait tell we gits dah, I's *so* thirsty."

"Well, you'll have to wait; and it won't do you no good, either, because there ain't no lake there, I tell you."

I says—

"Jim, don't you take your eye off of it, and I won't, either."

"'Deed I won't; en bless you, honey, I couldn't ef I wanted to."

We went a-tearing along toward it, piling the miles behind us like nothing, but never gaining an inch on it—and all of a sudden it was gone again! Jim staggered, and 'most fell down. When he got his breath he says, gasping like a fish—

"Mars Tom, hit's a *ghos'*, dat's what it is, en I hopes to goodness we ain't gwine to see it no mo'. Dey's *been* a lake, en suthin's happened, en de lake's dead, en we's seen its ghos'; we's seen it twiste, en dat's proof. De desert's ha'nted, it's ha'nted, sho; oh, Mars Tom, le' 's git outen it; I'd ruther die den have de night ketch us in it ag'in en de ghos' er dat lake come a-mournin' aroun' us en we asleep en doan' know de danger we's in."

"Ghost, you gander! It ain't anything but air and heat and thirstiness pasted together by a person's imagination. If I—gimme the glass!"

He grabbed it and begun to gaze off to the right.

"It's a flock of birds," he says. "It's getting toward sundown, and they're making a bee-line across our track for somewheres. They mean business—maybe they're going for food or water, or both. Let her go to starboard!—Port your hellum! Hard down! There—ease up—steady, as you go."

We shut down some of the power, so as not to outspeed them, and took out after them. We went skimming along a quarter of a mile behind them, and when we had followed them an hour and a half and was getting pretty discouraged, and was thirsty clean to unendurableness, Tom says—

"Take the glass, one of you, and see what that is, away ahead of the birds."

Jim got the first glimpse, and slumped down on the locker, sick. He was most crying, and says—

"She's dah ag'in, Mars Tom, she's dah ag'in, en I knows I's gwine to die, 'case when a body sees a ghos' de third time, dat's what it means. I wisht I'd never come in dis balloon, dat I does."

He wouldn't look no more, and what he said made me afraid, too, because I knowed it was true, for that has always been the way with ghosts; so then I wouldn't look any more, either. Both of us begged Tom to turn off and go some other way, but he wouldn't, and said we was ignorant superstitious blatherskites. Yes, and he'll git come up with, one of these days, I says to myself, insulting ghosts that way. They'll stand it for a while, maybe, but they won't stand it always, for anybody that knows about ghosts knows how easy they are hurt, and how revengeful they are.

So we was all quiet and still, Jim and me being scared, and Tom busy.

By-and-by Tom fetched the balloon to a standstill, and says—

"*Now* get up and look, you sapheads."

We done it, and there was the sure-enough water right under us!—clear, and blue, and cool, and deep, and wavy with the breeze, the loveliest sight that ever was. And all about it was grassy banks, and flowers, and shady groves of big trees, looped together with vines, and all looking so peaceful and comfortable—enough to make a body cry, it was so beautiful.

Jim *did* cry, and rip and dance and carry on, he was so thankful and out of his mind for joy. It was my watch, so I had to stay by the works, but Tom and Jim clumb down and drunk a barrel apiece, and fetched me up a lot, and I've tasted a many a good thing in my life, but nothing that ever begun with that water.

Then we went down and had a swim, and then Tom came up and spelled me, and me and Jim had a swim, and them Jim spelled Tom, and me and Tom had a foot-race and a boxing-mill, and I don't reckon I ever had such a good time in my life. It warn't so very hot, because it was close on to evening, and we hadn't any clothes on, anyway. Clothes is well enough in school, and in towns, and at balls, too, but there ain't no sense in them when there ain't no civilization nor other kinds of bothers and fussiness around.

"Lions a'comin'!—lions! Quick, Mars Tom! Jump for yo' life, Huck!"

Oh, and didn't we! We never stopped for clothes, but waltzed up the ladder just so. Jim lost his head straight off—he always done it whenever he got excited and scared; and so now, 'stead of just easing the ladder up from the ground a little, so the animals couldn't reach it, he turned on a raft of power, and we went whizzing up and was dangling in the sky before he got his wits together and seen what a foolish thing he was doing. Then he stopped her, but he had clean forgot what to do next; so there we was, so high that the lions looked like pups, and we was drifting off on the wind.

But Tom he shinned up and went for the works and begun to slant her down, and back toward the lake, where the animals was gathering like a camp-meeting, and I judged he had lost *his* head, too; for he knowed I was too scared to climb, and did he want to dump me among the tigers and things?

But no, his head was level, he knowed what he was about. He swooped down to within thirty or forty feet of the lake, and stopped right over the center, and sung out—

"Leggo, and drop!"

I done it, and shot down, feet first, and seemed to go about a mile toward the bottom; and when I come up, he says—

"Now lay on your back and float till you're rested and got your pluck back, then I'll dip the ladder in the water and you can climb aboard."

I done it. Now that was ever so smart in Tom, because if he had started off somewheres else to drop down on the sand, the menagerie would 'a' come along, too, and might 'a' kept us hunting a safe place till I got tuckered out and fell.

And all this time the lions and tigers was sorting out the clothes, and trying to divide them up so there would be some for all, but there was a

AND ALL THIS TIME THE LIONS AND TIGERS WAS
SORTING OUT THE CLOTHES.

misunderstanding about it somewheres, on account of some of them trying to hog more than their share; so there was another insurrection, and you never see anything like it in the world. There must 'a' been fifty of them, all mixed up together, snorting and roaring and snapping and biting and tearing, legs and tails in the air, and you couldn't tell which was which, and the sand and fur a-flying. And when they got done, some was dead, and some was limping off crippled, and the rest was setting around on the battle-field, some of them licking their sore places and the others looking up at us and seemed to be kind of inviting us to come down and have some fun, but which we didn't want any.

As for the clothes, they warn't any, any more. Every last rag of them was inside of the animals; and not agreeing with them very well, I don't reckon, for there was considerable many brass buttons on them, and there was knives in the pockets, too, and smoking-tobaccco, and nails and chalk and marbles and fish-hooks and things. But I wasn't caring. All that was bothering me was, that all we had, now, was the professor's clothes, a big enough assortment, but not suitable to go into company with, if we came across any, because the britches was as long as tunnels, and the coats and things according. Still, there was everything a tailor needed, and Jim was a kind of jack-legged tailor, and he allowed he could soon trim a suit or two down for us that would answer.

Chapter 9

TOM DISCOURSES ON THE DESERT

STILL, WE thought we would drop down there a minute, but on another errand. Most of the professor's cargo of food was put up in cans, in the new way that somebody had just invented; the rest was fresh. When you fetch Missouri beefsteak to the Great Sahara, you want to be particular and stay up in the coolish weather. So we reckoned we would drop down into the lion market and see how we could make out there.

We hauled in the ladder and dropped down till we was just above the reach of the animals, then we let down a rope with a slip-knot in it and hauled up a dead lion, a small tender one, then yanked up a cub tiger. We had to keep the congregation off with the revolver, or they would 'a' took a hand in the proceedings and helped.

We carved off a supply from both, and saved the skins, and hove the rest overboard. Then we baited some of the professor's hooks with the fresh meat and went a-fishing. We stood over the lake just a convenient distance above the water, and catched a lot of the nicest fish you ever see. It was a most amazing good supper we had; lion steak, tiger steak, fried fish, and hot corn-pone. I don't want nothing better than that.

We had some fruit to finish off with. We got it out of the top of a monstrous tall tree. It was a very slim tree that hadn't a branch on it from the bottom plumb to the top, and there it bursted out like a feather-duster. It was a pa'm-tree, of course; anybody knows a pa'm-tree the minute he see it, by the pictures. We went for coconuts in this one, but there warn't none. There was only big loose bunches of things like over-sized grapes, and Tom allowed they was dates, because he said they answered the description in the Arabian Nights and the other books. Of course they mightn't be, and they might be poison; so we had to wait a spell, and watch and see if the birds et them. They done it; so we done it too, and they was most amazing good.

By this time monstrous big birds begun to come and settle on the dead animals. They was plucky creturs; they would tackle one end of a lion that was being gnawed at the other end by another lion. If the lion drove the bird away, it didn't do no good; he was back again the minute the lion was busy.

The big birds come out of every part of the sky—you could make them out with the glass whilst they was still so far away you couldn't see them with your naked eye. Tom said the birds didn't find out the meat was there

WE CATCHED A LOT OF THE NICEST FISH YOU EVER SAW.

by the smell; they had to find it out by seeing it. Oh, but ain't that an eye for you! Tom said at the distance of five mile a patch of dead lions couldn't look any bigger than a person's finger-nail, and he couldn't imagine how the birds could notice such a little thing so far off.

It was strange and unnatural to see lion eat lion, and we thought maybe they warn't kin. But Jim said that didn't make no difference. He said a hog was fond of her own children, and so was a spider, and he reckoned maybe a lion was pretty near as unprincipled though maybe not quite. He thought likely a lion wouldn't eat his own father, if he knowed which was him, but reckoned he would eat his brother-in-law if he was uncommon hungry, and eat his mother-in-law any time. But *reckoning* don't settle nothing. You can reckon till the cows come home, but that don't fetch you to no decision. So we give it up and let it drop.

Generly it was very still in the Desert, nights, but this time there was music. A lot of other animals come to dinner; sneaking yelpers that Tom allowed was jackals, and roached-backed ones that he said was hyenas; and all the whole biling of them kept up a racket all the time. They made a picture in the moonlight that was more different than any picture I ever see. We had a line out and made fast to the top of a tree, and didn't stand no watch, but all turned in and slept; but I was up two or three times to look down at the animals and hear the music. It was like having a front seat at a menagerie for nothing, which I hadn't ever had before, and so it seemed foolish to sleep and not make the most of it; I mightn't ever have such a chance again.

We went a-fishing again in the early dawn, and then lazied around all day in the deep shade on an island, taking turn about to watch and see that none of the animals come a-snooping around there after erronorts for dinner. We was going to leave the next day, but couldn't, it was too lovely.

The day after, when we rose up toward the sky and sailed off eastward, we looked back and watched that place till it warn't nothing but just a speck in the Desert, and I tell you it was like saying good-by to a friend that you ain't ever going to see any more.

Jim was thinking to himself, and at last he says—

"Mars Tom, we's mos' to de end er de Desert now, I speck."

"Why?"

"Well, hit stan' to reason we is. You knows how long we's been a'skimmin' over it. Mus' be mos' out o' san'. Hit's a wonder to me dat it's hilt out as long as it has."

"Shucks, there's plenty sand, you needn't worry."

"Oh, I ain't a-worryin', Mars Tom, only wonderin', dat's all. De Lord's got plenty san', I ain't doubtin' dat; but nemmine, He ain' gwyne to *was'e* it jist on dat account; en I allows dat dis Desert's plenty big enough now, jist de way she is, en you can't spread her out no mo' 'dout was'in san'."

"Oh, go 'long! we ain't much more than fairly *started* across this Desert yet. The United States is a pretty big country, ain't it? Ain't it, Huck?"

"Yes," I says, "there ain't no bigger one, I don't reckon."

"Well," he says, "this Desert is about the shape of the United States, and if you was to lay it down on top of the United States, it would cover the land of the free out of sight like a blanket. There'd be a little corner sticking out, up at Maine and away up northwest, and Florida sticking out like a turtle's tail, and that's all. We've took California away from the Mexicans two or three years ago, so that part of the Pacific coast is ours, now, and if you laid the Great Sahara down with her edge on the Pacific, she would cover the United States and stick out past New York six hundred miles into the Atlantic Ocean.''

I say—

"Good land! have you got the documents for that, Tom Sawyer?''

"Yes, and they're right here, and I've been studying them. You can look for yourself. From New York to the Pacific is 2600 miles. From one end of the Great Desert to the other is 3200. The United States contains 3,600,000 square miles, the Desert contains 4,162,000. With the Desert's bulk you could cover up every last inch of the United States, and in under where the edges projected out, you could tuck England, Scotland, Ireland, France, Denmark, and all Germany. Yes, sir, you could hide the home of the brave and all of them countries clean out of sight under the Great Sahara, and you would still have 2000 square miles of sand left.''

"Well,'' I says, "it clean beats me. Why, Tom, it shows that the Lord took as much pains makin' this Desert as makin' the United States and all them other countries.''

Jim says—"Huck, dat don' stan' to reason. I reckon dis Desert wa'n't made at all. Now you take en look at it like dis—you look at it, and see ef I's right. What's a desert good for? 'Tain't good for nuthin'. Dey ain't no way to make it pay. Hain't dat so, Huck?''

"Yes, I reckon.''

"Hain't it so, Mars Tom?''

"I guess so. Go on.''

"Ef a thing ain't no good, it's made in vain, ain't it?''

"Yes.''

"*Now,* den! Do de Lord make anything in vain? You answer me dat.''

"Well—no, He don't.''

"Den how come He make a desert?''

"Well, go on. How *did* He come to make it?''

"Mars Tom, *I* b'lieve it uz just like when you's buildin' a house; dey's allays a lot o' truck en rubbish lef' over. What does you do wid it? Doan' you take en k'yart it off en dump it into a ole vacant back lot? 'Course. Now, den, it's my opinion hit was jes like dat—dat de Great Sahara warn't made at all, she jes *happen'.*''

I said it was real good argument, and I believed it was the best one Jim ever made. Tom he said the same, but said the trouble about arguments is, they ain't nothing but *theories,* after all, and theories don't prove nothing, they only give you a place to rest on, a spell, when you are tuckered out butting around and around trying to find out something there ain't no way *to* find out. And he says—

"There's another trouble about theories: there's always a hole in them somewheres, sure, if you look close enough. It's just so with this one of Jim's. Look what billions and billions of stars there is. How does it come that there was just exactly enough star-stuff, and none left over? How does it come there ain't no sand-pile up there?''

But Jim was fixed for him and says—

"What's de Milky Way?—dat's what *I* wants to know. What's de Milky Way? Answer me dat!"

In my opinion it was just a sockdologer. It's only an opinion, it's only *my* opinion and others may think different; but I said it then and I stand to it now—it was a sockdologer. And moreover, besides, it landed Tom Sawyer. He couldn't say a word. He had that stunned look of a person that's been shot in the back with a kag of nails. All he said was, as for people like me and Jim, he'd just as soon have intellectual intercourse with a catfish. But anybody can say that—and I notice they always do, when somebody has fetched them a lifter. Tom Sawyer was tired of that end of the subject.

So we got back to talking about the size of the Desert again, and the more we compared it with this and that and t'other thing, the more nobler and bigger and grander it got to look, right along. And so, hunting amongst the figgers, Tom found, by-and-by, that it was just the same size as the Empire of China. Then he showed us the spread the Empire of China made on the map, and the room she took up in the world. Well, it was wonderful to think of, and I says—

"Why, I've heard talk about this Desert plenty of times, but *I* never knowed, before, how important she was."

Then Tom says—

"Important! Sahara important! That's just the way with some people. If a thing's big, it's important. That's all the sense they've got. All they can see is *size*. Why, look at England. It's the most important country in the world; and yet you could put it in China's vest-pocket; and not only that, but you'd have the dickens's own time to find it again the next time you wanted it. And look at Russia. It spreads all around and everywhere, and yet ain't no more important in this world than Rhode Island is, and hasn't got half as much in it that's worth saving."

Away off, now, we see a little hill, a-standing up just on the edge of the world. Tom broke off his talk, and reached for a glass very much excited, and took a look, and says—

"That's it—it's the one I've been looking for, sure. If I'm right, it's the one the dervish took the man into and showed him all the treasures."

So we begun to gaze, and he begun to tell about it out of the Arabian Nights.

Chapter 10

THE TREASURE-HILL

TOM SAID it happened like this.

A dervish was stumping it along through the Desert, on foot, one blazing hot day, and he had come a thousand miles and was pretty poor, and hungry, and ornery and tired, and along about where we are now he run across a camel-driver with a hundred camels, and asked him for some a'ms. But the camel-driver he asked to be excused. The dervish says—

"Don't you own these camels?"

"Yes, they're mine."

"Are you in debt?"

"Who—me? No."

"Well, a man that owns a hundred camels and ain't in debt is rich— and not only rich, but very rich. Ain't it so?"

The camel-driver owned up that it was so. Then the dervish says—

"God has made you rich, and He has made me poor. He has His reasons, and they are wise, blessed be His name. But He has willed that His rich shall help His poor, and you have turned away from me, your brother, in my need, and He will remember this, and you will lose by it."

That made the camel-driver feel shaky, but all the same he was born hoggish after money and didn't like to let go a cent; so he begun to whine and explain, and said times was hard, and although he had took a full freight down to Balsora and got a fat rate for it, he couldn't git no return freight, and so he warn't making no great things out of his trip. So the dervish starts along again, and says—

"All right, if you want to take the risk; but I reckon you've made a mistake this time, and missed a chance."

Of course the camel-driver wanted to know what kind of a chance he had missed, because maybe there was money in it; so he run after the dervish, and begged him so hard and earnest to take pity on him that at last the dervish gave in, and says—

"Do you see that hill yonder? Well, in that hill is all the treasures of the earth, and I was looking around for a man with a particular good kind heart and a noble, generous disposition, because if I could find just that man, I've got a kind of a salve I could put on his eyes and he could see the treasures and get them out."

So then the camel-driver was in a sweat; and he cried, and begged, and took on, and went down on his knees, and said he was just that kind of a man, and said he could fetch a thousand people that would say he wasn't ever described so exact before.

"Well, then," says the dervish, "all right. If we load the hundred camels, can I have half of them?"

The driver was so glad he couldn't hardly hold in, and says—

"Now you're shouting."

So they shook hands on the bargain, and the dervish got out his box and rubbed the salve on the driver's right eye, and the hill opened and he went in, and there, sure enough, was piles and piles of gold and jewels sparkling like all the stars in heaven had fell down.

So him and the dervish laid into it, and they loaded every camel till he couldn't carry no more; then they said good-by, and each of them started off with his fifty. But pretty soon the camel-driver come a-running and overtook the dervish and says—

"You ain't in society, you know, and you don't really need all you've got. Won't you be good, and let me have ten of your camels?"

"Well," the dervish says, "I don't know but what you say is reasonable enough."

THE CAMEL-DRIVER IN THE TREASURE-CAVE.

So he done it, and they separated and the dervish started off again with his forty. But pretty soon here comes the camel-driver bawling after him again, and whines and slobbers around and begs another ten off of him, saying thirty camel loads of treasures was enough to see a dervish through, because they live very simple, you know, and don't keep house, but board around and give their note.

But that warn't the end yet. That ornery hound kept coming and coming till he had begged back all the camels and had the whole hundred. Then he was satisfied, and ever so grateful, and said he wouldn't ever forget the dervish as long as he lived, and nobody hadn't been so good to him before, and liberal. So they shook hands good-by, and separated and started off again.

But do you know, it warn't ten minutes till the camel-driver was unsatisfied again—he was the low-downest reptile in seven counties—and he come a-running again. And this time the thing he wanted was to get the dervish to rub some of the salve on his other eye.

"Why?" said the dervish.

"Oh, you know," says the driver.

"Know what?"

"Well, you can't fool me," says the driver. "You're trying to keep back something from me, you know it mighty well. You know, I reckon, that if I had the salve on the other eye I could see a lot more things that's valuable. Come—please put it on."

The dervish says—

"I wasn't keeping anything back from you. I don't mind telling you what would happen if I put it on. You'd never see again. You'd be stone-blind the rest of your days."

But do you know, that beat wouldn't believe him. No, he begged and begged, and whined and cried, till at last the dervish opened his box and told him to put it on, if he wanted to. So the man done it, and sure enough he was as blind as a bat in a minute.

Then the dervish laughed at him and mocked at him and made fun of him; and says—

"Good-by—a man that's blind hain't got no use for jewelry."

And he cleared out with the hundred camels, and left that man to wander around poor and miserable and friendless the rest of his days in the Desert.

Jim said he'd bet it was a lesson to him.

"Yes," Tom says, "and like a considerable many lessons a body gets. They ain't no account, because the thing don't ever happen the same way again—and can't. The time Hen Scovil fell down the chimbly and crippled his back for life, everybody said it would be a lesson to him. What kind of a lesson? How was he going to use it? He couldn't climb chimblies no more, and he hadn't no more backs to break."

"All de same, Mars Tom, dey *is* sich a thing as learnin' by expe'ence. De Good Book say de burnt chile shun de fire."

"Well, I ain't denying that a thing's a lesson if it's a thing that can happen twice just the same way. There's lots of such things, and *they* educate a person, that's what Uncle Abner always said; but there's forty *million* lots of the other kind—the kind that don't happen the same way twice—and they ain't no real use, they ain't no more instructive than the small-pox. When you've got it, it ain't no good to find out you ought to been vaccinated, and it ain't no good to git vaccinated afterwards, because the small-pox don't come but once. But on the other hand Uncle Abner said that the person that had took a bull by the tail once had learnt sixty or seventy times as much as a person that hadn't, and said a person that started in to carry a cat home by the tail was gitting knowledge that was always going to be useful to him, and warn't ever going to grow dim or doubtful. But I can tell you, Jim, Uncle Abner was down on them people that's all the time trying to dig a lesson out of everything that happens, no matter whether—"

But Jim was asleep. Tom looked kind of ashamed, because you know a person always feels bad when he is talking uncommon fine and thinks the other person is admiring, and that other person goes to sleep that way. Of course he oughtn't to go to sleep, because it's shabby; but the finer a person talks the certainer it is to make you sleep, and so when you come to look at it it ain't nobody's fault in particular; both of them's to blame.

Jim begun to snore—soft and blubbery at first, then a long rasp, then a stronger one, then a half a dozen horrible ones like the last water sucking down the plug-hole of a bath-tub, then the same with more power to it, and some big coughs and snorts flung in, the way a cow does that is choking to death; and when the person has got to that point he is at his level best, and can wake up a man that is in the next block with a dipperful of loddanum in him, but can't wake himself up although all that awful noise of his'n ain't but three inches from his own ears. And that is the curiosest thing in the world, seems to me. But you rake a match to light the candle, and that little bit of a noise will fetch him. I wish I knowed what was the reason of that, but there don't seem to be no way to find out. Now there was Jim alarming the whole Desert, and yanking the animals out, for miles and miles around, to see what in the nation was going on up there; there warn't nobody nor nothing that was as close to the noise as *he* was, and yet he was the only cretur that wasn't disturbed by it. We yelled at him and whooped at him, it never done no good; but the first time there come a little wee noise that wasn't of a usual kind it woke him up. No, sir, I've thought it all over, and so has Tom, and there ain't no way to find out why a snorer can't hear himself snore.

Jim said he hadn't been asleep; he just shut his eyes so he could listen better.

Tom said nobody warn't accusing him.

That made him look like he wished he hadn't said anything. And he wanted to git away from the subject, I reckon, because he begun to abuse the camel-driver, just the way a person does when he has got catched in something and wants to take it out of somebody else. He let into the camel-driver the hardest he knowed how, and I had to agree with him; and he praised up the dervish the highest he could, and I had to agree with him there, too. But Tom says—

"I ain't so sure. You call that dervish so dreadful liberal and good and unselfish, but I don't quite see it. He didn't hunt up another poor dervish, did he? No, he didn't. If he was so unselfish, why didn't he go in there himself and take a pocketful of jewels and go along and be satisfied? No, sir, the person he was hunting for was a man with a hundred camels. He wanted to get away with all the treasure he could."

"Why, Mars Tom, he was willin' to divide, fair and square; he only struck for fifty camels."

"Because he knowed how he was going to get all of them by-and-by."

"Mars Tom, he *tole* de man de truck would make him bline."

"Yes, because he knowed the man's character. It was just the kind of a man he was hunting for—a man that never believes in anybody's word or anybody's honorableness, because he ain't got none of his own. I reckon there's lots of people like that dervish. They swindle, right and left, but they always make the other person *seem* to swindle himself. They keep inside of the letter of the law all the time, and there ain't no way to git hold of them. *They* don't put the salve on—oh no, that would be sin; but they know how to fool *you* into putting it on, then it's you that blinds yourself. I reckon the dervish and the camel-driver was just a pair—a fine, smart, brainy rascal, and a dull, coarse, ignorant one, but both of them rascals, just the same."

"Mars Tom, does you reckon dey's any o' dat kind o' salve in de worl' now?"

"Yes, Uncle Abner says there is. He says they've got it in New York, and they put it on country people's eyes and show them all the railroads in the world, and they go in and git them, and then when they rub the salve on the other eye the other man bids them good-by and goes off with their railroads. Here's the treasure-hill, now. Lower away!"

We landed, but it warn't as interesting as I thought it was going to be, because we couldn't find the place where they went in to git the treasure. Still, it was plenty interesting enough, just to see the mere hill itself where such a wonderful thing happened. Jim said he wouldn't 'a' missed it for three dollars, and I felt the same way.

And to me and Jim, as wonderful a thing as any was the way Tom could come into a strange big country like this and go straight and find a little hump like that and tell it in a minute from a million other humps that was almost just like it, and nothing to help him but only his own learning and his own natural smartness. We talked and talked it over together, but couldn't make out how he done it. He had the best head on him I ever see; and all he lacked was age, to make a name for himself equal to Captain Kidd or George Washington. I bet you it would 'a' crowded either of *them* to find that hill, with all their gifts, but it warn't nothing to Tom Sawyer; he went across Sahara and put his finger on it as easy as you could pick a nigger out a bunch of angels.

We found a pond of salt water close by and scraped up a raft of salt around the edges, and loaded up the lion's skin and the tiger's so as they would keep till Jim could tan them.

Chapter 11

THE SAND-STORM

WE WENT a-fooling along for a day or two, and then just as the full moon was touching the ground on the other side of the desert, we see a string of little black figgers moving across its big silver face. You could see them as plain as if they was painted on the moon with ink. It was another caravan. We cooled down our speed and tagged along after it, just to have company, though it warn't going our way. It was a rattler, that caravan, and a most bully sight to look at, next morning when the sun come a-streaming across the desert and flung the long shadders of the camels on the gold sand like a thousand grand-daddy-longlegses marching in procession. We never went very near it, because we knowed better, now, than to act like that and scare people's camels and break up their caravans. It was the gayest outfit you ever see, for rich clothes and nobby style. Some of the chiefs rode on dromedaries, the first we ever see, and very tall, and they go plunging along like they was on stilts, and they rock the man that is on them pretty violent and churn up his dinner considerable, I bet you, but they make noble good time and a camel ain't nowheres with them for speed.

The caravan camped, during the middle part of the day, and then started again about the middle of the afternoon. Before long the sun begun to look very curious. First it kind of turned to brass, and then to copper, and after that it begun to look like a blood-red ball, and the air got hot and close, and pretty soon all the sky in the west darkened up and looked thick and foggy, but fiery and dreadful—like it looks through a piece of red glass, you know. We looked down and see a big confusion going on in the caravan, and a rushing every which way like they was scared; and then they all flopped down flat in the sand and laid there perfectly still.

Pretty soon we see something coming that stood up like an amazing wide wall, and reached from the desert up into the sky and hid the sun, and it was coming like the nation, too. Then a little faint breeze struck us, and then it come harder, and grains of sand begun to sift against our faces and sting like fire, and Tom sung out—

"It's a sand-storm—turn your backs to it!"

We done it; and in another minute it was blowing a gale, and the sand beat against us by the shovelful, and the air was so thick with it we couldn't see a thing. In five minutes the boat was level full, and we was setting on the lockers buried up to the chin in sand, and only our heads out and could hardly breathe.

Then the storm thinned, and we see that monstrous wall go a-sailing off across the desert, awful to look at, I tell you. We dug ourselves out and looked down, and where the caravan was before there wasn't anything but just the sand ocean now, and all still and quiet. All them people and camels was smothered and dead and buried—buried under ten foot of sand, we reckoned, and Tom allowed it might be years before the wind uncovered them, and all that time their friends wouldn't ever know what become of that caravan. Tom said—

"*Now* we know what it was that happened to the people we got the swords and pistols from."

Yes, sir, that was just it. It was as plain as day now. They got buried in a sand-storm, and the wild animals couldn't get at them, and the wind never uncovered them again until they was dried to leather and warn't fit to eat. It seemed to me we had felt as sorry for them poor people as a person could for anybody, and as mournful, too, but we was mistaken; this last caravan's death went harder with us, a good deal harder. You see, the others was total strangers, and we never got to feeling acquainted with them at all, except, maybe, a little with the man that was watching the girl, but it was different with this last caravan. We was huvvering around them a whole night and 'most a whole day, and had got to feeling real friendly with them, and acquainted. I have found out that there ain't no surer way to find out whether you like people or hate them than to travel with them. Just so with these. We kind of liked them from the start, and travelling with them put on the finisher. The longer we travelled with them, and the more we got used to their ways, the better and better we liked them, and the gladder and gladder we was that we run across them. We had come to know some of them so well that we called them by name

IN THE SAND-STORM.

when we was talking about them, and soon got so familiar and sociable that we even dropped the Miss and Mister and just used their plain names without any handle, and it did not seem unpolite, but just the right thing. Of course it wasn't their own names, but names we give them. There was Mr. Elexander Robinson and Miss Adaline Robinson, and Col. Jacob McDougal and Miss Harryet McDougal, and Judge Jeremia Butler and young Bushrod Butler, and these was big chiefs, mostly, that wore splendid great turbans and simmeters, and dressed like the Grand Mogul, and their families. But as soon as we come to know them good, and like them very much, it warn't Mister, nor Judge, nor nothing, any more, but only Elleck, and Addy, and Jake, and Hattie, and Jerry, and Buck, and so on.

And you know, the more you join in with people in their joys and their sorrows, the more nearer and dearer they come to be to you. Now we warn't cold and indifferent, the way most travellers is, we was right down friendly and sociable, and took a chance in everything that was going, and the caravan could depend on us to be on hand every time, it didn't make no difference what it was.

When they camped, we camped right over them, ten or twelve hundred feet up in the air. When they et a meal, we et ourn, and it made it ever so much home-liker to have their company. When they had a wedding, that night, and Buck and Addy got married, we got ourselves up in the very starchiest of the professor's duds for the blow-out, and when they danced we jined in and shook a foot up there.

But it is sorrow and trouble that brings you the nearest, and it was a funeral that done it with us. It was next morning, just in the still dawn. We didn't know the diseased, and he warn't in our set, but that never made no difference; he belonged to the caravan, and that was enough, and there warn't no more sincerer tears shed over him than the ones we dripped on him from up there eleven hundred foot on high.

Yes, parting with this caravan was much more bitterer than it was to part with them others, which was comparative strangers, and been dead so long, anyway. We had knowed these in their lives, and was fond of them, too, and now to have death snatch them from right before our faces

WHEN THEY DANCED WE JOINED IN AND SHOOK A FOOT UP THERE.

whilst we was looking, and leave us so lonesome and friendless in the middle of that big desert, it did hurt so, and we wished we mightn't ever make any more friends on that voyage if we was going to lose them again like that.

We couldn't keep from talking about them, and they was all the time coming up in our memory, and looking just the way they looked when we was all alive and happy together. We could see the line marching, and the shiny spearheads a-winking in the sun; we could see the dromedaries lumbering along; we could see the wedding and the funeral; and more oftener than anything else we could see them praying, because they don't allow nothing to prevent that; whenever the call come, several times a day, they would stop right there, and stand up and face to the east, and lift back their heads, and spread out their arms and begin, and four or five times they would go down on their knees, and then fall forwards and touch their forehead to the ground.

Well, it warn't good to go on talking about them, lovely as they was in their life, and dear to us in their life and death both, because it didn't do no good, and made us too downhearted. Jim allowed he was going to live as good a life as he could, so he could see them again in a better world; and Tom kept still and didn't tell him they was only Mohammedans; it warn't no use to disappoint him, he was feeling bad enough just as it was.

When we woke up next morning we was feeling a little cheerfuller, and had had a most powerful good sleep, because sand is the comfortablest bed there is, and I don't see why people that can afford it don't have it more. And it's terrible good ballast, too; I never see the balloon so steady before.

Tom allowed we had twenty tons of it, and wondered what we better do with it; it was good sand, and it didn't seem good sense to throw it away. Jim says—

"Mars Tom, can't we tote it back home en sell it? How long'll it take?"

"Depends on the way we go."

"Well, sah, she's wuth a quarter of a dollar a load at home, en I reckon we's got as much as twenty loads, hain't we? How much would dat be?"

THE WEDDING PROCESSION.

"Five dollars."

"By jings, Mars Tom, le's shove for home right on de spot! Hit's more'n a dollar en a half apiece, hain't it?"

"Yes."

"Well, ef dat ain't makin' money de easiest ever *I* struck! She jes' rained in—never cos' us a lick o' work. Le's mosey right along, Mars Tom."

But Tom was thinking and ciphering away so busy and excited he never heard him. Pretty soon he says—

"Five dollars—sho! Look here, this sand's worth—worth—why, it's worth no end of money."

"How is dat, Mars Tom? Go on, honey, go on!"

"Well, the minute people knows it's genuwyne sand from the genuwyne Desert of Sahara, they'll just be in a perfect state of mind to git hold of some of it to keep on the what-not in a vial with a label on it for a curiosity. All we got to do, is, to put it up in vials and float around all over the United States and peddle them out at ten cents apiece. We've got all of ten thousand dollars' worth of sand in this boat."

Me and Jim went all to pieces with joy, and begun to shout whoopjamboreehoo, and Tom says—

"And we can keep on coming back and fetching sand, and coming back and fetching more sand, and just keep it a-going till we've carted this whole Desert over there and sold it out; and there ain't ever going to be any opposition, either, because we'll take out a patent."

"My goodness," I says, "we'll be as rich as Creosote, won't we, Tom?"

"Yes—Creesus, you mean. Why, that dervish was hunting in that little hill for the treasures of the earth, and didn't know he was walking over the real ones for a thousand miles. He was blinder than he made the driver."

"Mars Tom, how much is we gwyne to be worth?"

"Well, I don't know, yet. It's got to be ciphered, and it ain't the easiest job to do, either, because it's over four million square miles of sand at ten cents a vial."

Jim was awful excited, but this faded it out considerable, and he shook his head and says—

"Mars Tom, we can't 'ford all dem vials—a king couldn't. We better not try to take de whole Desert, Mars Tom, de vials gwyne to bust us, sho'."

Tom's excitement died out, too, now, and I reckoned it was on account of the vials, but it wasn't. He set there thinking, and got bluer and bluer, and at last he says—

"Boys, it won't work; we got to give it up."

"Why, Tom?"

"On account of the duties."

I couldn't make nothing out of that, neither could Jim. I says—

"What *is* our duty, Tom? Because if we can't git around it, why can't we just *do* it? People often has to."

But he says—

"Oh, it ain't that kind of duty. The kind I mean is a tax. Whenever you strike a frontier—that's the border of a country, you know—you find a custom-house there, and the gov'ment officers comes and rummages amongst your things and charges a big tax, which they call a duty because it's their duty to bust you if they can, and if you don't pay the duty they'll hog your sand. They call it confiscating, but that don't deceive nobody, it's just hogging, and that's all it is. Now if we try to carry this sand home the way we're pointed now, we got to climb fences till we git tired—just frontier after frontier—Egypt, Arabia, Hindostan, and so on, and they'll all whack on a duty, and so you see, easy enough, we *can't* go *that* road."

"Why, Tom," I says, "we can sail right over their old frontiers; how are *they* going to stop us?"

He looked sorrowful at me, and says, very grave—

"Huck Finn, do you think that would be honest?"

I hate them kind of interruptions. I never said nothing, and he went on—

"Well, we're shut off the other way, too. If we go back the way we've come, there's the New York custom-house, and that is worse than all of them others put together, on account of the kind of cargo we've got."

"Why?"

"Well, they can't raise Sahara sand in America, of course, and when they can't raise a thing there, the duty is fourteen hundred thousand per cent on it if you try to fetch it in from where they do raise it."

"There ain't no sense in that, Tom Sawyer."

"Who said there *was*? What do you talk to me like that for, Huck Finn? You wait till I say a thing's got sense in it before you go to accusing me of saying it."

"All right, consider me crying about it, and sorry. Go on."

Jim says—

"Mars Tom, do dey dum dat duty onto everything we can't raise in America, en don't make no 'stinction 'twix' anything?"

"Yes, that's what they do."

"Mars Tom, ain't de blessin' o' de Lord de mos' valuable thing dey is?"

"Yes, it is."

"Don't de preacher stan' up in de pulpit en call it down on de people?"

"Yes."

"Whah do it come from?"

"From heaven."

"Yassir! you's jes' right, 'deed you is, honey—it come from heaven, en dat's a foreign country. *Now* den! do dey put a tax on dat blessin'?"

"No, they don't."

"Course dey don't; en so it stan' to reason dat you's mistaken, Mars Tom. Dey wouldn't put de tax on po' truck like san', dat everybody ain't 'bleeged to have, en leave if off'n de bes' thing dey is, which nobody can't git along widout."

Tom Sawyer was stumped; he see Jim had got him where he couldn't budge. He tried to wiggle out by saying they had *forgot* to put on that tax, but they'd be sure to remember about it, next session of Congress, and then they'd put it on, but that was a poor lame come-off, and he knowed it. He said there warn't nothing foreign that warn't taxed but just that one, and so they couldn't be consistent without taxing it, and to be consistent was the first law of politics. So he stuck to it that they'd left it out unintentional and would be certain to do their best to fix it before they got caught and laughed at.

But I didn't feel no more interest in such things, as long as we couldn't git our sand through, and it made me low-spirited, and Jim the same. Tom he tried to cheer us up by saying he would think up another speculation for us that would be just as good as this one and better, but it didn't do no good, we didn't believe there was any as big as this. It was mighty hard; such a little while ago we was so rich, and could 'a' bought a country and started a kingdom and been celebrated and happy, and now we was so poor and ornery again, and had our sand left on our hands. The sand was looking so lovely, before, just like gold and di'monds, and the feel of it was so soft and so silky and nice, but now I couldn't bear the sight of it, it made me sick to look at it, and I knowed I wouldn't ever feel comfortable again till we got shut of it, and I didn't have it there no more to remind us of what we had been and what we had got degraded down to. The others was feeling the same way about it that I was. I knowed it, because they cheered up so, the minute I says le's throw this truck overboard.

Well, it was going to be work, you know, and pretty solid work, too; so Tom he divided it up according to fairness and strength. He said me and him would clear out a fifth apiece, of the sand, and Jim three-fifths. Jim he didn't quite like that arrangement. He says—

"Course I's de stronges', en I's willin' to do a share accordin', but by jings you's kinder pilin' it onto ole Jim, Mars Tom, hain't you?"

"Well, I didn't think so, Jim, but you try your hand at fixing it, and let's see."

So Jim he reckoned it wouldn't be no more than fair if me and Tom done a *tenth* apiece. Tom he turned his back to git room and be private, and then he smole a smile that spread around and covered the whole Sahara to the westward, back to the Atlantic edge of it where we come from. Then he turned around again and said it was a good enough arrangement, and we was satisfied if Jim was. Jim said he was.

So then Tom measured off our two-tenths in the bow and left the rest for Jim, and it surprised Jim a good deal to see how much difference there was and what a raging lot of sand his share come to, and said he was powerful glad, now, that he had spoke up in time and got the first arrangement altered, for he said that even the way it was now, there was more sand than enjoyment in his end of the contract, he believed.

Then we laid into it. It was mighty hot work, and tough; so hot we had to move up into cooler weather or we couldn't 'a' stood it. Me and Tom took turn about, and one worked while t' other rested, but there warn't nobody to spell poor old Jim, and he made all that part of Africa damp, he sweated so. We couldn't work good, we was so full of laugh, and Jim he kept fretting and wanting to know what tickled us so, and we had to keep making up things to account for it, and they was pretty poor inventions, but they done well enough, Jim didn't see through them. At last when we got done we was 'most dead, but not with work but with laughing. By-and-by Jim was 'most dead too, but it was with work; then we took turns and spelled him, and he was as thankful as he could be, and would set on the gunnel and swab the sweat, and heave and pant, and say how good we was to a poor old nigger, and he wouldn't ever forgit us. He was always the gratefulest nigger I ever see, for any little thing you done for him. He was only nigger outside; inside he was as white as you be.

Chapter 12

JIM STANDING SIEGE

THE NEXT few meals was pretty sandy, but that don't make no difference when you are hungry; and when you ain't it ain't no satisfaction to eat, anyway, and so a little grit in the meat ain't no particular drawback, as far as I can see.

Then we struck the east end of the Desert at last, sailing on a northeast course. Away off on the edge of the sand, in a soft pinky light, we see three little sharp roofs like tents, and Tom says—

"It's the pyramids of Egypt."

It made my heart fairly jump. You see, I had seen a many and a many a picture of them, and heard tell about them a hundred times, and yet to come on them all of a sudden, that way, and find they was *real*, 'stead of imaginations, 'most knocked the breath out of me with surprise. It's a curious thing, that the more you hear about a grand and big and bully thing or person, the more it kind of dreamies out, as you may say, and gets to be a big dim wavery figger made out of moonshine and nothing solid to it. It's just so with George Washington, and the same with them pyramids.

And moreover besides, the thing they always said about them seemed to me to be stretchers. There was a feller come to the Sunday-school, once, and had a picture of them, and made a speech, and said the biggest pyramid covered thirteen acres, and was most five hundred foot high, just a steep mountain, all built out of hunks of stone as big as a bureau, and laid up in perfectly regular layers, like stair-steps. Thirteen acres, you see, for just one building; it's a farm. If it hadn't been in Sunday-school, I would 'a' judged it was a lie; and outside I was certain of it. And he said there was a hole in the pyramid, and you could go in there with candles, and go ever so far up a long slanting tunnel, and come to a large room in the stomach of that stone mountain, and there you would find a big stone chest with a king in it, four thousand years old. I said to myself, then, if that ain't a lie I will eat that king if they will fetch him, for even Methusalem warn't that old, and nobody claims it.

As we come a little nearer we see the yaller sand come to an end in a long straight edge like a blanket, and onto it was joined, edge to edge, a wide country of bright green, with a snaky stripe crooking through it, and Tom said it was the Nile. It made my heart jump again, for the Nile was another thing that wasn't real to me. Now I can tell you one thing which is dead certain: if you will fool along over three thousand miles of yaller sand, all glimmering with heat so that it makes your eyes water to look at it, and you've been a considerable part of a week doing it, the green country will look so like home and heaven to you that it will make your eyes water *again*.

It was just so with me, and the same with Jim.

And when Jim got so he could believe it *was* the land of Egypt he was looking at, he wouldn't enter it standing up, but got down on his knees and took off his hat, because he said it wasn't fitten' for a humble poor nigger to come any other way where such men had been as Moses and Joseph and Pharaoh and the other prophets. He was a Presbyterian, and had a most deep respect for Moses which was a Presbyterian too, he said. He was all stirred up, and says—

"Hit's de lan' of Egypt, de lan' of Egypt, en I's 'lowed to look at it wid my own eyes! En dah's de river dat was turn' to blood, en I's looking at de very same groun' whah de plagues was, en de lice, en de frogs; en de locus', en de hail, en whah dey marked de door-pos', en de angel o' de Lord come by in de darkness o' de night en slew de fust-born in all de lan' o' Egypt. Ole Jim ain't worthy to see dis day!"

And then he just broke down and cried, he was so thankful. So between him and Tom there was talk enough, Jim being excited because the land was so full of history—Joseph and his brethren, Moses in the bulrushes, Jacob coming down into Egypt to buy corn, the silver cup in the sack, and all them interesting things; and Tom just as excited too, because the land was so full of history that was in *his* line, about Noureddin, and Bedreddin, and such like monstrous giants, that made Jim's wool rise, and a raft of other Arabian Nights folks, which the half of them never done the things they let on they done, I don't believe.

Then we struck a disappointment, for one of them early morning fogs started up, and it warn't no use to sail over the top of it, because we would go by Egypt, sure, so we judged it was best to set her by compass straight for the place where the pyramids was gitting blurred and blotted out, and then drop low and skin along pretty close to the ground and keep a sharp lookout. Tom took the hellum, I stood by to let go the anchor, and Jim he straddled the bow to dig through the fog with his eyes and watch out for danger ahead. We went along a steady gait, but not very fast, and the fog got solider and solider, so solid that Jim looked dim and ragged and smoky through it. It was awful still, and we talked low and was anxious. Now and then Jim would say—

"Highst her a p'int, Mars Tom, highst her!" and up she would skip, a foot or two, and we would slide right over a flat-roofed mud cabin, with people that had been asleep on it just beginning to turn out and gap and stretch: and once when a feller was clear up on his hind legs so he could gap and stretch better, we took him a blip in the back and knocked him off. By-and-by, after about an hour, and everything dead still and we a-straining our ears for sounds and holding our breath, the fog thinned a little, very sudden, and Jim sung out in an awful scare—

"Oh, for de lan's sake, set her back, Mars Tom, here's de biggest giant outen de 'Rabian Nights a-comin' for us!" and he went over backwards in the boat.

Tom slammed on the back-action, and as we slowed to a standstill a man's face as big as our house at home looked in over the gunnel, same as a house looks out of its windows, and I laid down and died. I must 'a' been clear dead and gone for as much as a minute or more; then I come to, and Tom had hitched a boat-hook onto the lower lip of the giant and was holding the balloon steady with it whilst he canted his head back and got a good long look up at that awful face.

Jim was on his knees with his hands clasped, gazing up at the thing in a begging way, and working his lips but not getting anything out. I took only just a glimpse, and was fading out again, but Tom says—

"He ain't alive, you fools; it's the Sphinx!"

I never see Tom look so little and like a fly; but that was because the giant's head was so big and awful. Awful, yes, so it was, but not dreadful, any more, because you could see it was a noble face, and kind of sad, and not thinking about you, but about other things and larger. It was stone, reddish stone, and its nose and ears battered, and that give it an abused look, and you felt sorrier for it, for that.

We stood off a piece, and sailed around it and over it, and it was just grand. It was a man's head, or maybe a woman's, on a tiger's body a hundred and twenty-five foot long, and there was a dear little temple between its front paws. All but the head used to be under the sand, for hundreds of years, maybe thousands, but they had just lately dug the sand away and found that little temple. It took a power of sand to bury that cretur; most as much as it would to bury a steamboat, I reckon.

We landed Jim on top of the head, with an American flag to protect him, it being a foreign land; then we sailed off to this and that and t'other distance, to git what Tom called effects and perspectives and proportions, and Jim he done the best he could, striking all the different kinds of attitudes and positions he could study up, but standing on his head and working his legs the way a frog does was the best. The further we got away, the littler Jim got, and the grander the Sphinx got, till at last it was only a clothes-pin on a dome, as you might say. That's the way perspective brings out the correct proportions, Tom said; he said Julus Cesar's niggers didn't know how big he was, they was too close to him.

Then we sailed off further and further, till we couldn't see Jim at all, any more, and then that great figger was at its noblest, a-gazing out over the Nile Valley so still and solemn and lonesome, and all the little shabby huts and things that was scattered about clean disappeared and gone, and nothing around it now but a soft wide spread of yaller velvet, which was the sand.

That was the right place to stop, and we done it. We set there a-looking and a-thinking for a half an hour, nobody a-saying anything, for it made us feel quiet and kind of solemn to remember it had been looking over that valley just that same way, and thinking its awful thoughts all to itself for thousands of years, and nobody can't find out what they are to this day.

At last I took up the glass and see some little black things a-capering around on that velvet carpet, and some more a-climbing up the cretur's back, and then I see two or three wee puffs of white smoke, and told Tom to look. He done it, and says—

"They're bugs. No—hold on; they—why, I believe they're men. Yes, it's men—men and horses, both. They're hauling a long ladder up onto the Sphinx's back—now ain't that odd? And now they're trying to lean it up a—there's some more puffs of smoke—it's guns! Huck, they're after Jim!"

We clapped on the power, and went for them a-biling. We was there in no time, and come a-whizzing down amongst them, and they broke and scattered every which way, and some that was climbing the ladder after Jim let go all holts and fell. We soared up and found him laying on top of the head panting and most tuckered out, partly from howling for help and partly from scare. He had been standing a siege a long time—a week, *he* said, but it warn't so, it only just seemed so to him because they was crowding him so. They had shot at him, and rained the bullets all around him, but he warn't hit, and when they found he wouldn't stand up and the bullets couldn't git at him when he was laying down, they went for the ladder, and then he knowed it was all up with him if we didn't come pretty quick. Tom was very indignant, and asked him why he didn't show the flag and command them to *git,* in the name of the United States. Jim said he done it, but they never paid no attention. Tom said he would have this thing looked into at Washington, and says—

"You'll see that they'll have to apologize for insulting the flag, and pay an indemnity, too, on top of it, even if they git off *that* easy."

Jim says—

"What's an indemnity, Mars Tom?"

"It's cash, that's what it is."

"Who gits it, Mars Tom?"

"Why, *we* do."

"En who gits de apology?"

"The United States. Or, we can take whichever we please. We can take the apology, if we want to, and let the gov'ment take the money."

"How much money will it be, Mars Tom?"

"Well, in an aggravated case like this one, it will be at least three dollars apiece, and I don't know but more."

JIM STANDING A SIEGE.

"Well, den, we'll take de money, Mars Tom, blame de 'pology. Hain't dat yo' notion, too? En hain't it yourn, Huck?"

We talked it over a little and allowed that that was as good a way as any, so we agreed to take the money. It was a new business to me, and I asked Tom if countries always apologized when they had done wrong, and he says—

"Yes; the little ones does."

We was sailing around examining the pyramids, you know, and now we soared up and roosted on the flat top of the biggest one, and found it was just like what the man said in the Sunday-school. It was like four pairs of stairs that starts broad at the bottom and slants up and comes together in a point at the top, only these stair-steps couldn't be clumb the way you climb other stairs; no, for each step was as high as your chin, and you have to be boosted up from behind. The two other pyramids warn't far away, and the people moving about on the sand between looked like bugs crawling, we was so high above them.

Tom he couldn't hold himself he was so worked up with gladness and astonishment to be in such a celebrated place, and he just dripped history from every pore, seemed to me. He said he couldn't scarcely believe he was standing on the very identical spot the prince flew from on the Bronze Horse. It was in the Arabian Night times, he said. Somebody give the prince a bronze horse with a peg in its shoulder, and he could git on him and fly through the air like a bird, and go all over the world, and steer it by turning the peg, and fly high or low and land wherever he wanted to.

When he got done telling it there was one of them uncomfortable silences that comes, you know, when a person has been telling a whopper and you feel sorry for him and wish you could think of some way to change the subject and let him down easy, but git stuck and don't see no way, and before you can pull your mind together and *do* something, that silence has got in and spread itself and done the business. I was embarrassed, Jim he was embarrassed, and neither of us couldn't say a word. Well, Tom he glowered at me a minute, and says—

"Come, out with it. What do you think?"

RESCUE OF JIM.

I says—

"Tom Sawyer, *you* don't believe that, yourself."

"What's the reason I don't? What's to hender me?"

"There's one thing to hender you: it couldn't happen, that's all."

"What's the reason it couldn't happen?"

"You tell me the reason it *could* happen."

"This balloon is a good enough reason it could happen, I should reckon."

"*Why* is it?"

"*Why* is it? I never saw such an idiot. Ain't this balloon and the bronze horse the same thing under different names?"

"No, they're not. One is a balloon and the other's a horse. It's very different. Next you'll be saying a house and a cow is the same thing."

"By Jackson, Huck's got him ag'in! Dey ain't no wigglin' outer dat!"

"Shut your head, Jim; you don't know what you're talking about. And Huck don't. Look here, Huck, I'll make it plain to you, so you can understand. You see, it ain't the mere *form* that's got anything to do with their being similar or unsimilar, it's the *principle* involved; and the principle is the same in both. Don't you see, now?"

I turned it over in my mind, and says—

"Tom, it ain't no use. Principles is all very well, but they don't git around that one big fact, that the thing that a balloon can do ain't no sort of proof of what a horse can do."

"Shucks, Huck, you don't get the idea at all. Now look here a minute— it's perfectly plain. Don't we fly through the air?"

"Yes."

"Very well. Don't we fly high or fly low, just as we please?"

"Yes."

"Don't we steer whichever way we want to?"

"Yes."

"And don't we land when and where we please?"

"Yes."

"How do we move the balloon and steer it?"

"By touching the buttons."

"*Now* I reckon the thing is clear to you at last. In the other case the moving and steering was done by turning a peg. We touch a button, the prince turned a peg. There ain't an atom of difference, you see. I knowed I could git it through your head if I stuck to it long enough."

He felt so happy he begun to whistle. But me and Jim was silent, so he broke off surprised, and says—

"Looky here, Huck Finn, don't you see it *yet?*"

I says—

"Tom Sawyer, I want to ask you some questions."

"Go ahead," he says, and I see Jim chirk up to listen.

"As I understand it, the whole thing is in the buttons and the peg—the rest ain't of no consequence. A button is one shape, a peg is another shape, but that ain't any matter?"

"No, that ain't any matter, as long as they've both got the same power."

"All right, then. What is the power that's in a candle and in a match?"

"It's the fire."

"It's the same in both, then?"

"Yes, just the same in both."

"All right. Suppose I set fire to a carpenter shop with a match, what will happen to that carpenter shop?"

"She'll burn up."

"And suppose I set fire to this pyramid with a candle—will she burn up?"

"Of course she won't."

"All right. Now the fire's the same, both times. *Why* does the shop burn, and the pyramid don't?"

"Because the pyramid *can't* burn."

"Aha! and *a horse can't fly!*"

"My lan', ef Huck ain't got him ag'in! Huck's landed him high en dry dis time, *I* tell you! Hit's de smartes' trap I ever see a body walk inter—en ef I—"

But Jim was so full of laugh he got to strangling and couldn't go on, and Tom was that mad to see how neat I had floored him, and turned his own argument ag'in him and knocked him all to rags and flinders with it, that all he could manage to say was that whenever he heard me and Jim try to argue it made him ashamed of the human race. I never said nothing; I was feeling pretty well satisfied. When I have got the best of a person that way, it ain't my way to go around crowing about it the way some people does, for I consider that if I was in his place I wouldn't wish him to crow over me. It's better to be generous, that's what I think.

Chapter 13

GOING FOR TOM'S PIPE

By-and-by we left Jim to float around up there in the neighborhood of the pyramids, and we clumb down to the hole where you go into the tunnel, and went in with some Arabs and candles, and away in there in the middle of the pyramid we found a room and a big stone box in it where they used to keep that king, just as the man in the Sunday-school said; but he was gone, now; somebody had got him. But I didn't take no interest in the place, because there could be ghosts there, of course; not fresh ones, but I don't like no kind.

So then we come out and got some little donkeys and rode a piece, and then went in a boat another piece, and then more donkeys, and got to Cairo; and all the way the road was as smooth and beautiful a road as ever I see, and had tall date-pa'ms on both sides, and naked children everywhere, and the men was as red as copper, and fine and strong and handsome. And the city was a curiosity. Such narrow streets—why, they were just lanes, and crowded with people with turbans, and women with veils, and everybody rigged out in blazing bright clothes and all sorts of colors, and you wondered how the camels and the people got by each other in such narrow little cracks, but they done it—a perfect jam, you see, and everybody noisy. The stores warn't big enough to turn around in, but you didn't have to go in; the storekeeper sat tailor fashion on his counter, smoking his snaky long pipe, and had his things where he could reach them to sell, and he was just as good as in the street, for the camel-loads brushed him as they went by.

Now and then a grand person flew by in a carriage with fancy dressed men running and yelling in front of it and whacking anybody with a long rod that didn't get out of the way. And by-and-by along comes the Sultan riding horseback at the head of a procession, and fairly took your breath away his clothes was so splendid; and everybody fell flat and laid on his stomach while he went by. I forgot, but a feller helped me remember. He was one that had a rod and run in front.

There was churches, but they don't know enough to keep Sunday; they keep Friday and break the Sabbath. You have to take off your shoes when you go in. There was crowds of men and boys in the church, setting in groups on the stone floor and making no end of noise—getting their lessons by heart, Tom said, out of the Koran, which they think is a Bible, and people that knows better knows enough to not let on. I never see such a big church in my life before, and most awful high, it was; it made you dizzy to look up; our village church at home ain't a circumstance to it; if you was to put it in there, people would think it was a dry-goods box.

What I wanted to see was a dervish, because I was interested in dervishes on accounts of the one that played the trick on the camel-driver. So we found a lot in a kind of a church, and they called themselves Whirling Dervishes; and they did whirl, too, I never see anything like it. They had tall sugar-loaf hats on, and linen petticoats; and they spun and spun and spun, round and round like tops, and the petticoats stood out on a slant, and it was the prettiest thing I ever see, and made me drunk to look at it. They was all Moslems, Tom said, and when I asked him what a Moslem was, he said it was a person that wasn't a Presbyterian. So there is plenty of them in Missouri, though I didn't know it before.

We didn't see half there was to see in Cairo, because Tom was in such a sweat to hunt out places that was celebrated in history. We had a most tiresome time to find the granary where Joseph stored up the grain before the famine, and when we found it it warn't worth much to look at, being such an old tumble-down wreck, but Tom was satisfied, and made more fuss over it than I would make if I stuck a nail in my foot. How he ever found that place was too many for me. We passed as much as forty just like it before we come to it, and any of them would 'a' done for me, but none but just the right one would suit him; I never see anybody so particular as Tom Sawyer. The minute he struck the right one he reconnized it as easy as I would reconnize my other shirt if I had one, but how he done it he couldn't any more tell than he could fly; he said so himself.

Then we hunted a long time for the house where the boy lived that learned the cadi how to try the case of the old olives and the new ones, and said it was out of the Arabian Nights, and he would tell me and Jim about it when he got time. Well, we hunted and hunted till I was ready to drop, and I wanted Tom to give it up and come next day and git somebody that knowed the town and could talk Missourian and could go straight to the place; but no, he wanted to find it himself, and nothing else would answer. So on we went. Then at last the remarkablest thing happened I ever see. The house was gone—gone hundreds of years ago—every last rag of it gone but just one mud brick. Now a person wouldn't ever believe that a backwoods Missouri boy that hadn't ever been in that town before could go and hunt that place over and find that brick, but Tom Sawyer done it. I know he done it, because I see him do it. I was right by his very side at the time, and see him see the brick and see him reconnize it. Well, I says to myself, how *does* he do it? is it knowledge, or is it instink?

Now there's the facts, just as they happened: let everybody explain it their own way. I've ciphered over it a good deal, and it's my opinion that some of it is knowledge but the main bulk of it is instink. The reason is this. Tom put the brick in his pocket to give to a museum with his name on it and the facts when he went home, and I slipped it out and put another brick considerable like it in its place, and he didn't know the difference— but there was a difference, you see. I think that settles it—it's mostly instink, not knowledge. Instink tells him where the exact *place* is for the brick to be in, and so he reconnizes it by the place it's in, not by the look of the brick. If it was knowledge, not instink, he would know the brick again by the look of it the next time he seen it—which he didn't. So it shows that for all the brag you hear about knowledge being such a wonderful thing, instink is worth forty of it for real unerringness. Jim says the same.

When we got back Jim dropped down and took us in, and there was a young man there with a red skull-cap and tassel on and a beautiful blue silk jacket and baggy trousers with a shawl around his waist and pistols in it that could talk English and wanted to hire to us as guide and take us to Mecca and Medina and Central Africa and everywheres for a half a dollar a day and his keep, and we hired him and left, and piled on the power, and by the time we was through dinner we was over the place where the Israelites crossed the Red Sea when Pharaoh tried to overtake them and was caught by the waters. We stopped, then, and had a good look at the place, and it done Jim good to see it. He said he could see it all, now, just the way it happened; he could see the Israelites walking along between the walls of water, and the Egyptians coming, from away off yonder, hurrying all they could, and see them start in as the Israelites went out, and then when they was all in, see the walls tumble together and drown the last man of them. Then we piled on the power again and rushed away and huvvered over Mount Sinai and saw the place where Moses broke the tables of stone, and where the children of Israel camped in the plain and worshipped the golden calf, and it was all just as interesting as could be, and the guide knowed every place as well as I know the village at home.

But we had an accident, now, and it fetched all the plans to a standstill. Tom's old ornery corn-cob pipe had got so old and swelled and warped that she couldn't hold together any longer, notwithstanding the strings and bandages, but caved in and went to pieces. Tom he didn't know *what* to do. The professor's pipe wouldn't answer; it warn't anything but a mer- shum, and a person that's got used to a cob pipe knows it lays a long ways over all the other pipes in this world, and you can't git him to smoke any other. He wouldn't take mine, I couldn't persuade him. So there he was.

He thought it over, and said we must scour around and see if we could roust out one in Egypt or Arabia or around in some of these countries, but the guide said no, it warn't no use, they didn't have them. So Tom was pretty glum for a little while, then he chirked up and said he'd got the idea and knowed what to do. He says—

"I've got another corn-cob pipe, and it's a prime one, too, and nearly new. It's laying on the rafter that's right over the kitchen stove at home in the village. Jim, you and the guide will go and get it, and me and Huck will camp here on Mount Sinai till you come back."

"But, Mars Tom, we couldn't ever find de village. I could find de pipe, 'caze I knows de kitchen, but my lan', we can't ever find de village, nur Sent Louis, nur none o' dem places. We don't know de way, Mars Tom."

That was a fact, and it stumped Tom for a minute. Then he said—

"Looky here, it can be done, sure; and I'll tell you how. You set your compass and sail west as straight as a dart, till you find the United States. It ain't any trouble, because it's the first land you'll strike the other side of the Atlantic. If it's daytime when you strike it, bulge right on, straight west from the upper part of the Florida coast, and in an hour and three quarters you'll hit the mouth of the Mississippi—at the speed that I'm going to send you. You'll be so high up in the air that the earth will be curved considerable—sorter like a washbowl turned upside down—and you'll see a raft of rivers crawling around every which way, long before you get there, and you can pick out the Mississippi without any trouble. Then you can follow the river north nearly, an hour and three quarters, till you see the Ohio come in; then you want to look sharp, because you're getting near. Away up to your left you'll see another thread coming in— that's the Missouri and is a little above St. Louis. You'll come down low, then, so as you can examine the villages as you spin along. You'll pass about twenty-five in the next fifteen minutes, and you'll recognize ours when you see it—and if you don't, you can yell down and ask."

"Ef it's dat easy, Mars Tom, I reckon we kin do it—yassir, I knows we kin."

The guide was sure of it, too, and thought that he could learn to stand his watch in a little while.

"Jim can learn you the whole thing in a half an hour," Tom said. "This balloon's as easy to manage as a canoe."

Tom got out the chart and marked out the course and measured it, and says—

"To go back west is the shortest way, you see. It's only about seven thousand miles. If you went east, and so on around, it's over twice as far." Then he says to the guide, "I want you both to watch the tell-tale all through the watches, and whenever it don't mark three hundred miles an hour, you go higher or drop lower till you find a storm-current that's going your way. There's a hundred miles an hour in this old thing without any wind to help. There's two hundred-mile gales to be found, any time you want to hunt for them."

"We'll hunt for them, sir."

"See that you do. Sometimes you may have to go up a couple of miles, and it'll be p'ison cold, but most of the time you'll find your storm a good deal lower. If you can only strike a cyclone—that's the ticket for you! You'll see by the professor's books that they travel west in these latitudes; and they travel low, too."

HOMEWARD BOUND.

Then he ciphered on the time, and says—

"Seven thousand miles, three hundred miles an hour—you can make the trip in a day—twenty-four hours. This is Thursday; you'll be back here Saturday afternoon. Come, now, hustle out some blankets and food and books and things for me and Huck, and you can start right along. There ain't no occasion to fool around—I want a smoke, and the quicker you fetch that pipe the better."

All hands jumped for the things, and in eight minutes our things was out and the balloon was ready for America. So we shook hands good-by, and Tom gave his last orders:

"It's 10 minutes to 2 P.M. now, Mount Sinai time. In 24 hours you'll be home, and it'll be 6 to-morrow morning, village time. When you strike the village, land a little back of the top of the hill, in the woods, out of sight; then you rush down, Jim, and shove these letters in the post-office, and if you see anybody stirring, pull your slouch down over your face so they won't know you. Then you go and slip in the back way, to the kitchen and git the pipe, and lay this piece of paper on the kitchen table and put something on it to hold it, and then slide out and git away and don't let Aunt Polly catch a sight of you, nor nobody else. Then you jump for the balloon and shove for Mount Sinai three hundred miles an hour. You won't have lost more than an hour. You'll start back at 7 or 8 A.M., village time, and be here in 24 hours, arriving at 2 or 3 P.M., Mount Sinai time."

Tom he read the piece of paper to us. He had wrote on it—

> "THURSDAY AFTERNOON. *Tom Sawyer the Erronort sends his love to Aunt Polly from Mount Sinai where the Ark was, and so does Huck Finn, and she will get it tomorrow morning half-past six.**
>
> TOM SAWYER THE ERRONORT."

"That'll make her eyes bulge out and the tears come," he says. Then he says—

---

*This misplacing of the Ark is probably Huck's error, not Tom's.—M. T.

"Stand by! One—two—three—away you go!"

And away she *did* go! Why, she seemed to whiz out of sight in a second.

Then we found a most comfortable cave that looked out over the whole big plain, and there we camped to wait for the pipe.

The balloon come back all right, and brung the pipe; but Aunt Polly had catched Jim when he was getting it, and anybody can guess what happened: she sent for Tom. So Jim he says—

"Mars Tom, she's out on de porch wid her eye sot on de sky a-layin' for you, en she say she ain't gwyne to budge from dah tell she gits hold of you. Dey's gwyne to be trouble, Mars Tom, 'deed dey is."

So then we shoved for home, and not feeling very gay, neither.

Tom Sawyer, Detective

Chapter 1*

WELL, IT was the next spring after me and Tom Sawyer set our old nigger Jim free, the time he was chained up for a runaway slave down there on Tom's uncle Silas's farm in Arkansaw. The frost was working out of the ground, and out of the air too, and it was getting closer and closer onto barefoot time every day; and next it would be marble time, and next mumbletypeg, and next tops and hoops, and next kites, and then right away it would be summer and going in a-swimming. It just makes a boy homesick to look ahead like that and see how far off summer is. Yes, and it sets him to sighing and saddening around, and there's something the matter with him, he don't know what. But anyway, he gets out by himself and mopes and thinks; and mostly he hunts for a lonesome place high up on the hill in the edge of the woods, and sets there and looks away off on the big Mississippi down there a-reaching miles and miles around the points where the timber looks smoky and dim it's so far off and still, and everything's so solemn it seems like everybody you've loved is dead and gone, and you 'most wish you was dead and gone too, and done with it all.

Don't you know what that is? It's spring fever. That is what the name of it is. And when you've got it, you want—oh, you don't quite know what it is you *do* want, but it just fairly makes your heart ache, you want it so! It seems to you that mainly what you want is to get away; get away from the same old tedious things you're so used to seeing and so tired of, and see something new. That is the idea; you want to go and be a wanderer; you want to go wandering far away to strange countries where everything is mysterious and wonderful and romantic. And if you can't do that, you'll put up with considerable less; you'll go anywhere you *can* go, just so as to get away, and be thankful of the chance, too.

Well, me and Tom Sawyer had the spring fever, and had it bad, too; but it warn't any use to think about Tom trying to get away, because, as he said, his aunt Polly wouldn't let him quit school and go traipsing off somers wasting time; so we was pretty blue. We was setting on the front

*Strange as the incidents of this story are, they are not inventions, but facts—even to the public confession of the accused. I take them from an old-time Swedish criminal trial, change the actors, and transfer the scene to America. I have added some details, but only a couple of them are important ones.—M.T.

71

steps one day about sundown talking this way, when out comes his aunt
Polly with a letter in her hand and says—

"Tom, I reckon you've got to pack up and go down to Arkansaw—your
aunt Sally wants you."

I 'most jumped out of my skin for joy. I reckoned Tom would fly at his
aunt and hug her head off; but if you believe me he set there like a rock,
and never said a word. It made me fit to cry to see him act so foolish,
with such a noble chance as this opening up. Why, we might lose it if he
didn't speak up and show he was thankful and grateful. But he set there
and studied and studied till I was that distressed I didn't know what to do;
then he says, very ca'm, and I could a shot him for it:

"Well," he says, "I'm right down sorry, Aunt Polly, but I reckon I got
to be excused—for the present."

His aunt Polly was knocked so stupid and so mad at the cold impudence
of it that she couldn't say a word for as much as a half minute, and this
give me a chance to nudge Tom and whisper:

"Ain't you got any sense? Sp'iling such a noble chance as this and
throwing it away?"

But he warn't disturbed. He mumbled back:

"Huck Finn, do you want me to let her *see* how bad I want to go? Why,
she'd begin to doubt, right away, and imagine a lot of sicknesses and
dangers and objections, and first you know she'd take it all back. You
lemme alone; I reckon I know how to work her."

Now I never would 'a' thought of that. But he was right. Tom Sawyer
was always right—the levelest head I ever see, and always *at* himself and
ready for anything you might spring on him. By this time his aunt Polly
was all straight again, and she left fly. She says:

"You'll be excused! *You* will! Well, I never heard the like of it in all
my days! The idea of you talking like that to *me!* Now take yourself off
and pack your traps; and if I hear another word out of you about what
you'll be excused from and what you won't, I lay *I'll* excuse you—with a
hickory!"

She hit his head a thump with her thimble as we dodged by, and he let

I RECKON I GOT TO BE EXCUSED.

on to be whimpering as we struck for the stairs. Up in his room he hugged me, he was so out of his head for gladness because he was going travelling. And he says:

"Before we get away she'll wish she hadn't let me go, but she won't know any way to get around it now. After what she's said, her pride won't let her take it back."

Tom was packed in ten minutes, all except what his aunt and Mary would finish up for him; then we waited ten more for her to get cooled down and sweet and gentle again; for Tom said it took her ten minutes to unruffle in times when half of her feathers was up, but twenty when they was all up, and this was one of the times when they was all up. Then we went down, being in a sweat to know what the letter said.

She was setting there in a brown study, with it laying in her lap. We set down, and she says:

"They're in considerable trouble down there, and they think you and Huck'll be a kind of diversion for them—'comfort,' they say. Much of that they'll get out of you and Huck Finn, I reckon. There's a neighbor named Brace Dunlap that's been wanting to marry their Benny for three months, and at last they told him pine blank and once for all, he *couldn't;* so he has soured on them, and they're worried about it. I reckon he's somebody they think they better be on the good side of, for they've tried to please him by hiring his no-account brother to help on the farm when they can't hardly afford it, and don't want him around anyhow. Who are the Dunlaps?"

"They live about a mile from Uncle Silas's place, Aunt Polly—all the farmers live about a mile apart down there—and Brace Dunlap is a long sight richer than any of the others, and owns a whole grist of niggers. He's a widower, thirty-six years old, without any children, and is proud of his money and overbearing, and everybody is a little afraid of him. I judge he thought he could have any girl he wanted, just for the asking, and it must have set him back a good deal when he found he couldn't get Benny. Why, Benny's only half as old as he is, and just as sweet and lovely as—well, you've seen her. Poor old Uncle Silas—why, it's pitiful, him trying to curry favor that way—so hard pushed and poor, and yet hiring that useless Jubiter Dunlap to please his ornery brother."

"What a name—Jubiter! Where'd he get it?"

"It's only just a nickname. I reckon they've forgot his real name long before this. He's twenty-seven, now, and has had it ever since the first time he ever went in swimming. The school-teacher seen a round brown mole the size of a dime on his left leg above his knee, and four little bits of moles around it, when he was naked, and he said it minded him of Jubiter and his moons; and the children thought it was funny, and so they got to calling him Jubiter, and he's Jubiter yet. He's tall, and lazy, and sly, and sneaky, and ruther cowardly, too, but kind of good-natured, and wears long brown hair and no beard, and hasn't got a cent, and Brace boards him for nothing, and gives him his old clothes to wear, and despises him. Jubiter is a twin."

"What's t'other twin like?"

"Just exactly like Jubiter—so they say; used to was, anyway, but he hain't been seen for seven years. He got to robbing when he was nineteen or twenty, and they jailed him; but he broke jail and got away—up North here, somers. They used to hear about him robbing and burglaring now and then, but that was years ago. He's dead, now. At least that's what they say. They don't hear about him any more.''

"What was his name?''

"Jake.''

There wasn't anything more said for a considerable while; the old lady was thinking. At last she says:

"The thing that is mostly worrying your aunt Sally is the tempers that that man Jubiter gets your uncle into.''

Tom was astonished, and so was I. Tom says:

"Tempers? Uncle Silas? Land, you must be joking! I didn't know he *had* any temper.''

"Works him up into perfect rages, your aunt Sally says; says he acts as if he would really hit the man, sometimes.''

"Aunt Polly, it beats anything I ever heard of. Why, he's just as gentle as mush.''

"Well, she's worried, anyway. Says your uncle Silas is like a changed man, on account of all this quarrelling. And the neighbors talk about it, and lay all the blame on your uncle, of course, because he's a preacher and hain't got any business to quarrel. Your aunt Sally says he hates to go into the pulpit he's so ashamed; and the people have begun to cool toward him, and he ain't popular now as he used to was.''

"Well, ain't it strange? Why, Aunt Polly, he was always so good and kind and moony and absent-minded and chuckle-headed and lovable— why, he was just an angel! What *can* be the matter of him, do you reckon?''

Chapter 2

WE HAD powerful good luck; because we got a chance in a stern-wheeler from away North which was bound for one of them bayous or one-horse rivers away down Louisiana way, and so we could go all the way down the Upper Mississippi and all the way down the Lower Mississippi to that farm in Arkansaw without having to change steamboats at St. Louis: not so very much short of a thousand miles at one pull.

A pretty lonesome boat; there warn't but few passengers, and all old folks, that set around, wide apart, dozing, and was very quiet. We was four days getting out of the "upper river," because we got aground so much. But it warn't dull—couldn't be for boys that was travelling, of course.

From the very start me and Tom allowed that there was somebody sick in the state-room next to ourn, because the meals was always toted in there by the waiters. By-and-by we asked about it—Tom did—and the waiter said it was a man, but he didn't look sick.

"Well, but *ain't* he sick?''

"I don't know; maybe he is, but 'pears to me he's just letting on.''

"What makes you think that?"

"Because if he was sick he would pull his clothes off *some* time or other—don't you reckon he would? Well, this one don't. At least he don't ever pull off his boots, anyway."

"The mischief he don't! Not even when he goes to bed?"

"No."

It was always nuts for Tom Sawyer—a mystery was. If you'd lay out a mystery and a pie before me and him, you wouldn't have to say take your choice; it was a thing that would regulate itself. Because in my nature I have always run to pie, whilst in his nature he has always run to mystery. People are made different. And it is the best way. Tom says to the waiter:

"What's the man's name?"

"Phillips."

"Where'd he come aboard?"

"I think he got aboard at Elexandria, up on the Iowa line."

"What do you reckon he's a-playing?"

"I hain't any notion—I never thought of it."

I says to myself, here's another one that runs to pie.

"Anything peculiar about him?—the way he acts or talks?"

"No—nothing, except he seems so scary, and keeps his doors locked night and day both, and when you knock he won't let you in till he opens the door a crack and sees who it is."

"By jimminy, it's int'resting! I'd like to get a look at him. Say—the next time you're going in there, don't you reckon you could spread the door and—"

"No indeedy! He's always behind it. He would block that game."

Tom studied over it, and then he says:

"Looky here. You lend me your apern and let me take him his breakfast in the morning. I'll give you a quarter."

The boy was plenty willing enough, if the head steward wouldn't mind. Tom says that's all right, he reckoned he could fix it with the head steward; and he done it. He fixed it so as we could both go in with aperns on and toting vittles.

He didn't sleep much, he was in such a sweat to get in there and find out the mystery about Phillips; and moreover he done a lot of guessing about it all night, which warn't no use, for if you are going to find out the facts of a thing, what's the sense in guessing out what ain't the facts and wasting ammunition? I didn't lose no sleep. I wouldn't give a dern to know what's the matter of Phillips, I says to myself.

Well, in the morning we put on the aperns and got a couple of trays of truck, and Tom he knocked on the door. The man opened it a crack, and then he let us in and shut it quick. By Jackson, when we got a sight of him, we 'most dropped the trays! and Tom says:

"Why, Jubiter Dunlap, where'd *you* come from?"

Well, the man was astonished, of course; and first off he looked like he didn't know whether to be scared, or glad, or both, or which, but finally he settled down to being glad; and then his color come back, though at first his face had turned pretty white. So we got to talking together while he et his breakfast. And he says:

"But I ain't Jubiter Dunlap. I'd just as soon tell you who I am, though, if you'll swear to keep mum, for I ain't no Phillips, either.''

Tom says:

"We'll keep mum, but there ain't any need to tell who you are if you ain't Jubiter Dunlap.''

"Why?''

"Because if you ain't him you're t'other twin, Jake. You're the spit'n image of Jubiter.''

"Well, I *am* Jake. But looky here, how do you come to know us Dunlaps?''

Tom told about the adventures we'd had down there at his uncle Silas's last summer, and when he see that there warn't anything about his folks— or him either, for that matter—that we didn't know, he opened out and talked perfectly free and candid. He never made any bones about his own case; said he'd been a hard lot, was a hard lot yet, and reckoned he'd *be* a hard lot plumb to the end. He said of course it was a dangerous life, and—

He give a kind of gasp, and set his head like a person that's listening. We didn't say anything, and so it was very still for a second or so, and there warn't no sounds but the screaking of the wood-work and the chug-chugging of the machinery down below.

Then we got him comfortable again, telling him about his people, and how Brace's wife had been dead three years, and Brace wanted to marry Benny and she shook him, and Jubiter was working for Uncle Silas, and him and Uncle Silas quarrelling all the time—and then he let go and laughed.

"Land!'' he says, "it's like old times to hear all this tittle-tattle, and does me good. It's been seven years and more since I heard any. How do they talk about me these days?''

"Who?''

"The farmers—and the family.''

"Why, they don't talk about you at all—at least only just a mention, once in a long time.''

"The nation!'' he says, surprised; "why is that?''

"Because they think you are dead long ago.''

"No! Are you speaking true?—honor bright, now.'' He jumped up, excited.

"Honor bright. There ain't anybody thinks you are alive.''

"Then I'm saved, I'm saved, sure! I'll go home. They'll hide me and save my life. You keep mum. Swear you'll keep mum—swear you'll never, never tell on me. Oh, boys, be good to a poor devil that's being hunted day and night, and dasn't show his face! I've never done you any harm; I'll never do you any, as God is in the heavens; swear you'll be good to me and help me save my life.''

We'd a swore it if he'd been a dog; and so we done it. Well, he couldn't love us enough for it or be grateful enough, poor cuss; it was all he could do to keep from hugging us.

We talked along, and he got out a little hand-bag and begun to open it, and told us to turn our backs. We done it, and when he told us to turn again he was perfectly different to what he was before. He had on blue goggles and the naturalest-looking long brown whiskers and mustaches

SWEAR YOU'LL BE GOOD TO ME AND HELP ME SAVE MY LIFE.

you ever see. His own mother wouldn't 'a' knowed him. He asked us if he looked like his brother Jubiter, now.

"No," Tom said; "there ain't anything left that's like him except the long hair."

"All right, I'll get that cropped close to my head before I get there; then him and Brace will keep my secret, and I'll live with them as being a stranger, and the neighbors won't ever guess me out. What do you think?"

Tom he studied a while, then he says:

"Well, of course me and Huck are going to keep mum there, but if you don't keep mum yourself there's going to be a little bit of a risk—it ain't much, maybe, but it's a little. I mean, if you talk, won't people notice that your voice is just like Jubiter's; and mightn't it make them think of the twin they reckoned was dead, but maybe after all was hid all this time under another name?"

"By George," he says, "you're a sharp one! You're perfectly right. I've got to play deef and dumb when there's a neighbor around. If I'd a struck for home and forgot that little detail— However, I wasn't striking for home. I was breaking for any place where I could get away from these fellows that are after me; then I was going to put on this disguise and get some different clothes, and—"

He jumped for the outside door and laid his ear against it and listened, pale and kind of panting. Presently he whispers:

"Sounded like cocking a gun! Lord, what a life to lead!"

Then he sunk down in a chair all limp and sick like, and wiped the sweat off his face.

Chapter 3

FROM THAT time out, we was with him 'most all the time, and one or t'other of us slept in his upper berth. He said he had been so lonesome,

SOUNDED LIKE COCKING A GUN!

and it was such a comfort to him to have company, and somebody to talk
to in his troubles. We was in a sweat to find out what his secret was, but
Tom said the best way was not to seem anxious, then likely he would drop
into it himself in one of his talks, but if we got to asking questions he
would get suspicious and shet up his shell. It turned out just so. It warn't
no trouble to see that he *wanted* to talk about it, but always along at first
he would scare away from it when he got on the very edge of it, and go to
talking about something else. The way it come about was this: He got to
asking us, kind of indifferent like, about the passengers down on deck.
We told him about them. But he warn't satisfied; we warn't particular
enough. He told us to describe them better. Tom done it. At last, when
Tom was describing one of the roughest and raggedest ones, he gave a
shiver and a gasp and says:

"Oh, lordy, that's one of them! They're aboard sure—I just knowed it.
I sort of hoped I had got away, but I never believed it. Go on."

Presently when Tom was describing another mangy, rough deck passenger, he give that shiver again and says—

"That's him!—that's the other one. If it would only come a good black
stormy night and I could get ashore. You see, they've got spies on me.
They've got a right to come up and buy drinks at the bar yonder forrard,
and they take that chance to bribe somebody to keep watch on me—porter
or boots or somebody. If I was to slip ashore without anybody seeing me,
they would know it inside of an hour."

So then he got to wandering along, and pretty soon, sure enough, he
was telling! He was poking along through his ups and downs, and when
he come to that place he went right along. He says:

"It was a confidence game. We played it on a julery-shop in St. Louis.
What we was after was a couple of noble big di'monds as big as a hazel-
nuts, which everybody was running to see. We was dressed up fine, and
we played it on them in broad daylight. We ordered the di'monds sent to
the hotel for us to see if we wanted to buy, and when we was examining
them we had paste counterfeits all ready, and *them* was the things that

went back to the shop when we said the water wasn't quite fine enough for twelve thousand dollars.''

"Twelve—thousand—dollars!" Tom says. "Was they really worth all that money, do you reckon?''

"Every cent of it.''

"And you fellows got away with them?''

"As easy as nothing. I don't reckon the julery people know they've been robbed yet. But it wouldn't be good sense to stay around St. Louis, of course, so we considered where we'd go. One was for going one way, one another, so we throwed up, heads or tails, and the Upper Mississippi won. We done up the di'monds in a paper and put our names on it and put it in the keep of the hotel clerk, and told him not to ever let either of us have it again without the others was on hand to see it done; then we went down town, each by his own self—because I reckon maybe we all had the same notion. I don't know for certain, but I reckon maybe we had.''

"What notion?" Tom says.

"To rob the others.''

"What—one take everything, after all of you had helped to get it?''

"Cert'nly.''

It disgusted Tom Sawyer, and he said it was the orneriest, low-downest thing he ever heard of. But Jake Dunlap said it warn't unusual in the profession. Said when a person was in that line of business he'd got to look out for his own intrust, there warn't nobody else going to do it for him. And then he went on. He says:

"You see, the trouble was, you couldn't divide up two di'monds amongst three. If there'd been three— But never mind about that, there *warn't* three. I loafed along the back streets studying and studying. And I says to myself, I'll hog them di'monds the first chance I get, and I'll have a disguise all ready, and I'll give the boys the slip, and when I'm safe away I'll put it on, and then let them find me if they can. So I got the false whiskers and the goggles and this countrified suit of clothes, and fetched them along back in a hand-bag; and when I was passing a shop where they sell all sorts of things, I got a glimpse of one of my pals through the window. It was Bud Dixon. I was glad, you bet. I says to myself, I'll see what he buys. So I kept shady, and watched. Now what do you reckon it was he bought?''

"Whiskers?" said I.

"No.''

"Goggles?''

"No.''

"Oh, keep still, Huck Finn, can't you, you're only just hendering all you can. What *was* it he bought, Jake?''

"You'd never guess in the world. It was only just a screw-driver—just a wee little bit of a screw-driver.''

"Well, I declare! What did he want with that?''

"That's what *I* thought. It was curious. It clean stumped me. I says to myself, what can he want with that thing? Well, when he come out I stood back out of sight, and then tracked him to a second-hand slop-shop and

see him buy a red flannel shirt and some old ragged clothes—just the ones
he's got on now, as you've described. Then I went down to the wharf and
hid my things aboard the up-river boat that we had picked out, and then
started back and had another streak of luck. I seen our other pal lay in *his*
stock of old rusty second-handers. We got the di'monds and went aboard
the boat.

"But now we was up a stump, for we couldn't go to bed. We had to set
up and watch one another. Pity, that was; pity to put that kind of a strain
on us, because there was bad blood between us from a couple of weeks
back, and we was only friends in the way of business. Bad anyway, seeing
there was only two di'monds betwixt three men. First we had supper, and
then tramped up and down the deck together smoking till most midnight;
then we went and set down in my state-room and locked the doors and
looked in the piece of paper to see if the di'monds was all right, then laid
it on the lower berth right in full sight; and there we set, and set, and by-
and-by it got to be dreadful hard to keep awake. At last Bud Dixon
dropped off. As soon as he was snoring a good regular gait that was likely
to last, and had his chin on his breast and looked permanent, Hal Clayton
nodded towards the di'monds and then towards the outside door, and I
understood. I reached and got the paper, and then we stood up and waited
perfectly still; Bud never stirred; I turned the key of the outside door very
soft and slow, then turned the knob the same way, and we went tiptoeing
out onto the guard, and shut the door very soft and gentle.

"There warn't nobody stirring anywhere, and the boat was slipping
along, swift and steady, through the big water in the smoky moonlight.
We never said a word, but went straight up onto the hurricane-deck and
plumb back aft, and set down on the end of the skylight. Both of us
knowed what that meant, without having to explain to one another. Bud
Dixon would wake up and miss the swag, and would come straight for us,
for he ain't afeard of anything or anybody, that man ain't. He would come,
and we would heave him overboard, or get killed trying. It made me
shiver, because I ain't as brave as some people, but if I showed the white
feather—well, I knowed better than do that. I kind of hoped the boat

WE STOOD UP AND WAITED, PERFECTLY STILL.

would land somers, and we could skip ashore and not have to run the risk of this row, I was scared of Bud Dixon, but she was an upper-river tub and there warn't no real chance of that.

"Well, the time strung along and along, and that fellow never come! Why, it strung along till dawn begun to break, and still he never come. 'Thunder,' I says, 'what do you make out of this?—ain't it suspicious?' 'Land!' Hal says, 'do you reckon he's playing us?—open the paper!' I done it, and by gracious there warn't anything in it but a couple of little pieces of loaf-sugar! *That's* the reason he could set there and snooze all night so comfortable. Smart? Well, I reckon! He had had them two papers all fixed and ready, and he had put one of them in place of t'other right under our noses.

"We felt pretty cheap. But the thing to do, straight off, was to make a plan; and we done it. We would do up the paper again, just as it was, and slip in, very elaborate and soft, and lay it on the bunk again, and let on *we* didn't know about any trick, and hadn't any idea he was a-laughing at us behind them bogus snores of his'n; and we would stick by him, and the first night we was ashore we would get him drunk and search him, and get the di'monds; and *do* for him, too, if it warn't too risky. If we got the swag, we'd *got* to do for him, or he would hunt us down and do for us, sure. But I didn't have no real hope. I knowed we could get him drunk—he was always ready for that—but what's the good of it? You might search him a year and never find—

"Well, right there I catched my breath and broke off my thought! For an idea went ripping through my head that tore my brains to rags—and land, but I felt gay and good! You see, I had had my boots off, to unswell my feet, and just them I took up one of them to put it on, and I catched a glimpse of the heel-bottom, and it just took my breath away. You remember about that puzzlesome little screw-driver?"

"You bet I do," says Tom, all excited.

"Well, when I catched that glimpse of that boot heel, the idea that went smashing through my head was, *I* know where he's hid the di'monds! You look at this boot heel, now. See, it's bottomed with a steel plate, and the plate is fastened on with little screws. Now there wasn't a screw about that feller anywhere but in his boot heels; so, if he needed a screw-driver, I reckoned I knowed why."

"Huck, ain't it bully!" says Tom.

"Well, I got my boots on, and we went down and slipped in and laid the paper of sugar on the berth, and sat down soft and sheepish and went to listening to Bud Dixon snore. Hal Clayton dropped off pretty soon, but I didn't; I wasn't ever so wide-awake in my life. I was spying out from under the shade of my hat brim, searching the floor for leather. It took me a long time, and I begun to think maybe my guess was wrong, but at last I struck it. It laid over by the bulkhead, and was nearly the color of the carpet. It was a little round plug about as thick as the end of your little finger, and I says to myself there's a di'mond in the nest you've come from. Before long I spied out the plug's mate.

"Think of the smartness and coolness of that blatherskite! He put up that scheme on us and reasoned out what we would do, and we went ahead and done it perfectly exact, like a couple of pudd'n heads. He set there

and took his own time to unscrew his heel-plates and cut out his plugs
and stick in the di'monds and screw on his plates again. He allowed we
would steal the bogus swag and wait all night for him to come up and
get drownded, and by George it's just what we done! *I* think it was powerful smart.''

"You bet your life it was!'' says Tom, just full of admiration.

Chapter 4

"WELL, ALL day we went throught the humbug of watching one another,
and it was pretty sickly business for two of us and hard to act out, I can
tell you. About night we landed at one of them little Missouri towns high
up toward Iowa, and had supper at the tavern, and got a room upstairs
with a cot and a double bed in it, but I dumped my bag under a deal table
in the dark hall whilst we was moving along it to bed, single file, me last,
and the landlord in the lead with a tallow candle. We had up a lot of
whiskey, and went to playing high-low-jack for dimes, and as soon as the
whiskey begun to take hold of Bud we stopped drinking, but we didn't let
him stop. We loaded him till he fell out of his chair and laid there snoring.

"We was ready for business now. I said we better pull our boots off,
and his'n too, and not make any noise, then we could pull him and haul
him around and ransack him without any trouble. So we done it. I set my
boots and Bud's side by side, where they'd be handy. Then we stripped
him and searched his seams and his pockets and his socks and the inside
of his boots, and everything, and searched his bundle. Never found any
di'monds. We found the screw-driver, and Hal says, 'What do you reckon
he wanted with that?' I said I didn't know; but when he wasn't looking I
hooked it. At last Hal he looked beat and discouraged, and said we'd got
to give it up. That was what I was waiting for. I says:

" 'There's one place we hain't searched.'

SEARCHED HIS SEAMS AND HIS POCKETS AND HIS SOCKS.

" 'What place is that?' he says.

" 'His stomach.'

" 'By gracious, I never thought of that! *Now* we're on the homestretch, to a dead moral certainty. How'll we manage?'

" 'Well,' I says, 'just stay by him till I turn out and hunt up a drug-store, and I reckon I'll fetch something that'll make them di'monds tired of the company they're keeping.'

"He said that's the ticket, and with him looking straight at me I slid myself into Bud's boots instead of my own, and he never noticed. They was just a shade large for me, but that was considerable better than being too small. I got my bag as I went a-groping through the hall, and in about a minute I was out the back way and stretching up the river road at a five-mile gait.

"And not feeling so very bad, neither—walking on di'monds don't have no such effect. When I had gone fifteen minutes I says to myself, there's more'n a mile behind me, and everything quiet. Another five minutes and I says there's considerable more land behind me now, and there's a man back there that's begun to wonder what's the trouble. An-other five and I says to myself he's getting real uneasy—he's walking the floor now. Another five, and I says to myself, there's two miles and a half behind me, and he's *awful* uneasy—beginning to cuss, I reckon. Pretty soon I says to myself, forty minutes gone—he *knows* there's something up! Fifty minutes—the truth's a-busting on him now! he is reckoning I found the di'monds whilst we was searching, and shoved them in my pocket and never let on—yes, and he's starting out to hunt for me. He'll hunt for new tracks in the dust, and they'll as likely send him down the river as up.

"Just then I see a man coming down on a mule, and before I thought I jumped into the bush. It was stupid! When he got abreast he stopped and waited a little for me to come out; then he rode on again. But I didn't feel gay any more. I says to myself I've botched my chances by that; I surely have, if he meets up with Hal Clayton.

"Well, about three in the morning I fetched Elexandria and see this

WALKED ASHORE.

stern-wheeler laying there, and was very glad, because I felt perfectly safe, now, you know. It was just daybreak. I went aboard and got this state-room and put on these clothes and went up in the pilot-house—to watch, though I didn't reckon there was any need of it. I set there and played with my di'monds and waited and waited for the boat to start, but she didn't. You see, they was mending her machinery, but I didn't know anything about it, not being very much used to steamboats.

"Well, to cut the tale short, we never left there till plumb noon; and long before that I was hid in this state-room; for before breakfast I see a man coming, away off, that had a gait like Hal Clayton's, and it made me just sick. I says to myself, if he finds out I'm aboard this boat, he's got me like a rat in a trap. All he's got to do is to have me watched, and wait—wait till I slip ashore, thinking he is a thousand miles away, then slip after me and dog me to a good place and make me give up the di'monds, and then he'll—oh, *I* know what he'll do! Ain't it awful— awful! And now to think the *other* one's aboard, too! Oh, ain't it hard luck, boys—ain't it hard! But you'll help save me, *won't* you?—oh, boys, be good to a poor devil that's being hunted to death, and save me—I'll worship the very ground you walk on!"

We turned in and soothed him down and told him we would plan for him and help him, and he needn't be so afeard; and so by-and-by he got to feeling kind of comfortable again, and unscrewed his heel-plates and held up his di'monds this way and that, admiring them and loving them; and when the light struck into them they *was* beautiful, sure; why, they seemed to kind of bust, and snap fire out all around. But all the same I judged he was a fool. If I had been him I would a handed the di'monds to them pals and got them to go ashore and leave me alone. But he was made different. He said it was a whole fortune and he couldn't bear the idea.

Twice we stopped to fix the machinery and laid a good while, once in the night; but it wasn't dark enough, and he was afeard to skip. But the third time we had to fix it there was a better chance. We laid up at a country woodyard about forty mile above Uncle Silas's place a little after one at night, and it was thickening up and going to storm. So Jake he laid for a chance to slide. We begun to take in wood. Pretty soon the rain come a-drenching down, and the wind blowed hard. Of course every boat-hand fixed a gunny sack and put it on like a bonnet, the way they do when they are toting wood, and we got one for Jake, and he slipped down aft with his hand-bag and come tramping forrard just like the rest, and walked ashore with them, and when we see him pass out of the light of the torch-basket and get swallowed up in the dark, we got our breath again and just felt grateful and splendid. But it wasn't for long. Somebody told, I reckon; for in about eight or ten minutes them two pals come tearing forrard as tight as they could jump and darted ashore and was gone. We waited plumb till dawn for them to come back, and kept hoping they would, but they never did. We was awful sorry and low-spirited. All the hope we had was that Jake had got such a start that they couldn't get on his track, and he would get to his brother's and hide there and be safe.

He was going to take the river road, and told us to find out if Brace and Jubiter was to home and no strangers there, and then slip out about sun-down and tell him. Said he would wait for us in a little bunch of sycamores right back of Tom's uncle Silas's tobacker-field on the river road, a lonesome place.

We set and talked a long time about his chances, and Tom said he was all right if the pals struck up the river instead of down, but it wasn't likely, because maybe they knowed where he was from; more likely they would go right, and dog him all day, him not suspecting, and kill him when it come dark, and take the boots. So we was pretty sorrowful.

Chapter 5

WE DIDN'T get done tinkering the machinery till away late in the afternoon, and so it was so close to sundown when we got home that we never stopped on our road, but made a break for the sycamores as tight as we could go, to tell Jake what the delay was, and have him wait till we could go to Brace's and find out how things was there. It was getting pretty dim by the time we turned the corner of the woods, sweating and panting with that long run, and see the sycamores thirty yards ahead of us; and just then we see a couple of men run into the bunch and heard two or three terrible screams for help. "Poor Jake is killed, sure," we says. We was scared through and through, and broke for the tobacker-field and hid there, trembling so our clothes would hardly stay on; and just as we skipped in there, a couple of men went tearing by, and into the bunch they went, and in a second out jumps four men and took out up the road as tight as they could go, two chasing two.

We laid down, kind of weak and sick, and listened for more sounds, but didn't hear none for a good while but just our hearts. We was thinking of that awful thing laying yonder in the sycamores, and it seemed like being that close to a ghost, and it give me the cold shudders. The moon come a-swelling up out of the ground, now, powerful big and round and bright, behind a comb of trees, like a face looking through prison bars, and the black shadders and white places begun to creep around, and it was miserable quiet and still and night-breezy and graveyardy and scary. All of a sudden Tom whispers:

"Look!—what's that?"

"Don't!" I says. "Don't take a person by surprise that way. I'm 'most ready to die, anyway, without you doing that."

"Look, I tell you. It's something coming out of the sycamores."

"Don't, Tom!"

"It's terrible tall!"

"Oh, lordy-lordy! let's—"

"Keep still—it's a-coming this way."

He was so excited he could hardly get breath enough to whisper. I had to look. I couldn't help it. So now we was both on our knees with our chins on a fence-rail and gazing—yes, and gasping, too. It was coming down the road—coming in the shadder of the trees, and you couldn't see it good; not till it was pretty close to us; then it stepped into a bright splotch of moonlight and we sunk right down in our tracks—it was Jake

Dunlap's ghost! That was what we said to ourselves.

We couldn't stir for a minute or two; then it was gone. We talked about it in low voices. Tom says:

"They're mostly dim and smoky, or like they're made out of fog, but this one wasn't."

"No," I says; "I seen the goggles and the whiskers perfectly plain."

"Yes, and the very colors in them loud countrified Sunday clothes—plaid breeches, green and black—"

"Cotton-velvet westcot, fire-red and yaller squares—"

"Leather straps to the bottoms of the breeches legs and one of them hanging unbuttoned—"

"Yes, and that hat—"

"What a hat for a ghost to wear!"

You see it was the first season anybody wore that kind—a black stiff-brim stove-pipe, very high, and not smooth, with a round top—just like a sugar-loaf.

"Did you notice if its hair was the same, Huck?"

"No—seems to me I did, then again it seems to me I didn't."

"I didn't either; but it had its bag along, I noticed that."

"So did I. How can there be a ghost-bag, Tom?"

"Sho! I wouldn't be as ignorant as that if I was you, Huck Finn. Whatever a ghost has, turns to ghost-stuff. They've got to have their things, like anybody else. You see, yourself, that its clothes was turned to ghost-stuff. Well, then, what's to hender its bag from turning, too? Of course it done it."

That was reasonable. I couldn't find no fault with it. Bill Withers and his brother Jack come along by, talking, and Jack says:

"What do you recon he was toting?"

"I dunno; but it was pretty heavy."

"Yes, all he could lug. Nigger stealing corn from old Parson Silas, I judged."

"So did I. And so I allowed I wouldn't let on to see him."

"That's me, too."

IT WAS JAKE DUNLOP'S GHOST.

Then they both laughed, and went on out of hearing. It showed how unpopular old Uncle Silas had got to be, now. They wouldn't 'a' let a nigger steal anybody else's corn and never done anything to him.

We heard some more voices mumbling along towards us and getting louder, and sometimes a cackle of a laugh. It was Lem Beebe and Jim Lane. Jim Lane says:

"Who?—Jubiter Dunlap?"

"Yes."

"Oh, I don't know. I reckon so. I seen him spading up some ground along about an hour ago, just before sundown—him and the parson. Said he guessed he wouldn't go to-night, but we could have his dog if we wanted him."

"Too tired, I reckon."

"Yes—works so hard!"

"Oh, you bet!"

They cackled at that, and went on by. Tom said we better jump out and tag along after them, because they was going our way and it wouldn't be comfortable to run across the ghost all by ourselves. So we done it, and got home all right.

That night was the second of September—a Saturday. I sha'n't ever forget it. You'll see why, pretty soon.

Chapter 6

WE TRAMPED along behind Jim and Lem till we come to the back stile where old Jim's cabin was that he was captivated in, the time we set him free, and here come the dogs piling around us to say howdy, and there was the lights of the house, too; so we warn't afeard any more, and was going to climb over, but Tom says:

"Hold on; set down here a minute. By George!"

"What's the matter?" says I.

"Matter enough!" he says. "Wasn't you expecting we would be the first to tell the family who it is that's been killed yonder in the sycamores, and all about them rapscallions that done it, and about the di'monds they've smouched off of the corpse, and paint it up fine, and have the glory of being the ones that knows a lot more about it than anybody else?"

"Why, of course. It wouldn't be you, Tom Sawyer, if you was to let such a chance go by. I recon it ain't going to suffer none for lack of paint," I says, "when you start in to scollop the facts."

"Well, now," he says, perfectly ca'm, "what would you say if I was to tell you I ain't going to start in at all?"

I was astonished to hear him talk so. I says:

"I'd say it's a lie. You ain't in earnest, Tom Sawyer."

"You'll soon see. Was the ghost barefooted?"

"No, it wasn't. What of it?"

"You wait—I'll show you what. Did it have its boots on?"

"Yes. I seen them plain."

WAS THE GHOST BAREFOOTED?

"Swear it?"

"Yes, I swear it."

"So do I. Now do you know what that means?"

"No. What does it mean?"

"Means that them thieves *didn't get the di'monds.*"

"Jimminy! What makes you think that?"

"I don't only think it, I know it. Didn't the breeches and goggles and whiskers and hand-bag and every blessed thing turn to ghost-stuff? Everything it had on turned, didn't it? It shows that the reason its boots turned too was because it still had them on after it started to go ha'nting around, and if that ain't proof that them blatherskites didn't get the boots, I'd like to know what you'd *call* proof."

Think of that now. I never see such a head as that boy had. Why, *I* had eyes and could see things, but they never meant nothing to me. But Tom Sawyer was different. When Tom Sawyer seen a thing it just got up on its hind legs and *talked* to him—told him everything it knowed. I never see such a head.

"Tom Sawyer," I says, "I'll say it again as I've said it a many a time before: I ain't fitten to black your boots. But that's all right—that's neither here nor there. God Almighty made us all, and some He gives eyes that's blind, and some He gives eyes that can see, and I reckon it ain't none of our lookout what He done it for; it's all right, or He'd 'a' fixed it some other way. Go on—I see plenty plain enough, now, that them thieves didn't get way with the di'monds. Why didn't they, do you reckon?"

"Because they got chased away by them other two men before they could pull the boots off of the corpse."

"That's so! I see it now. But looky here, Tom, why ain't we to go and tell about it?"

"Oh, shucks, Huck Finn, can't you see? Look at it. What's a-going to happen? There's going to be an inquest in the morning. Them two men will tell how they heard the yells and rushed there just in time to not save the stranger. Then the jury'll twaddle and twaddle and twaddle, and finally they'll fetch in a verdict that he got shot or stuck or busted over the head with something, and come to his death by the inspiration of God. And after they've buried him they'll auction off his things for to pay the expenses, and then's *our* chance."

"How, Tom?"

"Buy the boots for two dollars!"

Well, it 'most took my breath.

"My land! Why, Tom, *we'll* get the di'monds!"

"You bet. Some day they'll be a big reward offered for them—a thousand dollars, sure. That's our money! Now we'll trot in and see the folks. And mind you we don't know anything about any murder, or any di'monds, or any thieves—don't you forget that."

I had to sigh a little over the way he had got it fixed. *I'd* 'a' *sold* them di'monds—yes, sir—for twelve thousand dollars; but I didn't say anything. It wouldn't done any good. I says:

"But what are we going to tell your aunt Sally has made us so long getting down here from the village, Tom?"

"Oh, I'll leave that to you," he says. "I reckon you can explain it somehow."

He was always just that strict and delicate. He never would tell a lie himself.

We struck across the big yard, noticing this, that, and t'other thing that was so familiar, and we so glad to see it again, and when we got to the roofed big passageway betwixt the double log house and the kitchen part, there was everything hanging on the wall just as it used to was, even to Uncle Silas's old faded green baize working-gown with the hood to it, and raggedy white patch between the shoulders that always looked like somebody had hit him with a snowball; and then we lifted the latch and walked in. Aunt Sally she was just a-ripping and a-tearing around, and the children was huddled in one corner, and the old man he was huddled in the other and praying for help in time of need. She jumped for us with joy and tears running down her face and give us a whacking box on the ear, and then hugged us and kissed us and boxed us again, and just couldn't seem to get enough of it, she was so glad to see us; and she says:

"Where *have* you been a-loafing to, you good-for-nothing trash! I've been that worried about you I didn't know what to do. Your traps has been here *ever* so long, and I've had supper cooked fresh about four times so as to have it hot and good when you come, till at last my patience is just plumb wore out, and I declare I—I—why I could skin you alive! You must be starving, poor things!—set down, set down, everybody; don't lose no more time."

It was good to be there again behind all that noble cornpone and spareribs, and everything that you could ever want in this world. Old Uncle Silas he peeled off one of his bulliest old-time blessings, with as many layers to it as an onion, and whilst the angels was hauling in the slack of it I was trying to study up what to say about what kept us so long. When our plates was all loadened and we'd got a-going, she asked me, and I says:

"Well, you see,—er—Mizzes—"

"Huck Finn! Since when am I Mizzes to you? Have I ever been stingy of cuffs or kisses for you since the day you stood in this room and I took you for Tom Sawyer and blessed God for sending you to me, though you told me four thousand lies and I believed every one of them like a simpleton? Call me Aunt Sally—like you always done.''

So I done it. And I says:

"Well, me and Tom allowed we would come along afoot and take a smell of the woods, and we run across Lem Beebe and Jim Lane, and they asked us to go with them blackberrying to-night, and said they could borrow Jubiter Dunlap's dog, because he had told them just that minute—''

"Where did they see him?'' says the old man; and when I looked up to see how *he* come to take an intrust in a little thing like that, his eyes was just burning into me, he was that eager. It surprised me so it kind of throwed me off, but I pulled myself together again and says:

"It was when he was spading up some ground along with you, towards sundown or along there.''

He only said, "Um,'' in a kind of a disappointed way, and didn't take no more intrust. So I went on. I says:

"Well, then, as I was a-saying—''

"That'll do, you needn't go no furder.'' It was Aunt Sally. She was boring right into me with her eyes, and very indignant. "Huck Finn,'' she says, "how'd them men come to talk about going a-blackberrying in September—in *this* region?''

I see I had slipped up, and I couldn't say a word. She waited, still a-gazing at me, then she says:

"And how'd they come to strike that idiot idea of going a-blackberrying in the night?''

"Well, m'm, they—er—they told us they had a lantern, and—''

"Oh, *shet* up—do! Looky here; what was they going to do with a dog?—hunt blackberries with it?''

"I think, m'm, they—''

"Now, Tom Sawyer, what kind of a lie are you fixing *your* mouth to contribit to this mess of rubbage? Speak out—and I warn you before you begin, that I don't believe a word of it. You and Huck's been up to something you no business to—*I* know it perfectly well; *I* know you, *both* of you. Now you explain that dog, and them blackberries, and the lantern, and the rest of that rot—and mind you talk as straight as a string—do you hear?''

Tom he looked considerable hurt, and says, very dignified:

"It is a pity if Huck is to be talked to that away, just for making a little bit of a mistake that anybody could make.''

"What mistake has he made?''

"Why, only the mistake of saying blackberries when of course he meant strawberries.''

"Tom Sawyer, I lay if you aggravate me a little more, I'll—''

"Aunt Sally, without knowing it—and of course without intending it— you are in the wrong. If you'd 'a' studied natural history the way you ought, you would know that all over the world except just here in Arkansaw they *always* hunt strawberries with a dog—and a lantern—''

But she busted in on him there and just piled into him and snowed him under. She was so mad she couldn't get the words out fast enough, and she gushed them out in one everlasting freshet. That was what Tom Sawyer was after. He allowed to work her up and get her started and then leave her alone and let her burn herself out. Then she would be so aggravated with that subject that she wouldn't say another word about it, nor let anybody else. Well, it happened just so. When she was tuckered out and had to hold up, he says, quite ca'm:

"And yet, all the same, Aunt Sally—"

"Shet up!" she says, "I don't want to hear another word out of you."

So we was perfectly safe, then, and didn't have no more trouble about that delay. Tom done it elegant.

Chapter 7

BENNY SHE was looking pretty sober, and she sighed some, now and then; but pretty soon she got to asking about Mary, and Sid, and Tom's aunt Polly, and then Aunt Sally's clouds cleared off and she got in a good humor and joined in on the questions and was her lovingest best self, and so the rest of the supper went along gay and pleasant. But the old man he didn't take any hand hardly, and was absent-minded and restless, and done a considerable amount of sighing; and it was kind of heart-breaking to see him so sad and troubled and worried.

By-and-by, a spell after supper, come a nigger and knocked on the door and put his head in with his old straw hat in his hand bowing and scraping, and said his Marse Brace was out at the stile and wanted his brother, and was getting tired waiting supper for him, and would Marse Silas please tell him where he was? I never see Uncle Silas speak up so sharp and fractious before. He says:

"Am *I* his brother's keeper?" And then he kind of wilted together, and looked like he wished he hadn't spoken so, and then he says, very gentle: "But you needn't say that, Billy; I was took sudden and irritable, and I ain't very well these days, and not hardly responsible. Tell him he ain't here."

And when the nigger was gone he got up and walked the floor, backwards and forwards, mumbling and muttering to himself and ploughing his hands through his hair. It was real pitiful to see him. Aunt Sally she whispered to us and told us not to take notice of him, it embarrassed him. She said he was always thinking and thinking, since these troubles come on, and she allowed he didn't more'n about half know what he was about when the thinking spells was on him; and she said he walked in his sleep considerable more now than he used to, and sometimes wandered around over the house and even outdoors in his sleep, and if we catched him at it we must let him alone and not disturb him. She said she reckoned it didn't do him no harm, and may be it done him good. She said Benny was the only one that was much help to him these days. Said Benny appeared to know just when to try to soothe him and when to leave him alone.

So he kept on tramping up and down the floor and muttering, till by-and-by he begun to look pretty tired; then Benny she went and snuggled up to his side and put one hand in his and one arm around his waist and walked with him; and he smiled down on her, and reached down and kissed her; and so, little by little the trouble went out of his face and she persuaded him off to his room. They had very petting ways together, and it was uncommon pretty to see.

Aunt Sally she was busy getting the children ready for bed; so by-and-by it got dull and tedious, and me and Tom took a turn in the moonlight, and fetched up in the watermelon-patch and et one, and had a good deal of talk. And Tom said he'd bet the quarrelling was all Jubiter's fault, and he was going to be on hand the first time he got a chance, and see; and if it was so, he was going to do his level best to get Uncle Silas to turn him off.

And so we talked and smoked and stuffed watermelon as much as two hours, and then it was pretty late, and when we got back the house was quiet and dark, and everybody gone to bed.

Tom he always seen everything, and now he see that the old green baize work-gown was gone, and said it wasn't gone when he went out; and so we allowed it was curious, and then we went up to bed.

We could hear Benny stirring around in her room, which was next to ourn, and judged she was worried a good deal about her father and couldn't sleep. We found we couldn't, neither. So we set up a long time, and smoked and talked in a low voice, and felt pretty dull and down-hearted. We talked the murder and the ghost over and over again, and got so creepy and crawly we couldn't get sleepy nohow and noway.

By-and-by, when it was away late in the night and all the sounds was late sounds and solemn, Tom nudged me and whispers to me to look, and I done it, and there we see a man poking around in the yard like he didn't know just what he wanted to do, but it was pretty dim and we couldn't see him good. Then he started for the stile, and as he went over it the moon came out strong, and he had a long-handled shovel over his shoulder and we see the white patch on the old work-gown. So Tom says:

"He's a-walking in his sleep. I wish we was allowed to follow him and

SMOKED AND STUFFED WATERMELON.

see where he's going to. There, he's turned down by the tobacker-field. Out of sight now. It's a dreadful pity he can't rest no better.''

We waited a long time, but he didn't come back any more, or if he did he come around the other way; so at last we was tuckered out and went to sleep and had nightmares, a million of them. But before dawn we was awake again, because meantime a storm had come up and been raging, and the thunder and lightning was awful, and the wind was a-thrashing the trees around, and the rain was driving down in slanting sheets, and the gullies was running rivers. Tom says:

"Looky here, Huck, I'll tell you one thing that's mighty curious. Up to the time we went out, last night, the family hadn't heard about Jake Dunlap being murdered. Now the men that chased Hal Clayton and Bud Dixon away would spread the thing around in a half an hour, and every neighbor that heard it would shin out and fly around from one farm to t'other and try to be the first to tell the news. Land, they don't have such a big thing as that to tell twice in thirty year! Huck, it's mighty strange; I don't understand it.''

So then he was in a fidget for the rain to let up, so we could turn out and run across some of the people and see if they would say anything about it to us. And he said if they did we must be horribly surprised and shocked.

We was out and gone the minute the rain stopped. It was just broad day, then. We loafed along up the road, and now and then met a person and stopped and said howdy, and told them when we come, and how we left the folks at home, and how long we was going to stay, and all that, but none of them said a word about that thing; which was just astonishing, and no mistake. Tom said he believed if we went to the sycamores we would find that body laying there solitary and alone, and not a soul around. Said he believed the men chased the thieves so far into the woods that the thieves prob'ly seen a good chance and turned on them at last, and maybe they all killed each other, and so there wasn't anybody left to tell.

First we knowed, gabbling along that away, we was right at the sycamores. The cold chills trickled down my back and I wouldn't budge another step, for all Tom's persuading. But he couldn't hold in; he'd *got* to see if the boots was safe on that body yet. So he crope in—and the next minute out he come again with his eyes bulging he was so excited, and says:

"Huck, it's gone!''

I *was* astonished! I says:

"Tom, you don't mean it.''

"It's gone, sure. There ain't a sign of it. The ground is trampled some, but if there was any blood it's all washed away by the storm, for it's all puddles and slush in there.''

At last I give in, and went and took a look myself; and it was just as Tom said—there wasn't a sign of a corpse.

"Dern it,'' I says, "the di'monds is gone. Don't you reckon the thieves slunk back and lugged him off, Tom?''

"Looks like it. It just does. Now where'd they hide him, do you reckon?''

HUCK, IT'S GONE!

"I don't know," I says, disgusted, "and what's more I don't care. They've got the boots, and that's all *I* cared about. He'll lay around these woods a long time before *I* hunt him up."

Tom didn't feel no more intrust in him neither, only curiosity to know what come of him; but he said we'd lay low and keep dark and it wouldn't be long till the dogs or somebody rousted him out.

We went back home to breakfast ever so bothered and put out and disappointed and swindled. I warn't ever so down on a corpse before.

Chapter 8

IT WARN'T very cheerful at breakfast. Aunt Sally she looked old and tired and let the children snarl and fuss at one another and didn't seem to notice it was going on, which wasn't her usual style; me and Tom had a plenty to think about without talking; Benny she looked like she hadn't had much sleep, and whenever she'd lift her head a little and steal a look towards her father you could see there was tears in her eyes; and as for the old man, his things stayed on his plate and got cold without him knowing they was there, I reckon, for he was thinking and thinking all the time, and never said a word and never et a bite.

By-and-by when it was stillest, that nigger's head was poked in at the door again, and he said his Marse Brace was getting powerful uneasy about Marse Jubiter, which hadn't come home yet, and would Marse Silas please—

He was looking at Uncle Silas, and he stopped there, like the rest of his words was froze; for Uncle Silas he rose up shaky and steadied himself leaning his fingers on the table, and he was panting, and his eyes was set on the nigger, and he kept swallowing, and put his other hand up to his throat a couple of times, and at last he got his words started, and says:

"Does he—does he—think—*what* does he think! Tell him—tell

him—" Then he sunk down in his chair limp and weak, and says, so as you could hardly hear him: "Go away—go away!"

The nigger looked scared, and cleared out, and we all felt—well, I don't know how we felt, but it was awful, with the old man panting there, and his eyes set and looking like a person that was dying. None of us could budge; but Benny she slid around soft, with her tears running down, and stood by his side, and nestled his old gray head up against her and begun to stroke it and pet it with her hands, and nodded to us to go away, and we done it, going out very quiet, like the dead was there.

Me and Tom struck out for the woods mighty solemn, and saying how different it was now to what it was last summer when we was here and everything was so peaceful and happy and everybody thought so much of Uncle Silas, and he was so cheerful and simple-hearted and pudd'n-headed and good—and now look at him. If he hadn't lost his mind he wasn't much short of it. That was what we allowed.

It was a most lovely day, now, and bright and sunshiny; and the further and further we went over the hill towards the prairie the lovelier and lovelier the trees and flowers got to be and the more it seemed strange and somehow wrong that there had to be trouble in such a world as this. And then all of a sudden I catched my breath and grabbed Tom's arm, and all my livers and lungs and things fell down into my legs.

"There it is!" I says. We jumped back behind a bush, shivering, and Tom says:

" 'Sh!—don't make a noise."

It was setting on a log right in the edge of the little prairie, thinking. I tried to get Tom to come away, but he wouldn't and I dasn't budge by myself. He said we mightn't ever get another chance to see one, and he was going to look his fill at this one if he died for it. So I looked too, though it give me the fan-tods to do it. Tom he *had* to talk, but he talked low. He says:

"Poor Jakey, it's got all its things on, just as he said he would. *Now* you see what we wasn't certain about—its hair. It's not long, now, the way it was; it's got it cropped close to its head, the way he said he would.

WHAT DOES HE THINK?

Huck, I never see anything look any more naturaler than what It does."

"Nor I neither," I says; "I'd recognize it anywheres."

"So would I. It looks perfectly solid and genuwyne, just the way it done before it died."

So we kept a-gazing. Pretty soon Tom says:

"Huck, there's something mighty curious about this one, don't you know? *It* oughtn't to be going around in the daytime."

"That's so, Tom—I never heard the like of it before."

"No, sir, they don't ever come out only at night—and then not till after twelve. There's something wrong about this one, now you mark my words. I don't believe it's got any right to be around in the daytime. But don't it look natural! Jake was going to play deef and dumb here, so the neighbors wouldn't know his voice. Do you reckon it would do that if we was to holler at it?"

"Lordy, Tom, don't talk so! If you was to holler at it I'd die in my tracks."

"Don't you worry, I ain't going to holler at it. Look, Huck, it's a-scratching its head—don't you see?"

"Well, what of it?"

"Why, this. What's the sense of it scratching its head? There ain't anything there to itch; its head is made out of fog or something like that, and *can't* itch. A fog can't itch; any fool knows that."

"Well, then, if it don't itch and can't itch, what in the nation is it scratching it for? Ain't it just habit, don't you reckon?"

"No, sir, I don't. I ain't a bit satisfied about the way this one acts. I've a blame good notion it's a bogus one—I have, as sure as I'm a-sitting here. Because, if it—Huck!"

"Well, what's the matter now?"

"You can't see the bushes through it!"

"Why, Tom, it's so, sure! It's as solid as a cow. I sort of begin to think—"

"Huck, it's biting off a chaw of tobacker! By George, *they* don't chaw—they hain't got anything to chaw *with*. Huck!"

"I'm a-listening."

"It ain't a ghost at all. It's Jake Dunlap his own self!"

"Oh, your granny!" I says.

"Huck Finn, did we find any corpse in the sycamores?"

"No."

"Or any sign of one?"

"No."

"Mighty good reason. Hadn't ever been any corpse there."

"Why, Tom, you know we heard—"

"Yes, we did—heard a howl or two. Does that prove anybody was killed? Course it don't. And we seen four men run, then this one come walking out and we took it for a ghost. No more ghost than you are. It was Jake Dunlap his own self, and it's Jake Dunlap now. He's been and got his hair cropped, the way he said he would, and he's playing himself for a stranger, just the same as he said he would. Ghost? Hum!—he's as sound as a nut."

Then I see it all, and how we had took too much for granted. I was powerful glad he didn't get killed, and so was Tom, and we wondered which he would like the best—for us to never let on to know him, or how? Tom reckoned the best way would be to go and ask him. So he started; but I kept a little behind, because I didn't know but it might be a ghost, after all. When Tom got to where he was, he says:

"Me and Huck's mighty glad to see you again, and you needn't be afeard we'll tell. And if you think it'll be safer for you if we don't let on to know you when we run across you, say the word and you'll see you can depend on us, and would ruther cut our hands off than get you into the least little bit of danger."

First off he looked surprised to see us, and not very glad, either; but as Tom went on he looked pleasanter, and when he was done he smiled, and nodded his head several times, and made signs with his hands, and says:

"Goo-goo—goo-goo," the way deef and dummies does.

Just then we see some of Steve Nickerson's people coming that lived t'other side of the prairie, so Tom says:

"You do it elegant; I never see anybody do it better. You're right; play it on us, too; play it on us same as the others; it'll keep you in practice and prevent you making blunders. We'll keep away from you and let on we don't know you, but any time we can be any help, you just let us know."

Then we loafed along past the Nickersons, and of course they asked if that was the new stranger yonder, and where'd he come from, and what was his name, and which communion was he, Babtis' or Methodis', and which politics, Whig or Democrat, and how long is he staying, and all them other questions that humans always asks when a stranger comes, and animals does too. But Tom said he warn't able to make anything out of deef and dumb signs, and the same with goo-gooing. Then we watched them go and bullyrag Jake; because we was pretty uneasy for him. Tom said it would take him days to get so he wouldn't forget he was a deef and dummy sometimes, and speak out before he thought. When we had watched

GOO-GOO—GOO-GOO.

long enough to see that Jake was getting along all right and working his signs very good, we loafed along again, allowing to strike the school-house about recess time, which was a three-mile tramp.

I was so disappointed not to hear Jake tell about the row in the syca-mores, and how near he come to getting killed, that I couldn't seem to get over it, and Tom he felt the same, but said if we was in Jake's fix we would want to go careful and keep still and not take any chances.

The boys and girls was all glad to see us again, and we had a real good time all through recess. Coming to school the Henderson boys had come across the new deef and dummy and told the rest; so all the scholars was chuck full of him and couldn't talk about anything else, and was in a sweat to get a sight of him because they hadn't ever seen a deef and dummy in their lives, and it made a powerful excitement.

Tom said it was tough to have to keep mum now; said we would be heroes if we could come out and tell all we knowed; but after all, it was still more heroic to keep mum, there warn't two boys in a million could do it. That was Tom Sawyer's idea about it, and I reckoned there warn't anybody could better it.

Chapter 9

IN THE next two or three days Dummy he got to be powerful popular. He went associating around with the neighbors, and they made much of him, and was proud to have such a rattling curiosity amongst them. They had him to breakfast, they had him to dinner, they had him to supper; they kept him loaded up with hog and hominy, and warn't ever tired staring at him and wondering over him, and wishing they knowed more about him, he was so uncommon and romantic. His signs warn't no good; people couldn't understand them and he prob'ly couldn't himself, but he done a sight of goo-gooing, and so everybody was satisfied, and admired to hear him go it. He toted a piece of slate around, and a pencil; and people wrote questions on it and he wrote answers; but there warn't anybody could read his writing but Brace Dunlap. Brace said he couldn't read it very good, but he could manage to dig out the meaning most of the time. He said Dummy said he belonged away off somers and used to be well off, but got busted by swindlers which he had trusted, and was poor now, and hadn't any way to make a living.

Everybody praised Brace Dunlap for being so good to that stranger. He let him have a little log-cabin all to himself, and had his niggers take care of it, and fetch him all the vittles he wanted.

Dummy was at our house some, because old Uncle Silas was so af-flicted himself, these days, that anybody else that was afflicted was a comfort to him. Me and Tom didn't let on that we had knowed him before, and he didn't let on that he had knowed us before. The family talked their troubles out before him the same as if he wasn't there, but we reckoned it wasn't any harm for him to hear what they said. Generly he didn't seem to notice, but sometimes he did.

Well, two or three days went along, and everybody got to getting uneasy about Jubiter Dunlap. Everybody was asking everybody if they had any idea what had become of him. No, they hadn't, they said; and they shook their heads and said there was something powerful strange about it. Another and another day went by; then there was a report got around that praps he was murdered. You bet it made a big stir! Everybody's tongue was clacking away after that. Saturday two or three gangs turned out and hunted the woods to see if they could run across his remainders. Me and Tom helped, and it was noble good times and exciting. Tom he was so brim full of it he couldn't eat nor rest. He said if we could find that corpse we would be celebrated, and more talked about than if we got drownded.

The others got tired and give it up; but not Tom Sawyer—that warn't his style. Saturday night he didn't sleep any, hardly, trying to think up a plan; and towards daylight in the morning he struck it. He snaked me out of bed and was all excited, and says—

"Quick, Huck, snatch on your clothes—I've got it! Blood-hound!"

In two minutes we was tearing up the river road in the dark towards the village. Old Jeff Hooker had a blood-hound, and Tom was going to borrow him. I says—

"The trail's too old, Tom—and, besides, it's rained, you know."

"It don't make any difference, Huck. If the body's hid in the woods anywhere around the hound will find it. If he's been murdered and buried, they wouldn't bury him deep, it ain't likely, and if the dog goes over the spot, he'll scent him, sure. Huck, we're going to be celebrated, sure as you're born!"

He was just a-blazing; and whenever he got afire he was most likely to get afire all over. That was the way this time. In two minutes he had got it all ciphered out, and wasn't only just going to find the corpse—no, he was going to get on the track of that murderer and hunt *him* down, too; and not only that, but he was going to stick to him till—

"Well," I says, "you better find the corpse first; I reckon that's a-plenty for to-day. For all we know, there *ain't* any corpse and nobody hain't been murdered. That cuss could 'a' gone off somers and not been killed at all."

That gravelled him, and he says—

"Huck Finn, I never see such a person as you to want to spoil everything. As long as *you* can't see anything hopeful in a thing, you won't let anybody else. What good can it do you to throw cold water on that corpse and get up that selfish theory that there ain't been any murder? None in the world. I don't see how you can act so. I wouldn't treat you like that, and you know it. Here we've got a noble good opportunity to make a ruputation, and—"

"Oh, go ahead," I says; "I'm sorry, and I take it all back. I didn't mean nothing. Fix it any way you want it. *He* ain't any consequence to me. If he's killed, I'm as glad of it as you are; and if he—"

"I never said anything about being glad; I only—"

"Well, then, I'm as *sorry* as you are. Any way you druther have it, that is the way *I* druther have it. He—"

"There ain't any druthers *about* it, Huck Finn; nobody said anything about druthers. And as for—"

He forgot he was talking, and went tramping along, studying. He begun to get excited again, and pretty soon he says—

"Huck, it'll be the bulliest thing that ever happened if we find the body after everybody else has quit looking, and then go ahead and hunt up the murderer. It won't only be an honor to us, but it'll be an honor to Uncle Silas because it was us that done it. It'll set him up again, you see if it don't."

But old Jeff Hooker he throwed cold water on the whole business when we got to his blacksmith-shop and told him what we come for.

"You can take the dog," he says, "but you ain't a-going to find any corpse, because there ain't any corpse to find. Everybody's quit looking, and they're right. Soon as they come to think, they knowed there warn't no corpse. And I'll tell you for why. What does a person kill another person *for,* Tom Sawyer?—answer me that."

"Why, he—er—"

"Answer up! You ain't no fool. What does he kill him *for?*"

"Well, sometimes it's for revenge, and—"

"Wait. One thing at a time. Revenge says you; and right you are. Now who ever had anything agin that poor trifling no-account? Who do you reckon would want to kill *him?*—that rabbit!"

Tom was stuck. I reckon he hadn't thought of a person having to have a *reason* for killing a person before, and now he sees it warn't likely anybody would have that much of a grudge against a lamb like Jubiter Dunlap. The blacksmith says, by-and-by—

"The revenge idea won't work, you see. Well, then, what's next? Robbery? B'gosh, that must 'a' been it, Tom! Yes, sirree, I reckon we've struck it this time. Some feller wanted his gallus-buckles, and so he—"

But it was so funny he busted out laughing, and just went *on* laughing and laughing and laughing till he was 'most dead, and Tom looked so put out and cheap that I knowed he was ashamed he had come, and he wished he hadn't. But old Hooker never let up on him. He raked up everything a person ever could want to kill another person about, and any fool could see they didn't any of them fit this case, and he just made no end of fun of the whole business and of the people that had been hunting the body; and he said—

"If they'd had any sense they'd 'a' knowed the lazy cuss slid out because he wanted a loafing spell after all this work. He'll come pottering back in a couple of weeks, and then how'll you fellers feel? But, laws bless you, take the dog, and go and hunt his remainders. Do, Tom."

Then he busted out, and had another of them forty-rod laughs of hisn. Tom couldn't back down after all this, so he said, "All right, unchain him;" and the blacksmith done it, and we started home and left that old man laughing yet.

It was a lovely dog. There ain't any dog that's got a lovelier disposition than a blood-hound, and this one knowed us and liked us. He capered and raced around ever so friendly, and powerful glad to be free and have a holiday; but Tom was so cut up he couldn't take any intrust in him, and said he wished he'd stopped and thought a minute before he ever started on such a fool errand. He said old Jeff Hooker would tell everybody, and we'd never hear the last of it.

So we loafed along home down the back lanes, feeling pretty glum and not talking. When we was passing the far corner of our tobacker-field we heard the dog set up a long howl in there, and we went to the place and he was scratching the ground with all his might, and every now and then canting up his head sideways and fetching another howl.

It was a long square, the shape of a grave; the rain had made it sink down and show the shape. The minute we come and stood there we looked at one another and never said a word. When the dog had dug down only a few inches he grabbed something and pulled it up, and it was an arm and a sleeve. Tom kind of gasped out, and says—

"Come away, Huck—it's found."

I just felt awful. We struck for the road and fetched the first men that come along. They got a spade at the crib and dug out the body, and you never see such an excitement. You couldn't make anything out of the face, but you didn't need to. Everybody said—

"Poor Jubiter; it's his clothes, to the last rag!"

Some rushed off to spread the news and tell the justice of the peace and have an inquest, and me and Tom lit out for the house. Tom was all afire and 'most out of breath when we come tearing in where Uncle Silas and Aunt Sally and Benny was. Tom sung out—

"Me and Huck's found Jubiter Dunlap's corpse all by ourselves with a blood-hound, after everybody else had quit hunting and given it up; and if it hadn't a been for us it never *would* 'a' been found; and he *was* murdered too—they done it with a club or something like that; and I'm going to start in and find the murderer, next, and I bet I'll do it!"

Aunt Sally and Benny sprung up pale and astonished, but Uncle Silas fell right forward out of his chair onto the floor and groans out—

"Oh, my God, you've found him *now!*"

FETCHING ANOTHER HOWL.

Chapter 10

THEM AWFUL words froze us solid. We couldn't move hand or foot for as much as half a minute. Then we kind of come to, and lifted the old man up and got him into his chair, and Benny petted him and kissed him and tried to comfort him, and poor old Aunt Sally she done the same; but, poor things, they was so broke up and scared and knocked out of their right minds that they didn't hardly know what they was about. With Tom it was awful; it 'most petrified him to think maybe he had got his uncle into a thousand times more trouble than ever, and maybe it wouldn't ever happened if he hadn't been so ambitious to get celebrated, and let the corpse alone the way the others done. But pretty soon he sort of come to himself again and says—

"Uncle Silas, don't you say another word like that. It's dangerous, and there ain't a shadder of truth in it."

Aunt Sally and Benny was thankful to hear him say that, and they said the same; but the old man he wagged his head sorrowful and hopeless, and the tears run down his face, and he says—

"No—I done it; poor Jubiter, I done it!"

It was dreadful to hear him say it. Then he went on and told about it, and said it happened the day me and Tom come—along about sundown. He said Jubiter pestered him and aggravated him till he was so mad he just sort of lost his mind and grabbed up a stick and hit him over the head with all his might, and Jubiter dropped in his tracks. Then he was scared and sorry, and got down on his knees and lifted his head up, and begged him to speak and say he wasn't dead; and before long he come to, and when he see who it was holding his head, he jumped like he was 'most scared to death, and cleared the fence and tore into the woods, and was gone. So he hoped he wasn't hurt bad.

"But laws," he says, "it was only just fear that gave him that last little spurt of strength, and of course it soon played out and he laid down in the bush, and there wasn't anybody to help him, and he died."

Then the old man cried and grieved, and said he was a murderer and the mark of Cain was on him, and he had disgraced his family and was going to be found out and hung. But Tom said—

"No, you ain't going to be found out. You *didn't* kill him. *One* lick wouldn't kill him. Somebody else done it."

"Oh yes," he says, "I done it—nobody else. Who else had anything against him? Who else *could* have anything against him?"

He looked up kind of like he hoped some of us could mention somebody that could have a grudge against that harmless no-account, but of course it warn't no use—he *had* us; we couldn't say a word. He noticed that, and he saddened down again, and I never see a face so miserable and so pitiful to see. Tom had a sudden idea, and says—

"But hold on!—somebody *buried* him. Now who—"

He shut off sudden. I knowed the reason. It give me the cold shudders when he said them words, because right away I remembered about us seeing Uncle Silas prowling around with a long-handled shovel away in the night that night. And I knowed Benny seen him, too, because she was talking about it one day. The minute Tom shut off he changed the subject and went to begging Uncle Silas to keep mum, and the rest of us done the same, and said he *must*, and said it wasn't his business to tell on himself, and if he kept mum nobody would ever know; but if it was found out and any harm come to him it would break the family's hearts and kill them, and yet never do anybody any good. So at last he promised. We was all of us more comfortable, then, and went to work to cheer up the old man. We told him all he'd got to do was to keep still, and it wouldn't be long till the whole thing would blow over and be forgot. We all said there wouldn't anybody ever suspect Uncle Silas, nor ever dream of such a thing, he being so good and kind, and having such a good character; and Tom says, cordial and hearty, he says—

"Why, just look at it a minute; just consider. Here is Uncle Silas, all these years a preacher—at his own expense, all these years doing good with all his might and every way he can think of—at his own expense, all the time; always been loved by everybody, and respected; always been peaceable and minding his own business, the very last man in this whole deestrict to touch a person, and everybody knows it. Suspect *him?* Why, it ain't any more possible than—"

"By authority of the State of Arkansaw, I arrest you for the murder of Jubiter Dunlap!" shouts the sheriff at the door.

It was awful. Aunt Sally and Benny flung themselves at Uncle Silas, screaming and crying, and hugged him and hung to him, and Aunt Sally said go away, she wouldn't ever give him up, they shouldn't have him, and the niggers they come crowding and crying to the door and—well, I couldn't stand it; it was enough to break a person's heart; so I got out.

They took him up to the little one-horse jail in the village, and we all went along to tell him good-by; and Tom was feeling elegant, and says to me, "We'll have a most noble good time and heaps of danger some dark night getting him out of there, Huck, and it'll be talked about everywheres and we will be celebrated;" but the old man busted that scheme up the minute he whispered to him about it. He said no, it was his duty to stand whatever the law done to him, and he would stick to the jail plumb through to the end, even if there warn't no door to it. It disappointed Tom and gravelled him a good deal, but he had to put up with it.

But he felt responsible and bound to get his uncle Silas free; and he told Aunt Sally, the last thing, not to worry, because he was going to turn in and work night and day and beat this game and fetch Uncle Silas out innocent; and she was very loving to him and thanked him and said she knowed he would do his very best. And she told us to help Benny take care of the house and children, and then we had a good-by cry all around and went back to the farm, and left her there to live with the jailer's wife a month till the trial in October.

Chapter 11

WELL, THAT was a hard month on us all. Poor Benny, she kept up the best she could, and me and Tom tried to keep things cheerful there at the

house, but it kind of went for nothing, as you may say. It was the same up
at the jail. We went up every day to see the old people, but it was awful
dreary, because the old man warn't sleeping much, and was walking in
his sleep considerable, and so he got to looking fagged and miserable, and
his mind got shaky, and we all got afraid his troubles would break him
down and kill him. And whenever we tried to persuade him to feel cheer-
fuler, he only shook his head and said if we only knowed what it was to
carry around a murderer's load on your heart we wouldn't talk that way.
Tom and all of us kept telling him it *wasn't* murder, but just accidental
killing, but it never made any difference—it was murder, and he wouldn't
have it any other way. He actu'ly begun to come out plain and square
towards trialtime and acknowledge that he *tried* to kill the man. Why, that
was awful, you know. It made things seem fifty times as dreadful, and
there warn't no more comfort for Aunt Sally and Benny. But he promised
he wouldn't say a word about his murder when others was around, and we
was glad of that.

Tom Sawyer racked the head off of himself all that month trying to plan
some way out for Uncle Silas, and many's the night he kept me up 'most
all night with this kind of tiresome work, but he couldn't seem to get on
the right track no way. As for me, I reckoned a body might as well give it
up, it all looked so blue and I was so downhearted; but he wouldn't. He
stuck to the business right along, and went on planning and thinking and
ransacking his head.

So at last the trial come on, towards the middle of October, and we was
all in the court. The place was jammed of course. Poor old Uncle Silas,
he looked more like a dead person than a live one, his eyes was so hollow
and he looked so thin and so mournful. Benny she set on one side of him
and Aunt Sally on the other, and they had veils on, and was full of trouble.
But Tom he set by our lawyer, and had his finger in everywheres, of
course. The lawyer let him, and the judge let him. He 'most took the
business out of the lawyer's hands sometimes; which was well enough,
because that was only a mud-turtle of a back-settlement lawyer and didn't
know enough to come in when it rains, as the saying is.

KEPT ME UP 'MOST ALL NIGHT.

They swore in the jury, and then the lawyer for the prostitution got up and begun. He made a terrible speech against the old man, that made him moan and groan, and made Benny and Aunt Sally cry. The way *he* told about the murder kind of knocked us all stupid it was so different from the old man's tale. He said he was going to prove that Uncle Silas was *seen* to kill Jubiter Dunlap by two good witnesses, and done it deliberate, and *said* he was going to kill him the very minute he hit him with the club; and they seen him hide Jubiter in the bushes, and they seen that Jubiter was stone-dead. And said Uncle Silas come later and lugged Jubiter down into the tobacker-field, and two men seen him do it. And said Uncle Silas turned out, away in the night, and buried Jubiter, and a man seen him at it.

I says to myself, poor old Uncle Silas has been lying about it because he reckoned nobody seen him and he couldn't bear to break Aunt Sally's heart and Benny's; and right he was: as for me, I would 'a' lied the same way, and so would anybody that had any feeling, to save them such misery and sorrow which *they* warn't no ways responsible for. Well, it made our lawyer look pretty sick; and it knocked Tom silly, too, for a little spell, but then he braced up and let on that he warn't worried—but I knowed he *was*, all the same. And the people—my, but it made a stir amongst them!

And when that lawyer was done telling the jury what he was going to prove, he set down and begun to work his witnesses.

First, he called a lot of them to show that there was bad blood betwixt Uncle Silas and the diseased; and they told how they had heard Uncle Silas threaten the diseased, at one time and another, and how it got worse and worse and everybody was talking about it, and how diseased got afraid of his life, and told two or three of them he was certain Uncle Silas would up and kill him some time or another.

Tom and our lawyer asked them some questions; but it warn't no use, they stuck to what they said.

Next, they called up Lem Beebe, and he took the stand. It come into my mind, then, Lem and Jim Lane had come along talking, that time, about borrowing a dog or something from Jubiter Dunlap; and that brought

OUR LAWYER.

up the blackberries and the lantern; and that brought up Bill and Jack Withers, and how *they* passed by, talking about a nigger stealing Uncle Silas's corn; and that fetched up our old ghost that come along about the same time and scared us so—and here *he* was too, and a privileged character, on accounts of his being deef and dumb and a stranger, and they had fixed him a chair inside the railing, where he could cross his legs and be comfortable, whilst the other people was all in a jam so they couldn't hardly breathe. So it all come back to me just the way it was that day; and it made me mournful to think how pleasant it was up to then, and how miserable ever since.

> *Lem Beebe*, sworn, said: "I was a-coming along, that day, second of September, and Jim Lane was with me, and it was towards sundown, and we heard loud talk, like quarrelling, and we was very close, only the hazel bushes between (that's along the fence); and we heard a voice say, 'I've told you more'n once I'd kill you,' and knowed it was this prisoner's voice; and then we see a club come up above the bushes and down out of sight again, and heard a smashing thump and then a groan or two; and then we crope soft to where we could see, and there laid Jubiter Dunlap dead, and this prisoner standing over him with the club; and the next he hauled the dead man into a clump of bushes and hid him, and then we stooped low, to be out of sight, and got away."

Well, it was awful. It kind of froze everybody's blood to hear it, and the house was 'most as still whilst he was telling it as if there warn't nobody in it. And when he was done, you could hear them gasp and sigh, all over the house, and look at one another the same as to say, "Ain't it perfectly terrible—ain't it awful!"

Now happened a thing that astonished me. All the time the first witnesses was proving the bad blood and the threats and all that, Tom Sawyer was alive and laying for them; and the minute they was through, he went for them, and done his level best to catch them in lies and spile their testimony. But now, how different. When Lem first begun to talk, and never said anything about speaking to Jubiter or trying to borrow a dog off of him, he was all alive and laying for Lem, and you could see he was getting ready to cross-question him to death pretty soon, and then I judged him and me would go on the stand by-and-by and tell what we heard him and Jim Lane say. But the next time I looked at Tom I got the cold shivers. Why, he was in the brownest study you ever see—miles and miles away. He warn't hearing a word Lem Beebe was saying; and when he got through he was still in that brown-study, just the same. Our lawyer joggled him, and then he looked up startled, and says, "Take the witness if you want him. Lemme alone—I want to think."

Well, that beat me. I couldn't understand it. And Benny and her mother—oh, they looked sick, they was so troubled. They shoved their veils to one side and tried to get his eye, but it warn't any use, and I couldn't get his eye either. So the mud-turtle he tackled the witness, but it didn't amount to nothing; and he made a mess of it.

Then they called up Jim Lane, and he told the very same story over again, exact. Tom never listened to this one at all, but set there thinking and thinking, miles and miles away. So the mud-turtle went in alone again and come out just as flat as he done before. The lawyer for the prostitution looked very comfortable, but the judge looked disgusted. You see, Tom was just the same as a regular lawyer, nearly, because it was Arkansaw law for a prisoner to choose anybody he wanted to help his lawyer, and Tom had had Uncle Silas shove him into the case, and now he was botching it and you could see the judge didn't like it much.

All that the mud-turtle got out of Lem and Jim was this: he asked them—

"Why didn't you go and tell what you saw?"

"We was afraid we would get mixed up in it ourselves. And we was just starting down the river a-hunting for all the week besides; but as soon as we come back we found out they'd been searching for the body, so then we went and told Brace Dunlap all about it."

"When was that?"

"Saturday night, September 9th."

The judge he spoke up and says—

"Mr. Sheriff, arrest these two witnesses on suspicions of being accessionary after the fact to the murder."

The lawyer for the prostitution jumps up all excited, and says—

"Your honor! I protest against this extraordi—"

"Set down!" says the judge, pulling his bowie and laying it on his pulpit. "I beg you to respect the Court."

So he done it. Then he called Bill Withers.

Bill Withers, sworn, said: "I was coming along about sundown, Saturday, September 2d, by the prisoner's field, and my brother Jack was with me, and we seen a man toting off something heavy on his back and allowed it was a nigger stealing corn; we couldn't see distinct; next we made out that it was one man carrying another; and the way it hung, so kind of limp, we judged it was

"SET DOWN!" SAYS THE JUDGE.

somebody that was drunk; and by the man's walk we said it was
Parson Silas, and we judged he had found Sam Cooper drunk in
the road, which he was always trying to reform him, and was
toting him out of danger.''

It made the people shiver to think of poor old Uncle Silas toting off the
diseased down to the place in his tobacker-field where the dog dug up the
body, but there warn't much sympathy around amongst the faces, and I
heard one cuss say, ''Tis the coldest-blooded work I ever struck, lugging
a murdered man around like that, and going to bury him like a animal,
and him a preacher at that.''

Tom he went on thinking, and never took no notice; so our lawyer took
the witness and done the best he could, and it was plenty poor enough.

Then Jack Withers he come on the stand and told the same tale, just
like Bill done.

And after him comes Brace Dunlap, and he was looking very mournful,
and most crying; and there was a rustle and a stir all around, and everybody got ready to listen, and lots of the women folks said, "Poor cretur,
poor cretur," and you could see a many of them wiping their eyes.

> *Brace Dunlap*, sworn, said: "I was in considerable trouble a
> long time about my poor brother, but I reckoned things warn't near
> so bad as he made out, and I couldn't make myself believe any-
> body would have the heart to hurt a poor harmless cretur like
> that''—[by jings, I was sure I seen Tom give a kind of a faint little
> start, and then look disappointed again]—''and you know I *couldn't*
> think a preacher would hurt him—it warn't natural to think such
> onlikely thing—so I never paid much attention, and now I sha'n't
> ever, ever forgive myself; for if I had a done different, my poor
> brother would be with me this day, and not laying yonder mur-
> dered, and him so harmless.'' He kind of broke down there and
> choked up, and waited to get his voice; and people all around said
> the most pitiful things, and women cried; and it was very still in
> there, and solemn, and old Uncle Silas, poor thing, he give a
> groan right out so everybody heard him. Then Brace he went on,
> "Saturday, September 2d, he didn't come home to supper. By-
> and-by I got a little uneasy, and one of my niggers went over to
> this prisoner's place, but come back and said he warn't there. So
> I got uneasier and uneasier, and couldn't rest. I went to bed, but I
> couldn't sleep; and turned out, away late in the night, and went
> wandering over to this prisoner's place and all around about there
> a good while, hoping I would run across my poor brother, and
> never knowing he was out of his troubles and gone to a better
> shore—'' So he broke down and choked up again, and most all
> the women was crying now. Pretty soon he got another start and
> says: "But it warn't no use; so at last I went home and tried to get
> some sleep, but couldn't. Well, in a day or two everybody was
> uneasy, and they got to talking about this prisoner's threats, and
> took to the idea, which I didn't take no stock in, that my brother

was murdered; so they hunted around and tried to find his body, but couldn't and give it up. And so I reckoned he was gone off somers to have a little peace, and would come back to us when his troubles was kind of healed. But late Saturday night, the 9th, Lem Beebe and Jim Lane come to my house and told me all—told me the whole awful 'sassination, and my heart was broke. And *then* I remembered something that hadn't took no hold of me at the time, because reports said this prisoner had took to walking in his sleep and doing all kind of things of no consequence, not knowing what he was about. I will tell you what that thing was that come back into my memory. Away late that awful Saturday night when I was wandering around about this prisoner's place, grieving and troubled, I was down by the corner of the tobacker-field and I heard a sound like digging in a gritty soil; and I crope nearer and peeped through the vines that hung on the rail fence and seen this prisoner *shovelling*—shovelling with a long-handled shovel—heaving earth into a big hole that was most filled up; his back was to me, but it was bright moonlight and I knowed him by his old green baize work-gown with a splattery white patch in the middle of the back like somebody had hit him with a snowball. *He was burying the man he'd murdered!*"

And he slumped down in his chair crying and sobbing, and 'most everybody in the house busted out wailing, and crying, and saying, "Oh, it's awful—awful—horrible!" and there was a most tremenduous excitement, and you couldn't hear yourself think; and right in the midst of it up jumps old Uncle Silas, white as a sheet, and sings out—

"It's true, every word—I murdered him in cold blood!"

By Jackson, it petrified them! People rose up wild all over the house, straining and staring for a better look at him, and the judge was hammering with his mallet and the sheriff yelling "Order—order in the court—order!"

And all the while the old man stood there a-quaking and his eyes a-burning, and not looking at his wife and daughter, which was clinging to him and begging him to keep still, but pawing them off with his hands and saying he *would* clear his black soul from crime, he *would* heave off this load that was more than he could bear, and he *wouldn't* bear it another hour! And then he raged right along with his awful tale, everybody a-staring and gasping, judge, jury, lawyers, and everybody, and Benny and Aunt Sally crying their hearts out. And by George, Tom Sawyer never looked at him once! Never once—just set there gazing with all his eyes at something else, I couldn't tell what. And so the old man raged right along, pouring his words out like a stream of fire:

"I killed him! I am guilty! But I never had the notion in my life to hurt him or harm him, spite of all them lies about my threatening him, till the very minute I raised the club—then my heart went cold!—then the pity all went out of it, and I struck to kill! In that one moment all my wrongs come into my mind; all the insults that that man and the scoundrel his brother, there, had put upon me, and how they laid in together to ruin me with the people, and take away my good name, and *drive* me to some

I STRUCK TO KILL.

deed that would destroy me and my family that hadn't ever done *them* no
harm, so help me God! And they done it in a mean revenge—for why?
Because my innocent pure girl here at my side wouldn't marry that rich,
insolent, ignorant coward, Brace Dunlap, who's been snivelling here over
a brother he never cared a brass farthing for''—[I see Tom give a jump
and look glad *this* time, to a dead certainty]—''and in that moment I've
told you about, I forgot my God and remembered only my heart's bitterness, God forgive me, and I struck to kill. In one second I was miserably
sorry—oh, filled with remorse; but I thought of my poor family, and I
must hide what I'd done for their sakes; and I did hide that corpse in the
bushes; and presently I carried it to the tobacker-field; and in the deep
night I went with my shovel and buried it where—''

Up jumps Tom and shouts—

''*Now*, I've got it!'' and waves his hand, oh, ever so fine and starchy,
towards the old man, and says—

''Set down! A murder *was* done, but you never had no hand in it!''

Well, sir, you could a heard a pin drop. And the old man he sunk down
kind of bewildered in his seat and Aunt Sally and Benny didn't know it,
because they was so astonished and staring at Tom with their mouths open
and not knowing what they was about. And the whole house the same. *I*
never seen people look so helpless and tangled up, and I hain't ever seen
eyes bug out and gaze without a blink the way theirn did. Tom says,
perfectly ca'm—

''Your honor, may I speak?''

''For God's sake, yes—go on!'' says the judge, so astonished and
mixed up he didn't know what he was about hardly.

Then Tom he stood there and waited a second or two—that was for to
work up an ''effect,'' as he calls it—then he started in just as ca'm as
ever, and says:

''For about two weeks, now, there's been a little bill sticking on the
front of this court-house offering two thousand dollars reward for a couple
of big di'monds—stole at St. Louis. Them di'monds is worth twelve

A MURDER WAS DONE.

thousand dollars. But never mind about that till I get to it. Now about this
murder. I will tell you all about it—how it happened—who done it—
every *de*tail.''

You could see everybody nestle, now, and begin to listen for all they
was worth.

"This man here, Brace Dunlap, that's been snivelling so about his dead
brother that *you* know he never cared a straw for, wanted to marry that
young girl there, and she wouldn't have him. So he told Uncle Silas he
would make him sorry. Uncle Silas knowed how powerful he was, and
how little chance he had against such a man, and he was scared and
worried, and done everything he could think of to smooth him over and
get him to be good to him: he even took his no-account brother Jubiter on
the farm and give him wages and stinted his own family to pay them; and
Jubiter done everything his brother could contrive to insult Uncle Silas,
and fret and worry him, and try to drive Uncle Silas into doing him a
hurt, so as to injure Uncle Silas with the people. And it done it. Everybody
turned against him and said the meanest kind of things about him, and it
graduly broke his heart—yes, and he was so worried and distressed that
often he warn't hardly in his right mind.

"Well, on that Saturday that we've had so much trouble about, two of
these witnesses here, Lem Beebe and Jim Lane, come along by where
Uncle Silas and Jubiter Dunlap was at work—and that much of what
they've said is true, the rest is lies. They didn't hear Uncle Silas say he
would kill Jubiter; they didn't hear no blow struck; they didn't see no dead
man, and they didn't see Uncle Silas hide anything in the bushes. Look at
them now—how they set there, wishing they hadn't been so handy with
their tongues; anyway, they'll wish it before I get done.

"That same Saturday evening Bill and Jack Withers *did* see one man
lugging off another one. That much of what they said is true, and the rest
is lies. First off they thought it was a nigger stealing Uncle Silas's corn—
you notice it makes them look silly, now, to find out somebody overheard
them say that. That's because they found out by-and-by who it was that

was doing the lugging, and *they* know best why they swore here that they took it for Uncle Silas by the gait—which it *wasn't*, and they knowed it when they swore to that lie.

"A man out in the moonlight *did* see a murdered person put under ground in the tobacker-field—but it wasn't Uncle Silas that done the burying. He was in his bed at that very time.

"Now, then, before I go on, I want to ask you if you've ever noticed this: that people, when they're thinking deep, or when they're worried, are most always doing something with their hands, and they don't know it, and don't notice what it is their hands are doing. Some stroke their chins; some stroke their noses; some stroke up *under* their chin with their hand; some twirl a chain, some fumble a button, then there's some that draws a figure or a letter with their finger on their cheek, or under their chin or on their under lip. That's *my* way. When I'm restless, or worried, or thinking hard, I draw capital V's on my cheek or on my under lip or under my chin, and never anything *but* capital V's—and half the time I don't notice it and don't know I am doing it."

That was odd. That is just what I do; only I make an O. And I could see people nodding to one another, same as they do when they mean "*that's* so."

"Now then, I'll go on. That same Saturday—no, it was the night before—there was a steamboat laying at Flagler's Landing, forty miles above here, and it was raining and storming like the nation. And there was a thief aboard, and he had them two big di'monds that's advertised out here on this court-house door; and he slipped ashore with his hand-bag and struck out into the dark and the storm, and he was a-hoping he could get to this town all right and be safe. But he had two pals aboard the boat, hiding, and he knowed they was going to kill him the first chance they got and take the di'monds; because all three stole them, and then this fellow he got hold of them and skipped.

"Well, he hadn't been gone more'n ten minutes before his pals found it out, and they jumped ashore and lit out after him. Prob'ly they burnt matches and found his tracks. Anyway, they dogged along after him all day Saturday and kept out of his sight; and towards sundown he come to the bunch of sycamores down by Uncle Silas's field, and he went in there to get a disguise out of his hand-bag and put it on before he showed himself here in the town—and mind you he done that just a little after the time that Uncle Silas was hitting Jubiter Dunlap over the head with a club—for he *did* hit him.

"But the minute the pals see that thief slide into the bunch of syca-mores, they jumped out of the bushes and slid in after him.

"They fell on him and clubbed him to death.

"Yes, for all he screamed and howled so, they never had no mercy on him, but clubbed him to death. And two men that was running along the road heard him yelling that way, and they made a rush into the sycamore bunch—which was where they was bound for, anyway—and when the pals saw them they lit out and the two new men after them a-chasing them as tight as they could go. But only a minute or two—then these two new men slipped back very quiet into the sycamores.

"*Then* what did they do? I will tell you what they done. They found where the thief had got his disguise out of his carpet-sack to put on; so one of them strips and puts on that disguise.''

Tom waited a little here, for some more "effect"—then he says, very deliberate—

"The man that put on that dead man's disguise was—*Jubiter Dunlap!*''

"Great Scott!'' everybody shouted, all over the house, and old Uncle Silas he looked perfectly astonished.

"Yes, it was Jubiter Dunlap. Not dead, you see. Then they pulled off the dead man's boots and put Jubiter Dunlap's old ragged shoes on the corpse and put the corpse's boots on Jubiter Dunlap. Then Jubiter Dunlap stayed where he was, and the other man lugged the dead body off in the twilight; and after midnight he went to Uncle Silas's house, and took his old green work-robe off of the peg where it always hangs in the passage betwixt the house and the kitchen and put it on, and stole the long-handled shovel and went off down into the tobacker-field and buried the murdered man.''

He stopped, and stood a half a minute. Then—

"And who do you reckon the murdered man *was?* It was—*Jake* Dunlap, the long-lost burglar!''

"Great Scott!''

"And the man that buried him was—*Brace* Dunlap, his brother!''

"Great Scott!''

"And who do you reckon is this mowing idiot here that's letting on all these weeks to be a deef and dumb stranger? It's—*Jubiter* Dunlap!''

My land, they all busted out in a howl, and you never see the like of that excitement since the day you was born. And Tom he made a jump for Jupiter and snaked off his goggles and his false whiskers, and there was the murdered man, sure enough, just as alive as anybody! And Aunt Sally and Benny they went to hugging and crying and kissing and smothering old Uncle Silas to that degree he was more muddled and confused and mushed up in his mind than he ever was before, and that is saying considerable. And next, people begun to yell—

"Tom Sawyer! Tom Sawyer! Shut up everybody, and let him go on! Go on, Tom Sawyer!''

Which made him feel uncommon bully, for it was nuts for Tom Sawyer to be a public character thataway, and a hero, as he calls it. So when it was all quiet, he says—

"There ain't much left, only this. When that man there, Brace Dunlap, had most worried the life and sense out of Uncle Silas till at last he plum lost his mind and hit this other blatherskite his brother with a club, I reckon he seen his chance. Jubiter broke for the woods to hide, and I reckon the game was for him to slide out, in the night, and leave the country. Then Brace would make everybody believe Uncle Silas killed him and hid his body somers; and that would ruin Uncle Silas and drive *him* out of the country—hang him, maybe; I dunno. But when they found their dead brother in the sycamores without knowing him, because he was so battered up, they see they had a better thing; disguise *both* and bury Jake and dig him up presently all dressed up in Jubiter's clothes, and hire Jim Lane and Bill Withers and the others to swear to some handy lies—which they done. And there they set, now, and I told them they would be

AND THERE WAS THE MURDERED MAN.

looking sick before I got done, and that is the way they're looking now.

"Well, me and Huck Finn here, we come down on the boat with the thieves, and the dead one told us all about the di'monds, and said the others would murder him if they got the chance; and we was going to help him all we could. We was bound for the sycamores when we heard them killing him in there; but we was in there in the early morning after the storm and allowed nobody hadn't been killed, after all. And when we see Jubiter Dunlap here spreading around in the very same disguise Jake told us *he* was going to wear, we thought it was Jake his own self—and he was goo-gooing deef and dumb, and *that* was according to agreement.

"Well, me and Huck went on hunting for the corpse after the others quit, and we found it. And was proud, too; but Uncle Silas he knocked us crazy by telling us *he* killed the man. So we was mighty sorry we found the body, and was bound to save Uncle Silas's neck if we could; and it was going to be tough work, too, because he wouldn't let us break him out of prison the way we done with our old nigger Jim.

"I done everything I could the whole month to think up some way to save Uncle Silas, but I couldn't strike a thing. So when we come into court to-day I come empty, and couldn't see no chance anywheres. But by-and-by I had a glimpse of something that set me thinking—just a little wee glimpse—only that, and not enough to make sure; but it set me thinking hard—and *watching,* when I was only letting on to think; and by-and-by, sure enough, when Uncle Silas was piling out that stuff about *him* killing Jubiter Dunlap, I catched that glimpse again, and this time I jumped up and shut down the proceedings, because I *knowed* Jubiter Dunlap was a-setting here before me. I knowed him by a thing which I seen him do—and I remembered it. I'd seen him do it when I was here a year ago."

He stopped then, and studied a minute—laying for an "effect"—I knowed it perfectly well. Then he turned off like he was going to leave the platform, and says, kind of lazy and indifferent—

"Well, I believe that is all."

Why, you never heard such a howl!—and it come from the whole house:

WHICH MADE HIM FEEL UNCOMMON BULLY.

"What *was* it you seen him do? Stay where you are, you little devil! You think you are going to work a body up till his mouth's a-watering and stop there? What *was* it he done?"

That was it, you see—he just done it to get an "effect"; you couldn't 'a' pulled him off of that platform with a yoke of oxen.

"Oh, it wasn't anything much," he says. "I seen him looking a little excited when he found Uncle Silas was actuly fixing to hang himself for a murder that warn't ever done; and he got more and more nervous and worried, I a-watching him sharp but not seeming to look at him—and all of a sudden his hands begun to work and fidget, and pretty soon his left crept up and *his finger drawed a cross on his check,* and then I *had* him!"

Well, then they ripped and howled and stomped and clapped their hands till Tom Sawyer was that proud and happy he didn't know what to do with himself. And then the judge he looked down over his pulpit and says—

"My boy, did you *see* all the various details of this strange conspiracy and tragedy that you've been describing?"

"No, your honor, I didn't see any of them."

"Didn't see any of them! Why, you've told the whole history straight through, just the same as if you'd seen it with your eyes. How did you manage that?"

Tom says, kind of easy and comfortable—

"Oh, just noticing the evidence and piecing this and that together, your honor; just an ordinary little bit of detective work; anybody could 'a' done it."

"Nothing of the kind! Not two in a million could 'a' done it. You are a very remarkable boy."

Then they let go and give Tom another smashing round, and he—well, he wouldn't 'a' sold out for a silver mine. Then the judge says—

"But are you certain you've got this curious history straight?"

"Perfectly, your honor. Here is Brace Dunlap—let him deny his share of it if he wants to take the chance; I'll engage to make him wish he hadn't said anything. . . . Well, you see *he's* pretty quiet. And his brother's pretty quiet, and them four witnesses that lied so and got paid for it, they're pretty quiet. And as for Uncle Silas, it ain't any use for him to put in his oar, I wouldn't believe him under oath!''

Well, sir, that fairly made them shout; and even the judge he let go and laughed. Tom he was just feeling like a rainbow. When they was done laughing he looks up at the judge and says—

"Your honor, there's a thief in this house.''

"A thief?''

"Yes, sir. And he's got them twelve-thousand-dollar di'monds on him.''

By gracious, but it made a stir! Everybody went shouting—

"Which is him? which is him? p'int him out!''

And the judge says—

"Point him out, my lad. Sheriff, you will arrest him. Which one is it?''

Tom says—

"This late dead man here—Jubiter Dunlap.''

Then there was another thundering let-go of astonishment and excitement; but Jubiter, which was astonished enough before, was just fairly putrefied with astonishment this time. And he spoke up, about half crying, and says—

"Now *that's* a lie! Your honor, it ain't fair; I'm plenty bad enough without that. I done the other things—Brace he put me up to it, and persuaded me, and promised he'd make me rich, some day, and I done it, and I'm sorry I done it, and I wisht I hadn't; but I hain't stole no di'monds, and I hain't *got* no di'monds; I wisht I may never stir if it ain't so. The sheriff can search me and see.''

Tom says—

"Your honor, it wasn't right to call him a thief, and I'll let up on that a little. He did steal the di'monds, but he didn't know it. He stole them from his brother Jake when he was laying dead, after Jake had stole them from the other thieves; but Jubiter didn't know he was stealing them; and he's been swelling around here with them a month; yes, sir, twelve thousand dollars' worth of di'monds on him—all that riches, and going around here every day just like a poor man. Yes, your honor, he's got them on him now.''

The judge spoke up and says—

"Search him, sheriff.''

Well, sir, the sheriff he ransacked him high and low, and everywhere: searched his hat, socks, seams, boots, everything—and Tom he stood there quiet, laying for another of them effects of hisn. Finally the sheriff he give it up, and everybody looked disappointed, and Jubiter says—

"There, now! what'd I tell you?''

And the judge says—

"It appears you were mistaken this time, my boy.''

Then Tom he took an attitude and let on to be studying with all his might, and scratching his head. Then all of a sudden he glanced up chipper, and says—

"Oh, now I've got it! I'd forgot.''

Which was a lie, and I knowed it. Then he says—

"Will somebody be good enough to lend me a little small screw-driver? There was one in your brother's hand-bag that you smouched, Jubiter, but I reckon you didn't fetch it with you.''

"No, I didn't. I didn't want it, and I give it away."

"That was because you didn't know what it was for."

Jubiter had his boots on again, by now, and when the thing Tom wanted was passed over the people's heads till it got to him, he says to Jubiter—

"Put up your foot on this chair." And he kneeled down and begun to unscrew the heel-plate, everybody watching; and when he got that big di'mond out of that boot-heel and held it up and let it flash and blaze and squirt sunlight everwhichaway, it just took everybody's breath; and Jubiter he looked so sick and sorry you never see the like of it. And when Tom held up the other di'mond he looked sorrier than ever. Land! he was thinking how he would 'a' skipped out and been rich and independent in a foreign land if he'd only had the luck to guess what the screw-driver was in the carpet-bag for.

Well, it was a most exciting time, take it all around, and Tom got cords of glory. The judge took the di'monds, and stood up in his pulpit, and cleared his throat, and shoved his spectacles back on his head, and says—

"I'll keep them and notify the owners; and when they send for them it will be a real pleasure to me to hand you the two thousand dollars, for you've earned the money—yes, and you've earned the deepest and most sincerest thanks of this community besides, for lifting a wronged and innocent family out of ruin and shame, and saving a good and honorable man from a felon's death, and for exposing to infamy and the punishment of the law a cruel and odious scoundrel and his miserable creatures!"

Well, sir, if there'd been a brass band to bust out some music, then, it would 'a' been just the perfectest thing I ever see, and Tom Sawyer he said the same.

Then the sheriff he nabbed Brace Dunlap and his crowd, and by-and-by next month the judge had them up for trial and jailed the whole lot. And everybody crowded back to Uncle Silas's little old church, and was ever so loving and kind to him and the family and couldn't do enough for them; and Uncle Silas he preached them the blamedest jumbledest idiotic sermons you ever struck, and would tangle you up so you couldn't find your way home in daylight; but the people never let on but 'what they thought it was the clearest and brightest and elegantest sermons that ever was; and they would set there and cry, for love and pity; but, by George, they give me the jim-jams and the fan-tods and caked up what brains I had, and turned them solid; but by-and-by they loved the old man's intellects back into him again and he was as sound in his skull as ever he was, which ain't no flattery, I reckon. And so the whole family was as happy as birds, and nobody could be gratefuler and lovinger than what they was to Tom Sawyer; and the same to me, though I hadn't done nothing. And when the two thousand dollars come, Tom give half of it to me, and never told anybody so, which didn't surprise me, because I knowed him.

The Stolen White Elephant

THE STOLEN WHITE ELEPHANT[1]

1

THE FOLLOWING curious history was related to me by a chance railway acquaintance. He was a gentleman more than seventy years of age, and his thoroughly good and gentle face and earnest and sincere manner imprinted the unmistakable stamp of truth upon every statement which fell from his lips. He said:—

You know in what reverence the royal white elephant of Siam is held by the people of that country. You know it is sacred to kings, only kings may possess it, and that it is indeed in a measure even superior to kings, since it receives not merely honor but worship. Very well; five years ago, when the troubles concerning the frontier line arose between Great Britain and Siam, it was presently manifest that Siam had been in the wrong. Therefore every reparation was quickly made, and the British representative stated that he was satisfied and the past should be forgotten. This greatly relieved the King of Siam, and partly as a token of gratitude, but partly also, perhaps, to wipe out any little remaining vestige of unpleasantness which England might feel toward him, he wished to send the Queen a present,—the sole sure way of propitiating an enemy, according to Oriental ideas. This present ought not only to be a royal one, but transcendently royal. Wherefore, what offering could be so meet as that of a white elephant? My position in the Indian civil service was such that I was deemed peculiarly worthy of the honor of conveying the present to her Majesty. A ship was fitted out for me and my servants and the officers and attendants of the elephant, and in due time I arrived in New York harbor and placed my royal charge in admirable quarters in Jersey City. It was necessary to remain awhile in order to recruit the animal's health before resuming the voyage.

All went well during a fortnight,—then my calamities began. The white elephant was stolen! I was called up at dead of night and informed of this fearful misfortune. For some moments I was beside myself with terror and

[1]Left out of "A Tramp Abroad," because it was feared that some of the particulars had been exaggerated, and that others were not true. Before these suspicions had been proven groundless, the book had gone to press.—M.T.

anxiety; I was helpless. Then I grew calmer and collected my faculties. I soon saw my course,—for indeed there was but the one course for an intelligent man to pursue. Late as it was, I flew to New York and got a policeman to conduct me to the headquarters of the detective force. Fortunately I arrived in time, though the chief of the force, the celebrated Inspector Blunt, was just on the point of leaving for his home. He was a man of middle size and compact frame, and when he was thinking deeply he had a way of knitting his brows and tapping his forehead reflectively with his finger, which impressed you at once with the conviction that you stood in the presence of a person of no common order. The very sight of him gave me confidence and made me hopeful. I stated my errand. It did not flurry him in the least; it had no more visible effect upon his iron self-possession than if I had told him somebody had stolen my dog. He motioned me to a seat, and said calmly,—

"Allow me to think a moment, please."

So saying, he sat down at his office table and leaned his head upon his hand. Several clerks were at work at the other end of the room; the scratching of their pens was all the sound I heard during the next six or seven minutes. Meantime the inspector sat there, buried in thought. Finally he raised his head, and there was that in the firm lines of his face which showed me that his brain had done its work and his plan was made. Said he,—and his voice was low and impressive,—

"This is no ordinary case. Every step must be warily taken; each step must be made sure before the next is ventured. And secrecy must be observed,—secrecy profound and absolute. Speak to no one about the matter, not even the reporters. I will take care of *them;* I will see that they get only what it may suit my ends to let them know." He touched a bell; a youth appeared. "Alaric, tell the reporters to remain for the present." The boy retired. "Now let us proceed to business,—and systematically. Nothing can be accomplished in this trade of mine without strict and minute method."

He took a pen and some paper. "Now—name of the elephant?"

"Hassan Ben Ali Selim Abdallah Mohammed Moisé Alhammal Jamsetjejeebhoy Dhuleep Sultan Ebu Bhudpoor."

"Very well. Given name?"

"Jumbo."

"Very well. Place of birth?"

"The capital city of Siam."

"Parents living?"

"No,—dead."

"Had they any other issue besides this one?"

"None. He was an only child."

"Very well. These matters are sufficient under that head. Now please describe the elephant, and leave out no particular, however insignificant,—that is, insignificant from *your* point of view. To men in my profession there *are* no insignificant particulars; they do not exist."

I described,—he wrote. When I was done, he said,—

"Now listen. If I have made any mistakes, correct me."

He read as follows:—

"Height, 19 feet; length from apex of forehead to insertion of tail, 26 feet; length of trunk, 16 feet; length of tail, 6 feet; total length, including trunk and tail, 48 feet; length of tusks, 9½ feet; ears in keeping with these dimensions; footprint resembles the mark left when one up-ends a barrel in the snow; color of the elephant, a dull white; has a hole the size of a plate in each ear for the insertion of jewelry, and possesses the habit in a remarkable degree of squirting water upon spectators and of maltreating with his trunk not only such persons as he is acquainted with, but even entire strangers; limps slightly with his right hind leg, and has a small scar in his left armpit cause by a former boil; had on, when stolen, a castle containing seats for fifteen persons, and a gold-cloth saddle-blanket the size of an ordinary carpet.''

There were no mistakes. The inspector touched the bell, handed the description to Alaric, and said,—

"Have fifty thousand copies of this printed at once and mailed to every detective office and pawnbroker's shop on the continent." Alaric retired. "There,—so far so good. Next, I must have a photograph of the property."

I gave him one. He examined it critically, and said,—

"It must do, since we can do no better; but he has his trunk curled up and tucked into his mouth. That is unfortunate, and is calculated to mislead, for of course he does not usually have it in that position." He touched his bell.

"Alaric, have fifty thousand copies of this photograph made, the first thing in the morning, and mail them with the descriptive circulars."

Alaric retired to execute his orders. The inspector said,—

"It will be necessary to offer a reward, of course. Now as to the amount?"

"What sum would you suggest?"

"To *begin* with, I should say,—well, twenty-five thousand dollars. It is an intricate and difficult business; there are a thousand avenues of escape and opportunities of concealment. These thieves have friends and pals everywhere—"

"Bless me, do you know who they are?"

The wary face, practised in concealing the thoughts and feelings within, gave me no token, nor yet the replying words, so quietly uttered:—

"Never mind about that. I may, and I may not. We generally gather a pretty shrewd inkling of who our man is by the manner of his work and the size of the game he goes after. We are not dealing with a pickpocket or a hall thief, now, make up your mind to that. This property was not 'lifted' by a novice. But, as I was saying, considering the amount of travel which will have to be done, and the diligence with which the thieves will cover up their traces as they move along, twenty-five thousand may be too small a sum to offer, yet I think it worth while to start with that."

So we determined upon that figure, as a beginning. Then this man, whom nothing escaped which could by any possibility be made to serve as a clue, said:—

"There are cases in detective history to show that criminals have been detected through peculiarities in their appetites. Now, what does this elephant eat, and how much?"

"Well, as to *what* he eats,—he will eat *anything*. He will eat a man, he will eat a Bible,—he will eat anything *between* a man and a Bible."

"Good,—very good indeed, but too general. Details are necessary,—

details are the only valuable things in our trade. Very well,—as to men. At one meal,—or, if you prefer, during one day,—how many men will he eat, if fresh?"

"He would not care whether they were fresh or not; at a single meal he would eat five ordinary men."

"Very good; five men; we will put that down. What nationalities would he prefer?"

"He is indifferent about nationalities. He prefers acquaintances, but is not prejudiced against strangers."

"Very good. Now, as to Bibles. How many Bibles would he eat at a meal?"

"He would eat an entire edition."

"It is hardly succinct enough. Do you mean the ordinary octavo, or the family illustrated?"

"I think he would be indifferent to illustrations; that is, I think he would not value illustrations above simple letter-press."

"No, you do not get my idea. I refer to bulk. The ordinary octavo Bible weighs about two pounds and a half, while the great quarto with the illustrations weighs ten or twelve. How many Doré Bibles would he eat at a meal?"

"If you knew this elephant, you could not ask. He would take what they had."

"Well, put it in dollars and cents, then. We must get at it somehow. The Doré costs a hundred dollars a copy, Russia leather, bevelled."

"He would require about fifty thousand dollars' worth,—say an edition of five hundred copies."

"Now that is more exact. I will put that down. Very well; he likes men and Bibles; so far, so good. What else will he eat? I want particulars."

"He will leave Bibles to eat bricks, he will leave bricks to eat bottles, he will leave bottles to eat clothing, he will leave clothing to eat cats, he will leave cats to eat oysters, he will leave oysters to eat ham, he will leave ham to eat sugar, he will leave sugar to eat pie, he will leave pie to eat potatoes, he will leave potatoes to eat bran, he will leave bran to eat hay, he will leave hay to eat oats, he will leave oats to eat rice, for he was mainly raised on it. There is nothing whatever that he will not eat but European butter, and he would eat that if he could taste it."

"Very good. General quantity at a meal,—say about—"

"Well, anywhere from a quarter to a half a ton."

"And he drinks—"

"Everything that is fluid. Milk, water, whiskey, molasses, castor oil, camphene, carbolic acid,—it is no use to go into particulars; whatever fluid occurs to you set it down. He will drink anything that is fluid, except European coffee."

"Very good. As to quantity?"

"Put it down five to fifteen barrels,—his thirst varies; his other appetites do not."

"These things are unusual. They ought to furnish quite good clues toward tracing him."

He touched the bell.

"Alaric, summon Captain Burns."

Burns appeared. Inspector Blunt unfolded the whole matter to him, detail by detail. Then he said in the clear, decisive tones of a man whose plans are clearly defined in his head, and who is accustomed to command,—

"Captain Burns, detail Detectives Jones, Davis, Halsey, Bates, and Hackett to shadow the elephant."

"Yes, sir."

"Detail Detectives Moses, Dakin, Murphy, Rogers, Tupper, Higgins, and Bartholomew to shadow the thieves."

"Yes, sir."

"Place a strong guard—a guard of thirty picked men, with a relief of thirty—over the place from whence the elephant was stolen, to keep strict watch there night and day, and allow none to approach—except reporters—without written authority from me."

"Yes, sir."

"Place detectives in plain clothes in the railway, steamship, and ferry depots, and upon all roadways leading out of Jersey City, with orders to search all suspicious persons."

"Yes, sir."

"Furnish all these men with photograph and accompanying description of the elephant, and instruct them to search all trains and outgoing ferryboats and other vessels."

"Yes, sir."

"If the elephant should be found, let him be seized, and the information forwarded to me by telegraph."

"Yes, sir."

"Let me be informed at once if any clues should be found,—footprints of the animal, or anything of that kind."

"Yes, sir."

"Get an order commanding the harbor police to patrol the frontages vigilantly."

"Yes, sir."

"Despatch detectives in plain clothes over all the railways, north as far as Canada, west as far as Ohio, south as far as Washington."

"Yes, sir."

"Place experts in all the telegraph offices to listen to all messages; and let them require that all cipher despatches be interpreted to them."

"Yes, sir."

"Let all these things be done with the utmost secrecy,—mind, the most impenetrable secrecy."

"Yes, sir."

"Report to me promptly at the usual hour."

"Yes, sir."

"Go!"

"Yes, sir."

He was gone.

Inspector Blunt was silent and thoughtful a moment, while the fire in his eye cooled down and faded out. Then he turned to me and said in a placid voice,—

"I am not given to boasting, it is not my habit; but—we shall find the elephant."

I shook him warmly by the hand and thanked him; and I *felt* my thanks, too. The more I had seen of the man the more I liked him, and the more I admired him and marvelled over the mysterious wonders of his profession. Then we parted for the night, and I went home with a far happier heart than I had carried with me to his office.

2

NEXT MORNING it was all in the newspapers, in the minutest detail. It even had additions,—consisting of Detective This, Detective That, and Detective The Other's "Theory" as to how the robbery was done, who the robbers were, and whither they had flown with their booty. There were eleven of these theories, and they covered all the possibilities; and this single fact shows what independent thinkers detectives are. No two theories were alike, or even much resembled each other, save in one striking particular, and in that one all the eleven theories were absolutely agreed. That was, that although the rear of my building was torn out and the only door remained locked, the elephant had not been removed through the rent, but by some other (undiscovered) outlet. All agreed that the robbers had made that rent only to mislead the detectives. That never would have occurred to me or to any other layman, perhaps, but it had not deceived the detectives for a moment. Thus, what I had supposed was the only thing that had no mystery about it was in fact the very thing I had gone furthest astray in. The eleven theories all named the supposed robbers, but no two named the same robbers; the total number of suspected persons was thirty-seven. The various newspaper accounts all closed with the most important opinion of all,—that of Chief Inspector Blunt. A portion of this statement read as follows:—

> "The chief knows who the two principals are, namely, 'Brick' Duffy and 'Red' McFadden. Ten days before the robbery was achieved he was already aware that it was to be attempted, and had quietly proceeded to shadow these two noted villains; but unfortunately on the night in question their track was lost, and before it could be found again the bird was flown,—that is, the elephant.
>
> "Duffy and McFadden are the boldest scoundrels in the profession; the chief has reasons for believing that they are the men who stole the stove out of the detective headquarters on a bitter night last winter,—in consequence of which the chief and every detective present were in the hands of the physicians before morning, some with frozen feet, others with frozen fingers, ears, and other members."

When I read the first half of that I was more astonished than ever at the wonderful sagacity of this strange man. He not only saw everything in the present with a clear eye, but even the future could not be hidden from him. I was soon at his office, and said I could not help wishing he had

had those men arrested, and so prevented the trouble and loss; but his reply was simple and unanswerable:—

"It is not our province to prevent crime, but to punish it. We cannot punish it until it is committed."

I remarked that the secrecy with which we had begun had been marred by the newspapers; not only all our facts but all our plans and purposes had been revealed; even all the suspected persons had been named; these would doubtless disguise themselves now, or go into hiding.

"Let them. They will find that when I am ready for them my hand will descend upon them, in their secret places, as unerringly as the hand of fate. As to the newspapers, we *must* keep in with them. Fame, reputation, constant public mention,—these are the detective's bread and butter. He must publish his facts, else he will be supposed to have none; he must publish his theory, for nothing is so strange or striking as a detective's theory, or brings him so much wondering respect; we must publish our plans, for these the journals insist upon having, and we could not deny them without offending. We must constantly show the public what we are doing, or they will believe we are doing nothing. It is much pleasanter to have a newspaper say, 'Inspector Blunt's ingenious and extraordinary theory is as follows,' than to have it say some harsh thing, or, worse still, some sarcastic one."

"I see the force of what you say. But I noticed that in one part of your remarks in the papers this morning you refused to reveal your opinion upon a certain minor point."

"Yes, we always do that; it has a good effect. Besides, I had not formed any opinion on that point, any way."

I deposited a considerable sum of money with the inspector, to meet current expenses, and sat down to wait for news. We were expecting the telegrams to begin to arrive at any moment now. Meantime I reread the newspapers and also our descriptive circular, and observed that our $25,000 reward seemed to be offered only to detectives. I said I thought it ought to be offered to anybody who would catch the elephant. The inspector said:—

"It is the detectives who will find the elephant, hence the reward will go to the right place. If other people found the animal, it would only be by watching the detectives and taking advantage of clues and indications stolen from them, and that would entitle the detectives to the reward, after all. The proper office of a reward is to stimulate the men who deliver up their time and their trained sagacities to this sort of work, and not to confer benefits upon chance citizens who stumble upon a capture without having earned the benefits by their own merits and labors."

This was reasonable enough, certainly. Now the telegraphic machine in the corner began to click, and the following despatch was the result:—

FLOWER STATION, N.Y., 7:30 A.M.

Have got a clue. Found a succession of deep tracks across a farm near here. Followed them two miles east without result; think elephant went west. Shall now shadow him in that direction.

DARLEY, *Detective.*

"Darley's one of the best men on the force," said the inspector. "We shall hear from him again before long."

Telegram No. 2 came:—

BARKER'S, N.J., 7:40 A.M.

Just arrived. Glass factory broken open here during night, and eight hundred bottles taken. Only water in large quantity near here is five miles distant. Shall strike for there. Elephant will be thirsty. Bottles were empty.

BAKER, *Detective.*

"That promises well, too," said the inspector. "I told you the creature's appetites would not be bad clues."

Telegram No. 3:—

TAYLORVILLE, L. I., 8:15 A.M.

A haystack near here disappeared during night. Probably eaten. Have got a clue, and am off.

HUBBARD, *Detective.*

"How he does move around!" said the inspector. "I knew we had a difficult job on hand, but we shall catch him yet."

FLOWER STATION, N.Y., 9 A.M.

Shadowed the tracks three miles westward. Large, deep, and ragged. Have just met a farmer who says they are not elephant tracks. Says they are holes where he dug up saplings for shade-trees when ground was frozen last winter. Give me orders how to proceed.

DARLEY, *Detective.*

"Aha! a confederate of the thieves! The thing grows warm," said the inspector.

He dictated the following telegram to Darley:—

Arrest the man and force him to name his pals. Continue to follow the tracks,—to the Pacific, if necessary.

Chief BLUNT.

Next telegram:—

CONEY POINT, PA., 8:45 A.M.

Gas office broken open here during night and three months' unpaid gas bills taken. Have got a clue and am away.

MURPHY, *Detective.*

"Heavens!" said the inspector; "would he eat gas bills?"

"Through ignorance,—yes; but they cannot support life. At least, un-assisted."

Now came this exciting telegram:—

IRONVILLE, N.Y., 9:30 A.M.

Just arrived. This village in consternation. Elephant passed through here at five this morning. Some say he went east, some say west, some north, some south,—but all say they did not wait to notice particularly. He killed a horse; have secured a piece of it for a clue. Killed it with his trunk; from style of blow, think he struck it left-handed. From position in which horse lies, think elephant traveled northward along line of Berkley railway. Has four and a half hours' start, but I move on his track at once.

HAWES, *Detective.*

I uttered exclamations of joy. The inspector was as self-contained as a graven image. He calmly touched his bell.

"Alaric, send Captain Burns here."

Burns appeared.

"How many men are ready for instant orders?"

"Ninety-six, sir."

"Send them north at once. Let them concentrate along the line of the Berkley road north of Ironville."

"Yes, sir."

"Let them conduct their movements with the utmost secrecy. As fast as others are at liberty, hold them for orders."

"Yes, sir."

"Go!"

"Yes, sir."

Presently came another telegram:—

SAGE CORNERS, N.Y., 10:30.

Just arrived. Elephant passed through here at 8:15. All escaped from the town but a policeman. Apparently elephant did not strike at policeman, but at the lamp-post, Got both. I have secured a portion of the policeman as clue.

STUMM, *Detective.*

"So the elephant has turned westward," said the inspector. "However, he will not escape, for my men are scattered all over that region."

The next telegram said:—

GLOVER'S, 11:15.

Just arrived. Village deserted, except sick and aged. Elephant passed through three quarters of an hour ago. The anti-temperance mass meeting was in session; he put his trunk in at a window and washed it out with water from cistern. Some swallowed it—since dead; several drowned. Detectives Cross and O'Shaughnessy were passing through town, but going south,—so missed elephant. Whole region for many miles around in terror,—people flying from their homes. Wherever they turn they meet elephant, and many are killed.

BRANT, Detective.

I could have shed tears, this havoc so distressed me. But the inspector only said,—

"You see,—we are closing in on him. He feels our presence; he has turned eastward again."

Yet further troublous news was in store for us. The telegraph brought this:—

HOGANPORT, 12:19.

Just arrived. Elephant passed through half an hour ago, creating wildest fright and excitement. Elephant raged around streets; two plumbers going by, killed one—other escaped. Regret general.

O'FLAHERTY, Detective.

"Now he is right in the midst of my men," said the inspector. "Nothing can save him."

A succession of telegrams came from detectives who were scattered through New Jersey and Pennsylvania, and who were following clues consisting of ravaged barns, factories, and Sunday school libraries, with high hopes,—hopes amounting to certainties, indeed. The inspector said,—

"I wish I could communicate with them and order them north, but that is impossible. A detective only visits a telegraph office to send his report; then he is off again, and you don't know where to put your hand on him."

Now came this despatch:—

BRIDGEPORT, CT., 12:15.

Barnum offers rate of $4,000 a year for exclusive privilege of using elephant as traveling advertising medium from now till detectives find him. Wants to paste circus-posters on him. Desires immediate answer.

BOGGS, Detective.

"That is perfectly absurd!" I exclaimed.

"Of course it is," said the inspector. "Evidently Mr. Barnum, who thinks he is so sharp, does not know me,—but I know him."

Then he dictated his answer to the despatch:—

Mr. Barnum's offer declined. Make it $7,000 or nothing.

Chief BLUNT.

"There. We shall not have to wait long for an answer. Mr. Barnum is not at home; he is in the telegraph office,—it is his way when he has business on hand. Inside of three—"

DONE.—P. T. BARNUM.

So interrupted the clicking telegraphic instrument. Before I could make a comment upon this extraordinary episode, the following despatch carried my thoughts into another and very distressing channel:—

BOLIVIA, N.Y., 12:50.

Elephant arrived here from the south and passed through toward the forest at 11:50, dispersing a funeral on the way, and diminishing the mourners by two. Citizens fired some small cannon-balls into him, and then fled. Detective Burke and I arrived ten minutes later, from the north, but mistook some excavations for footprints, and so lost a good deal of time; but at last we struck the right trail and followed it to the woods. We then got down on our hands and knees and continued to keep a sharp eye on the track, and so shadowed it into the brush. Burke was in advance. Unfortunately the animal had stopped to rest; therefore, Burke having his head down, intent upon the track, butted up against the elephant's hind legs before he was aware of his vicinity. Burke instantly rose to his feet, seized the tail, and exclaimed joyfully, "I claim the re——" but got no further, for a single blow of the huge trunk laid the brave fellow's fragments low in death. I fled rearward, and the elephant turned and shadowed me to the edge of the wood, making tremendous speed, and I should inevitably have been lost, but that the remains of the funeral providentially intervened again and diverted his attention. I have just learned that nothing of that funeral is now left; but this is no loss, for there is an abundance of material for another. Meantime, the elephant has disappeared again.

MULROONEY, *Detective*.

We heard no news except from the diligent and confident detectives scattered about New Jersey, Pennsylvania, Delaware, and Virginia,—who were all following fresh and encouraging clues,—until shortly after 2 P.M., when this telegram came:—

BAXTER CENTER, 2:15.

Elephant been here, plastered over with circus-bills, and broke up a revival, striking down and damaging many who were on the point of entering upon a better life. Citizens penned him up, and established a guard. When Detective Brown and I arrived, some time after, we entered enclosure and proceeded to identify elephant by photograph and description. All marks tallied exactly except one, which we could not see,—the boil-scar under armpit. To make sure, Brown crept under to look, and was immediately brained,—that is, head crushed and destroyed, though nothing issued from debris. All fled; so did elephant, striking right and left with much effect. Has escaped, but left bold blood-track from cannon-wounds. Rediscovery certain. He broke southward, through a dense forest.

BRENT, *Detective*.

That was the last telegram. At nightfall a fog shut down which was so dense that objects but three feet away could not be discerned. This lasted all night. The ferry-boats and even the omnibuses had to stop running.

3

NEXT MORNING the papers were as full of detective theories as before; they had all our tragic facts in detail also, and a great many more which they had received from their telegraphic correspondents. Column after column was occupied, a third of its way down, with glaring head-lines, which it made my heart sick to read. Their general tone was like this:—

"THE WHITE ELEPHANT AT LARGE! HE MOVES UPON HIS FA-TAL MARCH! WHOLE VILLAGES DESERTED BY THEIR FRIGHT-STRICKEN OCCUPANTS! PALE TERROR GOES BEFORE HIM, DEATH AND DEVASTATION FOLLOW AFTER! AFTER THESE, THE DETEC-TIVES. BARNS DESTROYED, FACTORIES GUTTED, HARVESTS DEVOURED, PUBLIC ASSEMBLAGES DISPERSED, ACCOMPANIED BY SCENES OF CARNAGE IMPOSSIBLE TO DESCRIBE! THEORIES OF THIRTY-FOUR OF THE MOST DISTINGUISHED DETECTIVES ON THE FORCE! THEORY OF CHIEF BLUNT!"

"There!" said Inspector Blunt, almost betrayed into excitement, "this is magnificent! This is the greatest windfall that any detective organization ever had. The fame of it will travel to the ends of the earth, and endure to the end of time, and my name with it."

But there was no joy for me. I felt as if I had committed all those red crimes, and that the elephant was only my irresponsible agent. And how the list had grown! In one place he had "interfered with an election and killed five repeaters." He had followed this act with the destruction of two poor fellows, named O'Donohue and McFlannigan, who had "found a refuge in the home of the oppressed of all lands only the day before, and were in the act of exercising for the first time the noble right of American citizens at the polls, when stricken down by the relentless hand of the Scourge of Siam." In another, he had "found a crazy sensation-preacher preparing his next season's heroic attacks on the dance, the theater, and other things which can't strike back, and had stepped on him.'' And in still another place he had ''killed a lightning-rod agent.'' And so the list went on, growing redder and redder, and more and more heart-breaking. Sixty persons had been killed, and two hundred and forty wounded. All the accounts bore just testimony to the activity and devotion of the detectives, and all closed with the remark that ''three hundred thousand citizens and four detectives saw the dread creature, and two of the latter he destroyed.''

I dreaded to hear the telegraphic instrument begin to click again. By and by the messages began to pour in, but I was happily disappointed in their nature. It was soon apparent that all trace of the elephant was lost. The fog had enabled him to search out a good hiding-place unobserved. Telegrams from the most absurdly distant points reported that a dim vast mass had been glimpsed there through the fog at such and such an hour, and was ''undoubtedly the elephant.'' This dim vast mass had been glimpsed in New Haven, in New Jersey, in Pennsylvania, in interior New York, in Brooklyn, and even in the city of New York itself! But in all cases the dim vast mass had vanished quickly and left no trace. Every detective of the large force scattered over this huge extent of country sent his hourly report, and each and every one of them had a clue, and was shadowing something, and was hot upon the heels of it.

But the day passed without other result.

The next day the same.

The next just the same.

The newspaper reports began to grow monotonous with facts that amounted to nothing, clues which led to nothing, and theories which had nearly exhausted the elements which surprise and delight and dazzle.

By advice of the inspector I doubled the reward.

Four more dull days followed. Then came a bitter blow to the poor, hard-working detectives,—the journalists declined to print their theories, and coldly said, ''Give us a rest.''

Two weeks after the elephant's disappearance I raised the reward to $75,000 by the inspector's advice. It was a great sum, but I felt that I would rather sacrifice my whole private fortune than lose my credit with my government. Now that the detectives were in adversity, the newspapers turned upon them, and began to fling the most stinging sarcasms at them. This gave the minstrels an idea, and they dressed themselves as detectives and hunted the elephant on the stage in the most extravagant way. The caricaturists made pictures of detectives scanning the country with spy-glasses, while the elephant, at their backs, stole apples out of their pockets. And they made all sorts of ridiculous pictures of the detective badge,—you have seen that badge printed in gold on the back of detective novels, no doubt,—it is a wide-staring eye, with the legend, ''WE NEVER SLEEP.'' When detectives called for a drink, the would-be facetious bar-keeper resurrected an obsolete form of expression and said, ''Will you have an eye-opener?'' All the air was thick with sarcasms.

But there was one man who moved calm, untouched, unaffected, through it all. It was that heart of oak, the Chief Inspector. His brave eye never drooped, his serene confidence never wavered. He always said,—

''Let them rail on; he laughs best who laughs last.''

My admiration for the man grew into a species of worship. I was at his side always. His office had become an unpleasant place to me, and now became daily more and more so. Yet if he could endure it I meant to do so also; at least, as long as I could. So I came regularly, and stayed,—the only outsider who seemed to be capable of it. Everybody wondered how I could; and often it seemed to me that I must desert, but at such times I looked into that calm and apparently unconscious face, and held my ground.

About three weeks after the elephant's disappearance I was about to say, one morning, that I should *have* to strike my colors and retire, when the great detective arrested the thought by proposing one more superb and masterly move.

This was to compromise with the robbers. The fertility of this man's invention exceeded anything I have ever seen, and I have had a wide intercourse with the world's finest minds. He said he was confident he could compromise for $100,000 and recover the elephant. I said I believed I could scrape the amount together, but what would become of the poor detectives who had worked so faithfully? He said,—

"In compromises they always get half."

This removed my only objection. So the inspector wrote two notes, in this form:—

> DEAR MADAM,—Your husband can make a large sum of money (and be entirely protected from the law) by making an immediate appointment with me.
>
> *Chief* BLUNT.

He sent one of these by his confidential messenger to the "reputed wife" of Brick Duffy, and the other to the reputed wife of Red McFadden. Within the hour these offensive answers came:—

> YE OWLD FOOL: brick McDuffys bin ded 2 yere.
>
> BRIDGET MAHONEY.

> CHIEF BAT,—Red McFadden is hung and in heving 18 month. Any Ass but a detective knose that.
>
> MARY O'HOOLIGAN.

"I had long suspected these facts," said the inspector; "this testimony proves the unerring accuracy of my instinct."

The moment one resource failed him he was ready with another. He immediately wrote an advertisement for the morning papers, and I kept a copy of it:—

> A.—xwblv. 242 N. Tjnd—fz328wmlg. Ozpo,—; 2 m! ogw. Mum.

He said that if the thief was alive this would bring him to the usual rendezvous. He further explained that the usual rendezvous was a place

where all business affairs between detectives and criminals were conducted. This meeting would take place at twelve the next night.

We could do nothing till then, and I lost no time in getting out of the
office, and was grateful indeed for the privilege.

At 11 the next night I brought $100,000 in banknotes and put them into
the chief's hands, and shortly afterward he took his leave, with the brave
old undimmed confidence in his eye. An almost intolerable hour dragged
to a close; then I heard his welcome tread, and rose gasping and tottered
to meet him. How his fine eyes flamed with triumph! He said,—

"We've compromised! The jokers will sing a different tune to-morrow!
Follow me!"

He took a lighted candle and strode down into the vast vaulted basement
where sixty detectives always slept, and where a score were now playing
cards to while the time. I followed close after him. He walked swiftly
down to the dim remote end of the place, and just as I succumbed to the
pangs of suffocation and was swooning away he stumbled and fell over
the outlying members of a mighty object, and I heard him exclaim as he
went down,—

"Our noble profession is vindicated. Here is your elephant!"

I was carried to the office above and restored with carbolic acid. The
whole detective force swarmed in, and such another season of triumphant
rejoicing ensued as I had never witnessed before. The reporters were
called, baskets of champagne were opened, toasts were drunk, the hand-
shakings and congratulations were continuous and enthusiastic. Naturally
the chief was the hero of the hour, and his happiness was so complete and
had been so patiently and worthily and bravely won that it made me happy
to see it, though I stood there a homeless beggar, my priceless charge
dead, and my position in my country's service lost to me through what
would always seem my fatally careless execution of a great trust. Many
an eloquent eye testified its deep admiration for the chief, and many a
detective's voice murmured, "Look at him,—just the king of the profession,—only give him a clue, it's all he wants, and there ain't anything hid
that he can't find." The dividing of the $50,000 made great pleasure;
when it was finished the chief made a little speech while he put his share
in his pocket, in which he said, "Enjoy it, boys, for you've earned it; and
more than that you've earned for the detective profession undying fame."

A telegram arrived, which read:—

MONROE, MICH., 10 P.M.

First time I've struck a telegraph office in over three weeks.
Have followed those footprints, horseback, through the woods, a
thousand miles to here, and they get stronger and bigger and
fresher every day. Don't worry—inside of another week I'll have
the elephant. This is dead sure.

DARLEY, *Detective*.

The chief ordered three cheers for "Darley, one of the finest minds on
the force," and then commanded that he be telegraphed to come home
and receive his share of the reward.

So ended that marvellous episode of the stolen elephant. The newspapers were pleasant with praises once more, the next day, with one contemptible exception. This sheet said, "Great is the detective! He may be a little slow in finding a little thing like a mislaid elephant,—he may hunt him all day and sleep with his rotting carcass all night for three weeks, but he will find him at last—if he can get the man who mislaid him to show him the place!"

Poor Hassan was lost to me forever. The cannonshots had wounded him fatally, he had crept to that unfriendly place in the fog, and there, surrounded by his enemies and in constant danger of detection, he had wasted away with hunger and suffering till death gave him peace.

The compromise cost me $100,000; my detective expenses were $42,000 more; I never applied for a place again under my government; I am a ruined man and a wanderer in the earth,—but my admiration for that man, whom I believe to be the greatest detective the world has ever produced, remains undimmed to this day, and will so remain unto the end.

SOME RAMBLING NOTES OF AN IDLE EXCURSION.

1

ALL THE journeyings I had ever done had been purely in the way of business. The pleasant May weather suggested a novelty, namely, a trip for pure recreation, the bread-and-butter element left out. The Reverend said he would go, too: a good man, one of the best of men, although a clergyman. By eleven at night we were in New Haven and on board the New York boat. We bought our tickets, and then went wandering around, here and there, in the solid comfort of being free and idle, and of putting distance between ourselves and the mails and telegraphs.

After a while I went to my state-room and undressed, but the night was too enticing for bed. We were moving down the bay now, and it was pleasant to stand at the window and take the cool night-breeze and watch the gliding lights on shore. Presently, two elderly men sat down under that window and began a conversation. Their talk was properly no business of mine, yet I was feeling friendly toward the world and willing to be entertained. I soon gathered that they were brothers, that they were from a small Connecticut village, and that the matter in hand concerned the cemetery. Said one,—

"Now, John, we talked it all over amongst ourselves, and this is what we've done. You see, everybody was a-movin' from the old buryin' ground, and our folks was most about left to theirselves, as you may say. They was crowded, too, as you know; lot wa'n't big enough in the first place; and last year, when Seth's wife died, we couldn't hardly tuck her in. She sort o' overlaid Deacon Shorb's lot, and he soured on her, so to speak, and on the rest of us, too. So we talked it over, and I was for a lay-out in the new simitery on the hill. They wa'n't unwilling, if it was cheap. Well, the two best and biggest plots was No. 8 and No. 9,—both of a size; nice comfortable room for twenty-six,—twenty-six full-growns, that is; but you reckon in children and other shorts, and strike an average, and I should say you might lay in thirty, or may be thirty-two or three, pretty genteel,—no crowdin' to signify.''

"That's a plenty, William. Which one did you buy?''

"Well, I'm a-comin' to that, John. You see, No. 8 was thirteen dollars, No. 9 fourteen—''

"I see. So's 't you took No. 8.''

"You wait. I took No. 9. And I'll tell you for why. In the first place, Deacon Shorb wanted it. Well, after the way he'd gone on about Seth's wife overlappin his prem'ses, I'd 'a' beat him out of that No. 9 if I'd 'a' had to stand two dollars extra, let alone one. That's the way I felt about it. Says I, what's a dollar, any way? Life's on'y a pilgrimage, says I; we ain't here for good, and we can't take it with us, says I. So I just dumped it down, knowin' the Lord don't suffer a good deed to go for nothin', and cal'latin' to take it out o' somebody in the course o' trade. Then there was another reason, John. No. 9's a long way the handiest lot in the simitery, and the likeliest for situation. It lays right on top of a knoll in the dead center of the buryin' ground; and you can see Millport from there, and Tracy's, and Hopper Mount, and a raft o' farms, and so on. There ain't no better outlook from a buryin' plot in the State. Si Higgins says so, and I reckon he ought to know. Well, and that ain't all. 'Course Shorb had to take No. 8; wa'n't no help for 't. Now, No. 8 jines on to No. 9, but it's on the slope of the hill, and every time it rains it'll soak right down on to the Shorbs. Si Higgins says 't when the deacon's time comes, he better take out fire and marine insurance both on his remains.''

Here there was the sound of a low, placid, duplicate chuckle of appreciation and satisfaction.

"Now, John, here's a little rough draft of the ground, that I've made on a piece of paper. Up here in the left-hand corner we've bunched the departed; took them from the old grave-yard and stowed them one along side o' t' other, on a first-come-first-served plan, no partialities, with Gran'ther Jones for a starter, on'y because it happened so, and windin' up indiscriminate with Seth's twins. A little crowded towards the end of the lay-out, may be, but we reckoned 't wa'n't best to scatter the twins. Well, next comes the livin'. Here, where it's marked A, we're goin' to put Mariar and her family, when they're called; B, that's for Brother Hosea and his'n; C, Calvin and tribe. What's left is these two lots here,—just the gem of the whole patch for general style and outlook; they're for me and my folks, and you and yourn. Which of them would you ruther be buried in?''

"I swan you've took me mighty unexpected, William! It sort of started the shivers. Fact is, I was thinkin' so busy about makin' things comfortable for the others, I hadn't thought about being buried myself.''

"Life's on'y a fleetin' show, John, as the sayin' is. We've all got to go, sooner or later. To go with a clean record's the main thing. Fact is, it's the on'y thing worth strivin' for, John.''

"Yes, that's so, William, that's so; there ain't no getting around it. Which of these lots would you recommend?''

"Well, it depends, John. Are you particular about outlook?''

"I don't say I am, William; I don't say I ain't. Reely, I don't know. But mainly, I reckon, I'd set store by a south exposure."

"That's easy fixed, John. They're both south exposure. They take the sun, and the Shorbs get the shade."

"How about sile, William?"

"D's a sandy sile, E's mostly loom."

"You may gimme E, then, William; a sandy sile caves in, more or less, and costs for repairs."

"All right; set your name down here, John, under E. Now, if you don't mind payin' me your share of the fourteen dollars, John, while we're on the business, everything's fixed."

After some higgling and sharp bargaining the money was paid, and John bade his brother good-night and took his leave. There was silence for some moments; then a soft chuckle welled up from the lonely William, and he muttered: "I declare for 't, if I haven't made a mistake! It's D that's mostly loom, not E. And John's booked for a sandy sile, after all."

There was another soft chuckle, and William departed to his rest, also.

The next day, in New York, was a hot one. Still we managed to get more or less entertainment out of it. Toward the middle of the afternoon we arrived on board the stanch steamship Bermuda, with bag and baggage, and hunted for a shady place. It was blazing summer weather, until we were half way down the harbor. Then I buttoned my coat closely; half an hour later I put on a spring overcoat and buttoned that. As we passed the light-ship I added an ulster and tied a handkerchief around the collar to hold it snug to my neck. So rapidly had the summer gone and winter come again!

By nightfall we were far out at sea, with no land in sight. No telegrams could come here, no letters, no news. This was an uplifting thought. It was still more uplifting to reflect that the millions of harassed people on shore behind us were suffering just as usual.

The next day brought us into the midst of the Atlantic solitudes,—out of smoke-colored soundings into fathomless deep blue; no ships visible anywhere over the wide ocean; no company but Mother Cary's chickens wheeling, darting, skimming the waves in the sun. There were some seafaring men among the passengers, and conversation drifted into matters concerning ships and sailors. One said that "true as the needle to the pole" was a bad figure, since the needle seldom pointed to the pole. He said a ship's compass was not faithful to any particular point, but was the most fickle and treacherous of the servants of man. It was forever changing. It changed every day in the year; consequently the amount of the daily variation had to be ciphered out and allowance made for it, else the mariner would go utterly astray. Another said there was a vast fortune waiting for the genius who should invent a compass that would not be affected by the local influences of an iron ship. He said there was only one creature more fickle than a wooden ship's compass, and that was the compass of an iron ship. Then came reference to the well-known fact that an experienced mariner can look at the compass of a new iron vessel, thousands of miles from her birthplace, and tell which way her head was pointing when she was in process of building.

Now an ancient whale-ship master fell to talking about the sort of crews they used to have in his early days. Said he,—

"Sometimes we'd have a batch of college students. Queer lot. Ignorant? Why, they didn't know the cat-heads from the main brace. But if you took them for fools you'd get bit, sure. They'd learn more in a month than another man would in a year. We had one, once, in the Mary Ann, that came aboard with gold spectacles on. And besides, he was rigged out from main truck to keelson in the nobbiest clothes that ever saw a fo'castle. He had a chest full, too: cloaks, and broadcloth coats, and velvet vests: everything swell, you know; and didn't the salt water fix them out for him? I guess not! Well, going to sea, the mate told him to go aloft and help shake out the fore-to'gallants'l. Up he shins to the foretop, with his spectacles on, and in a minute down he comes again, looking insulted. Says the mate, 'What did you come down for?' Says the chap, 'P'r'aps you didn't notice that there ain't any ladders above there.' You see we hadn't any shrouds above the foretop. The men bursted out in a laugh such as I guess you never heard the like of. Next night, which was dark and rainy, the mate ordered this chap to go aloft about something, and I'm dummed if he didn't start up with an umbrella and a lantern! But no matter; he made a mighty good sailor before the voyage was done, and we had to hunt up something else to laugh at. Years afterwards, when I had forgot all about him, I comes into Boston, mate of a ship, and was loafing around town with the second mate, and it so happened that we stepped into the Revere House, thinking may be we would chance the salt-horse in that big dining-room for a flyer, as the boys say. Some fellows were talking just at our elbow, and one says, 'Yonder's the new governor of Massachusetts,—at that table over there, with the ladies.' We took a good look, my mate and I, for we hadn't either of us ever seen a governor before. I looked and looked at that face, and then all of a sudden it popped on me! But I didn't give any sign. Says I, 'Mate, I've a notion to go over and shake hands with him.' Says he, 'I think I see you doing it, Tom.' Says I, 'Mate, I'm a-going to do it.' Says he, 'Oh, yes, I guess so! May be you don't want to bet you will, Tom?' Says I, 'I don't mind going a V on it, mate.' Says he, 'Put it up.' 'Up she goes,' says I, planking the cash. This surprised him. But he covered it, and says, pretty sarcastic, 'Hadn't you better take your grub with the governor and the ladies, Tom?' Says I, 'Upon second thoughts, I will.' Says he, 'Well, Tom, you *are* a dum fool.' Says I, 'May be I am, may be I ain't; but the main question is, do you want to risk two and half that I won't do it?' 'Make it a V,' says he. 'Done,' says I. I started, him a-giggling and slapping his hand on his thigh, he felt so good. I went over there and leaned my knuckles on the table a minute and looked the governor in the face, and says I, 'Mister Gardner, don't you know me?' He stared, and I stared, and he stared. Then all of a sudden he sings out, 'Tom Bowling, by the holy poker! Ladies, it's old Tom Bowling, that you've heard me talk about,—shipmate of mine in the Mary Ann.' He rose up and shook hands with me ever so hearty—I sort of glanced around and took a realizing sense of my mate's saucer eyes,—and then says the governor, 'Plant yourself, Tom, plant yourself; you can't cat your anchor again till you've had a feed with me and the ladies!' I planted myself alongside the governor, and canted my eye around towards my mate. Well, sir, his dead-lights were bugged out like tompions; and his mouth stood that wide open that you could have laid a ham in it without him noticing it."

There was great applause at the conclusion of the old captain's story; then, after a moment's silence, a grave, pale young man said,—

"Had you ever met the governor before?"

The old captain looked steadily at this inquirer a while, and then got up and walked aft without making any reply. One passenger after another stole a furtive glance at the inquirer, but failed to make him out, and so gave him up. It took some little work to get the talk-machinery to running smoothly again after this derangement; but at length a conversation sprang up about that important and jealously guarded instrument, a ship's time-keeper, its exceeding delicate accuracy, and the wreck and destruction that have sometimes resulted from its varying a few seemingly trifling moments from the true time; then, in due course, my comrade, the Reverend, got off on a yarn, with a fair wind and everything drawing. It was a true story, too,—about Captain Rounceville's shipwreck,—true in every detail. It was to this effect:—

Captain Rounceville's vessel was lost in mid-Atlantic, and likewise his wife and his two little children. Captain Rounceville and seven seamen escaped with life, but with little else. A small, rudely constructed raft was to be their home for eight days. They had neither provisions nor water. They had scarcely any clothing; no one had a coat but the captain. This coat was changing hands all the time, for the weather was very cold. Whenever a man became exhausted with the cold, they put the coat on him and laid him down between two shipmates until the garment and their bodies had warmed life into him again. Among the sailors was a Portuguese who knew no English. He seemed to have no thought of his own calamity, but was concerned only about the captain's bitter loss of wife and children. By day, he would look his dumb compassion in the captain's face; and by night, in the darkness and the driving spray and rain, he would seek out the captain and try to comfort him with caressing pats on the shoulder. One day, when hunger and thirst were making their sure inroads upon the men's strength and spirits, a floating barrel was seen at a distance. It seemed a great find, for doubtless it contained food of some sort. A brave fellow swam to it, and after long and exhausting effort got it to the raft. It was eagerly opened. It was a barrel of magnesia! On the fifth day an onion was spied. A sailor swam off and got it. Although perishing with hunger, he brought it in its integrity and put it into the captain's hand. The history of the sea teaches that among starving, ship-wrecked men selfishness is rare, and a wonder-compelling magnanimity the rule. The onion was equally divided into eight parts, and eaten with deep thanksgivings. On the eighth day a distant ship was sighted. Attempts were made to hoist an oar, with Captain Rounceville's coat on it for a signal. There were many failures, for the men were but skeletons now, and strengthless. At last success was achieved, but the signal brought no help. The ship faded out of sight and left despair behind her. By and by another ship appeared, and passed so near that the castaways, every eye eloquent with gratitude, made ready to welcome the boat that would be sent to save them. But this ship also drove on, and left these men staring their unutterable surprise and dismay into each other's ashen faces. Late in the day, still another ship came up out of the distance, but the men noted with a pang that her course was one which would not bring her

nearer. Their remnant of life was nearly spent; their lip
swollen, parched, cracked with eight days' thirst; their
here was their last chance gliding relentlessly from the
be alive when the next sun rose. For a day or two pas
their voices, but now Captain Rounceville whispered,
Portuguese patted him on the shoulder in sign of deep
at the base of the oar that was waving the signal-coat
their heads. The sea was tossing; the sun rested, a red, rayless disk, on
the sea-line in the west. When the men presently raised their heads they
would have roared a hallelujah if they had had a voice: the ship's sails lay
wrinkled and flapping against her masts, she was going about! Here was
rescue at last, and in the very last instant of time that was left for it. No,
not rescue yet,—only the imminent prospect of it. The red disk sank
under the sea and darkness blotted out the ship. By and by came a pleasant
sound,—oars moving in a boat's rowlocks. Nearer it came, and nearer,—
within thirty steps, but nothing visible. Then a deep voice: "Hol-*lo!*" The
castaways could not answer; their swollen tongues refused voice. The boat
skirted round and round the raft, started away—the agony of it!—returned, rested the oars, close at hand, listening, no doubt. The deep voice
again: "Hol-*lo!* Where are ye, shipmates?" Captain Rounceville whispered to his men, saying: "Whisper your best, boys! now—all at once!"
So they sent out an eightfold whisper in hoarse concert: "Here!" There
was life in it if it succeeded; death if it failed. After that supreme moment
Captain Rounceville was conscious of nothing until he came to himself
on board the saving ship. Said the Reverend, concluding,—

"There was one little moment of time in which that raft could be visible
from that ship, and only one. If that one little fleeting moment had passed
unfruitful, those men's doom was sealed. As close as that does God shave
events foreordained from the beginning of the world. When the sun reached
the water's edge that day, the captain of that ship was sitting on deck
reading his prayer-book. The book fell; he stooped to pick it up, and
happened to glance at the sun. In that instant that far-off raft appeared for
a second against the red disk, its needle-like oar and diminuitive signal
cut sharp and black against the bright surface, and in the next instant was
thrust away into the dusk again. But that ship, that captain, and that
pregnant instant had had their work appointed for them in the dawn of
time and could not fail of the performance. The chronometer of God
never errs!"

There was deep, thoughtful silence for some moments. Then the grave,
pale young man said,—

"What is the chronometer of God?"

2

At DINNER, six o'clock, the same people assembled whom we had talked
with on deck and seen at luncheon and breakfast this second day out, and
at dinner the evening before. That is to say, three journeying ship-masters,

ston merchant, and a returning Bermudian who had been absent from
Bermuda thirteen years; these sat on the starboard side. On the port
side sat the Reverend in the seat of honor; the pale young man next to
him; I next; next to me an aged Bermudian, returning to his sunny islands
after an absence of twenty-seven years. Of course our captain was at the
head of the table, the purser at the foot of it. A small company, but small
companies are pleasantest.

No racks upon the table; the sky cloudless, the sun brilliant, the blue
sea scarcely ruffled: then what had become of the four married couples,
the three bachelors, and the active and obliging doctor from the rural
districts of Pennsylvania?—for all these were on deck when we sailed
down New York harbor. This is the explanation. I quote from my note-
book:—

Thursday, 3:30 P.M. Under way, passing the Battery. The large party,
of four married couples, three bachelors, and a cheery, exhilarating doctor
from the wilds of Pennsylvania, are evidently travelling together. All but
the doctor grouped in camp-chairs on deck.

Passing principal fort. The doctor is one of those people who has an
infallible preventive of sea-sickness; is flitting from friend to friend admin-
istering it and saying, "Don't you be afraid; I *know* this medicine; absolutely infallible; prepared under my own supervision." Takes a dose himself, intrepidly.

4:15 P.M. Two of those ladies have struck their colors, notwithstanding
the "infallible." They have gone below. The other two begin to show
distress.

5 P.M. Exit one husband and one bachelor. These still had their infallible
in cargo when they started, but arrived at the companion-way without it.

5:10. Lady No. 3, two bachelors, and one married man have gone
below with their own opinion of the infallible.

5:20. Passing Quarantine Hulk. The infallible has done the business for
all the party except the Scotchman's wife and the author of that formidable
remedy.

Nearing the Light-Ship. Exit the Scotchman's wife, head drooped on
stewardess's shoulder.

Entering the open sea. Exit doctor!

The rout seems permanent; hence the smallness of the company at table
since the voyage began. Our captain is a grave, handsome Hercules of
thirty-five, with a brown hand of such majestic size that one cannot eat
for admiring it and wondering if a single kid or calf could furnish material
for gloving it.

Conversation not general; drones along between couples. One catches a
sentence here and there. Like this, from Bermudian of thirteen years'
absence: "It is the nature of women to ask trivial, irrelevant, and pursuing
questions,—questions that pursue you from a beginning in nothing to a
run-to-cover in nowhere." Reply of Bermudian of twenty-seven years'
absence: "Yes; and to think they have logical, analytical minds and argumentative ability. You see 'em begin to whet up whenever they smell
argument in the air." Plainly these be philosophers.

Twice since we left port our engines have stopped for a couple of minutes at a time. Now they stop again. Says the pale young man, meditatively, "There!—that engineer is sitting down to rest again."

Grave stare from the captain, whose mighty jaws cease to work, and whose harpooned potato stops in mid-air on its way to his open, paralyzed mouth. Presently says he in measured tones, "Is it your idea that the engineer of this ship propels her by a crank turned by his own hands?"

The pale young man studies over this a moment, then lifts up his guileless eyes, and says, "Don't he?"

Thus gently falls the death-blow to further conversation, and the dinner drags to its close in a reflective silence, disturbed by no sounds but the murmurous wash of the sea and the subdued clash of teeth.

After a smoke and a promenade on deck, where is no motion to discompose our steps, we think of a game of whist. We ask the brisk and capable stewardess from Ireland if there are any cards in the ship.

"Bless your soul, dear, indeed there is. Not a whole pack, true for ye, but not enough missing to signify."

However, I happened by accident to bethink me of a new pack in a morocco case, in my trunk, which I had placed there by mistake, thinking it to be a flask of something. So a party of us conquered the tedium of the evening with a few games and were ready for bed at six bells, mariner's time, the signal for putting out the lights.

There was much chat in the smoking-cabin on the upper deck after luncheon to-day, mostly whaler yarns from those old sea-captains. Captain Tom Bowling was garrulous. He had that garrulous attention to minor detail which is born of secluded farm life or life at sea on long voyages, where there is little to do and time no object. He would sail along till he was right in the most exciting part of a yarn, and then say, "Well, as I was saying, the rudder was fouled, ship driving before the gale, head-on, straight for the iceberg, all hands holding their breath, turned to stone, top-hamper giving way, sails blown to ribbons, first one stick going, then another, boom! smash! crash! duck your head and stand from under! when up comes Johnny Rogers, capstan bar in hand, eyes a-blazing, hair a-flying . . . no, 't wa'n't Johnny Rogers . . . lemme see . . . seems to me Johnny Rogers wa'n't along that voyage; he was along *one* voyage, I know that mighty well, but somehow it seems to me that he signed the articles for this voyage, but—but—whether he come along or not, or got left, or something happened—"

And so on and so on, till the excitement all cooled down and nobody cared whether the ship struck the iceberg or not.

In the course of his talk he rambled into a criticism upon New England degrees of merit in ship-building. Said he, "You get a vessel built away down Maineway; Bath, for instance; what's the result? First thing you do, you want to heave her down for repairs,—*that's* the result! Well, sir, she hain't been hove down a week till you can heave a dog through her seams. You send that vessel to sea, and what's the result? She wets her oakum the first trip! Leave it to any man if 't ain't so. Well, you let *our* folks build you a vessel—down New Bedford-way. What's the result? Well, sir, you might take that ship and heave her down, and keep her hove down six months, and she'll never shed a tear!"

Everybody, landsmen and all, recognized the descriptive neatness of that figure, and applauded, which greatly pleased the old man. A moment later, the meek eyes of the pale young fellow heretofore mentioned came up slowly, rested upon the old man's face a moment, and the meek mouth began to open.

"Shet your head!" shouted the old mariner.

It was a rather startling surprise to everybody, but it was effective in the matter of its purpose. So the conversation flowed on instead of perishing.

There was some talk about the perils of the sea, and a landsman delivered himself of the customary nonsense about the poor mariner wandering in far oceans, tempest-tossed, pursued by dangers, every storm-blast and thunderbolt in the home skies moving the friends by snug firesides to compassion for that poor mariner, and prayers for his succor. Captain Bowling put up with this for a while, and then burst out with a new view of the matter.

"Come, belay there! I have read this kind of rot all my life in poetry and tales and such like rubbage. Pity for the poor mariner! sympathy for the poor mariner! All right enough, but not in the way the poetry puts it. Pity for the mariner's wife! all right again, but not in the way the poetry puts it. Look-a-here! whose life's the safest in the whole world? The poor mariner's. You look at the statistics, you'll see. So don't you fool away any sympathy on the poor mariner's dangers and privations and sufferings. Leave that to the poetry muffs. Now you look at the other side a minute. Here is Captain Brace, forty years old, been at sea thirty. On his way now to take command of his ship and sail south from Bermuda. Next week he'll be under way: easy times; comfortable quarters; passengers, sociable company; just enough to do to keep his mind healthy and not tire him; king over his ship, boss of everything and everybody; thirty years' safety to learn him that his profession ain't a dangerous one. Now you look back at his home. His wife's a feeble woman; she's a stranger in New York; shut up in blazing hot or freezing cold lodgings, according to the season; don't know anybody hardly; no company but her lonesomeness and her thoughts; husband gone six months at a time. She has borne eight children; five of them she has buried without her husband ever setting eyes on them. She watched them all the long nights till they died,—he comfortable on the sea; she followed them to the grave, she heard the clods fall that broke her heart,—he comfortable on the sea; she mourned at home, weeks and weeks, missing them every day and every hour,—he cheerful at sea, knowing nothing about it. Now look at it a minute,—turn it over in your mind and size it: five children born, she among strangers, and him not by to hearten her; buried, and him not by to comfort her; think of that! Sympathy for the poor mariner's perils is rot; give it to his wife's hard lines, where it belongs! Poetry makes out that all the wife worries about is the dangers her husband's running. She's got substantialer things to worry over, I tell you. Poetry's always pitying the poor mariner on account of his perils at sea; better a blamed sight pity him for the nights he can't sleep for thinking of how he had to leave his wife in her very birth pains, lonesome and friendless, in the thick of disease and trouble and death. If there's one thing that can make me madder than another, it's this sappy, damned maritime poetry!"

Captain Brace was a patient, gentle, seldom-speaking man, with a pathetic something in his bronzed face that had been a mystery up to this time, but stood interpreted now, since we had heard his story. He had voyaged eighteen times to the Mediterranean, seven times to India, once to the arctic pole in a discovery-ship, and "between times" had visited all the remote seas and ocean corners of the globe. But he said that twelve years ago, on account of his family, he "settled down," and ever since then had ceased to roam. And what do you suppose was this simple-hearted, life-long wanderer's idea of settling down and ceasing to roam? Why, the making of two five-month voyages a year between Surinam and Boston for sugar and molasses!

Among other talk, to-day, it came out that whaleships carry no doctor. The captain adds the doctorship to his own duties. He not only gives medicines, but sets broken limbs after notions of his own, or saws them off and sears the stump when amputation seems best. The captain is provided with a medicine-chest, with the medicines numbered instead of named. A book of directions goes with this. It describes diseases and symptoms, and says, "Give a teaspoonful of No. 9 once an hour," or "Give ten grains of No. 12 every half hour," etc. One of our sea-captains came across a skipper in the North Pacific who was in a state of great surprise and perplexity. Said he,—

"There's something rotten about this medicine-chest business. One of my men was sick,—nothing much the matter. I looked in the book: it said, give him a teaspoonful of No. 15. I went to the medicine-chest, and I see I was out of No. 15. I judged I'd got to get up a combination somehow that would fill the bill; so I hove into the fellow half a teaspoonful of No. 8 and half a teaspoonful of No. 7, and I'll be hanged if it didn't kill him in fifteen minutes! There's something about this medicine-chest system that's too many for me!"

There was a good deal of pleasant gossip about old Captain "Hurricane" Jones, of the Pacific Ocean,—peace to his ashes! Two or three of us present had known him; I, particularly well, for I had made four sea-voyages with him. He was a very remarkable man. He was born in a ship; he picked up what little education he had among his shipmates; he began life in the forecastle, and climbed grade by grade to the captaincy. More than fifty years of his sixty-five were spent at sea. He had sailed all oceans, seen all lands, and borrowed a tint from all climates. When a man has been fifty years at sea he necessarily knows nothing of men, nothing of the world but its surface, nothing of the world's thought, nothing of the world's learning but its A B C, and that blurred and distorted by the unfocused lenses of an untrained mind. Such a man is only a gray and bearded child. That is what old Hurricane Jones was,— simply an innocent, lovable old infant. When his spirit was in repose he was as sweet and gentle as a girl; when his wrath was up he was a hurricane that made his nickname seem tamely descriptive. He was formidable in a fight, for he was of powerful build and dauntless courage. He was frescoed from head to heel with pictures and mottoes tattooed in red and blue India ink. I was with him one voyage when he got his last vacant space tattooed; this vacant space was around his left ankle. During three days he stumped about the ship with his ankle bare and swollen, and this legend gleaming red and angry out from a clouding of India ink: "Virtue is its own R'd." (There was a lack of room.) He was deeply and sincerely pious, and swore like a fish-woman. He considered swearing blameless, because sailors would not understand an order unillumined by it. He was a profound Biblical scholar,—that is, he thought he was. He believed everything in the Bible, but he had his own methods of arriving at his beliefs. He was of the "advanced" school of thinkers, and applied natural laws to the interpretation of all miracles, somewhat on the plan of the people who make the six days of creation six geological epochs, and so forth. Without being aware of it, he was a rather severe satire on modern scientific religionists. Such a man as I have been describing is rabidly fond of disquisition and argument; one knows that without being told it.

One trip the captain had a clergyman on board, but did not know he was a clergyman, since the passenger list did not betray the fact. He took a great liking to this Rev. Mr. Peters, and talked with him a great deal: told him yarns, gave him toothsome scraps of personal history, and wove a glittering streak of profanity through his garrulous fabric that was refreshing to a spirit weary of the dull neutralities of undecorated speech. One day the captain said, "Peters, do you ever read the Bible?"

"Well—yes."

"I judge it ain't often, by the way you say it. Now, you tackle it in dead earnest once, and you'll find it'll pay. Don't you get discouraged, but hang right on. First, you won't understand it; but by and by things will begin to clear up, and then you wouldn't lay it down to eat."

"Yes, I have heard that said."

"And it's so, too. There ain't a book that begins with it. It lays over 'em all, Peters. There's some pretty tough things in it,—there ain't any getting around that,—but you stick to them and think them out, and when once you get on the inside everything's plain as day."

"The miracles, too, captain?"

"Yes, sir! the miracles, too. Every one of them. Now, there's that business with the prophets of Baal; like enough that stumped you?"

"Well, I don't know but—"

"Own up, now; it stumped you. Well, I don't wonder. You hadn't had any experience in ravelling such things out, and naturally it was too many for you. Would you like to have me explain that thing to you, and show you how to get at the meat of these matters?"

"Indeed, I would, captain, if you don't mind."

Then the captain proceeded as follows: "I'll do it with pleasure. First, you see, I read and read, and thought and thought, till I got to understand what sort of people they were in the old Bible times, and then after that it was all clear and easy. Now, this was the way I put it up, concerning Isaac[1] and the prophets of Baal. There was some mighty sharp men amongst the public characters of that old ancient day, and Isaac was one of them. Isaac had his failings,—plenty of them, too; it ain't for me to apologize for Isaac; he played it on the prophets of Baal, and like enough he was justifiable, considering the odds that was against him. No, all I say is, 't

---

[1] This is the captain's own mistake.

wa'n't any miracle, and that I'll show you so's 't you can see it yourself.

"Well, times had been getting rougher and rougher for prophets,—that is, prophets of Isaac's denomination. There was four hundred and fifty prophets of Baal in the community, and only one Presbyterian; that is, if Isaac *was* a Presbyterian, which I reckon he was, but it don't say. Naturally, the prophets of Baal took all the trade. Isaac was pretty low-spirited, I reckon, but he was a good deal of a man, and no doubt he went a-prophesying around, letting on to be doing a land-office business, but 't wa'n't any use; he couldn't run any opposition to amount to anything. By and by things got desperate with him; he sets his head to work and thinks it all out, and then what does he do? Why, he begins to throw out hints that the other parties are this and that and t' other,—nothing very definite, may be, but just kind of undermining their reputation in a quiet way. This made talk, of course, and finally got to the king. The king asked Isaac what he meant by his talk. Says Isaac, 'Oh, nothing particular; only, can they pray down fire from heaven on an altar? It ain't much, may be, your majesty, only can they *do* it? That's the idea.' So the king was a good deal disturbed, and he went to the prophets of Baal, and they said, pretty airy, that if he had an altar ready, *they* were ready; and they intimated he better get it insured, too.

"So next morning all the children of Israel and their parents and the other people gathered themselves together. Well, here was that great crowd of prophets of Baal packed together on one side, and Isaac walking up and down all alone on the other, putting up his job. When time was called, Isaac let on to be comfortable and indifferent; told the other team to take the first innings. So they went at it, the whole four hundred and fifty, praying around the altar, very hopeful, and doing their level best. They prayed an hour,—two hours,—three hours,—and so on, plumb till noon. It wa'n't any use; they hadn't took a trick. Of course they felt kind of ashamed before all those people, and well they might. Now, what would a magnanimous man do? Keep still, wouldn't he? Of course. What did Isaac do? He gravelled the prophets of Baal every way he could think of. Says he, 'You don't speak up loud enough; your god's asleep, like enough, or may be he's taking a walk; you want to holler, you know,'—or words to that effect; I don't recollect the exact language. Mind, I don't apologize for Isaac; he had his faults.

"Well, the prophets of Baal prayed along the best they knew how all the afternoon, and never raised a spark. At last, about sundown, they were all tuckered out, and they owned up and quit.

"What does Isaac do, now? He steps up and says to some friends of his, there, 'Pour four barrels of water on the altar!' Everybody was astonished; for the other side had prayed at it dry, you know, and got white-washed. They poured it on. Says he, 'Heave on four more barrels.' Then he says, 'Heave on four more.' Twelve barrels, you see, altogether. The water ran all over the altar, and all down the sides, and filled up a trench around it that would hold a couple of hogsheads,—'measures,' it says; I reckon it means about a hogshead. Some of the people were going to put on their things and go, for they allowed he was crazy. They didn't know Isaac. Isaac knelt down and began to pray: he strung along, and strung along, about the heathen in distant lands, and about the sister churches,

and about the state and the country at large, and about those that's in
authority in the government, and all the usual program, you know, till
everybody had got tired and gone to thinking about something else, and
then, all of a sudden, when nobody was noticing, he outs with a match
and rakes it on the under side of his leg, and pff! up the whole thing blazes
like a house afire! Twelve barrels of *water? Petroleum,* sir, PETROLEUM!
that's what it was!''

"Petroleum, captain?"

"Yes, sir; the country was full of it. Isaac knew all about that. You read
the Bible. Don't you worry about the tough places. They ain't tough when
you come to think them out and throw light on them. There ain't a thing
in the Bible but what is true; all you want is to go prayerfully to work and
cipher out how 't was done.''

At eight o'clock on the third morning out from New York, land was
sighted. Away across the sunny waves one saw a faint dark stripe stretched
along under the horizon,— or pretended to see it, for the credit of his
eyesight. Even the Reverend said he saw it, a thing which was manifestly
not so. But I never have seen any one who was morally strong enough to
confess that he could not see land when others claimed that they could.

By and by the Bermuda Islands were easily visible. The principal one
lay upon the water in the distance, a long, dull-colored body, scalloped
with slight hills and valleys. We could not go straight at it, but had to
travel all the way around it, sixteen miles from shore, because it is fenced
with an invisible coral reef. At last we sighted buoys, bobbing here and
there, and then we glided into a narrow channel among them, "raised the
reef,'' and came upon shoaling blue water that soon further shoaled into
pale green, with a surface scarcely rippled. Now came the resurrection
hour: the berths gave up their dead. Who are these pale specters in plug
hats and silken flounces that file up the companion-way in melancholy
procession and step upon the deck? These are they which took the infallible preventive of sea-sickness in New York harbor and then disappeared
and were forgotten. Also there came two or three faces not seen before
until this moment. One's impulse is to ask, "Where did *you* come aboard?''

We followed the narrow channel a long time, with land on both sides,—
low hills that might have been green and grassy, but had a faded look
instead. However, the land-locked water was lovely, at any rate, with its
glittering belts of blue and green where moderate soundings were, and its
broad splotches of rich brown where the rocks lay near the surface. Everybody was feeling so well that even the grave, pale young man (who, by a
sort of kindly common consent, had come latterly to be referred to as "the
Ass'') received frequent and friendly notice,—which was right enough,
for there was no harm in him.

At last we steamed between two island points whose rocky jaws allowed only just enough room for the vessel's body, and now before us
loomed Hamilton on her clustered hillsides and summits, the whitest mass
of terraced architecture that exists in the world, perhaps.

It was Sunday afternoon, and on the pier were gathered one or two
hundred Bermudians, half of them black, half of them white, and all of
them nobbily dressed, as the poet says.

Several boats came off to the ship, bringing citizens. One of these citizens was a faded, diminutive old gentleman, who approached our most ancient passenger with a childlike joy in his twinkling eyes, halted before him, folded his arms, and said, smiling with all his might and with all the simple delight that was in him, "You don't know me, John! Come, out with it, now; you know you don't!"

The ancient passenger scanned him perplexedly, scanned the napless, threadbare costume of venerable fashion that had done Sunday-service no man knows how many years, contemplated the marvellous stovepipe hat of still more ancient and venerable pattern, with its poor pathetic old stiff brim canted up "gallusly" in the wrong places, and said, with a hesitation that indicated strong internal effort to "place" the gentle old apparition, "Why . . . let me see . . . plague on it . . . there's *something* about you that . . . er . . . er . . . but I've been gone from Bermuda for twenty-seven years, and . . . hum, hum . . . I don't seem to get at it, somehow, but there's something about you that is just as familiar to me as—"

"Likely it might be his hat," murmured the Ass, with innocent, sympathetic interest.

3

SO THE Reverend and I had at last arrived at Hamilton, the principal town in the Bermuda Islands. A wonderfully white town; white as snow itself. White as marble; white as flour. Yet looking like none of these, exactly. Never mind, we said; we shall hit upon a figure by and by that will describe this peculiar white.

It was a town that was compacted together upon the sides and tops of a cluster of small hills. Its outlying borders fringed off and thinned away among the cedar forests, and there was no woody distance of curving coast, or leafy islet sleeping upon the dimpled, painted sea, but was flecked with shining white points,—half-concealed houses peeping out of the foliage. The architecture of the town was mainly Spanish, inherited from the colonists of two hundred and fifty years ago. Some ragged-topped cocoa-palms, glimpsed here and there, gave the land a tropical aspect.

There was an ample pier of heavy masonry; upon this, under shelter, were some thousands of barrels containing that product which has carried the fame of Bermuda to many lands, the potato. With here and there an onion. That last sentence is facetious; for they grow at least two onions in Bermuda to one potato. The onion is the pride and joy of Bermuda. It is her jewel, her gem of gems. In her conversation, her pulpit, her literature, it is her most frequent and eloquent figure. In Bermudian metaphor it stands for perfection,—perfection absolute.

The Bermudian weeping over the departed exhausts praise when he says, "He was an onion!" The Bermudian extolling the living hero bankrupts applause when he says, "He is an onion!" The Bermudian setting his son upon the stage of life to dare and do for himself climaxes all counsel, supplication, admonition, comprehends all ambition, when he says, "Be an onion!"

When parallel with the pier, and ten or fifteen steps outside it, we anchored. It was Sunday, bright and sunny. The groups upon the pier— men, youths, and boys—were whites and blacks in about equal proportion. All were well and neatly dressed, many of them nattily, a few of them very stylishly. One would have to travel far before he would find another town of twelve thousand inhabitants that could represent itself so respectably, in the matter of clothes, on a freight-pier, without premeditation or effort. The women and young girls, black and white, who occasionally passed by, were nicely clad, and many were elegantly and fashionably so. The men did not affect summer clothing much, but the girls and women did, and their white garments were good to look at, after so many months of familiarity with somber colors.

Around one isolated potato barrel stood four young gentlemen, two black, two white, becomingly dressed, each with the head of a slender cane pressed against his teeth, and each with a foot propped up on the barrel. Another young gentleman came up, looked longingly at the barrel, but saw no rest for his foot there, and turned pensively away to seek another barrel. He wandered here and there, but without result. Nobody sat upon a barrel, as is the custom of the idle in other lands, yet all the isolated barrels were humanly occupied. Whosoever had a foot to spare put it on a barrel, if all the places on it were not already taken. The habits of all peoples are determined by their circumstances. The Bermudians lean upon barrels because of the scarcity of lamp-posts.

Many citizens came on board and spoke eagerly to the officers,— inquiring about the Turco-Russian war news, I supposed. However, by listening judiciously I found that this was not so. They said, "What is the price of onions?" or, "How's onions?" Naturally enough this was their first interest; but they dropped into the war the moment it was satisfied.

We went ashore and found a novelty of a pleasant nature: there were no hackmen, hacks, or omnibuses on the pier or about it anywhere, and nobody offered his services to us, or molested us in any way. I said it was like being in heaven. The Reverend rebukingly and rather pointedly advised me to make the most of it, then. We knew of a boarding-house, and what we needed now was somebody to pilot us to it. Presently a little barefooted colored boy came along, whose raggedness was conspicuously un-Bermudian. His rear was so marvellously bepatched with colored squares and triangles that one was half persuaded he had got it out of an atlas. When the sun struck him right, he was as good to follow as a lightning-bug. We hired him and dropped into his wake. He piloted us through one picturesque street after another, and in due course deposited us where we belonged. He charged nothing for his map, and but a trifle for his services; so the Reverend doubled it. The little chap received the money with a beaming applause in his eye which plainly said, "This man's an onion!"

We had brought no letters of introduction; our names had been misspelt in the passenger list; nobody knew whether we were honest folk or otherwise. So we were expecting to have a good private time in case there was nothing in our general aspect to close boarding-house doors against us. We had no trouble. Bermuda has had but little experience of rascals, and is not suspicious. We got large, cool, well-lighted rooms on a second floor, overlooking a bloomy display of flowers and flowering shrubs,—calla and annunciation lilies, lantanas, heliotrope, jessamine, roses, pinks, double geraniums, oleanders, pomegranates, blue morning-glories of a great size, and many plants that were unknown to me.

We took a long afternoon walk, and soon found out that that exceedingly white town was built of blocks of white coral. Bermuda is a coral island, with a six-inch crust of soil on top of it, and every man has a quarry on his own premises. Everywhere you go you see square recesses cut into the hillsides, with perpendicular walls unmarred by crack or crevice, and perhaps you fancy that a house grew out of the ground there, and has been removed in a single piece from the mold. If you do, you err. But the material for a house has been quarried there. They cut right down through the coral, to any depth that is convenient,—ten to twenty feet,—and take it out in great square blocks. This cutting is done with a chisel that has a handle twelve or fifteen feet long, and is used as one uses a crowbar when he is drilling a hole, or a dasher when he is churning. Thus soft is this stone. Then with a common handsaw they saw the great blocks into handsome, huge bricks that are two feet long, a foot wide, and about six inches thick. These stand loosely piled during a month to harden; then the work of building begins. The house is built of these blocks; it is roofed with broad coral slabs an inch thick, whose edges lap upon each other, so that the roof looks like a succession of shallow steps or terraces; the chimneys are built of the coral blocks, and sawed into graceful and picturesque patterns; the ground-floor veranda is paved with coral blocks; also the walk to the gate; the fence is built of coral blocks,—built in massive panels, with broad capstones and heavy gate-posts, and the whole trimmed into easy lines and comely shape with the saw. Then they put a hard coat of whitewash, as thick as your thumb nail, on the fence and all over the house, roof, chimneys, and all; the sun comes out and shines on this spectacle, and it is time for you to shut your unaccustomed eyes, lest they be put out. It is the whitest white you can conceive of, and the blindingest. A Bermuda house does not look like marble; it is a much intenser white than that; and besides, there is a dainty, indefinable something else about its look that is not marble-like. We put in a great deal of solid talk and reflection over this matter of trying to find a figure that would describe the unique white of a Bermuda house, and we contrived to hit upon it at last. It is exactly the white of the icing of a cake, and has the same unemphasized and scarcely perceptible polish. The white of marble is modest and retiring compared with it.

After the house is cased in its hard scale of whitewash, not a crack, or sign of a seam, or joining of the blocks, is detectable, from base-stone to chimney-top; the building looks as if it had been carved from a single block of stone, and the doors and windows sawed out afterwards. A white marble house has a cold, tomb-like, unsociable look, and takes the conversation out of a body and depresses him. Not so with a Bermuda house. There is something exhilarating, even hilarious, about its vivid whiteness when the sun plays upon it. If it be of picturesque shape and graceful contour,—and many of the Bermudian dwellings are,—it will so fascinate you that you will keep your eyes on it until they ache. One of those clean-cut, fanciful chimneys,—too pure and white for this world,—with one side glowing in the sun and the other touched with a soft shadow, is an object that will charm one's gaze by the hour. I know of no other country that has chimneys worthy to be gazed at and gloated over. One of those snowy houses, half-concealed and half-glimpsed through green foliage, is a pretty thing to see; and if it takes one by surprise and suddenly, as he turns a sharp corner of a country road, it will wring an exclamation from him, sure.

Wherever you go, in town or country, you find those snowy houses, and always with masses of bright-colored flowers about them, but with no vines climbing their walls; vines cannot take hold of the smooth, hard whitewash. Wherever you go, in the town or along the country roads, among little potato farms and patches or expensive country-seats, these stainless white dwellings, gleaming out from flowers and foliage, meet you at every turn. The least little bit of a cottage is as white and blemish-less as the stateliest mansion. Nowhere is there dirt or stench, puddle or hog-wallow, neglect, disorder, or lack of trimness and neatness. The roads, the streets, the dwellings, the people, the clothes,—this neatness extends to everything that falls under the eye. It is the tidiest country in the world. And very much the tidiest, too.

Considering these things, the question came up, Where do the poor live? No answer was arrived at. Therefore, we agreed to leave this conun-drum for future statesmen to wrangle over.

What a bright and startling spectacle one of those blazing white country palaces, with its brown-tinted window caps and ledges, and green shut-ters, and its wealth of caressing flowers and foliage, would be in black London! And what a gleaming surprise it would be in nearly any Ameri-can city one could mention, too!

Bermuda roads are made by cutting down a few inches into the solid white coral—or a good many feet, where a hill intrudes itself—and smoothing off the surface of the road-bed. It is a simple and easy process. The grain of the coral is coarse and porous; the road-bed has the look of being made of coarse white sugar. Its excessive cleanness and whiteness are a trouble in one way: the sun is reflected into your eyes with such energy as you walk along, that you want to sneeze all the time. Old Captain Tom Bowling found another difficulty. He joined us in our walk, but kept wandering unrestfully to the roadside. Finally he explained. Said he, "Well, I chew, you know, and the road's so plaguy clean."

We walked several miles that afternoon in the bewildering glare of the sun, the white roads, and the white buildings. Our eyes got to paining us a good deal. By and by a soothing, blessed twilight spread its cool balm around. We looked up in pleased surprise and saw that it proceeded from an intensely black negro who was going by. We answered his military salute in the grateful gloom of his near presence, and then passed on into the pitiless white glare again.

The colored women whom we met usually bowed and spoke; so did the children. The colored men commonly gave the military salute. They bor-row this fashion from the soldiers, no doubt; England has kept a garrison here for generations. The younger men's custom of carrying small canes is also borrowed from the soldiers, I suppose, who always carry a cane, in Bermuda as everywhere else in Britain's broad dominions.

The country roads curve and wind hither and thither in the delightfulest way, unfolding pretty surprises at every turn: billowy masses of oleander that seem to float out from behind distant projections like the pink cloud-banks of sunset; sudden plunges among cottages and gardens, life and activity, followed by as sudden plunges into the somber twilight and still-ness of the woods; flitting visions of white fortresses and beacon towers pictured against the sky on remote hill-tops; glimpses of shining green sea caught for a moment through opening headlands, then lost again; more woods and solitude; and by and by another turn lays bare, without warn-ing, the full sweep of the inland ocean, enriched with its bars of soft color, and graced with its wandering sails.

Take any road you please, you may depend upon it you will not stay in it half a mile. Your road is everything that a road ought to be: it is bordered with trees, and with strange plants and flowers; it is shady and pleasant, or sunny and still pleasant; it carries you by the prettiest and peacefulest and most homelike of homes, and through stretches of forest that lie in a deep hush sometimes, and sometimes are alive with the music of birds; it curves always, which is a continual promise, whereas straight roads reveal everything at a glance and kill interest. Your road is all this, and yet you will not stay in it half a mile, for the reason that little seductive, mysterious roads are always branching out from it on either hand, and as these curve sharply also and hide what is beyond, you cannot resist the temptation to desert your own chosen road and explore them. You are usually paid for your trouble; consequently, your walk inland always turns out to be one of the most crooked, involved, purposeless, and interesting experiences a body can imagine. There is enough of variety. Sometimes you are in the level open, with marshes thick grown with flag-lances that are ten feet high on the one hand, and potato and onion orchards on the other; next, you are on a hill-top, with the ocean and the Islands spread around you; presently the road winds through a deep cut, shut in by perpendicular walls thirty or forty feet high, marked with the oddest and abruptest stratum lines, suggestive of sudden and eccentric old upheavals, and gar-nished with here and there a clinging adventurous flower, and here and there a dangling vine; and by and by your way is along the sea edge, and you may look down a fathom or two through the transparent water and watch the diamond-like flash and play of the light upon the rocks and sands on the bottom until you are tired of it,—if you are so constituted as to be able to get tired of it.

You may march the country roads in maiden meditation, fancy free, by field and farm, for no dog will plunge out at you from unsuspected gate, with breathtaking surprise of ferocious bark, notwithstanding it is a Chris-tian land and a civilized. We saw upwards of a million cats in Bermuda, but the people are very abstemious in the matter of dogs. Two or three nights we prowled the country far and wide, and never once were accosted by a dog. It is a great privilege to visit such a land. The cats were no offence when properly distributed, but when piled they obstructed travel.

As we entered the edge of the town that Sunday afternoon, we stopped at a cottage to get a drink of water. The proprietor, a middle-aged man with a good face, asked us to sit down and rest. His dame brought chairs,

and we grouped ourselves in the shade of the trees by the door. Mr.
Smith—that was not his name, but it will answer—questioned us about
ourselves and our country, and we answered him truthfully, as a general
thing, and questioned him in return. It was all very simple and pleasant
and sociable. Rural, too; for there was a pig and a small donkey and a hen
anchored out, close at hand, by cords to their legs, on a spot that purported
to be grassy. Presently, a woman passed along, and although she coldly
said nothing she changed the drift of our talk. Said Smith:—

"She didn't look this way, you noticed? Well, she is our next neighbor
on one side, and there's another family that's our next neighbors on the
other side; but there's a general coolness all around now, and we don't
speak. Yet these three families, one generation and another, have lived
here side by side and been as friendly as weavers for a hundred and fifty
years, till about a year ago."

"Why, what calamity could have been powerful enough to break up so
old a friendship?"

"Well, it was too bad, but it couldn't be helped. It happened like this:
About a year or more ago, the rats got to pestering my place a good deal,
and I set up a steel-trap in the back yard. Both of these neighbors run
considerable to cats, and so I warned them about the trap, because their
cats were pretty sociable around here nights, and they might get into
trouble without my intending it. Well, they shut up their cats for a while,
but you know how it is with people; they got careless, and sure enough
one night the trap took Mrs. Jones's principal tomcat into camp, and
finished him up. In the morning Mrs. Jones comes here with the corpse
in her arms, and cries and takes on the same as if it was a child. It was a
cat by the name of Yelverton,—Hector G. Yelverton,—a troublesome old
rip, with no more principle than an Injun, though you couldn't make *her*
believe it. I said all a man could to comfort her, but no, nothing would do
but I must pay for him. Finally, I said I warn't investing in cats now as
much as I was, and with that she walked off in a huff, carrying the remains
with her. That closed our intercourse with the Joneses. Mrs. Jones joined
another church and took her tribe with her. She said she would not hold
fellowship with assassins. Well, by and by comes Mrs. Brown's turn,—
she that went by here a minute ago. She had a disgraceful old yellow cat
that she thought as much of as if he was twins, and one night he tried that
trap on his neck, and it fitted him so, and was so sort of satisfactory, that
he laid down and curled up and stayed with it. Such was the end of Sir
John Baldwin."

"Was that the name of the cat?"

"The same. There's cats around here with names that would surprise
you. Maria" (to his wife), "what was that cat's name that eat a keg of
ratsbane by mistake over at Hooper's, and started home and got struck by
lightning and took the blind staggers and fell in the well and was most
drowned before they could fish him out?"

"That was that colored Deacon Jackson's cat. I only remember the last
end of its name, which was Hold-The-Fort-For-I-Am-Coming Jackson."

"Sho! that ain't the one. That's the one that eat up an entire box of
Seidlitz powders, and then hadn't any more judgment than to go and take
a drink. He was considered to be a great loss, but I never could see it.

Well, no matter about the names. Mrs. Brown wanted to be reasonable, but Mrs. Jones wouldn't let her. She put her up to going to law for damages. So to law she went, and had the face to claim seven shillings and sixpence. It made a great stir. All the neighbors went to court. Everybody took sides. It got hotter and hotter, and broke up all the friendships for three hundred yards around,—friendships that had lasted for generations and generations.

"Well, I proved by eleven witnesses that the cat was of a low character and very ornery, and warn't worth a cancelled postage-stamp, any way, taking the average of cats here; but I lost the case. What could I expect? The system is all wrong here, and is bound to make revolution and bloodshed some day. You see, they give the magistrate a poor little starvation salary, and then turn him loose on the public to gouge for fees and costs to live on. What is the natural result? Why he never looks into the justice of a case,—never once. All he looks at is which client has got the money. So this one piled the fees and costs and everything on to me. I could pay specie, don't you see? and he knew mighty well that if he put the verdict on to Mrs. Brown, where it belonged, he'd have to take his swag in currency."

"Currency? Why, has Bermuda a currency?"

"Yes,—onions. And they were forty per cent discount, too, then, because the season had been over as much as three months. So I lost my case. I had to pay for that cat. But the general trouble the case made was the worst thing about it. Broke up so much good feeling. The neighbors don't speak to each other now. Mrs. Brown had named a child after me. But she changed its name right away. She is a Baptist. Well, in the course of baptizing it over again, it got drowned. I was hoping we might get to be friendly again some time or other, but of course this drowning the child knocked that all out of the question. It would have saved a world of heartbreak and ill blood if she had named it dry."

I knew by the sigh that this was honest. All this trouble and all this destruction of confidence in the purity of the bench on account of a seven-shilling lawsuit about a cat! Somehow, it seemed to "size" the country.

At this point we observed that an English flag had just been placed at half-mast on a building a hundred yards away. I and my friends were busy in an instant trying to imagine whose death, among the island dignitaries, could command such a mark of respect as this. Then a shudder shook them and me at the same moment, and I knew that we had jumped to one and the same conclusion: "The governor has gone to England; it is for the British admiral!"

At this moment Mr. Smith noticed the flag. He said with emotion,—

"That's on a boarding-house. I judge there's a boarder dead."

A dozen other flags within view went to half-mast.

"It's a boarder, sure," said Smith.

"But would they half-mast the flags here for a boarder, Mr. Smith?"

"Why, certainly they would, if he was *dead*."

That seemed to size the country again.

4

THE EARLY twilight of a Sunday evening in Hamilton, Bermuda, is an alluring time. There is just enough of whispering breeze, fragrance of flowers, and sense of repose to raise one's thoughts heavenward; and just enough amateur piano music to keep him reminded of the other place. There are many venerable pianos in Hamilton, and they all play at twilight. Age enlarges and enriches the powers of some musical instruments,—notably those of the violin,—but it seems to set a piano's teeth on edge. Most of the music in vogue there is the same that those pianos prattled in their innocent infancy; and there is something very pathetic about it when they go over it now, in their asthmatic second childhood, dropping a note here and there, where a tooth is gone.

We attended evening service at the stately Episcopal church on the hill, where were five or six hundred people, half of them white and the other half black, according to the usual Bermudian proportions; and all well dressed,—a thing which is also usual in Bermuda and to be confidently expected. There was good music, which we heard, and doubtless a good sermon, but there was a wonderful deal of coughing, and so only the high parts of the argument carried over it. As we came out, after service, I overheard one young girl say to another,—

"Why, you don't mean to say you pay duty on gloves and laces! I only pay postage; have them done up and sent in the 'Boston Advertiser.' "

There are those who believe that the most difficult thing to create is a woman who can comprehend that it is wrong to smuggle; and that an impossible thing to create is a woman who will not smuggle, whether or no, when she gets a chance. But these may be errors.

We went wandering off toward the country, and were soon far down in the lonely black depths of a road that was roofed over with the dense foliage of a double rank of great cedars. There was no sound of any kind, there; it was perfectly still. And it was so dark that one could detect nothing but somber outlines. We strode farther and farther down this tunnel, cheering the way with chat.

Presently the chat took this shape: "How insensibly the character of a people and of a government makes its impress upon a stranger, and gives him a sense of security or of insecurity without his taking deliberate thought upon the matter or asking anybody a question! We have been in this land half a day; we have seen none but honest faces; we have noted the British flag flying, which means efficient government and good order; so without inquiry we plunge unarmed and with perfect confidence into this dismal place, which in almost any other country would swarm with thugs and garroters—"

'Sh! What was that? Stealthy footsteps! Low voices! We gasp, we close up together, and wait. A vague shape glides out of the dusk and confronts us. A voice speaks—demands money!

"A shilling, gentlemen, if you please, to help build the new Methodist church."

Blessed sound! Holy sound! We contribute with thankful avidity to the new Methodist church, and are happy to think how lucky it was that those little colored Sunday-school scholars did not seize upon everything we had with violence, before we recovered from our momentary helpless condition. By the light of cigars we write down the names of weightier philanthropists than ourselves on the contribution-cards, and then pass on into the farther darkness, saying, What sort of a government do they call this, where they allow little black pious children, with contribution-cards, to plunge out upon peaceable strangers in the dark and scare them to death?

We prowled on several hours, sometimes by the seaside, sometimes inland, and finally managed to get lost, which is a feat that requires talent in Bermuda. I had on new shoes. They were No. 7's when I started, but were not more than 5's now, and still diminishing. I walked two hours in those shoes after that, before we reached home. Doubtless I could have the reader's sympathy for the asking. Many people have never had the headache or the toothache, and I am one of those myself; but everybody has worn tight shoes for two or three hours, and known the luxury of taking them off in a retired place and seeing his feet swell up and obscure the firmament. Once when I was a callow, bashful cub, I took a plain, unsentimental country girl to a comedy one night. I had known her a day; she seemed divine; I wore my new boots. At the end of the first half-hour she said, "Why do you fidget so with your feet?" I said, "Did I?" Then I put my attention there and kept still. At the end of another half-hour she said, "Why do you say, 'Yes, oh yes!' and 'Ha, ha, oh, certainly! very true!' to everything I say, when half the time those are entirely irrelevant answers?" I blushed, and explained that I had been a little absent-minded. At the end of another half-hour she said, "Please, why do you grin so steadfastly at vacancy, and yet look so sad?" I explained that I always did that when I was reflecting. An hour passed, and then she turned and contemplated me with her earnest eyes and said, "Why do you cry all the time?" I explained that very funny comedies always made me cry. At last human nature surrendered, and I secretly slipped my boots off. This was a mistake. I was not able to get them on any more. It was a rainy night; there were no omnibuses going our way; and as I walked home, burning up with shame, with the girl on one arm and my boots under the other, I was an object worthy of some compassion,—especially in those moments of martyrdom when I had to pass through the glare that fell upon the pavement from street lamps. Finally, this child of the forest said, "Where are your boots?" and being taken unprepared, I put a fitting finish to the follies of the evening with the stupid remark, "The higher classes do not wear them to the theater."

The Reverend had been an army chaplain during the war, and while we were hunting for a road that would lead to Hamilton he told a story about two dying soldiers which interested me in spite of my feet. He said that in the Potomac hospitals rough pine coffins were furnished by government, but that it was not always possible to keep up with the demand; so, when a man died, if there was no coffin at hand he was buried without one. One night, late, two soldiers lay dying in a ward. A man came in with a coffin on his shoulder, and stood trying to make up his mind which of these two poor fellows would be likely to need it first. Both of them begged for it with their fading eyes,—they were past talking. Then one of them protruded a wasted hand from his blankets and made a feeble beck-oning sign with the fingers, to signify, "Be a good fellow; put it under my bed, please." The man did it, and left. The lucky soldier painfully turned himself in his bed until he faced the other warrior, raised himself partly on his elbow, and began to work up a mysterious expression of some kind in his face. Gradually, irksomely, but surely and steadily, it developed, and at last it took definite form as a pretty successful *wink*. The sufferer fell back exhausted with his labor, but bathed in glory. Now entered a personal friend of No. 2, the despoiled soldier. No. 2 pleaded with him with eloquent eyes, till presently he understood, and removed the coffin from under No. 1's bed and put it under No. 2's. No. 2 indicated his joy, and made some more signs; the friend understood again, and put his arm under No. 2's shoulders and lifted him partly up. Then the dying hero turned the dim exultation of his eye upon No. 1, and began a slow and labored work with his hands; gradually he lifted one hand up toward his face; it grew weak and dropped back again; once more he made the effort, but failed again. He took a rest; he gathered all the remnant of his strength, and this time he slowly but surely carried his thumb to the side of his nose, spread the gaunt fingers wide in triumph, and dropped back dead. That picture sticks by me yet. The "situation" is unique.

The next morning, at what seemed a very early hour, the little white table-waiter appeared suddenly in my room and shot a single word out of himself: "Breakfast!"

This was a remarkable boy in many ways. He was about eleven years old; he had alert, intent black eyes; he was quick of movement; there was no hesitation, no uncertainty about him anywhere; there was a military decision in his lip, his manner, his speech, that was an astonishing thing to see in a little chap like him; he wasted no words; his answers always came so quick and brief that they seemed to be part of the question that had been asked instead of a reply to it. When he stood at table with his fly-brush, rigid, erect, his face set in a cast-iron gravity, he was a statue till he detected a dawning want in somebody's eye; then he pounced down, supplied it, and was instantly a statue again. When he was sent to the kitchen for anything, he marched upright till he got to the door; he turned hand-springs the rest of the way.

"Breakfast!"

I thought I would make one more effort to get some conversation out of this being.

"Have you called the Reverend, or are—"

"Yes s'r!"

"Is it early, or is—"

"Eight-five!"

"Do you have to do all the 'chores,' or is there somebody to give you a l—"

"Colored girl!"

"Is there only one parish in this island, or are there—"

"Eight!"

"Is the big church on the hill a parish church, or is it—"

"Chapel-of-ease!"

"Is taxation here classified into poll, parish, town, and—"

"Don't know!"

Before I could cudgel another question out of my head, he was below, hand-springing across the back yard. He had slid down the balusters, head-first. I gave up trying to provoke a discussion with him. The essential element of discussion had been left out of him; his answers were so final and exact that they did not leave a doubt to hang conversation on. I suspect that there is the making of a mighty man or a mighty rascal in this boy,— according to circumstances,—but they are going to apprentice him to a carpenter. It is the way the world uses its opportunities.

During this day and the next we took carriage drives about the island and over to the town of St. George's, fifteen or twenty miles away. Such hard, excellent roads to drive over are not to be found elsewhere out of Europe. An intelligent young colored man drove us, and acted as guide-book. In the edge of the town we saw five or six mountain-cabbage palms (atrocious name!) standing in a straight row, and equidistant from each other. These were not the largest or the tallest trees I have ever seen, but they were the statliest, the most majestic. That row of them must be the nearest that nature has ever come to counterfeiting a colonnade. These trees are all the same height, say sixty feet; the trunks as gray as granite, with a very gradual and perfect taper; without sign of branch or knot or flaw; the surface not looking like bark, but like granite that has been dressed and not polished. Thus all the way up the diminishing shaft for fifty feet; then it begins to take the appearance of being closely wrapped, spool-fashion, with gray cord, or of having been turned in a lathe. Above this point there is an outward swell, and thence upwards, for six feet or more, the cylinder is a bright, fresh green, and is formed of wrappings like those of an ear of green Indian corn. Then comes the great, spraying palm plume, also green. Other palm-trees always lean out of the perpendicular, or have a curve in them. But the plumb-line could not detect a deflection in any individual of this stately row; they stand as straight as the colonnade of Baalbec; they have its great height, they have its grace-fulness, they have its dignity; in moonlight or twilight, and shorn of their plumes, they would duplicate it.

The birds we came across in the country were singularly tame; even that wild creature, the quail, would pick around in the grass at ease while we inspected it and talked about it at leisure. A small bird of the canary species had to be stirred up with the butt-end of the whip before it would move, and then it moved only a couple of feet. It is said that even the suspicious flea is tame and sociable in Bermuda, and will allow himself to be caught and caressed without misgivings. This should be taken with allowance, for doubtless there is more or less brag about it. In San Francisco they used to claim that their native flea could kick a child over, as if it were a merit in a flea to be able to do that; as if the knowledge of it trumpeted abroad ought to entice immigration. Such a thing in nine cases out of ten would be almost sure to deter a thinking man from coming.

We saw no bugs or reptiles to speak of, and so I was thinking of saying in print, in a general way, that there were none at all; but one night after I had gone to bed, the Reverend came into my room carrying something, and asked, "Is this your boot?" I said it was, and he said he had met a spider going off with it. Next morning he stated that just at dawn the same spider raised his window and was coming in to get a shirt, but saw him and fled.

I inquired, "Did he get the shirt?"

"No."

"How did you know it was a shirt he was after?"

"I could see it in his eye."

We inquired around, but could hear of no Bermudian spider capable of doing these things. Citizens said that their largest spiders could not more than spread their legs over an ordinary saucer, and that they had always been considered honest. Here was testimony of a clergyman against the testimony of mere worldlings,—interested ones, too. On the whole, I judged it best to lock up my things.

Here and there on the country roads we found lemon, papaia, orange, lime, and fig trees; also several sorts of palms, among them the cocoa, the date, and the palmetto. We saw some bamboos forty feet high, with stems as thick as a man's arm. Jungles of the mangrove-tree stood up out of swamps, propped on their interlacing roots as upon a tangle of stilts. In dryer places the noble tamarind sent down its grateful cloud of shade. Here and there the blossomy tamarisk adorned the roadside. There was a curious gnarled and twisted black tree, without a single leaf on it. It might have passed itself off for a dead apple-tree but for the fact that it had a star-like, red-hot flower sprinkled sparsely over its person. It had the scattery red glow that a constellation might have when glimpsed through smoked glass. It is possible that our constellations have been so constructed as to be invisible through smoked glass; if this is so it is a great mistake.

We saw a tree that bears grapes, and just as calmly and unostentatiously as a vine would do it. We saw an India-rubber tree, but out of season, possibly, so there were no shoes on it, nor suspenders, nor anything that a person would properly expect to find there. This gave it an impressively fraudulent look. There was exactly one mahogany-tree on the island. I know this to be reliable, because I saw a man who said he had counted it many a time and could not be mistaken. He was a man with a hare lip and a pure heart, and everybody said he was as true as steel. Such men are all too few.

One's eye caught near and far the pink cloud of the oleander and the red blaze of the pomegranate blossom. In one piece of wild wood the morning-glory vines had wrapped the trees to their very tops, and decorated them all over with couples and clusters of great blue bells,—a fine and striking spectacle, at a little distance. But the dull cedar is everywhere, and its is the prevailing foliage. One does not appreciate how dull it is until the varnished, bright green attire of the infrequent lemon-tree pleasantly intrudes its contrast. In one thing Bermuda is eminently tropical,—was in May, at least,—the unbrilliant, slightly faded, unrejoicing look of the landscape. For forests arrayed in a blemishless magnificence of glowing green foliage that seems to exult in its own existence and can move the beholder to an enthusiasm that will make him either shout or cry, one must go to countries that have malignant winters.

We saw scores of colored farmers digging their crops of potatoes and onions, their wives and children helping,—entirely contented and comfortable, if looks go for anything. We never met a man, or woman, or child anywhere in this sunny island who seemed to be unprosperous, or discontented, or sorry about anything. This sort of monotony became very tiresome presently, and even something worse. The spectacle of an entire nation grovelling in contentment is an infuriating thing. We felt the lack of something in this community,—a vague, an undefinable, an elusive something, and yet a lack. But after considerable thought we made out what it was,—tramps. Let them go there, right now, in a body. It is utterly virgin soil. Passage is cheap. Every true patriot in America will help buy tickets. Whole armies of these excellent beings can be spared from our midst and our polls; they will find a delicious climate and a green, kind-hearted people. There are potatoes and onions for all, and a generous welcome for the first batch that arrives, and elegant graves for the second.

It was the Early Rose potato the people were digging. Later in the year they have another crop, which they call the Garnet. We buy their potatoes (retail) at fifteen dollars a barrel; and those colored farmers buy ours for a song, and live on them. Havana might exchange cigars with Connecticut in the same advantageous way, if she thought of it.

We passed a roadside grocery with a sign up, "Potatoes Wanted." An ignorant stranger, doubtless. He could not have gone thirty steps from his place without finding plenty of them.

In several fields the arrowroot crop was already sprouting. Bermuda used to make a vast annual profit out of this staple before fire-arms came into such general use.

The island is not large. Somewhere in the interior a man ahead of us had a very slow horse. I suggested that we had better go by him; but the driver said the man had but a little way to go. I waited to see, wondering how he could know. Presently the man did turn down another road. I asked, "How did you know he would?"

"Because I knew the man, and where he lived."

I asked him, satirically, if he knew everybody in the island; he answered, very simply, that he did. This gives a body's mind a good substantial grip on the dimensions of the place.

At the principal hotel in St. George's, a young girl, with a sweet, serious face, said we could not be furnished with dinner, because we had not been expected, and no preparation had been made. Yet it was still an hour before dinner time. We argued, she yielded not; we supplicated, she was serene. The hotel had not been expecting an inundation of two people, and so it seemed that we should have to go home dinnerless. I said we were not very hungry; a fish would do. My little maid answered, it was not the marketday for fish. Things began to look serious; but presently the boarder who sustained the hotel came in, and when the case was laid before him he was cheerfully willing to divide. So we had much pleasant chat at table about St. George's chief industry, the repairing of damaged ships; and in between we had a soup that had something in it that seemed to taste like the hereafter, but it proved to be only pepper of a particularly vivacious kind. And we had an iron-clad chicken that was deliciously cooked, but not in the right way. Baking was not the thing to convince his sort. He ought to have been put through a quartz mill until the "tuck" was taken out of him, and then boiled till we came again. We got a good deal of sport out of him, but not enough sustenance to leave the victory on our side. No matter; we had potatoes and a pie and a sociable good time. Then a ramble through the town, which is a quaint one, with interesting, crooked streets, and narrow, crooked lanes, with here and there a grain of dust. Here, as in Hamilton, the dwellings had Venetian blinds of a very sensible pattern. They were not double shutters, hinged at the sides, but a single broad shutter, hinged at the top; you push it outward, from the bottom, and fasten it at any angle required by the sun or desired by yourself.

All about the island one sees great white scars on the hill-slopes. These are dished spaces where the soil has been scraped off and the coral exposed and glazed with hard whitewash. Some of these are a quarter-acre in size. They catch and carry the rainfall to reservoirs; for the wells are few and poor, and there are no natural springs and no brooks.

They say that the Bermuda climate is mild and equable, with never any snow or ice, and that one may be very comfortable in spring clothing the year round, there. We had delightful and decided summer weather in May, with a flaming sun that permitted the thinnest of raiment, and yet there was a constant breeze; consequently we were never discomforted by heat. At four or five in the afternoon the mercury began to go down, and then it became necessary to change to thick garments. I went to St. George's in the morning clothed in the thinnest of linen, and reached home at five in the afternoon with two overcoats on. The nights are said to be always cool and bracing. We had mosquito nets, and the Reverend said the mosquitoes persecuted him a good deal. I often heard him slapping and banging at these imaginary creatures with as much zeal as if they had been real. There are no mosquitoes in the Bermudas in May.

The poet Thomas Moore spent several months in Bermuda more than seventy years ago. He was sent out to be registrar of the admiralty. I am not quite clear as to the function of a registrar of the admiralty of Bermuda, but I think it is his duty to keep a record of all the admirals born there. I will inquire into this. There was not much doing in admirals, and Moore got tired and went away. A reverently preserved souvenir of him is still one of the treasures of the islands. I gathered the idea, vaguely, that it was a jug, but was persistently thwarted in the twenty-two efforts I made to visit it. However, it was no matter, for I found afterwards that it was only a chair.

There are several "sights" in the Bermudas, of course, but they are easily avoided. This is a great advantage,—one cannot have it in Europe. Bermuda is the right country for a jaded man to "loaf" in. There are no harassments; the deep peace and quiet of the country sink into one's body and bones and give his conscience a rest, and chloroform the legion of invisible small devils that are always trying to whitewash his hair. A good many Americans go there about the first of March and remain until the early spring weeks have finished their villanies at home.

The Bermudians are hoping soon to have telegraphic communication with the world. But even after they shall have acquired this curse it will still be a good country to go to for a vacation, for there are charming little islets scattered about the enclosed sea where one could live secure from interruption. The telegraph boy would have to come in a boat, and one could easily kill him while he was making his landing.

We had spent four days in Bermuda,—three bright ones out of doors and one rainy one in the house, we being disappointed about getting a yacht for a sail; and now our furlough was ended, and we entered into the ship again and sailed homeward.

Among the passengers was a most lean and lank and forlorn invalid, whose weary look and patient eyes and sorrowful mien awoke every one's kindly interest and stirred every one's compassion. When he spoke— which was but seldom—there was a gentleness in his tones that made each hearer his friend. The second night of the voyage—we were all in the smoking cabin at the time—he drifted, little by little, into the general conversation. One thing brought on another, and so, in due course, he happened to fall into the biographical vein, and the following strange narrative was the result.

THE INVALID'S STORY[1]

I SEEM sixty and married, but these effects are due to my condition and sufferings, for I am a bachelor, and only forty-one. It will be hard for you to believe that I, who am now but a shadow, was a hale, hearty man two short years ago,—a man of iron, a very athlete!—yet such is the simple truth. But stranger still than this fact is the way in which I lost my health. I lost it through helping to take care of a box of guns on a two-hundred-mile railway journey one winter's night. It is the actual truth, and I will tell you about it.

I belong in Cleveland, Ohio. One winter's night, two years ago, I reached home just after dark, in a driving snow-storm, and the first thing I heard when I entered the house was that my dearest boyhood friend and schoolmate, John B. Hackett, had died the day before, and that his last utterance had been a desire that I would take his remains home to his poor old father and mother in Wisconsin. I was greatly shocked and grieved, but there was no time to waste in emotions; I must start at once. I took the card, marked "Deacon Levi Hackett, Bethlehem, Wisconsin," and hurried off through the whistling storm to the railway station. Arrived there I found the long white-pine box which had been described to me; I fastened the card to it with some tacks, saw it put safely aboard the express car, and then ran into the eating-room to provide myself with a sandwich and some cigars. When I returned, presently, there was my coffin-box *back again,* apparently, and a young fellow examining around it, with a card in his hand, and some tacks and a hammer! I was astonished and puzzled. He began to nail on his card, and I rushed out to the express car, in a good deal of a state of mind, to ask for an explanation. But no— there was my box, all right, in the express car; it hadn't been disturbed. [The fact is that without my suspecting it a prodigious mistake had been made. I was carrying off a box of *guns* which that young fellow had come to the station to ship to a rifle company in Peoria, Illinois, and *he* had got

---

[1] Left out of these "Rambling Notes," when originally published in the "Atlantic Monthly," because it was feared that the story was not true, and at that time there was no way of proving that it was not.—M.T.

my corpse!] Just then the conductor sung out "All aboard," and I jumped into the express car and got a comfortable seat on a bale of buckets. The expressman was there, hard at work,—a plain man of fifty, with a simple, honest, good-natured face, and a breezy, practical heartiness in his general style. As the train moved off a stranger skipped into the car and set a package of peculiarly mature and capable Limburger cheese on one end of my coffin-box—I mean my box of guns. That is to say, I know *now* that it was Limburger cheese, but at that time I never had heard of the article in my life, and of course was wholly ignorant of its character. Well, we sped through the wild night, the bitter storm raged on, a cheerless misery stole over me, my heart went down, down, down! The old express-man made a brisk remark or two about the tempest and the arctic weather, slammed his sliding doors to, and bolted them, closed his window down tight, and then went bustling around, here and there and yonder, setting things to rights, and all the time contentedly humming "Sweet By and By," in a low tone, and flatting a good deal. Presently I began to detect a most evil and searching odor stealing about on the frozen air. This de-pressed my spirits still more, because of course I attributed it to my poor departed friend. There was something infinitely saddening about his call-ing himself to my remembrance in this dumb pathetic way, so it was hard to keep the tears back. Moreover, it distressed me on account of the old expressman, who, I was afraid, might notice it. However, he went hum-ming tranquilly on, and gave no sign; and for this I was grateful. Grateful, yes, but still uneasy; and soon I began to feel more and more uneasy every minute, for every minute that went by that odor thickened up the more, and got to be more and more gamey and hard to stand. Presently, having got things arranged to his satisfaction, the expressman got some wood and made up a tremendous fire in his stove. This distressed me more than I can tell, for I could not but feel that it was a mistake. I was sure that the effect would be deleterious upon my poor departed friend. Thompson—the expressman's name was Thompson, as I found out in the course of the night—now went poking around his car, stopping up what-ever stray cracks he could find, remarking that it didn't make any differ-ence what kind of a night it was outside, he calculated to make *us* com-fortable, anyway. I said nothing, but I believed he was not choosing the right way. Meantime he was humming to himself just as before; and meantime, too, the stove was getting hotter and hotter, and the place closer and closer. I felt myself growing pale and qualmish, but grieved in silence and said nothing. Soon I noticed that the "Sweet By and By" was gradually fading out; next it ceased altogether, and there was an ominous stillness. After a few moments Thompson said,—

"Pfew! I reckon it ain't no cinnamon 't I've loaded up thish-yer stove with!"

He gasped once or twice, then moved toward the cof— gun-box, stood over that Limburger cheese part of a moment, then came back and sat down near me, looking a good deal impressed. After a contemplative pause, he said, indicating the box with a gesture,—

"Friend of yourn?"

"Yes," I said with a sigh.

"He's pretty ripe, *ain't* he!"

Nothing further was said for perhaps a couple of minutes, each being busy with his own thoughts; then Thompson said, in a low, awed voice,—

"Sometimes it's uncertain whether they're really gone or not,—*seem* gone, you know—body warm, joints limber—and so, although you *think* they're gone, you don't really know. I've had cases in my car. It's perfectly awful, becuz *you* don't know what minute they'll rise right up and look at you!" Then, after a pause, and slightly lifting his elbow toward the box,—"But *he* ain't in no trance! No, sir, I go bail for *him!*"

We sat some time, in meditative silence, listening to the wind and the roar of the train; then Thompson said, with a good deal of feeling,—

"Well-a-well, we've all got to go, they ain't no getting around it. Man that is born of woman is of few days and far between, as Scriptur' says. Yes, you look at it any way you want to, it's awful solemn and cur'us: they ain't *nobody* can get around it; *all's* got to go—just *everybody,* as you may say. One day you're hearty and strong"—here he scrambled to his feet and broke a pane and stretched his nose out at it a moment or two, then sat down again while I struggled up and thrust my nose out at the same place, and this we kept on doing every now and then—"and next day he's cut down like the grass, and the places which knowed him then knows him no more forever, as Scriptur' says. Yes-'ndeedy, it's awful solemn and cur'us; but we've all got to go, one time or another; they ain't no getting around it."

There was another long pause; then,—

"What did he die of?"

I said I didn't know.

"How long has he ben dead?"

It seemed judicious to enlarge the facts to fit the probabilities; so I said,—

"Two or three days."

But it did no good; for Thompson received it with an injured look which plainly said. "Two or three *years,* you mean." Then he went right along, placidly ignoring my statement, and gave his views at considerable length upon the unwisdom of putting off burials too long. Then he lounged off toward the box, stood a moment, then came back on a sharp trot and visited the broken pane, observing,—

"'T would 'a' ben a dum sight better, all around, if they'd started him along last summer."

Thompson sat down and buried his face in his red silk handkerchief, and began to slowly sway and rock his body like one who is doing his best to endure the almost unendurable. By this time the fragrance—if you may call it fragrance—was just about suffocating, as near as you can come at it. Thompson's face was turning gray; I knew mine hadn't any color left in it. By and by Thompson rested his forehead in his left hand, and his elbow on his knee, and sort of waved his red handkerchief towards the box with his other hand, and said,—

"I've carried a many a one of 'em,—some of 'em considerable overdue, too,—but, lordy, he just lays over 'em all!—and does it *easy.* Cap., they was heliotrope to *him!*"

This recognition of my poor friend gratified me, in spite of the sad circumstances, because it had so much the sound of a compliment.

Pretty soon it was plain that something had got to be done. I suggested cigars. Thompson thought it was a good idea. He said,—

"Likely it'll modify him some."

We puffed gingerly along for a while, and tried hard to imagine that things were improved. But it wasn't any use. Before very long, and without any consultation, both cigars were quietly dropped from our nerveless fingers at the same moment. Thompson said, with a sigh,—

"No, Cap., it don't modify him worth a cent. Fact is, it makes him worse, becuz it appears to stir up his ambition. What do you reckon we better do now?"

I was not able to suggest anything; indeed, I had to be swallowing and swallowing, all the time, and did not like to trust myself to speak. Thompson fell to maundering, in a desultory and low-spirited way, about the miserable experiences of this night; and he got to referring to my poor friend by various titles,—sometimes military ones, sometimes civil ones; and I noticed that as fast as my poor friend's effectiveness grew, Thompson promoted him accordingly,—gave him a bigger title. Finally he said,—

"I 've got an idea. Suppos'n' we buckle down to it and give the Colonel a bit of a shove towards t'other end of the car?—about ten foot, say. He wouldn't have so much influence, then, don't you reckon?"

I said it was a good scheme. So we took in a good fresh breath at the broken pane, calculating to hold it till we got through; then we went there and bent down over that deadly cheese and took a grip on the box. Thompson nodded "All ready," and then we threw ourselves forward with all our might; but Thompson slipped, and slumped down with his nose on the cheese, and his breath got loose. He gagged and gasped, and floundered up and made a break for the door, pawing the air and saying, hoarsely, "Don't hender me!—gimme the road! I'm a-dying; gimme the road!" Out on the cold platform I sat down and held his head a while, and he revived. Presently he said,—

"Do you reckon we started the Gen'rul any?"

I said no; we hadn't budged him.

"Well, then, *that* idea's up the flume. We got to think up something else. He's suited wher' he is, I reckon; and if that's the way he feels about it, and has made up his mind that he don't wish to be disturbed, you bet you he 's a-going to have his own way in the business. Yes, better leave him right wher' he is, long as he wants it so; becuz he holds all the trumps, don't you know, and so it stands to reason that the man that lays out to alter his plans for him is going to get left."

But we couldn't stay out there in that mad storm; we should have frozen to death. So we went in again and shut the door, and began to suffer once more and take turns at the break in the window. By and by, as we were starting away from a station where we had stopped a moment Thompson pranced in cheerily, and exclaimed,—

"We're all right, now! I reckon we've got the Commodore this time. I judge I've got the stuff here that'll take the tuck out of him."

It was carbolic acid. He had a carboy of it. He sprinkled it all around everywhere; in fact he drenched everything with it, rifle-box, cheese, and all. Then we sat down, feeling pretty hopeful. But it wasn't for long. You see the two perfumes began to mix, and then—well, pretty soon we made

a break for the door; and out there Thompson swabbed his face with his
bandanna and said in a kind of disheartened way,—

"It ain't no use. We can't buck agin *him*. He just utilizes everything
we put up to modify him with, and gives it his own flavor and plays it
back on us. Why, Cap., don't you know, it's as much as a hundred times
worse in there now than it was when he first got a-going. I never *did* see
one of 'em warm up to his work so, and take such a dumnation interest in
it. No, sir, I never did, as long as I've ben on the road; and I've carried a
many of one of 'em, as I was telling you."

We went in again, after we were frozen pretty stiff; but my, we couldn't
stay in, now. So we just waltzed back and forth, freezing, and thawing,
and stifling, by turns. In about an hour we stopped at another station; and
as we left it Thompson came in with a bag, and said,—

"Cap., I'm a-going to chance him once more,—just this once; and if
we don't fetch him this time, the thing for us to do, is to just throw up the
sponge and withdraw from the canvass. That's the way *I* put it up."

He had brought a lot of chicken feathers, and dried apples, and leaf
tobacco, and rags, and old shoes, and sulphur, and assafœtida, and one
thing or another; and he piled them on a breadth of sheet iron in the
middle of the floor, and set fire to them. When they got well started, I
couldn't see, myself, how even the corpse could stand it. All that went
before was just simply poetry to that smell,—but mind you, the original
smell stood up out of it just as sublime as ever,—fact is, these other
smells just seemed to give it a better hold; and my, how rich it was! I
didn't make these reflections there—there wasn't time—made them on
the platform. And breaking for the platform, Thompson got suffocated and fell; and before I got him dragged out, which I did by the
collar, I was mighty near gone myself. When we revived, Thompson
said dejectedly,—

"We got to stay out here, Cap. We got to do it. They ain't no other
way. The Governor wants to travel alone, and he's fixed so he can out
vote us."

And presently he added,—

"And don't you know, we're *pisoned*. It's *our* last trip, you can make
up your mind to it. Typhoid fever is what's going to come of this. I feel it
a-coming right now. Yes, sir, we're elected, just as sure as you're born."

We were taken from the platform an hour later, frozen and insensible,
at the next station, and I went straight off into a virulent fever, and never
knew anything again for three weeks. I found out, then, that I had spent
that awful night with a harmless box of rifles and a lot of innocent cheese;
but the news was too late to save *me;* imagination had done its work, and
my health was permanently shattered; neither Bermuda nor any other land
can ever bring it back to me. This is my last trip; I am on my way home
to die.

We made the run home to New York quarantine in three days and five
hours, and could have gone right along up to the city if we had had a
health permit. But health permits are not granted after seven in the evening,
partly because a ship cannot be inspected and overhauled with exhaustive

thoroughness except in daylight, and partly because health officers are liable to catch cold if they expose themselves to the night air. Still, you can *buy* a permit after hours for five dollars extra, and the officer will do the inspecting next week. Our ship and passengers lay under expense and in humiliating captivity all night, under the very nose of the little official reptile who is supposed to protect New York from pestilence by his vigilant "inspections." This imposing rigor gave everybody a solemn and awful idea of the beneficent watchfulness of our government, and there were some who wondered if anything finer could be found in other countries.

In the morning we were all a-tiptoe to witness the intricate ceremony of inspecting the ship. But it was a disappointing thing. The health officer's tug ranged alongside for a moment, our purser handed the lawful three-dollar permit fee to the health officer's bootblack, who passed us a folded paper in a forked stick, and away we went. The entire "inspection" did not occupy thirteen seconds.

The health officer's place is worth a hundred thousand dollars a year to him. His system of inspection is perfect, and therefore cannot be improved on; but it seems to me that his system of collecting his fees might be amended. For a great ship to lie idle all night is a most costly loss of time; for her passengers to have to do the same thing works to them the same damage, with the addition of an amount of exasperation and bitterness of soul that the spectacle of that health officer's ashes on a shovel could hardly sweeten. Now why would it not be better and simpler to let the ships pass in unmolested, and the fees and permits be exchanged once a year by post?

THE FACTS CONCERNING THE RECENT CARNIVAL OF CRIME IN CONNECTICUT

I WAS feeling blithe, almost jocund. I put a match to my cigar, and just then the morning's mail was handed in. The first superscription I glanced at was in a handwriting that sent a thrill of pleasure through and through me. It was Aunt Mary's; and she was the person I loved and honored most in all the world, outside of my own household. She had been my boyhood's idol; maturity, which is fatal to so many enchantments, had not been able to dislodge her from her pedestal; no, it had only justified her right to be there, and placed her dethronement permanently among the impossibilities. To show how strong her influence over me was, I will observe that long after everybody else's "*do*-stop-smoking" had ceased to affect me in the slightest degree, Aunt Mary could still stir my torpid conscience into faint signs of life when she touched upon the matter. But all things have their limit, in this world. A happy day came at last, when even Aunt Mary's words could no longer move me. I was not merely glad to see that day arrive; I was more than glad—I was grateful; for when its sun had set, the one alloy that was able to mar my enjoyment of my aunt's society was gone. The remainder of her stay with us that winter was in every way a delight. Of course she pleaded with me just as earnestly as ever, after that blessed day, to quit my pernicious habit, but to no purpose whatever; the moment she opened the subject I at once became calmly, peacefully, contentedly indifferent—absolutely, adamantinely indifferent. Consequently the closing weeks of that memorable visit melted away as pleasantly as a dream, they were so freighted, for me, with tranquil satisfaction. I could not have enjoyed my pet vice more if my gentle tormentor had been a smoker herself, and an advocate of the practice. Well, the sight of her handwriting reminded me that I was getting very hungry to see her again. I easily guessed what I should find in her letter. I opened it. Good! just as I expected; she was coming! Coming this very day, too, and by the morning train; I might expect her any moment.

I said to myself, "I am thoroughly happy and content, now. If my most pitiless enemy could appear before me at this moment, I would freely right any wrong I may have done him."

Straightway the door opened, and a shrivelled, shabby dwarf entered. He was not more than two feet high. He seemed to be about forty years old. Every feature and every inch of him was a trifle out of shape; and so, while one could not put his finger upon any particular part and say, "This is a conspicuous deformity," the spectator perceived that this little person was a deformity as a whole,—a vague, general, evenly blended, nicely adjusted deformity. There was a foxlike cunning in the face and the sharp little eyes, and also alertness and malice. And yet, this vile bit of human rubbish seemed to bear a sort of remote and ill-defined resemblance to me! It was dully perceptible in the mean form, the countenance, and even the clothes, gestures, manner, and attitudes of the creature. He was a far-fetched, dim suggestion of a burlesque upon me, a caricature of me in little. One thing about him struck me forcibly, and most unpleasantly: he was covered all over with a fuzzy, greenish mold, such as one sometimes sees upon mildewed bread. The sight of it was nauseating.

He stepped along with a chipper air, and flung himself into a doll's chair in a very free and easy way, without waiting to be asked. He tossed his hat into the waste basket. He picked up my old chalk pipe from the floor, gave the stem a wipe or two on his knee, filled the bowl from the tobacco-box at his side, and said to me in a tone of pert command,—

"Gimme a match!"

I blushed to the roots of my hair; partly with indignation, but mainly because it somehow seemed to me that this whole performance was very like an exaggeration of conduct which I myself had sometimes been guilty of in my intercourse with familiar friends,—but never, never with strangers, I observed to myself. I wanted to kick the pygmy into the fire, but some incomprehensible sense of being legally and legitimately under his authority forced me to obey his order. He applied the match to the pipe, took a contemplative whiff or two, and remarked, in an irritatingly familiar way,—

"Seems to me it's devilish odd weather for this time of year."

I flushed again, and in anger and humiliation as before; for the language was hardly an exaggeration of some that I have uttered in my day, and moreover was delivered in a tone of voice and with an exasperating drawl that had the seeming of a deliberate travesty of my style. Now there is nothing I am quite so sensitive about as a mocking imitation of my drawling infirmity of speech. I spoke up sharply and said,—

"Look here, you miserable ash-cat! you will have to give a little more attention to your manners, or I will throw you out of the window!"

The manikin smiled a smile of malicious content and security, puffed a whiff of smoke contemptuously toward me, and said, with a still more elaborate drawl,—

"Come—go gently, now; don't put on *too* many airs with your betters."

This cool snub rasped me all over, but it seemed to subjugate me, too, for a moment. The pygmy contemplated me awhile with his weasel eyes, and then said, in a peculiarly sneering way,—

"You turned a tramp away from your door this morning."

I said crustily,—

"Perhaps I did, perhaps I didn't. How do *you* know?"

"Well, I know. It isn't any matter *how* I know."

"Very well. Suppose I *did* turn a tramp away from the door—what of it?"

"Oh, nothing; nothing in particular. Only you lied to him."

"I *didn't!* That is, I—".

"Yes, but you did; you lied to him."

I felt a guilty pang,—in truth I had felt it forty times before that tramp had travelled a block from my door,—but still I resolved to make a show of feeling slandered; so I said,—

"This is a baseless impertinence. I said to the tramp—"

"There—wait. You were about to lie again. *I* know what you said to him. You said the cook was gone down town and there was nothing left from breakfast. Two lies. You knew the cook was behind the door, and plenty of provisions behind *her.*"

This astonishing accuracy silenced me; and it filled me with wondering speculations, too, as to how this cub could have got his information. Of course he could have culled the conversation from the tramp, but by what sort of magic had he contrived to find out about the concealed cook? Now the dwarf spoke again:—

"It was rather pitiful, rather small, in you to refuse to read that poor young woman's manuscript the other day, and give her an opinion as to its literary value; and she had come so far, too, and *so* hopefully. Now *wasn't* it?"

I felt like a cur! And I had felt so every time the thing had recurred to my mind, I may as well confess. I flushed hotly and said,—

"Look here, have you nothing better to do than prowl around prying into other people's business? Did that girl tell you that?"

"Never mind whether she did or not. The main thing is, you did that contemptible thing. And you felt ashamed of it afterwards. Aha! you feel ashamed of it *now*!"

This with a sort of devilish glee. With fiery earnestness I responded,—

"I told that girl, in the kindest, gentlest way, that I could not consent to deliver judgment upon *any* one's manuscript, because an individual's verdict was worthless. It might underrate a work of high merit and lose it to the world, or it might overrate a trashy production and so open the way for its infliction upon the world. I said that the great public was the only tribunal competent to sit in judgment upon a literary effort, and therefore it must be best to lay it before that tribunal in the outset, since in the end it must stand or fall by that mighty court's decision any way.''

"Yes, you said all that. So you did, you juggling, small-souled shuffler! And yet when the happy hopefulness faded out of that poor girl's face, when you saw her furtively slip beneath her shawl the scroll she had so patiently and honestly scribbled at,—so ashamed of her darling now, so proud of it before,—when you saw the gladness go out of her eyes and the tears come there, when she crept away so humbly who had come so—''

"Oh, peace! peace! peace! Blister your merciless tongue, haven't all these thoughts tortured me enough, without *your* coming here to fetch them back again?''

Remorse! remorse! It seemed to me that it would eat the very heart out of me! And yet that small fiend only sat there leering at me with joy and contempt, and placidly chuckling. Presently he began to speak again. Every sentence was an accusation, and every accusation a truth. Every clause was freighted with sarcasm and derision, every slow-dropping word burned like vitriol. The dwarf reminded me of times when I had flown at my children in anger and punished them for faults which a little inquiry would have taught me that others, and not they, had committed. He reminded me of how I had disloyally allowed old friends to be traduced in my hearing, and been too craven to utter a word in their defence. He reminded me of many dishonest things which I had done; of many which I had procured to be done by children and other irresponsible persons; of some which I had planned, thought upon, and longed to do, and been kept from the performance by fear of consequences only. With exquisite cruelty he recalled to my mind, item by item, wrongs and unkindnesses I had inflicted and humiliations I had put upon friends since dead, "who died thinking of those injuries, maybe, and grieving over them,'' he added, by way of poison to the stab.

"For instance,'' said he, "take the case of your younger brother, when you two were boys together, many a long year ago. He always lovingly trusted in you with a fidelity that your manifold treacheries were not able to shake. He followed you about like a dog, content to suffer wrong and abuse if he might only be with you; patient under these injuries so long as it was your hand that inflicted them. The latest picture you have of him in health and strength must be such a comfort to you! You pledged your honor that if he would let you blindfold him no harm should come to him; and then, giggling and choking over the rare fun of the joke, you led him to a brook thinly glazed with ice, and pushed him in; and how you did laugh! Man, you will never forget the gentle, reproachful look he gave you as he struggled shivering out, if you live a thousand years! Oho! you see it now, you see it *now*!''

"Beast, I have seen it a million times, and shall see it a million more! and may you rot away piecemeal, and suffer till doomsday what I suffer now, for bringing it back to me again!''

The dwarf chuckled contentedly, and went on with his accusing history of my career. I dropped into a moody, vengeful state, and suffered in silence under the merciless lash. At last this remark of his gave me a sudden rouse:—

"Two months ago, on a Tuesday, you woke up, away in the night, and fell to thinking, with shame, about a peculiarly mean and pitiful act of yours toward a poor ignorant Indian in the wilds of the Rocky Mountains in the winter of eighteen hundred and—"

"Stop a moment, devil! Stop! Do you mean to tell me that even my very *thoughts* are not hidden from you?"

"It seems to look like that. Didn't you think the thoughts I have just mentioned?"

"If I didn't, I wish I may never breathe again! Look here, friend—look me in the eye. Who *are* you?"

"Well, who do you think?"

"I think you are Satan himself. I think you are the devil."

"No."

"No? Then who *can* you be?"

"Would you really like to know?"

"*Indeed* I would."

"Well, I am your *Conscience*!"

In an instant I was in a blaze of joy and exultation. I sprang at the creature, roaring,—

"Curse you, I have wished a hundred million times that you were tangible, and that I could get my hands on your throat once! Oh, but I will wreak a deadly vengeance on—"

Folly! Lightning does not move more quickly than my Conscience did! He darted aloft so suddenly that in the moment my fingers clutched the empty air he was already perched on the top of the high book-case, with his thumb at his nose in token of derision. I flung the poker at him, and missed. I fired the bootjack. In a blind rage I flew from place to place, and snatched and hurled any missile that came handy; the storm of books, inkstands, and chunks of coal gloomed the air and beat about the mani-kin's perch relentlessly, but all to no purpose; the nimble figure dodged every shot; and not only that, but burst into a cackle of sarcastic and triumphant laughter as I sat down exhausted. While I puffed and gasped with fatigue and excitement, my Conscience talked to this effect:—

"My good slave, you are curiously witless—no, I mean characteristi-cally so. In truth, you are always consistent, always yourself, always an ass. Otherwise it must have occurred to you that if you attempted this murder with a sad heart and a heavy conscience, I would droop under the burdening influence instantly. Fool, I should have weighed a ton, and could not have budged from the floor; but instead, you are so cheerfully anxious to kill me that your conscience is as light as a feather; hence I am away up here out of your reach. I can almost respect a mere ordinary sort of fool; but *you*—pah!"

I would have given anything, then, to be heavy-hearted, so that I could get this person down from there and take his life, but I could no more be heavy-hearted over such a desire than I could have sorrowed over its accomplishment. So I could only look longingly up at my master, and rave at the ill-luck that denied me a heavy conscience the one only time that I

had ever wanted such a thing in my life. By and by I got to musing over
the hour's strange adventure, and of course my human curiosity began to
work. I set myself to framing in my mind some questions for this fiend to
answer. Just then one of my boys entered, leaving the door open behind
him, and exclaimed,—

"My! what *has* been going on, here? The book-case is all one riddle
of—"

I sprang up in consternation, and shouted,—

"Out of this! Hurry! Jump! Fly! Shut the door! Quick, or my Conscience will get away!"

The door slammed to, and I locked it. I glanced up and was grateful,
to the bottom of my heart, to see that my owner was still my prisoner.
I said,—

"Hang you, I might have lost you! Children are the heedlessest creatures. But look here, friend, the boy did not seem to notice you at all; how
is that?"

"For a very good reason. I am invisible to all but you."

I made mental note of that piece of information with a good deal of
satisfaction. I could kill this miscreant now, if I got a chance, and no one
would know it. But this very reflection made me so light-hearted that my
Conscience could hardly keep his seat, but was like to float aloft toward
the ceiling like a toy balloon. I said, presently,—

"Come, my Conscience, let us be friendly. Let us fly a flag of truce for
a while. I am suffering to ask you some questions."

"Very well. Begin."

"Well, then, in the first place, why were you never visible to me
before?"

"Because you never asked to see me before; that is, you never asked in
the right spirit and the proper form before. You were just in the right spirit
this time, and when you called for your most pitiless enemy I was that
person by a very large majority, though you did not suspect it."

"Well, did that remark of mine turn you into flesh and blood?"

"No. It only made me visible to you. I am unsubstantial, just as other
spirits are."

This remark prodded me with a sharp misgiving. If he was unsubstantial, how was I going to kill him? But I dissembled, and said persua-
sively,—

"Conscience, it isn't sociable of you to keep at such a distance. Come
down and take another smoke."

This was answered with a look that was full of derision, and with this
observation added:—

"Come where you can get at me and kill me? The invitation is declined
with thanks."

"All right," said I to myself; "so it seems a spirit *can* be killed, after
all; there will be one spirit lacking in this world, presently, or I lose my
guess." Then I said aloud,—

"Friend—"

"There; wait a bit. I am not your friend, I am your enemy; I am not
your equal, I am your master. Call me 'my lord,' if you please. You are
too familiar."

"I don't like such titles. I am willing to call you *sir*. That is as far as—"

"We will have no argument about this. Just obey; that is all. Go on with your chatter."

"Very well, my lord,—since nothing but my lord will suit you,—I was going to ask you how long you will be visible to me?"

"Always!"

I broke out with strong indignation: "This is simply an outrage. That is what I think of it. You have dogged, and dogged, and *dogged* me, all the days of my life, invisible. That was misery enough; now to have such a looking thing as you tagging after me like another shadow all the rest of my days is an intolerable prospect. You have my opinion, my lord; make the most of it."

"My lad, there was never so pleased a conscience in this world as I was when you made me visible. It gives me an inconceivable advantage. *Now,* I can look you straight in the eye, and call you names, and leer at you, jeer at you, sneer at you; and *you* know what eloquence there is in visible gesture and expression, more especially when the effect is heightened by audible speech. I shall always address you henceforth in your o-w-n s-n-i-v-e-l-l-i-n-g d-r-a-w-l—baby!"

I let fly with the coal-hod. No result. My lord said,—

"Come, come! Remember the flag of truce!"

"Ah, I forgot that. I will try to be civil; and *you* try it, too, for a novelty. The idea of a *civil* conscience! It is a good joke; an excellent joke. All the consciences *I* have ever heard of were nagging, badgering, fault-finding, execrable savages! Yes; and always in a sweat about some poor little insignificant trifle or other—destruction catch the lot of them, *I* say! I would trade mine for the small-pox and seven kinds of consumption, and be glad of the chance. Now tell me, why *is* it that a conscience can't haul a man over the coals once, for an offence, and then let him alone? Why is it that it wants to keep on pegging at him, day and night and night and day, week in and week out, forever and ever, about the same old thing? There is no sense in that, and no reason in it. I think a conscience that will act like that is meaner than the very dirt itself."

"Well, *we* like it; that suffices."

"Do you do it with the honest intent to improve a man?"

That question produced a sarcastic smile, and this reply:—

"No, sir. Excuse me. We do it simply because it is 'business.' It is our trade. The *purpose* of it *is* to improve the man, but *we* are merely disinterested agents. We are appointed by authority, and haven't anything to say in the matter. We obey orders and leave the consequences where they belong. But I am willing to admit this much: we *do* crowd the orders a trifle when we get a chance, which is most of the time. We enjoy it. We are instructed to remind a man a few times of an error; and I don't mind acknowledging that we try to give pretty good measure. And when we get hold of a man of a peculiarly sensitive nature, oh, but we do haze him! I have known consciences to come all the way from China and Russia to see a person of that kind put through his paces, on a special occasion. Why, I knew a man of that sort who had accidentally crippled a mulatto baby; the news went abroad, and I wish you may never commit another sin if the consciences didn't flock from all over the earth to enjoy the fun and help his master exercise him. That man walked the floor in torture for forty-eight hours, without eating or sleeping, and then blew his brains out. The child was perfectly well again in three weeks.''

"Well, you are a precious crew, not to put it too strong. I think I begin to see, now, why you have always been a trifle inconsistent with me. In your anxiety to get all the juice you can out of a sin, you make a man repent of it in three or four different ways. For instance, you found fault with me for lying to that tramp, and I suffered over that. But it was only yesterday that I told a tramp the square truth to wit, that, it being regarded as bad citizenship to encourage vagrancy, I would give him nothing. What did you do *then?* Why, you made me say to myself, 'Ah, it would have been so much kinder and more blameless to ease him off with a little white lie, and send him away feeling that if he could not have bread, the gentle treatment was at least something to be grateful for!' Well, I suffered all day about *that*. Three days before, I had fed a tramp, and fed him freely, supposing it a virtuous act. Straight off you said, 'O false citizen, to have fed a tramp!' and I suffered as usual. I gave a tramp work; you objected to it,—*after* the contract was made, of course; you never speak up beforehand. Next, I *refused* a tramp work; you objected to *that*. Next, I proposed to kill a tramp; you kept me awake all night, oozing remorse at every pore. Sure I was going to be right *this* time, I sent the next tramp away with my benediction; and I wish you may live as long as I do, if you didn't make me smart all night again because I didn't kill him. Is there *any* way of satisfying that malignant invention which is called a conscience?"

"Ha, ha! this is luxury! Go on!"

"But come, now, answer me that question. *Is* there any way?"

"Well, none that I propose to tell *you*, my son. Ass! I don't care *what* act you may turn your hand to, I can straightway whisper a word in your ear and make you think you have committed a dreadful meanness. It is my *business*—and my joy—to make you repent of *every*thing you do. If I have fooled away any opportunities it was not intentional; I beg to assure you it was not intentional!''

"Don't worry; you haven't missed a trick that *I* know of. I never did a thing in all my life, virtuous or otherwise, that I didn't repent of within twenty-four hours. In church last Sunday I listened to a charity sermon. My first impulse was to give three hundred and fifty dollars; I repented of that and reduced it a hundred; repented of that and reduced it another hundred; repented of that and reduced it another hundred; repented of that and reduced the remaining fifty to twenty-five; repented of that and came down to fifteen; repented of that and dropped to two dollars and a half; when the plate came around at last, I repented once more and contributed ten cents. Well, when I got home, I did wish to goodness I had that ten cents back again! You never *did* let me get through a charity sermon without having something to sweat about.''

"Oh, and I never shall, I never shall. You can always depend on me.''

"I think so. Many and many's the restless night I've wanted to take you by the neck. If I could only get hold of you now!''

"Yes, no doubt. But I am not an ass; I am only the saddle of an ass.

But go on, go on. You entertain me more than I like to confess."

"I am glad of that. (You will not mind my lying a little, to keep in practice.) Look here; not to be too personal, I think you are about the shabbiest and most contemptible little shrivelled-up reptile that can be imagined. I am grateful enough that you are invisible to other people, for I should die with shame to be seen with such a mildewed monkey of a conscience as *you* are. Now if you were five or six feet high, and—"

"Oh, come! who is to blame?"

"*I* don't know."

"Why, you are; nobody else."

"Confound you, I wasn't consulted about your personal appearance."

"I don't care, you had a good deal to do with it, nevertheless. When you were eight or nine years old, I was seven feet high, and as pretty as a picture."

"I wish you had died young! So you have grown the wrong way, have you?"

"Some of us grow one way and some the other. You had a large conscience once; if you've a small conscience now, I reckon there are reasons for it. However, both of us are to blame, you and I. You see, you used to be conscientious about a great many things; morbidly so, I may say. It was a great many years ago. You probably do not remember it, now. Well, I took a great interest in my work, and I so enjoyed the anguish which certain pet sins of yours afflicted you with, that I kept pelting at you until I rather overdid the matter. You began to rebel. Of course I began to lose ground, then, and shrivel a little,—diminish in stature, get moldy, and grow deformed. The more I weakened, the more stubbornly you fastened on to those particular sins; till at last the places on my person that represent those vices became as callous as shark skin. Take smoking, for instance. I played that card a little too long, and I lost. When people plead with you at this late day to quit that vice, that old callous place seems to enlarge and cover me all over like a shirt of mail. It exerts a mysterious, smothering effect; and presently I, your faithful hater, your devoted Conscience, go sound asleep! Sound? It is no name for it. I couldn't hear it thunder at such a time. You have some few other vices— perhaps eighty, or maybe ninety—that affect me in much the same way."

"This is flattering; you must be asleep a good part of your time."

"Yes, of late years. I should be asleep *all* the time, but for the help I get."

"Who helps you?"

"Other consciences. Whenever a person whose conscience I am acquainted with tries to plead with you about the vices you are callous to, I get my friend to give his client a pang concerning some villany of his own, and that shuts off his meddling and starts him off to hunt personal consolation. My field of usefulness is about trimmed down to tramps, budding authoresses, and that line of goods, now; but don't you worry— I'll harry you on *them* while they last! Just you put your trust in me."

"I think I can. But if you had only been good enough to mention these facts some thirty years ago, I should have turned my particular attention to sin, and I think that by this time I should not only have had you pretty permanently asleep on the entire list of human vices, but reduced to the size of a homœopathic pill, at that. That is about the style of conscience *I* am pining for. If I only had you shrunk down to a homœopathic pill, and could get my hands on you, would I put you in a glass case for a keepsake? No, sir. I would give you to a yellow dog! That is where *you* ought to be—you and all your tribe. You are not fit to be in society, in my opinion. Now another question. Do you know a good many consciences in this section?"

"Plenty of them."

"I would give anything to see some of them! Could you bring them here? And would they be visible to me?"

"Certainly not."

"I suppose I ought to have known that, without asking. But no matter, you can describe them. Tell me about my neighbor Thompson's conscience, please."

"Very well. I know him intimately; have known him many years. I knew him when he was eleven feet high and of a faultless figure. But he is very rusty and tough and misshapen, now, and hardly ever interests himself about anything. As to his present size—well, he sleeps in a cigar box."

"Likely enough. There are few smaller, meaner men in this region than Hugh Thompson. Do you know Robinson's conscience?"

"Yes. He is a shade under four and a half feet high; used to be a blonde; is a brunette, now, but still shapely and comely."

"Well, Robinson is a good fellow. Do you know Tom Smith's conscience?"

"I have known him from childhood. He was thirteen inches high, and rather sluggish, when he was two years old—as nearly all of us are, at that age. He is thirty-seven feet high, now, and the stateliest figure in America. His legs are still racked with growing-pains, but he has a good time, nevertheless. Never sleeps. He is the most active and energetic member of the New England Conscience Club; is president of it. Night and day you can find him pegging away at Smith, panting with his labor, sleeves rolled up, countenance all alive with enjoyment. He has got his victim splendidly dragooned, now. He can make poor Smith imagine that the most innocent little thing he does is an odious sin; and then he sets to work and almost tortures the soul out of him about it."

"Smith is the noblest man in all this section, and the purest; and yet is always breaking his heart because he cannot be good! Only a conscience *could* find pleasure in heaping agony upon a spirit like that. Do you know my aunt Mary's conscience?"

"I have seen her at a distance, but am not acquainted with her. She lives in the open air altogether, because no door is large enough to admit her."

"I can believe that. Let me see. Do you know the conscience of that publisher who once stole some sketches of mine for a 'series' of his, and then left me to pay the law expenses I had to incur in order to choke him off?"

"Yes. He has a wide fame. He was exhibited, a month ago, with some other antiquities, for the benefit of a recent Member of the Cabinet's conscience, that was starving in exile. Tickets and fares were high, but I travelled for nothing by pretending to be the conscience of an editor, and got in for half price by representing myself to be the conscience of a clergyman. However, the publisher's conscience, which was to have been the main feature of the entertainment, was a failure—as an exhibition. He was there, but what of that? The management had provided a microscope with a magnifying power of only thirty thousand diameters, and so nobody got to see him, after all. There was great and general dissatisfaction, of course, but—"

Just here there was an eager footstep on the stair; I opened the door, and my aunt Mary burst into the room. It was a joyful meeting, and a cheery bombardment of questions and answers concerning family matters ensued. By and by my aunt said,—

"But I am going to abuse you a little now. You promised me, the day I saw you last, that you would look after the needs of the poor family around the corner as faithfully as I had done it myself. Well, I found out by accident that you failed of your promise. *Was* that right?"

In simple truth, I never had thought of that family a second time! And now such a splintering pang of guilt shot through me! I glanced up at my Conscience. Plainly, my heavy heart was affecting him. His body was drooping forward; he seemed about to fall from the book-case. My aunt continued:—

"And think how you have neglected my poor *protégée* at the almshouse, you dear, hard-hearted promise-breaker!" I blushed scarlet, and my tongue was tied. As the sense of my guilty negligence waxed sharper and stronger, my Conscience began to sway heavily back and forth; and when my aunt, after a little pause, said in a grieved tone, "Since you never once went to see her, maybe it will not distress you now to know that that poor child died, months ago, utterly friendless and forsaken!" my Conscience could no longer bear up under the weight of my sufferings, but tumbled headlong from his high perch and struck the floor with a dull, leaden thump. He lay there writhing with pain and quaking with apprehension, but straining every muscle in frantic efforts to get up. In a fever of expectancy I sprang to the door, locked it, placed my back against it, and bent a watchful gaze upon my struggling master. Already my fingers were itching to begin their murderous work.

"Oh, what *can* be the matter!" exclaimed my aunt, shrinking from me, and following with her frightened eyes the direction of mine. My breath was coming in short, quick gasps now, and my excitement was almost uncontrollable. My aunt cried out,—

"Oh, do not look so! You appall me! Oh, what can the matter be? What is it you see? Why do you stare so? Why do you work your fingers like that?"

"Peace, woman!" I said, in a hoarse whisper. "Look elsewhere; pay no attention to me; it is nothing—nothing. I am often this way. It will pass in a moment. It comes from smoking too much."

My injured lord was up, wild-eyed with terror, and trying to hobble toward the door. I could hardly breathe, I was so wrought up. My aunt wrung her hands, and said,—

"Oh, I knew how it would be; I knew it would come to this at last! Oh,

tude of clamorous and beseeching dogs, he said, "I might as well acknowledge it, I have been fooled by the books; they only tell the pretty part of the story, and then stop. Fetch me the shot-gun; this thing has gone along far enough."

He issued forth with his weapon, and chanced to step upon the tail of the original poodle, who promptly bit him in the leg. Now the great and good work which this poodle had been engaged in had engendered in him such a mighty and augmenting enthusiasm as to turn his weak head at last and drive him mad. A month later, when the benevolent physician lay in the death throes of hydrophobia, he called his weeping friends about him, and said,—

"Beware of the books. They tell but half of the story. Whenever a poor wretch asks you for help, and you feel a doubt as to what result may flow from your benevolence, give yourself the benefit of the doubt and kill the applicant."

And so saying he turned his face to the wall and gave up the ghost.

THE BENEVOLENT AUTHOR.

A POOR and young literary beginner had tried in vain to get his manuscripts accepted. At last, when the horrors of starvation were staring him in the face, he laid his sad case before a celebrated author, beseeching his counsel and assistance. This generous man immediately put aside his own matters and proceeded to peruse one of the despised manuscripts. Having completed his kindly task, he shook the poor young man cordially by the hand, saying, "I perceive merit in this; come again to me on Monday." At the time specified, the celebrated author, with a sweet smile, but saying nothing, spread open a magazine which was damp from the press. What was the poor young man's astonishment to discover upon the printed page his own article. "How can I ever," said he, falling upon his knees and bursting into tears, "testify my gratitude for this noble conduct!" The celebrated author was the renowned Snodgrass; the poor young beginner thus rescued from obscurity and starvation was the afterwards equally renowned Snagsby. Let this pleasing incident admonish us to turn a charitable ear to all beginners that need help.

SEQUEL.

THE NEXT week Snagsby was back with five rejected manuscripts. The celebrated author was a little surprised, because in the books the young struggler had needed but one lift, apparently. However, he ploughed through these papers, removing unnecessary flowers and digging up some acres of adjective-stumps, and then succeeded in getting two of the articles accepted.

A week or so drifted by, and the grateful Snagsby arrived with another cargo. The celebrated author had felt a mighty glow of satisfaction within himself the first time he had successfully befriended the poor young struggler, and had compared himself with the generous people in the books with high gratification; but he was beginning to suspect now that he had struck upon something fresh in the noble-episode line. His enthusiasm took a chill. Still, he could not bear to repulse this struggling young author, who clung to him with such pretty simplicity and trustfulness.

Well, the upshot of it all was that the celebrated author presently found himself permanently freighted with the poor young beginner. All his mild efforts to unload his cargo went for nothing. He had to give daily counsel, daily encouragement; he had to keep on procuring magazine acceptances, and then revamping the manuscripts to make them presentable. When the young aspirant got a start at last, he rode into sudden fame by describing the celebrated author's private life with such a caustic humor and such minuteness of blistering detail that the book sold a prodigious edition, and broke the celebrated author's heart with mortification. With his latest gasp he said, "Alas, the books deceived me; they do not tell the whole story. Beware of the struggling young author, my friends. Whom God sees fit to starve, let not man presumptuously rescue to his own undoing."

THE GRATEFUL HUSBAND.

ONE DAY a lady was driving through the principal street of a great city with her little boy, when the horses took fright and dashed madly away, hurling the coachman from his box and leaving the occupants of the carriage paralyzed with terror. But a brave youth who was driving a grocery wagon threw himself before the plunging animals, and succeeded in arresting their flight at the peril of his own.[1] The grateful lady took his number, and upon arriving at her home she related the heroic act to her husband (who had read the books), who listened with streaming eyes to the moving recital, and who, after returning thanks, in conjunction with his restored loved ones, to Him who suffereth not even a sparrow to fall to the ground unnoticed, sent for the brave young person, and, placing a check for five hundred dollars in his hand, said, "Take this as a reward for your noble act, William Ferguson, and if ever you shall need a friend, remember that Thompson McSpadden has a grateful heart." Let us learn from this that a good deed cannot fail to benefit the doer, however humble he may be.

SEQUEL.

WILLIAM FERGUSON called the next week and asked Mr. McSpadden to use his influence to get him a higher employment, he feeling capable of better things than driving a grocer's wagon. Mr. McSpadden got him an under-clerkship at a good salary.

Presently William Ferguson's mother fell sick, and William—Well, to cut the story short, Mr. McSpadden consented to take her into his house. Before long she yearned for the society of her younger children; so Mary and Julia were admitted also, and little Jimmy, their brother. Jimmy had a pocket-knife, and he wandered into the drawing-room with it one day, alone, and reduced ten thousand dollars' worth of furniture to an indeterminable value in rather less than three quarters of an hour. A day or two later he fell downstairs and broke his neck, and seventeen of his family's

[1]This is probably a misprint.—M.T.

relatives came to the house to attend the funeral. This made them acquainted, and they kept the kitchen occupied after that, and likewise kept the McSpaddens busy hunting up situations of various sorts for them, and hunting up more when they wore these out. The old woman drank a good deal and swore a good deal; but the grateful McSpaddens knew it was their duty to reform her, considering what her son had done for them, so they clave nobly to their generous task. William came often and got decreasing sums of money, and asked for higher and more lucrative employments,—which the grateful McSpadden more or less promptly procured for him. McSpadden consented also, after some demur, to fit William for college; but when the first vacation came and the hero requested to be sent to Europe for his health, the persecuted McSpadden rose against the tyrant and revolted. He plainly and squarely refused. William Ferguson's mother was so astounded that she let her gin-bottle drop, and her profane lips refused to do their office. When she recovered she said in a half-gasp, "Is this your gratitude? Where would your wife and boy be now, but for my son?"

William said, "Is this your gratitude? Did I save your wife's life or not? tell me that!"

Seven relations swarmed in from the kitchen and each said, "And this is his gratitude!"

William's sisters stared, bewildered, and said, "And this is his grat—" but were interrupted by their mother, who burst into tears and exclaimed, "To think that my sainted little Jimmy threw away his life in the service of such a reptile!"

Then the pluck of the revolutionary McSpadden rose to the occasion, and he replied with fervor, "Out of my house, the whole beggarly tribe of you! I was beguiled by the books, but shall never be beguiled again,—once is sufficient for me." And turning to William he shouted, "Yes, you did save my wife's life, and the next man that does it shall die in his tracks!"

Not being a clergyman, I place my text at the end of my sermon instead of at the beginning. Here it is, from Mr. Noah Brooks's Recollections of President Lincoln, in "Scribner's Monthly":—

"J. H. Hackett, in his part of Falstaff, was an actor who gave Mr. Lincoln great delight. With his usual desire to signify to others his sense of obligation, Mr. Lincoln wrote a genial little note to the actor, expressing his pleasure at witnessing his performance. Mr. Hackett, in reply, sent a book of some sort; perhaps it was one of his own authorship. He also wrote several notes to the President. One night, quite late, when the episode had passed out of my mind, I went to the White House in answer to a message. Passing into the President's office, I noticed, to my surprise, Hackett sitting in the anteroom as if waiting for an audience. The President asked me if any one was outside. On being told, he said, half sadly, 'Oh, I can't see him, I can't see him; I was in hopes he had gone away.' Then he added, 'Now this just illustrates the difficulty of having pleasant friends and acquaintances in this place. You know how I liked Hackett as an actor, and how I wrote to tell him so. He sent me that book, and there I thought the matter would end. He is a master of his place in the profession, I suppose, and well fixed in it; but just because we had a little friendly correspondence, such as any two men might have, he wants something. What do you suppose he wants?' I could not guess, and Mr. Lincoln added, 'Well, he wants to be consul to London. Oh, dear!' ''

I will observe, in conclusion, that the William Ferguson incident occurred, and within my personal knowledge,—though I have changed the nature of the details, to keep William from recognizing himself in it.

All the readers of this article have in some sweet and gushing hour of their lives played the rôle of Magnanimous-Incident hero. I wish I knew how many there are among them who are willing to talk about that episode and like to be reminded of the consequences that flowed from it.

PUNCH, BROTHERS, PUNCH

WILL THE reader please to cast his eye over the following verses, and see if he can discover anything harmful in them?

> "Conductor, when you receive a fare,
> Punch in the presence of the passenjare!
> A blue trip slip for an eight-cent fare,
> A buff trip slip for a six-cent fare,
> A pink trip slip for a three-cent fare,
> Punch in the presence of the passenjare!
>   CHORUS.
> Punch, brothers! punch with care!
> Punch in the presence of the passenjare!''

I came across these jingling rhymes in a newspaper, a little while ago, and read them a couple of times. They took instant and entire possession of me. All through breakfast they went waltzing through my brain; and when, at last, I rolled up my napkin, I could not tell whether I had eaten anything or not. I had carefully laid out my day's work the day before,— a thrilling tragedy in the novel which I am writing. I went to my den to begin my deed of blood. I took up my pen, but all I could get it to say was, "Punch in the presence of the passenjare." I fought hard for an hour, but it was useless. My head kept humming, "A blue trip slip for an eight-cent fare, a buff trip slip for a six-cent fare," and so on and so on, without peace or respite. The day's work was ruined—I could see that plainly enough. I gave up and drifted down town, and presently discovered that my feet were keeping time to that relentless jingle. When I could stand it no longer I altered my step. But it did no good; those rhymes accommodated themselves to the new step and went on harassing me just as before. I returned home, and suffered all the afternoon; suffered all through an unconscious and unrefreshing dinner; suffered, and cried, and jingled all through the evening; went to bed and rolled, tossed, and jingled right along, the same as ever; got up at midnight frantic, and tried to read; but there was nothing visible upon the whirling page except "Punch! punch in the presence of the passenjare." By sunrise I was out of my mind, and everybody marvelled and was distressed at the idiotic burden of my ravings,—"Punch! oh, punch! punch in the presence of the passenjare!"

Two days later, on Saturday morning, I arose, a tottering wreck, and went forth to fulfil an engagement with a valued friend, the Rev. Mr. ——, to walk to the Talcott Tower, ten miles distant. He stared at me, but asked no questions. We started. Mr. —— talked, talked, talked— as is his wont. I said nothing; I heard nothing. At the end of a mile, Mr. —— said,—

"Mark, are you sick? I never saw a man look so haggard and worn and absent-minded. Say something; do!"

Drearily, without enthusiasm, I said: "Punch, brothers, punch with care! Punch in the presence of the passenjare!"

My friend eyed me blankly, looked perplexed, then said,—

"I do not think I get your drift, Mark. There does not seem to be any relevancy in what you have said, certainly nothing sad; and yet—maybe it was the way you *said* the words—I never heard anything that sounded so pathetic. What is —"

But I heard no more. I was already far away with my pitiless, heart-breaking "blue trip slip for an eight-cent fare, buff trip slip for a six-cent fare, pink trip slip for a three-cent fare; punch in the presence of the passenjare." I do not know what occurred during the other nine miles. However, all of a sudden Mr. —— laid his hand on my shoulder and shouted,—

"Oh, wake up! wake up! wake up! Don't sleep all day! Here we are at the Tower, man! I have talked myself deaf and dumb and blind, and never got a response. Just look at this magnificent autumn landscape! Look at it! look at it! Feast your eyes on it! you have travelled; you have seen boasted landscapes elsewhere. Come, now, deliver an honest opinion. What do you say to this?"

I sighed wearily, and murmured, —

"A buff trip slip for a six-cent fare, a pink trip slip for a three-cent fare, punch in the presence of the passenjare."

Rev. Mr. —— stood there, very grave, full of concern, apparently, and looked long at me; then he said, —

"Mark, there is something about this that I cannot understand. Those are about the same words you said before; there does not seem to be anything in them, and yet they nearly break my heart when you say them. Punch in the—how is it they go?"

I began at the beginning and repeated all the lines. My friend's face lighted with interest. He said,—

"Why, what a captivating jingle it is! It is almost music. It flows along so nicely. I have nearly caught the rhymes myself. Say them over just once more, and then I'll have them, sure."

I said them over. Then Mr. —— said them. He made one little mistake, which I corrected. The next time and the next he got them right. Now a great burden seemed to tumble from my shoulders. That torturing jingle departed out of my brain, and a grateful sense of rest and peace descended upon me. I was light-hearted enough to sing; and I did sing for half an hour, straight along, as we went jogging homeward. Then my freed tongue found blessed speech again, and the pent talk of many a weary hour began to gush and flow. It flowed on and on, joyously, jubilantly, until the fountain was empty and dry. As I wrung my friend's hand at parting, I said,—

"Haven't we had a royal good time! But now I remember, you haven't said a word for two hours. Come, come, out with something!"

The Rev. Mr. —— turned a lack-luster eye upon me, drew a deep sigh, and said, without animation, without apparent consciousness,—

"Punch, brothers, punch with care! Punch in the presence of the passenjare!"

A pang shot through me as I said to myself, "Poor fellow, poor fellow! *he* has got it, now."

I did not see Mr. —— for two or three days after that. Then, on Tuesday evening, he staggered into my presence and sank dejectedly into a seat. He was pale, worn; he was a wreck. He lifted his faded eyes to my face and said,—

"Ah, Mark, it was a ruinous investment that I made in those heartless rhymes. They have ridden me like a nightmare, day and night, hour after hour, to this very moment. Since I saw you I have suffered the torments of the lost. Saturday evening I had a sudden call, by telegraph, and took the night train for Boston. The occasion was the death of a valued old friend who had requested that I should preach his funeral sermon. I took my seat in the cars and set myself to framing the discourse. But I never got beyond the opening paragraph; for then the train started and the car-wheels began their 'clack, clack—clack-clack-clack! clack, clack—clack-clack-clack!' and right away those odious rhymes fitted themselves to that accompaniment. For an hour I sat there and set a syllable of those rhymes to every separate and distinct clack the car-wheels made. Why, I was as fagged out, then, as if I had been chopping wood all day. My skull was splitting with headache. It seemed to me that I must go mad if I sat there any longer; so I undressed and went to bed. I stretched myself out in my berth, and—well, you know what the result was. The thing went right along, just the same. 'Clack-clack-clack, a blue trip slip, clack-clack-clack, for an eight-cent fare; clack-clack-clack, a buff trip slip, clack-clack-clack, for a six-cent fare, and so on, and so on, and so on—*punch*, in the presence of the passenjare!' Sleep? Not a single wink! I was almost a lunatic when I got to Boston. Don't ask me about the funeral. I did the best I could, but every solemn individual sentence was meshed and tangled and woven in and out with 'Punch, brothers, punch with care, punch in the presence of the passenjare.' And the most distressing thing was that my *delivery* dropped into the undulating rhythm of those pulsing rhymes, and I could actually catch absent-minded people nodding *time* to the swing of it with their stupid heads. And, Mark, you may believe it or not, but before I got through, the entire assemblage were placidly bobbing their heads in solemn unison, mourners, undertaker, and all. The moment I had finished, I fled to the anteroom in a state bordering on frenzy. Of course it would be my luck to find a sorrowing and aged maiden aunt of the deceased there, who had arrived from Springfield too late to get into the church. She began to sob, and said,—

" 'Oh, oh, he is gone, he is gone, and I didn't see him before he died!'

" 'Yes!' I said, 'he *is* gone, he *is* gone, he *is* gone—Oh, *will* this suffering never cease!'

" '*You* loved him, then! Oh, you too loved him!'

" 'Loved him! Loved *who?*'

" 'Why, my poor George! my poor nephew!'

" 'Oh—*him!* Yes—oh, yes, yes. Certainly—certainly. Punch—punch—oh, this misery will kill me!'

" 'Bless you! bless you, sir, for these sweet words! *I*, too, suffer in this dear loss. Were you present during his last moments?'

" 'Yes! I—*whose* last moments?'

" '*His*. The dear departed's.'

" 'Yes! Oh, yes—yes—*yes!* I suppose so, I think so, *I* don't know! Oh, certainly—I was there—*I* was there!'

" 'Oh, what a privilege! what a precious privilege! And his last words—oh, tell me, tell me his last words! What did he say?'

" 'He said—he said—oh, my head, my head, my head! He said—he said—he never said *any*thing but Punch, punch, *punch* in the presence of the passenjare! Oh, leave me, madam! In the name of all that is generous, leave me to my madness, my misery, my despair!—a buff trip slip for a six-cent fare, a pink trip slip for a three-cent fare—endu-rance *can* no further go!—PUNCH in the presence of the passenjare!' "

My friend's hopeless eyes rested upon mine a pregnant minute, and then he said impressively,—

"Mark, you do not say anything. You do not offer me any hope. But, ah me, it is just as well—it is just as well. You could not do me any good. The time has long gone by when words could comfort me. Something tells me that my tongue is doomed to wag forever to the jigger of that remorseless jingle. There—there it is coming on me again: a blue trip slip for an eight-cent fare, a buff trip slip for a—"

Thus murmuring faint and fainter, my friend sank into a peaceful trance and forgot his sufferings in a blessed respite.

How did I finally save him from the asylum? I took him to a neighboring university and made him discharge the burden of his persecuting rhymes into the eager ears of the poor, unthinking students. How is it with *them,* now? The result is too sad to tell. Why did I write this article? It was for a worthy, even a noble, purpose. It was to warn you, reader, if you should come across those merciless rhymes, to avoid them—avoid them as you would a pestilence!

A CURIOUS EXPERIENCE

THIS IS the story which the Major told me, as nearly as I can recall it:—

In the winter of 1862–3, I was commandant of Fort Trumbull, at New London, Conn. Maybe our life there was not so brisk as life at "the front"; still it was brisk enough, in its way—one's brains didn't cake together there for lack of something to keep them stirring. For one thing, all the Northern atmosphere at that time was thick with mysterious rumors—rumors to the effect that rebel spies were flitting everywhere, and getting ready to blow up our Northern forts, burn our hotels, send infected clothing into our towns, and all that sort of thing. You remember it. All this had a tendency to keep us awake, and knock the traditional dulness out of garrison life. Besides, ours was a recruiting station—which is the same as saying we hadn't any time to waste in dozing, or dreaming, or fooling around. Why, with all our watchfulness, fifty per cent of a day's recruits would leak out of our hands and give us the slip the same night. The bounties were so prodigious that a recruit could pay a sentinel three or four hundred dollars to let him escape, and still have enough of his bounty-money left to constitute a fortune for a poor man. Yes, as I said before, our life was not drowsy.

Well, one day I was in my quarters alone, doing some writing, when a pale and ragged lad of fourteen or fifteen entered, made a neat bow, and said,—

"I believe recruits are received here?"

"Yes."

"Will you please enlist me, sir?"

"Dear me, no! You are too young, my boy, and too small."

A disappointed look came into his face, and quickly deepened into an expression of despondency. He turned slowly away, as if to go; hesitated, then faced me again, and said, in a tone which went to my heart,—

"I have no home, and not a friend in the world. If you *could* only enlist me!"

But of course the thing was out of the question, and I said so as gently as I could. Then I told him to sit down by the stove and warm himself, and added,—

"You shall have something to eat presently. You are hungry?"

He did not answer; he did not need to; the gratitude in his big soft eyes was more eloquent than any words could have been. He sat down by the stove, and I went on writing. Occasionally I took a furtive glance at him. I noticed that his clothes and shoes, although soiled and damaged, were of good style and material. This fact was suggestive. To it I added the facts that his voice was low and musical; his eyes deep and melancholy; his carriage and address gentlemanly; evidently the poor chap was in trouble. As a result, I was interested.

However, I became absorbed in my work, by and by, and forgot all about the boy. I don't know how long this lasted; but, at length, I happened to look up. The boy's back was toward me, but his face was turned in such a way that I could see one of his cheeks—and down that cheek a rill of noiseless tears was flowing.

"God bless my soul!" I said to myself; "I forgot the poor rat was starving." Then I made amends for my brutality by saying to him, "Come along, my lad; you shall dine with *me;* I am alone to-day."

He gave me another of those grateful looks, and a happy light broke in his face. At the table he stood with his hand on his chair-back until I was seated, then seated himself. I took up my knife and fork and—well, I simply held them, and kept still; for the boy had inclined his head and was saying a silent grace. A thousand hallowed memories of home and my childhood poured in upon me, and I sighed to think how far I had drifted from religion and its balm for hurt minds, its comfort and solace and support.

As our meal progressed, I observed that young Wicklow—Robert Wicklow was his full name—knew what to do with his napkin; and—well, in a word, I observed that he was a boy of good breeding; never mind the details. He had a simple frankness, too, which won upon me. We talked mainly about himself, and I had no difficulty in getting his history out of him. When he spoke of his having been born and reared in Louisiana, I warmed to him decidedly, for I had spent some time down there. I knew all of the "coast" region of the Mississippi, and loved it, and had not been long enough away from it for my interest in it to begin to pale. The very names that fell from his lips sounded good to me,—so good that I steered the talk in directions that would bring them out. Baton Rouge, Plaquemine, Donaldsonville, Sixtymile Point, Bonnet-Carre, the Stock-Landing, Carrollton, the Steamship Landing, the Steamboat Landing, New Orleans, Tchoupitoulas Street, the Esplanade, the Rue des Bons Enfants, the St. Charles Hotel, the Tivoli Circle, the Shell Road, Lake Pontchartrain; and it was particularly delightful to me to hear once more of the "R. E. Lee," the "Natchez," the "Eclipse," the "General Quitman," the "Duncan F. Kenner," and other old familiar steamboats. It was almost as good as being back there, these names so vividly reproduced in my mind the look of the things they stood for. Briefly, this was little Wicklow's history:—

When the war broke out, he and his invalid aunt and his father were living near Baton Rouge, on a great and rich plantation which had been in the family for fifty years. The father was a Union man. He was persecuted in all sorts of ways, but clung to his principles. At last, one night, masked men burned his mansion down, and the family had to fly for their lives. They were hunted from place to place, and learned all there was to know about poverty, hunger, and distress. The invalid aunt found relief at last: misery and exposure killed her; she died in an open field, like a tramp, the rain beating upon her and the thunder booming overhead. Not long afterward, the father was captured by an armed band; and while the son begged and pleaded, the victim was strung up before his face. [At this point a baleful light shone in the youth's eyes, and he said, with the manner of one who talks to himself: "If I cannot be enlisted, no matter—I shall find a way—I shall find a way."] As soon as the father was pronounced dead, the son was told that if he was not out of that region within twenty-four hours, it would go hard with him. That night he crept to the riverside and hid himself near a plantation landing. By and by the "Duncan F. Kenner," stopped there, and he swam out and concealed himself in the yawl that was dragging at her stern. Before daylight the boat reached the Stock-Landing, and he slipped ashore. He walked the three miles which lay between that point and the house of an uncle of his in Good-Children Street, in New Orleans, and then his troubles were over for the time being. But this uncle was a Union man, too, and before very long he concluded that he had better leave the South. So he and young Wicklow slipped out of the country on board a sailing vessel, and in due time reached New York. They put up at the Astor House. Young Wicklow had a good time of it for a while, strolling up and down Broadway, and observing the strange Northern sights; but in the end a change came,—and not for the better. The uncle had been cheerful at first, but now he began to look troubled and despondent; moreover, he became moody and irritable; talked of money giving out, and no way to get more,—"not enough left for one, let alone two." Then, one morning, he was missing—did not come to breakfast. The boy inquired at the office, and was told that the uncle had paid his bill the night before and gone away—to Boston, the clerk believed, but was not certain.

The lad was alone and friendless. He did not know what to do, but concluded he had better try to follow and find his uncle. He went down to the steamboat landing; learned that the trifle of money in his pocket would not carry him to Boston; however, it would carry him to New London; so he took passage for that port, resolving to trust to Providence to furnish him means to travel the rest of the way. He had now been wandering about the streets of New London three days and nights, getting a bite and a nap here and there for charity's sake. But he had given up at last; courage and hope were both gone. If he could enlist, nobody could be more thankful; if he could not get in as a soldier, couldn't he be a drummer-boy? Ah, he would work *so* hard to please, and would be so grateful!

Well, there's the history of young Wicklow, just as he told it to me, barring details. I said,—

"My boy, you're among friends, now,—don't you be troubled any more." How his eyes glistened! I called in Sergeant John Rayburn,—he was from Hartford; lives in Hartford yet; maybe you know him,—and said, "Rayburn, quarter this boy with the musicians. I am going to enroll him as a drummer-boy, and I want you to look after him and see that he is well treated."

Well, of course, intercourse between the commandant of the post and the drummer-boy came to an end, now; but the poor little friendless chap lay heavy on my heart, just the same. I kept on the lookout, hoping to see him brighten up and begin to be cheery and gay; but no, the days went by, and there was no change. He associated with nobody; he was always absent-minded, always thinking; his face was always sad. One morning Rayburn asked leave to speak to me privately. Said he,—

"I hope I don't offend, sir; but the truth is, the musicians are in such a sweat it seems as if somebody's *got* to speak."

"Why, what is the trouble?"

"It's the Wicklow boy, sir. The musicians are down on him to an extent you can't imagine."

"Well, go on, go on. What has he been doing?"

"Prayin', sir."

"Praying!"

"Yes, sir; the musicians haven't any peace of their life for that boy's prayin'. First thing in the morning he's at it; noons he's at it; and nights—well, *nights* he just lays into 'em like all possessed! Sleep? Bless you, they *can't* sleep: he's got the floor, as the sayin' is, and then when he once gets his supplication-mill agoin', there just simply ain't any let-up *to* him. He starts in with the band-master, and he prays for him; next he takes the head bugler, and he prays for him; next the bass drum, and he scoops *him* in; and so on, right straight through the band, given' them all a show, and takin' that amount of interest in it which would make you think he thought he warn't but a little while for this world, and believed he couldn't be happy in heaven without he had a brass band along, and wanted to pick 'em out for himself, so he could depend on 'em to do up the national tunes in a style suitin' to the place. Well, sir, heavin' boots at him don't have no effect; it's dark in there; and, besides, he don't pray fair, anyway, but kneels down behind the big drum; so it don't make no difference if they *rain* boots at him, *he* don't give a dern—warbles right along, same as if it was applause. They sing out, 'Oh, dry up!' 'Give us a rest!' 'Shoot him!' 'Oh, take a walk!' and all sorts of such things. But what of it? It don't phaze him. *He* don't mind it." After a pause: "Kind of a good little fool, too; gits up in the mornin' and carts all that stock of boots back, and sorts 'em out and sets each man's pair where they belong. And they've been throwed at him so much now, that he knows every boot in the band,—can sort 'em out with his eyes shut."

After another pause, which I forbore to interrupt,—

"But the roughest thing about it is, that when he's done prayin', —when he ever *does* get done,—he pipes up and begins to *sing*. Well, you know what a honey kind of a voice he's got when he talks; you know how it would persuade a cast-iron dog to come down off of a doorstep and lick his hand. Now if you'll take my word for it, sir, it ain't a circumstance to his singin'! Flute music is harsh to that boy's singin'. Oh, he just gurgles it out so soft and sweet and low, there in the dark, that it makes you think you are in heaven."

"What is there 'rough' about that?"

"Ah, that's just it, sir. You hear him sing

" 'Just as I am—poor, wretched, blind,'

—just you hear him sing that, once, and see if you don't melt all up and the water come into your eyes! I don't care *what* he sings, it goes plum straight home to you—it goes deep down to where you *live*—and it fetches you every time! Just you hear him sing:—

" 'Child of sin and sorrow, filled with dismay,
  Wait not till to-morrow, yield thee to-day;
    Grieve not that love
    Which, from above'—

and so on. It makes a body feel like the wickedest, ungratefulest brute that walks. And when he sings them songs of his about home, and mother, and childhood, and old memories, and things that's vanished, and old friends dead and gone, it fetches everything before your face that you've ever loved and lost in all your life—and it's just beautiful, it's just divine to listen to, sir—but, Lord, Lord, the heart-break of it! The band—well, they all cry—every rascal of them blubbers, and don't try to hide it, either; and first you know, that very gang that's been slammin' boots at that boy will skip out of their bunks all of a sudden, and rush over in the dark and hug him! Yes, they do—and slobber all over him, and call him pet names, and beg him to forgive them. And just at that time, if a regiment was to offer to hurt a hair of that cub's head, they'd go for that regiment, if it was a whole army corps!''

Another pause.

"Is that all?'' said I.

"Yes, sir.''

"Well, dear me, what is the complaint? What do they want done?''

"Done? Why, bless you, sir, they want you to stop him from *singin'*.''

"What an idea! You said his music was divine.''

"That's just it. It's *too* divine. Mortal man can't stand it. It stirs a body up so; it turns a body inside out; it racks his feelin's all to rags; it makes him feel bad and wicked, and not fit for any place but perdition. It keeps a body in such an everlastin' state of repentin', that nothin' don't taste good and there ain't no comfort in life. And then the *cryin'*, you see— every mornin' they are ashamed to look one another in the face.''

"Well, this is an odd case, and a singular complaint. So they really want the singing stopped?''

"Yes, sir, that is the idea. They don't wish to ask too much; they would like powerful well to have the prayin' shut down on, or leastways trimmed off around the edges; but the main thing's the singin'. If they can only get the singin' choked off, they think they can stand the prayin', rough as it is to be bullyragged so much that way.''

I told the sergeant I would take the matter under consideration. That night I crept into the musicians' quarters and listened. The sergeant had not overstated the case. I heard the praying voice pleading in the dark; I heard the execrations of the harassed men; I heard the rain of boots whiz through the air, and bang and thump around the big drum. The thing touched me, but it amused me, too. By and by, after an impressive silence, came the singing. Lord, the pathos of it, the enchantment of it! Nothing in the world was ever so sweet, so gracious, so tender, so holy, so moving. I made my stay very brief; I was beginning to experience emotions of a sort not proper to the commandant of a fortress.

Next day I issued orders which stopped the praying and singing. Then followed three or four days which were so full of bounty-jumping excitements and irritations that I never once thought of my drummer-boy. But now comes Sergeant Rayburn, one morning, and says,—

"That new boy acts mighty strange, sir.''

"How?''

"Well, sir, he's all the time writing.''

"Writing? What does he write—letters?''

"I don't know, sir; but whenever he's off duty, he is always poking and nosing around the fort, all by himself,—blest if I think there's a hole or corner in it he hasn't been into,—and every little while he outs with pencil and paper and scribbles something down.''

This gave me a most unpleasant sensation. I wanted to scoff at it, but it was not a time to scoff at *anything* that had the least suspicious tinge about it. Things were happening all around us, in the North, then, that warned us to be always on the alert, and always suspecting. I recalled to mind the suggestive fact that this boy was from the South,—the extreme

South, Louisiana,—and the thought was not of a reassuring nature, under the circumstances. Nevertheless, it cost me a pang to give the orders which I now gave to Rayburn. I felt like a father who plots to expose his own child to shame and injury. I told Rayburn to keep quiet, bide his time, and get me some of those writings whenever he could manage it without the boy's finding it out. And I charged him not to do anything which might let the boy discover that he was being watched. I also ordered that he allow the lad his usual liberties, but that he be followed at a distance when we went out into the town.

During the next two days, Rayburn reported to me several times. No success. The boy was still writing, but he always pocketed his paper with a careless air whenever Rayburn appeared in his vicinity. He had gone twice to an old deserted stable in the town, remained a minute or two, and come out again. One could not pooh-pooh these things—they had an evil look. I was obliged to confess to myself that I was getting uneasy. I went into my private quarters and sent for my second in command,—an officer of intelligence and judgment, son of General James Watson Webb. He was surprised and troubled. We had a long talk over the matter, and came to the conclusion that it would be worth while to institute a secret search. I determined to take charge of that myself. So I had myself called at two in the morning; and, pretty soon after, I was in the musicians' quarters, crawling along the floor on my stomach among the snorers. I reached my slumbering waif's bunk at last, without disturbing anybody, captured his clothes and kit, and crawled stealthily back again. When I got to my own quarters, I found Webb there, waiting and eager to know the result. We made search immediately. The clothes were a disappointment. In the pockets we found blank paper and a pencil; nothing else, except a jack-knife and such queer odds and ends and useless trifles as boys hoard and value. We turned to the kit hopefully. Nothing there but a rebuke for us!—a little Bible with this written on the fly-leaf: "Stranger, be kind to my boy, for his mother's sake."

I looked at Webb—he dropped his eyes; he looked at me—I dropped mine. Neither spoke. I put the book reverently back in its place. Presently Webb got up and went away, without remark. After a little I nerved myself up to my unpalatable job, and took the plunder back to where it belonged, crawling on my stomach as before. It seemed the peculiarly appropriate attitude for the business I was in. I was most honestly glad when it was over and done with.

About noon next day Rayburn came, as usual, to report. I cut him short. I said,—

"Let this nonsense be dropped. We are making a bugaboo out of a poor little cub who has got no more harm in him than a hymn-book."

The sergeant looked surprised, and said,—

"Well, you know it was your orders, sir, and I've got some of the writing."

"And what does it amount to? How did you get it?"

"I peeped through the key-hole, and see him writing. So when I judged he was about done, I made a sort of a little cough, and I see him crumple it up and throw it in the fire, and look all around to see if anybody was coming. Then he settled back as comfortable and careless as anything.

Then I comes in, and passes the time of day pleasantly, and sends him of an errand. He never looked uneasy, but went right along. It was a coal-fire and new-built; the writing had gone over behind a chunk, out of sight; but I got it out; there it is; it ain't hardly scorched, you see.''

I glanced at the paper and took in a sentence or two. Then I dismissed the sergeant and told him to send Webb to me. Here is the paper in full:—

> "Fort Trumbull, the 8th.
>
> "COLONEL,—I was mistaken as to the caliber of the three guns I ended my list with. They are 18-pounders; all the rest of the armament is as I stated. The garrison remains as before reported, except that the two light infantry companies that were to be de-tached for service at the front are to stay here for the present—can't find out for how long, just now, but will soon. We are satisfied that, all things considered, matters had better be post-poned un—"

There it broke off—there is where Rayburn coughed and interrupted the writer. All my affection for the boy, all my respect for him and charity for his forlorn condition, withered in a moment under the blight of this revelation of cold-blooded baseness.

But never mind about that. Here was business,—business that required profound and immediate attention, too. Webb and I turned the subject over and over, and examined it all around. Webb said,—

"What a pity he was interrupted! Something is going to be postponed until—when? And what *is* the something? Possibly he would have men-tioned it, the pious little reptile!''

"Yes," I said, "we have missed a trick. And who is 'we', in the letter? Is it conspirators inside the fort or outside?''

That "we" was uncomfortably suggestive. However, it was not worth while to be guessing around that, so we proceeded to matters more prac-tical. In the first place, we decided to double the sentries and keep the strictest possible watch. Next, we thought of calling Wicklow in and making him divulge everything; but that did not seem wisest until other methods should fail. We must have some more of the writings; so we began to plan to that end. And now we had an idea: Wicklow never went to the post-office,—perhaps the deserted stable was his post-office. We sent for my confidential clerk—a young German named Sterne, who was a sort of natural detective—and told him all about the case, and ordered him to go to work on it. Within the hour we got word that Wicklow was writing again. Shortly afterward, word came that he had asked leave to go out into the town. He was detained awhile, and meantime Sterne hurried off and concealed himself in the stable. By and by he saw Wicklow saunter in, look about him, then hide something under some rubbish in a corner, and take leisurely leave again. Sterne pounced upon the hidden article—a letter—and brought it to us. It had no superscription and no signature. It repeated what we had already read, and then went on to say:—

> "We think it best to postpone till the two companies are gone. I mean the four inside think so; have not communicated with the

others—afraid of attracting attention. I say four because we have lost two; they had hardly enlisted and got inside when they were shipped off to the front. It will be absolutely necessary to have two in their places. The two that went were the brothers from Thirtymile Point. I have something of the greatest importance to reveal, but must not trust it to this method of communication; will try the other.''

"The little scoundrel!'' said Webb; "who *could* have supposed he was a spy? However, never mind about that; let us add up our particulars, such as they are, and see how the case stands to date. First, we've got a rebel spy in our midst, whom we know; secondly, we've got three more in our midst whom we don't know; thirdly, these spies have been introduced among us through the simple and easy process of enlisting as soldiers in the Union army—and evidently two of them have got sold at it, and been shipped off to the front; fourthly, there are assistant spies 'outside'— number indefinite; fifthly, Wicklow has very important matter which he is afraid to communicate by the 'present method'—will 'try the other.' That is the case, as it now stands. Shall we collar Wicklow and make him confess? Or shall we catch the person who removes the letters from the stable and make *him* tell? Or shall we keep still and find out more?''

We decided upon the last course. We judged that we did not need to proceed to summary measures now, since it was evident that the conspirators were likely to wait till those two light infantry companies were out of the way. We fortified Sterne with pretty ample powers, and told him to use his best endeavors to find out Wicklow's "other method" of communication. We meant to play a bold game; and to this end we proposed to keep the spies in an unsuspecting state as long as possible. So we ordered Sterne to return to the stable immediately, and, if he found the coast clear, to conceal Wicklow's letter where it was before, and leave it there for the conspirators to get.

The night closed down without further event. It was cold and dark and sleety, with a raw wind blowing; still I turned out of my warm bed several times during the night, and went the rounds in person, to see that all was right and that every sentry was on the alert. I always found them wide awake and watchful; evidently whispers of mysterious dangers had been floating about, and the doubling of the guards had been a kind of indorsement of those rumors. Once, toward morning, I encountered Webb, breasting his way against the bitter wind, and learned then that he, also, had been the rounds several times to see that all was going right.

Next day's events hurried things up somewhat. Wicklow wrote another letter; Sterne preceded him to the stable and saw him deposit it; captured it as soon as Wicklow was out of the way, then slipped out and followed the little spy at a distance, with a detective in plain clothes at his own heels, for we thought it judicious to have the law's assistance handy in case of need. Wicklow went to the railway station, and waited around till the train from New York came in, then stood scanning the faces of the crowd as they poured out of the cars. Presently an aged gentleman, with green goggles and a cane, came limping along, stopped in Wicklow's neighborhood, and began to look about him expectantly. In an instant

Wicklow darted forward, thrust an envelope into his hand, then glided away and disappeared in the throng. The next instant Sterne had snatched the letter; and as he hurried past the detective, he said: "Follow the old gentleman—don't lose sight of him." Then Sterne skurried out with the crowd, and came straight to the fort.

We sat with closed doors, and instructed the guard outside to allow no interruption.

First we opened the letter captured at the stable. It read as follows:—

> "HOLY ALLIANCE,—Found, in the usual gun, commands from the Master, left there last night, which set aside the instructions heretofore received from the subordinate quarter. Have left in the gun the usual indication that the commands reached the proper hand—"

Webb, interrupting: "Isn't the boy under constant surveillance now?"

I said yes; he had been under strict surveillance ever since the capturing of his former letter.

"Then how could he put anything into a gun, or take anything out of it, and not get caught?"

"Well," I said, "I don't like the look of that very well."

"I don't, either," said Webb. "It simply means that there are conspirators among the very sentinels. Without their connivance in some way or other, the thing couldn't have been done."

I sent for Rayburn, and ordered him to examine the batteries and see what he could find. The reading of the letter was then resumed:—

> "The new commands are peremptory, and require that the MMMM shall be FFFFF at 3 o'clock to-morrow morning. Two hundred will arrive, in small parties, by train and otherwise, from various directions, and will be at appointed place at right time. I will distribute the sign to-day. Success is apparently sure, though something must have got out, for the sentries have been doubled, and the chiefs went the rounds last night several times. W. W. comes from southerly to-day and will receive secret orders—by the other method. All six of you must be in 166 at sharp 2 A.M. You will find B. B. there, who will give you detailed instructions. Password same as last time, only reversed—put first syllable last and last syllable first. REMEMBER XXXX. Do not forget. Be of good heart; before the next sun rises you will be heroes; your fame will be permanent; you will have added a deathless page to history. Amen."

"Thunder and Mars," said Webb, "but we are getting into mighty hot quarters, as I look at it!"

I said there was no question but that things were beginning to wear a most serious aspect. Said I,—

"A desperate enterprise is on foot, that is plain enough. To-night is the time set for it,—that, also, is plain. The exact nature of the enterprise— I mean the manner of it—is hidden away under those blind bunches of

M's and F's, but the end and aim, I judge, is the surprise and capture of the post. We must move quick and sharp now. I think nothing can be gained by continuing our clandestine policy as regards Wicklow. We *must* know, and as soon as possible, too, where '166' is located, so that we can make a descent upon the gang there at 2 A.M.; and doubtless the quickest way to get that information will be to force it out of that boy. But first of all, and before we make any important move, I must lay the facts before the War Department, and ask for plenary powers."

The despatch was prepared in cipher to go over the wires; I read it, approved it, and sent it along.

We presently finished discussing the letter which was under consideration, and then opened the one which had been snatched from the lame gentleman. It contained nothing but a couple of perfecoly blank sheets of note-paper! It was a chilly check to our hot eagerness and expectancy. We felt as blank as the paper, for a moment, and twice as foolish. But it was for a moment only; for, of course, we immediately afterward thought of "sympathetic ink." We held the paper close to the fire and watched for the characters to come out, under the influence of the heat; but nothing appeared but some faint tracings, which we could make nothing of. We then called in the surgeon, and sent him off with orders to apply every test he was acquainted with till he got the right one, and report the contents of the letter to me the instant he brought them to the surface. This check was a confounded annoyance, and we naturally chafed under the delay; for we had fully expected to get out of that letter some of the most important secrets of the plot.

Now appeared Sergeant Rayburn, and drew from his pocket a piece of twine string about a foot long, with three knots tied in it, and held it up.

"I got it out of a gun on the water-front," said he. "I took the tompions out of all the guns and examined close; this string was the only thing that was in any gun."

So this bit of string was Wicklow's "sign" to signify that the "Master's" commands had not miscarried. I ordered that every sentinel who had served near that gun during the past twenty-four hours be put in confinement at once and separately, and not allowed to communicate with any one without my privity and consent.

A telegram now came from the Secretary of War. It read as follows:—

"Suspend *habeus corpus*. Put town under martial law. Make necessary arrests. Act with vigor and promptness. Keep the Department informed."

We were now in shape to go to work. I sent out and had the lame gentleman quietly arrested and as quietly brought into the fort; I placed him under guard, and forbade speech to him or from him. He was inclined to bluster at first, but he soon dropped that.

Next came word that Wicklow had been seen to give something to a couple of our new recruits; and that, as soon as his back was turned, these had been seized and confined. Upon each was found a small bit of paper, bearing these words and signs in pencil:—

EAGLE'S THIRD FLIGHT.

REMEMBER XXXX.

166.

In accordance with instructions, I telegraphed to the Department, in cipher, the progress made, and also described the above ticket. We seemed to be in a strong enough position now to venture to throw off the mast as regarded Wicklow; so I sent for him. I also sent for and received back the letter written in sympathetic ink, the surgeon accompanying it with the information that thus far it had resisted his tests, but that there were others he could apply when I should be ready for him to do so.

Presently Wicklow entered. He had a somewhat worn and anxious look, but he was composed and easy, and if he suspected anything it did not appear in his face or manner. I allowed him to stand there a moment or two, then I said pleasantly,—

"My boy, why do you go to that old stable so much?"

He answered, with simple demeanor and without embarrassment,—

"Well, I hardly know, sir; there isn't any particular reason, except that I like to be alone, and I amuse myself there."

"You amuse yourself there, do you?"

"Yes, sir," he replied, as innocently and simply as before.

"Is that all you do there?"

"Yes, sir," he said, looking up with childlike wonderment in his big soft eyes.

"You are *sure?*"

"Yes, sir, sure."

After a pause, I said,—

"Wicklow, why do you write so much?"

"I? I do not write much, sir."

"You don't?"

"No, sir. Oh, if you mean scribbling, I *do* scribble some, for amusement."

"What do you do with your scribblings?"

"Nothing, sir—throw them away."

"Never send them to anybody?"

"No, sir."

I suddenly thrust before him the letter to the "Colonel." He started slightly, but immediately composed himself. A slight tinge spread itself over his cheek.

"How came you to send *this* piece of scribbling, then?"

"I nev-never meant any harm, sir."

"Never meant any harm! You betray the armament and condition of the post, and mean no harm by it?"

He hung his head and was silent.

"Come, speak up, and stop lying. Whom was this letter intended for?"

He showed signs of distress, now; but quickly collected himself, and replied, in a tone of deep earnestness,—

"I will tell you the truth, sir—the whole truth. The letter was never intended for anybody at all. I wrote it only to amuse myself. I see the error and foolishness of it, now,—but it is the only offence, sir, upon my honor."

"Ah, I am glad of that. It is dangerous to be writing such letters. I hope you are sure this is the only one you wrote?"

"Yes, sir, perfectly sure."

His hardihood was stupefying. He told that lie with as sincere a countenance as any creature ever wore. I waited a moment to soothe down my rising temper, and then said,—

"Wicklow, jog your memory now, and see if you can help me with two or three little matters which I wish to inquire about."

"I will do my very best, sir."

"Then, to begin with—who is 'the Master'?"

It betrayed him into darting a startled glance at our faces, but that was all. He was serene again in a moment, and tranquilly answered,—

"I do not know, sir."

"You do not know?"

"I do not know."

"You are *sure* you do not know?"

He tried hard to keep his eyes on mine, but the strain was too great; his chin sunk slowly toward his breast and he was silent; he stood there nervously fumbling with a button, an object to command one's pity, in spite of his base acts. Presently I broke the stillness with the question,—

"Who are the 'Holy Alliance'?"

His body shook visibly, and he made a slight random gesture with his hands, which to me was like the appeal of a despairing creature for compassion. But he made no sound. He continued to stand with his face bent toward the ground. As we sat gazing at him, waiting for him to speak, we saw the big tears begin to roll down his cheeks. But he remained silent. After a little, I said,—

"You must answer me, my boy, and you must tell me the truth. Who are the Holy Alliance?"

He wept on in silence. Presently I said, somewhat sharply,—

"Answer the question!"

He struggled to get command of his voice; and then, looking up appealingly, forced the words out between his sobs,—

"Oh, have pity on me, sir! I cannot answer it, for I do not know."

"What!"

"Indeed, sir, I am telling the truth. I never have heard of the Holy Alliance till this moment. On my honor, sir, this is so."

"Good heavens! Look at this second letter of yours; there, do you see those words, *'Holy Alliance'?* What do you say now?"

He gazed up into my face with the hurt look of one upon whom a great wrong has been wrought, then said, feelingly,—

"This is some cruel joke, sir; and how could they play it upon me, who have tried all I could to do right, and have never done harm to anybody?

Some one has counterfeited my hand; I never wrote a line of this; I have never seen this letter before!''

"Oh, you unspeakable liar! Here, what do you say to *this?*''—and I snatched the sympathetic-ink letter from my pocket and thrust it before his eyes.

His face turned white!—as white as a dead person's. He wavered slightly in his tracks, and put his hand against the wall to steady himself. After a moment he asked, in so faint a voice that it was hardly audible,—

"Have you—read it?"

Our faces must have answered the truth before my lips could get out the false "yes," for I distinctly saw the courage come back into that boy's eyes. I waited for him to say something, but he kept silent. So at last I said,—

"Well, what have you to say as to the revelations in this letter?"

He answered, with perfect composure,—

"Nothing, except that they are entirely harmless and innocent; they can hurt nobody.''

I was in something of a corner now, as I couldn't disprove his assertion. I did not know exactly how to proceed. However, an idea came to my relief, and I said,—

"You are sure you know nothing about the Master and the Holy Alliance, and did not write the letter which you say is a forgery?"

"Yes, sir—sure.''

I slowly drew out the knotted twine string and held it up without speaking. He gazed at it indifferently, then looked at me inquiringly. My patience was sorely taxed. However, I kept my temper down, and said in my usual voice,—

"Wicklow, do you see this?"

"Yes, sir.''

"What is it?"

"It seems to be a piece of string.''

"*Seems?* It *is* a piece of string. Do you recognize it?"

"No, sir," he replied, as calmly as the words could be uttered.

His coolness was perfectly wonderful! I paused now for several seconds, in order that the silence might add impressiveness to what I was about to say; then I rose and laid my hand on his shoulder, and said gravely,—

"It will do you no good, poor boy, none in the world. This sign to the 'Master,' this knotted string, found in one of the guns on the water-front—"

"Found *in* the gun! Oh, no, no, no! do not say *in* the gun, but in a crack in the tompion!—it *must* have been in the crack!" and down he went on his knees and clasped his hands and lifted up a face that was pitiful to see, so ashy it was, and so wild with terror.

"No, it was *in* the gun.''

"Oh, something has gone wrong! My God, I am lost!" and he sprang up and darted this way and that, dodging the hands that were put out to catch him, and doing his best to escape from the place. But of course escape was impossible. Then he flung himself on his knees again, crying with all his might, and clasped me around the legs; and so he clung to me and begged and pleaded, saying, "Oh, have pity on me! Oh, be merciful to me! Do not betray me; they would not spare my life a moment! Protect me, save me. I will confess everything!"

It took us some time to quiet him down and modify his fright, and get him into something like a rational frame of mind. Then I began to question him, he answering humbly, with downcast eyes, and from time to time swabbing away his constantly flowing tears.

"So you are at heart a rebel?"

"Yes, sir."

"And a spy?"

"Yes, sir."

"And have been acting under distinct orders from outside?"

"Yes, sir."

"Willingly?"

"Yes, sir."

"*Gladly,* perhaps?"

"Yes, sir; it would do no good to deny it. The South is my country; my heart is Southern, and it is all in her cause."

"Then the tale you told me of your wrongs and the persecution of your family was made up for the occasion?"

"They—they told me to say it, sir."

"And you would betray and destroy those who pitied and sheltered you. Do you comprehend how base you are, you poor misguided thing?"

He replied with sobs only.

"Well, let that pass. To business. Who is the 'Colonel,' and where is he?"

He began to cry hard, and tried to beg off from answering. He said he would be killed if he told. I threatened to put him in the dark cell and lock him up if he did not come out with the information. At the same time I promised to protect him from all harm if he made a clean breast. For all answer, he closed his mouth firmly and put on a stubborn air which I could not bring him out of. At last I started with him; but a single glance into the dark cell converted him. He broke into a passion of weeping and supplicating, and declared he would tell everything.

So I brought him back, and he named the "Colonel," and described him particularly. Said he would be found at the principal hotel in the town, in citizen's dress. I had to threaten him again, before he would describe and name the "Master." Said the Master would be found at No. 15 Bond Street, New York, passing under the name of R. F. Gaylord. I telegraphed name and description to the chief of police of the metropolis, and asked that Gaylord be arrested and held till I could send for him.

"Now," said I, "it seems that there are several of the conspirators 'outside,'—presumably in New London. Name and describe them."

He named and described three men and two women,—all stopping at the principal hotel. I sent out quietly, and had them and the "Colonel" arrested and confined in the fort.

"Next, I want to know all about your three fellow-conspirators who are here in the fort."

He was about to dodge me with a falsehood, I thought; but I produced the mysterious bits of paper which had been found upon two of them, and this had a salutary effect upon him. I said we had possession of two of the men, and he must point out the third. This frightened him badly, and he cried out,—

"Oh, please don't make me; he would kill me on the spot!"

I said that that was all nonsense; I would have somebody near by to protect him, and, besides, the men should be assembled without arms. I ordered all the raw recruits to be mustered, and then the poor trembling little wretch went out and stepped along down the line, trying to look as indifferent as possible. Finally he spoke a single word to one of the men, and before he had gone five steps the man was under arrest.

As soon as Wicklow was with us again, I had those three men brought in. I made one of them stand forward, and said,—

"Now, Wicklow, mind, not a shade's divergence from the exact truth. Who is this man, and what do you know about him?"

Being "in for it," he cast consequences aside, fastened his eyes on the man's face, and spoke straight along without hesitation,—to the following effect.

"His real name is George Bristow. He is from New Orleans; was second mate of the coast-packet 'Capitol,' two years ago; is a desperate character, and has served two terms for manslaughter,—one for killing a deck-hand named Hyde with a capstan-bar, and one for killing a roustabout for refusing to heave the lead, which is no part of a roustabout's business. He is a spy, and was sent here by the Colonel, to act in that capacity. He was third mate of the 'St. Nicholas,' when she blew up in the neighborhood of Memphis, in '58, and came near being lynched for robbing the dead and wounded while they were being taken ashore in an empty wood-boat."

And so forth and so on—he gave the man's biography in full. When he had finished, I said to the man,—

"What have you to say to this?"

"Barring your presence, sir, it is the infernalest lie that ever was spoke!"

I sent him back into confinement, and called the others forward in turn. Same result. The boy gave a detailed history of each, without ever hesitating for a word or a fact; but all I could get out of either rascal was the indignant assertion that it was all a lie. They would confess nothing. I returned them to captivity, and brought out the rest of my prisoners, one by one. Wicklow told all about them—what towns in the South they were from, and every detail of their connection with the conspiracy.

But they all denied his facts, and not one of them confessed a thing. The men raged, the women cried. According to their stories, they were all innocent people from out West, and loved the Union above all things in this world. I locked the gang up, in disgust, and fell to catechizing Wicklow once more.

"Where is No. 166, and who is B.B.?"

But *there* he was determined to draw the line. Neither coaxing nor threats had any effect upon him. Time was flying—it was necessary to institute sharp measures. So I tied him up a-tiptoe by the thumbs. As the pain increased, it wrung screams from him which were almost more than I could bear. But I held my ground, and pretty soon he shrieked out,—

"Oh, *please* let me down, and I will tell!"

"No—you'll tell *before* I let you down."

Every instant was agony to him, now, so out it came:—

"No. 166, Eagle Hotel!"—naming a wretched tavern down by the water, a resort of common laborers, 'longshoremen, and less reputable folk.

So I released him, and then demanded to know the object of the conspiracy.

"To take the fort to-night," said he, doggedly and sobbing.

"Have I got all the chiefs of the conspiracy?"

"No, you've got all except those that are to meet at 166."

"What does 'Remember XXXX' mean?"

No reply.

"What is the password to No. 166?"

No reply.

"What do those bunches of letters mean,—'FFFFF' and 'MMMM'? Answer! or you will catch it again."

"I never *will* answer! I will die first. Now do what you please."

"Think what you are saying, Wicklow. Is it final?"

He answered steadily, and without a quiver in his voice,—

"It is final. As sure as I love my wronged country and hate everything this Northern sun shines on, I will die before I will reveal those things."

I triced him up by the thumbs again. When the agony was full upon him, it was heart-breaking to hear the poor thing's shrieks, but we got nothing else out of him. To every question he screamed the same reply: "I can die, and I *will* die; but I will never tell."

Well, we had to give it up. We were convinced that he certainly would die rather than confess. So we took him down and imprisoned him, under strict guard.

Then for some hours we busied ourselves with sending telegrams to the War Department, and with making preparations for a descent upon No. 166.

It was stirring times, that black and bitter night. Things had leaked out, and the whole garrison was on the alert. The sentinels were trebled, and nobody could move, outside or in, without being brought to a stand with a musket levelled at his head. However, Webb and I were less concerned now than we had previously been, because of the fact that the conspiracy must necessarily be in a pretty crippled condition, since so many of its principals were in our clutches.

I determined to be at No. 166 in good season, capture and gag B. B., and be on hand for the rest when they arrived. At about a quarter past one in the morning I crept out of the fortress with half a dozen stalwart and gamy U.S. regulars at my heels—and the boy Wicklow, with his hands tied behind him. I told him we were going to No. 166, and that if I found he had lied again and was misleading us, he would have to show us the right place or suffer the consequences.

We approached the tavern stealthily and reconnoitered. A light was burning in the small bar-room, the rest of the house was dark. I tried the front door; it yielded, and we softly entered, closing the door behind us. Then we removed our shoes, and I led the way to the bar-room. The German landlord sat there, asleep in his chair. I woke him gently, and told him to take off his boots and precede us; warning him at the same time to utter no sound. He obeyed without a murmur, but evidently he was badly frightened. I ordered him to lead the way to 166. We ascended two or three flights of stairs as softly as a file of cats; and then, having arrived near the farther end of a long hall, we came to a door through the glazed transom of which we could discern the glow of a dim light from within. The landlord felt for me in the dark and whispered me that that was 166. I tried the door—it was locked on the inside. I whispered an order to one of my biggest soldiers; we set our ample shoulders to the door and with one heave we burst it from its hinges. I caught a half-glimpse of a figure in a bed—saw its head dart toward the candle; out went the light, and we were in pitch darkness. With one big bound I lit on that bed and pinned its occupant down with my knees. My prisoner struggled fiercely, but I got a grip on his throat with my left hand, and that was a good assistance to my knees in holding him down. Then straightaway I snatched out my revolver, cocked it, and laid the cold barrel warningly against his cheek.

"Now somebody strike a light!" said I. "I've got him safe."

It was done. The flame of the match burst up. I looked at my captive, and, by George, it was a young woman!

I let go and got off the bed, feeling pretty sheepish. Everybody stared stupidly at his neighbor. Nobody had any wit or sense left, so sudden and overwhelming had been the surprise. The young woman began to cry, and covered her face with the sheet. The landlord said, meekly,—

"My daughter, she has been doing something that is not right, nicht wahr?"

"Your daughter? Is she your daughter?"

"Oh, yes, she is my daughter. She is just to-night come home from Cincinnati a little bit sick."

"Confound it, that boy has lied again. This is not the right 166; this is not B. B. Now, Wicklow, you will find the correct 166 for us, or—hello! where is that boy?"

Gone, as sure as guns! And, what is more, we failed to find a trace of him. Here was an awkward predicament. I cursed my stupidity in not tying him to one of the men; but it was of no use to bother about that now. What should I do in the present circumstances?—that was the question. That girl might be B. B., after all. I did not believe it, but still it would not answer to take unbelief for proof. So I finally put my men in a vacant room across the hall from 166, and told them to capture anybody and everybody that approached the girl's room, and to keep the landlord with them, and under strict watch, until further orders. Then I hurried back to the fort to see if all was right there yet.

Yes, all was right. And all remained right. I stayed up all night to make sure of that. Nothing happened. I was unspeakably glad to see the dawn come again, and be able to telegraph the Department that the Stars and Stripes still floated over Fort Trumbull.

An immense pressure was lifted from my breast. Still I did not relax vigilance, of course, nor effort either; the case was too grave for that. I had up my prisoners, one by one, and harried them by the hour, trying to get them to confess, but it was a failure. They only gnashed their teeth and tore their hair, and revealed nothing.

About noon came tidings of my missing boy. He had been seen on the road, tramping westward, some eight miles out, at six in the morning. I started a cavalry lieutenant and a private on his track at once. They came in sight of him twenty miles out. He had climbed a fence and was wearily dragging himself across a slushy field toward a large old-fashioned mansion in the edge of a village. They rode through a bit of woods, made a detour, and closed up on the house from the opposite side; then dismounted and skurried into the kitchen. Nobody there. They slipped into the next room, which was also unoccupied; the door from that room into the front or sitting room was open. They were about to step through it when they heard a low voice; it was somebody praying. So they halted reverently, and the lieutenant put his head in and saw an old man and an old woman kneeling in a corner of that sitting-room. It was the old man that was praying, and just as he was finishing his prayer, the Wicklow boy opened the front door and stepped in. Both of those old people sprang at him and smothered him with embraces, shouting,—

"Our boy! our darling! God be praised. The lost is found! He that was dead is alive again!"

Well, sir, what do you think! That young imp was born and reared on that homestead, and had never been five miles away from it in all his life, till the fortnight before he loafed into my quarters and gulled me with that maudlin yarn of his! It's as true as gospel. That old man was his father— a learned old retired clergyman; and that old lady was his mother.

Let me throw in a word or two of explanation concerning that boy and his performances. It turned out that he was a ravenous devourer of dime novels and sensation-story papers—therefore, dark mysteries and gaudy heroisms were just in his line. Then he had read newspaper reports of the stealthy goings and comings of rebel spies in our midst, and of their lurid purposes and their two or three startling achievements, till his imagination was all aflame on that subject. His constant comrade for some months had been a Yankee youth of much tongue and lively fancy, who had served for a couple of years as "mud clerk" (that is, subordinate purser) on certain of the packet-boats plying between New Orleans and points two or three hundred miles up the Mississippi—hence his easy facility in handling the names and other details pertaining to that region. Now I had spent two or three months in that part of the country before the war; and I knew just enough about it to be easily taken in by that boy, whereas a born Louisianian would probably have caught him tripping before he had talked fifteen minutes. Do you know the reason he said he would rather die than explain certain of his treasonable enigmas? Simply because he *couldn't* explain them!—they had no meaning; he had fired them out of his imagination without forethought or afterthought; and so, upon sudden call, he wasn't able to invent an explanation of them. For instance, he couldn't reveal what was hidden in the "sympathetic ink" letter, for the ample reason that there wasn't anything hidden in it; it was blank paper only. He hadn't put anything into a gun, and had never intended to—for his letters were all written to imaginary persons, and when he hid one in the stable he always removed the one he had put there the day before; so he was not acquainted with that knotted string, since he was seeing it for the first time when I showed it to him; but as soon as I had let him find out where it came from, he straightway adopted it, in his romantic fashion, and got some fine effects out of it. He invented Mr. "Gaylord;" there wasn't any 15 Bond Street, just then—it had been pulled down three months before. He invented the "Colonel;" he invented the glib histories of those unfortunates whom I captured and confronted with him; he invented "B. B.;" he even invented No. 166, one may say, for he didn't know there *was* such a number in the Eagle Hotel until we went there. He stood ready to invent anybody or anything whenever it was wanted. If I called for "outside" spies, he promptly described strangers whom he had seen at the hotel, and whose names he had happened to hear. Ah, he lived in a gorgeous, mysterious, romantic world during those few stirring days, and I think it was *real* to him, and that he enjoyed it clear down to the bottom of his heart.

But he made trouble enough for us, and just no end of humiliation. You see, on account of him we had fifteen or twenty people under arrest and confinement in the fort, with sentinels before their doors. A lot of the captives were soldiers and such, and to them I didn't have to apologize; but the rest were first-class citizens, from all over the country, and no amount of apologies was sufficient to satisfy them. They just fumed and raged and made no end of trouble! And those two ladies,—one was an Ohio Congressman's wife, the other a Western bishop's sister,—well, the scorn and ridicule and angry tears they poured out on me made up a keepsake that was likely to make me remember them for a considerable time,—and I shall. That old lame gentleman with the goggles was a college president from Philadelphia, who had come up to attend his nephew's funeral. He had never seen young Wicklow before, of course. Well, he not only missed the funeral, and got jailed as a rebel spy, but Wicklow had stood up there in my quarters and coldly described him as a counterfeiter, nigger-trader, horse-thief, and fire-bug from the most notorious rascal-nest in Galveston; and this was a thing which that poor old gentleman couldn't seem to get over at all.

And the War Department! But, O my soul, let's draw the curtain over that part!*

THE GREAT REVOLUTION IN PITCAIRN

LET ME refresh the reader's memory a little. Nearly a hundred years ago the crew of the British ship "Bounty" mutinied, set the captain and his officers adrift upon the open sea, took possession of the ship, and sailed southward. They procured wives for themselves among the natives of Tahiti, then proceeded to a lonely little rock in mid-Pacific, called Pitcairn's Island, wrecked the vessel, stripped her of everything that might

*NOTE.—I showed my manuscript to the Major, and he said: "Your unfamiliarity with military matters has betrayed you into some little mistakes. Still, they are picturesque ones— let them go; military men will smile at them, the rest won't detect them. You have got the main facts of the history right, and have set them down just about as they occurred."—M.T.

be useful to a new colony, and established themselves on shore.

Pitcairn's is so far removed from the track of commerce that it was many years before another vessel touched there. It had always been considered an uninhabited island; so when a ship did at last drop its anchor there, in 1808, the captain was greatly surprised to find the place peopled. Although the mutineers had fought among themselves, and gradually killed each other off until only two or three of the orginal stock remained, these tragedies had not occurred before a number of children had been born; so in 1808 the island had a population of twenty-seven persons. John Adams, the chief mutineer, still survived, and was to live many years yet, as governor and patriarch of the flock. From being mutineer and homicide, he had turned Christian and teacher, and his nation of twenty-seven persons was now the purest and devoutest in Christendom. Adams had long ago hoisted the British flag and constituted his island an appanage of the British crown.

To-day the population numbers ninety persons,—sixteen men, nineteen women, twenty-five boys, and thirty girls,—all descendants of the mutineers, all bearing the family names of those mutineers, and all speaking English, and English only. The island stands high up out of the sea, and has precipitous walls. It is about three quarters of a mile long, and in places is as much as half a mile wide. Such arable land as it affords is held by the several families, according to a division made many years ago. There is some live stock,—goats, pigs, chickens, and cats; but no dogs, and no large animals. There is one church building,—used also as a capitol, a school-house, and a public library. The title of the governor has been, for a generation or two, "Magistrate and Chief Ruler, in subordination to her Majesty the Queen of Great Britain." It was his province to *make* the laws, as well as execute them. His office was elective; everybody over seventeen years old had a vote,—no matter about the sex.

The sole occupations of the people were farming and fishing; their sole recreation, religious services. There has never been a shop in the island, nor any money. The habits and dress of the people have always been primitive, and their laws simple to puerility. They have lived in a deep Sabbath tranquillity, far from the world and its ambitions and vexations, and neither knowing nor caring what was going on in the mighty empires that lie beyond their limitless ocean solitudes. Once in three or four years a ship touched there, moved them with aged news of bloody battles, devastating epidemics, fallen thrones, and ruined dynasties, then traded them some soap and flannel for some yams and bread-fruit, and sailed away, leaving them to retire into their peaceful dreams and pious dissipations once more.

On the 8th of last September, Admiral de Horsey, commander-in-chief of the British fleet in the Pacific, visited Pitcairn's Island, and speaks as follows in his offical report to the admiralty:—

"They have beans, carrots, turnips, cabbages, and a little maize; pineapples, fig-trees, custard apples, and oranges; lemons and cocoa-nuts. Clothing is obtained alone from passing ships, in barter for refreshments. There are no springs on the island, but as it rains generally once a month they have plenty of water, although at times, in former years, they have suffered from drought. No alcoholic liquors, except for medicinal purposes, are used, and a drunkard is unknown. . . .

"The necessary articles required by the islanders are best shown by those we furnished in barter for refreshments: namely, flannel, serge, drill, half-boots, combs, tobacco, and soap. They also stand much in need of maps and slates for their school, and tools of any kind are most acceptable. I caused them to be supplied from the public stores with a union-jack for display on the arrival of ships, and a pit saw, of which they were greatly in need. This, I trust, will meet the approval of their lordships. If the munificent people of England were only aware of the wants of this most deserving little colony, they would not long go unsupplied. . . .

"Divine service is held every Sunday at 10:30 A.M. and 3 P.M., in the house built and used by John Adams for that purpose until he died in 1829. It is conducted strictly in accordance with the liturgy of the Church of England, by Mr. Simon Young, their selected pastor, who is much respected. A Bible class is held every Wednesday, when all who conveniently can, attend. There is also a general meeting for prayer on the first Friday in every month. Family prayers are said in every house the first thing in the morning and the last thing in the evening, and no food is partaken of without asking God's blessing before and afterwards. Of these islanders' religious attributes no one can speak without deep respect. A people whose greatest pleasure and privilege is to commune in prayer with their God, and to join in hymns of praise, and who are, moreover, cheerful, diligent, and probably freer from vice than any other community, need no priest among them."

Now I come to a sentence in the admiral's report which he dropped carelessly from his pen, no doubt, and never gave the matter a second thought. He little imagined what a freight of tragic prophecy it bore! This is the sentence:—

"One stranger, an American, has settled on the island,—*a doubtful acquisition*."

A doubtful acquisition indeed! Captain Ormsby, in the American ship "Hornet," touched at Pitcairn's nearly four months after the admiral's visit, and from the facts which he gathered there we now know all about that American. Let us put these facts together, in historical form. The American's name was Butterworth Stavely. As soon as he had become well acqainted with all the people,—and this took but a few days, of course,—he began to ingratiate himself with them by all the arts he could command. He became exceedingly popular, and much looked up to; for one of the first things he did was to forsake his worldly way of life, and throw all his energies into religion. He was always reading his Bible, or praying, or singing hymns, or asking blessings. In prayer, no one had such "liberty" as he, no one could pray so long or so well.

At last, when he considered the time to be ripe, he began secretly to sow the seeds of discontent among the people. It was his deliberate purpose, from the beginning, to subvert the government, but of course he kept that to himself for a time. He used different arts with different individuals. He awakened dissatisfaction in one quarter by calling attention to the shortness of the Sunday services; he argued that there should be three three-hour services on Sunday instead of only two. Many had secretly held this opinion before; they now privately banded themselves into a party to work for it. He showed certain of the women that they were not allowed sufficient voice in the prayer-meetings; thus another party was formed. No weapon was beneath his notice; he even descended to the children, and awoke discontent in their breasts because—as *he* discovered for them— they had not enough Sunday-school. This created a third party.

Now, as the chief of these parties, he found himself the strongest power in the community. So he proceeded to his next move,—a no less important one than the impeachment of the chief magistrate, James Russell Nickoy; a man of character and ability, and possessed of great wealth, he being the owner of a house with a parlor to it, three acres and a half of yam land, and the only boat in Pitcairn's, a whale-boat; and, most unfortunately, a pretext for this impeachment offered itself at just the right time. One of the earliest and most precious laws of the island was the law against trespass. It was held in great reverence, and was regarded as the palladium of the people's liberties. About thirty years ago an important case came before the courts under this law, in this wise: a chicken belonging to Elizabeth Young (aged, at that time, fifty-eight, a daughter of John Mills, one of the mutineers of the "Bounty") trespassed upon the grounds of Thursday October Christian (aged twenty-nine, a grandson of Fletcher Christian, one of the mutineers). Christian killed the chicken. According to the law, Christian could keep the chicken; or, if he preferred, he could restore its remains to the owner, and receive damages in "produce" to an amount equivalent to the waste and injury wrought by the trespasser. The court records set forth that "the said Christian aforesaid did deliver the aforesaid remains to the said Elizabeth Young, and did demand one bushel of yams in satisfaction of the damage done." But Elizabeth Young considered the demand exorbitant; the parties could not agree; therefore Christian brought suit in the courts. He lost his case in the justice's court; at least, he was awarded only a half-peck of yams, which he considered insufficient, and in the nature of a defeat. He appealed. The case lingered several years in an ascending grade of courts, and always resulted in decrees sustaining the original verdict; and finally the thing got into the supreme court, and there it stuck for twenty years. But last summer, even the supreme court managed to arrive at a decision at last. Once more the original verdict was sustained. Christian then said he was satisfied; but Stavely was present, and whispered to him and to his lawyer, suggesting, "as a mere form," that the original law be exhibited, in order to make sure that it still existed. It seemed an odd idea, but an ingenious one. So the demand was made. A messenger was sent to the magistrate's house; he presently returned with the tidings that it had disappeared from among the state archives.

The court now pronounced its late decision void, since it had been made under a law which had no actual existence.

Great excitement ensued, immediately. The news swept abroad over the whole island that the palladium of the public liberties was lost,—may be treasonably destroyed. Within thirty minutes almost the entire nation were in the court-room,—that is to say, the church. The impeachment of the chief magistrate followed, upon Stavely's motion. The accused met his misfortune with the dignity which became his great office. He did not plead, or even argue: he offered the simple defence that he had not meddled with the missing law; that he had kept the state archives in the same candle-box that had been used as their depository from the beginning; and that he was innocent of the removal or destruction of the lost document.

But nothing could save him; he was found guilty of misprision of treason, and degraded from his office, and all his property was confiscated.

The lamest part of the whole shameful matter was the *reason* suggested by his enemies for his destruction of the law, to wit: that he did it to favor Christian, because Christian was his cousin! Whereas Stavely was the only individual in the entire nation who was *not* his cousin. The reader must remember that all of these people are the descendants of half a dozen men; that the first children intermarried together and bore grandchildren to the mutineers; that these grandchildren intermarried; after them, great and great-great-grandchildren intermarried: so that to-day everybody is blood kin to everybody. Moreover, the relationships are wonderfully, even astoundingly, mixed up and complicated. A stranger, for instance, says to an islander,—

"You speak of that young woman as your cousin; a while ago you called her your aunt."

"Well, she *is* my aunt, and my cousin too. And also my step-sister, my niece, my fourth cousin, my thirty-third cousin, my forty-second cousin, my great-aunt, my grandmother, my widowed sister-in-law,—and next week she will be my wife."

So the charge of nepotism against the chief magistrate was weak. But no matter; weak or strong, it suited Stavely. Stavely was immediately elected to the vacant magistracy; and, oozing reform from every pore, he went vigorously to work. In no long time religious services raged everywhere and unceasingly. By command, the second prayer of the Sunday morning service, which had customarily endured some thirty-five or forty minutes, and had pleaded for the world, first by continent and then by national and tribal detail, was extended to an hour and a half, and made to include supplications in behalf of the possible peoples in the several planets. Everybody was pleased with this; everybody said, "Now *this* is something *like*." By command, the usual three-hour sermons were doubled in length. The nation came in a body to testify their gratitude to the new magistrate. The old law forbidding cooking on the Sabbath was extended to the prohibition of eating, also. By command, Sunday-school was privileged to spread over into the week. The joy of all classes was complete. In one short month the new magistrate had become the people's idol!

The time was ripe for this man's next move. He began, cautiously at first, to poison the public mind against England. He took the chief citizens aside, one by one, and conversed with them on this topic. Presently he grew bolder, and spoke out. He said the nation owed it to itself, to its honor, to its great traditions, to rise in its might and throw off "this galling English yoke."

But the simple islanders answered,—

"We had not noticed that it galled. How does it gall? England sends a ship once in three or four years to give us soap and clothing, and things which we sorely need and gratefully receive; but she never troubles us; she lets us go our own way.''

"She lets you go your own way! So slaves have felt and spoken in all the ages! This speech shows how fallen you are, how base, how brutalized, you have become, under this grinding tyranny! What! has all manly pride forsaken you? Is liberty nothing? Are you content to be a mere appendage to a foreign and hateful sovereignty, when you might rise up and take your rightful place in the august family of nations, great, free, enlightened, independent, the minion of no sceptered master, but the arbiter of your own destiny, and a voice and a power in decreeing the destinies of your sister-sovereignties of the world?''

Speeches like this produced an effect by and by. Citizens began to feel the English yoke; they did not know exactly how or whereabouts they felt it, but they were perfectly certain they did feel it. They got to grumbling a good deal, and chafing under their chains, and longing for relief and release. They presently fell to hating the English flag, that sign and symbol of their nation's degradation; they ceased to glance up at it as they passed the capitol, but averted their eyes and grated their teeth; and one morning, when it was found trampled into the mud at the foot of the staff, they left it there, and no man put his hand to it to hoist it again. A certain thing which was sure to happen sooner or later happened now. Some of the chief citizens went to the magistrate by night, and said,—

"We can endure this hated tyranny no longer. How can we cast it off?''

"By a *coup d'état*.''

"How?''

"A coup d'état. It is like this: everything is got ready, and at the appointed moment I, as the official head of the nation, publicly and solemnly proclaim its independence, and absolve it from allegiance to any and all other powers whatsoever.''

"That sounds simple and easy. We can do that right away. Then what will be the next thing to do?''

"Seize all the defences and public properties of all kinds, establish martial law, put the army and navy on a war footing, and proclaim the empire!''

This fine program dazzled these innocents. They said,—

"This is grand,—this is splendid; but will not England resist?''

"Let her. This rock is a Gibraltar.''

"True. But about the empire? Do we *need* an empire, and an emperor?''

"What you *need*, my friends, is unification. Look at Germany; look at Italy. They are unified. Unification is the thing. It makes living dear. That constitutes progress. We must have a standing army, and a navy. Taxes follow, as a matter of course. All these things summed up make grandeur. With unification and grandeur, what more can you want? Very well,— only the empire can confer these boons.''

So on the 8th day of December Pitcairn's Island was proclaimed a free and independent nation; and on the same day the solemn coronation of Butterworth I., emperor of Pitcairn's Island, took place, amid great rejoicings and festivities. The entire nation, with the exception of fourteen persons, mainly little children, marched past the throne in single file, with banners and music, the procession being upwards of ninety feet long; and some said it was as much as three quarters of a minute passing a given point. Nothing like it had ever been seen in the history of the island before. Public enthusiasm was measureless.

Now straightway imperial reforms began. Orders of nobility were instituted. A minister of the navy was appointed, and the whale-boat put in commission. A minister of war was created, and ordered to proceed at once with the formation of a standing army. A first lord of the treasury was named, and commanded to get up a taxation scheme, and also open negotiations for treaties, offensive, defensive, and commercial, with foreign powers. Some generals and admirals were appointed; also some chamberlains, some equerries in waiting, and some lords of the bed-chamber.

At this point all the material was used up. The Grand Duke of Galilee, minister of war, complained that all the sixteen grown men in the empire had been given great offices, and consequently would not consent to serve in the ranks; wherefore his standing army was at a stand-still. The Marquis of Ararat, minister of the navy, made a similar complaint. He said he was willing to steer the whale-boat himself, but he *must* have somebody to man her.

The emperor did the best he could in the circumstances: he took all the boys above the age of ten years away from their mothers, and pressed them into the army, thus constructing a corps of seventeen privates, officered by one lieutenant-general and two major-generals. This pleased the minister of war, but procured the enmity of all the mothers in the land; for they said their precious ones must now find bloody graves in the fields of war, and he would be answerable for it. Some of the more heart-broken and inappeasable among them lay constantly in wait for the emperor and threw yams at him, unmindful of the body-guard.

On account of the extreme scarcity of material, it was found necessary to require the Duke of Bethany, postmaster-general, to pull stroke-oar in the navy, and thus sit in the rear of a noble of lower degree, namely, Viscount Canaan, lord-justice of the common pleas. This turned the Duke of Bethany into a tolerably open malcontent and secret conspirator,—a thing which the emperor foresaw, but could not help.

Things went from bad to worse. The emperor raised Nancy Peters to the peerage on one day, and married her the next, notwithstanding, for reasons of state, the cabinet had strenuously advised him to marry Emmeline, eldest daughter of the Archbishop of Bethlehem. This caused trouble in a powerful quarter,—the church. The new empress secured the support and friendship of two thirds of the thirty-six grown women in the nation by absorbing them into her court as maids of honor; but this made deadly enemies of the remaining twelve. The families of the maids of honor soon began to rebel, because there was now nobody at home to keep house. The twelve snubbed women refused to enter the imperial kitchen as servants; so the empress had to require the Countess of Jericho and other great court dames to fetch water, sweep the palace, and perform other menial and equally distasteful services. This made bad blood in that department.

Everybody fell to complaining that the taxes levied for the support of the army, the navy, and the rest of the imperial establishment were intolerably burdensome, and were reducing the nation to beggary. The emperor's reply—"Look at Germany; look at Italy. Are you better than they? and haven't you unification?"—did not satisfy them. They said, "People can't *eat* unification, and we are starving. Agriculture has ceased. Everybody is in the army, everybody is in navy, everybody is in the public service, standing around in a uniform, with nothing whatever to do, nothing to eat, and nobody to till the fields—"

"Look at Germany; look at Italy. It is the same there. Such is unification, and there's no other way to get it,—no other way to keep it after you've got it," said the poor emperor always.

But the grumblers only replied, "We can't *stand* the taxes,—we can't *stand* them."

Now right on top of this the cabinet reported a national debt amounting to upwards of forty-five dollars,—half a dollar to every individual in the nation. And they proposed to fund something. They had heard that this was always done in such emergencies. They proposed duties on exports; also on imports. And they wanted to issue bonds; also paper money, redeemable in yams and cabbages in fifty years. They said the pay of the army and of the navy and of the whole governmental machine was far in arrears, and unless something was done, and done immediately, national bankruptcy must ensue, and possibly insurrection and revolution. The emperor at once resolved upon a high-handed measure, and one of a nature never before heard of in Pitcairn's Island. He went in state to the church on Sunday morning, with the army at his back, and commanded the minister of the treasury to take up a collection.

That was the feather that broke the camel's back. First one citizen, and then another, rose and refused to submit to this unheard-of outrage,—and each refusal was followed by the immediate confiscation of the malcontent's property. This vigor soon stopped the refusals, and the collection proceeded amid a sullen and ominous silence. As the emperor withdrew with the troops, he said, "I will teach you who is master here." Several persons shouted, "Down with unification!" They were at once arrested and torn from the arms of their weeping friends by the soldiery.

But in the mean time, as any prophet might have foreseen, a Social Democrat had been developed. As the emperor stepped into the gilded imperial wheelbarrow at the church door, the social democrat stabbed at him fifteen or sixteen times with a harpoon, but fortunately with such a peculiarly social democratic unprecision of aim as to do no damage.

That very night the convulsion came. The nation rose as one man,—though forty-nine of the revolutionists were of the other sex. The infantry threw down their pitchforks; the artillery cast aside their cocoa-nuts; the navy revolted; the emperor was seized, and bound hand and foot in his palace. He was very much depressed. He said,—

"I freed you from a grinding tyranny; I lifted you up out of your degradation, and made you a nation among nations; I gave you a strong, compact, centralized government; and, more than all, I gave you the blessing of blessings,—unification. I have done all this, and my reward is hatred, insult, and these bonds. Take me; do with me as ye will. I here resign my crown and all my dignities, and gladly do I release myself from their too heavy burden. For your sake I took them up; for your sake I lay them down. The imperial jewel is no more; now bruise and defile as ye will the useless setting.''

By a unanimous voice the people condemned the ex-emperor and the social democrat to perpetual banishment from church services, or to perpetual labor as galley-slaves in the whale-boat,—whichever they might prefer. The next day the nation assembled again, and rehoisted the British flag, reinstated the British tyranny, reduced the nobility to the condition of commoners again, and then straightway turned their diligent attention to the weeding of the ruined and neglected yam patches, and the rehabilitation of the old useful industries and the old healing and solacing pieties. The ex-emperor restored the lost trespass law, and explained that he had stolen it,—not to injure any one, but to further his political projects. Therefore the nation gave the late chief magistrate his office again, and also his alienated property.

Upon reflection, the ex-emperor and the social democrat chose perpetual banishment from religious services, in preference to perpetual labor as galley-slaves ''*with* perpetual religious services,'' as they phrased it; wherefore the people believed that the poor fellows' troubles had unseated their reason, and so they judged it best to confine them for the present. Which they did.

Such is the history of Pitcairn's ''doubtful acquisition.''

MRS. McWILLIAMS AND THE LIGHTNING

WELL, SIR, —continued Mr. McWilliams, for this was not the beginning of his talk,—the fear of lightning is one of the most distressing infirmities a human being can be afflicted with. It is mostly confined to women; but now and then you find it in a little dog, and sometimes in a man. It is a particularly distressing infirmity, for the reason that it takes the sand out of a person to an extent which no other fear can, and it can't be *reasoned* with, and neither can it be shamed out of a person. A woman who could face the very devil himself—or a mouse—loses her grip and goes all to pieces in front of a flash of lightning. Her fright is something pitiful to see.

Well, as I was telling you, I woke up, with that smothered and unlocatable cry of ''Mortimer! Mortimer!'' wailing in my ears; and as soon as I could scrape my faculties together I reached over in the dark and then said,—

''Evangeline, is that you calling? What is the matter? Where are you?''

''Shut up in the boot-closet. You ought to be ashamed to lie there and sleep so, and such an awful storm going on.''

''Why, how *can* one be ashamed when he is asleep? It is unreasonable; a man *can't* be ashamed when he is asleep, Evangeline.''

''You never try, Mortimer,—you know very well you never try.''

I caught the sound of muffled sobs.

That sound smote dead the sharp speech that was on my lips, and I changed it to—

"I'm sorry, dear,—I'm truly sorry. I never meant to act so. Come back and—"

"MORTIMER!"

"Heavens! what is the matter, my love?"

"Do you mean to say you are in that bed yet?"

"Why, of course."

"Come out of it instantly. I should think you would take some *little* care of your life, for *my* sake and the children's, if you will not for your own."

"But my love—"

"Don't talk to me, Mortimer. You *know* there is no place so dangerous as a bed, in such a thunderstorm as this,—all the books say that; yet there you would lie, and deliberately throw away your life,—for goodness knows what, unless for the sake of arguing and arguing, and—"

"But, confound it, Evangeline, I'm *not* in the bed, *now*. I'm—"

[Sentence interrupted by a sudden glare of lightning, followed by a terrified little scream from Mrs. McWilliams and a tremendous blast of thunder.]

"There! You see the result. Oh, Mortimer, how *can* you be so profligate as to swear at such a time as this?"

"I *didn't* swear. And that *wasn't* a result of it, any way. It would have come, just the same, if I hadn't said a word; and you know very well, Evangeline,—at least you ought to know,—that when the atmosphere is charged with electricity—"

"Oh, yes, now argue it, and argue it, and argue it!—I don't see how you can act so, when you *know* there is not a lightning-rod on the place, and your poor wife and children are absolutely at the mercy of Providence. What *are* you doing?—lighting a match at such a time as this! Are you stark mad?"

"Hang it, woman, where's the harm? The place is as dark as the inside of an infidel, and—"

"Put it out! put it out instantly! Are you determined to sacrifice us all? You *know* there is nothing attracts lightning like a light. [*Fzt!—crash! boom—boloom-boom-boom!*] Oh, just hear it! Now you see what you've done!"

"No, I *don't* see what I've done. A match may attract lightning, for all I know, but it don't *cause* lightning,—I'll go odds on that. And it didn't attract it worth a cent this time; for if that shot was levelled at my match, it was blessed poor marksmanship,—about an average of none out of a possible million, I should say. Why, at Dollymount, such marksmanship as that—"

"For shame, Mortimer! Here we are standing right in the very presence of death, and yet in so solemn a moment you are capable of using such language as that. If you have no desire to—Mortimer!"

"Well?"

"Did you say your prayers to-night?"

"I—I—meant to, but I got to trying to cipher out how much twelve times thirteen is, and—"

[*Fzt!—boom-berroom-boom! bumble-umble bang-*SMASH!]

"Oh, we are lost, beyond all help! How *could* you neglect such a thing at such a time as this?"

"But it *wasn't* 'such a time as this.' There wasn't a cloud in the sky. How could *I* know there was going to be all this rumpus and pow-wow about a little slip like that? And I don't think it's just fair for you to make so much out of it, any way, seeing it happens so seldom; I haven't missed before since I brought on that earthquake, four years ago."

"MORTIMER! How you talk! Have you forgotten the yellow fever?"

"My dear, you are always throwing up the yellow fever to me, and I think it is perfectly unreasonable. You can't even send a telegraphic message as far as Memphis without relays, so how is a little devotional slip of mine going to carry so far? I'll *stand* the earthquake, because it was in the neighborhood; but I'll be hanged if I'm going to be responsible for every blamed—"

[*Fzt!—*BOOM *beroom-*boom! boom!—BANG!]

"Oh, dear, dear, dear! I *know* it struck something, Mortimer. We never shall see the light of another day; and if it will do you any good to remember, when we are gone, that your dreadful language—*Mortimer!*"

"WELL! What now?"

"Your voice sounds as if—Mortimer, are you actually standing in front of that open fireplace?"

"That is the very crime I am committing."

"Get away from it, this moment. You do seem determined to bring destruction on us all. Don't you *know* that there is no better conductor for lightning than an open chimney? *Now* where have you got to?"

"I'm here by the window."

"Oh, for pity's sake, have you lost your mind? Clear out from there, this moment. The very children in arms know it is fatal to stand near a window in a thunder-storm. Dear, dear, I know I shall never see the light of another day. Mortimer?"

"Yes?"

"What is that rustling?"

"It's me."

"What are you doing?"

"Trying to find the upper end of my pantaloons."

"Quick! throw those things away! I do believe you would deliberately put on those clothes at such a time as this; yet you know perfectly well that *all* authorities agree that woollen stuffs attract lightning. Oh, dear, dear, it isn't sufficient that one's life must be in peril from natural causes, but you must do everything you can possibly think of to augment the danger. Oh, *don't* sing! What *can* you be thinking of?"

"Now where's the harm in it?"

"Mortimer, if I have told you once, I have told you a hundred times, that singing causes vibrations in the atmosphere which interrupt the flow of the electric fluid, and—What on *earth* are you opening that door for?"

"Goodness gracious, woman, is there any harm in *that?*"

"*Harm?* There's *death* in it. Anybody that has given this subject any attention knows that to create a draft is to invite the lightning. You haven't half shut it; shut it *tight,*—and do hurry, or we are all destroyed. Oh, it is an awful thing to be shut up with a lunatic at such a time as this. Mortimer, what *are* you doing?"

"Nothing. Just turning on the water. This room is smothering hot and close. I want to bathe my face and hands."

"You have certainly parted with the remnant of your mind! Where lightning strikes any other substance once, it strikes water fifty times. Do turn it off. Oh, dear, I am sure that nothing in this world can save us. It does seem to me that—Mortimer, what was that?"

"It was a da—it was a picture. Knocked it down."

"Then you are close to the wall! I never heard of such imprudence! Don't you *know* that there's no better conductor for lightning than a wall? Come away from there! And you came as near as anything to swearing, too. Oh, how can you be so desperately wicked, and your family in such peril? Mortimer, did you order a feather bed, as I asked you to do?"

"No. Forgot it."

"Forgot it! It may cost you your life. If you had a feather bed, now, and could spread it in the middle of the room and lie on it, you would be perfectly safe. Come in here,—come quick, before you have a chance to commit any more frantic indiscretions."

I tried, but the little closet would not hold us both with the door shut, unless we could be content to smother. I gasped awhile, then forced my way out. My wife called out,—

"Mortimer, something *must* be done for your preservation. Give me that German book that is on the end of the mantel-piece, and a candle; but don't light it; give me a match; I will light it in here. That book has some directions in it."

I got the book,—at cost of a vase and some other brittle things; and the madam shut herself up with her candle. I had a moment's piece; then she called out,—

"Mortimer, what was that?"

"Nothing but the cat."

"The cat! Oh, destruction! Catch her, and shut her up in the wash-stand. Do be quick, love; cats are *full* of electricity. I just know my hair will turn white with this night's awful perils."

I heard the muffled sobbings again. But for that, I should not have moved hand or foot in such a wild enterprise in the dark.

However, I went at my task,—over chairs, and against all sorts of obstructions, all of them hard ones, too, and most of them with sharp edges,—and at last I got kitty cooped up in the commode, at an expense of over four hundred dollars in broken furniture and shins. Then these muffled words came from the closet:—

"It says the safest thing is to stand on a chair in the middle of the room, Mortimer; and the legs of the chair must be insulated, with non-conductors. That is, you must set the legs of the chair in glass tumblers. [*Fzt!— boom—bang!—smash!*] Oh, hear that! Do hurry, Mortimer, before you are struck."

I managed to find and secure the tumblers. I got the last four,—broke all the rest. I insulated the chair legs, and called for further instructions.

"Mortimer, it says, 'Während eines Gewitters entferne man Metalle, wie z. B., Ringe, Uhren, Schlüssel, etc., von sich und halte sich auch nicht an solchen Stellen auf, wo viele Metalle bei einander liegen, oder mit andern Körpern verbunden sind, wie an Herden, Oefen, Eisengittern u. dgl.' What does that mean, Mortimer? does it mean that you must keep metals *about* you, or keep them *away* from you?''

''Well, I hardly know. It appears to be a little mixed. All German advice is more or less mixed. However, I think that that sentence is mostly in the dative case, with a little genitive and accusative sifted in, here and there, for luck; so I reckon it means that you must keep some metals *about* you.''

''Yes, that must be it. It stands to reason that it is. They are in the nature of lightning-rods, you know. Put on your fireman's helmet, Mortimer; that is mostly metal.''

I got it and put it on,—a very heavy and clumsy and uncomfortable thing on a hot night in a close room. Even my night-dress seemed to be more clothing than I strictly needed.

''Mortimer, I think your middle ought to be protected. Won't you buckle on your militia sabre, please?''

I complied.

''Now, Mortimer, you ought to have some way to protect your feet. Do please put on your spurs.''

I did it,—in silence,—and kept my temper as well as I could.

''Mortimer, it says, 'Das Gewitteer läuten ist sehr gefährlich, weil die Glocke selbst, sowie der durch das Läuten veranlasste Luftzug und die Höhe des Thurmes den Blitz anziehen könnten.' Mortimer, does that mean that it is dangerous not to ring the church bells during a thunder-storm?''

''Yes, it seems to mean that,—if that is the past participle of the nominative case singular, and I reckon it is. Yes, I think it means that on account of the height of the church tower and the absence of *Luftzug* it would be very dangerous (*sehr gefährlich*) not to ring the bells in time of a storm; and moreover, don't you see, the very wording—''

''Never mind that, Mortimer; don't waste the precious time in talk. Get the large dinner-bell; it is right there in the hall. Quick, Mortimer dear; we are almost safe. Oh, dear, I do believe we are going to be saved, at last!''

Our little summer establishment stands on top of a high range of hills, overlooking a valley. Several farm-houses are in our neighborhood,—the nearest some three or four hundred yards away.

When I, mounted on the chair, had been clanging that dreadful bell a matter of seven or eight minutes, our shutters were suddenly torn open from without, and a brilliant bull's-eye lantern was thrust in at the window, followed by a hoarse inquiry:—

''What in the nation is the matter here?''

The window was full of men's heads, and the heads were full of eyes that stared wildly at my night-dress and my warlike accoutrements.

I dropped the bell, skipped down from the chair in confusion, and said,—

''There is nothing the matter, friends,—only a little discomfort on account of the thunder-storm. I was trying to keep off the lightning.''

''Thunder-storm? Lightning? Why, Mr. McWilliams, have you lost your mind? It is a beautiful starlight night; there has been no storm.''

I looked out, and I was so astonished I could hardly speak for a while. Then I said,—

"I do not understand this. We distinctly saw the glow of the flashes through the curtains and shutters, and heard the thunder."

One after another of those people lay down on the ground to laugh,— and two of them died. One of the survivors remarked,—

"Pity you didn't think to open your blinds and look over to the top of the high hill yonder. What you heard was cannon; what you saw was the flash. You see, the telegraph brought some news, just at midnight: Garfield's nominated,—and that's what's the matter!"

Yes, Mr. Twain, as I was saying in the beginning (said Mr. McWilliams), the rules for preserving people against lightning are so excellent and so innumerable that the most incomprehensible thing in the world to me is how anybody ever manages to get struck.

So saying, he gathered up his satchel and umbrella, and departed; for the train had reached his town.

ON THE DECAY OF THE ART OF LYING

Essay, for discussion, read at a meeting of the Historical and Antiquarian Club of Hartford, and offered for the Thirty-dollar Prize. Now first published.[1]

OBSERVE, I do not mean to suggest that the *custom* of lying has suffered any decay or interruption,—no, for the Lie, as a Virtue, a Principle, is eternal; the Lie, as a recreation, a solace, a refuge in time of need, the fourth Grace, the tenth Muse, man's best and surest friend, is immortal, and cannot perish from the earth while this Club remains. My complaint simply concerns the decay of the *art* of lying. No high-minded man, no man of right feeling, can contemplate the lumbering and slovenly lying of the present day without grieving to see a noble art so prostituted. In this veteran presence I naturally enter upon this theme with diffidence; it is like an old maid trying to teach nursery matters to the mothers in Israel. It would not become me to criticize you, gentlemen, who are nearly all my elders—and my superiors, in this thing—and so, if I should here and there *seem* to do it, I trust it will in most cases be more in a spirit of admiration than of fault-finding; indeed if this finest of the fine arts had everywhere received the attention, encouragement, and conscientious practice and development which this Club has devoted to it, I should not need to utter this lament, or shed a single tear. I do not say this to flatter: I say it in a spirit of just and appreciative recognition. [It had been my intention, at this point, to mention names and give illustrative specimens, but indi-

[1] Did not take the prize.

cations observable about me admonished me to beware of particulars and confine myself to generalities.]

No fact is more firmly established than that lying is a necessity of our circumstances,—the deduction that it is then a Virtue goes without saying. No virtue can reach its highest usefulness without careful and diligent cultivation,—therefore, it goes without saying, that this one ought to be taught in the public schools—at the fireside—even in the newspapers. What chance has the ignorant, uncultivated liar against the educated expert? What chance have I against Mr. Per—against a lawyer? *Judicious* lying is what the world needs. I sometimes think it were even better and safer not to lie at all than to lie injudiciously. An awkward, unscientific lie is often as ineffectual as the truth.

Now let us see what the philosophers say. Note that venerable proverb: Children and fools *always* speak the truth. The deduction is plain,—adults and wise persons *never* speak it. Parkman, the historian, says, "The principle of truth may itself be carried into an absurdity." In another place in the same chapter he says, "The saying is old that truth should not be spoken at all times; and those whom a sick conscience worries into habitual violation of the maxim are imbeciles and nuisances." It is strong language, but true. None of us could *live* with an habitual truth-teller; but thank goodness none of us has to. An habitual truth-teller is simply an impossible creature; he does not exist; he never has existed. Of course there are people who *think* they never lie, but it is not so,—and this ignorance is one of the very things that shame our so-called civilization. Everybody lies—every day; every hour; awake; asleep; in his dreams; in his joy; in his mourning; if he keeps his tongue still, his hands, his feet, his eyes, his attitude, will convey deception—and purposely. Even in sermons—but that is a platitude.

In a far country where I once lived the ladies used to go around paying calls, under the humane and kindly pretence of wanting to see each other; and when they returned home, they would cry out with a glad voice, saying, "We made sixteen calls and found fourteen of them out,"—not meaning that they found out anything against the fourteen,—no, that was only a colloquial phrase to signify that they were not at home,—and their manner of saying it expressed their lively satisfaction in that fact. Now their pretence of wanting to see the fourteen—and the other two whom they had been less lucky with—was that commonest and mildest form of lying which is sufficiently described as a deflection from the truth. Is it justifiable? Most certainly. It is beautiful, it is noble; for its object is, *not* to reap profit, but to convey a pleasure to the sixteen. The iron-souled truth-monger would plainly manifest, or even utter the fact that he didn't want to see those people,—and he would be an ass, and inflict a totally unnecessary pain. And next, those ladies in that far country—but never mind, they had a thousand pleasant ways of lying, that grew out of gentle impulses, and were a credit to their intelligence and an honor to their hearts. Let the particulars go.

The men in that far country were liars, every one. Their mere howdy-do was a lie, because *they* didn't care how you did, except they were undertakers. To the ordinary inquirer you lied in return; for you made no conscientious diagnosis of your case, but answered at random, and usually missed it considerably. You lied to the undertaker, and said your health was failing—a wholly commendable lie, since it cost you nothing and pleased the other man. If a stranger called and interrupted you, you said with your hearty tongue, "I'm glad to see you," and said with your heartier soul, "I wish you were with the cannibals and it was dinner time." When he went, you said regretfully, "*Must* you go?" and followed it with a "Call again;" but you did no harm, for you did not deceive anybody nor inflict any hurt, whereas the truth would have made you both unhappy.

I think that all this courteous lying is a sweet and loving art, and should be cultivated. The highest perfection of politeness is only a beautiful edifice, built, from the base to the dome, of graceful and gilded forms of charitable and unselfish lying.

What I bemoan is the growing prevalence of the brutal truth. Let us do what we can to eradicate it. An injurious truth has no merit over an injurious lie. Neither should ever be uttered. The man who speaks an injurious truth lest his soul be not saved if he do otherwise, should reflect that that sort of a soul is not strictly worth saving. The man who tells a lie to help a poor devil out of trouble, is one of whom the angels doubtless say, "Lo, here is an heroic soul who casts his own welfare into jeopardy to succor his neighbor's; let us exalt this magnanimous liar."

An injurious lie is an uncommendable thing; and so, also, and in the same degree, is an injurious truth,—a fact which is recognized by the law of libel.

Among other common lies, we have the *silent* lie,—the deception which one conveys by simply keeping still and concealing the truth. Many obstinate truth-mongers indulge in this dissipation, imagining that if they *speak* no lie, they lie not at all. In that far country where I once lived, there was a lovely spirit, a lady whose impulses were always high and pure, and whose character answered to them. One day I was there at dinner, and remarked, in a general way, that we are all liars. She was amazed, and said, "Not *all?*" It was before Pinafore's time, so I did not make the response which would naturally follow in our day, but frankly said, "Yes, *all*—we are all liars; there are no exceptions." She looked almost offended, and said, "Why, do you include *me?*" "Certainly," I said, "I think you even rank as an expert." She said, "Sh—sh! the children!" So the subject was changed in deference to the children's presence, and we went on talking about other things. But as soon as the young people were out of the way, the lady came warmly back to the matter and said, "I have made it the rule of my life to never tell a lie; and I have never departed from it in a single instance." I said, "I don't mean the least harm or disrespect, but really you have been lying like smoke ever since I've been sitting here. It has caused me a good deal of pain, because I am not used to it." She required of me an instance—just a single instance. So I said,—

"Well, here is the unfilled duplicate of the blank which the Oakland hospital people sent to you by the hand of the sick-nurse when she came here to nurse your little nephew through his dangerous illness. This blank asks all manner of questions as to the conduct of that sick-nurse: 'Did she ever sleep on her watch? Did she ever forget to give the medicine?' and so forth and so on. You are warned to be very careful and explicit in your answers, for the welfare of the service requires that the nurses be promptly fined or otherwise punished for derelictions. You told me you were perfectly delighted with that nurse—that she had a thousand perfections and only one fault: you found you never could depend on her wrapping Johnny up half sufficiently while he waited in a chilly chair for her to rearrange the warm bed. You filled up the duplicate of this paper, and sent it back to the hospital by the hand of the nurse. How did you answer this question,—'Was the nurse at any time guilty of a negligence which was likely to result in the patient's taking cold?' Come—everything is decided by a bet here in California: ten dollars to ten cents you lied when you answered that question.'' She said, ''I didn't; I *left it blank!''* ''Just so—you have told a *silent* lie; you have left it to be inferred that you had no fault to find in that matter.'' She said, ''Oh, was that a lie? And how *could* I mention her one single fault, and she so good?—it would have been cruel.'' I said, ''One ought always to lie, when one can do good by it; your impulse was right, but your judgment was crude; this comes of unintelligent practice. Now observe the result of this inexpert deflection of yours. You know Mr. Jones's Willie is lying very low with scarlet fever; well, your recommendation was so enthusiastic that that girl is there nursing him, and the worn-out family have all been trustingly sound asleep for the last fourteen hours, leaving their darling with full confidence in those fatal hands, because you, like young George Washington, have a reputa— However, if you are not going to have anything to do, I will come around to-morrow and we'll attend the funeral together, for of course you'll naturally feel a peculiar interest in Willie's case,—as personal a one, in fact, as the undertaker.''

But that was all lost. Before I was half-way through she was in a carriage and making thirty miles an hour toward the Jones mansion to save what was left of Willie and tell all she knew about the deadly nurse. All of which was unnecessary, as Willie wasn't sick; I had been lying myself. But that same day, all the same, she sent a line to the hospital which filled up the neglected blank, and stated the *facts,* too, in the squarest possible manner.

Now, you see, this lady's fault was *not* in lying, but only in lying injudiciously. She should have told the truth, *there,* and made it up to the nurse with a fraudulent compliment further along in the paper. She could have said, ''In one respect this sick-nurse is perfection,—when she is on watch, she never snores.'' Almost any little pleasant lie would have taken the sting out of that troublesome but necessary expression of the truth.

Lying is universal—we *all* do it; we all *must* do it. Therefore, the wise thing is for us diligently to train ourselves to lie thoughtfully, judiciously; to lie with a good object, and not an evil one; to lie for others' advantage, and not our own; to lie healingly, charitably, humanely, not cruelly, hurtfully, maliciously; to lie gracefully and graciously, not awkwardly and clumsily; to lie firmly, frankly, squarely, with head erect, not haltingly, tortuously, with pusillanimous mien, as being ashamed of our high calling. Then shall we be rid of the rank and pestilent truth that is rotting the land; then shall we be great and good and beautiful, and worthy dwellers in a world where even benign Nature habitually lies, except when she promises execrable weather. Then— But I am but a new and feeble student in this gracious art; I cannot instruct *this* Club.

Joking aside, I think there is much need of wise examination into what sorts of lies are best and wholesomest to be indulged, seeing we *must* all lie and *do* all lie, and what sorts it may be best to avoid,—and this is a thing which I feel I can confidently put into the hands of this experienced Club,—a ripe body, who may be termed, in this regard, and without undue flattery, Old Masters.

THE CANVASSER'S TALE

POOR, SAD-EYED stranger! There was that about his humble mien, his tired look, his decayed-gentility clothes, that almost reached the mustard-seed of charity that still remained, remote and lonely, in the empty vastness of my heart, notwithstanding I observed a portfolio under his arm, and said to myself, Behold, Providence hath delivered his servant into the hands of another canvasser.

Well, these people always get one interested. Before I well knew how it came about, this one was telling me his history, and I was all attention and sympathy. He told it something like this:—

My parents died, alas, when I was a little, sinless child. My uncle Ithuriel took me to his heart and reared me as his own. He was my only relative in the wide world; but he was good and rich and generous. He reared me in the lap of luxury. I knew no want that money could satisfy.

In the fulness of time I was graduated, and went with two of my servants—my chamberlain and my valet—to travel in foreign countries. During four years I flitted upon careless wing amid the beauteous gardens of the distant strand, if you will permit this form of speech in one whose tongue was ever attuned to poesy; and indeed I so speak with confidence, as one unto his kind, for I perceive by your eyes that you too, sir, are gifted with the divine inflation. In those far lands I revelled in the ambrosial food that fructifies the soul, the mind, the heart. But of all things, that which most appealed to my inborn aesthetic taste was the prevailing custom there, among the rich, of making collections of elegant and costly rarities, dainty *objets de vertu,* and in an evil hour I tried to uplift my uncle Ithuriel to a plane of sympathy with this exquisite employment.

I wrote and told him of one gentleman's vast collection of shells; another's noble collection of meerschaum pipes; another's elevating and refining collection of undecipherable autographs; another's priceless collection of old china; another's enchanting collection of postage stamps,— and so forth and so on. Soon my letters yielded fruit. My uncle began to look about for something to make a collection of. You may know, perhaps, how fleetly a taste like this dilates. His soon became a raging fever, though I knew it not. He began to neglect his great pork business; presently he wholly retired and turned an elegant leisure into a rabid search for curious things. His wealth was vast, and he spared it not. First he tried cow-bells. He made a collection which filled five large *salons,* and comprehended all the different sorts of cow-bells that ever had been contrived, save one. That one—an antique, and the only specimen extant—was possessed by another collector. My uncle offered enormous sums for it, but the gentleman would not sell. Doubtless you know what necessarily resulted. A true collector attaches no value to a collection that is not complete. His great heart breaks, he sells his hoard, he turns his mind to some field that seems unoccupied.

Thus did my uncle. He next tried brickbats. After piling up a vast and intensely interesting collection, the former difficulty supervened; his great heart broke again; he sold out his soul's idol to the retired brewer who possessed the missing brick. Then he tried flint hatchets and other implements of Primeval Man, but by and by discovered that the factory where they were made was supplying other collectors as well as himself. He tried Aztec inscriptions and stuffed whales—another failure, after incredible labor and expense. When his collection seemed at last perfect, a stuffed whale arrived from Greenland and an Aztec inscription from the Cundurango regions of Central America that made all former specimens insignificant. My uncle hastened to secure these noble gems. He got the stuffed whale, but another collector got the inscription. A real Cundurango, as possibly you know, is a possession of such supreme value that, when once a collector gets it, he will rather part with his family than with it. So my uncle sold out, and saw his darlings go forth, never more to return; and his coal-black hair turned white as snow in a single night.

Now he waited, and thought. He knew another disappointment might kill him. He was resolved that he would choose things next time that no other man was collecting. He carefully made up his mind, and once more entered the field—this time to make a collection of echoes.

"Of what?" said I.

Echoes, sir. His first purchase was an echo in Georgia that repeated four times; his next was a six-repeater in Maryland; his next was a thirteen-repeater in Maine; his next was a nine-repeater in Kansas; his next was a twelve-repeater in Tennessee, which he got cheap, so to speak, because it was out of repair, a portion of the crag which reflected it having tumbled down. He believed he could repair it at a cost of a few thousand dollars, and, by increasing the elevation with masonry, treble the repeating capacity; but the architect who undertook the job had never built an echo before, and so he utterly spoiled this one. Before he meddled with it, it used to talk back like a mother-in-law, but now it was only fit for the deaf and dumb asylum. Well, next he bought a lot of cheap little double-barrelled echoes, scattered around over various States and Territories; he got them at twenty per cent off by taking the lot. Next he bought a perfect Gatling gun of an echo in Oregon, and it cost a fortune, I can tell you. You may know, sir, that in the echo market the scale of prices is cumulative, like the carat-scale in diamonds; in fact, the same phraseology is used. A single-carat echo is worth but ten dollars over and above the value of the land it is on; a two-carat or double-barrelled echo is worth thirty dollars; a five-carat is worth nine hundred and fifty; a ten-carat is worth thirteen thousand. My uncle's Oregon echo, which he called the Great Pitt Echo, was a twenty-two carat gem, and cost two hundred and sixteen thousand dollars—they threw the land in, for it was four hundred miles from a settlement.

Well, in the mean time my path was a path of roses. I was the accepted suitor of the only and lovely daughter of an English earl, and was beloved to distraction. In that dear presence I swam in seas of bliss. The family were content, for it was known that I was sole heir to an uncle held to be worth five millions of dollars. However, none of us knew that my uncle had become a collector, at least in anything more than a small way, for aesthetic amusement.

Now gathered the clouds above my unconscious head. That divine echo, since known throughout the world as the Great Koh-i-noor, or Mountain of Repetitions, was discovered. It was a sixty-five-carat gem. You could utter a word and it would talk back at you for fifteen minutes, when the day was otherwise quiet. But behold, another fact came to light at the same time: another echo-collector was in the field. The two rushed to make the peerless purchase. The property consisted of a couple of small hills with a shallow swale between, out yonder among the back settlements of New York State. Both men arrived on the ground at the same time, and neither knew the other was there. The echo was not all owned by one man; a person by the name of Williamson Bolivar Jarvis owned the east hill, and a person by the name of Harbison J. Bledso owned the west hill; the swale between was the dividing line. So while my uncle was buying Jarvis's hill for three million two hundred and eighty-five thousand dollars, the other party was buying Bledso's hill for a shade over three million.

Now, do you perceive the natural result? Why, the noblest collection of echoes on earth was forever and ever incomplete, since it possessed but the one half of the king echo of the universe. Neither man was content with this divided ownership, yet neither would sell to the other. There were jawings, bickerings, heart-burnings. And at last, that other collector, with a malignity which only a collector can ever feel toward a man and a brother, proceeded to cut down his hill!

You see, as long as he could not have the echo, he was resolved that nobody should have it. He would remove his hill, and then there would be nothing to reflect my uncle's echo. My uncle remonstrated with him, but the man said, "I own one end of this echo; I choose to kill my end; you must take care of your own end yourself."

Well, my uncle got an injunction put on him. The other man appealed and fought it in a higher court. They carried it on up, clear to the Supreme Court of the United States. It made no end of trouble there. Two of the judges believed that an echo was personal property, because it was impalpable to sight and touch, and yet was purchasable, salable, and consequently taxable; two others believed that an echo was real estate, because it was manifestly attached to the land, and was not removable from place to place; other of the judges contended that an echo was not property at all.

It was finally decided that the echo was property; that the hills were property; that the two men were separate and independent owners of the two hills, but tenants in common in the echo; therefore defendant was at full liberty to cut down his hill, since it belonged solely to him, but must give bonds in three million dollars as indemnity for damages which might result to my uncle's half of the echo. This decision also debarred my uncle from using defendant's hill to reflect his part of the echo, without defendant's consent; he must use only his own hill; if his part of the echo would not go, under these circumstances, it was sad, of course, but the court could find no remedy. The court also debarred defendant from using my uncle's hill to reflect *his* end of the echo, without consent. You see the grand result! Neither man would give consent, and so that astonishing and most noble echo had to cease from its great powers; and since that day that magnificent property is tied up and unsalable.

A week before my wedding day, while I was still swimming in bliss and the nobility were gathering from far and near to honor our espousals, came news of my uncle's death, and also a copy of his will, making me his sole heir. He was gone; alas, my dear benefactor was no more. The thought surcharges my heart even at this remote day. I handed the will to the earl; I could not read it for the blinding tears. The earl read it; then he sternly said, "Sir, do you call this wealth?—but doubtless you do in your inflated country. Sir, you are left sole heir to a vast collection of echoes— if a thing can be called a collection that is scattered far and wide over the huge length and breadth of the American continent; sir, this is not all; you are head and ears in debt; there is not an echo in the lot but has a mortgage on it; sir, I am not a hard man, but I must look to my child's interest; if you had but one echo which you could honestly call your own, if you had but one echo which was free from incumbrance, so that you could retire to it with my child, and by humble, painstaking industry, cultivate and improve it, and thus wrest from it a maintenance, I would not say you nay; but I cannot marry my child to a beggar. Leave his side, my darling; go, sir; take your mortgage-ridden echoes and quit my sight forever."

My noble Celestine clung to me in tears, with loving arms, and swore she would willingly, nay, gladly marry me, though I had not an echo in the world. But it could not be. We were torn asunder, she to pine and die within the twelvemonth, I to toil life's long journey sad and lone, praying daily, hourly, for that release which shall join us together again in that dear realm where the wicked cease from troubling and the weary are at rest. Now, sir, if you will be so kind as to look at these maps and plans in my portfolio, I am sure I can sell you an echo for less money than any man in the trade. Now this one, which cost my uncle ten dollars, thirty years ago, and is one of the sweetest things in Texas, I will let you have for—

"Let me interrupt you," I said. "My friend, I have not had a moment's respite from canvassers this day. I have bought a sewing-machine which I did not want; I have bought a map which is mistaken in all its details; I have bought a clock which will not go; I have bought a moth poison which the moths prefer to any other beverage; I have bought no end of useless inventions, and now I have had enough of this foolishness. I would not have one of your echoes if you were even to give it to me. I would not let it stay on the place. I always hate a man that tries to sell me echoes. You see this gun? Now take your collection and move on; let us not have bloodshed."

But he only smiled a sad, sweet smile, and got out some more diagrams. You know the result perfectly well, because you know that when you have once opened the door to a canvasser, the trouble is done and you have got to suffer defeat.

I compromised with this man at the end of an intolerable hour. I bought two double-barrelled echoes in good condition, and he threw in another, which he said was not salable because it only spoke German. He said, "She was a perfect polyglot once, but somehow her palate got down."

AN ENCOUNTER WITH AN INTERVIEWER

THE NERVOUS, dapper, "peart" young man took the chair I offered him, and said he was connected with the "Daily Thunderstorm," and added,—

"Hoping it's no harm, I've come to interview you."

"Come to what?"

"*Interview* you."

"Ah! I see. Yes—yes. Um! Yes—yes."

I was not feeling bright that morning. Indeed, my powers seemed a bit under a cloud. However, I went to the bookcase, and when I had been looking six or seven minutes, I found I was obliged to refer to the young man. I said,—

"How do you spell it?"

"Spell what?"

"Interview."

"Oh my goodness! what do you want to spell it for?"

"I don't want to spell it; I want to see what it means."

"Well, this is astonishing, I must say. *I* can tell you what it means, if you—if you—"

"Oh, all right! That will answer, and much obliged to you, too."

"In, *in*, ter, *ter*, *in*ter—"

"Then you spell it with an *I?*"

"Why, certainly!"

"Oh, that is what took me so long."

"Why, my *dear* sir, what did *you* propose to spell it with?"

"Well, I—I—hardly know. I had the Unabridged, and I was ciphering around in the back end, hoping I might tree her among the pictures. But it's a very old edition."

"Why, my friend, they wouldn't have a *picture* of it in even the latest e— My dear sir, I beg your pardon, I mean no harm in the world, but you do not look as—as—intelligent as I had expected you would. No harm— I mean no harm at all."

"Oh, don't mention it! It has often been said, and by people who would not flatter and who could have no inducement to flatter, that I am quite remarkable in that way. Yes—yes; they always speak of it with rapture."

"I can easily imagine it. But about this interview. You know it is the custom, now, to interview any man who has become notorious."

"Indeed, I had not heard of it before. It must be very interesting. What do you do it with?"

"Ah, well—well—well—this is disheartening. It *ought* to be done with a club in some cases; but customarily it consists in the interviewer asking questions and the interviewed answering them. It is all the rage now. Will you let me ask you certain questions calculated to bring out the salient points of your public and private history?''

"Oh, with pleasure,—with pleasure. I have a very bad memory, but I hope you will not mind that. That is to say, it is an irregular memory,—singularly irregular. Sometimes it goes in a gallop, and then again it will be as much as a fortnight passing a given point. This is a great grief to me.''

"Oh, it is no matter, so you will try to do the best you can.''

"I will. I will put my whole mind on it.''

"Thanks. Are you ready to begin?''

"Ready.''

Q.   How old are you?

A.   Nineteen, in June.

Q.   Indeed! I would have taken you to be thirty-five or six. Where were you born?

A.   In Missouri.

Q.   When did you begin to write?

A.   In 1836.

Q.   Why, how could that be, if you are only nineteen now?

A.   I don't know. It does seem curious, somehow.

Q.   It does, indeed. Whom do you consider the most remarkable man you ever met?

A.   Aaron Burr.

Q.   But you never could have met Aaron Burr, if you are only nineteen years—

A.   Now, if you know more about me than I do, what do you ask me for?

Q.   Well, it was only a suggestion; nothing more. How did you happen to meet Burr?

A.   Well, I happened to be at his funeral one day, and he asked me to make less noise, and—

Q.   But, good heavens! if you were at his funeral, he must have been dead; and if he was dead, how could he care whether you made a noise or not?

A.   I don't know. He was always a particular kind of a man that way.

Q.   Still, I don't understand it at all. You say he spoke to you, and that he was dead.

A.   I didn't say he was dead.

Q.   But wasn't he dead?

A.   Well, some said he was, some said he wasn't.

Q.   What did you think?

A.   Oh, it was none of my business! It wasn't any of my funeral.

Q.   Did you— However, we can never get this matter straight. Let me ask about something else. What was the date of your birth?

A.   Monday, October 31st, 1693.

Q.   What! Impossible! That would make you a hundred and eighty years old. How do you account for that?

A.   I don't account for it at all.

Q.   But you said at first you were only nineteen, and now you make yourself out to be one hundred and eighty. It is an awful discrepancy.

A. Why, have you noticed that? (Shaking hands.) Many a time it has seemed to me like a discrepancy, but somehow I couldn't make up my mind. How quick you notice a thing!

Q. Thank you for the compliment, as far as it goes. Had you, or have you, any brothers or sisters?

A. Eh! I—I—I think so—yes—but I don't remember.

Q. Well, that's the most extraordinary statement I ever heard!

A. Why, what makes you think that?

Q. How could I think otherwise? Why, look here! Who is this a picture of on the wall? Isn't that a brother of yours?

A. Oh! yes, yes, yes! Now you remind me of it; that *was* a brother of mine. That's William—*Bill* we called him. Poor old Bill!

Q. Why? Is he dead, then?

A. Ah! well, I suppose so. We never could tell. There was a great mystery about it.

Q. That is sad, very sad. He disappeared, then?

A. Well, yes, in a sort of general way. We buried him.

Q. *Buried* him! *Buried* him, without knowing whether he was dead or not?

A. Oh, no! Not that. He was dead enough.

Q. Well, I confess that I can't understand this. If you buried him, and you knew he was dead—

A. No! no! We only thought he was.

Q. Oh, I see! He came to life again?

A. I bet he didn't.

Q. Well, I never heard anything like this. *Somebody* was dead. *Somebody* was buried. Now, where was the mystery?

A. Ah! that's just it! That's it exactly. You see, we were twins,—defunct and I,—and we got mixed in the bath-tub when we were only two weeks old, and one of us was drowned. But we didn't know which. Some think it was Bill. Some think it was me.

Q. Well, that *is* remarkable. What do *you* think?

A. Goodness knows! I would give whole worlds to know. This solemn, this awful mystery has cast a gloom over my whole life. But I will tell you a secret now, which I never have revealed to any creature before. One of us had a peculiar mark—a large mole on the back of his left hand; that was *me*. *That child was the one that was drowned!*

Q. Very well, then, I don't see that there is any mystery about it, after all.

A. You don't? Well, *I* do. Anyway, I don't see how they could ever have been such a blundering lot as to go and bury the wrong child. But, 'sh!—don't mention it where the family can hear of it. Heaven knows they have heart-breaking troubles enough without adding this.

Q. Well, I believe I have got material enough for the present, and I am very much obliged to you for the pains you have taken. But I was a good deal interested in that account of Aaron Burr's funeral. Would you mind telling me what particular circumstance it was that made you think Burr was such a remarkable man?

A. Oh! it was a mere trifle! Not one man in fifty would have noticed it at all. When the sermon was over, and the procession all ready to start for the cemetery, and the body all arranged nice in the hearse, he said he wanted to take a last look at the scenery, and so he *got up and rode with the driver*.

Then the young man reverently withdrew. He was very pleasant company, and I was sorry to see him go.

PARIS NOTES[1]

THE PARISIAN travels but little, he knows no language but his own, reads no literature but his own, and consequently he is pretty narrow and pretty self-sufficient. However, let us not be too sweeping; there are Frenchmen who know languages not their own: these are the waiters. Among the rest, they know English; that is, they know it on the European plan,—which is to say, they can speak it, but can't understand it. They easily make themselves understood, but it is next to impossible to word an English sentence in such a way as to enable them to comprehend it. They think they comprehend it; they pretend they do; but they don't. Here is a conversation which I had with one of these beings; I wrote it down at the time, in order to have it exactly correct.

I.   These are fine oranges. Where are they grown?

He.   More? Yes, I will bring them.

I.   No, do not bring any more; I only want to know where they are from—where they are raised.

He.   Yes? (with imperturbable mien, and rising inflection.)

I.   Yes. Can you tell me what country they are from?

He.   Yes? (blandly, with rising inflection.)

I.   (disheartened). They are very nice.

He.   Good night. (Bows, and retires, quite satisfied with himself.)

That young man could have become a good English scholar by taking the right sort of pains, but he was French, and wouldn't do that. How different is the case with our people; they utilize every means that offers. There are some alleged French Protestants in Paris, and they built a nice little church on one of the great avenues that lead away from the Arch of Triumph, and proposed to listen to the correct thing, preached in the correct way, there, in their precious French tongue, and be happy. But their little game does not succeed. Our people are always there ahead of them, Sundays, and take up all the room. When the minister gets up to preach, he finds his house full of devout foreigners, each ready and waiting, with his little book in his hand,—a morocco-bound Testament, apparently. But only apparently; it is Mr. Bellows's admirable and exhaustive little French-English dictionary, which in look and binding and size is just like a Testament,—and those people are there to study French. The building has been nicknamed "The Church of the Gratis French Lesson."

These students probably acquire more language than general information, for I am told that a French sermon is like a French speech,—it never

---

[1] Crowded out of "A Tramp Abroad" to make room for more vital statistics.—M. T.

names an historical event, but only the date of it; if you are not up in
dates, you get left. A French speech is something like this:—

"Comrades, citizens, brothers, noble parts of the only sublime and
perfect nation, let us not forget that the 21st January cast off our chains;
that the 10th August relieved us of the shameful presence of foreign spies;
that the 5th September was its own justification before Heaven and humanity; that the 18th Brumaire contained the seeds of its own punishment;
that the 14th July was the mighty voice of liberty proclaiming the resurrection, the new day, and inviting the oppressed peoples of the earth to
look upon the divine face of France and live; and let us here record our
everlasting curse against the man of the 2d December, and declare in
thunder tones, the native tones of France, that but for him there had been
no 17th March in history, no 12th October, no 19th January, no 22d April,
no 16th November, no 30th September, no 2d July, no 14th February,
no 29th June, no 15th August, no 31st May,—that but for him, France,
the pure, the grand, the peerless, had had a serene and vacant almanac
to-day!"

I have heard of one French sermon which closed in this odd yet eloquent
way:—

"My hearers, we have sad cause to remember the man of the 13th
January. The results of the vast crime of the 13th January have been in
just proportion to the magnitude of the act itself. But for it there had been
no 30th November,—sorrowful spectacle! The grisly deed of the 16th
June had not been done but for it, nor had the man of the 16th June known
existence; to it alone the 3d September was due, also the fatal 12th
October. Shall we, then, be grateful for the 13th January, with its freight
of death for you and me and all that breathe? Yes, my friends, for it gave
us also that which had never come but for it, and it alone,—the blessed
25th December."

It may be well enough to explain, though in the case of many of my
readers this will hardly be necessary. The man of the 13th January is
Adam; the crime of that date was the eating of the apple; the sorrowful
spectacle of the 30th November was the expulsion from Eden; the grisly
deed of the 16th June was the murder of Abel; the act of the 3d September
was the beginning of the journey to the land of Nod; the 12th day of
October, the last mountain-tops disappeared under the flood. When you
go to church in France, you want to take your almanac with you,—
annotated.

LEGEND OF SAGENFELD, IN GERMANY[1]

1

MORE THAN a thousand years ago this small district was a kingdom,—a
little bit of a kingdom, a sort of dainty little toy kingdom, as one might

---

[1]Left out of "A Tramp Abroad" because its authenticity seemed doubtful, and could not at
that time be proved.—M.T.

say. It was far removed from the jealousies, strifes, and turmoils of that
old warlike day, and so its life was a simple life, its people a gentle and
guileless race; it lay always in a deep dream of peace, a soft Sabbath
tranquillity; there was no malice, there was no envy, there was no ambition, consequently there were no heart-burnings, there was no unhappiness in the land.

In the course of time the old king died and his little son Hubert came
to the throne. The people's love for him grew daily; he was so good and
so pure and so noble, that by and by this love became a passion, almost a
worship. Now at his birth the soothsayers had diligently studied the stars
and found something written in that shining book to this effect:—

> In Hubert's fourteenth year a pregnant event will happen; the
> animal whose singing shall sound sweetest in Hubert's ear shall
> save Hubert's life. So long as the king and the nation shall honor
> this animal's race for this good deed, the ancient dynasty shall not
> fail of an heir, nor the nation know war or pestilence or poverty.
> But beware an erring choice!

All through the king's thirteenth year but one thing was talked of by
the soothsayers, the statesmen, the little parliament, and the general people. That one thing was this: How is the last sentence of the prophecy to
be understood? What goes before seems to mean that the saving animal
will choose *itself*, at the proper time; but the closing sentence seems to
mean that the *king* must choose beforehand, and say what singer among
the animals pleases him best, and that if he choose wisely the chosen
animal will save his life, his dynasty, his people, but that if he should
make "an erring choice"—beware!

By the end of the year there were as many opinions about this matter as
there had been in the beginning; but a majority of the wise and the simple
were agreed that the safest plan would be for the little king to make choice
beforehand, and the earlier the better. So an edict was sent forth commanding all persons who owned singing creatures to bring them to the
great hall of the palace in the morning of the first day of the new year.
This command was obeyed. When everything was in readiness for the
trial, the king made his solemn entry with the great officers of the crown,
all clothed in their robes of state. The king mounted his golden throne and
prepared to give judgment. But he presently said,—

"These creatures all sing at once; the noise is unendurable; no one can
choose in such a turmoil. Take them all away, and bring back one at
a time."

This was done. One sweet warbler after another charmed the young
king's ear and was removed to make way for another candidate. The
precious minutes slipped by; among so many bewitching songsters he
found it hard to choose, and all the harder because the promised penalty
for an error was so terrible that it unsettled his judgment and made him
afraid to trust his own ears. He grew nervous and his face showed distress.
His ministers saw this, for they never took their eyes from him a moment.
Now they began to say in their hearts,—

"He has lost courage—the cool head is gone—he will err—he and his dynasty and his people are doomed!"

At the end of an hour the king sat silent awhile, and then said,—

"Bring back the linnet."

The linnet trilled forth her jubilant music. In the midst of it the king was about to uplift his scepter in sign of choice, but checked himself and said,—

"But let us be sure. Bring back the thrush; let them sing together."

The thrush was brought, and the two birds poured out their marvels of song together. The king wavered, then his inclination began to settle and strengthen—one could see it in his countenance. Hope budded in the hearts of the old ministers, their pulses began to beat quicker, the scepter began to rise slowly, when—

There was a hideous interruption! It was a sound like this—just at the door:—

"Waw. . . . . .*he!*—waw. . . . . .*he!*—waw-he! waw-he!—waw-he!"

Everybody was sorely startled—and enraged at himself for showing it.

The next instant the dearest, sweetest, prettiest little peasant maid of nine years came tripping in, her brown eyes glowing with childish eagerness; but when she saw that august company and those angry faces she stopped and hung her head and put her poor coarse apron to her eyes. Nobody gave her welcome, none pitied her. Presently she looked up timidly through her tears, and said,—

"My lord the king, I pray you pardon me, for I meant no wrong. I have no father and no mother, but I have a goat and a donkey, and they are all in all to me. My goat gives me the sweetest milk, and when my dear good donkey brays it seems to me there is no music like to it. So when my lord the king's jester said the sweetest singer among all the animals should save the crown and nation, and moved me to bring him here—"

All the court burst into a rude laugh, and the child fled away crying, without trying to finish her speech. The chief minister gave a private order that she and her disastrous donkey be flogged beyond the precincts of the palace and commanded to come within them no more.

Then the trial of the birds was resumed. The two birds sang their best, but the scepter lay motionless in the king's hand. Hope died slowly out in the breasts of all. An hour went by; two hours; still no decision. The day waned to its close, and the waiting multitudes outside the palace grew crazed with anxiety and apprehension. The twilight came on, the shadows fell deeper and deeper. The king and his court could no longer see each other's faces. No one spoke—none called for lights. The great trial had been made; it had failed; each and all wished to hide their faces from the light and cover up their deep trouble in their own hearts.

Finally—hark! A rich, full strain of the divinest melody streamed forth from a remote part of the hall,—the nightingale's voice!

"Up!" shouted the king, "let all the bells make proclamation to the people, for the choice is made and we have not erred. King, dynasty, and nation are saved. From henceforth let the nightingale be honored throughout the land forever. And publish it among all the people that whosoever shall insult a nightingale, or injure it, shall suffer death. The king hath spoken."

All that little world was drunk with joy. The castle and the city blazed with bonfires all night long, the people danced and drank and sang, and the triumphant clamor of the bells never ceased.

From that day the nightingale was a sacred bird. Its song was heard in every house; the poets wrote its praises; the painters painted it; its sculptured image adorned every arch and turret and fountain and public building. It was even taken into the king's councils; and no grave matter of state was decided until the soothsayers had laid the thing before the state nightingale and translated to the ministry what it was that the bird had sung about it.

2

THE YOUNG king was very fond of the chase. When the summer was come he rode forth with hawk and hound, one day, in a brilliant company of his nobles. He got separated from them, by and by, in a great forest, and took what he imagined a near cut, to find them again; but it was a mistake. He rode on and on, hopefully at first, but with sinking courage finally. Twilight came on, and still he was plunging through a lonely and unknown land. Then came a catastrophe. In the dim light he forced his horse through a tangled thicket overhanging a steep and rocky declivity. When horse and rider reached the bottom, the former had a broken neck and the latter a broken leg. The poor little king lay there suffering agonies of pain, and each hour seemed a long month to him. He kept his ear strained to hear any sound that might promise hope of rescue; but he heard no voice, no sound of horn or bay of hound. So at last he gave up all hope, and said, "Let death come, for come it must."

Just then the deep, sweet song of a nightingale swept across the still wastes of the night.

"Saved!" the king said. "Saved! It is the sacred bird, and the prophecy is come true. The gods themselves protected me from error in the choice."

He could hardly contain his joy; he could not word his gratitude. Every few moments, now, he thought he caught the sound of approaching succor. But each time it was a disappointment; no succor came. The dull hours drifted on. Still no help came,—but still the sacred bird sang on. He began to have misgivings about his choice, but he stifled them. Toward dawn the bird ceased. The morning came, and with it thirst and hunger; but no succor. The day waxed and waned. At last the king cursed the nightingale.

Immediately the song of the thrush came from out the wood. The king said in his heart, "This was the true bird—my choice was false—succor will come now."

But it did not come. Then he lay many hours insensible. When he came to himself, a linnet was singing. He listened—with apathy. His faith was gone. "These birds," he said, "can bring no help; I and my house and my people are doomed." He turned him about to die; for he was grown very feeble from hunger and thirst and suffering, and felt that his end was near. In truth, he wanted to die, and be released from pain. For long hours he lay without thought or feeling or motion. Then his senses returned. The dawn of the third morning was breaking. Ah, the world seemed very beautiful to those worn eyes. Suddenly a great longing to live rose up in the lad's heart, and from his soul welled a deep and fervent prayer that Heaven would have mercy upon him and let him see his home and his friends once more. In that instant a soft, a faint, a far-off sound, but oh, how inexpressibly sweet to his waiting ear, came floating out of the distance,—

"Waw . . . . . . he!—waw . . . . . . he!—waw-he!—waw-he!—waw-he!"

"*That*, oh, *that* song is sweeter, a thousand times sweeter, than the voice of nightingale, thrush, or linnet, for it brings not mere hope, but *certainty* of succor; and now indeed am I saved! The sacred singer has chosen itself, as the oracle intended; the prophecy is fulfilled, and my life, my house, and my people are redeemed. The ass shall be sacred from this day!"

The divine music grew nearer and nearer, stronger and stronger,—and ever sweeter and sweeter to the perishing sufferer's ear. Down the declivity the docile little donkey wandered, cropping herbage and singing as he went; and when at last he saw the dead horse and the wounded king, he came and snuffed at them with simple and marvelling curiosity. The king petted him, and he knelt down as had been his wont when his little mistress desired to mount. With great labor and pain the lad drew himself upon the creature's back, and held himself there by aid of the generous ears. The ass went singing forth from the place and carried the king to the little peasant maid's hut. She gave him her pallet for a bed, refreshed him with goat's milk, and then flew to tell the great news to the first scouting party of searchers she might meet.

The king got well. His first act was to proclaim the sacredness and inviolability of the ass; his second was to add this particular ass to his cabinet and make him chief minister of the crown; his third was to have all the statues and effigies of nightingales throughout his kingdom destroyed, and replaced by statues and effigies of the sacred donkey; and his fourth was to announce that when the little peasant maid should reach her fifteenth year he would make her his queen,—and he kept his word.

Such is the legend. This explains why the moldering image of the ass adorns all these old crumbling walls and arches; and it explains why, during many centuries, an ass was always the chief minister in that royal cabinet, just as is still the case in most cabinets to this day; and it also explains why, in that little kingdom, during many centuries, all great poems, all great speeches, all great books, all public solemnities, and all royal proclamations, always began with these stirring words,—

"Waw . . . . . . he!—waw! . . . . . . he!—waw-he!—waw-he!—waw-he!

SPEECH ON THE BABIES

At the Banquet, in Chicago, given by the Army of the
Tennessee to their first Commander, General U. S. Grant,
November, 1879.

[The fifteenth regular toast was "The Babies.—As they comfort
us in our sorrows, let us not forget them in our festivities."]

I LIKE that. We have not all had the good fortune to be ladies. We have
not all been generals, or poets, or statesmen; but when the toast works
down to the babies, we stand on common ground. It is a shame that for a
thousand years the world's banquets have utterly ignored the baby, as if he
didn't amount to anything. If you will stop and think a minute,—if you
will go back fifty or one hundred years to your early married life and
recontemplate your first baby,—you will remember that he amounted to a
good deal, and even something over. You soldiers all know that when that
little fellow arrived at family headquarters you had to hand in your resignation. He took entire command. You became his lackey, his mere body-
servant, and you had to stand around too. He was not a commander who
made allowances for time, distance, weather, or anything else. You had to
execute his order whether it was possible or not. And there was only one
form of marching in his manual of tactics, and that was the double-quick.
He treated you with every sort of insolence and disrespect, and the bravest
of you didn't dare to say a word. You could face the death-storm at
Donelson and Vicksburg, and give back blow for blow; but when he
clawed your whiskers, and pulled your hair, and twisted your nose, you
had to take it. When the thunders of war were sounding in your ears you
set your faces toward the batteries, and advanced with steady tread; but
when he turned on the terrors of his war-whoop you advanced in the other
direction, and mighty glad of the chance too. When he called for soothing-
syrup, did you venture to throw out any side remarks about certain services
being unbecoming an officer and a gentleman? No. You got up and *got* it.
When he ordered his pap bottle and it was not warm, did you talk back?
Not you. You went to work and *warmed* it. You even descended so far in
your menial office as to take a suck at that warm, insipid stuff yourself,
to see if it was right,—three parts water to one of milk, a touch of sugar
to modify the colic, and a drop of peppermint to kill those immortal
hiccoughs. I can taste that stuff yet. And how many things you learned as
you went along! Sentimental young folks still take stock in that beautiful
old saying that when the baby smiles in his sleep, it is because the angels
are whispering to him. Very pretty, but too thin,—simply wind on the
stomach, my friends. If the baby proposed to take a walk at his usual
hour, two o'clock in the morning, didn't you rise up promptly and remark,
with a mental addition which would not improve a Sunday-school book
much, that that was the very thing you were about to propose yourself?
Oh! you were under good discipline, and as you went fluttering up and
down the room in your undress uniform, you not only prattled undignified

baby-talk, but even tuned up your martial voices and tried to *sing*!—
"Rock-a-by baby in the tree-top," for instance. What a spectacle for an
Army of the Tennessee! And what an affliction for the neighbors, too; for
it is not everybody within a mile around that likes military music at three
in the morning. And when you had been keeping this sort of thing up two
or three hours, and your little velvet-head intimated that nothing suited
him like exercise and noise, what did you do? [*"Go on"!*] You simply
went on until you dropped in the last ditch. The idea that a *baby* doesn't
amount to anything! Why, *one* baby is just a house and a front yard full
by itself. *One* baby can furnish more business than you and your whole
Interior Department can attend to. He is enterprising, irrepressible, brim-
ful of lawless activities. Do what you please, you can't make him stay on
the reservation. Sufficient unto the day is one baby. As long as you are in
your right mind don't you ever pray for twins. Twins amount to a permanent riot. And there ain't any real difference between triplets and an
insurrection.

Yes, it was high time for a toast-master to recognize the importance of
the babies. Think what is in store for the present crop! Fifty years from
now we shall all be dead, I trust, and then this flag, if it still survive (and
let us hope it may), will be floating over a Republic numbering 200,000,000
souls, according to the settled laws of our increase. Our present schooner
of State will have grown into a political leviathan,—a Great Eastern. The
cradled babies of to-day will be on deck. Let them be well trained, for we
are going to leave a big contract on their hands. Among the three or four
million cradles now rocking in the land are some which this nation would
preserve for ages as sacred things, if we could know which ones they are.
In one of these cradles the unconscious Farragut of the future is at this
moment teething,—think of it!—and putting in a world of dead earnest,
unarticulated, but perfectly justifiable profanity over it, too. In another the
future renowned astronomer is blinking at the shining Milky Way with but
a languid interest,—poor little chap!—and wondering what has become
of that other one they call the wet-nurse. In another the future great
historian is lying,—and doubtless will continue to lie until his earthly
mission is ended. In another the future President is busying himself with
no profounder problem of state than what the mischief has become of his
hair so early; and in a mighty array of other cradles there are now some
60,000 future office-seekers, getting ready to furnish him occasion to
grapple with that same old problem a second time. And in still one more
cradle, somewhere under the flag, the future illustrious commander-in-
chief of the American armies is so little burdened with his approaching
grandeurs and responsibilities as to be giving his whole strategic mind at
this moment to trying to find out some way to get his big toe into his
mouth,—an achievement which, meaning no disrespect, the illustrious
guest of this evening turned *his* entire attention to some fifty-six years
ago; and if the child is but a prophecy of the man, there are mighty few
who will doubt that he *succeeded*.

SPEECH ON THE WEATHER

*At the New England Society's Seventy-first Annual Dinner,
New York City.*

The next toast was: "The Oldest Inhabitant—The Weather of
New England."

> Who can lose it and forget it?
> Who can have it and regret it?

"Be interposer 'twixt us Twain."

Merchant of Venice.

To this Samuel L. Clemens (Mark Twain) replied as follows:—

I REVERENTLY believe that the Maker who made us all makes everything
in New England but the weather. I don't know who makes that, but I think
it must be raw apprentices in the weather clerk's factory who experiment
and learn how, in New England, for board and clothes, and then are
promoted to make weather for countries that require a good article, and
will take their custom elsewhere if they don't get it. There is a sumptuous
variety about the New England weather that compels the stranger's admiration—and regret. The weather is always doing something there; always
attending strictly to business; always getting up new designs and trying
them on the people to see how they will go. But it gets through more
business in spring than in any other season. In the spring I have counted
one hundred and thirty-six different kinds of weather inside of four-and-
twenty hours. It was I that made the fame and fortune of that man that
had that marvellous collection of weather on exhibition at the Centennial,
that so astounded the foreigners. He was going to travel all over the world
and get specimens from all the climes. I said, "Don't you do it; you come
to New England on a favorable spring day." I told him what we could do
in the way of style, variety, and quantity. Well, he came and he made his
collection in four days. As to variety, why, he confessed that he got
hundreds of kinds of weather that he had never heard of before. And as to
quantity—well, after he had picked out and discarded all that was blem-
ished in any way, he not only had weather enough, but weather to spare;
weather to hire out; weather to sell; to deposit; weather to invest; weather
to give to the poor. The people of New England are by nature patient and
forbearing, but there are some things which they will not stand. Every
year they kill a lot of poets for writing about "Beautiful Spring." These
are generally casual visitors, who bring their notions of spring from somewhere else, and cannot, of course, know how the natives feel about spring.
And so the first thing they know the opportunity to inquire how they feel
has permanently gone by. Old Probabilities has a mighty reputation for
accurate prophecy, and thoroughly well deserves it. You take up the paper

and observe how crisply and confidently he checks off what to-day's weather is going to be on the Pacific, down South, in the Middle States, in the Wisconsin region. See him sail along in the joy and pride of his power till he gets to New England, and then see his tail drop. *He* doesn't know what the weather is going to be in New England. Well, he mulls over it, and by and by he gets out something about like this: Probable northeast to southwest winds, varying to the southward and westward and eastward, and points between, high and low barometer swapping around from place to place; probable areas of rain, snow, hail, and drought, succeeded or preceded by earthquakes, with thunder and lightning. Then he jots down this postscript from his wandering mind, to cover accidents. "But it is possible that the program may be wholly changed in the mean time." Yes, one of the brightest gems in the New England weather is the dazzling uncertainty of it. There is only one thing certain about it: you are certain there is going to be plenty of it—a perfect grand review; but you never can tell which end of the procession is going to move first. You fix up for the drought; you leave your umbrella in the house and sally out, and two to one you get drowned. You make up your mind that the earthquake is due; you stand from under, and take hold of something to steady yourself, and the first thing you know you get struck by lightning. These are great disappointments; but they can't be helped. The lightning there is peculiar; it is so convincing, that when it strikes a thing it doesn't leave enough of that thing behind for you to tell whether— Well, you'd think it was something valuable, and a Congressman had been there. And the thunder. When the thunder begins to merely tune up and scrape and saw, and key up the instruments for the performance, strangers say, "Why, what awful thunder you have here!" But when the baton is raised and the real concert begins, you'll find that stranger down in the cellar with his head in the ash-barrel. Now as to the *size* of the weather in New England,—lengthways, I mean. It is utterly disproportioned to the size of that little country. Half the time, when it is packed as full as it can stick, you will see that New England weather sticking out beyond the edges and projecting around hundreds and hundreds of miles over the neighboring States. She can't hold a tenth part of her weather. You can see cracks all about where she has strained herself trying to do it. I could speak volumes about the inhuman perversity of the New England weather, but I will give but a single specimen. I like to hear rain on a tin roof. So I covered part of my roof with tin, with an eye to that luxury. Well, sir, do you think it ever rains on that tin? No, sir: skips it every time. Mind, in this speech I have been trying merely to do honor to the New England weather,—no language could do it justice. But, after all, there is at least one or two things about that weather (or, if you please, effects produced by it) which we residents would not like to part with. If we hadn't our bewitching autumn foliage, we should still have to credit the weather with one feature which compensates for all its bullying vagaries,—the ice-storm: when a leafless tree is clothed with ice from the bottom to the top,—ice that is as bright and clear as crystal; when every bough and twig is strung with ice-beads, frozen dew-drops, and the whole tree sparkles cold and white, like the Shah of Persia's diamond plume. Then the wind waves the branches and the sun comes out and turns all those myriads of beads and drops to prisms that glow and burn and flash with all manner of colored fires, which change and change again with inconceivable rapidity from blue to red, from red to green, and green to gold,—the tree becomes a spraying fountain, a very explosion of dazzling jewels; and it stands there the acme, the climax, the supremest possibility in art or nature, of bewildering, intoxicating, intolerable magnificence. One cannot make the words too strong.

CONCERNING THE AMERICAN LANGUAGE[1]

THERE WAS an Englishman in our compartment, and he complimented me on—on what? But you would never guess. He complimented me on my English. He said Americans in general did not speak the English language as correctly as I did. I said I was obliged to him for his compliment, since I knew he meant it for one, but that I was not fairly entitled to it, for I didn't speak English at all,—I only spoke American.

He laughed, and said it was a distinction without a difference. I said no, the difference was not prodigious, but still it was considerable. We fell into a friendly dispute over the matter. I put my case as well as I could, and said,—

"The languages were identical several generations ago, but our changed conditions and the spread of our people far to the south and far to the west have made many alterations in our pronunciation, and have introduced new words among us and changed the meanings of many old ones. English people talk through their noses; we do not. We say *know,* English people say *näo;* we say *cow,* the Briton says *käow;* we—"

"Oh, come! that is pure Yankee; everybody knows that."

"Yes, it is pure Yankee; that is true. One cannot hear it in America outside of the little corner called New England, which is Yankee land. The English themselves planted it there, two hundred and fifty years ago, and there it remains; it has never spread. But England talks through her nose yet; the Londoner and the backwoods New-Englander pronounce 'know' and 'cow' alike, and then the Briton unconsciously satirizes himself by making fun of the Yankee's pronunciation."

We argued this point at some length; nobody won; but no matter, the fact remains,—Englishmen say *näo* and *käow* for "know" and "cow," and that is what the rustic inhabitant of a very small section of America does.

"You conferred your *a* upon New England, too, and there it remains; it has not travelled out of the narrow limits of those six little States in all these two hundred and fifty years. All England uses it, New England's small population—say four millions—use it, but we have forty-five millions who do not use it. You say 'glahs of wawtah,' so does New England; at least, New England says *glahs.* America at large flattens the *a,* and says

---

[1]Being part of a chapter which was crowded out of "A Tramp Abroad."—M. T.

'glass of water.' These sounds are pleasanter than yours; you may think they are not right,—well, in English they are *not* right, but in 'American' they are. You say *flahsk,* and *bahsket,* and *jackahss;* we say 'flask,' 'basket,' 'jackass,'—sounding the *a* as it is in 'tallow,' 'fallow,' and so on. Up to as late as 1847 Mr. Webster's Dictionary had the impudence to still pronounce 'basket' *bahsket,* when he knew that outside of his little New England all America shortened the *a* and paid no attention to his English broadening of it. However, it called itself an English Dictionary, so it was proper enough that it should stick to English forms, perhaps. It still calls itself an English Dictionary to-day, but it has quietly ceased to pronounce 'basket' as if it were spelt *bahsket.* In the American language the *h* is respected; the *h* is not dropped or added improperly.''

"The same is the case in England,—I mean among the educated classes, of course.''

"Yes, that is true; but a nation's language is a very large matter. It is not simply a manner of speech obtaining among the educated handful; the manner obtaining among the vast uneducated multitude must be considered also. Your uneducated masses speak English, you will not deny that; our uneducated masses speak American,—it won't be fair for you to deny that, for you can see, yourself, that when your stable-boy says, 'It isn't the 'unting that 'urts the 'orse, but the 'ammer, 'ammer, 'ammer on the 'ard 'ighway,' and our stable-boy makes the same remark without suffocating a single *h,* these two people are manifestly talking two different languages. But if the signs are to be trusted, even your educated classes used to drop the *h.* They say *humble,* now, and *heroic,* and *historic,* etc., but I judge that they used to drop those *h*'s because your writers still keep up the fashion of putting *an* before those words, instead of *a.* This is what Mr. Darwin might call a 'rudimentary' sign that that *an* was justifiable once, and useful,—when your educated classes used to say *'umble,* and *'eroic,* and *'istorical.* Correct writers of the American language do not put *an* before those words.''

The English gentleman had something to say upon this matter, but never mind what he said,—I'm not arguing his case. I have him at a disadvantage, now. I proceeded:—

"In England you encourage an orator by exclaiming 'H'yaah! h'yaah!' We pronounce it *heer* in some sections, 'h'*yer*' in others, and so on; but our whites do not say 'h'yaah,' prouncing the *a*'s like the *a* in *ah.* I have heard English ladies say 'don't you'—making two separate and distinct words of it; your Mr. Bernand has satirized it. But we always say 'dontchu.' This is much better. Your ladies say, 'Oh, it's *o*ful nice!'' Ours say, 'Oh, it's *aw*ful nice!' We say, '*Four* hundred,' you say '*For*'—as in the word *or.* Your clergymen speak of 'the Lawd,' ours of 'the Lord'; yours speak of 'the gawds of the heathen,' ours of 'the gods of the heathen.' When you are exhausted, you say you are 'knocked up.' We don't. When you say you will do a thing 'directly,' you mean 'immediately'; in the American language—generally speaking—the word signifies 'after a little.' When you say 'clever,' you mean 'capable'; with us the word used to mean 'accommodating,' but I don't know what it means now. Your word 'stout' means 'fleshy'; our word 'stout' usually means 'strong.' Your words 'gentleman' and 'lady' have a very restricted meaning; with us they include the bar-maid, butcher, burglar, harlot, and horse-thief. You say, 'I haven't *got* any stockings on,' 'I haven't *got* any memory,' 'I haven't *got* any money in my purse'; we usually say, 'I haven't any stockings on,' 'I haven't any memory,' 'I haven't any money in my purse.' You say 'out of window'; we always put in a *the*. If one asks 'How old is that man?' the Briton answers, 'He will be about forty;' in the American language, we should say, 'He *is* about forty.' However, won't tire you, sir; but if I wanted to, I could pile up differences here until I not only convinced you that English and American are separate languages, but that when I speak my native tongue in its utmost purity an Englishman can't understand me at all.''

"I don't wish to flatter you, but it is about all I can do to understand you *now*."

That was a very pretty compliment, and it put us on the pleasantest terms directly,—I use the word in the English sense.

[*Later*—1882. Aesthetes in many of our schools are now beginning to teach the pupils to broaden the *a,* and to say "don't you," in the elegant foreign way.]

ROGERS

THIS MAN Rogers happened upon me and introduced himself at the town of————, in the South of England, where I stayed awhile. His stepfather had married a distant relative of mine who was afterwards hanged, and so he seemed to think a blood relationship existed between us. He came in every day and sat down and talked. Of all the bland, serene human curiosities I ever saw, I think he was the chiefest. He desired to look at my new chimney-pot hat. I was very willing, for I thought he would notice the name of the great Oxford Street hatter in it, and respect me accordingly. But he turned it about with a sort of grave compassion, pointed out two or three blemishes, and said that I, being so recently arrived, could not be expected to know where to supply myself. Said he would send me the address of *his* hatter. Then he said, "Pardon me," and proceeded to cut a neat circle of red tissue-paper; daintily notched the edges of it; took the mucilage and pasted it in my hat so as to cover the manufacturer's name. He said, "No one will know now where you got it. I will send you a hat-tip of my hatter, and you can paste it over this tissue circle." It was the calmest, coolest thing,—I never admired a man so much in my life. Mind, he did this while his own hat sat offensively near our noses, on the table,—an ancient extinguisher of the "slouch" pattern, limp and shapeless with age, discolored by vicissitudes of the weather, and banded by an equator of bear's grease that had stewed through.

Another time he examined my coat. I had no terrors, for over my tailor's door was the legend, "By Special Appointment Tailor to H. R. H. the Prince of Wales," etc. I did not know at the time that the most of the tailor shops had the same sign out, and that whereas it takes nine tailors to make an ordinary man, it takes a hundred and fifty to make a prince. He was full of compassion for my coat. Wrote down the address of his tailor for me. Did not tell me to mention my *nom de plume* and the tailor would put his best work on my garment, as complimentary people sometimes do, but said his tailor would hardly trouble himself for an unknown person (unknown person, when I thought I was so celebrated in England!—that was the cruelest cut), but cautioned me to mention *his* name, and it would be all right. Thinking to be facetious, I said,—

"But he might sit up all night and injure his health."

"Well, *let* him," said Rogers; "I've done enough for him, for him to show some appreciation of it."

I might as well have tried to disconcert a mummy with my facetiousness. Said Rogers: "I get all my coats there,—they're the only coats fit to be seen in."

I made one more attempt. I said, "I wish you had brought one with you—I would like to look at it."

"Bless your heart, haven't I got one on?—*this* article is Morgan's make."

I examined it. The coat had been bought ready-made, of a Chatham Street Jew, without any question—about 1848. It probably cost four dollars when it was new. It was ripped, it was frayed, it was napless and greasy. I could not resist showing him where it was ripped. It so affected him that I was almost sorry I had done it. First he seemed plunged into a bottomless abyss of grief. Then he roused himself, made a feint with his hands as if waving off the pity of a nation, and said,—with what seemed to me a manufactured emotion,—"No matter; no matter; don't mind me; do not bother about it. I can get another."

When he was thoroughly restored, so that he could examine the rip and command his feelings, he said, ah, *now* he understood it,—his servant must have done it while dressing him that morning.

His servant! There was something awe-inspiring in effrontery like this.

Nearly every day he interested himself in some article of my clothing. One would hardly have expected this sort of infatuation in a man who always wore the same suit, and it a suit that seemed coeval with the Conquest.

It was an unworthy ambition, perhaps, but I *did* wish I could make this man admire *something* about me or something I did,—you would have felt the same way. I saw my opportunity: I was about to return to London, and had "listed" my soiled linen for the wash. It made quite an imposing mountain in the corner of the room,—fifty-four pieces. I hoped he would fancy it was the accumulation of a single week. I took up the wash-list, as if to see that it was all right, and then tossed it on the table, with pretended forgetfulness. Sure enough, he took it up and ran his eye along down the grand total. Then he said, "You get off easy," and laid it down again.

His gloves were the saddest ruin, but he told me where I could get some like them. His shoes would hardly hold walnuts without leaking, but he liked to put his feet up on the mantel-piece and contemplate them. He wore a dim glass breastpin, which he called a "morphylitic diamond,"—

whatever that may mean,—and said only two of them had ever been found,—the Emperor of China had the other one.

Afterward, in London, it was a pleasure to me to see this fantastic vagabond come marching into the lobby of the hotel in his grand-ducal way, for he always had some new imaginary grandeur to develop—there was nothing stale about him but his clothes. If he addressed me when strangers were about, he always raised his voice a little and called me "Sir Richard," or "General," or "Your Lordship,"—and when people began to stare and look deferential, he would fall to inquiring in a casual way why I disappointed the Duke of Argyll the night before; and then remind me of our engagement at the Duke of Westminister's for the following day. I think that for the time being these things were realities to him. He once came and invited me to go with him and spend the evening with the Earl of Warwick at his town house. I said I had received no formal invitation. He said that that was of no consequence, the Earl had no formalities for him or his friends. I asked if I might go just as I was. He said no, that would hardly do; evening dress was requisite at night in any gentleman's house. He said he would wait while I dressed, and then we would go to his apartments and I could take a bottle of champagne and a cigar while he dressed. I was very willing to see how this enterprise would turn out, so I dressed, and we started to his lodgings. He said if I didn't mind we would walk. So we tramped some four miles through the mud and fog, and finally found his "apartments:" they consisted of a single room over a barber's shop in a back street. Two chairs, a small table, an ancient valise, a wash-basin and pitcher (both on the floor in a corner), an unmade bed, a fragment of a looking-glass, and a flower-pot with a perishing little rose geranium in it, which he called a century plant, and said it had not bloomed now for upwards of two centuries—given to him by the late Lord Palmerston—been offered a prodigious sum for it)—these were the contents of the room. Also a brass candlestick and part of a candle. Rogers lit the candle, and told me to sit down and make myself at home. He said he hoped I was thirsty, because he would surprise my palate with an article of champagne that seldom got into a commoner's system; or would I prefer sherry, or port? Said he had port in bottles that were swathed in stratified cobwebs, every stratum representing a generation. And as for his cigars,—well, I should judge of them myself. Then he put his head out at the door and called,—

"Sackville!" No answer.

"Hi!—Sackville!" No answer.

"Now what the devil can have become of that butler? I *never* allow a servant to—Oh, confound that idiot, he's got the *keys*. Can't get into the other rooms without the keys."

(I was just wondering at his intrepidity in still keeping up the delusion of the champagne, and trying to imagine how he was going to get out of the difficulty.)

Now he stopped calling Sackville and began to call "Anglesy." But Anglesy didn't come. He said, "This is the *second* time that that equerry has been absent without leave. To-morrow I'll discharge him."

Now he began to whoop for "Thomas," but Thomas didn't answer. Then for "Theodore," but no Theodore replied.

"Well, I give it up," said Rogers. "The servants never expect me at this hour, and so they're all off on a lark. Might get along without the equerry and the page, but can't have any wine or cigars without the butler, and can't dress without my valet."

I offered to help him dress, but he would not hear of it; and besides, he said he would not feel comfortable unless dressed by a practised hand. However, he finally concluded that he was such old friends with the Earl that it would not make any difference how he was dressed. So we took a cab, he gave the driver some directions, and we started. By and by we stopped before a large house and got out. I never had seen this man with a collar on. He now stepped under a lamp and got a venerable paper collar out of his coat pocket, along with a hoary cravat, and put them on. He ascended the stoop, and entered. Presently he reappeared, descended rapidly, and said,—

"Come—quick!"

We hurried away, and turned the corner.

"Now we're safe," he said, and took off his collar and cravat and returned them to his pocket.

"Made a mighty narrow escape," said he.

"How?" said I.

"B' George, the Countess was there!"

"Well, what of that?—don't she know you?"

"Know me? Absolutely worships me. I just did happen to catch a glimpse of her before she saw me—and out I shot. Haven't seen her for two months—to rush in on her without any warning might have been fatal. She could *not* have stood it. I didn't know *she* was in town—thought she was at the castle. Let me lean on you—just a moment—there; now I am better—thank you; thank you ever so much. Lord bless me, what an escape!"

So I never got to call on the Earl after all. But I marked his house for future reference. It proved to be an ordinary family hotel, with about a thousand plebeians roosting in it.

In most things Rogers was by no means a fool. In some things it was plain enough that he was a fool, but he certainly did not know it. He was in the "deadest" earnest in these matters. He died at sea, last summer, as the "Earl of Ramsgate."

THE LOVES of ALONZO FITZ CLARENCE and ROSANNAH ETHELTON

IT WAS well along in the forenoon of a bitter winter's day. The town of Eastport, in the State of Maine, lay buried under a deep snow that was newly fallen. The customary bustle in the streets was wanting. One could look long distances down them and see nothing but a dead-white emptiness, with silence to match. Of course I do not mean that you could *see* the silence,—no, you could only hear it. The sidewalks were merely long, deep ditches, with steep snow walls on either side. Here and there you might hear the faint, far scrape of a wooden shovel, and if you were quick enough you might catch a glimpse of a distant black figure stooping and disappearing in one of those ditches, and reappearing the next moment with a motion which you would know meant the heaving out of a shovelful of snow. But you needed to be quick, for that black figure would not linger, but would soon drop that shovel and scud for the house, thrashing itself with its arms to warm them. Yes, it was too venomously cold for snow-shovellers or anybody else to stay out long.

Presently the sky darkened; then the wind rose and began to blow in fitful, vigorous gusts, which sent clouds of powdery snow aloft, and straight ahead, and everywhere. Under the impulse of one of these gusts, great white drifts banked themselves like graves across the streets; a moment later, another gust shifted them around the other way, driving a fine spray of snow from their sharp crests, as the gale drives the spume flakes from wave-crests at sea; a third gust swept that place as clean as your hand, if it saw fit. This was fooling, this was play; but each and all of the gusts dumped some snow into the sidewalk ditches, for that was business.

Alonzo Fitz Clarence was sitting in his snug and elegant little parlor, in a lovely blue silk dressing-gown, with cuffs and facings of crimson satin, elaborately quilted. The remains of his breakfast were before him, and the dainty and costly little table service added a harmonious charm to the grace, beauty, and richness of the fixed appointments of the room. A cheery fire was blazing on the hearth.

A furious gust of wind shook the windows, and a great wave of snow washed against them with a drenching sound, so to speak. The handsome young bachelor murmured,—

"That means, no going out to-day. Well, I am content. But what to do for company? Mother is well enough, Aunt Susan is well enough; but these, like the poor, I have with me always. On so grim a day as this, one needs a new interest, a fresh element, to whet the dull edge of captivity. That was very neatly said, but it doesn't mean anything. One doesn't *want* the edge of captivity sharpened up, you know, but just the reverse."

He glanced at his pretty French mantel-clock.

"That clock's wrong again. That clock hardly ever knows what time it is; and when it does know, it lies about it,—which amounts to the same thing. Alfred!"

There was no answer.

"Alfred! . . . Good servant, but as uncertain as the clock."

Alonzo touched an electric bell-button in the wall. He waited a moment, then touched it again; waited a few moments more, and said,—

"Battery out of order, no doubt. But now that I have started, I *will* find out what time it is." He stepped to a speaking-tube in the wall, blew its whistle, and called, "Mother!" and repeated it twice.

"Well, *that's* no use. Mother's battery is out of order, too. Can't raise anybody down-stairs,—that is plain."

He sat down at a rosewood desk, leaned his chin on the left-hand edge of it, and spoke, as if to the floor: "Aunt Susan!"

A low, pleasant voice answered, "Is that you, Alonzo?"

"Yes. I'm too lazy and comfortable to go downstairs; I am in extremity, and I can't seem to scare up any help."

"Dear me, what is the matter?"

"Matter enough, I can tell you!"

"Oh, don't keep me in suspense, dear! What *is* it?"

"I want to know what time it is."

"You abominable boy, what a turn you did give me! Is that all?"

"All,—on my honor. Calm yourself. Tell me the time, and receive my blessing."

"Just five minutes after nine. No charge,—keep your blessing."

"Thanks. It wouldn't have impoverished me, aunty, nor so enriched you that you could live without other means." He got up, murmuring, "Just five minutes after nine," and faced his clock. "Ah," said he, "you are doing better than usual. You are only thirty-four minutes wrong. Let me see. . . . let me see. . . . Thirty-three and twenty-one are fifty-four; four times fifty-four are two hundred and thirty-six. One off, leaves two hundred and thirty-five. That's right."

He turned the hands of his clock forward till they marked twenty-five minutes to one, and said, "Now see if you can't keep right for a while . . . else I'll raffle you!"

He sat down at the desk again, and said, "Aunt Susan!"

"Yes, dear."

"Had breakfast?"

"Yes indeed, an hour ago."

"Busy?"

"No,—except sewing. Why?"

"Got any company?"

"No, but I expect some at half past nine."

"I wish *I* did. I'm lonesome. I want to talk to somebody."

"Very well, talk to me."

"But this is very private."

"Don't be afraid,—talk right along; there's nobody here but me."

"I hardly know whether to venture or not, but—"

"But what? Oh, don't stop there! You *know* you can trust me, Alonzo,— you know you can."

"I feel it, aunt, but this is very serious. It affects me deeply,—me, and all the family,—even the whole community."

"Oh, Alonzo, tell me! I will never breathe a word of it. What is it?"

"Aunt, if I might dare—"

"Oh, please go on! I love you, and can feel for you. Tell me all. Confide in me. What *is* it?"

"The weather!"

"Plague take the weather! I don't see how you can have the heart to serve me so, Lon."

"There, there, aunty dear, I'm sorry; I am, on my honor! I won't do it again. Do you forgive me?"

"Yes, since you seem so sincere about it, though I know I oughtn't to. You will fool me again as soon as I have forgotten this time."

"No, I won't, honor bright. But such weather, oh, such weather! You've *got* to keep your spirits up artificially. It is snowy, and blowy, and gusty, and bitter cold! How is the weather with you?"

"Warm and rainy and melancholy. The mourners go about the streets with their umbrellas running streams from the end of every whalebone. There's an elevated double pavement of umbrellas stretching down the sides of the streets as far as I can see. I've got a fire for cheerfulness, and the windows open to keep cool. But it is vain, it is useless: nothing comes in but the balmy breath of December, with its burden of mocking odors from the flowers that possess the realm outside, and rejoice in their lawless profusion whilst the spirit of man is low, and flaunt their gaudy splendors in his face whilst his soul is clothed in sackcloth and ashes and his heart breaketh."

Alonzo opened his lips to say, "You ought to print that, and get it framed," but checked himself, for he heard his aunt speaking to some one else. He went and stood at the window and looked out upon the wintry prospect. The storm was driving the snow before it more furiously than ever; window shutters were slamming and banging; a forlorn dog, with bowed head and tail withdrawn from service, was pressing his quaking body against a windward wall for shelter and protection; a young girl was ploughing knee-deep through the drifts, with her face turned from the blast, and the cape of her water-proof blowing straight rearward over her head. Alonzo shuddered, and said with a sigh, "Better the slop, and the sultry rain, and even the insolent flowers, than this!"

He turned from the window, moved a step, and stopped in a listening attitude. The faint, sweet notes of a familiar song caught his ear. He remained there, with his head unconsciously bent forward, drinking in the melody, stirring neither hand nor foot, hardly breathing. There was a blemish in the execution of the song, but to Alonzo it seemed an added charm instead of a defect. This blemish consisted of a marked flatting of the third, fourth, fifth, sixth, and seventh notes of the refrain or chorus of the piece. When the music ended, Alonzo drew a deep breath, and said, "Ah, I never have heard 'In the Sweet By and By' sung like that before!"

He stepped quickly to the desk, listened a moment, and said in a guarded, confidential voice, "Aunty, who is this divine singer?"

"She is the company I was expecting. Stays with me a month or two. I will introduce you. Miss—"

"For goodness' sake, wait a moment, Aunt Susan! You never stop to think what you are about!"

He flew to his bed-chamber, and returned in a moment perceptibly changed in his outward appearance, and remarking, snappishly,—

"Hang it, she would have introduced me to this angel in that sky-blue dressing-gown with red-hot lapels! Women never think, when they get a-going."

He hastened and stood by the desk, and said eagerly, "Now, Aunty, I am ready," and fell to smiling and bowing with all the persuasiveness and elegance that were in him.

"Very well. Miss Rosannah Ethelton, let me introduce to you my favorite nephew, Mr. Alonzo Fitz Clarence. There! You are both good people, and I like you; so I am going to trust you together while I attend to a few household affairs. Sit down, Rosannah; sit down, Alonzo. Good-by; I shan't be gone long."

Alonzo had been bowing and smiling all the while, and motioning

imaginary young ladies to sit down in imaginary chairs, but now he took
a seat himself, mentally saying, "Oh, this is luck! Let the winds blow
now, and the snow drive, and the heavens frown! Little I care!"

While these young people chat themselves into an acquaintanceship, let
us take the liberty of inspecting the sweeter and fairer of the two. She sat
alone, at her graceful ease, in a richly furnished apartment which was
manifestly the private parlor of a refined and sensible lady, if signs and
symbols may go for anything. For instance, by a low, comfortable chair
stood a dainty, top-heavy work-stand, whose summit was a fancifully
embroidered shallow basket, with varicolored crewels, and other strings
and odds and ends, protruding from under the gaping lid and hanging
down in negligent profusion. On the floor lay bright shreds of Turkey red,
Prussian blue, and kindred fabrics, bits of ribbon, a spool or two, a pair
of scissors, and a roll or so of tinted silken stuffs. On a luxurious sofa,
upholstered with some sort of soft Indian goods wrought in black and gold
threads interwebbed with other threads not so pronounced in color, lay a
great square of coarse white stuff, upon whose surface a rich bouquet of
flowers was growing, under the deft cultivation of the crochet needle. The
household cat was asleep on this work of art. In a bay window stood an
easel with an unfinished picture on it, and a palette and brushes on a chair
beside it. There were books everywhere: Robertson's Sermons, Tennyson,
Moody and Sankey, Hawthorne, "Rab and his Friends," cook-books,
prayer-books, pattern-books,—and books about all kinds of odious and
exasperating pottery, of course. There was a piano, with a deckload of
music, and more in a tender. There was a great plenty of pictures on the
walls, on the shelves of the mantel-piece, and around generally; where
coigns of vantage offered were statuettes, and quaint and pretty gim-
cracks, and rare and costly specimens of peculiarly devilish china. The
bay-window gave upon a garden that was ablaze with foreign and domestic
flowers and flowering shrubs.

But the sweet young girl was the daintiest thing those premises, within
or without, could offer for contemplation: delicately chiselled features, of
Grecian cast; her complexion the pure snow of a japonica that is receiving
a faint reflected enrichment from some scarlet neighbor of the garden;
great, soft blue eyes fringed with long, curving lashes; an expression made
up of the trustfulness of a child and the gentleness of a fawn; a beautiful
head crowned with its own prodigal gold; a lithe and rounded figure,
whose every attitude and movement were instinct with native grace.

Her dress and adornment were marked by that exquisite harmony that
can come only of a fine natural taste perfected by culture. Her gown was
of a simple magenta tulle, cut bias, traversed by three rows of light blue
flounces, with the selvage edges turned up with ashes-of-roses chenille;
overdress of dark bay tarlatan, with scarlet satin lambrequins; corn-colored
polonaise, *en panier,* looped with mother-of-pearl buttons and silver cord,
and hauled aft and made fast by buff-velvet lashings; basque of lavender
reps, picked out with valenciennes; low neck, short sleeves; maroon-velvet
necktie edged with delicate pink silk; inside handkerchief of some simple
three-ply ingrain fabric of the soft saffron tint; coral bracelets and locket-
chain; coiffure of forget-me-nots and lilies of the valley massed around a
noble calla.

This was all; yet even in this subdued attire she was divinely beautiful. Then what must she have been when adorned for the festival or the ball?

All this time she has been busily chatting with Alonzo, unconscious of our inspection. The minutes still sped, and still she talked. But by and by she happened to look up, and saw the clock. A crimson blush sent its rich flood through her cheeks, and she exclaimed,—

"There, good-by, Mr. Fitz Clarence; I must go now!"

She sprang from her chair with such haste that she hardly heard the young man's answered good-by. She stood radiant, graceful, beautiful, and gazed, wondering, upon the accusing clock. Presently her pouting lips parted, and she said,—

"Five minutes after eleven! Nearly two hours, and it did not seem twenty minutes! Oh, dear, what will he think of me!"

At the self-same moment Alonzo was staring at *his* clock. And presently he said,—

"Twenty-five minutes to three! Nearly two hours, and I didn't believe it was two minutes! Is it possible that this clock is humbugging again? Miss Ethelton! Just one moment, please. Are you there yet?"

"Yes, but be quick; I'm going right away."

"Would you be so kind as to tell me what time it is?"

The girl blushed again, murmured to herself, "It's right down cruel of him to ask me!" and then spoke up and answered with admirably counterfeited unconcern, "Five minutes after eleven."

"Oh, thank you! You have to go, now, have you?"

"Yes."

"I'm sorry."

No reply.

"Miss Ethelton!"

"Well?"

"You—you're there yet, *ain't* you?"

"Yes; but please hurry. What did you want to say?"

"Well, I—well, nothing in particular. It's very lonesome here. It's asking a great deal, I know, but would you mind talking with me again by and by,—that is, if it will not trouble you too much?"

"I don't know—but I'll think about it. I'll try."

"Oh, thanks! Miss Ethelton? . . . Ah me, she's gone, and here are the black clouds and the whirling snow and the raging winds come again! But she said *good-by!* She didn't say good-morning, she said good-by! . . . The clock was right, after all. What a lightning-winged two hours it was!"

He sat down, and gazed dreamily into his fire for a while, then heaved a sigh and said,—

"How wonderful it is! Two little hours ago I was a free man, and now my heart's in San Francisco!"

About that time Rosannah Ethelton, propped in the window-seat of her bed-chamber, book in hand, was gazing vacantly out over the rainy seas that washed the Golden Gate, and whispering to herself, "How different he is from poor Burley, with his empty head and his single little antic talent of mimicry!"

2

FOUR WEEKS later Mr. Sidney Algernon Burley was entertaining a gay luncheon company, in a sumptuous drawing-room on Telegraph Hill, with some capital imitations of the voices and gestures of certain popular actors and San Franciscan literary people and Bonanza grandees. He was elegantly upholstered, and was a handsome fellow, barring a trifling cast in his eye. He seemed very jovial, but nevertheless he kept his eye on the door with an expectant and uneasy watchfulness. By and by a nobby lackey appeared, and delivered a message to the mistress, who nodded her head understandingly. That seemed to settle the thing for Mr. Burley; his vivacity decreased little by little, and a dejected look began to creep into one of his eyes and a sinister one into the other.

The rest of the company departed in due time, leaving him with the mistress, to whom he said,—

"There is no longer any question about it. She avoids me. She continually excuses herself. If I could see her, if I could speak to her only a moment,—but this suspense—"

"Perhaps her seeming avoidance is mere accident, Mr. Burley. Go to the small drawing-room up-stairs and amuse yourself a moment. I will despatch a household order that is on my mind, and then I will go to her room. Without doubt she will be persuaded to see you."

Mr. Burley went up-stairs, intending to go to the small drawing-room, but as he was passing "Aunt Susan's" private parlor, the door of which stood slightly ajar, he heard a joyous laugh which he recognized; so without knock or announcement he stepped confidently in. But before he could make his presence known he heard words that harrowed up his soul and chilled his young blood. He heard a voice say,—

"Darling, it has come!"

Then he heard Rosannah Ethelton, whose back was toward him, say,—

"So has yours, dearest!"

He saw her bowed form bend lower; he heard her kiss something,—not merely once, but again and again! His soul raged within him. The heartbreaking conversation went on,—

"Rosannah, I knew you must be beautiful, but this is dazzling, this is blinding, this is intoxicating!"

"Alonzo, it is such happiness to hear you say it. I know it is not true, but I am *so* grateful to have you think it is, nevertheless! I knew you must have a noble face, but the grace and majesty of the reality beggar the poor creation of my fancy."

Burley heard that rattling shower of kisses again.

"Thank you, my Rosannah! The photograph flatters me, but you must not allow yourself to think of that. Sweetheart?"

"Yes, Alonzo."

"I am so happy, Rosannah."

"Oh, Alonzo, none that have gone before me knew what love was, none that come after me will ever know what happiness is. I float in a gorgeous cloud-land, a boundless firmament of enchanted and bewildering ecstasy!"

"Oh, my Rosannah!—for you are mine, are you not?"

"Wholly, oh, wholly yours, Alonzo, now and forever! All the day long, and all through my nightly dreams, one song sings itself, and its sweet burden is, 'Alonzo Fitz Clarence, Alonzo Fitz Clarence, Eastport, State of Maine!'"

"Curse him, I've got his address, any way!" roared Burley, inwardly, and rushed from the place.

Just behind the unconscious Alonzo stood his mother, a picture of astonishment. She was so muffled from head to heel in furs that nothing of herself was visible but her eyes and nose. She was a good allegory of winter, for she was powdered all over with snow.

Behind the unconscious Rosannah stood "Aunt Susan," another picture of astonishment. She was a good allegory of summer, for she was lightly clad, and was vigorously cooling the perspiration on her face with a fan.

Both of these women had tears of joy in their eyes.

"So ho!" exclaimed Mrs. Fitz Clarence, "this explains why nobody has been able to drag you out of your room for six weeks, Alonzo!"

"So ho!" exclaimed Aunt Susan, "this explains why you have been a hermit for the past six weeks, Rosannah!"

The young couple were on their feet in an instant, abashed, and standing like detected dealers in stolen goods awaiting Judge Lynch's doom.

"Bless you, my son! I am happy in your happiness. Come to your mother's arms, Alonzo!"

"Bless you, Rosannah, for my dear nephew's sake! Come to my arms!"

Then was there a mingling of hearts and of tears of rejoicing on Telegraph Hill and in Eastport Square.

Servants were called by the elders, in both places. Unto one was given the order, "Pile this fire high with hickory wood, and bring me a roasting-hot lemonade."

Unto the other was given the order, "Put out this fire, and bring me two palm-leaf fans and a pitcher of ice-water."

Then the young people were dismissed, and the elders sat down to talk the sweet surprise over and make the wedding plans.

Some minutes before this Mr. Burley rushed from the mansion on Telegraph Hill without meeting or taking formal leave of anybody. He hissed through his teeth, in unconscious imitation of a popular favorite in melodrama, "Him shall she never wed! I have sworn it! Ere great Nature shall have doffed her winter's ermine to don the emerald gauds of spring, she shall be mine!"

3

Two weeks later. Every few hours, during some three or four days, a very prim and devout-looking Episcopal clergyman, with a cast in his eye, had visited Alonzo. According to his card, he was the Rev. Melton Hargrave, of Cincinnati. He said he had retired from the ministry on account of his health. If he had said on account of ill health, he would probably have erred, to judge by his wholesome looks and firm build. He was the inventor of an improvement in telephones, and hoped to make his bread by selling the privilege of using it. "At present," he continued, "a man may go and tap a telegraph wire which is conveying a song or a concert from one State to another, and he can attach his private telephone and steal a hearing of that music as it passes along. My invention will stop all that."

"Well," answered Alonzo, "if the owner of the music could not miss what was stolen, why should he care?"

"He shouldn't care," said the Reverend.

"Well?" said Alonzo inquiringly.

"Suppose," replied the Reverend, "suppose that, instead of music that was passing along and being stolen, the burden of the wire was loving endearments of the most private and sacred nature?"

Alonzo shuddered from head to heel. "Sir, it is a priceless invention," said he; "I must have it at any cost."

But the invention was delayed somewhere on the road from Cincinnati, most unaccountably. The impatient Alonzo could hardly wait. The thought of Rosannah's sweet words being shared with him by some ribald thief was galling to him. The Reverend came frequently and lamented the delay, and told of measures he had taken to hurry things up. This was some little comfort to Alonzo.

One forenoon the Reverend ascended the stairs and knocked at Alonzo's door. There was no response. He entered, glanced eagerly around, closed the door softly, then ran to the telephone. The exquisitely soft and remote strains of the "Sweet By and By" came floating through the instrument. The singer was flatting, as usual, the five notes that follow the first two in the chorus, when the Reverend interrupted her with this word, in a voice which was an exact imitation of Alonzo's, with just the faintest flavor of impatience added,—

"Sweetheart?"

"Yes, Alonzo?"

"Please don't sing that any more this week,—try something modern."

The agile step that goes with a happy heart was heard on the stairs, and the Reverend, smiling diabolically, sought sudden refuge behind the heavy folds of the velvet window curtains. Alonzo entered and flew to the telephone. Said he,—

"Rosannah, dear, shall we sing something together?"

"Something *modern?*" asked she, with sarcastic bitterness.

"Yes, if you prefer."

"Sing it yourself, if you like!"

This snappishness amazed and wounded the young man. He said,—

"Rosannah, that was not like you."

"I suppose it becomes me as much as your very polite speech became you, Mr. Fitz Clarence."

"*Mister* Fitz Clarence! Rosannah, there was nothing impolite about my speech."

"Oh, indeed! Of course, then, I misunderstood you, and I most humbly beg your pardon, ha-ha-ha! No doubt you said, 'Don't sing it any more *to-day.*' ''

"Sing *what* any more to-day?"

"The song you mentioned, of course. How very obtuse we are, all of a sudden!"

"I never mentioned any song."

"Oh, you *didn't!*"

"No, I *didn't!*"

"I am compelled to remark that you *did.*"

"And I am obliged to reiterate that I *didn't.*"

"A second rudeness! That is sufficient, sir. I will never forgive you. All is over between us."

Then came a muffled sound of crying. Alonzo hastened to say,—

"Oh, Rosannah, unsay those words! There is some dreadful mystery here, some hideous mistake. I am utterly earnest and sincere when I say I never said anything about any song. I would not hurt you for the whole world . . . Rosannah, dear? . . . Oh, speak to me, won't you?"

There was a pause; then Alonzo heard the girl's sobbings retreating, and knew she had gone from the telephone. He rose with a heavy sigh and hastened from the room, saying to himself, "I will ransack the charity missions and the haunts of the poor for my mother. She will persuade her that I never meant to wound her."

A minute later, the Reverend was crouching over the telephone like a cat that knoweth the ways of the prey. He had not very many minutes to wait. A soft, repentant voice, tremulous with tears, said,—

"Alonzo, dear, I have been wrong. You *could* not have said so cruel a thing. It must have been some one who imitated your voice in malice or in jest."

The Reverend coldly answered, in Alonzo's tones,—

"You have said all was over between us. So let it be. I spurn your proffered repentance, and despise it!"

Then he departed, radiant with fiendish triumph, to return no more with his imaginary telephonic invention forever.

Four hours afterward, Alonzo arrived with his mother from her favorite haunts of poverty and vice. They summoned the San Francisco household; but there was no reply. They waited, and continued to wait, upon the voiceless telephone.

At length, when it was sunset in San Francisco, and three hours and a half after dark in Eastport, an answer came to the oft-repeated cry of "Rosannah!"

But, alas, it was Aunt Susan's voice that spake. She said,—

"I have been out all day; just got in. I will go and find her."

The watchers waited two minutes—five minutes—ten minutes. Then came these fatal words, in a frightened tone,—

"She is gone, and her baggage with her. To visit another friend, she told the servants. But I found this note on the table in her room. Listen: 'I am gone; seek not to trace me out; my heart is broken; you will never see me more. Tell him I shall always think of him when I sing my poor "Sweet By and By," but never of the unkind words he said about it.' That is her note. Alonzo, Alonzo, what does it mean? What has happened?"

But Alonzo sat white and cold as the dead. His mother threw back the velvet curtains and opened a window. The cold air refreshed the sufferer, and he told his aunt his dismal story. Meantime his mother was inspecting a card which had disclosed itself upon the floor when she cast the curtains back. It read, "Mr. Sidney Algernon Burley, San Francisco."

"The miscreant!" shouted Alonzo, and rushed forth to seek the false Reverend and destroy him; for the card explained everything, since in the course of the lovers' mutual confessions they had told each other all about all the sweethearts they had ever had, and thrown no end of mud at their failings and foibles,—for lovers always do that. It has a fascination that ranks next after billing and cooing.

4

DURING THE next two months many things happened. It had early transpired that Rosannah, poor suffering orphan, had neither returned to her grandmother in Portland, Oregon, nor sent any word to her save a duplicate of the woeful note she had left in the mansion on Telegraph Hill. Whosoever was sheltering her—if she was still alive—had been persuaded not to betray her whereabouts, without doubt; for all efforts to find trace of her had failed.

Did Alonzo give her up? Not he. He said to himself, "She will sing that sweet song when she is sad; I shall find her." So he took his carpet sack and a portable telephone, and shook the snow of his native city from his arctics, and went forth into the world. He wandered far and wide and in many States. Time and again, strangers were astounded to see a wasted, pale, and woe-worn man laboriously climb a telegraph pole in wintry and lonely places, perch sadly there an hour, with his ear at a little box, then come sighing down, and wander wearily away. Sometimes they shot at him, as peasants do at aeronauts, thinking him mad and dangerous. Thus his clothes were much shredded by bullets and his person grievously lacerated. But he bore it all patiently.

In the beginning of his pilgrimage he used often to say, "Ah, if I could but hear the 'Sweet By and By'!" But toward the end of it he used to shed tears of anguish and say, "Ah, if I could but hear something else!"

Thus a month and three weeks drifted by, and at last some humane people seized him and confined him in a private mad-house in New York. He made no moan, for his strength was all gone, and with it all heart and all hope. The superintendent, in pity, gave up his own comfortable parlor and bed-chamber to him and nursed him with affectionate devotion.

At the end of a week the patient was able to leave his bed for the first time. He was lying, comfortably pillowed, on a sofa, listening to the plaintive Miserere of the bleak March winds, and the muffled sound of tramping feet in the street below,—for it was about six in the evening, and New York was going home from work. He had a bright fire and the added cheer of a couple of student lamps. So it was warm and snug within, though bleak and raw without; it was light and bright within, though outside it was as dark and dreary as if the world had been lit with Hartford gas. Alonzo smiled feebly to think how his loving vagaries had made him a maniac in the eyes of the world, and was proceeding to pursue his line of thought further, when a faint, sweet strain, the very ghost of sound, so remote and attenuated it seemed, struck upon his ear. His pulses stood still; he listened with parted lips and bated breath. The song flowed on,— he waiting, listening, rising slowly and unconsciously from his recumbent position. At last he exclaimed,—

"It is! it is she! Oh, the divine flatted notes!"

He dragged himself eagerly to the corner whence the sounds proceeded, tore aside a curtain, and discovered a telephone. He bent over, and as the last note died away he burst forth with the exclamation,—

"Oh, thank Heaven, found at last! Speak to me, Rosannah, dearest! The cruel mystery has been unravelled; it was the villain Burley who mimicked my voice and wounded you with insolent speech!"

There was a breathless pause, a waiting age to Alonzo; then a faint sound came, framing itself into language,—

"Oh, say those precious words again, Alonzo!"

"They are the truth, the veritable truth, my Rosannah, and you shall have the proof, ample and abundant proof!"

"Oh, Alonzo, stay by me! Leave me not for a moment! Let me feel that you are near me! Tell me we shall never be parted more! Oh, this happy hour, this blessed hour, this memorable hour!"

"We will make a record of it, my Rosannah; every year, as this dear hour chimes from the clock, we will celebrate it with thanksgivings, all the years of our life."

"We will, we will, Alonzo!"

"Four minutes after six, in the evening, my Rosannah, shall hence- forth—"

"Twenty-three minutes after twelve, afternoon, shall—"

"Why, Rosannah, darling, where are you?"

"In Honolulu, Sandwich Islands. And where are you? Stay by me; do not leave me for a moment. I cannot bear it. Are you at home?"

"No, dear, I am in New York,—a patient in the doctor's hands."

An agonizing shriek came buzzing to Alonzo's ear, like the sharp buzzing of a hurt gnat; it lost power in travelling five thousand miles. Alonzo hastened to say,—

"Calm yourself, my child. It is nothing. Already I am getting well under the sweet healing of your presence. Rosannah?"

"Yes, Alonzo? Oh, how you terrified me! Say on."

"Name the happy day, Rosannah!"

There was a little pause. Then a diffident small voice replied, "I blush— but it is with pleasure, it is with happiness. Would—would you like to have it soon?"

"This very night, Rosannah! Oh, let us risk no more delays. Let it be now!—this very night, this very moment!"

"Oh, you impatient creature! I have nobody here but my good old uncle, a missionary for a generation, and now retired from service,—nobody but him and his wife. I would so dearly like it if your mother and your aunt Susan—"

"*Our* mother and *our* aunt Susan, my Rosannah."

"Yes, *our* mother and *our* aunt Susan,—I am content to word it so if it pleases you; I would so like to have them present."

"So would I. Suppose you telegraph Aunt Susan. How long would it take her to come?"

"The steamer leaves San Francisco day after tomorrow. The passage is eight days. She would be here the 31st of March."

"Then name the 1st of April: do, Rosannah, dear."

"Mercy, it would make us April fools, Alonzo!"

"So we be the happiest ones that that day's sun looks down upon in the whole broad expanse of the globe, why need we care? Call it the 1st of April, dear."

"Then the 1st of April it shall be, with all my heart!"

"Oh, happiness! Name the hour, too, Rosannah."

"I like the morning, it is so blithe. Will eight in the morning do, Alonzo?"

"The loveliest hour in the day,—since it will make you mine."

There was a feeble but frantic sound for some little time, as if wool-lipped, disembodied spirits were exchanging kisses; then Rosannah said, "Excuse me just a moment, dear; I have an appointment, and am called to meet it."

The young girl sought a large parlor and took her place at a window which looked out upon a beautiful scene. To the left one could view the charming Nuuana Valley, fringed with its ruddy flush of tropical flowers and its plumed and graceful cocoa palms; its rising foot-hills clothed in the shining green of lemon, citron, and orange groves; its storied precipice beyond, where the first Kamehameha drove his defeated foes over to their destruction,—a spot that had forgotten its grim history, no doubt, for now it was smiling, as almost always at noonday, under the glowing arches of a succession of rainbows. In front of the window one could see the quaint town, and here and there a picturesque group of dusky natives, enjoying the blistering weather; and far to the right lay the restless ocean, tossing its white mane in the sunshine.

Rosannah stood there, in her filmy white raiment, fanning her flushed and heated face, waiting. A Kanaka boy, clothed in a damaged blue neck-tie and part of a silk hat, thrust his head in at the door, and announced, " 'Frisco *haole!*"

"Show him in," said the girl, straightening herself up and assuming a meaning dignity. Mr. Sidney Algernon Burley entered, clad from head to heel in dazzling snow,—that is to say, in the lightest and whitest of Irish linen. He moved eagerly forward, but the girl made a gesture and gave him a look which checked him suddenly. She said coldly, "I am here, as I promised. I believed your assertions, I yielded to your importunities, and said I would name the day. I name the 1st of April,—eight in the morning. Now go!"

"Oh, my dearest, if the gratitude of a life-time—"

"Not a word. Spare me all sight of you, all communication with you, until that hour. No,—no supplications; I will have it so."

When he was gone, she sank exhausted in a chair, for the long siege of troubles she had undergone had wasted her strength. Presently she said, "What a narrow escape! If the hour appointed had been an hour earlier— Oh, horror, what an escape I have made! And to think I had come to imagine I was loving this beguiling, this truthless, this treacherous monster! Oh, he shall repent his villany!"

Let us now draw this history to a close, for little more needs to be told. On the 2d of the ensuing April, the Honolulu "Advertiser" contained this notice:—

> MARRIED.—In this city, by telephone, yesterday morning, at eight o'clock, by Rev. Nathan Hays, assisted by Rev. Nathaniel Davis, of New York, Mr. Alonzo Fitz Clarence, of Eastport, Maine, U.S., and Miss Rosannah Ethelton, of Portland, Oregon, U.S. Mrs. Susan Howland, of San Francisco, a friend of the bride, was present, she being the guest of the Rev. Mr. Hays and wife, uncle and aunt of the bride. Mr. Sidney Algernon Burley, of San Francisco, was also present, but did not remain till the conclusion of the marriage service. Captain Hawthorne's beautiful yacht, tastefully decorated, was in waiting, and the happy bride and her friends immediately departed on a bridal trip to Lahaina and Haleakala.

The New York papers of the same date contained this notice:—

> MARRIED.—In this city, yesterday, by telephone, at half past two in the morning, by Rev. Nathaniel Davis, assisted by Rev. Nathan Hays, of Honolulu, Mr. Alonzo Fitz Clarence, of Eastport, Maine, and Miss Rosannah Ethelton, of Portland, Oregon. The parents and several friends of the bridegroom were present, and enjoyed a sumptuous breakfast and much festivity until nearly sunrise, and then departed on a bridal trip to the Aquarium, the bridegroom's state of health not admitting of a more extended journey.

Toward the close of that memorable day, Mr. and Mrs. Alonzo Fitz Clarence were buried in sweet converse concerning the pleasures of their several bridal tours, when suddenly the young wife exclaimed: "Oh, Lonny, I forgot! I did what I said I would."

"Did you, dear?"

"Indeed I did. I made *him* the April fool! And I told him so, too! Ah, it was a charming surprise! There he stood, sweltering in a black dress suit, with the mercury leaking out of the top of the thermometer, waiting to be married. You should have seen the look he gave when I whispered it in his ear! Ah, his wickedness cost me many a heartache and many a tear, but the score was all squared up, then. So the vengeful feeling went right out of my heart, and I begged him to stay, and said I forgave him everything. But he wouldn't. He said he would live to be avenged; said he would make our lives a curse to us. But he can't, *can* he, dear?''

''Never in this world, my Rosannah!''

Aunt Susan, the Oregonian grandmother, and the young couple and their Eastport parents, are all happy at this writing, and likely to remain so. Aunt Susan brought the bride from the Islands, accompanied her across our continent, and had the happiness of witnessing the rapturous meeting between an adoring husband and wife who had never seen each other until that moment.

A word about the wretched Burley, whose wicked machinations came so near wrecking the hearts and lives of our poor young friends, will be sufficient. In a murderous attempt to seize a crippled and helpless artisan who he fancied had done him some small offence, he fell into a caldron of boiling oil and expired before he could be extinguished.

The £1,000,000 Bank-Note
& Other New Stories

GIVE ME THE CHANGE, PLEASE.

THE £1,000,000 BANK-NOTE

WHEN I was twenty-seven years old, I was a mining-broker's clerk in San Francisco, and an expert in all the details of stock traffic. I was alone in the world, and had nothing to depend upon but my wits and a clean reputation; but these were setting my feet in the road to eventual fortune, and I was content with the prospect.

My time was my own after the afternoon board, Saturdays, and I was accustomed to put it in on a little sail-boat on the bay. One day I ventured too far, and was carried out to sea. Just at nightfall, when hope was about gone, I was picked up by a small brig which was bound for London. It was a long and stormy voyage, and they made me work my passage without pay, as a common sailor. When I stepped ashore in London my clothes were ragged and shabby, and I had only a dollar in my pocket. This money fed and sheltered me twenty-four hours. During the next twenty-four I went without food and shelter.

About ten o'clock on the following morning, seedy and hungry, I was dragging myself along Portland Place, when a child that was passing, towed by a nursemaid, tossed a luscious big pear—minus one bite—into the gutter. I stopped, of course, and fastened my desiring eye on that muddy treasure. My mouth watered for it, my stomach craved it, my whole being begged for it. But every time I made a move to get it some passing eye detected my purpose, and of course I straightened up, then, and looked indifferent, and pretended that I hadn't been thinking about the pear at all. This same thing kept happening and happening, and I couldn't get the pear. I was just getting desperate enough to brave all the shame, and to seize it, when a window behind me was raised, and a gentleman spoke out of it, saying:

"Step in here, please."

I was admitted by a gorgeous flunkey, and shown into a sumptuous room where a couple of elderly gentlemen were sitting. They sent away the servant, and made me sit down. They had just finished their breakfast, and the sight of the remains of it almost overpowered me. I could hardly keep my wits together in the presence of that food, but as I was not asked to sample it, I had to bear my trouble as best I could.

Now, something had been happening there a little before, which I did not know anything about until a good many days afterward, but I will tell you about it now. Those two old brothers had been having a pretty hot argument a couple of days before, and had ended by agreeing to decide it by a bet, which is the English way of settling everything.

You will remember that the Bank of England once issued two notes of a million pounds each, to be used for a special purpose connected with some public transaction with a foreign country. For some reason or other only one of these had been used and canceled; the other still lay in the vaults of the Bank. Well, the brothers, chatting along, happened to get to wondering what might be the fate of a perfectly honest and intelligent stranger who should be turned adrift in London without a friend, and with no money but that million-pound bank-note, and no way to account for his being in possession of it. Brother A said he would starve to death; Brother B said he wouldn't. Brother A said he couldn't offer it at a bank or anywhere else, because he would be arrested on the spot. So they went on disputing till Brother B said he would bet twenty thousand pounds that the man would live thirty days, *anyway,* on that million, and keep out of jail, too. Brother A took him up. Brother B went down to the Bank and bought that note. Just like an Englishman, you see; pluck to the backbone. Then he dictated a letter, which one of his clerks wrote out in a beautiful round hand, and then the two brothers sat at the window a whole day watching for the right man to give it to.

They saw many honest faces go by that were not intelligent enough; many that were intelligent, but not honest enough; many that were both, but the possessors were not poor enough, or, if poor enough, were not strangers. There was always a defect, until I came along; but they agreed that I filled the bill all around; so they elected me unanimously, and there I was, now, waiting to know why I was called in. They began to ask me questions about myself, and pretty soon they had my story. Finally they told me I would answer their purpose. I said I was sincerely glad, and asked what it was. Then one of them handed me an envelope, and said I would find the explanation inside. I was going to open it, but he said no; take it to my lodgings, and look it over carefully, and not be hasty or rash. I was puzzled, and wanted to discuss the matter a little further, but they didn't; so I took my leave, feeling hurt and insulted to be made the butt of what was apparently some kind of a practical joke, and yet obliged to put up with it, not being in circumstances to resent affronts from rich and strong folk.

I would have picked up the pear, now, and eaten it before all the world, but it was gone; so I had lost that by this unlucky business, and the thought of it did not soften my feeling toward those men. As soon as I was out of sight of that house I opened my envelope, and saw that it contained money! My opinion of those people changed, I can tell you! I lost not a moment, but shoved note and money into my vest-pocket, and broke for the nearest cheap eating-house. Well, how I did eat! When at last I couldn't hold any more, I took out my money and unfolded it, took one glimpse and nearly fainted. Five millions of dollars! Why, it made my head swim.

I must have sat there stunned and blinking at the note as much as a minute before I came rightly to myself again. The first thing I noticed, then, was the landlord. His eye was on the note, and he was petrified. He was worshiping, with all his body and soul, but he looked as if he couldn't stir hand or foot. I took my cue in a moment, and did the only rational thing there was to do. I reached the note toward him, and said carelessly:

"Give me the change, please."

Then he was restored to his normal condition, and made a thousand apologies for not being able to break the bill, and I couldn't get him to touch it. He wanted to look at it, and keep on looking at it; he couldn't seem to get enough of it to quench the thirst of his eye, but he shrank from touching it as if it had been something too sacred for poor common clay to handle. I said:

"I am sorry if it is an inconvenience, but I must insist. Please change it; I haven't anything else."

But he said that wasn't any matter; he was quite willing to let the trifle stand over till another time. I said I might not be in his neighborhood again for a good while; but he said it was of no consequence, he could wait, and, morever, I could have anything I wanted, any time I chose, and let the account run as long as I pleased. He said he hoped he wasn't afraid to trust as rich a gentleman as I was, merely because I was of a merry disposition, and chose to play larks on the public in the matter of dress. By this time another customer was entering, and the landlord hinted to me to put the monster out of sight; then he bowed me all the way to the door, and I started straight for that house and those brothers, to correct the mistake which had been made before the police should hunt me up, and help me do it. I was pretty nervous, in fact pretty badly frightened, though, of course, I was no way in fault; but I knew men well enough to know that when they find they've given a tramp a million-pound bill when they thought it was a one-pounder, they are in a frantic rage against *him* instead of quarreling with their own near-sightedness, as they ought. As I approached the house my excitement began to abate, for all was quiet there, which made me feel pretty sure the blunder was not discovered yet. I rang. The same servant appeared. I asked for those gentlemen.

"They are gone." This in the lofty, cold way of that fellow's tribe.

"Gone? Gone where?"

"On a journey."

"But whereabouts?"

"To the Continent, I think."

"The Continent?"

"Yes, sir."

"Which way—by what route?"

"I can't say, sir."

"When will they be back?"

"In a month, they said."

"A month! Oh, this is awful! Give me *some* sort of idea of how to get a word to them. It's of the last importance."

"I can't, indeed. I've no idea where they've gone, sir."

"Then I must see some member of the family."

"Family's away too; been abroad months—in Egypt and India, I think."

"Man, there's been an immense mistake made. They'll be back before night. Will you tell them I've been here, and that I will keep coming till it's all made right, and they needn't be afraid?"

"I'll tell them, if they come back, but I am not expecting them. They said you would be here in an hour to make inquiries, but I must tell you it's all right, they'll be here on time and expect you.''

So I had to give it up and go away. What a riddle it all was! I was like to lose my mind. They would be here "on time." What could that mean? Oh, the letter would explain, maybe. I had forgotten the letter; I got it out and read it. This is what it said:

> You are an intelligent and honest man, as one may see by your face. We conceive you to be poor and a stranger. Enclosed you will find a sum of money. It is lent to you for thirty days, without interest. Report at this house at the end of that time. I have a bet on you. If I win it you shall have any situation that is in my gift— any, that is, that you shall be able to prove yourself familiar with and competent to fill.

No signature, no address, no date.

Well, here was a coil to be in! You are posted on what had preceded all this, but I was not. It was just a deep, dark puzzle to me. I hadn't the least idea what the game was, nor whether harm was meant me or a kindness. I went into a park, and sat down to try to think it out, and to consider what I had best do.

At the end of an hour, my reasonings had crystallized into this verdict.

Maybe those men mean me well, maybe they mean me ill; no way to decide that—let it go. They've got a game, or a scheme, or an experiment, of some kind on hand; no way to determine what it is—let it go. There's a bet on me; no way to find out what it is—let it go. That disposes of the indeterminable quantities; the remainder of the matter is tangible, solid, and may be classed and labeled with certainty. If I ask the Bank of England to place this bill to the credit of the man it belongs to, they'll do it, for they know him, although I don't; but they will ask me how I came in possession of it, and if I tell the truth, they'll put me in the asylum, naturally, and a lie will land me in jail. The same result would follow if I tried to bank the bill anywhere or to borrow money on it. I have got to carry this immense burden around until those men come back, whether I want to or not. It is useless to me, as useless as a handful of ashes, and yet I must take care of it, and watch over it, while I beg my living. I couldn't *give* it away, if I should try, for neither honest citizen nor high-wayman would accept it or meddle with it for anything. Those brothers are safe. Even if I lose their bill, or burn it, they are still safe, because they can stop payment, and the Bank will make them whole; but mean-time, I've got to do a month's suffering without wages or profit—unless I help win that bet, whatever it may be, and get that situation that I am promised. I *should* like to get that; men of their sort have situations in their gift that are worth having.

I got to thinking a good deal about that situation. My hopes began to rise high. Without doubt the salary would be large. It would begin in a month; after that I should be all right. Pretty soon I was feeling first rate. By this time I was tramping the streets again. The sight of a tailor-shop gave me a sharp longing to shed my rags, and to clothe myself decently once more. Could I afford it? No; I had nothing in the world but a million pounds. So I forced myself to go on by. But soon I was drifting back again. The temptation persecuted me cruelly. I must have passed that shop back and forth six times during that manful struggle. At last I gave in; I had to. I asked if they had a misfit suit that had been thrown on their hands. The fellow I spoke to nodded his head toward another fellow, and gave me no answer. I went to the indicated fellow, and he indicated another fellow with *his* head, and no words. I went to him, and he said:

"'Tend to you presently."

I waited till he was done with what he was at, then he took me into a back room, and overhauled a pile of rejected suits, and selected the rattiest one for me. I put it on. It didn't fit, and wasn't in any way attractive, but it was new, and I was anxious to have it; so I didn't find any fault, but said with some diffidence:

"It would be an accommodation to me if you could wait some days for the money. I haven't any small change about me."

The fellow worked up a most sarcastic expression of countenance, and said:

"Oh, you haven't? Well, of course, I didn't expect it. I'd only expect gentlemen like you to carry large change."

I was nettled, and said:

"My friend, you shouldn't judge a stranger always by the clothes he wears. I am quite able to pay for this suit; I simply didn't wish to put you to the trouble of changing a large note."

He modified his style a little at that, and said, though still with something of an air:

"I didn't mean any particular harm, but as long as rebukes are going, I might say it wasn't quite your affair to jump to the conclusion that we couldn't change any note that you might happen to be carrying around. On the contrary, we *can*."

I handed the note to him, and said:

"Oh, very well; I apologize."

He received it with a smile, one of those large smiles which goes all around over, and has folds in it, and wrinkles, and spirals, and looks like the place where you have thrown a brick in a pond; and then in the act of his taking a glimpse of the bill this smile froze solid, and turned yellow, and looked like those wavy, wormy spreads of lava which you find hardened on little levels on the side of Vesuvius. I never before saw a smile caught like that, and perpetuated. The man stood there holding the bill, and looking like that, and the proprietor hustled up to see what was the matter, and said briskly:

"Well, what's up? what's the trouble? what's wanting?"

I said: "There isn't any trouble. I'm waiting for my change."

"Come, come; get him his change, Tod; get him his change."

Tod retorted: "Get him his change! It's easy to say, sir; but look at the bill yourself."

The proprietor took a look, gave a low, eloquent whistle, then made a dive for the pile of rejected clothing, and began to snatch it this way and that, talking all the time excitedly, and as if to himself:

"Sell an eccentric millionaire such an unspeakable suit as that! Tod's a fool—a born fool. Always doing something like this. Drives every millionaire away from this place, because he can't tell a millionaire from a tramp, and never could. Ah, here's the thing I'm after. Please get those things off, sir, and throw them in the fire. Do me the favor to put on this shirt and this suit; it's just the thing, the very thing—plain, rich, modest, and just ducally nobby; made to order for a foreign prince—you may know him, sir, his Serene Highness the Hospodar of Halifax; had to leave it with us and take a mourning-suit because his mother was going to die—which she didn't. But that' all right; we can't always have things the way we—that is, the way they—there! trousers all right, they fit you to a charm, sir; now the waistcoat; aha, right again! now the coat—lord! look at that, now! Perfect—the whole thing! I never saw such a triumph in all my experience.''

I expressed my satisfaction.

"Quite right, sir, quite right; it'll do for a makeshift, I'm bound to say. But wait till you see what we'll get up for you on your own measure. Come, Tod, book and pen; get at it. Length of leg, 32″—and so on. Before I could get in a word he had measured me, and was giving orders for dress-suits, morning suits, shirts, and all sorts of things. When I got a chance I said:

"But, my dear sir, I *can't* give these orders, unless you can wait indefinitely, or change the bill.''

"Indefinitely! It's a weak word, sir, a weak word. Eternally—*that's* the word, sir. Tod, rush these things through, and send them to the gentleman's address without any waste of time. Let the minor customers wait. Set down the gentleman's address and—''

"I'm changing my quarters. I will drop in and leave the new address.''

"Quite right, sir, quite right. One moment—let me show you out, sir. There—good day, sir, good day.''

Well, don't you see what was bound to happen? I drifted naturally into buying whatever I wanted, and asking for change. Within a week I was sumptuously equipped with all needful comforts and luxuries, and was housed in an expensive private hotel in Hanover Square. I took my dinners there, but for breakfast I stuck by Harris's humble feedinghouse, where I had got my first meal on my million-pound bill. I was the making of Harris. The fact had gone all abroad that the foreign crank who carried million-pound bills in his vest-pocket was the patron saint of the place. That was enough. From being a poor, struggling, little hand-to-mouth enterprise, it had become celebrated, and overcrowded with customers. Harris was so grateful that he forced loans upon me, and would not be denied; and so, pauper as I was, I had money to spend, and was living like the rich and the great. I judged that there was going to be a crash by and by, but I was in, now, and must swim across or drown. You see there was just that element of impending disaster to give a serious side, a sober side, yes, a tragic side, to a state of things which would otherwise have been purely ridiculous. In the night, in the dark, the tragedy part was always to the front, and always warning, always threatening; and so I moaned and tossed, and sleep was hard to find. But in the cheerful daylight the tragedy element faded out and disappeared, and I walked on air, and was happy to giddiness, to intoxication, you may say.

And it was natural; for I had become one of the notorieties of the metropolis of the world, and it turned my head, not just a little, but a good deal. You could not take up a newspaper, English, Scotch, or Irish, without finding in it one or more references to the "vest-pocket million-pounder" and his latest doings and sayings. At first, in these mentions, I was at the bottom of the personal-gossip column; next, I was listed above the knights, next above the baronets, next above the barons, and so on, and so on, climbing steadily, as my notoriety augmented, until I reached the highest altitude possible, and there I remained, taking precedence of all dukes not royal, and of all ecclesiastics except the primate of all England. But mind, this was not fame; as yet I had achieved only notoriety. Then came the climaxing stroke—the accolade, so to speak—which in a single instance transmuted the perishable dross of notoriety into the enduring gold of fame: "Punch" caricatured me! Yes, I was a made man, now; my place was established. I might be joked about still, but reverently, not hilariously, not rudely; I could be smiled at, but not laughed at. The time for that had gone by. "Punch" pictured me all a-flutter with rags, dickering with a beef-eater for the Tower of London. Well, you can imagine how it was with a young fellow who had never been taken notice of before, and now all of a sudden couldn't say a thing that wasn't taken up and repeated everywhere; couldn't stir abroad without constantly overhearing the remark flying from lip to lip, "There he goes; that's him!" couldn't take his breakfast without a crowd to look on; couldn't appear in an opera-box without concentrating there the fire of a thousand lorgnettes. Why, I just swam in glory all day long—that is the amount of it.

You know, I even kept my old suit of rags, and every now and then appeared in them, so as to have the old pleasure of buying trifles, and being insulted, and then shooting the scoffer dead with the million-pound bill. But I couldn't keep that up. The illustrated papers made the outfit so familiar that when I went out in it I was at once recognized and followed by a crowd, and if I attempted a purchase the man would offer me his whole shop on credit before I could pull my note on him.

About the tenth day of my fame I went to fulfill my duty to my flag by paying my respects to the American minister. He received me with the enthusiasm proper in my case, upbraided me for being so tardy in my duty, and said that there was only one way to get his forgiveness, and that was to take the seat at his dinner-party that night made vacant by the illness of one of his guests. I said I would, and we got to talking. It turned out that he and my father had been schoolmates in boyhood, Yale students together later, and always warm friends up to my father's death. So then he required me to put in at his house all the odd time I might have to spare, and I was very willing, of course.

In fact I was more than willing; I was glad. When the crash should come, he might somehow be able to save me from total destruction; I didn't know how, but he might think of a way, maybe. I couldn't venture to unbosom myself to him at this late date, a thing which I would have been quick to do in the beginning of this awful career of mine in London. No, I couldn't venture it now; I was in too deep; that is, too deep for me to be risking revelations to so new a friend, though not clear beyond my depth, as *I* looked at it. Because, you see, with all my borrowing, I was carefully keeping within my means—I mean within my salary. Of course I couldn't *know* what my salary was going to be, but I had a good enough

basis for an estimate in the fact that, if I won the bet, I was to have *choice*
of any situation in that rich old gentleman's gift provided I was competent—and I should certainly prove competent; I hadn't any doubt about
that. And as to the bet, I wasn't worrying about that; I had always been
lucky. Now my estimate of the salary was six hundred to a thousand a
year; say, six hundred for the first year, and so on up year by year, till I
struck the upper figure by proved merit. At present I was only in debt for
my first year's salary. Everybody had been trying to lend me money, but I
had fought off the most of them on one pretext or another; so this indebt-
edness represented only £300 borrowed money, the other £300 represented
my keep and my purchases. I believed my second year's salary would
carry me through the rest of the month if I went on being cautious and
economical, and I intended to look sharply out for that. My month ended,
my employer back from his journey, I should be all right once more, for I
should at once divide the two years' salary among my creditors by assign-
ment, and get right down to my work.

It was a lovely dinner-party of fourteen. The Duke and Duchess of
Shoreditch, and their daughter the Lady Anne-Grace-Eleanor-Celeste-and-
so-forth-and-so-forth-de-Bohun, the Earl and Countess of Newgate, Viscount Cheapside, Lord and Lady Blatherskite, some untitled people of
both sexes, the minister and his wife and daughter, and his daughter's
visiting friend, an English girl of twenty-two, named Portia Langham,
whom I fell in love with in two minutes, and she with me—I could see it
without glasses. There was still another guest, an American—but I am a
little ahead of my story. While the people were still in the drawing-room,
whetting up for dinner, and coldly inspecting the late comers, the servant
announced:

"Mr. Lloyd Hastings."

The moment the usual civilities were over, Hastings caught sight of me,
and came straight with cordially outstretched hand; then stopped short
when about to shake, and said with an embarrassed look:

"I beg your pardon, sir, I thought I knew you."

"Why, you do know me, old fellow."

"No! Are *you* the—the—"

"Vest-pocket monster? I am, indeed. Don't be afraid to call me by my
nickname; I'm used to it."

"Well, well, well, this is a surprise. Once or twice I've seen your own
name coupled with the nickname, but it never occurred to me that *you*
could be the Henry Adams referred to. Why, it isn't six months since you
were clerking away for Blake Hopkins in Frisco on a salary, and sitting up
nights on an extra allowance, helping me arrange and verify the Gould
and Curry Extension papers and statistics. The idea of your being in
London, and a vast millionaire, and a colossal celebrity! Why, it's the
Arabian Nights come again. Man, I can't take it in at all; can't realize it;
give me time to settle the whirl in my head."

"The fact is, Lloyd, you are no worse off than I am. I can't realize it
myself."

"Dear me, it *is* stunning, now isn't it? Why, it's just three months to-
day since we went to the Miners' restaurant—"

"No; the What Cheer."

"Right, it *was* the What Cheer; went there at two in the morning, and had a chop and coffee after a hard six hours' grind over those Extension papers, and I tried to persuade you to come to London with me, and offered to get leave of absence for you and pay all your expenses, and give you something over if I succeeded in making the sale; and you would not listen to me, said I wouldn't succeed, and you couldn't afford to lose the run of business and be no end of time getting the hang of things again when you got back home. And yet here you are. How odd it all is! How did you happen to come, and whatever *did* give you this incredible start?"

"Oh, just an accident. It 's a long story—a romance, a body may say. I'll tell you all about it, but not now."

"When?"

"The end of this month."

"That's more than a fortnight yet. It's too much of a strain on a person's curiosity. Make it a week."

"I can't. You'll know why, by and by. But how's the trade getting along?"

His cheerfulness vanished like a breath, and he said with a sigh:

"You were a true prophet, Hal, a true prophet. I wish I hadn't come. I don't want to talk about it."

"But you must. You must come and stop with me to-night, when we leave here, and tell me all about it."

"Oh, may I? Are you in earnest?" and the water showed in his eyes.

"Yes; I want to hear the whole story, every word."

"I'm so grateful! Just find a human interest once more, in some voice and in some eye, in me and affairs of mine, after what I've been through here—lord! I could go down on my knees for it!"

He gripped my hand hard, and braced up, and was all right and lively after that for the dinner—which didn't come off. No; the usual thing happened, the thing that is always happening under that vicious and aggravating English system—the matter of precedence couldn't be settled, and so there was no dinner. Englishmen always eat dinner before they go out to dinner, because *they* know the risks they are running; but nobody ever warns the stranger, and so he walks placidly into the trap. Of course nobody was hurt this time, because we had all been to dinner, none of us being novices except Hastings, and he having been informed by the minister at the time that he invited him that in deference to the English custom he had not provided any dinner. Everybody took a lady and processioned down to the dining-room, because it is usual to go through the motions; but there the dispute began. The Duke of Shoreditch wanted to take precedence, and sit at the head of the table, holding that he outranked a minister who represented merely a nation and not a monarch; but I stood for my rights, and refused to yield. In the gossip column I ranked all dukes not royal, and said so, and claimed precedence of this one. It couldn't be settled, of course, struggle as we might and did, he finally (and injudiciously) trying to play birth and antiquity, and I "seeing" his Conqueror and "raising" him with Adam, whose direct posterity I was, as shown by my name, while *he* was of a collateral branch, as shown by *his*, and by his recent Norman origin; so we all processioned back to the drawing-room again and had a perpendicular lunch—plate of sardines and a strawberry, and you group yourself and stand up and eat it. Here the religion of precedence is not so strenuous; the two persons of highest rank chuck up a shilling, the one that wins has first go at his strawberry, and the loser gets the shilling. The next two chuck up, then the next two, and so on. After refreshment, tables were brought, and we all played cribbage, six-pence a game. The English never play any game for amusement. If they can't make something or lose something,—they don't care which,—they won't play.

We had a lovely time; certainly two of us had, Miss Langham and I. I was so bewitched with her that I couldn't count my hands if they went above a double sequence; and when I struck home I never discovered it, and started up the outside row again, and would have lost the game every time, only the girl did the same, she being in just my condition, you see; and consequently neither of us ever got out, or cared to wonder why we didn't; we only just knew we were happy, and didn't wish to know any-thing else, and didn't want to be interrupted. And I *told* her—I did indeed—told her I loved her; and she—well, she blushed till her hair turned red, but she liked it; she *said* she did. Oh, there was never such an evening! Every time I pegged I put on a postscript; every time she pegged she acknowledged receipt of it, counting the hands the same. Why, I couldn't even say "Two for his heels" without adding, "*My*, how sweet you do look!" and she would say, "Fifteen two, fifteen four, fifteen six, and a pair are eight, and eight are sixteen—*do* you think so?"—peeping out aslant from under her lashes, you know, so sweet and cunning. Oh, it was just *too*-too!

Well, I was perfectly honest and square with her; told her I hadn't a cent in the world but just the million-pound note she'd heard so much talk about, and *it* didn't belong to me; and that started her curiosity, and then I talked low, and told her the whole history right from the start, and it nearly killed her, laughing. What in the nation she could find to laugh about, *I* couldn't see, but there it was; every half minute some new detail would fetch her, and I would have to stop as much as a minute and a half to give her a chance to settle down again. Why, she laughed herself lame, she did indeed; I never saw anything like it. I mean I never saw a painful story—a story of a person's troubles and worries and fears—produce just *that* kind of effect before. So I loved her all the more, seeing she could be so cheerful when there wasn't anything to be cheerful about; for I might soon need that kind of wife, you know, the way things looked. Of course I told her we should have to wait a couple of years, till I could catch up on my salary; but she didn't mind that, only she hoped I would be as careful as possible in the matter of expenses, and not let them run the least risk of trenching on our third year's pay. Then she began to get a little worried, and wondered if we were making any mistake, and starting the salary on a higher figure for the first year than I would get. This was good sense, and it made me feel a little less confident than I had been feeling before; but it gave me a good business idea, and I brought it frankly out.

"Portia, dear, would you mind going with me that day, when I confront those old gentlemen?"

She shrank a little, but said:

"N-o; if my being with you would help hearten you. But—would it be quite proper, do you think?"

"No, I don't know that it would; in fact I'm afraid it wouldn't: but you see, there's so *much* dependent upon it that—"

"Then I'll go anyway, proper or improper," she said, with a beautiful and generous enthusiasm. "Oh, I shall be so happy to think I'm helping."

"Helping, dear? Why, you'll be doing it all. You're so beautiful and so lovely and so winning, that with you there I can pile our salary up till I break those good old fellows, and they'll never have the heart to struggle."

Sho! you should have seen the rich blood mount, and her happy eyes shine!

"You wicked flatterer! There isn't a word of truth in what you say, but still I'll go with you. Maybe it will teach you not to expect other people to look with your eyes."

Were my doubts dissipated? Was my confidence restored? You may judge by this fact: privately I raised my salary to twelve hundred the first year on the spot. But I didn't tell her; I saved it for a surprise.

All the way home I was in the clouds, Hastings talking, I not hearing a word. When he and I entered my parlor, he brought me to myself with his fervent appreciations of my manifold comforts and luxuries.

"Let me just stand here a little and look my fill! Dear me, it's a palace; it's just a palace! And in it everything a body *could* desire, including cozy coal fire and supper standing ready. Henry, it doesn't merely make me realize how rich you are; it makes me realize, to the bone, to the marrow, how poor I am—how poor I am, and how miserable, how defeated, routed, annihilated!"

Plague take it! this language gave me the cold shudders. It scared me broad awake, and made me comprehend that I was standing on a half-inch crust, with a crater underneath. *I* didn't know I had been dreaming—that is, I hadn't been allowing myself to know it for a while back; but *now*—oh, dear! Deep in debt, not a cent in the world, a lovely girl's happiness or woe in my hands, and nothing in front of me but a salary which might never—oh, *would* never—materialize! Oh, oh, oh, I am ruined past hope; nothing can save me!

"Henry, the mere unconsidered drippings of your daily income would—"

"Oh, my daily income! Here, down with this hot Scotch, and cheer up your soul. Here's with you! Or, no—you're hungry; sit down and—"

"Not a bite for me; I'm past it. I can't eat, these days; but I'll drink with you till I drop. Come!"

"Barrel for barrel, I'm with you! Ready? Here we go! Now, then, Lloyd, unreel your story while I brew."

"Unreel it? What, again?"

"Again? What do you mean by that?"

"Why, I mean do you want to hear it *over* again?"

"Do I want to hear it *over* again? This *is* a puzzler. Wait; don't take any more of that liquid. You don't need it."

"Look here, Henry, you alarm me. Didn't I tell you the whole story on the way here?"

"You?"

"Yes, I."

"I'll be hanged if I heard a word of it."

"Henry, this is a serious thing. It troubles me. What did you take up yonder at the minister's?"

Then it all flashed on me, and I owned up, like a man.

"I took the dearest girl in this world—prisoner!"

So then he came with a rush, and we shook, and shook, and shook till our hands ached; and he didn't blame me for not having heard a word of a story which had lasted while we walked three miles. He just sat down then, like the patient, good fellow he was, and told it all over again. Synopsized, it amounted to this: He had come to England with what he thought was a grand opportunity; he had an "option" to sell the Gould and Curry Extension for the "locators" of it, and keep all he could get over a million dollars. He had worked hard, had pulled every wire he knew of, had left no honest expedient untried, had spent nearly all the money he had in the world, had not been able to get a solitary capitalist to listen to him, and his option would run out at the end of the month. In a word, he was ruined. Then he jumped up and cried out:

"Henry, you can save me! You can save me, and you're the only man in the universe that can. Will you do it? *Won't* you do it?"

"Tell me how. Speak out, my boy."

"Give me a million and my passage home for my 'option'! Don't, *don't* refuse!"

I was in a kind of agony. I was right on the point of coming out with the words, "Lloyd, I'm a pauper myself—absolutely penniless, and in *debt!*" But a white-hot idea came flaming through my head, and I gripped my jaws together, and calmed myself down till I was as cold as a capitalist. Then I said, in a commercial and self-possessed way:

"I will save you, Lloyd—"

"Then I'm already saved! God be merciful to you forever! If ever I—"

"Let me finish, Lloyd. I will save you, but not in that way; for that would not be fair to you, after your hard work, and the risks you've run. I don't need to buy mines; I can keep my capital moving, in a commercial center like London without that; it's what I'm at, all the time; but here is what I'll do. I know all about that mine, of course; I know its immense value, and can swear to it if anybody wishes it. You shall sell out inside of the fortnight for three millions cash, using my name freely, and we'll divide, share and share alike."

Do you know, he would have danced the furniture to kindling-wood in his insane joy, and broken everything on the place, if I hadn't tripped him up and tied him.

Then he lay there, perfectly happy, saying:

"I may use your name! Your name—think of it! Man, they'll flock in droves, these rich Londoners; they'll *fight* for that stock! I'm a made man, I'm a made man forever, and I'll never forget you as long as I live!"

In less than twenty-four hours London was abuzz! I hadn't anything to do, day after day, but sit at home, and say to all comers:

"Yes; I told him to refer to me. I know the man, and I know the mine. His character is above reproach, and the mine is worth far more than he asks for it."

Meantime I spent all my evenings at the minister's with Portia. I didn't say a word to her about the mine; I saved it for a surprise. We talked salary; never anything but salary and love; sometimes love, sometimes salary, sometimes love and salary together. And my! the interest the minister's wife and daughter took in our little affair, and the endless ingenuities they invented to save us from interruption, and to keep the minister in the dark and unsuspicious—well, it was just lovely of them!

When the month was up, at last, I had a million dollars to my credit in the London and County Bank, and Hastings was fixed in the same way. Dressed at my level best, I drove by the house in Portland Place, judged by the look of things that my birds were home again, went on toward the minister's and got my precious, and we started back, talking salary with all our might. She was so excited and anxious that it made her just intolerably beautiful. I said:

"Dearie, the way you're looking it's a crime to strike for a salary a single penny under three thousand a year."

"Henry, Henry, you'll ruin us!"

"Don't you be afraid. Just keep up those looks, and trust to me. It'll all come out right."

So as it turned out, I had to keep bolstering up *her* courage all the way. She kept pleading with me, and saying:

"Oh, please remember that if we ask for too much we may get no salary at all; and then what will become of us, with no way in the world to earn our living?"

We were ushered in by that same servant, and there they were, the two old gentlemen. Of course they were surprised to see that wonderful creature with me, but I said:

"It's all right, gentlemen; she is my future stay and helpmate."

And I introduced them to her, and called them by name. It didn't surprise them; they knew I would know enough to consult the directory. They seated us, and were very polite to me, and very solicitous to relieve her from embarrassment, and put her as much at her ease as they could. Then I said:

"Gentlemen, I am ready to report."

"We are glad to hear it," said *my* man, "for now we can decide the bet which my brother Abel and I made. If you have won for me, you shall have any situation in my gift. Have you the million-pound note?"

"Here it is, sir," and I handed it to him.

"I've won!" he shouted, and slapped Abel on the back. "*Now* what do you say, brother?"

"I say he *did* survive, and I've lost twenty thousand pounds. I never would have believed it."

"I've a further report to make," I said, "and a pretty long one. I want you to let me come soon, and detail my whole month's history; and I promise you it's worth hearing. Meantime, take a look at that."

"What, man! Certificate of deposit for £200,000? Is it yours?"

"Mine. I earned it by thirty days' judicious use of that little loan you let me have. And the only use I made of it was to buy trifles and offer the bill in change."

"Come, this is astonishing! It's incredible, man!"

"Never mind, I'll prove it. Don't take my word unsupported."

But now Portia's turn was come to be surprised. Her eyes were spread wide, and she said:

"Henry, is that really your money? Have you been fibbing to me?"

"I have indeed, dearie. But you'll forgive me, *I* know."

She put up an arch pout, and said:

"Don't you be so sure. You are a naughty thing to deceive me so!"

"Oh, you'll get over it, sweetheart, you'll get over it; it was only fun, you know. Come, let's be going."

"But wait, wait! The situation, you know. I want to give you the situation," said my man.

"Well," I said, 'I'm just as grateful as I can be, but really I don't want one."

"But you can have the very choicest one in my gift."

"Thanks again, with all my heart; but I don't even want *that* one."

"Henry, I'm ashamed of you. You don't half thank the good gentleman. May I do if for you?"

"Indeed you shall, dear, if you can improve it. Let us see you try."

She walked to my man, got up in his lap, put her arm round his neck, and kissed him right on the mouth. Then the two old gentlemen shouted with laughter, but I was dumbfounded, just petrified, as you may say. Portia said:

"Papa, he has said you haven't a situation in your gift that he'd take; and I feel just as hurt as—"

"My darling! is that your papa?"

"Yes; he's my steppapa, and the dearest one that ever was. You understand now, don't you, why I was able to laugh when you told me at the minister's, not knowing my relationships, what trouble and worry papa's and Uncle Abel's scheme was giving you?"

Of course I spoke right up, now, without any fooling, and went straight to the point.

"Oh, my dearest dear sir, I want to take back what I said. You *have* got a situation open that I want."

"Name it."

"Son-in-law."

"Well, well, well! But you know, if you haven't ever served in that capacity, you of course can't furnish recommendations of a sort to satisfy the conditions of the contract, and so—"

"Try me—oh, do, I beg of you! Only just try me thirty or forty years, and if—"

"Oh, well, all right; it's but a little thing to ask. Take her along."

Happy, we two? There are not words enough in the unabridged to describe it. And when London got the whole history, a day or two later, of my month's adventures with that bank-note, and how they ended, did London talk, and have a good time? Yes.

My Portia's papa took that friendly and hospitable bill back to the Bank of England and cashed it; then the Bank canceled it and made him a present of it, and he gave it to us at our wedding, and it has always hung in its frame in the sacredest place in our home, ever since. For it gave me my Portia. But for it I could not have remained in London, would not have appeared at the minister's, never should have met her. And so I always say, "Yes, it's a million-pounder, as you see; but it never made but one purchase in its life, and *then* got the article for only about a tenth part of its value."

MENTAL TELEGRAPHY

A MANUSCRIPT WITH A HISTORY

NOTE TO THE EDITOR.—By glancing over the enclosed bundle of rusty old manuscript, you will perceive that I once made a great discovery: the discovery that certain sorts of things which, from the beginning of the world, had always been regarded as merely "curious coincidences"—that is to say, accidents—were no more accidental than is the sending and receiving of a telegram an accident. I made this discovery sixteen or seventeen years ago, and gave it a name—"Mental Telegraphy." It is the same thing around the outer edges of which the Psychical Society of England began to grope (and play with) four or five years ago, and which they named "Telepathy." Within the last two or three years they have penetrated toward the heart of the matter, however, and have found out that mind can act upon mind in a quite detailed and elaborate way over vast stretches of land and water. And they have succeeded in doing, by their great credit and influence, what I could never have done—they have convinced the world that mental telegraphy is not a jest, but a fact, and that it is a thing not rare, but exceedingly common. They have done our age a service—and a very great service, I think.

In this old manuscript you will find mention of an extraordinary experience of mine in the mental telegraphic line, of date about the year 1874 or 1875—the one concerning the Great Bonanza book. It was this experience that called my attention to the matter under consideration. I began to keep a record, after that, of such experiences of mine as seemed explicable by the theory that minds telegraph thoughts to each other. In 1878 I went to Germany and began to write the book called *A Tramp Abroad*. The bulk of this old batch of manuscript was written at that time and for that book. But I removed it when I came to revise the volume for the press; for I feared that the public would treat the thing as a joke and throw it aside, whereas I was in earnest.

At home, eight or ten years ago, I tried to creep in under shelter of an authority grave enough to protect the article from ridicule—

the *North American Review*. But Mr. Metcalf was too wary for me. He said that to treat these mere "coincidences" seriously was a thing which the *Review* couldn't dare to do; that I must put either my name or my *nom de plume* to the article, and thus save the *Review* from harm. But I couldn't consent to that; it would be the surest possible way to defeat my desire that the public should receive the thing seriously, and be willing to stop and give it some fair degree of attention. So I pigeonholed the MS., because I could not get it published anonymously.

Now see how the world has moved since then. These small experiences of mine, which were too formidable at that time for admission to a grave magazine—if the magazine must allow them to appear as something above and beyond "accidents" and "coincidences"—are trifling and commonplace now, since the flood of light recently cast upon mental telegraphy by the intelligent labors of the Psychical Society. But I think they are worth publishing, just to show what harmless and ordinary matters were considered dangerous and incredible eight or ten years ago.

As I have said, the bulk of this old manuscript was written in 1878; a later part was written from time to time two, three, and four years afterward. The "Postscript" I add to-day.

MAY, '78. —Another of those apparently trifling things has happened to me which puzzle and perplex all men every now and then, keep them thinking an hour or two, and leave their minds barren of explanation or solution at last. Here it is—and it looks inconsequential enough, I am obliged to say. A few days ago I said: "It must be that Frank Millet doesn't know we are in Germany, or he would have written long before this. I have been on the point of dropping him a line at least a dozen times during the past six weeks, but I always decided to wait a day or two longer, and see if we shouldn't hear from him. But now I *will* write." And so I did. I directed the letter to Paris, and thought, "*Now* we shall hear from him before this letter is fifty miles from Heidelberg—it always happens so."

True enough; but *why* should it? That is the puzzling part of it. We are always talking about letters "crossing" each other, for that is one of the very commonest accidents of this life. We call it "accident," but perhaps we misname it. We have the instinct a dozen times a year that the letter we are writing is going to "cross" the other person's letter; and if the reader will rack his memory a little he will recall the fact that this presentiment had strength enough to it to make him cut his letter down to a decided briefness, because it would be a waste of time to write a letter which was going to "cross," and hence be a useless letter. I think that in my experience this instinct has generally come to me in cases where I had put off my letter a good while in the hope that the other person would write.

Yes, as I was saying, I had waited five or six weeks; then I wrote but three lines, because I felt and seemed to know that a letter from Millet would cross mine. And so it did. He wrote the same day that I wrote. The letters crossed each other. His letter went to Berlin, care of the American minister, who sent it to me. In this letter Millet said he had been trying for six weeks to stumble upon somebody who knew my German address, and at last the idea had occurred to him that a letter sent to the care of the embassy at Berlin might possibly find me.

Maybe it was an "accident" that he finally determined to write me at the same moment that I finally determined to write him, but I think not.

With me the most irritating thing has been to wait a tedious time in a purely business matter, hoping that the other party will do the writing, and then sit down and do it myself, perfectly satisfied that that other man is sitting down at the same moment to write a letter which will "cross" mine. And yet one must go on writing, just the same; because if you get up from your table and postpone, that other man will do the same thing, exactly as if you two were harnessed together like the Siamese twins, and must duplicate each other's movements.

Several months before I left home a New York firm did some work about the house for me, and did not make a success of it, as it seemed to me. When the bill came, I wrote and said I wanted the work perfected before I paid. They replied that they were very busy, but that as soon as they could spare the proper man the thing should be done. I waited more than two months, enduring as patiently as possible the companionship of bells which would fire away of their own accord sometimes when nobody was touching them, and at other times wouldn't ring though you struck the button with a sledgehammer. Many a time I got ready to write and then postponed it; but at last I sat down one evening and poured out my grief to the extent of a page or so, and then cut my letter suddenly short, because a strong instinct told me that the firm had begun to move in the matter. When I came down to breakfast next morning the postman had not yet taken my letter away, but the electrical man had been there, done his work, and was gone again! He had received his orders the previous evening from his employers, and had come up by the night train.

If that was an "accident," it took about three months to get it up in good shape.

One evening last summer I arrived in Washington, registered at the Arlington Hotel, and went to my room. I read and smoked until ten o'clock; then, finding I was not yet sleepy, I thought I would take a breath of fresh air. So I went forth in the rain, and tramped through one street after another in an aimless and enjoyable way. I knew that Mr. O——, a friend of mine, was in town, and I wished I might run across him; but I did not propose to hunt for him at midnight, especially as I did not know where he was stopping. Toward twelve o'clock the streets had become so deserted that I felt lonesome; so I stepped into a cigar shop far up the Avenue, and remained there fifteen minutes, listening to some bummers discussing national politics. Suddenly the spirit of prophecy came upon me, and I said to myself, "Now I will go out at this door, turn to the left, walk ten steps, and meet Mr. O—— face to face." I did it, too! I could not see his face, because he had an umbrella before it, and it was pretty dark anyhow, but he interrupted the man he was walking and talking with, and I recognized his voice and stopped him.

That I should step out there and stumble upon Mr. O—— was nothing, but that I should know beforehand that I was going to do it was a good deal. It is a very curious thing when you come to look at it. I stood far within the cigar shop when I delivered my prophecy; I walked about five steps to the door, opened it, closed it after me, walked down a flight of three steps to the sidewalk, then turned to the left and walked four or five more, and found my man. I repeat that in itself the thing was nothing; but to know it would happen so *beforehand,* wasn't that really curious?

I have criticised absent people so often, and then discovered, to my humiliation, that I was talking with their relatives, that I have grown superstitious about that sort of thing and dropped it. How like an idiot one feels after a blunder like that!

We are always mentioning people, and in that very instant they appear before us. We laugh, and say, "Speak of the devil," and so forth, and there we drop it, considering it an "accident." It is a cheap and convenient way of disposing of a grave and very puzzling mystery. The fact is it does seem to happen too often to be an accident.

Now I come to the oddest thing that ever happened to me. Two or three years ago I was lying in bed, idly musing, one morning—it was the 2d of March—when suddenly a red-hot new idea came whistling down into my camp, and exploded with such comprehensive effectiveness as to sweep the vicinity clean of rubbishy reflections, and fill the air with their dust and flying fragments. This idea, stated in simple phrase, was that the time was ripe and the market ready for a certain book; a book which ought to be written at once; a book which must command attention and be of peculiar interest—to wit, a book about the Nevada silver mines. The "Great Bonanza" was a new wonder then, and everybody was talking about it. It seemed to me that the person best qualified to write this book was Mr. William H. Wright, a journalist of Virginia, Nevada, by whose side I had scribbled many months when I was a reporter there ten or twelve years before. He might be alive still; he might be dead; I could not tell; but I would write him, anyway. I began by merely and modestly suggesting that he make such a book; but my interest grew as I went on, and I ventured to map out what I thought ought to be the plan of the work, he being an old friend, and not given to taking good intentions for ill. I even dealt with details, and suggested the order and sequence which they should follow. I was about to put the manuscript in an envelope, when the thought occurred to me that if this book should be written at my suggestion, and then no publisher happened to want it, I should feel uncomfortable; so I concluded to keep my letter back until I should have secured a publisher. I pigeonholed my document, and dropped a note to my own publisher, asking him to name a day for a business consultation. He was out of town on a far journey. My note remained unanswered, and at the end of three or four days the whole matter had passed out of my mind. On the 9th of March the postman brought three or four letters, and among them a thick one whose superscription was in a hand which seemed dimly familiar to me. I could not "place" it at first, but presently I succeeded. Then I said to a visiting relative who was present:

"Now I will do a miracle. I will tell you everything this letter contains—date, signature, and all—without breaking the seal. It is from a Mr. Wright, of Virginia, Nevada, and is dated the 2d of March—seven days ago. Mr. Wright proposes to make a book about the silver mines and the Great Bonanza, and asks what I, as a friend, think of the idea. He says his subjects are to be so and so, their order and sequence so and so, and he will close with a history of the chief feature of the book, the Great Bonanza.''

I opened the letter, and showed that I had stated the date and the contents correctly. Mr. Wright's letter simply contained what my own letter, written on the same date, contained, and mine still lay in its pigeonhole, where it had been lying during the seven days since it was written.

There was no clairvoyance about this, if I rightly comprehend what clairvoyance is. I think the clairvoyant professes to actually *see* concealed writing, and read it off word for word. This was not my case. I only seemed to know, and to know absolutely, the contents of the letter in detail and due order, but I had to *word* them myself. I translated them, so to speak, out of Wright's language into my own.

Wright's letter and the one which I had written to him but never sent were in substance the same.

Necessarily this could not come by accident; such elaborate accidents cannot happen. Chance might have duplicated one or two of the details, but she would have broken down on the rest. I could not doubt—there was no tenable reason for doubting—that Mr. Wright's mind and mine had been in close and crystal-clear communication with each other across three thousand miles of mountain and desert on the morning of the 2d of March. I did not consider that both minds *originated* that succession of ideas, but that one mind originated them, and simply telegraphed them to the other. I was curious to know which brain was the telegrapher and which the receiver, so I wrote and asked for particulars. Mr. Wright's reply showed that his mind had done the originating and telegraphing and mine the receiving. Mark that significant thing, now; consider for a moment how many a splendid "original" idea has been unconsciously stolen from a man three thousand miles away! If one should question that this is so, let him look into the cyclopedia and con once more that curious thing in the history of inventions which has puzzled everyone so much—that is, the frequency with which the same machine or other contrivance has been invented at the same time by several persons in different quarters of the globe. The world was without an electric telegraph for several thousand years; then Professor Henry, the American, Wheatstone in England, Morse on the sea, and a German in Munich, all invented it at the same time. The discovery of certain ways of applying steam was made in two or three countries in the same year. Is it not possible that inventors are constantly and unwittingly stealing each other's ideas whilst they stand thousands of miles asunder?

Last spring a literary friend of mine,* who lived a hundred miles away, paid me a visit, and in the course of our talk he said he had made a discovery—conceived an entirely new idea—one which certainly had never been used in literature. He told me what it was. I handed him a manuscript, and said he would find substantially the same idea in that—a manuscript which I had written a week before. The idea had been in my

---

*W. D. Howells.

mind since the previous November; it had only entered his while I was putting it on paper, a week gone by. He had not yet written his; so he left it unwritten, and gracefully made over all his right and title in the idea to me.

The following statement, which I have clipped from a newspaper, is true. I had the facts from Mr. Howells's lips when the episode was new:

> "A remarkable story of a literary coincidence is told of Mr. Howells's *Atlantic Monthly* serial 'Dr. Breen's Practice.' A lady of Rochester, New York, contributed to the magazine, after 'Dr. Breen's Practice' was in type, a short story which so much resembled Mr. Howells's that he felt it necessary to call upon her and explain the situation of affairs in order that no charge of plagiarism might be preferred against him. He showed her the proof-sheets of his story, and satisfied her that the similarity between her work and his was one of those strange coincidences which have from time to time occurred in the literary world."

I had read portions of Mr. Howells's story, both in MS. and in proof, before the lady offered her contribution to the magazine.

Here is another case. I clip it from a newspaper:

> "The republication of Miss Alcott's novel *Moods* recalls to a writer in the Boston *Post* a singular coincidence which was brought to light before the book was first published: 'Miss Anna M. Crane, of Baltimore, published *Emily Chester,* a novel which was pronounced a very striking and strong story. A comparison of this book with *Moods* showed that the two writers, though entire strangers to each other, and living hundreds of miles apart, had both chosen the same subject for their novels, had followed almost the same line of treatment up to a certain point, where the parallel ceased, and the dénouements were entirely opposite. And even more curious, the leading characters in both books had identically the same names, so that the names in Miss Alcott's novel had to be changed. Then the book was published by Loring.' "

Four or five times within my recollection there has been a lively newspaper war in this country over poems whose authorship was claimed by two or three different people at the same time. There was a war of this kind over "Nothing to Wear," "Beautiful Snow," "Rock Me to Sleep, Mother," and also over one of Mr. Will Carleton's early ballads, I think. These were all blameless cases of unintentional and unwitting mental telegraphy, I judge.

A word more as to Mr. Wright. He had had his book in his mind some time; consequently he, and not I, had originated the idea of it. The subject was entirely foreign to my thoughts; I was wholly absorbed in other things. Yet this friend, whom I had not seen and had hardly thought of for eleven years, was able to shoot his thoughts at me across three thousand miles of country, and fill my head with them, to the exclusion of every other interest, in a single moment. He had begun his letter after finishing his work on the morning paper—a little after three o'clock, he said. When it was three in the morning in Nevada it was about six in Hartford, where I lay awake thinking about nothing in particular; and just about that time his ideas came pouring into my head from across the continent, and I got up and put them on paper, under the impression that they were my own original thoughts.

I have never seen any mesmeric or clairvoyant performances or spiritual manifestations which were in the least degree convincing—a fact which is not of consequence, since my opportunities have been meager; but I am forced to believe that one human mind (still inhabiting the flesh) can communicate with another, over any sort of a distance, and without any *artificial* preparation of "sympathetic conditions" to act as a transmitting agent. I suppose that when the sympathetic conditions happen to exist the two minds communicate with each other, and that otherwise they don't; and I suppose that if the sympathetic conditions could be kept up right along, the two minds would continue to correspond without limit as to time.

Now there is that curious thing which happens to everybody: suddenly a succession of thoughts or sensations flocks in upon you, which startles you with the weird idea that you have ages ago experienced just this succession of thoughts or sensations in a previous existence. The previous existence is possible, no doubt, but I am persuaded that the solution of this hoary mystery lies not there, but in the fact that some far-off stranger has been telegraphing his thoughts and sensations into your conscious-ness, and that he stopped because some counter-current or other obstruc-tion intruded and broke the line of communication. Perhaps they seem repetitions to you because they *are* repetitions, got at second hand from the other man. Possibly Mr. Brown, the "mind-reader," reads other peo-ple's minds, possibly he does not; but I know of a surety that I have read another man's mind, and therefore I do not see why Mr. Brown shouldn't do the like also.

I wrote the foregoing about three years ago, in Heidelberg, and laid the manuscript aside, purposing to add to it instances of mind-telegraphing from time to time as they should fall under my experience. Meantime the "crossing" of letters has been so frequent as to become monotonous. However, I have managed to get something useful out of this hint; for now, when I get tired of waiting upon a man whom I very much wish to hear from, I sit down and *compel* him to write, whether he wants to or not; that is to say, I sit down and write him, and then tear my letter up, satisfied that my act has forced him to write me at the same moment. I do not need to mail my letter—the writing it is the only essential thing.

Of course I have grown superstitious about this letter-crossing busi-ness—this was natural. We stayed awhile in Venice after leaving Heidel-berg. One day I was going down the Grand Canal in a gondola, when I heard a shout behind me, and looked around to see what the matter was; a gondola was rapidly following, and the gondolier was making signs to me to stop. I did so, and the pursuing boat ranged up alongside. There was an American lady in it—a resident of Venice. She was in a good deal of distress. She said:

"There's a New York gentleman and his wife at the Hotel Britannia who arrived a week ago, expecting to find news of their son, whom they have heard nothing about during eight months. There was no news. The lady is down sick with despair; the gentleman can't sleep or eat. Their son arrived at San Francisco eight months ago, and announced the fact in a letter to his parents the same day. That is the last trace of him. The parents have been in Europe ever since; but their trip has been spoiled, for they have occupied their time simply in drifting restlessly from place to place, and writing letters everywhere and to everybody, begging for news of their son; but the mystery remains as dense as ever. Now the gentleman wants to stop writing and go to cabling. He wants to cable San Francisco. He has never done it before, because he is afraid of—of he doesn't know what—death of his son, no doubt. But he wants somebody to *advise* him to cable; wants me to do it. Now I simply can't; for if no news came, that mother yonder would die. So I have chased you up in order to get you to support me in urging him to be patient, and put the thing off a week or two longer; it may be the saving of this lady. Come along; let's not lose any time."

So I went along, but I had a program of my own. When I was introduced to the gentleman I said: "I have some superstitions, but they are worthy of respect. If you will cable San Francisco immediately, you will hear news of your son inside of twenty-four hours. I don't know that you will get the news from San Francisco, but you will get it from somewhere. The only necessary thing is to *cable*—that is all. The news will come within twenty-four hours. Cable Peking, if you prefer; there is no choice in this matter. This delay is all occasioned by your not cabling long ago, when you were first moved to do it."

It seems absurd that this gentleman should have been cheered up by this nonsense, but he was; he brightened up at once, and sent his cablegram; and next day, at noon, when a long letter arrived from his lost son, the man was as grateful to me as if I had really had something to do with the hurrying up of that letter. The son had shipped from San Francisco in a sailing vessel, and his letter was written from the first port he touched at, months afterward.

This incident argues nothing, and is valueless. I insert it only to show how strong is the superstition which "letter-crossing" has bred in me. I was so sure that a cablegram sent to anyplace, no matter where, would defeat itself by "crossing" the incoming news, that my confidence was able to raise up a hopeless man, and make him cheery and hopeful.

But here are two or three incidents which come strictly under the head of mind-telegraphing. One Monday morning, about a year ago, the mail came in, and I picked up one of the letters and said to a friend: "Without opening this letter I will tell you what it says. It is from Mrs. ——, and she says she was in New York last Saturday, and was purposing to run up here in the afternoon train and surprise us, but at the last moment changed her mind and returned westward to her home."

I was right; my details were exactly correct. Yet we had had no suspicion that Mrs. —— was coming to New York, or that she had even a remote intention of visiting us.

I smoke a good deal—that is to say, all the time—so, during seven years, I have tried to keep a box of matches handy, behind a picture on the mantelpiece; but I have had to take it out in trying, because George (colored), who makes the fires and lights the gas, always uses my matches, and never replaces them. Commands and persuasions have gone for nothing with him all these seven years. One day last summer, when our family had been away from home several months, I said to a member of the household:

"Now, with all this long holiday, and nothing in the way to interrupt—"

"I can finish the sentence for you," said the member of the household.

"Do it, then," said I.

"George ought to be able, by practicing, to learn to let those matches alone."

It was correctly done. That was what I was going to say. Yet until that moment George and the matches had not been in my mind for three months, and it is plain that the part of the sentence which I uttered offers not the least cue or suggestion of what I was purposing to follow it with.

My mother* is descended from the younger of two English brothers named Lambton, who settled in this country a few generations ago. The tradition goes that the elder of the two eventually fell heir to a certain estate in England (now an earldom), and died right away. This has always been the way with our family. They always die when they could make anything by not doing it. The two Lambtons left plenty of Lambtons behind them; and when at last, about fifty years ago, the English baronetcy was exalted to an earldom, the great tribe of American Lambtons began to bestir themselves—that is, those descended from the elder branch. Ever since that day one or another of these has been fretting his life uselessly away with schemes to get at his "rights." The present "rightful earl"—I mean the American one—used to write me occasionally, and try to interest me in his projected raids upon the title and estates by offering me a share in the latter portion of the spoil; but I have always managed to resist his temptations.

Well, one day last summer I was lying under a tree, thinking about nothing in particular, when an absurd idea flashed into my head, and I said to a member of the household, "Suppose I should live to be ninety-two, and dumb and blind and toothless, and just as I was gasping out what was left of me on my death-bed—"

"Wait, I will finish the sentence," said the member of the household.

"Go on," said I.

"Somebody should rush in with a document, and say, 'All the other heirs are dead, and you are the Earl of Durham!' "

That is truly what I was going to say. Yet until that moment the subject had not entered my mind or been referred to in my hearing for months before. A few years ago this thing would have astounded me, but the like could not much surprise me now, though it happened every week; for I

---

*She was still living when this was written.

think I *know* now that mind can communicate accurately with mind without the aid of the slow and clumsy vehicle of speech.

This age does seem to have exhausted invention nearly; still, it has one important contract on its hands yet—the invention of the *phrenophone;* that is to say, a method whereby the communicating of mind with mind may be brought under command and reduced to certainty and system. The telegraph and the telephone are going to become too slow and wordy for our needs. We must have the *thought* itself shot into our minds from a distance; then, if we need to put it into words, we can do that tedious work at our leisure. Doubtless the something which conveys our thoughts through the air from brain to brain is a finer and subtler form of electricity, and all we need do is to find out how to capture it and how to force it to do its work, as we have had to do in the case of the electric currents. Before the day of telegraphs neither one of these marvels would have seemed any easier to achieve than the other.

While I am writing this, doubtless somebody on the other side of the globe is writing it too. The question is, am I inspiring him or is he inspiring me? I cannot answer that; but that these thoughts have been passing through somebody else's mind all the time I have been setting them down I have no sort of doubt.

I will close this paper with a remark which I found some time ago in Boswell's *Johnson:*

"Voltaire's *Candide* is wonderfully similar in its plan and conduct to Johnson's *Rasselas;* insomuch that I have heard Johnson say that if they had not been published so closely one after the other that there was not time for imitation, *it would have been in vain to deny that the scheme of that which came latest was taken from the other.*"

The two men were widely separated from each other at the time, and the sea lay between.

POSTSCRIPT

IN THE *Atlantic* for June, 1882, Mr. John Fiske refers to the often-quoted Darwin-and-Wallace "co-incidence":

> "I alluded, just now, to the 'unforeseen circumstance' which led Mr. Darwin in 1859 to break his long silence, and to write and publish the *Origin of Species*. This circumstance served, no less than the extraordinary success of his book, to show how ripe the minds of men had become for entertaining such views as those which Mr. Darwin propounded. In 1858 Mr. Wallace, who was then engaged in studying the natural history of the Malay Archipelago, sent to Mr. Darwin (as to the man most likely to understand him) a paper in which he sketched the outlines of a theory identical with that upon which Mr. Darwin had so long been at work. The same sequence of observed facts and inferences that had led Mr. Darwin to the discovery of natural selection and its consequences had led Mr. Wallace to the very threshold of the same discovery; but in Mr. Wallace's mind the theory had by no means been wrought out to the same degree of completeness to

which it had been wrought in the mind of Mr. Darwin. In the preface to his charming book on Natural Selection, Mr. Wallace, with rare modesty and candor, acknowledges that whatever value his speculations may have had, they have been utterly surpassed in richness and cogency of proof by those of Mr. Darwin. This is no doubt true, and Mr. Wallace has done such good work in further illustration of the theory that he can well afford to rest content with the second place in the first announcement of it.

"The coincidence, however, between Mr. Wallace's conclusions and those of Mr. Darwin was very remarkable. But, after all, coincidences of this sort have not been uncommon in the history of scientific inquiry. Nor is it at all surprising that they should occur now and then, when we remember that a great and pregnant discovery must always be concerned with some question which many of the foremost minds in the world are busy thinking about. It was so with the discovery of the differential calculus, and again with the discovery of the planet Neptune. It was so with the interpretation of the Egyptian hieroglyphics, and with the establishment of the undulatory theory of light. It was so, to a considerable extent, with the introduction of the new chemistry, with the discovery of the mechanical equivalent of heat, and the whole doctrine of the correlation of forces. It was so with the invention of the electric telegraph and with the discovery of spectrum analysis. And it is not at all strange that it should have been so with the doctrine of the origin of species through natural selection."

He thinks these "coincidences" were apt to happen because the matters from which they sprang were matters which many of the foremost minds in the world were busy thinking about. But perhaps *one* man in each case did the telegraphing to the others. The aberrations which gave Leverrier the idea that there must be a planet of such and such mass and such and such an orbit hidden from sight out yonder in the remote abysses of space were not new; they had been noticed by astronomers for generations. Then why should it happen to occur to three people, widely separated—Leverrier, Mrs. Somerville, and Adams—to suddenly go to worrying about those aberrations all at the same time, and set themselves to work to find out what caused them, and to measure and weigh an invisible planet, and calculate its orbit, and hunt it down and catch it?—a strange project which nobody but they had ever thought of before. If one astronomer had invented that odd and happy project fifty years before, don't you think he would have telegraphed it to several others without knowing it?

But now I come to a puzzler. How is it that *inanimate* objects are able to affect the mind? They seem to do that. However, I wish to throw in a parenthesis first—just a reference to a thing everybody is familiar with—the experience of receiving a clear and particular *answer* to your telegram before your telegram has reached the sender of the answer. That is a case where your telegram has gone straight from your brain to the man it was meant for, far outstripping the wire's slow electricity, and it is an exercise of mental telegraphy which is as common as dining. To return to the influence of inanimate things. In the cases of non-professional clairvoyance examined by the Psychical Society the clairvoyant has usually been blindfolded, then some object which has been touched or worn by a person is placed in his hand; the clairvoyant immediately describes that person, and goes on and gives a history of some event with which the text object has been connected. If the inanimate object is able to affect and inform the clairvoyant's mind, maybe it can do the same when it is working in the interest of mental telegraphy. Once a lady in the West wrote me that her son was coming to New York to remain three weeks, and would pay me a visit if invited, and she gave me his address. I mislaid the letter, and forgot all about the matter till the three weeks were about up. Then a sudden and fiery irrupton of remorse burst up in my brain that illuminated all the region round about, and I sat down at once and wrote to the lady and asked for that lost address. But, upon reflection, I judged that the stirring up of my recollection had not been an accident, so I added a postscript to say, never mind, I should get a letter from her son before night. And I did get it; for the letter was already in the town, although not delivered yet. It had influenced me somehow. I have had so many experiences of this sort—a dozen of them at least—that I am nearly persuaded that inanimate objects do not confine their activities to helping the clairvoyant, but do every now and then give the mental telegraphist a lift.

The case of mental telegraphy which I am coming to now comes under I don't exactly know what head. I clipped it from one of our local papers six or eight years ago. I know the details to be right and true, for the story was told to me in the same form by one of the two persons concerned (a clergyman of Hartford) at the time that the curious thing happened:

"A REMARKABLE COINCIDENCE.—Strange coincidences make the most interesting of stories and most curious of studies. Nobody can quite say how they come about, but everybody appreciates the fact when they do come, and it is seldom that any more complete and curious coincidence is recorded of minor importance than the following, which is absolutely true, and occurred in this city:

"At the time of the building of one of the finest residences of Hartford, which is still a very new house, a local firm supplied the wall-paper for certain rooms, contracting both to furnish and to put on the paper. It happened that they did not calculate the size of one room exactly right, and the paper of the design selected for it fell short just half a roll. They asked for delay enough to send on to the manufacturers for what was needed, and were told that there was no especial hurry. It happened that the manufacturers had none on hand, and had destroyed the blocks from which it was printed. They wrote that they had a full list of the dealers to whom they had sold that paper, and that they would write to each of these, and get from some of them a roll. It might involve a delay of a couple of weeks, but they would surely get it.

"In the course of time came a letter saying that, to their great surprise, they could not find a single roll. Such a thing was very unusual, but in this case it had so happened. Accordingly the local firm asked for further time, saying they would write to their own customers who had bought of that pattern, and would get the piece from them. But, to their surprise, this effort also failed. A long time had now elapsed, and there was no use of delaying any longer. They had contracted to paper the room, and their only course was to take off that which was insufficient and put on some other of which there was enough to go around. Accordingly at length a man was sent out to remove the paper. He got his apparatus ready, and was about to begin work, under the direction of the owner of the building, when the latter was for the moment called away. The house was large and very interesting, and so many people had rambled about it that finally admission had been refused by a sign at the door. On the occasion, however, when a gentleman had knocked and asked for leave to look about, the owner, being on the premises, had been sent for to reply to the request in person. That was the call that for the moment delayed the final preparations. The gentleman went to the door and admitted the stranger, saying he would show him about the house, but first must return for a moment to that room to finish his directions there, and he told the curious story about the paper as they went on. They entered the room together, and the first thing the stranger, who lived fifty miles away, said on looking about was, 'Why, I have that very paper on a room in my house, and I have an extra roll of it laid away, which is at your service.' In a few days the wall was papered according to the original contract. Had not the owner been at the house, the stranger would not have been admitted; had he called a day later, it would have been too late; had not the facts been almost accidentally told to him, he would probably have said nothing of the paper, and so on. The exact fitting of all the circumstances is something very remarkable, and makes one of those stories that seem hardly accidental in their nature."

Something that happened the other day brought my hoary MS. to mind, and that is how I came to dig it out from its dusty pigeonhole grave for publication. The thing that happened was a question. A lady asked it: "Have you ever had a vision—when awake?" I was about to answer promptly, when the last two words of the question began to grow and spread and swell, and presently they attained to vast dimensions. She did not know that they were important; and I did not at first, but I soon saw that they were putting me on the track of the solution of a mystery which had perplexed me a good deal. You will see what I mean when I get down to it. Ever since the English Society for Psychical Research began its searching investigations of ghost stories, haunted houses, and apparitions of the living and the dead, I have read their pamphlets with avidity as fast as they arrived. Now one of their commonest inquiries of a dreamer or a vision-seer is, "Are you sure you were awake at the time?" If the man can't say he is sure he was awake, a doubt falls upon his tale right there. But if he is positive he was awake, and offers reasonable evidence to substantiate it, the fact counts largely for the credibility of his story. It does with the society, and it did with me until that lady asked me the above question the other day.

The question set me to considering, and brought me to the conclusion that you can be asleep—at least wholly unconscious—for a time, and not suspect that it has happened, and not have any way to prove that it *has* happened. A memorable case was in my mind. About a year ago I was standing on the porch one day, when I saw a man coming up the walk. He was a stranger, and I hoped he would ring and carry his business into the house without stopping to argue with me; he would have to pass the front door to get to me, and I hoped he wouldn't take the trouble; to help, I tried to look like a stranger myself—it often works. I was looking straight at that man; he had got to within ten feet of the door and within twenty-five feet of me—and suddenly he disappeared. It was as astounding as if a church should vanish from before your face and leave nothing behind it but a vacant lot. I was unspeakably delighted. I had seen an apparition at last, with my own eyes, in broad daylight. I made up my mind to write an account of it to the society. I ran to where the specter had been, to make sure he was playing fair, then I ran to the other end of the porch, scanning the open grounds as I went. No, everything was perfect; he couldn't have escaped without my seeing him; he was an apparition, without the slightest doubt, and I would write him up before he was cold. I ran, hot with excitement, and let myself in with a latch-key. When I stepped into the hall my lungs collapsed and my heart stood still. For there sat that same apparition in a chair, all alone, and as quiet and reposeful as if he had come to stay a year! The shock kept me dumb for a moment or two, then I said, "Did you come in at that door?"

"Yes."

"Did *you* open it, or did you ring?"

"I rang, and the colored man opened it."

I said to myself: "This is astonishing. It takes George all of two minutes to answer the door-bell when he is in a hurry, and I have never seen him in a hurry. How *did* this man stand two minutes at that door, within five steps of me, and I not see him?"

I should have gone to my grave puzzling over that riddle but for that lady's chance question last week: "Have you ever had a vision—when awake?" It stands explained now. During at least sixty seconds that day I was asleep, or at least totally unconscious, without suspecting it. In that interval the man came to my immediate vicinity, rang, stood there and waited, then entered and closed the door, and I did not see him and did not hear the door slam.

If he had slipped around the house in that interval and gone into the cellar—he had time enough—I should have written him up for the society, and magnified him, and gloated over him, and hurrahed about him, and thirty yoke of oxen could not have pulled the belief out of me that I was of the favored ones of the earth, and had seen a vision—while wide awake.

Now how are you to tell when you are awake? What are you to go by? People bite their fingers to find out. Why, you can do that in a dream.

A CURE FOR THE BLUES

BY COURTESY of Mr. Cable I came into possession of a singular book eight or ten years ago. It is likely that mine is now the only copy in existence. Its title-page, unabbreviated, reads as follows:

"The Enemy Conquered; or, Love Triumphant. By G. Ragsdale Mc-Clintock,* author of 'An Address,' etc., delivered at Sunflower Hill, South Carolina, and member of the Yale Law School. New Haven: published by T. H. Pease, 83 Chapel Street, 1845."

No one can take up this book, and lay it down again unread. Whoever reads one line of it is caught, is chained; he has become the contented slave of its fascinations; and he will read and read, devour and devour, and will not let it go out of his hand till it is finished to the last line, though the house be on fire over his head. And after a first reading, he will not throw it aside, but will keep it by him, with his Shakespeare and his Homer, and will take it up many and many a time, when the world is dark, and his spirits are low, and be straightway cheered and refreshed. Yet this work has been allowed to lie wholly neglected, unmentioned, and apparently unregretted, for nearly half a century.

The reader must not imagine that he is to find in it wisdom, brilliancy, fertility of invention, ingenuity of construction, excellence of form, purity of style, perfection of imagery, truth to nature, clearness of statement, humanly possible situations, humanly possible people, fluent narrative, connected sequence of events—or philosophy, or logic, or sense. No; the rich, deep, beguiling charm of the book lies in the total and miraculous *absence* from it of all these qualities—a charm which is completed and perfected by the evident fact that the author, whose naïve innocence easily and surely wins our regard, and almost our worship, does not know that they are absent, does not even suspect that they are absent. When read by the light of these helps to an understanding of the situation, the book is delicious—profoundly and satisfyingly delicious.

I call it a book because the author calls it a book, I call it a work because he calls it a work; but in truth it is merely a duodecimo pamphlet of thirty-one pages. It was written for fame and money as the author very frankly—yes, and very hopefully, too, poor fellow—says in his preface. The money never came; no penny of it ever came; and how long, how pathetically long, the fame has been deferred—forty-seven years! He was young then, it would have been so much to him then; but will he care for it now?

As time is measured in America, McClintock's epoch is antiquity. In his long-vanished day the Southern author had a passion for "eloquence"; it was his pet, his darling. He would be eloquent, or perish. And he recognized only one kind of eloquence, the lurid, the tempestuous, the volcanic. He liked words; big words, fine words, grand words, rumbling, thundering, reverberating words—with sense attaching if it could be got in without marring the sound, but not otherwise. He loved to stand up before a dazed world, and pour forth flame, and smoke, and lava, and pumice-stone, into the skies, and work his subterranean thunders, and shake himself with earthquakes, and stench himself with sulphur fumes. If he consumed his own fields and vineyards, that was a pity, yes; but he would have his eruption at any cost. Mr. McClintock's eloquence—and he is always eloquent, his crater is always spouting—is of the pattern common to his day, but he departs from the custom of the time in one

*The name here given is a substitute for the one actually attached to the pamphlet.

respect: his brethren allowed sense to intrude when it did not mar the sound, but he does not allow it to intrude at all. For example, consider this figure, which he uses in the village "Address" referred to with such candid complacency in the title-page above quoted—"like the topmost topaz of an ancient tower." Please read it again; contemplate it; measure it; walk around it; climb up it; try to get at an approximate realization of the size of it. Is the fellow to that to be found in literature, ancient or modern, foreign or domestic, living or dead, drunk or sober? One notices how fine and grand it sounds. We know that if it was loftily uttered, it got a noble burst of applause from the villagers; yet there isn't a ray of sense in it, or meaning to it.

McClintock finished his education at Yale in 1843, and came to Hartford on a visit that same year. I have talked with men who at that time talked with him, and felt of him, and knew he was real. One needs to remember that fact, and to keep fast hold of it; it is the only way to keep McClintock's book from undermining one's faith in McClintock's actuality.

As to the book. The first four pages are devoted to an inflamed eulogy of Woman,—simply Woman in general, or perhaps as an Institution,—wherein, among other compliments to her details, he pays a unique one to her voice. He says it "fills the breast with fond alarms, echoed by every rill." It sounds well enough, but it is not true. After the eulogy he takes up his real work, and the novel begins. It begins in the woods, near the village of Sunflower Hill.

> Brightening clouds seemed to rise from the mist of the fair Chattahoochee, to spread their beauty over the thick forest, to guide the hero whose bosom beats with aspirations to conquer the enemy that would tarnish his name, and to win back the admiration of his long tried friend.

It seems a general remark, but it is not general; the hero mentioned is the to-be hero of the book; and in this abrupt fashion, and without name or description, he is shoveled into the tale. "With aspirations to conquer the enemy that would tarnish his name" is merely a phrase flung in for the sake of the sound—let it not mislead the reader. No one is trying to tarnish this person; no one has thought of it. The rest of the sentence is also merely a phrase; the man has no friend as yet, and of course has had no chance to try him, or win back his admiration, or disturb him in any other way.

The hero climbs up over "Sawney's Mountain," and down the other side, making for an old Indian "castle"—which becomes "the red man's hut" in the next sentence; and when he gets there at last, he "surveys with wonder and astonishment" the invisible structure, "which time had buried in the dust; and thought to himself his happiness was not yet complete." One doesn't know why it wasn't, nor how near it came to being complete, nor what was still wanting to round it up and make it so. Maybe it was the Indian; but the book does not say. At this point we have an episode:

Beside the shore of the brook sat a young man, about eighteen or twenty, who seemed to be reading some favorite book, and who had a remarkably noble countenance—eyes which betrayed more than a common mind. This of course made the youth a welcome guest, and gained him friends in whatever condition of life he might be placed. The traveler observed that he was a well built figure which showed strength and grace in every moment. He accordingly addressed him in quite a gentlemanly manner, and inquired of him the way to the village. After he had received the desired information, and was about taking his leave, the youth said, "Are you not Major Elfonzo, the great musician*—the champion of a noble cause—the modern Achilles, who gained so many victories in the Florida War?" "I bear that name," said the Major, "and those titles, trusting at the same time, that the ministers of grace will carry me triumphantly through all my laudable undertakings, and if," continued the Major, "you sir, are the patronizer of noble deeds, I should like to make you my confidant, and learn your address." The youth looked somewhat amazed, bowed low, mused for a moment, and began: "My name is Roswell. I have been recently admitted to the bar, and can only give a faint outline of my future success in that honorable profession; but I trust, sir, like the Eagle, I shall look down from lofty rocks upon the dwellings of man, and shall ever be ready to give you any assistance in my official capacity, and whatever this muscular arm of mine can do, whenever it shall be called from its buried greatness." The Major grasped him by the hand, and exclaimed: "O! thou exalted spirit of inspiration—thou flame of burning prosperity, may the Heaven directed blaze be the glare of thy soul, and battle down every rampart that seems to impede your progress!"

There is a strange sort of originality about McClintock; he imitates other people's styles, but nobody can imitate his, not even an idiot. Other people can be windy, but McClintock blows a gale; other people can blubber sentiment, but McClintock spews it; other people can mishandle metaphors, but only McClintock knows how to make a business of it. McClintock is always McClintock, he is always consistent, his style is always his own style. He does not make the mistake of being relevant on one page and irrelevant on another; he is irrelevant on all of them. He does not make the mistake of being lucid in one place and obscure in another; he is obscure all the time. He does not make the mistake of slipping in a name here and there that is out of character with his work; he always uses names that exactly and fantastically fit his lunatics. In the matter of undeviating consistency he stands alone in authorship. It is this that makes his style unique, and entitles it to a name of its own—McClintockian. It is this that protects it from being mistaken for anybody else's. Uncredited quotations from other writers often leave a reader in

---

*Further on it will be seen that he is a country expert on the fiddle, and has a three-township fame.

doubt as to their authorship, but McClintock is safe from that accident; an uncredited quotation from him would always be recognizable. When a boy nineteen years old, who had just been admitted to the bar, says, "I trust, sir, like the Eagle, I shall look down from lofty rocks upon the dwellings of man," we know who is speaking through that boy; we should recognize that note anywhere. There be myriads of instruments in this world's literary orchestra, and a multitudinous confusion of sounds that they make, wherein fiddles are drowned, and guitars smothered, and one sort of drum mistaken for another sort; but whensoever the brazen note of the McClintockian trombone breaks through that fog of music, that note is recognizable, and about it there can be no blur of doubt.

The novel now arrives at the point where the Major goes home to see his father. When McClintock wrote this interview, he probably believed it was pathetic.

The road which led to the town, presented many attractions. Elfonzo had bid farewell to the youth of deep feeling, and was now wending his way to the dreaming spot of his fondness. The south winds whistled through the woods, as the waters dashed against the banks, as rapid fire in the pent furnace roars. This brought him to remember while alone, that he quietly left behind the hospitality of a father's house, and gladly entered the world, with higher hopes than are often realized. But as he journeyed onward, he was mindful of the advice of his father, who had often looked sadly on the ground, when tears of cruelly deceived hope, moistened his eyes. Elfonzo had been somewhat of a dutiful son; yet fond of the amusements of life—had been in distant lands— had enjoyed the pleasure of the world, and had frequently returned to the scenes of his boyhood, almost destitute of many of the comforts of life. In this condition, he would frequently say to his father, "Have I offended you, that you look upon me as a stranger, and frown upon me with stinging looks? Will you not favor me with the sound of your voice? If I have trampled upon your veneration, or have spread a humid veil of darkness around your expectations, send me back into the world, where no heart beats for me—where the foot of man has never yet trod; but give me at least one kind word—allow me to come into the presence sometimes of thy winter-worn locks." "Forbid it, Heaven, that I should be angry with thee," answered the father, "my son, and yet I send thee back to the children of the world—to the cold charity of the combat, and to a land of victory. I read another destiny in thy countenance—I learn thy inclinations from the flame that has already kindled in my soul a strange sensation. It will seek thee, my dear Elfonzo, it will find thee—thou canst not escape that lighted torch, which shall blot out from the remembrance of men a long train of prophecies which they have foretold against thee. I once thought not so. Once, I was blind; but now the path of life is plain before me, and my sight is clear; yet Elfonzo, return to thy worldly occupation—take again in thy hand, that chord of sweet sounds— struggle with the civilized world, and with your own heart; fly

swiftly to the enchanted ground—let the night-owl send forth its
screams from the stubborn oak—let the sea sport upon the beach,
and the stars sing together; but learn of these, Elfonzo, thy doom,
and thy hiding-place. Our most innocent as well as our most
lawful desires must often be denied us, that we may learn to
sacrifice them to a Higher will."

Remembering such admonitions with gratitude, Elfonzo was
immediately urged by the recollection of his father's family to
keep moving.

McClintock has a fine gift in the matter of surprises; but as a rule they
are not pleasant ones, they jar upon the feelings. His closing sentence in
the last quotation is of that sort. It brings one down out of the tinted clouds
in too sudden and collapsed a fashion. It incenses one against the author
for a moment. It makes the reader want to take him by his winter-worn
locks, and trample on his veneration, and deliver him over to the cold
charity of combat, and blot him out with his own lighted torch. But the
feeling does not last. The master takes again in his hand that concord of
sweet sounds of his, and one is reconciled, pacified.

His steps became quicker and quicker—he hastened through
the piny woods, dark as the forest was, and with joy he very soon
reached the little village of repose, in whose bosom rested the
boldest chivalry. His close attention to every important object—
his modest questions about whatever was new to him—his reverence for wise old age, and his ardent desire to learn many of the
fine arts, soon brought him into respectable notice.

One mild winter day, as he walked along the streets toward the
Academy, which stood upon a small eminence, surrounded by
native growth—some venerable in its appearance, others young
and prosperous—all seemed inviting, and seemed to be the very
place for learning as well as for genius to spend its research beneath its spreading shades. He entered its classic walls in the usual
mode of southern manners.

The artfulness of this man! None knows so well as he how to pique the
curiosity of the reader—and how to disappoint it. He raises the hope,
here, that he is going to tell all about how one enters a classic wall in the
usual mode of Southern manners; but does he? No; he smiles in his sleeve,
and turns aside to other matters.

The principal of the Institution begged him to be seated, and
listen to the recitations that were going on. He accordingly obeyed
the request, and seemed to be much pleased. After the school was
dismissed, and the young hearts regained their freedom, with the
songs of the evening, laughing at the anticipated pleasures of a
happy home, while others tittered at the actions of the past day, he
addressed the teacher in a tone that indicated a resolution—with
an undaunted mind. He said he had determined to become a
student, if he could meet with his approbation, "Sir," said he, "I

have spent much time in the world. I have traveled among the
uncivilized inhabitants of America. I have met with friends, and
combated with foes; but none of these gratify my ambition, or
decide what is to be my destiny. I see the learned world have an
influence with the voice of the people themselves. The despoilers
of the remotest kingdoms of the earth, refer their differences to
this class of persons. This the illiterate and inexperienced little
dream of; and now if you will receive me as I am, with these
deficiencies—with all my misguided opinions, I will give you my
honor, sir, that I will never disgrace the Institution, or those who
have placed you in this honorable station.'' The instructor, who
had met with many disappointments, knew how to feel for a stranger
who had been thus turned upon the charities of an unfeeling community. He looked at him earnestly, and said: "Be of good cheer—
look forward, sir, to the high destination you may attain. Remember, the more elevated the mark at which you aim, the more sure,
the more glorious, the more magnificent the prize.'' From wonder
to wonder, his encouragement led the impatient listener. A strange
nature bloomed before him—giant streams promised him success—gardens of hidden treasures opened to his view. All this, so
vividly described, seemed to gain a new witchery from his glowing fancy.

It seems to me that this situation is new in romance. I feel sure it has
not been attempted before. Military celebrities have been disguised and
set at lowly occupations for dramatic effect, but I think McClintock is the
first to send one of them to school. Thus, in this book, you pass from
wonder to wonder, through gardens of hidden treasure, where giant streams
bloom before you, and behind you, and all around, and you feel as happy,
and groggy, and satisfied, with your quart of mixed metaphor aboard, as
you would if it had been mixed in a sample-room, and delivered from
a jug.

Now we come upon some more McClintockian surprises—a sweetheart
who is sprung upon us without any preparation, along with a name for her
which is even a little more of a surprise than she herself is.

In 1842, he entered the class, and made rapid progress in the
English and Latin departments. Indeed, he continued advancing
with such rapidity that he was like to become the first in his class,
and made such unexpected progress, and was so studious, that he
had almost forgotten the pictured saint of his affections. The fresh
wreaths of the pine and cypress, had waited anxiously to drop
once more the dews of Heaven upon the heads of those who had
so often poured forth the tender emotions of their souls under its
boughs. He was aware of the pleasure that he had seen there. So
one evening, as he was returning from his reading, he concluded
he would pay a visit to this enchanting spot. Little did he think of
witnessing a shadow of his former happiness, though no doubt, he
wished it might be so. He continued sauntering by the road-side,
meditating on the past. The nearer he approached the spot, the

more anxious he became. At that moment, a tall female figure
flitted across his path, with a bunch of roses in her hand; her
countenance showed uncommon vivacity, with a resolute spirit;
her ivory teeth already appeared as she smiled beautifully, promenading,—while her ringlets of hair, dangled unconsciously around
her snowy neck. Nothing was wanting to complete her beauty. The
tinge of the rose was in full bloom upon her cheek; the charms of
sensibility and tenderness were always her associates. In Ambulinia's bosom dwelt a noble soul—one that never faded—one that
never was conquered.

Ambulinia! It can hardly be matched in fiction. The full name is Ambulinia Valeer. Marriage will presently round it out and perfect it. Then it
will be Mrs. Ambulinia Valeer Elfonzo. It takes the chromo.

Her heart yielded to no feeling but the love of Elfonzo, on whom
she gazed with intense delight, and to whom she felt herself more
closely bound, because he sought the hand of no other. Elfonzo
was roused from his apparent revery. His books no longer were his
inseparable companions—his thoughts arrayed themselves to encourage him to the field of victory. He endeavored to speak to his
supposed Ambulinia, but his speech appeared not in words. No,
his effort was a stream of fire, that kindled his soul into a flame of
admiration, and carried his senses away captive. Ambulinia had
disappeared, to make him more mindful of his duty. As she walked
speedily away through the piny woods, she calmly echoed: "O!
Elfonzo, thou wilt now look from thy sunbeams. Thou shalt now
walk in a new path—perhaps thy way leads through darkness; but
fear not, the stars foretell happiness."

To McClintock that jingling jumble of fine words meant something, no
doubt, or seemed to mean something; but it is useless for us to try to
divine what it was. Ambulinia comes—we don't know whence nor why;
she mysteriously intimates—we don't know what; and then she goes
echoing away—we don't know whither; and down comes the curtain.
McClintock's art is subtle; McClintock's art is deep.

Not many days afterwards, as surrounded by fragrant flowers,
she sat one evening at twilight, to enjoy the cool breeze that
whispered notes of melody along the distant groves, the little birds
perched on every side, as if to watch the movements of their new
visitor. The bells were tolling, when Elfonzo silently stole along
by the wild wood flowers, holding in his hand his favorite instrument of music—his eye continually searching for Ambulinia, who
hardly seemed to perceive him, as she played carelessly with the
songsters that hopped from branch to branch. Nothing could be
more striking than the difference between the two. Nature seemed
to have given the more tender soul to Elfonzo, and the stronger
and more courageous to Ambulinia. A deep feeling spoke from
the eyes of Elfonzo,—such a feeling as can only be expressed by

those who are blessed as admirers, and by those who are able to return the same with sincerity of heart. He was a few years older than Ambulinia: she had turned a little into her seventeenth. He had almost grown up in the Cherokee country, with the same equal proportions as one of the natives. But little intimacy had existed between them until the year forty-one—because the youth felt that the character of such a lovely girl was too exalted to inspire any other feeling than that of quiet reverence. But as lovers will not always be insulted, at all times and under all circumstances, by the frowns and cold looks of crabbed old age, which should continually reflect dignity upon those around, and treat the unfortunate as well as the fortunate with a graceful mien, he continued to use diligence and perseverance. All this lighted a spark in his heart that changed his whole character, and like the unyielding Deity that follows the storm to check its rage in the forest, he resolves for the first time to shake off his embarrassment, and return where he had before only worshiped.

At last we begin to get the major's measure. We are able to put this and that casual fact together, and build the man up before our eyes, and look at him. And after we have got him built, we find him worth the trouble. By the above comparison between his age and Ambulinia's, we guess the warworn veteran to be twenty-two; and the other facts stand thus: he had grown up in the Cherokee country with the same equal proportions as one of the natives—how flowing and graceful the language, and yet how tantalizing as to meaning!—he had been turned adrift by his father, to whom he had been "somewhat of a dutiful son"; he wandered in distant lands; came back frequently "to the scenes of his boyhood, almost destitute of many of the comforts of life," in order to get into the presence of his father's winter-worn locks, and spread a humid veil of darkness around his expectations; but he was always promptly sent back to the cold charity of the combat again; he learned to play the fiddle, and made a name for himself in that line; he had dwelt among the wild tribes; he had philosophized about the despoilers of the kingdoms of the earth, and found out— the cunning creature—that they refer their differences to the learned for settlement; he had achieved a vast fame as a military chieftain, the Achilles of the Florida campaigns, and then had got him a spelling-book and started to school; he had fallen in love with Ambulinia Valeer while she was teething, but had kept it to himself awhile, out of the reverential awe which he felt for the child; but now at last, like the unyielding deity who follows the storm to check its rage in the forest, he resolves to shake off his embarrassment, and to return where before he had only worshiped. The major, indeed, has made up his mind to rise up and shake his faculties together, and to see if *he* can't do that thing himself. This is not clear. But no matter about that: there stands the hero, compact and visible; and he is no mean structure, considering that his creator had never created anything before, and hadn't anything but rags and wind to build with this time. It seems to me that no one can contemplate this odd creature, this quaint and curious blatherskite, without admiring McClintock, or, at any rate, loving him and feeling grateful to him; for McClintock made him, he gave-him to us; without McClintock we could not have had him, and would now be poor.

But we must come to the feast again. Here is a courtship scene, down there in the romantic glades among the raccoons, alligators, and things, that has merit, peculiar literary merit. See how Achilles woos. Dwell upon the second sentence (particularly the close of it), and the beginning of the third. Never mind the new personage, Leos, who is intruded upon us unheralded and unexplained. That is McClintock's way; it is his habit; it is a part of his genius; he cannot help it; he never interrupts the rush of his narrative to make introductions:

It could not escape Ambulinia's penetrating eye, that he sought an interview with her, which she as anxiously avoided, and assumed a more distant calmness than before, seemingly to destroy all hope. After many efforts and struggles with his own person, with timid steps the Major approached the damsel, with the same caution as he would have done in a field of battle. "Lady Ambulinia," said he, trembling, "I have long desired a moment like this. I dare not let it escape. I fear the consequences; yet I hope your indulgence will at least hear my petition. Can you not anticipate what I would say, and what I am about to express? Will you not, like Minerva, who sprung from the brain of Jupiter, release me from thy winding chains or cure me—" "Say no more, Elfonzo," answered Ambulinia, with a serious look, raising her hand as if she intended to swear eternal hatred against the whole world,—"another lady in my place would have perhaps answered your question in bitter coldness. I know not the little arts of my sex. I care but little for the vanity of those who would chide me, and am unwilling, as well as ashamed to be guilty of any thing that would lead you to think 'all is not gold that glitters': so be not rash in your resolution. It is better to repent now, than to do it in a more solemn hour. Yes, I know what you would say. I know you have a costly gift for me—the noblest that man can make—your heart! you should not offer it to one so unworthy. Heaven, you know, has allowed my father's house to be made a house of solitude, a home of silent obedience, which my parents say is more to be admired than big names and high sounding titles. Notwithstanding all this, let me speak the emotions of an honest heart—allow me to say in the fullness of my hopes that I anticipate better days. The bird may stretch its wings toward the sun, which it can never reach; and flowers of the field appear to ascend in the same direction, because they cannot do otherwise: but man confides his complaints to the saints in whom he believes; for in their abodes of light they know no more sorrow. From your confession and indicative looks, I must be that person: if so, deceive not yourself."

Elfonzo replied, "Pardon me, my dear madam, for my frankness. I have loved you from my earliest days—everything grand and beautiful hath borne the image of Ambulinia: while precipices on every hand surrounded me, your guardian angel stood and beckoned me away from the deep abyss. In every trial—in every misfortune, I have met with your helping hand; yet I never dreamed or dared to cherish thy love, till a voice impaired with age encouraged the cause, and declared they who acquired thy favor, should win a victory. I saw how Leos worshiped thee. I felt my own unworthiness. I began to know jealousy, a strong guest indeed, in my bosom, yet I could see if I gained your admiration, Leos was to be my rival. I was aware that he had the influence of your parents, and the wealth of a deceased relative, which is too often mistaken for permanent and regular tranquillity; yet I have determined by your permission to beg an interest in your prayers—to ask you to animate my drooping spirits by your smiles and your winning looks; for, if you but speak, I shall be conqueror, my enemies shall stagger like Olympus shakes. And though earth and sea may tremble, and the charioteer of the sun may forget his dashing steed; yet I am assured that it is only to arm me with divine weapons, which will enable me to complete my long tried intention." "Return to yourself, Elfonzo," said Ambulinia, pleasantly, "a dream of vision has disturbed your intellect—you are above the atmosphere, dwelling in the celestial regions, nothing is there that urges or hinders, nothing that brings discord into our present litigation. I entreat you to condescend a little, and be a man, and forget it all. When Homer describes the battle of the gods and noble men, fighting with giants and dragons, they represent under this image, our struggles with the delusions of our passions. You have exalted me, an unhappy girl, to the skies,— you have called me a saint, and portrayed in your imagination, an angel in human form. Let her remain such to you,—let her continue to be as you have supposed, and be assured that she will consider a share in your esteem, as her highest treasure. Think not that I would allure you from the path in which your conscience leads you; for you know I respect the conscience of others, as I would die for my own. Elfonzo, if I am worthy of thy love, let such conversation never again pass between us. Go, seek a nobler theme! we will seek it in the stream of time, as the sun set in the Tigris." As she spake these words, she grasped the hand of Elfonzo, saying at the same time—"peace and prosperity attend you my hero: be up and doing." Closing her remarks with this expression, she walked slowly away, leaving Elfonzo astonished and amazed. He ventured not to follow, or detain her. Here he stood alone, gazing at the stars;—confounded as he was, here he stood.

Yes; there he stood. There seems to be no doubt about that. Nearly half of this delirious story has now been delivered to the reader. It seems a pity to reduce the other half to a cold synopsis. Pity! it is more than a pity, it is a crime; for, to synopsize McClintock is to reduce a sky-flushing conflagration to dull embers, it is to reduce barbaric splendor to ragged poverty. McClintock never wrote a line that was not precious; he never wrote one that could be spared; he never framed one from which a word could be removed without damage. Every sentence that this master has produced may be likened to a perfect set of teeth, white, uniform, beautiful. If you pull one, the charm is gone.

Still, it is now necessary to begin to pull, and to keep it up; for lack of space requires us to synopsize.

We left Elfonzo standing there, amazed. At what, we do not know. Not at the girl's speech. No; we ourselves should have been amazed at it, of course, for none of us has ever heard anything resembling it: but Elfonzo was used to speeches made up of noise and vacancy, and could listen to them with undaunted mind like the "topmost topaz of an ancient tower"; he was used to making them himself; he—but let it go, it cannot be guessed out; we shall never know what it was that astonished him. He stood there awhile; then he said, "Alas! am I now Grief's disappointed son at last." He did not stop to examine his mind, and to try to find out what he probably meant by that, because, for one reason, "a mixture of ambition and greatness of soul moved upon his young heart," and started him for the village. He resumed his bench in school, "and reasonably progressed in his education." His heart was heavy, but he went into society, and sought surcease of sorrow in its light distractions. He made himself popular with his violin, "which seemed to have a thousand chords—more symphonious than the Muses of Apollo, and more enchanting than the ghost of the Hills." This is obscure, but let it go.

During this interval Leos did some unencouraged courting, but at last, "choked by his undertaking," he desisted.

Presently "Elfonzo again wends his way to the stately walls and new built village." He goes to the house of his beloved; she opens the door herself. To my surprise—for Ambulinia's heart had still seemed free at the time of their last interview—love beamed from the girl's eyes. One sees that Elfonzo was surprised, too; for when he caught that light, "a halloo of smothered shouts ran through every vein." A neat figure—a very neat figure, indeed! Then he kissed her. "The scene was overwhelming." They went into the parlor. The girl said it was safe, for her parents were abed, and would never know. Then we have this fine picture—flung upon the canvas with hardly an effort, as you will notice.

> Advancing toward him she gave a bright display of her rosy neck, and from her head the ambrosial locks breathed divine fragrance; her robe hung waving to his view, while she stood like a goddess confessed before him.

There is nothing of interest in the couple's interview. Now at this point the girl invites Elfonzo to a village show, where jealousy is the motive of the play, for she wants to teach him a wholesome lesson, if he is a jealous person. But this is a sham, and pretty shallow. McClintock merely wants a pretext to drag in a plagiarism of his upon a scene or two in "Othello."

The lovers went to the play. Elfonzo was one of the fiddlers. He and Ambulinia must not be seen together, lest trouble follow with the girl's malignant father; we are made to understand that clearly. So the two sit together in the orchestra, in the midst of the musicians. This does not seem to be good art. In the first place, the girl would be in the way, for orchestras are always packed closely together, and there is no room to spare for people's girls; in the next place, one cannot conceal a girl in an orchestra without everybody taking notice of it. There can be no doubt, it seems to me, that this is bad art.

Leos is present. Of course one of the first things that catches his eye is the maddening spectacle of Ambulinia "leaning upon Elfonzo's chair." This poor girl does not seem to understand even the rudiments of concealment. But she is "in her seventeenth," as the author phrases it, and that is her justification.

Leos meditates, constructs a plan—with personal violence as a basis, of course. It was their way, down there. It is a good plain plan, without any imagination in it. He will go out and stand at the front door, and when these two come out he will "arrest Ambulinia from the hands of the insolent Elfonzo," and thus make for himself a "more prosperous field of immortality than ever was decreed by Omnipotence, or ever pencil drew or artist imagined." But dear me, while he is waiting there the couple climb out at the back window and scurry home! This is romantic enough, but there is a lack of dignity in the situation.

At this point McClintock puts in the whole of his curious play—which we skip.

Some correspondence follows now. The bitter father and the distressed lovers write the letters. Elopements are attempted. They are all idiotically planned, and they fail. Then we have several pages of romantic powwow and confusion signifying nothing. Another elopement is planned; it is to take place on Sunday, when everybody is at church. But the "hero" cannot keep the secret; he tells everybody. Another author would have found another instrument when he decided to defeat this elopement; but that is not McClintock's way. He uses the person that is nearest at hand.

The evasion failed, of course. Ambulinia, in her flight, takes refuge in a neighbor's house. Her father drags her home. The villagers gather, attracted by the racket.

> Elfonzo was moved at this sight. The people followed on to see what was going to become of Ambulinia, while he, with downcast looks, kept at a distance, until he saw them enter the abode of the father, thrusting her, that was the sigh of his soul, out of his presence into a solitary apartment, when she exclaimed, "Elfonzo! Elfonzo! oh, Elfonzo! where art thou, with all thy heroes? haste, oh! haste, come thou to my relief. Ride on the wings of the wind! Turn thy force loose like a tempest, and roll on thy army like a whirlwind, over this mountain of trouble and confusion. Oh, friends! if any pity me, let your last efforts throng upon the green hills, and come to the relief of Ambulinia, who is guilty of nothing but innocent love." Elfonzo called out with a loud voice, "my God, can I stand this! arouse up, I beseech you, and put an end to this tyranny. Come, my brave boys," said he, "are you ready to go forth to your duty?" They stood around him. "Who," said he, "will call us to arms? Where are my thunderbolts of war? Speak ye, the first who will meet the foe! Who will go forth with me in this ocean of grievous temptation? If there is one who desires to go, let him come and shake hands upon the altar of devotion, and

swear that he will be a hero; yes, a Hector in a cause like this, which calls aloud for a speedy remedy.'' ''Mine be the deed,'' said a young lawyer, ''and mine alone; Venus alone shall quit her station before I will forsake one jot or tittle of my promise to you; what is death to me? what is all this warlike army, if it is not to win a victory? I love the sleep of the lover and the mighty: nor would I give it over till the blood of my enemies should wreak with that of my own. But God forbid that our fame should soar on the blood of the slumberer.'' Mr. Valeer stands at his door with the frown of a demon upon his brow, with his dangerous weapon* ready to strike the first man who should enter his door. ''Who will arise and go forward through blood and carnage to the rescue of my Ambulinia?'' said Elfonzo. ''All,'' exclaimed the multitude; and onward they went, with their implements of battle. Others, of a more timid nature, stood among the distant hills to see the result of the contest.

It will hardly be believed that after all this thunder and lightning not a drop of rain fell; but such is the fact. Elfonzo and his gang stood up and blackguarded Mr. Valeer with vigor all night, getting their outlay back with interest; then in the early morning the army and its general retired from the field, leaving the victory with their solitary adversary and his crowbar. This is the first time this has happened in romantic literature. The invention is original. Everything in this book is original; there is nothing hackneyed about it anywhere. Always, in other romances, when you find the author leading up to a climax, you know what is going to happen. But in this book it is different; the thing which seems inevitable and unavoidable never happens; it is circumvented by the art of the author every time.

Another elopement was attempted. It failed.

We have now arrived at the end. But it is not exciting. McClintock thinks it is; but it isn't. One day Elfonzo sent Ambulinia another note—a note proposing elopement No. 16. This time the plan is admirable; admirable, sagacious, ingenious, imaginative, deep—oh, everything, and perfectly easy. One wonders why it was never thought of before. This is the scheme. Ambulinia is to leave the breakfast-table, ostensibly to ''attend to the placing of those flowers, which ought to have been done a week ago,''—artificial ones, of course; the others wouldn't keep so long,—and then, instead of fixing the flowers, she is to walk out to the grove, and go off with Elfonzo. The invention of this plan overstrained the author, that is plain, for he straightway shows failing powers. The details of the plan are not many or elaborate. The author shall state them himself—this good soul, whose intentions are always better than his English:

You walk carelessly towards the academy grove, where you will find me with a lightning steed, elegantly equipped to bear you off where we shall be joined in wedlock with the first connubial rights.

*It is a crowbar.

Last scene of all, which the author, now much enfeebled, tries to smarten up and make acceptable to his spectacular heart by introducing some new properties,—silver bow, golden harp, olive branch,—things that can all come good in an elopement, no doubt, yet are not to be compared to an umbrella for real handiness and reliability in an excursion of that kind.

> And away she ran to the sacred grove, surrounded with glittering pearls, that indicated her coming. Elfonzo hails her with his silver bow and his golden harp. They meet—Ambulinia's countenance brightens—Elfonzo leads up his winged steed. "Mount," said he, "ye true hearted, ye fearless soul—the day is ours." She sprang upon the back of the young thunderbolt, a brilliant star sparkles upon her head, with one hand she grasps the reins, and with the other she holds an olive-branch. "Lend thy aid, ye strong winds," they exclaimed, "ye moon, ye sun, and all ye fair host of heaven, witness the enemy conquered." "Hold," said Elfonzo, "thy dashing steed." "Ride on," said Ambulinia, "the voice of thunder is behind us." And onward they went, with such rapidity, that they very soon arrived at Rural Retreat, where they dismounted, and were united with all the solemnities that usually attend such divine operations.

There is but one Homer, there was but one Shakespeare, there is but one McClintock—and his immortal book is before you. Homer could not have written this book, Shakespeare could not have written it, I could not have done it myself. There is nothing just like it in the literature of any country or of any epoch. It stands alone; it is monumental. It adds G. Ragsdale McClintock's to the sum of the republic's imperishable names.

THE
CURIOUS BOOK
COMPLETE

[The foregoing review of the great work of G. Ragsdale Mc-Clintock is liberally illuminated with sample extracts, but these cannot appease the appetite. Only the complete book, unabridged, can do that. Therefore it is here printed.—M.T.]

THE ENEMY CONQUERED; OR, LOVE TRIUMPHANT

Sweet girl, thy smiles are full of charms,
   Thy voice is sweeter still,
It fills the breast with fond alarms,
   Echoed by every rill.

I BEGIN this little work with an eulogy upon woman, who has ever been distinguished for her perseverance, her constancy, and her devoted attention to those upon whom she has been pleased to place her *affections*. Many have been the themes upon which writers and public speakers have dwelt with intense and increasing interest. Among these delightful themes stands that of woman, the balm to all our sighs and disappointments, and the most preëminent of all other topics. Here the poet and orator have stood and gazed with wonder and with admiration; they have dwelt upon her innocence, the ornament of all her virtues. First viewing her external charms, such as are set forth in her form and her benevolent countenance, and then passing to the deep hidden springs of loveliness and disinterested devotion. In every clime, and in every age, she has been the pride of her *nation*. Her watchfulness is untiring; she who guarded the sepulchre was the first to approach it, and the last to depart from its awful yet sublime scene. Even here, in this highly-favored land, we look to her for the security of our institutions, and for our future greatness as a nation. But, strange as it may appear, woman's charms and virtues are but slightly appreciated by thousands. Those who should raise the standard of female worth, and paint her value with her virtues, in living colors, upon the banners that are fanned by the zephyrs of heaven, and hand them down to posterity as emblematical of a rich inheritance, do not properly estimate them.

Man is not sensible, at all times, of the nature and the emotions which bear that name; he does not understand, he will not comprehend; his intelligence has not expanded to that degree of glory which drinks in the vast revolution of humanity, its end, its mighty destination, and the causes which operated, and are still operating, to produce a more elevated station, and the objects which energize and enliven its consummation. This he is a stranger to; he is not aware that woman is the recipient of celestial love, and that man is dependent upon her to perfect his character; that without her, philosophically and truly speaking, the brightest of his intelligence is but the coldness of a winter moon, whose beams can produce no fruit, whose solar light is not its own, but borrowed from the great dispenser of effulgent beauty. We have no disposition in the world to flatter the fair sex, we would raise them above those dastardly principles which only exist in little souls, contracted hearts, and a distracted brain. Often does she unfold herself in all her fascinating loveliness, presenting the most captivating charms; yet we find man frequently treats such purity of purpose with indifference. Why does he do it? Why does he baffle that which is inevitably the source of his better days? Is he so much of a stranger to those excellent qualities, as not to appreciate woman, as not to have respect to her dignity? Since her art and beauty first capti- vated man, she has been his delight and his comfort; she has shared alike in his misfortunes and in his prosperity.

Whenever the billows of adversity and the tumultuous waves of trouble beat high, her smiles subdue their fury. Should the tear of sorrow and the mournful sigh of grief interrupt the peace of his mind, her voice removes them all, and she bends from her circle to encourage him onward. When darkness would obscure his mind, and a thick cloud of gloom would bewilder its operations, her intelligent eye darts a ray of streaming light into his heart. Mighty and charming is that disinterested devotion which she is ever ready to exercise toward man, not waiting till the last moment of his danger, but seeks to relieve him in his early afflictions. It gushes forth from the expansive fullness of a tender and devoted heart, where the noblest, the purest, and the most elevated and refined feelings are matured, and developed in those many kind offices which invariably make her character.

In the room of sorrow and sickness, this unequaled character- istic may always be seen, in the performance of the most charita- ble acts; nothing that she can do to promote the happiness of him who she claims to be her protector, will be omitted; all is invigo- rated by the animating sunbeams which awaken the heart to songs of gaiety. Leaving this point, to notice another prominent consid- eration, which is generally one of great moment and of vital im- portance. Invariably she is firm and steady in all her pursuits and aims. There is required a combination of forces and extreme op- position to drive her from her position; she takes her stand, not to be moved by the sound of Apollo's lyre, or the curved bow of pleasure.

Firm and true to what she undertakes, and that which she re- quires by her own aggrandizement, and regards as being within the strict rules of propriety, she will remain stable and unflinching to the last. A more genuine principle is not to be found in the most determined, resolute heart of man. For this she deserves to be held in the highest commendation, for this she deserves the purest of all other blessings, and for this she deserves the most laudable reward of all others. It is a noble characteristic, and is worthy the imitation of any age. And when we look at it in one particular aspect, it is still magnified, and grows brighter and brighter the more we reflect upon its eternal duration. What will she not do, when her word as well as her affections and *love* are pledged to her lover? Everything that is dear to her on earth, all the hospitalities of kind and loving parents, all the sincerity and loveliness of sisters, and the benevolent devotion of brothers, who have surrounded her with every comfort; she will forsake them all, quit the harmony and sweet sound of the lute and the harp, and throw herself upon the affections of some devoted admirer, in whom she fondly hopes to find more than she has left behind, which is not often realized by many. Truth and virtue all combined! How deserving our admiration and love! Ah! cruel would it be in man, after she has thus manifested such an unshaken confidence in him, and said by her determination to abandon all the endearments and blandishments of home, to act a villainous part, and prove a traitor in the revolution of his mission, and then turn Hector over the innocent victim whom he swore to protect, in the presence of Heaven, recorded by the pen of an angel.

Striking as this trait may unfold itself in her character, and as preëminent as it may stand among the fair display of her other qualities, yet there is another, which struggles into existence, and adds an additional luster to what she already possesses. I mean that disposition in woman which enables her, in sorrow, in grief, and in distress, to bear all with enduring patience. This she has done, and can and will do, amid the din of war and clash of arms. Scenes and occurrences which, to every appearance, are calculated to rend the heart with the profoundest emotions of trouble, do not fetter that exalted principle imbued in her very nature. It is true, her tender and feeling heart may often be moved, (as she is thus constituted,) but still she is not conquered, she has not given up to the harlequin of disappointments, her energies have not become clouded in the last moment of misfortune, but she is continually invigorated by the archetype of her affections. She may bury her face in her hands, and let the tear of anguish roll, she may promenade the delightful walks of some garden, decorated with all the flowers of nature, or she may steal out along some gently rippling stream, and there, as the silver waters uninterruptedly move forward, sheds her silent tears, they mingle with the waves, and take a last farewell of their agitated home, to seek a peaceful dwelling among the rolling floods; yet there is a voice rushing from her breast, that proclaims *victory* along the whole line and battlement of her affections. That voice is the voice of patience and resignation; that voice is one that bears everything calmly and dispassionately; amid the most distressing scenes, when the fates are arrayed against her peace, and apparently plotting for her destruction, still she is resigned.

Woman's affections are deep, consequently her troubles may be made to sink deep. Although you may not be able to mark the traces of her grief and the furrowings of her anguish upon her winning countenance, yet be assured they are nevertheless preying upon her inward person, sapping the very foundation of that heart which alone was made for the weal and not the woe of man. The deep recesses of the soul are fields for their operation. But they are not destined simply to take the regions of the heart for their dominion, they are not satisfied merely with interrupting her better feelings; but after a while you may see the blooming cheek beginning to droop and fade, her intelligent eye no longer sparkles with the starry light of heaven, her vibrating pulse long since changed its regular motion, and her palpitating bosom beats once more for the mid-day of her glory. Anxiety and care ultimately throw her into the arms of the haggard and grim monster death. But, oh, how patient, under every pining influence! Let us view the matter in bolder colors; see her when the dearest object of her affections recklessly seeks every bacchanalian pleasure, contents himself with the last rubbish of creation. With what solicitude she awaits his return! Sleep fails to perform its office—she weeps while the nocturnal shades of the night triumph in the stillness. Bending over some favorite book, whilst the author throws before her mind the most beautiful imagery, she startles at every sound. The midnight silence is broken by the solemn announcement of the return of another morning. He is still absent: she listens for that voice which has so often been greeted by the melodies of her own; but, alas! stern silence is all that she receives for her vigilance.

Mark her unwearied watchfullness, as the night passes away. At last, brutalized by the accursed thing, he staggers along with rage, and shivering with cold, he makes his appearance. Not a murmur is heard from her lips. On the contrary, she meets him with a smile—she caresses him with her tender arms, with all the gentleness and softness of her sex. Here then, is seen her disposition, beautifully arrayed. Woman, thou art more to be admired than the spicy gales of Arabia, and more sought for than the gold of Golconda. We believe that Woman should associate freely with man, and we believe that it is for the preservation of her rights. She should become acquainted with the metaphysical designs of those who condescend to sing the siren song of flattery. This, we think, should be according to the unwritten law of decorum, which is stamped upon every innocent heart. The precepts of prudery are often steeped in the guilt of contamination, which blasts the expectations of better moments. Truth, and beautiful dreams—loveliness, and delicacy of character, with cherished affections of the ideal woman—gentle hopes and aspirations, are enough to uphold her in the storms of darkness, without the transferred colorings of a stained sufferer. How often have we seen it in our public prints, that woman occupies a false station in the world! and some have gone so far as to say it was an unnatural one. So long has she been regarded a weak creature, by the rabble and illiterate—they have looked upon her as an insufficient actress on the great stage of human life—a mere puppet, to fill up the drama of human exis-

tence—a thoughtless inactive being,—that she has too often come
to the same conclusion herself, and has sometimes forgotten her
high destination, in the meridian of her glory. We have but little
sympathy or patience for those who treat her as a mere Rosy
Melindi—who are always fishing for pretty compliments—who
are satisfied by the gossamer of Romance, and who can be allured
by the verbosity of high-flown words, rich in language, but poor
and barren in sentiment. Beset, as she has been, by the intellectual
vulgar, the selfish, the designing, the cunning, the hidden, and the
artful—no wonder she has sometimes folded her wings in despair,
and forgotten her *heavenly* mission in the derlirium of imagination;
no wonder she searches out some wild desert, to find a peaceful
home. But this cannot always continue. A new era is moving
gently onward, old things are rapidly passing away; old superstitions, old prejudices, and old notions are now bidding farewell to
their old associates and companions, and giving way to one whose
wings are plumed with the light of heaven, and tinged by the dews
of the morning. There is a remnant of blessedness that clings to
her in spite of all evil influence—there is enough of the Divine
Master left, to accomplish the noblest work ever achieved under
the canopy of the vaulted skies; and that time is fast approaching,
when the picture of the true woman will shine from its frame of
glory, to captivate, to win back, to restore, and to call into being
once more, *the object of her mission*.

> Star of the brave! thy glory shed,
> O'er all the earth, thy army led—
> Bold meteor of immortal birth!
> Why come from Heaven to dwell on Earth?

Mighty and glorious are the days of youth; happy the moments
of the *lover,* mingled with smiles and tears of his devoted, and
long to be remembered are the achievements which he gains with
a palpitating heart and a trembling hand. A bright and lovely
dawn, the harbinger of a fair and prosperous day, had arisen over
the beautiful little village of Cumming, which is surrounded by
the most romantic scenery in the Cherokee country. Brightening
clouds seemed to rise from the mist of the fair Chattahoochee, to
spread their beauty over the thick forest, to guide the hero whose
bosom beats with aspirations to conquer the enemy that would
tarnish his name, and to win back the admiration of his long tried
friend. He endeavored to make his way through Sawney's Mountain, where many meet to catch the gales that are continually
blowing for the refreshment of the stranger and the traveler. Surrounded as he was, by hills on every side, naked rocks dared the
efforts of his energies. Soon the sky became overcast, the sun
buried itself in the clouds, and the fair day gave place to gloomy
twilight, which lay heavily on the Indian Plains. He remembered
an old Indian Castle, that once stood at the foot of the Mountain.
He thought if he could make his way to this, he would rest con-

tented for a short time. The mountain air breathed fragrance—a
rosy tinge rested on the glassy waters that murmured at its base.
His resolution soon brought him to the remains of the red man's
hut: he surveyed with wonder and astonishment, the decayed
building, which time had buried in the dust, and thought to himself, his happiness was not yet complete. Beside the shore of the
brook sat a young man, about eighteen or twenty, who seemed to
be reading some favorite book, and who had a remarkably noble
countenance—eyes which betrayed more than a common mind.
This of course made the youth a welcome guest, and gained him
friends in whatever condition of life he might be placed. The
traveler observed that he was a well built figure which showed
strength and grace in every movement. He accordingly addressed
him in quite a gentlemanly manner, and inquired of him the way
to the village. After he had received the desired information, and
was about taking his leave, the youth said, "Are you not Major
Elfonzo, the great musician—the champion of a noble cause—the
modern Achilles, who gained so many victories in the Florida
War?" "I bear that name," said the Major, "and those titles,
trusting at the same time, that the ministers of grace will carry me
triumphantly through all my laudable undertakings, and if," continued the Major, "you sir, are the patronizer of noble deeds, I
should like to make you my confidant, and learn your address."
The youth looked somewhat amazed, bowed low, mused for a
moment, and began: "My name is Roswell. I have been recently
admitted to the bar, and can only give a faint outline of my future
success in that honorable profession; but I trust, sir, like the Eagle,
I shall look down from lofty rocks upon the dwellings of man, and
shall ever be ready to give you any assistance in my official capacity, and whatever this muscular arm of mine can do, whenever it
shall be called from its buried *greatness*." The Major grasped him
by the hand, and exclaimed: "O! thou exalted spirit of inspiration—thou flame of burning prosperity, may the Heaven directed
blaze be the glare of thy soul, and battle down every rampart that
seems to impede your progress!"

The road which led to the town, presented many attractions.
Elfonzo had bid farewell to the youth of deep feeling, and was
now wending his way to the dreaming spot of his fondness. The
south winds whistled through the woods, as the waters dashed
against the banks, as rapid fire in the pent furnace roars. This
brought him to remember while alone, that he quietly left behind
the hospitality of a father's house, and gladly entered the world,
with higher hopes than are often realized. But as he journeyed
onward, he was mindful of the advice of his father, who had often
looked sadly on the ground, when tears of cruelly deceived hope,
moistened his eye. Elfonzo had been somewhat of a dutiful son;
yet fond of the amusements of life—had been in distant lands—
had enjoyed the pleasure of the world, and had frequently returned
to the scenes of his boyhood, almost destitute of many of the
comforts of life. In this condition, he would frequently say to his

father,-"Have I offended you, that you look upon me as a stranger, and frown upon me with stinging looks? Will you not favor me with the sound of your voice? If I have trampled upon your veneration, or have spread a humid veil of darkness around your expectations, send me back into the world where no heart beats for me—where the foot of man has never yet trod; but give me at least one kind word—allow me to come into the presence sometimes of thy winter-worn locks." "Forbid it, Heaven, that I should be angry with thee," answered the father, "my son, and yet I send thee back to the children of the world—to the cold charity of the combat, and to a land of victory. I read another destiny in thy countenance—I learn thy inclinations from the flame that has already kindled in my soul a strange sensation. It will seek thee, my dear *Elfonzo*, it will find thee—thou canst not escape that lighted torch, which shall blot out from the remembrance of men a long train of prophecies which they have foretold against thee. I once thought not so. Once, I was blind; but now the path of life is plain before me, and my sight is clear; yet Elfonzo, return to thy worldly occupation—take again in thy hand, that chord of sweet sounds—struggle with the civilized world, and with your own heart; fly swiftly to the enchanted ground—let the night-*Owl* send forth its screams from the stubborn oak—let the sea sport upon the beach, and the stars sing together; but learn of these, Elfonzo, thy doom, and thy hiding place. Our most innocent as well as our most lawful *desires* must often be denied us, that we may learn to sacrifice them to a Higher will."

Remembering such admonitions with gratitude, Elfonzo was immediately urged by the recollection of his father's family to keep moving. His steps became quicker and quicker—he hastened through the *piny* woods, dark as the forest was, and with joy he very soon reached the little village of repose, in whose bosom rested the boldest chivalry. His close attention to every important object—his modest questions about whatever was new to him—his reverence for wise old age, and his ardent desire to learn many of the fine arts, soon brought him into respectable notice.

One mild winter day, as he walked along the streets toward the Academy, which stood upon a small eminence, surrounded by native growth—some venerable in its appearance, others young and prosperous—all seemed inviting, and seemed to be the very place for learning as well as for genius to spend its research beneath its spreading shades. He entered its classic walls in the usual mode of southern manners. The principal of the Institution begged him to be seated, and listen to the recitations that were going on. He accordingly obeyed the request, and seemed to be much pleased. After the school was dismissed, and the young hearts regained their freedom, with the songs of the evening, laughing at the anticipated pleasures of a happy home, while others tittered at the actions of the past day, he addressed the teacher in a tone that indicated a resolution—with an undaunted mind. He said he had determined to become a student, if he could meet with his approbation. "Sir," said he, "I have spent much time in the world. I have traveled among the uncivilized inhabitants of America. I have met with friends, and combated with foes; but none of these gratify my ambition, or decide what is to be my destiny. I see the learned world have an influence with the voice of the people themselves. The despoilers of the remotest kingdoms of the earth, refer their differences to this class of persons. This the illiterate and inexperienced little dream of; and now if you will receive me as I am, with these deficiencies—with all my misguided opinions, I will give you my honor, sir, that I will never disgrace the Institution, or those who have placed you in this honorable station." The instructor, who had met with many disappointments, knew how to feel for a stranger who had been thus turned upon the charities of an unfeeling community. He looked at him earnestly, and said: "Be of good cheer—look forward, sir, to the high destination you may attain. Remember, the more elevated the mark at which you aim, the more sure, the more glorious, the more magnificent the prize." From wonder to wonder, his encouragement led the impatient listener. A strange nature bloomed before him—giant streams promised him success—gardens of hidden treasures opened to his view. All this, so vividly described, seemed to gain a new witchery from his glowing fancy.

In 1842, he entered the class, and made rapid progress in the English and Latin departments. Indeed, he continued advancing with such rapidity that he was like to become the first in his class, and made such unexpected progress, and was so studious, that he had almost forgotten the pictured saint of his affections. The fresh wreaths of the pine and cypress, had waited anxiously to drop once more the dews of Heaven upon the heads of those who had so often poured forth the tender emotions of their souls under its boughs. He was aware of the pleasure that he had seen there. So one evening, as he was returning from his reading, he concluded he would pay a visit to this enchanting spot. Little did he think of witnessing a shadow of his former happiness, though no doubt, he wished it might be so. He continued sauntering by the road-side, meditating on the past. The nearer he approached the spot, the more anxious he became. At that moment, a tall female figure flitted across his path, with a bunch of roses in her hand; her countenance showed uncommon vivacity, with a resolute spirit; her ivory teeth already appeared as she smiled beautifully, promenading,—while her ringlets of hair, dangled unconsciously around her snowy neck. Nothing was wanting to complete her beauty. The tinge of the rose was in full bloom upon her cheek; the charms of sensibility and tenderness were always her associates. In Ambulinia's bosom dwelt a noble soul—one that never faded—one that never was conquered. Her heart yielded to no feeling but the love of Elfonzo, on whom she gazed with intense delight, and to whom she felt herself more closely bound, because he sought the hand of no other. Elfonzo was roused from his apparent revery. His books no longer were his inseparable companions—his thoughts arrayed themselves to encourage him to the field of victory. He endeavored to speak to his supposed Ambulinia, but his speech appeared not in words. No, his effort was a stream of fire, that kindled his soul into a flame of admiration, and carried his senses away captive. Ambulinia had disappeared, to make him more mindful of his duty. As she walked speedily away through the piny woods, she calmly echoed: "O! Elfonzo, thou wilt now look from thy sunbeams. Thou shalt now walk in a new path—perhaps thy way leads through darkness; but fear not, the stars foretell happiness."

Not many days afterwards, as surrounded by fragrant flowers, she sat one evening at twilight, to enjoy the cool breeze that whispered notes of melody along the distant groves, the little birds perched on every side, as if to watch the movements of their new visitor. The bells were tolling, when Elfonzo silently stole along by the wild wood flowers, holding in his hand his favorite instrument of music—his eye continually searching for Ambulinia, who hardly seemed to perceive him, as she played carelessly with the songsters that hopped from branch to branch. Nothing could be more striking than the difference between the two. Nature seemed to have given the more tender soul to Elfonzo, and the stronger and more courageous to Ambulinia. A deep feeling spoke from the eyes of Elfonzo,—such a feeling as can only be expressed by those who are blessed as admirers, and by those who are able to return the same with sincerity of heart. He was a few years older than Ambulinia: she had turned a little into her seventeenth. He had almost grown up in the Cherokee country, with the same equal proportions as one of the natives. But little intimacy had existed between them until the year forty-one—because the youth felt that the character of such a lovely girl was too exalted to inspire any other feeling than that of quiet reverence. But as lovers will not always be insulted, at all times and under all circumstances, by the frowns and cold looks of crabbed old age, which should continually reflect dignity upon those around, and treat the unfortunate as well as the fortunate with a graceful mien, he continued to use diligence and perseverance. All this lighted a spark in his heart that changed his whole character, and like the unyielding Deity that follows the storm to check its rage in the forest, he resolves for the first time to shake off his embarrassment, and return where he had before only worshiped.

It could not escape Ambulinia's penetrating eye, that he sought an interview with her, which she as anxiously avoided, and assumed a more distant calmness than before, seemingly to destroy all hope. After many efforts and struggles with his own person, with timid steps the Major approached the damsel, with the same caution as he would have done in a field of battle. "Lady Ambulinia," said he, trembling, "I have long desired a moment like this. I dare not let it escape. I fear the consequences; yet I hope your indulgence will at least hear my petition. Can you not anticipate what I would say, and what I am about to express? Will you not, like Minerva, who sprung from the brain of Jupiter, release

me from thy winding chains or cure me——" "Say no more,
Elfonzo," answered Ambulinia, with a serious look, raising her
hand as if she intended to swear eternal hatred against the whole
world,—"another lady in my place, would have perhaps answered
your question in bitter coldness. I know not the little arts of my
sex. I care but little for the vanity of those who would chide me,
and am unwilling, as well as ashamed to be guilty of anything that
would lead you to think 'all is not gold that glitters:' so be not
rash in your resolution. It is better to repent now, than to do it in
a more solemn hour. Yes, I know what you would say. I know you
have a costly gift for me—the noblest that man can make—*your
heart!* you should not offer it to one so unworthy. Heaven, you
know, has allowed my father's house to be made a house of solitude, a home of silent obedience, which my parents say, is more
to be admired than big names and high sounding titles. Notwithstanding all this, let me speak the emotions of an honest heart—
allow me to say in the fullness of my hopes that I anticipate better
days. The bird may stretch its wings toward the sun, which it can
never reach; and flowers of the field appear to ascend in the same
direction, because they cannot do otherwise: but man confides his
complaints to the saints in whom he believes; for in their abodes
of light they know no more sorrow. From your confession and
indicative looks, I must be that person: if so, deceive not yourself."

Elfonzo replied, "Pardon me, my dear madam, for my frankness. I have loved you from my earliest days—everything grand
and beautiful hath borne the image of Ambulinia: while precipices
on every hand surrounded me, your *guardian angel* stood and
beckoned me away from the deep abyss. In every trial—in every
misfortune, I have met with your helping hand; yet I never dreamed
or dared to cherish thy love, till a voice impaired with age encouraged the cause, and declared they who acquired thy favor, should
win a victory. I saw how Leos worshiped thee. I felt my own
unworthiness. I began to *know jealousy,* a strong guest indeed, in
my bosom, yet I could see if I gained your admiration, Leos was
to be my rival. I was aware that he had the influence of your
parents, and the wealth of a deceased relative, which is too often
mistaken for permanent and regular tranquillity; yet I have determined by your permission to beg an interest in your prayers—to
ask you to animate my drooping spirits by your smiles and your
winning looks; for, if you but speak, I shall be conqueror, my
enemies shall stagger like Olympus shakes. And though earth and
sea may tremble, and the charioteer of the sun may forget his
dashing steed; yet I am assured that it is only to arm me with
divine weapons, which will enable me to complete my long tried
intention." "Return to yourself, Elfonzo," said Ambulinia, pleasantly, "a dream of vision has disturbed your intellect—you are
above the atmosphere, dwelling in the celestial regions, nothing is
there that urges or hinders, nothing that brings discord into our
present litigation. I entreat you to condescend a little, and be a

man, and forget it all. When Homer describes the battle of the gods and noble men, fighting with giants and dragons, they represent under this image, our struggles with the delusions of our passions. You have exalted me, an unhappy girl, to the skies,— you have called me a saint, and portrayed in your imagination, an angel in human form. Let her remain such to you,—let her continue to be as you have supposed, and be assured that she will consider a share in your esteem, as her highest treasure. Think not that I would allure you from the path in which your conscience leads you; for you know I respect the conscience of others, as I would die for my own. Elfonzo, if I am worthy of thy love, let such conversation never again pass between us. Go, seek a nobler theme! we will seek it in the stream of time, as the sun set in the Tigris.'' As she spake these words, she grasped the hand of Elfonzo, saying at the same time—''peace and prosperity attend you my hero: be up and doing.'' Closing her remarks with this expression, she walked slowly away, leaving Elfonzo astonished and amazed. He ventured not to follow, or detain her. Here he stood alone, gazing at the stars;—confounded as he was, here he stood. The rippling stream rolled on at his feet. Twilight had already begun to draw her sable mantle over the earth, and now and then, the fiery smoke would ascend from the little town which lay spread out before him. The citizens seemed to be full of life and good humor; but poor Elfonzo saw not a brilliant scene. No, his future life stood before him, stripped of the hopes that once adorned all his sanguine desires. ''Alas!'' said he, ''am I now Grief's disappointed son at last.'' Ambulinia's image rose before his fancy. A mixture of ambition and greatness of soul, moved upon his young heart, and encouraged him to bear all his crosses with the patience of a Job, notwithstanding he had to encounter with so many obstacles. He still endeavored to prosecute his studies, and reasonably progressed in his education. Still, he was not content; there was something yet to be done, before his happiness was complete. He would visit his friends and acquaintances. They would invite him to social parties, insisting that he should partake of the amusements that were going on. This he enjoyed tolerably well. The ladies and gentlemen were generally well pleased with the Major; as he delighted all with his violin, which seemed to have a thousand chords—more symphonious than the Muses of Apollo, and more enchanting than the ghost of the Hills. He passed some days in the country. During that time Leos had made many calls upon Ambulinia, who was generally received with a great deal of courtesy by the family. They thought him to be a young man worthy of attention, though he had but little in his soul to attract the attention, or even win the affections of her whose graceful manners had almost made him a slave to every bewitching look that fell from her eyes. Leos made several attempts to tell her of his fair prospects—how much he loved her, and how much it would add to his bliss if he could but think she would be willing to share these blessings with him; but choked by his undertaking, he made himself more like an inactive drone, than he did like one who bowed at beauty's shrine.

Elfonzo again wends his way to the stately walls and new-built village. He now determines to see the end of the prophecy which had been foretold to him. The clouds burst from his sight; he believes if he can but see his Ambulinia, he can open to her view the bloody altars that have been misrepresented to stigmatize his name. He knows that her breast is transfixed with the sword of reason, and ready at all times to detect the hidden villainy of her enemies. He resolves to see her in her own home, with the consoling theme; " 'I can but perish if I go.' Let the consequences be what they may," said he, "if I die, it shall be contending and struggling for my own rights."

Night had almost overtaken him when he arrived in town. Col. Elder, a noble-hearted, high-minded and independent man, met him at his door as usual, and seized him by the hand. "Well, Elfonzo," said the Col., "how does the world use you in your efforts?" "I have no objection to the world," said Elfonzo; "but the people are rather singular in some of their opinions." "Aye, well," said the Col., "you must remember that creation is made up of many mysteries: just take things by the right handle—be always sure you know which is the smooth side, before you attempt your polish—be reconciled to your fate, be it what it may, and never find fault with your condition, unless your complaining will benefit it. Perseverance is a principle that should be commendable in those who have judgment to govern it. I should never have been so successful in my hunting excursions, had I waited till the deer by some magic dream had been drawn to the muzzle of the gun, before I made an attempt to fire at the game that dared my boldness in the wild forest. The great mystery in hunting seems to be,—a good marksman, a resolute mind, a fixed determination, and my word for it, you will never return home without sounding your horn with the breath of a new victory. And so with every other undertaking. Be confident that your ammunition is of the right kind—always pull your trigger with a steady hand, and so soon as you perceive a calm, touch her off, and the spoils are yours."

This filled him with redoubled vigor, and he set out with a stronger anxiety than ever to the home of Ambulinia. A few short steps soon brought him to the door, half out of breath. He rapped gently. Ambulinia, who sat in the parlor alone, suspecting Elfonzo was near, ventured to the door, opened it, and beheld the hero, who stood in an humble attitude, bowed gracefully, and as they caught each other's looks, the light of peace beamed from the eyes of Ambulinia. Elfonzo caught the expression; a halloo of smothered shouts ran through every vein, and for the first time he dared to impress a kiss upon her cheek. The scene was overwhelming; had the temptation been less animating, he would not have ventured to have acted so contrary to the desired wish of his Ambulinia; but who could have withstood the irresistible temptation! What society condemns the practice, but a cold, heartless, uncivilized people, that know nothing of the warm attachments of refined society? Here the dead was raised to his long cherished hopes, and the lost was found. Here all doubt and danger were buried in the vortex of oblivion; sectional differences no longer disunited their opinions; like the freed bird from the cage, sportive claps its rustling wings, wheels about to Heaven in a joyful strain, and raises its notes to the upper sky. Ambulinia insisted upon Elfonzo to be seated, and give her a history of his unnecessary absence; assuring him the family had retired, consequently they would ever remain ignorant of his visit. Advancing toward him, she gave a bright display of her rosy neck, and from her head the ambrosial locks breathed divine fragrance; her robe hung waving to his view, while she stood like a goddess confessed before him.

"It does seem to me, my dear sir," said Ambulinia, "that you have been gone an age. Oh, the restless hours I have spent since I last saw you, in yon beautiful grove. There is where I trifled with your feelings for the express purpose of trying your attachment for me. I now find you are devoted; but ah! I trust you live not unguarded by the powers of Heaven. Though oft did I refuse to join my hand with thine, and as oft did I cruelly mock thy entreaties with borrowed shapes: yes, I feared to answer thee by terms, in words sincere and undissembled. O! could I pursue, and you had leisure to hear the annals of my woes, the evening star would shut Heaven's gates upon the impending day, before my tale would be finished, and this night would find me soliciting your forgiveness." "Dismiss thy fears and thy doubts," replied Elfonzo. "Look O! look: that angelic look of thine,—bathe not thy visage in tears; banish those floods that are gathering; let my confession and my presence bring thee some relief." "Then, indeed, I will be cheerful," said Ambulinia, "and I think if we will go to the exhibition this evening, we certainly will see something worthy of our attention. One of the most tragical scenes is to be acted that has ever been witnessed, and one that every jealous-hearted person should learn a lesson from. It cannot fail to have a good effect, as it will be performed by those who are young and vigorous, and learned as well as enticing. You are aware, Major Elfonzo, who are to appear on the stage, and what the characters are to represent." "I am acquainted with the circumstances," replied Elfonzo, "and as I am to be one of the musicians upon that interesting occasion, I should be much gratified if you would favor me with your company during the hours of the exercises."

"What strange notions are in your mind?" inquired Ambulinia. "Now I know you have something in view, and I desire you to tell me why it is that you are so anxious that I should continue with you while the exercises are going on; though if you think I can add to your happiness and predilections, I have no particular objection to acquiesce in your request. Oh, I think I foresee, now, what you anticipate." "And will you have the goodness to tell me what you think it to be?" inquired Elfonzo. "By all means," answered

Ambulinia; "a rival, sir, you would fancy in your own mind; but let me say to you, fear not! fear not! I will be one of the last persons to disgrace my sex, by thus encouraging everyone who may feel disposed to visit me, who may honor me with their graceful bows and their choicest compliments. It is true, that young men too often mistake civil politeness for the finer emotions of the heart, which is tantamount to courtship; but, ah! how often are they deceived, when they come to test the weight of sunbeams, with those on whose strength hangs the future happiness of an untried life."

The people were now rushing to the Academy with impatient anxiety; the band of music was closely followed by the students; then the parents and guardians; nothing interrupted the glow of spirits which ran through every bosom, tinged with the songs of a Virgil and the tide of a Homer. Elfonzo and Ambulinia soon repaired to the scene, and fortunately for them both, the house was so crowded that they took their seats together in the music department, which was not in view of the auditory. This fortuitous circumstance added more to the bliss of the major than a thousand such exhibitions would have done. He forgot that he was man; music had lost its charms for him; whenever he attempted to carry his part, the string of the instrument would break, the bow became stubborn, and refused to obey the loud calls of the audience. Here, he said, was the paradise of his home, the long sought for opportunity; he felt as though he could send a million supplications to the throne of heaven, for such an exalted privilege. Poor Leos, who was somewhere in the crowd, looking as attentively as if he was searching for a needle in a haystack; here he stood, wondering to himself why Ambulinia was not there. "Where can she be? Oh! if she was only here, how I could relish the scene! Elfonzo is certainly not in town; but what if he is? I have got the wealth, if I have not the dignity, and I am sure that the squire and his lady have always been particular friends of mine, and I think with this assurance I shall be able to get upon the blind side of the rest of the family, and make the heaven-born Ambulinia the mistress of all I possess." Then, again, he would drop his head, as if attempting to solve the most difficult problem in Euclid. While he was thus conjecturing in his own mind, a very interesting part of the exhibition was going on, which called the attention of all present. The curtains of the stage waved continually by the repelled forces that were given to them, which caused Leos to behold Ambulinia leaning upon the chair of Elfonzo. Her lofty beauty, seen by the glimmering of the chandelier, filled his heart with rapture, he knew not how to contain himself; to go where they were, would expose him to ridicule; to continue where he was, with such an object before him, without being allowed an explanation in that trying hour, would be to the great injury of his mental as well as of his physical powers; and, in the name of high heaven, what must he do? Finally, he resolved to contain himself as well as he conveniently could, until the scene was over, and then he would plant himself at the door, to arrest Ambulinia from the hands of the insolent Elfonzo, and thus make for himself a more prosperous field of immortality than ever was decreed by Omnipotence, or ever pencil drew or artist imagined. Accordingly he made himself sentinel, immediately after the performance of the evening,— retained his position apparently in defiance of all the world, he waited, he gazed at every lady, his whole frame trembled; here he stood, until everything like human shape had disappeared from the institution, and he had done nothing; he had failed to accomplish that which he so eagerly sought for. Poor, unfortunate crea-' ture! he had not the eyes of an Argus, or he might have seen his Juno and Elfonzo, assisted by his friend Sigma, make their escape from the window, and, with the rapidity of a racehorse, hurry through the blast of the storm, to the residence of her father, without being recognized. He did not tarry long, but assured Ambulinia the endless chain of their existence was more closely connected than ever, since he had seen the virtuous, innocent, imploring, and the constant Amelia murdered by the jealous-hearted Farcillo, the accursed of the land.

The following is the tragical scene, which is only introduced to show the subject matter that enabled Elfonzo to come to such a determinate resolution, that nothing of the kind should ever dispossess him of his true character, should he be so fortunate as to succeed in his present undertaking.

Amelia was the wife of Farcillo, and a virtuous woman; Gracia, a young lady, was her particular friend and confidant. Farcillo grew jealous of Amelia, murders her, finds out that he was deceived, *and stabs himself.* Amelia appears alone, talking to herself.

A. Hail, ye solitary ruins of antiquity, ye sacred tombs and silent walks! it is your aid I invoke; it is to you, my soul, wrapt in deep meditation, pours forth its prayer. Here I wander upon the stage of mortality, since the world hath turned against me. Those whom I believed to be my friends, alas! are now my enemies, planting thorns in all my paths, poisoning all my pleasures, and turning the past to pain. What a lingering catalogue of sighs and tears lies just before me, crowding my aching bosom with the fleeting dream of humanity, which must shortly terminate. And to what purpose will all this bustle of life, these agitations and emotions of the heart have conduced, if it leave behind it nothing of utility, if it leave no traces of improvement! Can it be that I am deceived in my conclusion? No, I see that I have nothing to hope for, but everything to fear, which tends to drive me from the walks of time.

> Oh! in this dead night, if loud winds arise,
> To lash the surge and bluster in the skies,
> May the west its furious rage display,
> Toss me with storms in the watery way.

(Enter Gracia.)

G.   Oh, Amelia, is it you, the object of grief, the daughter of opulence, of wisdom and philosophy, that thus complaineth? It cannot be you are the child of misfortune, speaking of the monuments of former ages, which were allotted not for the reflection of the distressed, but for the fearless and bold.

A.   Not the child of poverty, Gracia, or the heir of glory and peace, but of fate. Remember, I have wealth more than wit can number; I have had power more than kings could encompass; yet the world seems a desert; all nature appears an afflictive spectacle of warring passions. This blind fatality, that capriciously sports with the rules and lives of mortals, tells me that the mountains will never again send forth the water of their springs to my thirst. Oh, that I might be freed and set at liberty from wretchedness! But I fear, I fear this will never be.

G.   Why, Amelia, this untimely grief? What has caused the sorrows that bespeak better and happier days, to thus lavish out such heaps of misery? You are aware that your instructive lessons embellish the mind with holy truths, by wedding its attention to none but great and noble affections.

A.   This, of course, is some consolation. I will ever love my own species with feelings of a fond recollection, and while I am studying to advance the universal philanthropy, and the spotless name of my own sex, I will try to build my own upon the pleasing belief, that I have accelerated the advancement of one who whispers of departed confidence.

> And I, like some poor peasant fated to reside
> Remote from friends, in a forest wide.
> Oh, see what woman's woes and human wants require,
> Since that great day hath spread the seed of sinful fire.

G.   Look up, thou poor disconsolate; you speak of quitting earthly enjoyments. Unfold thy bosom to a friend, who would be willing to sacrifice every enjoyment for the restoration of that dignity and gentleness of mind, which used to grace your walks, and which is so natural to yourself; not only that, but your paths were strewed with flowers of every hue and of every order.

> With verdant green the mountains glow,
> For thee, for thee, the lilies grow;
> Far stretched beneath the tented hills,
> A fairer flower the valley fills.

A.   Oh, would to Heaven I could give you a short narrative of my former prospects for happiness, since you have acknowledged to be an unchangeable confidant—the richest of all other blessings. Oh, ye names forever glorious, ye celebrated scenes, ye renowned spot of my hymeneal moments; how replete is your chart with sublime reflections! How many profound vows, decorated with immaculate deeds, are written upon the surface of that precious spot of earth, where I yielded up my life of celibacy, bade youth with all its beauties a final adieu, took a last farewell of the laurels that had accompanied me up the hill of my juvenile career. It was then I began to descend toward the valley of disappointment and sorrow; it was then I cast my little bark upon a mysterious ocean of wedlock, with him who then smiled and caressed me, but, alas! now frowns with bitterness, and has grown jealous and cold towards me, because the ring he gave me is misplaced or lost. Oh, bear me, ye flowers of memory, softly through the eventful history of past times; and ye places that have witnessed the progression of man in the circle of so many societies, aid, oh aid my recollection, while I endeavor to trace the vicissitudes of a life devoted in endeavoring to comfort him that I claim as the object of my wishes.

> Ah! ye mysterious men, of all the world, how few
> Act just to Heaven and to your promise true!
> But He who guides the stars with a watchful eye,
> The deeds of men lay open without disguise;
> Oh, this alone will avenge the wrongs I bear,
> For all the oppressed are his peculiar care.

(F. makes a slight noise.)

A.   Who is there—Farcillo?

G.   Then I must be gone. Heaven protect you. Oh, Amelia, farewell, be of good cheer.

> May you stand, like Olympus' towers,
> Against earth and all jealous powers!
> May you, with loud shouts ascend on high,
> Swift as an eagle in the upper sky.

A.   Why so cold and distant to-night, Farcillo? Come, let us each other greet, and forget all the past, and give security for the future.

F.   Security! talk to me about giving security for the future— what an insulting requisition! Have you said your prayers to-night, Madam Amelia?

A.   Farcillo, we sometimes forget our duty, particularly when we expect to be caressed by others.

F.   If you bethink yourself of any crime, or of any fault, that is yet concealed from the courts of Heaven and the thrones of grace, I bid you ask and solicit forgiveness for it now.

A.   Oh, be kind, Farcillo, don't treat me so. What do you mean by all this?

F.   Be kind, you say; you, madam, have forgot that kindness you owe to me, and bestowed it upon another; you shall suffer for your conduct when you make your peace with your God. I would not slay thy unprotected spirit. I call to Heaven to be my guard and my watch—I would not kill thy soul, in which all once seemed just, right, and perfect; but I must be brief, woman.

A. What, talk you of killing? Oh, Farcillo, Farcillo, what is the matter?

F. Aye, I do, without doubt; mark what I say, Amelia.

A. Then, O God, O Heaven, and Angels, be propitious, and have mercy upon me.

F. Amen, to that, madam, with all my heart, and with all my soul.

A. Farcillo, listen to me one moment; I hope you will not kill me.

F. Kill you, aye, that I will; attest it, ye fair host of light, record it, ye dark imps of hell!

A. Oh, I fear you—you are fatal when darkness covers your brow; yet I know not why I should fear, since I never wronged you in all my life. I stand, sir, guiltless before you.

F. You pretend to say you are guiltless! Think of thy sins, Amelia; think, oh think, hidden woman.

A. Wherein have I not been true to you? That death is unkind, cruel, and unnatural, that kills for loving.

F. Peace, and be still while I unfold to thee.

A. I will, Farcillo, and while I am thus silent, tell me the cause of such cruel coldness in an hour like this.

F. That *ring,* oh that ring I so loved, and gave thee as the ring of my heart; the allegiance you took to be faithful, when it was presented; the kisses and smiles with which you honored it. You became tired of the donor, despised it as a plague, and finally gave it to Malos, the hidden, the vile traitor.

A. No, upon my word and honor, I never did; I appeal to the Most High to bear me out in this matter. Send for Malos, and ask him.

F. Send for Malos, aye! Malos you wish to see; I thought so. I knew you could not keep his name concealed. Amelia, sweet Amelia, take heed, take heed of perjury; you are on the stage of death, to suffer for *your sins.*

A. What, not to die I hope, my Farcillo, my ever beloved.

F. Yes, madam, to die a traitor's death. Shortly your spirit shall take its exit; therefore confess freely thy sins, for to deny tends only to make me groan under the bitter cup thou hast made for me. Thou art to die with the name of traitor on thy brow!

A. Then, O Lord, have mercy upon me; give me courage, give me grace and fortitude to stand this hour of trial.

F. Amen, I say, with all my heart.

A. And, oh, Farcillo, will you have mercy, too? I never intentionally offended you in all my life; never *loved* Malos, never gave him cause to think so, as the high court of Justice will acquit me before its tribunal.

F.   Oh, false, perjured woman, thou dost chill my blood, and makest me a demon like thyself. I saw the ring.

A.   He found it, then, or got it clandestinely; send for him, and let him confess the truth; let his confession be sifted.

F.   And you still wish to see him! I tell you, madam, he hath already confessed, and thou knowest the darkness of thy heart.

A.   What, my deceived Farcillo, that I gave him the ring, in which all my affections were concentrated? Oh, surely not.

F.   Aye, he did. Ask thy conscience, and it will speak with a voice of thunder to thy soul.

A.   He will not say so, he dare not, he cannot.

F.   No, he will not say so now, because his mouth, I trust, is hushed in death, and his body stretched to the four winds of heaven, to be torn to pieces by carnivorous birds.

A.   What, is he dead, and gone to the world of spirits with that declaration in his mouth? Oh, unhappy man! Oh, insupportable hour!

F.   Yes, and had all his sighs and looks and tears been lives, my great revenge could have slain them all, without the least condemnation.

A.   Alas! he is ushered into eternity without testing the matter for which I am abused and sentenced and condemned to die.

F.   Cursed, infernal woman! Weepest thou for him to my face? He that hath robbed me of my peace, my energy, the whole love of my life? Could I call the fabled Hydra, I would have him live and perish, survive and die, until the sun itself would grow dim with age. I would make him have the thirst of a Tantalus, and roll the wheel of an Ixion, until the stars of heaven should quit their brilliant stations.

A.   Oh, invincible God, save me! Oh, unsupportable moment! Oh, heavy hour! Banish me, Farcillo—send me where no eye can ever see me, where no sound shall ever greet my ear; but, oh, slay me not, Farcillo; vent thy rage and thy spite upon this emaciated frame of mine, only spare my life.

F.   Your petitions avail nothing, cruel Amelia.

A.   Oh, Farcillo, perpetrate the dark deed to-morrow; let me live till then, for my past kindness to you, and it may be some kind angel will show to you that I am not only the object of innocence, but one who never loved another but your noble self.

F.   Amelia, the decree has gone forth, it is to be done, and that quickly; thou art to die, madam.

A.   But half an hour allow me, to see my father and my only child, to tell her the treachery and vanity of this world.

F.   There is no alternative, there is no pause; my daughter shall not see its deceptive mother die; your father shall not know that his daughter fell disgraced, despised by all but her enchanting Malos.

A.   Oh, Farcillo, put up thy threatening dagger into its scabbard; let it rest and be still, just while I say one prayer for thee and for my child.

F. It is too late, thy doom is fixed, thou hast not confessed to Heaven or to me, my child's protector—thou art to die. Ye powers of earth and heaven, protect and defend me in this alone. (Stabs her, while imploring for mercy.)

A. Oh, Farcillo, Farcillo, a guiltless death I die.

F. Die! die! die!

(Gracia enters running, falls to her knees weeping, and kisses Amelia.)

G. Oh, Farcillo, Farcillo! oh, Farcillo!

F. I am here, the genius of the age, and the avenger of my wrongs.

G. Oh, lady, speak once more; sweet Amelia, oh speak again. Gone, gone—yes, forever gone! Farcillo, oh, coldhearted Farcillo, some evil fiend hath urged you to do this, Farcillo.

F. Say you not so again, or you shall receive the same fate. I did the glorious deed, madam—beware, then, how you talk.

G. I fear not your implements of war; I will let you know you have not the power to do me harm. If you have a heart of triple brass, it shall be reached and melted, and thy blood shall chill thy veins and grow stiff in thy arteries. Here is the ring of the virtuous and innocent murdered Amelia; I obtained it from Malos, who yet lives, in hopes that he will survive the wound given him, and says he got it clandestinely—declares Amelia to be the princess of truth and virtue, invulnerable to anything like forgetting her first devotion to thee. The world has heard of your conduct and your jealousy, and with one universal voice declare her to be the best of all in piety; that she is the star of this great universe, and a more virtuous woman never lived since the wheels of time began. Oh, had you waited till to-morrow, or until I had returned, some kind window would have been opened to her relief. But, alas! she is gone—yes, forever gone, to try the realities of an unknown world!

(Farcillo leaning over the body of Amelia.)

F. Malos not dead, and here is my ring! Oh, Amelia! falsely, falsely murdered! Oh, bloody deed! Oh, wretch that I am! Oh, angels forgive me! Oh, God, withhold thy vengeance! Oh, Amelia! if Heaven would make a thousand worlds like this, set with diamonds, and all of one perfect chrysolite, I would not have done this for them all, I would not have frowned and cursed as I did. Oh, she was heavenly true, nursed in the very lap of bright angels! Cursed slave that I am! Jealousy, oh! thou infernal demon! Lost, lost to every sense of honor! Oh! Amelia—heaven-born Amelia— dead, dead! Oh! oh! oh!—then let me die with thee. Farewell! farewell! ye world that deceived me! (Stabs himself.)

Soon after the excitement of this tragical scene was over, and the enlisted feeling for Amelia had grown more buoyant with Elfonzo and Ambulinia, he determined to visit his retired home, and make the necessary improvements to enjoy a better day; consequently he conveyed the following lines to Ambulinia:

> Go tell the world that hope is glowing,
> Go bid the rocks their silence break,
> Go tell the stars that love is glowing,
> Then bid the hero his lover take.

In the region where scarcely the foot of man hath ever trod, where the woodman hath not found his way, lies a blooming grove, seen only by the sun when he mounts his lofty throne, visited only by the light of the stars, to whom are entrusted the guardianship of earth, before the sun sinks to rest in his rosy bed. High cliffs of rocks surround the romantic place, and in the small cavity of the rocky wall grows the daffodil clear and pure; and as the wind blows along the enchanting little mountain which surrounds the lonely spot, it nourishes the flowers with the dew-drops of heaven. Here is the seat of Elfonzo; darkness claims but little victory over this dominion, and in vain does she spread out her gloomy wings. Here the waters flow perpetually, and the trees lash their tops together to bid the welcome visitor a happy muse. Elfonzo during his short stay in the country, had fully persuaded himself that it was his duty to bring this solemn matter to an issue. A duty that he individually owed, as a gentleman, to the parents of Ambulinia, a duty in itself involving not only his own happiness and his own standing in society, but one that called aloud the act of the parties to make it perfect and complete. How he should communicate his intentions to get a favorable reply, he was at a loss to know; he knew not whether to address Esq. Valeer in prose or in poetry, in a jocular or an argumentative manner, or whether he should use moral suasion, legal injunction, or seize and take by reprisal; if it was to do the latter, he would have no difficulty in deciding in his own mind, but his gentlemanly honor was at stake; so he concluded to address the following letter to the father and mother of Ambulinia, as his address in person he knew would only aggravate the old gentleman, and perhaps his lady.

Cumming, Ga., January 22, 1844.

MR. AND MRS. VALEER—

Again, I resume the pleasing task of addressing you, and once more beg an immediate answer to my many salutations. From every circumstance that has taken place, I feel in duty bound to comply with my obligations; to forfeit my word would be more than I dare do; to break my pledge, and my vows that have been witnessed, sealed, and delivered in the presence of an unseen Deity, would be disgraceful on my part, as well as ruinous to Ambulinia. I wish no longer to be kept in suspense about this matter. I wish to act gentlemanly in every particular. It is true, the promises I have made, are unknown to any but Ambulinia, and I

think it unnecessary to here enumerate them, as they who promise
the most, generally perform the least. Can you for a moment doubt
my sincerity, or my character? My only wish is, sir, that you may
calmly and dispassionately look at the situation of the case, and if
your better judgment should dictate otherwise, my obligations may
induce me to pluck the flower that you so diametrically opposed.
We have sworn by the saints—by the gods of battle, and by that
faith whereby just men are made perfect, to be united. I hope, my
dear sir, you will find it convenient as well as agreeable, to give
me a favorable answer, with the signature of Mrs. Valeer, as well
as yourself.

> With very great esteem,
> your humble servant,
> J. I. ELFONZO.

The moon and stars had grown pale, when Ambulinia had retired to rest. A crowd of unpleasant thoughts passed through her
bosom. Solitude dwelt in her chamber—no sound from the neighboring world penetrated its stillness; it appeared a temple of silence, of repose, and of mystery. At that moment she heard a still
voice calling her father. In an instant, like the flash of lightning, a
thought ran through her mind, that it must be the bearer of Elfonzo's communication. "It is not a dream!" she said, "no, I cannot
read dreams. Oh! I would to Heaven I was near that glowing
eloquence—that poetical language,—it charms the mind in an
inexpressible manner, and warms the coldest heart." While consoling herself with this strain, her father rushed into her room
almost frantic with rage, exclaiming: "O, Ambulinia! Ambulinia!!
undutiful, ungrateful daughter! What does this mean? Why does
this letter bear such heartrending intelligence? Will you quit a
father's house with this debased wretch, without a place to lay his
distracted head; going up and down the country, with every novel
object that may chance to wander through this region. He is a
pretty man to make love known to his superiors, and you, Ambulinia, have done but little credit to yourself by honoring his visits.
O wretchedness! can it be, that my hopes of happiness are forever
blasted! Will you not listen to a father's entreaties, and pay some
regard to a mother's tears. I know, and I do pray that God will
give me fortitude to bear with this sea of troubles, and rescue my
daughter, my Ambulinia, as a brand from the eternal burning."
"Forgive me, father. Oh! forgive thy child," replied Ambulinia.
"My heart is ready to break, when I see you in this grieved state
of agitation. Oh! think not so meanly of me, as that I mourn for
my own danger. Father, I am only woman. Mother, I am only the
templement of thy youthful years; but will suffer courageously
whatever punishment you think proper to inflict upon me, if you
will but allow me to comply with my most sacred promises—if
you will but give me my personal right, and my personal liberty.
Oh father! if your generosity will but give me these, I ask nothing

more. When Elfonzo offered me his heart, I gave him my hand, never to forsake him, and now may the mighty God banish me, before I leave him in adversity. What a heart must I have to rejoice in prosperity with him whose offers I have accepted, and then, when poverty comes, haggard as it may be,—for me to trifle with the oracles of Heaven, and change with every fluctuation that may interrupt our happiness,—like the politician who runs the political gauntlet for office one day, and the next day, because the horizon is darkened a little, he is seen running for his life, for fear he might perish in its ruins. Where is the philosophy; where is the consistency; where is the charity; in conduct like this? Be happy then, my beloved father, and forget me; let the sorrow of parting break down the wall of separation and make us equal in our feeling; let me now say how ardently I love you; let me kiss that age-worn cheek, and should my tears bedew thy face, I will wipe them away. Oh, I never can forget you; no, never, never!''

"Weep not,'' said the father, "Ambulinia. I will forbid Elfonzo my house, and desire that you may keep retired a few days. I will let him know, that my friendship for my family is not linked together by cankered chains; and if he ever enters upon my premises again, I will send him to his long home.'' "Oh, father! let me entreat you to be calm upon this occasion, and though Elfonzo may be the sport of the clouds and winds; yet I feel assured, that no fate will send him to the silent tomb, until the God of the Universe calls him hence with a triumphant voice.''

Here the father turned away, exclaiming: "I will answer his letter in a very few words, and you, madam, will have the goodness to stay at home with your mother: and remember, I am determined to protect you from the consuming fire that looks so fair to your view.''

Cumming, January 22, 1844.

SIR—In regard to your request, I am as I ever have been, utterly opposed to your marrying into my family; and if you have any regard for yourself, or any gentlemanly feeling, I hope you will mention it to me no more; but seek some other one who is not so far superior to you in standing.

W. W. VALEER.

When Elfonzo read the above letter, he became so much depressed in spirits, that many of his friends thought it advisable to use other means to bring about the happy union. "Strange,'' said he, "that the contents of this diminutive letter should cause me to have such depressed feelings; but there is a nobler theme than this. I know not why my *military title* is not as great as that of *Squire Valeer*. For my life I cannot see that my ancestors are inferior to those who are so bitterly opposed to my marriage with Ambulinia. I know I have seen huge mountains before me, yet, when I think that I know gentlemen will insult me upon this delicate matter, should I become angry at fools and babblers, who pride themselves in their impudence and ignorance. No. My equals! I know not where to find them. My inferiors! I think it beneath me; and my superiors! I think it presumption: therefore, if this youthful heart is protected by any of the divine rights, I never will betray my trust."

He was aware that Ambulinia had a confidence, that was indeed, as firm and as resolute, as she was beautiful and interesting. He hastened to the cottage of Louisa, who received him in her usual mode of pleasantness, and informed him that Ambulinia had just that moment left. "Is it possible?" said Elfonzo. "Oh murdered hour! Why did she not remain and be the guardian of my secrets? But hasten and tell me, how she has stood this trying scene, and what are her future determinations." "You know," said Louisa, "Maj. Elfonzo, that you have Ambulinia's first love, which is of no small consequence. She came here about twilight, and shed many precious tears in consequence of her own fate with yours. We walked silently, in yon little valley you see, where we spent a momentary repose. She seemed to be quite as determined as ever, and before we left that beautiful spot she offered up a prayer to Heaven for thee." "I will see her then," replied Elfonzo, "though legions of enemies may oppose. She is mine by foreordination—she is mine by prophecy—she is mine by her own free will, and I will rescue her from the hands of her oppressors. Will you not, Miss Louisa, assist me in my capture?" "I will certainly, by the aid of Divine Providence," answered Louisa, "endeavor to break those slavish chains that bind the richest of prizes; though allow me, Major, to entreat you to use no harsh means on this important occasion; take a decided stand, and write freely to Ambulinia upon this subject, and I will see that no intervening cause hinders its passage to her. God alone will save a mourning people. Now is the day, and now is the hour to obey a command of such valuable worth." The Major felt himself grow stronger after this short interview with Louisa. He felt as if he could whip his weight in wild-cats—he knew he was master of his own feelings, and could now write a letter that would bring this litigation to *an issue*.

Cumming, January 24, 1844.

DEAR AMBULINIA—

We have now reached the most trying moment of our lives; we are pledged not to forsake our trust; we have waited for a favorable hour to come, thinking your friends would settle the matter agreeably among themselves, and finally be reconciled to our marriage; but as I have waited in vain, and looked in vain, I have determined in my own mind to make a proposition to you, though you may think it not in accordance with your station, or compatible with your rank; yet, "sub hoc signo vinces." You know I cannot resume my visits, in consequence of the utter hostility that your father has to me; therefore the consummation of our union will have to be sought for in a more sublime sphere, at the residence of a respectable friend of this village. You cannot have any scruples upon this mode of proceeding, if you will but remember it emanates from one who loves you better than his own life—who is more than anxious to bid you welcome to a new and a happy home. Your warmest associates say come; the talented, the learned, the wise and the experienced say come;—all these with their friends say, come. Viewing these, with many other inducements, I flatter myself that you will come to the embraces of your Elfonzo; for now is the time of your acceptance and the day of your liberation. You cannot be ignorant, Ambulinia, that thou art the desire of my heart; its thoughts are too noble, and too pure, to conceal themselves from you. I shall wait for your answer to this impatiently, expecting that you will set the time to make your departure, and to be in readiness at a moment's warning to share the joys of a more preferable life. This will be handed you by Louisa, who will take a pleasure in communicating anything to you that may relieve your dejected spirits, and will assure you that I now stand ready, willing and waiting to make good my vows.

I am, dear Ambulinia, yours
truly, and forever,
J. I. ELFONZO.

Louisa made it convenient to visit Mr. Valeer's, though they did not suspect her in the least, the bearer of love epistles: consequently, she was invited in the room to console Ambulinia, where they were left alone. Ambulinia was seated by a small table—her head resting on her hand—her brilliant eyes were bathed in tears. Louisa handed her the letter of Elfonzo, when another spirit animated her features—the spirit of renewed confidence that never fails to strengthen the female character in an hour of grief and sorrow like this, and as she pronounced the last accent of his name, she exclaimed, "and does he love me yet! I never will forget your generosity, Louisa. Oh, unhappy and yet blessed Louisa! may you never feel what I have felt—may you never know the pangs of love. Had I never loved, I never would have been unhappy; but I turn to Him who can save, and if His wisdom does not will my expected union, I know He will give me strength to bear my lot. Amuse yourself with this little book, and take it as an apology for my silence," said Ambulinia, "while I attempt to answer this volume of consolation." "Thank you," said Louisa, "you are excusable upon this occasion; but I pray you, Ambulinia, to be expert upon this momentous subject, that there may be nothing mistrustful upon my part." "I will," said Ambulinia, and immediately resumed her seat and addressed the following to Elfonzo:—

Cumming, Ga., January 28, 1844.

DEVOTED ELFONZO—

I hail your letter as a welcome messenger of faith, and can now say truly and firmly, that my feelings correspond with yours. Nothing shall be wanting on my part to make my obedience your fidelity. Courage and perseverance will accomplish success. Receive this as my oath, that while I grasp your hand in my own imagination, we stand united before a higher tribunal than any on earth. All the powers of my life, soul, and body, I devote to thee. Whatever dangers may threaten me, I fear not to encounter them. Perhaps I have determined upon my own destruction, by leaving the house of the best of parents; be it so, I flee to you; I share your destiny, faithful to the end. The day that I have concluded upon for this task, is *Sabbath* next, when the family with the citizens are generally at church. For Heaven's sake let not that day pass unimproved: trust not till to-morrow, it is the cheat of life—the future that never comes—the grave of many noble births—the cavern of ruined enterprise: which like the lightning's flash is born, and dies, and perishes, ere the voice of him who sees, can cry, *behold! behold!!* You may trust to what I say, no power shall tempt me to betray confidence. Suffer me to add one word more.

> I will soothe thee, in all thy grief,
>   Beside the gloomy river;
> And though thy love may yet be brief;
>   Mine is fixed forever.

Receive the deepest emotions of my heart for thy constant love, and may the power of inspiration be thy guide, thy portion, and thy all. In great haste,   Yours faithfully,

                                                        AMBULINIA.

"I now take my leave of you, sweet girl," said Louisa, "sincerely wishing you success on Sabbath next." When Ambulinia's letter was handed to Elfonzo, he perused it without doubting its contents. Louisa charged him to make but few confidants; but like most young men who happened to win the heart of a beautiful girl, he was so elated with the idea, that he felt as a commanding general on parade, who had confidence in all, consequently gave orders to all. The appointed Sabbath, with a delicious breeze and cloudless sky, made its appearance. The people gathered in crowds to the church—the streets were filled with the neighboring citizens, all marching to the house of worship. It is entirely useless for me to attempt to describe the feelings of Elfonzo and Ambulinia, who were silently watching the movements of the multitude, apparently counting them as they entered the house of God, looking for the last one to darken the door. The impatience and anxiety with which they waited, and the bliss they anticipated on the eventful day, is altogether indescribable. Those that have been so fortunate as to embark in such a noble enterprise, know all its realities; and those who have not had this inestimable privilege, will have to taste its sweets, before they can tell to others its joys, its comforts, and its Heaven-born worth. Immediately after Ambulinia had assisted the family off to church, she took the advantage of that opportunity to make good her promises. She left a home of enjoyment to be wedded to one whose love had been justifiable. A few short steps brought her to the presence of Louisa, who urged her to make good use of her time, and not to delay a moment, but to go with her to her brother's house, where Elfonzo would forever make her happy. With lively speed, and yet a graceful air, she entered the door and found herself protected by the champion of her confidence. The necessary arrangements were fast making to have the two lovers united—everything was in readiness except the Parson; and as they are generally very sanctimonious on such occasions, the news got to the parents of Ambulinia, before the everlasting knot was tied, and they both came running, with uplifted hands and injured feelings, to arrest their daughter from an unguarded and hasty resolution. Elfonzo desired to maintain his ground, but Ambulinia thought it best for him to leave, to prepare for a greater contest. He accordingly obeyed, as it would have been a vain endeavor for him to have battled against a man who was armed with deadly weapons; and besides, he could not resist the request of such a pure heart. Ambulinia concealed herself in the upper story of the house, fearing the rebuke of her father; the door was locked, and no chastisement was now expected. Esq. Valeer, whose pride was already touched, resolved to preserve the dignity of his family. He entered the house almost exhausted, looking wildly for Ambulinia. "Amazed and astonished indeed I am," said he, "at a people who call themselves civilized, to allow such behavior as this. Ambulinia, Ambulinia!" he cried, "come to the calls of your first, your best, and your only friend. I appeal to you, sir," turning to the gentleman of the house, "to know where Ambulinia has gone, or where is she?" "Do you mean to insult me, sir, in my own house?" inquired the confounded gentleman. "I will burst," said Mr. V., "asunder every door in your dwelling, in search of my daughter, if you do not speak quickly, and tell me where she is. I care nothing about that outcast rubbish of creation, that mean, low-lived Elfonzo, if I can but obtain Ambulinia. Are you not going to open this door?" said he. "By the Eternal that made Heaven and earth! I will go about the work instantly, if it is not done." The confused citizens gathered from all parts of the village, to know the cause of this commotion. Some rushed into the house; the door that was locked flew open, and there stood Ambulinia, weeping. "Father, be still," said she, "and I will follow thee home." But the agitated man seized her, and bore her off through the gazing multitude. "Father!" she exclaimed, "I humbly beg your pardon—I will be dutiful—I will obey thy commands. Let the sixteen years I have lived in obedience to thee, be my future security." "I don't like to be always giving credit, when the old score is not paid up, madam;" said the father. The mother followed almost in a state of derangement, crying and imploring her to think beforehand, and ask advice from experienced persons, and they would tell her it was a rash undertaking. "Oh!" said she, "Ambulinia, my daughter, did you know what I have suffered—did you know how many nights I have whiled away in agony, in pain, and in fear, you would pity the sorrows of a heartbroken mother."

"Well, mother," replied Ambulinia, "I know I have been disobedient; I am aware that what I have done might have been done much better; but oh! what shall I do with my honor? it is so dear to me; I am pledged to Elfonzo. His high moral worth is certainly worth some attention; moreover, my vows, I have no doubt, are recorded in the book of life, and must I give these all up? must my fair hopes be forever blasted? Forbid it father, oh! forbid it mother, forbid it heaven." "I have seen so many beautiful skies overclouded," replied the mother, "so many blossoms nipped by the frost, that I am afraid to trust you to the care of those fair days, which may be interrupted by thundering and tempestuous nights. You no doubt think as I did—life's devious ways were strewed with sweet scented flowers, but ah! how long they have lingered around me and took their flight in the vivid hopes that laughs at the drooping victims it has murdered." Elfonzo was moved at this sight. The people followed on to see what was going to become of Ambulinia, while he, with downcast looks, kept at a distance, until he saw them enter the abode of the father, thrusting her, that was the sigh of his soul, out of his presence into a solitary apartment, when she exclaimed, "Elfonzo! Elfonzo! oh, Elfonzo! where are thou, with all thy heroes? haste, oh! haste, come thou to my relief. Ride on the wings of the wind! Turn thy force loose like a tempest, and roll on thy army like a whirlwind, over this mountain of trouble and confusion. Oh, friends! if any pity me, let your last efforts throng upon the green hills, and come to the relief of Ambulinia, who is guilty of nothing but innocent love." Elfonzo called out with a loud voice, "my God, can I stand this! arouse up, I beseech you, and put an end to this tyranny. Come, my brave boys," said he, "are you ready to go forth to your duty?" They stood around him. "Who," said he, "will call us to arms? Where are my thunderbolts of war? Speak ye, the first who will meet the foe! Who will go forward with me in this ocean of grievous temptation? If there is one who desires to go, let him come and shake hands upon the altar of devotion, and swear that he will be a hero; yes, a Hector in a cause like this, which calls aloud for a speedy remedy." "Mine be the deed." said a young lawyer, "and mine alone; Venus alone shall quit her station before I will forsake one jot or tittle of my promise to you; what is death to me? what is all this warlike army, if it is not to win a victory? I love the sleep of the lover and the mighty; nor would I give it over till the blood of my enemies should wreak with that of my own. But God forbid that our fame should soar on the blood of the slumberer." Mr. Valeer stands at his door with the frown of a demon upon his brow, with his dangerous weapon ready to strike the first man who should enter his door. "Who will arise and go forward through blood and

carnage to the rescue of my Ambulinia?'' said Elfonzo. "All,''
exclaimed the multitude; and onward they went, with their implements of battle. Others, of a more timid nature, stood among the
distant hills to see the result of the contest.

Elfonzo took the lead of his band. Night arose in clouds; darkness concealed the heavens; but the blazing hopes that stimulated
them gleamed in every bosom. All approached the anxious spot;
they rushed to the front of the house, and with one exclamation
demanded Ambulinia. "Away, begone, and disturb my peace no
more,'' said Mr. Valeer. "You are a set of base, insolent, and
infernal rascals. Go, the northern star points your path through the
dim twilight of the night; go, and vent your spite upon the lonely
hills; pour forth your love, you poor, weak minded wretch, upon
your idleness and upon your guitar, and your fiddle; they are fit
subjects for your admiration, for let me assure you, though this
sword and iron lever are cankered, yet they frown in sleep, and let
one of you dare to enter my house this night and you shall have
the contents and the weight of these instruments.'' "Never yet did
base dishonor blur my name,'' said Elfonzo; "mine is a cause of
renown; here are my warriors, fear and tremble, for this night,
though hell itself should oppose, I will endeavor to avenge her
whom thou hast banished in solitude. The voice of Ambulinia shall
be heard from that dark dungeon.'' At that moment Ambulinia
appeared at the window above, and with a tremulous voice said,
"live, Elfonzo! oh! live to raise my stone of moss! why should
such language enter your heart? why should thy voice rend the air
with such agitation? I bid thee live, once more remembering these
tears of mine are shed alone for thee, in this dark and gloomy
vault, and should I perish under this load of trouble, join the song
of thrilling accents with the raven above my grave, and lay this
tattered frame beside the banks of the Chattahoochee, or the stream
of Sawney's brook; sweet will be the song of death to your Ambulinia. My ghost shall visit you in the smiles of Paradise, and tell
your high fame to the minds of that region, which is far more
preferable than this lonely cell. My heart shall speak for thee till
the latest hour; I know faint and broken are the sounds of sorrow,
yet our souls, Elfonzo, shall hear the peaceful songs together. One
bright name shall be ours on high, if we are not permitted to be
united here; bear in mind that I still cherish my old sentiments,
and the poet will mingle the names of Elfonzo and Ambulinia in
the tide of other days.'' "Fly, Elfonzo,'' said the voices of his
united band, "to the wounded heart of your beloved. All enemies
shall fall beneath thy sword. Fly through the clefts, and the dim
spark shall sleep in death.'' Elfonzo rushes forward and strikes his
shield against the door, which was barricaded, to prevent any
intercourse. His brave sons throng around him. The people pour
along the streets, both male and female, to prevent or witness the
melancholy scene.

"To arms, to arms!'' cried Elfonzo, "here is a victory to be
won, a prize to be gained, that is more to me than the whole world

beside." "It cannot be done to-night," said Mr. Valeer. "I bear
the clang of death; my strength and armor shall prevail. My Ambulinia shall rest in this hall until the break of another day, and if
we fall, we fall together. If we die, we die clinging to our tattered
rights, and our blood alone shall tell the mournful tale of a murderer daughter and a ruined father." Sure enough, he kept watch
all night, and was successful in defending his house and family.
The bright morning gleamed upon the hills, night vanished away,
the major and his associates felt somewhat ashamed, that they had
not been as fortunate as they expected to have been; however, they
still leaned upon their arms in dispersed groups; some were walking the streets, others were talking in the major's behalf. Many of
the citizens suspended business, as the town presented nothing but
consternation. A novelty that might end in the destruction of some
worthy and respectable citizens. Mr. Valeer ventured in the streets,
though not without being well armed. Some of his friends congratulated him on the decided stand he had taken, and hoped he
would settle the matter amicably with Elfonzo, without any serious
injury. "Me," he replied, "what, me, condescend to fellowship
with a coward, and a low-live, lazy, undermining villain? no,
gentlemen, this cannot be; I had rather be borne off, like the
bubble upon the dark blue ocean, with Ambulinia by my side, than
to have him in the ascending or descending line of relationship.
Gentlemen," continued he, "if Elfonzo is so much of a distinguished character, and is so learned in the fine arts, why do you
not patronize such men? why not introduce him into your families,
as a gentleman of taste and of unequaled magnanimity? why are
you so very anxious that he should become a relative of mine? Oh,
gentlemen, I fear you yet are tainted with the curiosity of our first
parents, who were beguiled by the poisonous kiss of an old ugly
serpent, and who, for one *apple, damned* all mankind. I wish to
divest myself, as far as possible, of that untutored custom. I have
long since learned that the perfection of wisdom, and the end of
true philosophy is to proportion our wants to our possessions, our
ambition to our capacities; we will then be a happy and a virtuous
people." Ambulinia was sent off to prepare for a long and tedious
journey. Her new acquaintances had been instructed by her father
how to treat her, and in what manner, and to keep the anticipated
visit entirely secret. Elfonzo was watching the movements of everybody; some friends had told him of the plot that was laid to
carry off Ambulinia. At night, he rallied some two or three of his
forces, and went silently along to the stately mansion; a faint and
glimmering light showed through the windows; lightly he steps to
the door, there were many voices rallying fresh in fancy's eye; he
tapped the shutter, it was opened instantly and he beheld once
more seated beside several ladies, the hope of all his toils; he
rushed toward her, she rose from her seat, rejoicing: he made one
mighty grasp, when Ambulinia exclaimed, "huzza for Major Elfonzo! I will defend myself and you too, with this conquering
instrument I hold in my hand; huzza, I say, I now invoke time's

broad wing to shed around us some dewdrops of verdant spring.''

But the hour had not come for this joyous reunion; her friends struggled with Elfonzo for some time, and finally succeeded in arresting her from his hands. He dared not injure them, because they were matrons whose courage needed no spur; she was snatched from the arms of Elfonzo, with so much eagerness, and yet with such expressive signification, that he calmly withdrew from this lovely enterprise, with an ardent hope that he should be lulled to repose by the zephyrs which whispered peace to his soul. Several long days and nights passed unmolested, all seemed to have grounded their arms of rebellion, and no callidity appeared to be going on with any of the parties. Other arrangements were made by Ambulinia; she feigned herself to be entirely the votary of a mother's care, and said, by her graceful smiles, that manhood might claim his stern dominion in some other region, where such boisterous love was not so prevalent. This gave the parents a confidence that yielded some hours of sober joy; they believed that Ambulinia would now cease to love Elfonzo, and that her stolen affections would now expire with her misguided opinions. They therefore declined the idea of sending her to a distant land. But oh! they dreamed not of the rapture that dazzled the fancy of Ambulinia, who would say, when alone, youth should not fly away on his rosy pinions, and leave her to grapple in the conflict with unknown admirers.

> No frowning age shall control
> The constant current of my soul,
> Nor a tear from pity's eye
> Shall check my sympathetic sigh.

With this resolution fixed in her mind, one dark and dreary night, when the winds whistled and the tempest roared, she received intelligence that Elfonzo was then waiting, and every preparation was then ready, at the residence of Dr. Tully, and for her to make a quick escape while the family were reposing. Accordingly she gathered her books, went to the wardrobe supplied with a variety of ornamental dressing, and ventured alone in the streets to make her way to Elfonzo, who was near at hand, impatiently looking and watching her arrival. "What forms," said she, "are those rising before me? What is that dark spot on the clouds? I do wonder what frightful ghost that is, gleaming on the red tempest? Oh, be merciful and tell me what region you are from. O tell me, ye strong spirits, or ye dark and fleeting clouds, that I yet have a friend." "A friend," said a low, whispering voice. "I am thy unchanging, thy aged, and thy disappointed mother. Oh, Ambulinia, why hast thou deceived me? Why brandish in that hand of thine a javelin of pointed steel? Why suffer that lip I have kissed a thousand times, to equivocate? My daughter, let these tears sink deep into thy soul, and no longer persist in that which may be your destruction and ruin. Come, my dear child, retract your steps, and

bear me company to your welcome home." Without one retorting
word, or frown from her brow, she yielded to the entreaties of her
mother, and with all the mildness of her former character she went
along with the silver lamp of age, to the home of candor and
benevolence. Her father received her cold and formal politeness—
"Where has Ambulinia been, this blustering evening, Mrs. Valeer?" inquired he. "Oh, she and I have been taking a solitary
walk," said the mother; "all things, I presume, are now working
for the best."

Elfonzo heard this news shortly after it happened. "What,"
said he, "has heaven and earth turned against me? I have been
disappointed times without number. Shall I despair?—must I give
it over? Heaven's decrees will not fade; I will write again—I will
try again; and if it traverses a gory field, I pray forgiveness at the
altar of justice."

Desolate Hill, Cumming, Geo., 1844.

UNCONQUERED AND BELOVED AMBULINIA—

I have only time to say to you, not to despair; thy fame shall
not perish; my visions are brightening before me. The whirlwind's
rage is past, and we now shall subdue our enemies without doubt.
On Monday morning, when your friends are at breakfast, they will
not suspect your departure, or even mistrust me being in town, as
it has been reported advantageously, that I have left for the west.
You walk carelessly toward the academy grove, where you will
find me with a lightning steed, elegantly equipped to bear you off
where we shall be joined in wedlock with the first connubial rights.
Fail not to do this—think not of the tedious relations of our wrongs—
be invincible. You alone occupy all my ambition, and I alone will
make you my happy spouse, with the same unimpeached veracity.
I remain, forever, your devoted friend and admirer,

J. I. ELFONZO.

The appointed day ushered in undisturbed by any clouds; nothing disturbed Ambulinia's soft beauty. With serenity and loveliness she obeys the request of Elfonzo. The moment the family
seated themselves at the table—"Excuse my absence for a short
time," said she, "while I attend to the placing of those flowers,
which should have been done a week ago." And away she ran to
the sacred grove, surrounded with glittering pearls, that indicated
her coming. Elfonzo hails her with his silver bow and his golden
harp. They meet—Ambulinia's countenance brightens—Elfonzo
leads up his winged steed. "Mount," said he, "ye true hearted,
ye fearless soul—the day is ours." She sprang upon the back of
the young thunderbolt, a brilliant star sparkles upon her head, with
one hand she grasps the reins, and with the other she holds an
olive-branch. "Lend thy aid, ye strong winds," they exclaimed,
"ye moon, ye sun, and all ye fair host of heaven, witness the
enemy conquered." "Hold," said Elfonzo, "thy dashing steed."

"Ride on," said Ambulinia, "the voice of thunder is behind us."
And onward they went, with such rapidity, that they very soon
arrived at Rural Retreat, where they dismounted, and were united
with all the solemnities that usually attend such divine operations.
They passed the day in thanksgiving and great rejoicing, and on
that evening they visited their uncle, where many of their friends
and acquaintances had gathered to congratulate them in the field
of untainted bliss. The kind old gentleman met them in the yard:
"Well," said he, "I wish I may die, Elfonzo, if you and Ambulinia haven't tied a knot with your tongue that you can't untie with
your teeth. But come in, come in, never mind, all is right—the
world still moves on, and no one has fallen in this great battle."

Happy now is their lot! Unmoved by misfortune, they live among
the fair beauties of the South. Heaven spreads their peace and
fame upon the arch of the rainbow, and smiles propitiously at their
triumph, *through the tears of the storm*.

ABOUT ALL KINDS OF SHIPS

THE MODERN STEAMER AND THE OBSOLETE
STEAMER

WE ARE victims of one common superstition—the superstition that we
realize the changes that are daily taking place in the world because we
read about them and know what they are. I should not have supposed that
the modern ship could be a surprise to me, but it is. It seems to be as
much of a surprise to me as it could have been if I had never read anything
about it. I walk about this great vessel, the "Havel," as she plows her
way through the Atlantic, and every detail that comes under my eye brings
up the miniature counterpart of it as it existed in the little ships I crossed
the ocean in, fourteen, seventeen, eighteen, and twenty years ago.

In the "Havel" one can be in several respects more comfortable than
he can be in the best hotels on the continent of Europe. For instance, she
has several bathrooms, and they are as convenient and as nicely equipped
as the bathrooms in a fine private house in America; whereas in the hotels
of the continent one bathroom is considered sufficient, and it is generally
shabby and located in some out of the way corner of the house; moreover,
you need to give notice so long beforehand that you get over wanting a
bath by the time you get it. In the hotels there are a good many different
kinds of noises, and they spoil sleep; in my room in the ship I hear no
sounds. In the hotels they usually shut off the electric light at midnight; in
the ship one may burn it in one's room all night.

In the steamer "Batavia," twenty years ago, one candle, set in the
bulkhead between two staterooms, was there to light both rooms, but did
not light either of them. It was extinguished at 11 at night, and so were
all the saloon lamps except one or two, which were left burning to help

the passenger see how to break his neck trying to get around in the dark. The passengers sat at table on long benches made of the hardest kind of wood; in the "Havel" one sits on a swivel chair with a cushioned back to it. In those old times the dinner bill of fare was always the same: a pint of some simple, homely soup or other, boiled codfish and potatoes, slab of boiled beef, stewed prunes for dessert—on Sundays "dog in a blanket," on Thursdays "plum duff." In the modern ship the menu is choice and elaborate, and is changed daily. In the old times dinner was a sad occasion; in our day a concealed orchestra enlivens it with charming music. In the old days the decks were always wet, in our day they are usually dry, for the promenade-deck is roofed over, and a sea seldom comes aboard. In a moderately disturbed sea, in the old days, a landsman could hardly keep his legs, but in such a sea in our day, the decks are as level as a table. In the old days the inside of a ship was the plainest and barrenest thing, and the most dismal and uncomfortable that ingenuity could devise; the modern ship is a marvel of rich and costly decoration and sumptuous appointment, and is equipped with every comfort and convenience that money can buy. The old ships had no place of assembly but the dining-room, the new ones have several spacious and beautiful drawing-rooms. The old ships offered the passenger no chance to smoke except in the place that was called the "fiddle." It was a repulsive den made of rough boards (full of cracks) and its office was to protect the main hatch. It was grimy and dirty; there were no seats; the only light was a lamp of the rancid-oil-and-rag kind; the place was very cold, and never dry, for the seas broke in through the cracks every little while and drenched the cavern thoroughly. In the modern ship there are three or four large smoking-rooms, and they have card tables and cushioned sofas, and are heated by steam and lighted by electricity. There are few European hotels with such smoking-rooms.

The former ships were built of wood, and had two or three water-tight compartments in the hold with doors in them which were often left open, particularly when the ship was going to hit a rock. The modern leviathan is built of steel, and the water-tight bulkheads have no doors in them; they divide the ship into nine or ten water-tight compartments and endow her with as many lives as a cat. Their complete efficiency was established by the happy results following the memorable accident to the City of Paris a year or two ago.

One curious thing which is at once noticeable in the great modern ship is the absence of hubbub, clatter, rush of feet, roaring of orders. That is all gone by. The elaborate maneuvers necessary in working the vessel into her dock are conducted without sound; one sees nothing of the processes, hears no commands. A Sabbath stillness and solemnity reign, in place of the turmoil and racket of the earlier days. The modern ship has a spacious bridge fenced chin-high with sail-cloth, and floored with wooden gratings; and this bridge, with its fenced fore-and-aft annexes, could accommodate a seated audience of a hundred and fifty men. There are three steering equipments, each competent if the others should break. From the bridge the ship is steered, and also handled. The handling is not done by shout or whistle, but by signaling with patent automatic gongs. There are three tell-tales, with plainly lettered dials—for steering, handling the engines, and for communicating orders to the invisible mates who are conducting the landing of the ship or casting off. The officer who is astern is out of sight and too far away to hear trumpet calls; but the gongs near him tell him to haul in, pay out, make fast, let go, and so on; he hears, but the passengers do not, and so the ship seems to land herself without human help.

This great bridge is thirty or forty feet above the water, but the sea climbs up there sometimes; so there is another bridge twelve or fifteen feet higher still, for use in these emergencies. The force of water is a strange thing. It slips between one's fingers like air, but upon occasion it acts like a solid body and will bend a thin iron rod. In the "Havel" it has splintered a heavy oaken rail into broom-straws instead of merely breaking it in two as would have been the seemingly natural thing for it to do. At the time of the awful Johnstown disaster, according to the testimony of several witnesses, rocks were carried some distance on the surface of the stupendous torrent; and at St. Helena, many years ago, a vast sea-wave carried a battery of cannon forty feet up a steep slope and deposited the guns there in a row. But the water has done a still stranger thing, and it is one which is credibly vouched for. A marlinspike is an implement about a foot long which tapers from its butt to the other extremity and ends in a sharp point. It is made of iron and is heavy. A wave came aboard a ship in a storm and raged aft, breast high, carrying a marlinspike point-first with it, and with such lightning-like swiftness and force as to drive it three or four inches into a sailor's body and kill him.

In all ways the ocean greyhound of to-day is imposing and impressive to one who carries in his head no ship-pictures of a recent date. In bulk she comes near to rivaling the Ark; yet this monstrous mass of steel is driven five hundred miles through the waves in twenty-four hours. I remember the brag run of a steamer which I traveled in once on the Pacific— it was two hundred and nine miles in twenty-four hours; a year or so later I was a passenger in the excursion-tub "Quaker City," and on one occasion in a level and glassy sea, it was claimed that she reeled off two hundred and eleven miles between noon and noon, but it was probably a campaign lie. That little steamer had seventy passengers, and a crew of forty men, and seemed a good deal of a bee-hive. But in this present ship we are living in a sort of solitude, these soft summer days, with sometimes a hundred passengers scattered about the spacious distances, and sometimes nobody in sight at all; yet, hidden somewhere in the vessel's bulk, there are (including crew,) near eleven hundred people.

The stateliest lines in the literature of the sea are these:

> "Britannia needs no bulwark, no towers along the steep—
> Her march is o'er the mountain wave, her home is on the
>   deep!"

There it is. In those old times the little ships climbed over the waves and wallowed down into the trough on the other side; the giant ship of our day does not climb over the waves, but crushes her way through them. Her formidable weight and mass and impetus give her mastery over any but extraordinary storm-waves.

The ingenuity of man! I mean in this passing generation. To-day I found in the chart-room a frame of removable wooden slats on the wall, and on the slats was painted uninforming information like this:

Trim-Tank ....Empty
Double-Bottom No. 1 ....Full
Double-Bottom No. 2 ....Full
Double-Bottom No. 3 ....Full
Double-Bottom No. 4 ....Full

While I was trying to think out what kind of a game this might be and how a stranger might best go to work to beat it, a sailor came in and pulled out the "Empty" end of the first slat and put it back with its reverse side to the front, marked "Full." He made some other change, I did not notice what. The slat-frame was soon explained. Its function was to indicate how the ballast in the ship was distributed. The striking thing was, that that ballast was water. I did not know that a ship had ever been ballasted with water. I had merely read, some time or other, that such an experiment was to be tried. But that is the modern way: between the experimental trial of a new thing and its adoption, there is no wasted time, if the trial proves its value.

On the wall, near the slat-frame, there was an outline drawing of the ship, and this betrayed the fact that this vessel has twenty-two considerable lakes of water in her. These lakes are in her bottom; they are imprisoned between her real bottom and a false bottom. They are separated from each other, thwartships, by water-tight bulkheads, and separated down the middle by a bulkhead running from the bow four-fifths of the way to the stern. It is a chain of lakes four hundred feet long and from five to seven feet deep. Fourteen of the lakes contain fresh water brought from shore, and the aggregate weight of it is four hundred tons. The rest of the lakes contain salt water—six hundred and eighteen tons. Upwards of a thousand tons of water, altogether.

Think how handy this ballast is. The ship leaves port with the lakes all full. As she lightens forward through consumption of coal, she loses trim—her head rises, her stern sinks down. Then they spill one of the sternward lakes into the sea, and the trim is restored. This can be repeated right along as occasion may require. Also, a lake at one end of the ship can be moved to the other end by pipes and steam pumps. When the sailor changed the slat-frame to-day, he was posting a transference of that kind. The seas had been increasing, and the vessel's head needed more weighting, to keep it from rising on the waves instead of plowing through them; therefore, twenty-five tons of water had been transferred to the bow from a lake situated well toward the stern.

A water compartment is kept either full or empty. The body of water must be compact, so that it cannot slosh around. A shifting ballast would not do, of course.

The modern ship is full of beautiful ingenuities, but it seems to me that this one is the king. I would rather be the originator of that idea than of any of the others. Perhaps the trim of a ship was never perfectly ordered and preserved until now. A vessel out of trim will not steer, her speed is maimed, she strains and labors in the seas. Poor creature, for six thousand years she has had no comfort until these latest days. For six thousand years she swam through the best and cheapest ballast in the world, the only perfect ballast, but she couldn't tell her master and he had not the wit to find it out for himself. It is odd to reflect that there is nearly as much water inside of this ship as there is outside, and yet there is no danger.

NOAH'S ARK

THE PROGRESS made in the great art of shipbuilding since Noah's time is quite noticeable. Also, the looseness of the navigation laws in the time of Noah is in quite striking contrast with the strictness of the navigation laws of our time. It would not be possible for Noah to do in our day what he was permitted to do in his own. Experience has taught us the necessity of being more particular, more conservative, more careful of human life. Noah would not be allowed to sail from Bremen in our day. The inspectors would come and examine the Ark, and make all sorts of objections. A person who knows Germany can imagine the scene and the conversation without difficulty and without missing a detail. The inspector would be in a beautiful military uniform; he would be respectful, dignified, kindly, the perfect gentleman, but steady as the north star to the last requirement of his duty. He would make Noah tell him where he was born, and how old he was, and what religious sect he belonged to, and the amount of his income, and the grade and position he claimed socially, and the name and style of his occupation, and how many wives and children he had, and how many servants, and the name, sex and age of the whole of them; and if he hadn't a passport he would be courteously required to get one right away. Then he would take up the matter of the Ark:

"What is her length?"

"Six hundred feet."

"Depth?"

"Sixty-five."

"Beam?"

"Fifty or sixty."

"Built of—"

"Wood."

"What kind?"

"Shittim and gopher."

"Interior and exterior decorations?"

"Pitched within and without."

"Passengers?"

"Eight."

"Sex?"

"Half male, the others female."

"Ages?"

"From a hundred years up."

"Up to where?"

"Six hundred."

"Ah—going to Chicago; good idea, too. Surgeon's name?"

"We have no surgeon."

"Must provide a surgeon. Also an undertaker—particularly the undertaker. These people must not be left without the necessities of life at their
age. Crew?"

"The same eight."

"The same eight?"

"The same eight."

"And half of them women?"

"Yes, sir."

"Have they ever served as seamen?"

"No, sir."

"Have the men?"

"No, sir."

"Have any of you ever been to sea?"

"No, sir."

"Where were you reared?"

"On a farm—all of us."

"This vessel requires a crew of eight hundred men, she not being a
steamer. You must provide them. She must have four mates and nine
cooks. Who is captain?"

"I am, sir."

"You must get a captain. Also a chambermaid. Also sick nurses for the
old people. Who designed this vessel?"

"I did, sir."

"Is it your first attempt?"

"Yes, sir."

"I partly suspected it. Cargo?"

"Animals."

"Kind?"

"All kinds."

"Wild, or tame?"

"Mainly wild."

"Foreign, or domestic?"

"Mainly foreign."

"Principal wild ones?"

"Megatherium, elephant, rhinoceros, lion, tiger, wolf, snakes—all the
wild things of all climes—two of each."

"Securely caged?"

"No, not caged."

"They must have iron cages. Who feeds and waters the menagerie?"

"We do."

"The old people?"

"Yes, sir."

"It is dangerous—for both. The animals must be cared for by a competent force. How many animals are there?"

"Big ones, seven thousand; big and little together, ninety-eight thousand."

"You must provide twelve hundred keepers. How is the vessel lighted?"

"By two windows."

"Where are they?"

"Up under the eaves."

"Two windows for a tunnel six hundred feet long and sixty-five feet deep? You must put in the electric light—a few arc lights and fifteen hundred incandescents. What do you do in case of leaks? How many pumps have you?"

"None, sir."

"You must provide pumps. How do you get water for the passengers and the animals?"

"We let down the buckets from the windows."

"It is inadequate. What is your motive power?"

"What is my which?"

"Motive power. What power do you use in driving the ship?"

"None."

"You must provide sails or steam. What is the nature of your steering apparatus?"

"We haven't any."

"Haven't you a rudder?"

"No, sir."

"How do you steer the vessel?"

"We don't."

"You must provide a rudder, and properly equip it. How many anchors have you?"

"None."

"You must provide six. One is not permitted to sail a vessel like this without that protection. How many life boats have you?"

"None, sir."

"Provide twenty-five. How many life preservers?"

"None."

"You will provide two thousand. How long are you expecting your voyage to last?"

"Eleven or twelve months."

"Eleven or twelve months. Pretty slow—but you will be in time for the Exposition. What is your ship sheathed with—copper?"

"Her hull is bare—not sheathed at all."

"Dear man, the wood-boring creatures of the sea would riddle her like a sieve and send her to the bottom in three months. She *cannot* be allowed to go away, in this condition; she must be sheathed. Just a word more: Have you reflected that Chicago is an inland city and not reachable with a vessel like this?"

"Shecargo? What is Shecargo? I am not going to Shecargo."

"Indeed? Then may I ask what the animals are for?"

"Just to breed others from."

"Others? Is it possible that you haven't enough?"

"For the present needs of civilization, yes; but the rest are going to be drowned in a flood, and these are to renew the supply."

"A flood?"

"Yes, sir."

"Are you sure of that?"

"Perfectly sure. It is going to rain forty days and forty nights."

"Give yourself no concern about that, dear sir, it often does that, here."

"Not this kind of rain. This is going to cover the mountain tops, and the earth will pass from sight."

"Privately—but of course not officially—I am sorry you revealed this, for it compels me to withdraw the option I gave you as to sails or steam. I must require you to use steam. Your ship cannot carry the hundredth part of an eleven-months' water supply for the animals. You will have to have condensed water."

"But I tell you I am going to dip water from outside with buckets."

"It will not answer. Before the flood reaches the mountain tops the fresh waters will have joined the salt seas, and it will all be salt. You must put in steam and condense your water. I will now bid you good-day, sir. Did I understand you to say that this was your very first attempt at ship-building?"

"My very first, sir, I give you the honest truth. I built this Ark without having ever had the slightest training or experience or instruction in marine architecture."

"It is a remarkable work, sir, a most remarkable work. I consider that it contains more features that are new—absolutely new and unhackneyed—than are to be found in any other vessel that swims the seas."

"This compliment does me infinite honor, dear sir, infinite; and I shall cherish the memory of it while life shall last. Sir, I offer my duty, and most grateful thanks. Adieu!"

No, the German inspector would be limitlessly courteous to Noah, and would make him feel that he was among friends, but he wouldn't let him go to sea with that Ark.

COLUMBUS'S CRAFT

BETWEEN NOAH'S time and the time of Columbus, naval architecture underwent some changes, and from being unspeakably bad was improved to a point which may be described as less unspeakably bad. I have read somewhere, some time or other, that one of Columbus's ships was a ninety-ton vessel. By comparing that ship with the ocean greyhounds of our time one is able to get down to a comprehension of how small that Spanish bark was, and how little fitted she would be to run opposition in the Atlantic passenger trade to-day. It would take seventy-four of her to match the tonnage of the "Havel" and carry the "Havel's" trip. If I remember rightly, it took her ten weeks to make the passage. With our ideas this would now be considered an objectionable gait. She probably had a captain, a mate, and a crew consisting of four seamen and a boy. The crew of a modern greyhound numbers two hundred and fifty persons.

Columbus's ship being small and very old, we know that we may draw from these two facts several absolute certainties in the way of minor details which history has left unrecorded. For instance: being small, we know that she rolled and pitched and tumbled, in any ordinary sea, and stood on her head or her tail, or lay down with her ear in the water when storm-seas ran high; also, that she was used to having billows plunge aboard and wash her decks from stem to stern; also, that the storm-racks were on the table all the way over, and that nevertheless a man's soup was oftener landed in his lap than in his stomach; also, that the dining-saloon was about ten feet by seven, dark, airless, and suffocating with oil-stench; also, that there was only about one stateroom—the size of a grave—with a tier of two or three berths in it of the dimensions and comfortableness of coffins, and that when the light was out, the darkness in there was so thick and real that you could bite into it and chew it like gum; also, that the only promenade was on the lofty poop-deck astern (for the ship was shaped like a high-quarter shoe)—a streak sixteen feet long by three feet wide, all the rest of the vessel being littered with ropes and flooded by the seas.

We know all these things to be true, from the mere fact that we know the vessel was small. As the vessel was old, certain other truths follow, as matters of course. For instance: she was full of rats; she was full of cockroaches; the heavy seas made her seams open and shut like your fingers, and she leaked like a basket; where leakage is, there also, of necessity, is bilgewater; and where bilgewater is, only the dead can enjoy life. This is on account of the smell. In the presence of bilgewater, Limburger cheese becomes odorless and ashamed.

From these absolutely sure data we can competently picture the daily life of the great discoverer. In the early morning he paid his devotions at the shrine of the Virgin. At eight bells he appeared on the poop-deck promenade. If the weather was chilly he came up clad from plumed helmet to spurred heel in magnificent plate armor inlaid with arabesques of gold, having previously warmed it at the galley fire. If the weather was warm, he came up in the ordinary sailor toggery of the time: great slouch hat of blue velvet with a flowing brush of snowy ostrich plumes, fastened on with a flashing cluster of diamonds and emeralds; gold-embroidered doublet of green velvet with slashed sleeves exposing under-sleeves of crimson satin; deep collar and cuff-ruffles of rich limp lace; trunk hose of pink velvet, with big knee-knots of brocaded yellow ribbon; pearl-tinted silk stockings, clocked and daintily embroidered; lemon-colored buskins of unborn kid, funnel-topped, and drooping low to expose the pretty stockings; deep gauntlets of finest white heretic skin, from the factory of the Holy Inquisition, formerly part of the person of a lady of rank; rapier with sheath crusted with jewels, and hanging from a broad baldric upholstered with rubies and sapphires.

He walked the promenade thoughtfully, he noted the aspects of the sky and the course of the wind; he kept an eye out for drifting vegetation and other signs of land; he jawed the man at the wheel for pastime; he got out an imitation egg and kept himself in practice on his old trick of making it stand on its end; now and then he hove a life-line below and fished up a sailor who was drowning on the quarter-deck; the rest of his watch he gaped and yawned and stretched and said he wouldn't make the trip again to discover six Americas. For that was the kind of natural human person Columbus was when not posing for posterity.

At noon he took the sun and ascertained that the good ship had made three hundred yards in twenty-four hours, and this enabled him to win the pool. Anybody can win the pool when nobody but himself has the privilege of straightening out the ship's run and getting it right.

The Admiral has breakfasted alone, in state: bacon, beans, and gin; at noon he dines alone in state: bacon, beans, and gin; at six he sups alone in state: bacon, beans, and gin; at eleven P.M. he takes a night-relish, alone, in state: bacon, beans, and gin. At none of these orgies is there any music; the ship-orchestra is modern. After his final meal he returned thanks for his many blessings, a little over-rating their value, perhaps, and then he laid off his silken splendors or his gilded hardware, and turned in, in his little coffin-bunk, and blew out his flickering stencher and began to refresh his lungs with inverted sighs freighted with the rich odors of rancid oil and bilgewater. The sighs returned as snores, and then the rats and the cockroaches swarmed out in brigades and divisions and army corps and had a circus all over him. Such was the daily life of the great discoverer in his marine basket during several historic weeks; and the difference between his ship and his comforts and ours is visible almost at a glance.

When he returned, the King of Spain, marveling, said—as history records:

"This ship seems to be leaky. Did she leak badly?"

"You shall judge for yourself, sire. I pumped the Atlantic ocean through her sixteen times on the passage."

This is General Horace Porter's account. Other authorities say fifteen.

It can be shown that the differences between that ship and the one I am writing these historical contributions in, are in several respects remarkable. Take the matter of decoration, for instance. I have been looking around again, yesterday and to-day, and have noted several details which I conceive to have been absent from Columbus's ship, or at least slurred over and not elaborated and perfected. I observe state-room doors three inches thick, of solid oak and polished. I note companionway vestibules with walls, doors and ceilings paneled in polished hard woods, some light, some dark, all dainty and delicate joiner-work, and yet every joint compact and tight; with beautiful pictures inserted, composed of blue tiles—some of the pictures containing as many as sixty tiles—and the joinings of those tiles perfect. These are daring experiments. One would have said that the first time the ship went straining and laboring through a storm-tumbled sea those tiles would gape apart and drop out. That they have not done so is evidence that the joiner's art has advanced a good deal since the days when ships were so shackly that when a giant sea gave them a wrench the doors came unbolted. I find the walls of the dining-saloon upholstered with mellow pictures wrought in tapestry, and the ceiling aglow with pictures done in oil. In other places of assembly I find great panels filled with embossed Spanish leather, the figures rich with gilding and bronze. Everywhere I find sumptuous masses of color—color, color, color—color all about, color of every shade and tint and variety; and as a result, the ship is bright and cheery to the eye, and this cheeriness invades one's spirit and contents it. To fully appreciate the force and spiritual value of this radiant and opulent dream of color, one must stand outside at night in the pitch dark and the rain, and look in through a port, and observe it in the lavish splendor of the electric lights. The old-time ships were dull, plain, graceless, gloomy, and horribly depressing. They compelled the blues; one could not escape the blues in them. The modern idea is right: to surround the passenger with conveniences, luxuries, and abundance of inspiriting color. As a result, the ship is the pleasantest place one can be in, except, perhaps, one's home.

A VANISHED SENTIMENT

ONE THING is gone, to return no more forever—the romance of the sea. Soft sentimentality about the sea has retired from the activities of this life, and is but a memory of the past, already remote and much faded. But within the recollection of men still living, it was in the breast of every individual; and the further any individual lived from salt water the more of it he kept in stock. It was as pervasive, as universal, as the atmosphere itself. The mere mention of the sea, the romantic sea, would make any company of people sentimental and mawkish at once. The great majority of the songs that were sung by the young people of the back settlements had the melancholy wanderer for subject and his mouthings about the sea for refrain. Picnic parties paddling down a creek in a canoe when the twilight shadows were gathering, always sang

> Homeward bound, homeward bound
> From a foreign shore;

and this was also a favorite in the West with the passengers on sternwheel steamboats. There was another—

> My boat is by the shore
>   And my bark is on the sea,
> But before I go, Tom Moore,
>   Here's a double health to thee.

And this one, also—

> O, pilot, 'tis a fearful night,
> There's danger on the deep.

And this—

> A life on the ocean wave
>   And a home on the rolling deep,
> Where the scattered waters rave
>   And the winds their revels keep!

And this—

> A wet sheet and a flowing sea,
> And a wind that follows fair.

And this—

> My foot is on my gallant deck,
> Once more the rover is free!

And the "Larboard Watch"—the person referred to below is at the masthead, or somewhere up there—

O, who can tell what joy he feels,
As o'er the foam his vessel reels,
And his tired eyelids slumb'ring fall,
He rouses at the welcome call
     Of "Larboard watch—ahoy!"

Yes, and there was forever and always some jackass-voiced person braying out—

Rocked in the cradle of the deep,
I lay me down in peace to sleep!

Other favorites had these suggestive titles: "The Storm at Sea;" "The Bird at Sea;" "The Sailor Boy's Dream;" "The Captive Pirate's Lament;" "We are far from Home on the Stormy Main"—and so on, and so on, the list is endless. Everybody on a farm lived chiefly amid the dangers of the deep on those days, in fancy.

But all that is gone, now. Not a vestige of it is left. The iron-clad, with her unsentimental aspect and frigid attention to business, banished romance from the war-marine, and the unsentimental steamer has banished it from the commercial marine. The dangers and uncertainties which made sea life romantic have disappeared and carried the poetic element along with them. In our day the passengers never sing sea-songs on board a ship, and the band never plays them. Pathetic songs about the wanderer in strange lands far from home, once so popular and contributing such fire and color to the imagination by reason of the rarity of that kind of wanderer, have lost their charm and fallen silent, because everybody is a wanderer in the far lands now, and the interest in that detail is dead. Nobody is worried about the wanderer; there are no perils of the sea for him, there are no uncertainties. He is safer in the ship than he would probably be at home, for there he is always liable to have to attend some friend's funeral and stand over the grave in the sleet, bareheaded—and that means pneumonia for him, if he gets his deserts; and the uncertainties of his voyage are reduced to whether he will arrive on the other side in the appointed afternoon, or have to wait till morning.

The first ship I was ever in was a sailing vessel. She was twenty-eight days going from San Francisco to the Sandwich Islands. But the main reason for this particularly slow passage was, that she got becalmed and lay in one spot fourteen days in the center of the Pacific two thousand miles from land. I hear no sea-songs in this present vessel, but I heard the entire layout in that one. There were a dozen young people—they are pretty old now, I reckon—and they used to group themselves on the stern, in the starlight or the moonlight, every evening, and sing sea-songs till after midnight, in that hot, silent, motionless calm. They had no sense of humor, and they always sang "Homeward Bound," without reflecting that that was practically ridiculous, since they were standing still and not proceeding in any direction at all; and they often followed that song with "Are we almost there, are we almost there, said the dying girl as she drew near home?"

It was a very pleasant company of young people, and I wonder where they are now. Gone, oh, none knows whither; and the bloom and grace and beauty of their youth, where is that? Among them was a liar; all tried to reform him, but none could do it. And so, gradually, he was left to himself, none of us would associate with him. Many a time since, I have seen in fancy that forsaken figure, leaning forlorn against the taffrail, and have reflected that perhaps if we had tried harder, and been more patient, we might have won him from his fault and persuaded him to relinquish it. But it is hard to tell; with him the vice was extreme, and was probably incurable. I like to think—and indeed I do think—that I did the best that in me lay to lead him to higher and better ways.

There was a singular circumstance. The ship lay becalmed that entire fortnight in exactly the same spot. Then a handsome breeze came fanning over the sea, and we spread our white wings for flight. But the vessel did not budge. The sails bellied out, the gale strained at the ropes, but the vessel moved not a hair's breadth from her place. The captain was surprised. It was some hours before we found out what the cause of the detention was. It was barnacles. They collect very fast in that part of the Pacific. They had fastened themselves to the ship's bottom; then others had fastened themselves to the first bunch, others to these, and so on, down and down and down, and the last bunch had glued the column hard and fast to the bottom of the sea, which is five miles deep at that point. So the ship was simply become the handle of a walking cane five miles long—yes, and no more movable by wind and sail than a continent is. It was regarded by everyone as remarkable.

Well, the next week—however, Sandy Hook is in sight.

PLAYING COURIER

A TIME would come when we must go from Aix-les-Bains to Geneva, and from thence, by a series of day-long and tangled journeys, to Bayreuth in Bavaria. I should have to have a courier of course to take care of so considerable a party as mine.

But I procrastinated. The time slipped along, and at last I woke up one day to the fact that we were ready to move and had no courier. I then resolved upon what I felt was a foolhardy thing, but I was in the humor of it. I said I would make the first stage without help—I did it.

I brought the party from Aix to Geneva by myself—four people. The distance was two hours and more, and there was one change of cars. There was not an accident of any kind, except leaving a valise and some other matters on the platform, a thing which can hardly be called an accident, it is so common. So I offered to conduct the party all the way to Bayreuth.

This was a blunder, though it did not seem so at the time. There was more detail than I thought there would be: 1. Two persons whom we had left in a Genevan pension some weeks before, must be collected and brought to the hotel; 2. I must notify the people on the Grand Quay who store trunks to bring seven of our stored trunks to the hotel and carry back seven which they would find piled in the lobby; 3. I must find out what part of Europe Bayreuth was in and buy seven railway tickets for that point; 4. I must send a telegram to a friend in the Netherlands; 5. It was now 2 in the afternoon, and we must look sharp and be ready for the first night train and make sure of sleeping-car tickets; 6. I must draw money at the bank.

It seemed to me that the sleeping-car tickets must be the most important thing, so I went to the station myself to make sure; hotel messengers are not always brisk people. It was a hot day and I ought to have driven, but it seemed better economy to walk. It did not turn out so, because I lost my way and trebled the distance. I applied for the tickets, and they asked me which route I wanted to go by, and that embarrassed me and made me lose my head, there were so many people standing around, and I not knowing anything about the routes and not supposing there were going to be two; so I judged it best to go back and map out the road and come again.

I took a cab this time, but on my way upstairs at the hotel I remembered that I was out of cigars, so I thought it would be well to get some while the matter was in my mind. It was only round the corner and I didn't need the cab. I asked the cabman to wait where he was. Thinking of the telegram and trying to word it in my head, I forgot the cigars and the cab, and walked on indefinitely. I was going to have the hotel people send the telegram, but as I could not be far from the Post Office by this time, I thought I would do it myself. But it was further than I had supposed. I found the place at last and wrote the telegram and handed it in. The clerk was a severe-looking, fidgety man, and he began to fire French questions at me in such a liquid form that I could not detect the joints between his words, and this made me lose my head again. But an Englishman stepped up and said the clerk wanted to know where he was to send the telegram. I could not tell him, because it was not my telegram, and I explained that I was merely sending it for a member of my party. But nothing would pacify the clerk but the address; so I said that if he was so particular I would go back and get it.

However, I thought I would go and collect those lacking two persons first, for it would be best to do everything systematically and in order, and one detail at a time. Then I remembered the cab was eating up my substance down at the hotel yonder; so I called another cab and told the man to go down and fetch it to the Post Office and wait till I came.

I had a long hot walk to collect those people, and when I got there they couldn't come with me because they had heavy satchels and must have a cab. I went away to find one, but before I ran across any I noticed that I had reached the neighborhood of the Grand Quay—at least I thought I had—so I judged I could save time by stepping around and arranging about the trunks. I stepped around about a mile, and although I did not find the Grand Quay, I found a cigar shop, and remembered about the cigars. I said I was going to Bayreuth, and wanted enough for the journey. The man asked me which route I was going to take. I said I did not know. He said he would recommend me to go by Zurich and various other places which he named, and offered to sell me seven second-class through tickets for $22 apiece, which would be throwing off the discount which the railroads allowed him. I was already tired of riding second-class on first-class tickets, so I took him up.

By and by I found Natural & Co.'s storage office, and told them to send seven of our trunks to the hotel and pile them up in the lobby. It seemed to me that I was not delivering the whole of the message, still it was all I could find in my head.

Next I found the bank and asked for some money, but I had left my letter of credit somewhere and was not able to draw. I remembered now that I must have left it lying on the table where I wrote my telegram: so I got a cab and drove to the Post Office and went upstairs, and they said that a letter of credit had indeed been left on the table, but that it was now in the hands of the police authorities, and it would be necessary for me to go there and prove property. They sent a boy with me, and we went out the back way and walked a couple of miles and found the place; and then I remembered about my cabs, and asked the boy to send them to me when he got back to the Post Office. It was nightfall now, and the Mayor had gone to dinner. I thought I would go to dinner myself, but the officer on duty thought differently, and I stayed. The Mayor dropped in at half past 10, but said it was too late to do anything to-night—come at 9:30 in the morning. The officer wanted to keep me all night, and said I was a suspicious-looking person, and probably did not own the letter of credit, and didn't know what a letter of credit was, but merely saw the real owner leave it lying on the table, and wanted to get it because I was probably a person that would want anything he could get, whether it was valuable or not. But the Mayor said he saw nothing suspicious about me, and that I seemed a harmless person and nothing the matter with me but a wandering mind, and not much of that. So I thanked him and he set me free, and I went home in my three cabs.

As I was dog-tired and in no condition to answer questions with discretion, I thought I would not disturb the Expedition at that time of night, as there was a vacant room I knew of at the other end of the hall; but I did not quite arrive there, as a watch had been set, the Expedition being anxious about me. I was placed in a galling situation. The Expedition sat stiff and forbidding on four chairs in a row, with shawls and things all on, satchels and guide books in lap. They had been sitting like that for four hours, and the glass going down all the time. Yes, and they were waiting—waiting for me. It seemed to me that nothing but a sudden, happily contrived, and brilliant *tour de force* could break this iron front and make a diversion in my favor; so I shied my hat into the arena and followed it with a skip and a jump, shouting blithely:

"Ha, ha, here we all are, Mr. Merryman!"

Nothing could be deeper or stiller than the absence of applause which followed. But I kept on; there seemed no other way, though my confidence, poor enough before, had got a deadly check and was in effect gone.

I tried to be jocund out of a heavy heart, I tried to touch the other hearts there and soften the bitter resentment in those faces by throwing off bright and airy fun and making of the whole ghastly thing a joyously humorous incident, but this idea was not well conceived. It was not the right atmosphere for it. I got not one smile; not one line in those offended faces relaxed; I thawed nothing of the winter that looked out of those frosty eyes. I started one more breezy, poor effort, but the head of the Expedition cut into the center of it and said:

"Where have you been?"

I saw by the manner of this that the idea was to get down to cold business now. So I began my travels but was cut short again.

"Where are the two others? We have been in frightful anxiety about them."

"Oh, they're all right. I was to fetch a cab. I will go straight off, and——"

"Sit down! Don't you know it is 11 o'clock? Where did you leave them?"

"At the pension."

"Why didn't you bring them?"

"Because we couldn't carry the satchels. And so I thought——"

"Thought! You should not try to think. One cannot think without the proper machinery. It is two miles to that pension. Did you go there without a cab?"

"I—well I didn't intend to; it only happened so."

"How did it happen so?"

"Because I was at the Post Office and I remembered that I had left a cab waiting here, and so, to stop that expense, I sent another cab to—to——"

"To what?"

"Well, I don't remember now, but I think the new cab was to have the hotel pay the old cab, and send it away."

"What good would that do?"

"What good would it do? It would stop the expense, wouldn't it?"

"By putting the new cab in its place to continue the expense?"

I didn't say anything.

"Why didn't you have the new cab come back for you?"

"Oh, that is what I did. I remember now. Yes, that is what I did. Because I recollect that when I——"

"Well, then, why didn't it come back for you?"

"To the Post Office? Why, it did."

"Very well, then, how did you come to walk to the pension?"

"I—I don't quite remember how that happened. Oh, yes, I do remember now. I wrote the despatch to send to the Netherlands, and——"

"Oh, thank goodness, you did accomplish something! I wouldn't have had you fail to send—what makes you look like that! You are trying to avoid my eye. That despatch is the most important thing that——You haven't sent that despatch!"

"I haven't said I didn't send it."

"You don't need to. Oh, dear, I wouldn't have had that telegram fail for anything. Why didn't you send it?"

"Well, you see, with so many things to do and think of, I—they're very particular there, and after I had written the telegram——"

"Oh, never mind, let it go, explanations can't help the matter now—what will he think of us?"

"Oh, that's all right, that's all right, he'll think we gave the telegram to the hotel people, and that they——"

"Why, certainly! Why didn't you do that? There was no other rational way."

"Yes, I know, but then I had it on my mind that I must be sure and get to the bank and draw some money——"

"Well, you are entitled to some credit, after all, for thinking of that, and I don't wish to be too hard on you, though you must acknowledge yourself that you have cost us all a good deal of trouble, and some of it not necessary. How much did you draw?"

"Well, I—I had an idea that—that——"

"That what?"

"That—well, it seems to me that in the circumstances—so many of us, you know, and—and——"

"What are you mooning about? Do turn your face this way and let me—why, you haven't drawn any money!"

"Well, the banker said——"

"Never mind what the banker said. You must have had a reason of your own. Not a reason, exactly, but something which——"

"Well, then, the simple fact was that I hadn't my letter of credit."

"Hadn't your letter of credit?"

"Hadn't my letter of credit."

"Don't repeat me like that. Where was it?"

"At the Post Office."

"What was it doing there?"

"Well, I forgot it and left it there."

"Upon my word, I've seen a good many couriers, but of all the couriers that ever I——"

"I've done the best I could."

"Well, so you have, poor thing, and I'm wrong to abuse you so when you've been working yourself to death while we've been sitting here only thinking of our vexations instead of feeling grateful for what you were trying to do for us. It will all come out right. We can take the 7:30 train in the morning just as well. You've bought the tickets?"

"I have—and it's a bargain, too. Second class."

"I'm glad of it. Everybody else travels second class, and we might just as well save that ruinous extra charge. What did you pay?"

"Twenty-two dollars apiece—through to Bayreuth."

"Why, I didn't know you could buy through tickets anywhere but in London and Paris."

"Some people can't, maybe; but some people can—of whom I am one of which, it appears."

"It seems a rather high price."

"On the contrary, the dealer knocked off his commission."

"Dealer?"

"Yes—I bought them at a cigar shop."

"That reminds me. We shall have to get up pretty early, and so there should be no packing to do. Your umbrella, your rubbers, your cigars—what is the matter?"

"Hang it, I've left the cigars at the bank."

"Just think of it! Well, your umbrella?"

"I'll have that all right. There's no hurry."

"What do you mean by that?"

"Oh, that's all right; I'll take care of——"

"Where is that umbrella?"

"It's just the merest step—it won't take me——"

"Where is it?"

"Well, I think I left it at the cigar shop; but anyway——"

"Take your feet out from under that thing. It's just as I expected! Where are your rubbers?"

"They—well——"

"Where are your rubbers?"

"It's got so dry now—well, everybody says there's not going to be another drop of——"

"Where—are—your—rubbers?"

"Well, you see—well, it was this way. First, the officer said——"

"What officer?"

"Police officer; but the Mayor, he——"

"What Mayor?"

"Mayor of Geneva; but I said——"

"Wait. What is the matter with you?"

"Who, me? Nothing. They both tried to persuade me to stay, and——"

"Stay where?"

"Well—the fact is——"

"Where have you been? What's kept you out till half-past ten at night?"

"O, you see, after I lost my letter of credit, I——"

"You are beating around the bush a good deal. Now, answer the question in just one straightforward word. Where are those rubbers?"

"They—well; they're in the county jail."

I started a placating smile, but it petrified. The climate was unsuitable. Spending three or four hours in jail did not seem to the Expedition humorous. Neither did it to me, at bottom.

I had to explain the whole thing, and of course it came out then that we couldn't take the early train, because that would leave my letter of credit in hock still. It did look as if we had all got to go to bed estranged and unhappy, but by good luck that was prevented. There happened to be mention of the trunks, and I was able to say I had attended to that feature.

"There, you are just as good and thoughtful and painstaking and intelligent as you can be, and it's a shame to find so much fault with you, and there sha'nt be another word of it. You've done beautifully, admirably, and I'm sorry I ever said one ungrateful word to you."

This hit deeper than some of the other things and made me uncomfortable, because I wasn't feeling as solid about that trunk errand as I wanted to. There seemed somehow to be a defect about it somewhere, though I couldn't put my finger on it, and didn't like to stir the matter just now, it being late and maybe well enough to let well enough alone.

Of course there was music in the morning, when it was found that we couldn't leave by the early train. But I had no time to wait; I got only the opening bars of the overture, and then started out to get my letter of credit.

It seemed a good time to look into the trunk business and rectify it if it needed it, and I had a suspicion that it did. I was too late. The concierge said he had shipped the trunks to Zurich the evening before. I asked him how he could do that without exhibiting passage tickets.

"Not necessary in Switzerland. You pay for your trunks and send them where you please. Nothing goes free but your hand baggage."

"How much did you pay on them?"

"A hundred and forty francs."

"Twenty-eight dollars. There's something wrong about that trunk business, sure."

Next I met the porter. He said:

"You have not slept well, is it not. You have the worn look. If you would like a courier, a good one has arrived last night, and is not engaged for five days already, by the name of Ludi. We recommend him; dass heiss, the Grande Hotel Beau Rivage recommends him."

I declined with coldness. My spirit was not broken yet. And I did not like having my condition taken notice of in this way. I was at the county jail by 9 o'clock, hoping that the Mayor might chance to come before his regular hour; but he didn't. It was dull there. Every time I offered to touch anything, or look at anything, or do anything, or refrain from doing anything, the policeman said it was "defendu." I thought I would practise my French on him, but he wouldn't have that either. It seemed to make him particularly bitter to hear his own tongue.

The Mayor came at last, and then there was no trouble; for the minute he had convened the Supreme Court—which they always do whenever there is valuable property in dispute—and got everything shipshape and sentries posted, and had prayer, by the chaplain, my unsealed letter was brought and opened, and there wasn't anything in it but some photographs: because, as I remembered now, I had taken out the letter of credit so as to make room for the photographs, and had put the letter in my other pocket, which I proved to everybody's satisfaction by fetching it out and showing it with a good deal of exultation. So then the court looked at each other in a vacant kind of way, and then at me, and then at each other again, and finally let me go, but said it was imprudent for me to be at large, and asked me what my profession was. I said I was a courier. They lifted up their eyes in a kind of reverent way and said, "Du lieber Gott!" and I said a word of courteous thanks for their apparent admiration and hurried off to the bank.

However, being a courier was already making me a great stickler for order and system and one thing at a time and each thing in its own proper turn; so I passed by the bank and branched off and started for the two lacking members of the Expedition. A cab lazied by and I took it upon persuasion. I gained no speed by this, but it was a reposeful turnout and I liked reposefulness. The week-long jubilations over the six hundredth anniversary of the birth of Swiss liberty and the Signing of the Compact was at flood tide, and all the streets were clothed in fluttering flags.

The horse and the driver had been drunk three days and nights, and had known no stall nor bed meantime. They looked as I felt—dreamy and seedy. But we arrived in course of time. I went in and rang, and asked a housemaid to rush out the lacking members. She said something which I did not understand, and I returned to the chariot. The girl had probably told me that those people did not belong on her floor, and that it would be judicious for me to go higher, and ring from floor to floor till I found them; for in those Swiss flats there does not seem to be any way to find the right family but to be patient and guess your way along up. I calculated that I must wait fifteen minutes, there being three details inseparable from an occasion of this sort: 1, put on hats and come down and climb in; 2, return of one to get "my other glove;" 3, presently, return of the other one to fetch "my French Verbs at a Glance." I would muse during the fifteen minutes and take it easy.

A very still and blank interval ensued, and then I felt a hand on my shoulder and started. The intruder was a policeman. I glanced up and perceived that there was new scenery. There was a good deal of a crowd, and they had that pleased and interested look which such a crowd wears when they see that somebody is out of luck. The horse was asleep, and so was the driver, and some boys had hung them and me full of gaudy decorations stolen from the innumerable banner poles. It was a scandalous spectacle. The officer said:

"I'm sorry, but we can't have you sleeping here all day."

I was wounded and said with dignity:

"I beg your pardon, I was not sleeping; I was thinking."

"Well, you can think if you want to, but you've got to think to yourself; you disturb the whole neighborhood."

It was a poor joke, and it made the crowd laugh. I snore at night sometimes, but it is not likely that I would do such a thing in the daytime and in such a place. The officer undecorated us, and seemed sorry for our friendlessness, and really tried to be humane, but he said we mustn't stop there any longer or he would have to charge us rent—it was the law, he said, and he went on to say in a sociable way that I was looking pretty moldy, and we wished he knew——

I shut him off pretty austerely, and said I hoped one might celebrate a little, these days, especially when one was personally concerned.

"Personally?" he asked. "How?"

"Because 600 years ago an ancestor of mine signed the compact."

He reflected a moment, then looked me over and said:

"Ancestor! It's my opinion you signed it yourself. For of all the old ancient relics that ever I—but never mind about that. What is it you are waiting here for so long?"

I said:

"I'm not waiting here so long at all. I'm waiting fifteen minutes till they forget a glove and a book and go back and get them." Then I told him who they were that I had come for.

He was very obliging, and began to shout inquiries to the tiers of heads and shoulders projecting from the windows above us. Then a woman away up there sung out:

"Oh, they? Why I got them a cab and they left here long ago—half-past 8, I should say."

It was annoying. I glanced at my watch, but didn't say anything. The officer said:

"It is a quarter of 12, you see. You should have inquired better. You have been asleep three-quarters of an hour, and in such a sun as this. You are baked—baked black. It is wonderful. And you will miss your train, perhaps. You interest me greatly. What is your occupation?''

I said I was a courier. It seemed to stun him, and before he could come to we were gone.

When I arrived in the third story of the hotel I found our quarters vacant. I was not surprised. The moment a courier takes his eye off his tribe they go shopping. The nearer it is to train time the surer they are to go. I sat down to try and think out what I had best do next, but presently the hall boy found me there, and said the expedition had gone to the station half an hour before. It was the first time I had known them to do a rational thing, and it was very confusing. This is one of the things that make a courier's life so difficult and uncertain. Just as matters are going the smoothest, his people will strike a lucid interval, and down go all his arrangements to wreck and ruin.

The train was to leave at 12 noon sharp. It was now ten minutes after 12. I could be at the station in ten minutes. I saw I had no great amount of leeway, for this was the lightning express, and on the Continent the lightning expresses are pretty fastidious about getting away sometime during the advertised day. My people were the only ones remaining in the waiting room; everybody else had passed through and "mounted the train," as they say in those regions. They were exhausted with nervousness and fret, but I comforted them and heartened them up, and we made our rush.

But no; we were out of luck again. The doorkeeper was not satisfied with the tickets. He examined them cautiously, deliberately, suspiciously; then glared at me awhile, and after that he called another official. The two examined the tickets and called another official. These called others, and the convention discussed and discussed, and gesticulated and carried on until I begged that they would consider how time was flying, and just pass a few resolutions and let us go. Then they said very courteously that there was a defect in the tickets, and asked me where I got them.

I judged I saw what the trouble was, now. You see, I had bought the tickets in a cigar shop, and of course the tobacco smell was on them; without doubt the thing they were up to was to work the tickets through the Custom House and to collect duty on that smell. So I resolved to be perfectly frank; it is sometimes the best way. I said:

"Gentlemen, I will not deceive you. These railway tickets——"

"Ah, pardon, monsieur! These are not railway tickets."

"Oh," I said, "is that the defect?"

"Ah, truly yes, monsieur. These are lottery tickets, yes; and it is a lottery which has been drawn two years ago."

I affected to be greatly amused; it is all one can do in such circumstances; it is all one can do, and yet there is no value in it; it deceives nobody, and you can see that everybody around pities you and is ashamed of you. One of the hardest situations in life, I think, is to be full of grief and a sense of defeat and shabbiness that way, and yet have to put on an outside of archness and gaiety, while all the time you know that your own expedition, the treasures of your heart, and whose love and reverence you are by the custom of our civilization entitled to, are being consumed with humiliation before strangers to see you earning and getting a compassion, which is a stigma, a brand—a brand which certifies you to be—oh, anything and everything which is fatal to human respect.

I said cheerily, it was all right, just one of those little accidents that was likely to happen to anybody—I would have the right tickets in two minutes, and we would catch the train yet, and, moreover, have something to laugh about all through the journey. I did get the tickets in time, all stamped and complete, but then it turned out that I couldn't take them, because in taking so much pains about the two missing members, I had skipped the bank and hadn't the money. So then the train left, and there didn't seem to be anything to do but go back to the hotel, which we did; but it was kind of melancholy and not much said. I tried to start a few subjects, like scenery and transubstantiation, and those sorts of things, but they didn't seem to hit the weather right.

We had lost our good rooms, but we got some others which were pretty scattering, but would answer. I judged things would brighten now, but the Head of the Expedition said "Send up the trunks." It made me feel pretty cold. There was a doubtful something about that trunk business. I was almost sure of it. I was going to suggest——

But a wave of the hand sufficiently restrained me, and I was informed that we would now camp for three days and see if we could rest up.

I said all right, never mind ringing; I would go down and attend to the trunks myself. I got a cab and went straight to Mr. Charles Natural's place, and asked what order it was I had left there.

"To send seven trunks to the hotel."

"And were you to bring any back?"

"No."

"You are sure I didn't tell you to bring back seven that would be found piled in the lobby?"

"Absolutely sure you didn't."

"Then the whole fourteen are gone to Zurich or Jericho or somewhere, and there is going to be more débris around that hotel when the Expedition——"

I didn't finish, because my mind was getting to be in a good deal of a whirl, and when you are that way you think you have finished a sentence when you haven't, and you go mooning and dreaming away, and the first thing you know you get run over by a dray or a cow or something.

I left the cab there—I forgot it—and on my way back I thought it all out and concluded to resign, because otherwise I should be nearly sure to be discharged. But I didn't believe it would be a good idea to resign in person; I could do it by message. So I sent for Mr. Ludi and explained that there was a courier going to resign on account of incompatibility or fatigue or something, and as he had four or five vacant days, I would like to insert him into that vacancy if he thought he could fill it. When everything was arranged I got him to go up and say to the Expedition that, owing to an error made by Mr. Natural's people, we were out of trunks here, but would have plenty in Zurich, and we'd better take the first train, freight, gravel, or construction, and move right along.

He attended to that and came down with an invitation for me to go up— yes, certainly; and, while we walked along over to the bank to get money, and collect my cigars and tobacco, and to the cigar shop to trade back the lottery tickets and get my umbrella, and to Mr. Natural's to pay that

cab and send it away, and to the county jail to get my rubbers and leave
p. p. c. cards for the Mayor and Supreme Court, he described the weather
to me that was prevailing on the upper levels there with the Expedition,
and I saw that I was doing very well where I was.

I stayed out in the woods till 4 P. M., to let the weather moderate, and
then turned up at the station just in time to take the 3 o'clock express for
Zurich along with the Expedition, now in the hands of Ludi, who conducted its complex affairs with little apparent effort or inconvenience.

Well, I had worked like a slave while I was in office, and done the very
best I knew how; yet all that these people dwelt upon or seemed to care
to remember was the defects of my administration, not its creditable
features. They would skip over a thousand creditable features to remark
upon and reiterate and fuss about just one fact, till it seemed to me they
would wear it out; and not much of a fact, either, taken by itself—the fact
that I elected myself courier in Geneva, and put in work enough to carry
a circus to Jerusalem, and yet never even got my gang out of the town. I
finally said I didn't wish to hear any more about the subject, it made me
tired. And I told them to their faces that I would never be a courier again
to save anybody's life. And if I live long enough I'll prove it. I think it's
a difficult, brain racking, overworked, and thoroughly ungrateful office,
and the main bulk of its wages is a sore heart and a bruised spirit.

THE GERMAN CHICAGO

I FEEL lost, in Berlin. It has no resemblance to the city I had supposed it
was. There was once a Berlin which I would have known, from descrip-
tions in books—the Berlin of the last century and the beginning of the
present one: a dingy city in a marsh, with rough streets, muddy and
lantern-lighted, dividing straight rows of ugly houses all alike, compacted
into blocks as square and plain and uniform and monotonous and serious
as so many dry-goods boxes. But that Berlin has disappeared. It seems to
have disappeared totally, and left no sign. The bulk of the Berlin of to-
day has about it no suggestion of a former period. The site it stands on
has traditions and a history, but the city itself has no traditions and no
history. It is a new city; the newest I have ever seen. Chicago would seem
venerable beside it; for there are many old-looking districts in Chicago,
but not many in Berlin. The main mass of the city looks as if it had been
built last week, the rest of it has a just perceptibly graver tone, and looks
as if it might be six or even eight months old.

The next feature that strikes one is the spaciousness, the roominess of
the city. There is no other city, in any country, whose streets are so
generally wide. Berlin is not merely *a* city of wide streets, it is *the* city of
wide streets. As a wide-street city it has never had its equal, in any age of
the world. "Unter den Linden" is three streets in one; the Potsdamer-
strasse is bordered on both sides by sidewalks which are themselves wider
than some of the historic thoroughfares of the old European capitals; there
seem to be no lanes or alleys; there are no short-cuts; here and there,

where several important streets empty into a common center, that center's circumference is of a magnitude calculated to bring that word spaciousness into your mind again. The park in the middle of the city is so huge that it calls up that expression once more.

The next feature that strikes one is the straightness of the streets. The short ones haven't so much as a waver in them; the long ones stretch out to prodigious distances and then tilt a little to the right or left, then stretch out on another immense reach as straight as a ray of light. A result of this arrangement is, that at night Berlin is an inspiring sight to see. Gas and the electric light are employed with a wasteful liberality, and so, wherever one goes, he has always double ranks of brilliant lights stretching far down into the night on every hand, with here and there a wide and splendid constellation of them spread out over an intervening "Platz;" and between the interminable double procession of street lamps one has the swarming and darting cab lamps, a lively and pretty addition to the fine spectacle, for they counterfeit the rush and confusion and sparkle of an invasion of fire-flies.

There is one other noticeable feature—the absolutely level surface of the site of Berlin. Berlin—to capitulate—is newer to the eye than is any other city and also blonder of complexion and tidier; no other city has such an air of roominess, freedom from crowding; no other city has so many straight streets; and with Chicago it contests the chromo for flatness of surface and for phenomenal swiftness of growth. Berlin is the European Chicago. The two cities have about the same population—say a million and a half. I cannot speak in exact terms, because I only know what Chicago's population was week before last; but at that time it was about a million and a half. Fifteen years ago Berlin and Chicago were large cities, of course, but neither of them was the giant it now is.

But now the parallels fail. Only parts of Chicago are stately and beautiful, whereas all of Berlin is stately and substantial, and it is not merely in parts but uniformly beautiful. There are buildings in Chicago that are architecturally finer than any in Berlin, I think, but what I have just said above is still true. These two flat cities would lead the world for phenomenal good health if London were out of the way. As it is, London leads, by a point or two. Berlin's death rate is only nineteen in the thousand. Fourteen years ago the rate was a third higher.

Berlin is a surprise in a great many ways—in a multitude of ways, to speak strongly and be exact. It seems to be the most governed city in the world, but one must admit that it also seems to be the best governed. Method and system are observable on every hand—in great things, in little things, in all details, of whatsoever size. And it is not method and system on paper, and there an end—it is method and system in practice. It has a rule for everything, and puts the rule in force; puts it in force against the poor and powerful alike, without favor or prejudice. It deals with great matters and minute particulars with equal faithfulness, and with a plodding and painstaking diligence and persistency which compel admiration—and sometimes regret. There are several taxes, and they are collected quarterly. Collected is the word; they are not merely levied, they are collected—every time. This makes light taxes. It is in cities and countries where a considerable part of the community shirk payment that taxes have to be lifted to a burdensome rate. Here the police keep coming, calmly and patiently until you pay your tax. They charge you five or ten cents per visit, after the first call. By experiment you will find that they will presently collect that money.

In one respect the million and a half of Berlin's population are like a family: the head of this large family knows the names of its several members, and where the said members are located, and when and where they were born, and what they do for a living, and what their religious brand is. Whoever comes to Berlin must furnish these particulars to the police immediately; moreover, if he knows how long he is going to stay, he must say so. If he take a house he will be taxed on the rent and taxed also on his income. He will not be asked what his income is, and so he may save some lies for home consumption. The police will estimate his income from the house-rent he pays, and tax him on that basis.

Duties on imported articles are collected with inflexible fidelity, be the sum large or little; but the methods are gentle, prompt, and full of the spirit of accommodation. The postman attends to the whole matter for you, in cases where the article comes by mail, and you have no trouble and suffer no inconvenience. The other day a friend of mine was informed that there was a package in the post office for him, containing a lady's silk belt with gold clasp, and a gold chain to hang a bunch of keys on. In his first agitation he was going to try to bribe the postman to chalk it through, but acted upon his sober second thought and allowed the matter to take its proper and regular course. In a little while the postman brought the package and made these several collections: duty on the silk belt, 7½ cents; duty on the gold chain, 10 cents; charge for fetching the package, 5 cents. These devastating imposts are exacted for the protection of German home industries.

The calm, quiet, courteous, cussed persistence of the police is the most admirable thing I have encountered on this side. They undertook to per- suade me to send and get a passport for a Swiss maid whom we had brought with us, and at the end of six weeks of patient, tranquil, angelic daily effort they succeeded. I was not intending to give them trouble, but I was lazy and I thought they would get tired. Meanwhile they probably thought I would be the one. It turned out just so.

One is not allowed to build unstable, unsafe or unsightly houses in Berlin; the result is this comely and conspicuously stately city, with its security from conflagrations and break-downs. It is built of architectural Gibraltars. The Building Commissioners inspect while the building is going up. It has been found that this is better than to wait till it falls down. These people are full of whims.

One is not allowed to cram poor folk into cramped and dirty tenement houses. Each individual must have just so many cubic feet of room-space, and sanitary inspections are systematic and frequent.

Everything is orderly. The fire brigade march in rank, curiously uni- formed, and so grave is their demeanor that they look like a Salvation Army under conviction of sin. People tell me that when a fire alarm is sounded, the firemen assemble calmly, answer to their names when the roll is called, then proceed to the fire. There they are ranked up, military fashion, and told off in detachments by the chief, who parcels out to the detachments the several parts of the work which they are to undertake in putting out that fire. This is all done with low-voiced propriety, and strangers think these people are working a funeral. As a rule the fire is confined to a single floor in these great masses of bricks and masonry, and consequently there is little or no interest attaching to a fire here for the rest of the occupants of the house.

There are abundance of newspapers in Berlin, and there was also a newsboy, but he died. At intervals of half a mile on the thoroughfares there are booths, and it is at these that you buy your papers. There are plenty of theaters, but they do not advertise in a loud way. There are no big posters of any kind, and the display of vast type and of pictures of actors and performance framed on a big scale and done in rainbow colors is a thing unknown. If the big show-bills existed there would be no place to exhibit them; for there are no poster-fences, and one would not be allowed to disfigure dead walls with them. Unsightly things are forbidden here; Berlin is a rest to the eye.

And yet the saunterer can easily find out what is going on at the theaters. All over the city, at short distances apart, there are neat round pillars eighteen feet high and about as thick as a hogshead, and on these the little black and white theater bills and other notices are posted. One generally finds a group around each pillar reading these things. There are plenty of things in Berlin worth importing to America. It is these that I have particularly wished to make a note of. When Buffalo Bill was here his biggest poster was probably not larger than the top of an ordinary trunk.

There is a multiplicity of clean and comfortable horse-cars, but whenever you think you know where a car is going to, you would better stop ashore, because that car is not going to that place at all. The car-routes are marvelously intricate, and often the drivers get lost and are not heard of for years. The signs on the cars furnish no details as to the course of the journey; they name the end of it, and then experiment around to see how much territory they can cover before they get there. The conductor will collect your fare over again, every few miles, and give you a ticket which he hasn't apparently kept any record of, and you keep it till an inspector comes aboard by and by and tears a corner off it (which he does not keep,) then you throw the ticket away and get ready to buy another. Brains are of no value when you are trying to navigate Berlin in a horse car. When the ablest of Brooklyn's editors was here on a visit he took a horse car in the early morning and wore it out trying to go to a point in the center of the city. He was on board all day and spent many dollars in fares, and then did not arrive at the place which he had started to go to. This is the most thorough way to see Berlin, but it is also the most expensive.

But there are excellent features about the car system, nevertheless. The car will not stop for you to get on or off, except at certain places a block or two apart where there is a sign to indicate that that is a halting station. This system saves many bones. There are twenty places inside the car; when these seats are filled, no more can enter. Four or five persons may stand on each platform—the law decrees the number—and when these standing places are all occupied the next applicant is refused. As there is no crowding, and as no rowdyism is allowed, women stand on the platforms as well as men; they often stand there when there are vacant seats inside, for these places are comfortable, there being little or no jolting. A native tells me that when the first car was put on, thirty or forty years ago, the public had such a terror of it that they didn't feel safe inside of it or outside either. They made the company keep a man at every crossing with a red flag in his hand. Nobody would travel in the car except convicts on the way to the gallows. This made business in only one direction, and the car had to go back light. To save the company, the city government transferred the convict cemetery to the other end of the line. This made traffic in both directions and kept the company from going under. This sounds like some of the information which traveling foreigners are furnished with in America. To my mind is has a doubtful ring about it.

The first-class cab is neat and trim, and has leather-cushion seats and a swift horse. The second-class cab is an ugly and lubberly vehicle, and is always old. It seems a strange thing that they have never built any new ones. Still, if such a thing were done everybody that had time to flock would flock to see it, and that would make a crowd, and the police do not like crowds and disorder here. If there were an earthquake in Berlin the police would take charge of it and conduct it in that sort of orderly way that would make you think it was a prayer meeting. That is what an earthquake generally ends in, but this one would be different from those others; it would be kind of soft and self-contained, like a republican praying for a mugwump.

For a course (a quarter of an hour or less), one pays twenty-five cents in a first-class cab, and fifteen cents in a second-class. The first-class will take you along faster, for the second-class horse is old—always old—as old as his cab, some authorities say—and ill-fed and weak. He has been a first-class once, but has been degraded to second-class for long and faithful service.

Still, he must take you as *far* for 15 cents as the other horse takes you for 25. If he can't do his fifteen-minute distance in 15 minutes, he must still do the distance for the 15 cents. Any stranger can check the distance off—by means of the most curious map I am acquainted with. It is issued by the city government and can be bought in any shop for a trifle. In it every street is sectioned off like a string of long beads of different colors. Each long bead represents a minute's travel, and when you have covered fifteen of the beads you have got your money's worth. This map of Berlin is a gay-colored maze, and looks like pictures of the circulation of the blood.

The streets are very clean. They are kept so—not by prayer and talk and the other New York methods, but by daily and hourly work with scrapers and brooms; and when an asphalted street has been tidily scraped after a rain or a light snowfall, they scatter clean sand over it. This saves some of the horses from falling down. In fact this is a city government which seems to stop at no expense where the public convenience, comfort and health are concerned—except in one detail. That is the naming of the streets and the numbering of the houses. Sometimes the name of a street will change in the middle of a block. You will not find it out till you get to the next corner and discover the new name on the wall, and of course you don't know just when the change happened.

The names are plainly marked on the corners—on all the corners—there are no exceptions. But the numbering of the houses—there has never been anything like it since original chaos. It is not possible that it was done by this wise city government. At first one thinks it was done by an idiot; but there is too much variety about it for that; an idiot could not think of so many different ways of making confusion and propagating blasphemy. The numbers run up one side the street and down the other. That is endurable, but the rest isn't. They often use one number for three or four houses—and sometimes they put the number on only one of the houses and let you guess at the others. Sometimes they put a number on a house—4, for instance—then put *4a, 4b, 4c* on the succeeding houses, and one becomes old and decrepit before he finally arrives at 5. A result of this systemless system is, that when you are at No. 1 in a street, you haven't any idea how far it may be to No. 150; it may be only six or eight blocks, it may be a couple of miles. Frederick street is long, and is one of the great thoroughfares. The other day a man put up his money behind the assertion that there were more refreshment-places in that street than numbers on the houses—and he won. There were 254 numbers and 257 refreshment-places. Yet as I have said, it is a long street.

But the worst feature of all this complex business is, that in Berlin the numbers do not travel in any one direction; no, they travel along until they get to 50 or 60, perhaps, then suddenly you find yourself up in the hundreds—140, maybe; the next will be 139—then you perceive by that sign that the numbers are now traveling toward you from the opposite direction. They will keep that sort of insanity up as long as you travel that street; every now and then the numbers will turn and run the other way. As a rule there is an arrow under the number, to show by the direction of its flight which way the numbers are proceeding. There are a good many suicides in Berlin; I have seen six reported in a single day. There is always a deal of learned and laborious arguing and ciphering going on as to the cause of this state of things. If they will set to work and number their houses in a rational way perhaps they will find out what was the matter.

More than a month ago Berlin began to prepare to celebrate Professor Virchow's seventieth birthday. When the birthday arrived, the middle of October, it seemed to me that all the world of science arrived with it; deputation after deputation came, bringing the homage and reverence of far cities and centers of learning, and during the whole of a long day the hero of it sat and received such witness of his greatness as has seldom been vouchsafed to any man in any walk of life in any time ancient or modern. These demonstrations were continued in one form or another day after day, and were presently merged in similar demonstrations to his twin in science and achievement, Professor Helmholtz, whose seventieth birthday is separated from Virchow's, by only about three weeks; so nearly as this did these two extraordinary men come to being born together. Two such births have seldom signalized a single year in human history.

But perhaps the final and closing demonstration was peculiarly grateful to them. This was a Commers given in their honor the other night, by 1,000 students. It was held in a huge hall, very long and very lofty, which had five galleries, far above everybody's head, which were crowded with ladies—four or five hundred, I judged.

It was beautifully decorated with clustered flags and various ornamental devices, and was brilliantly lighted. On the spacious floor of this place were ranged, in files, innumerable tables, seating twenty-four persons each, extending from one end of the great hall clear to the other and with narrow aisles between the files. In the center on one side was a high and tastefully decorated platform twenty or thirty feet long, with a long table on it behind which sat the half dozen chiefs of the givers of the Commers in the rich medieval costumes of as many different college corps. Behind these youths a band of musicians was concealed. On the floor directly in front of this platform were half a dozen tables which were distinguished from the outlying continent of tables by being covered instead of left naked. Of these the central table was reserved for the two heroes of the occasion and twenty particularly eminent professors of the Berlin University, and the other covered tables were for the occupancy of a hundred less distinguished professors.

I was glad to be honored with a place at the table of the two heroes of the occasion, although I was not really learned enough to deserve it. Indeed there was a pleasant strangeness in being in such company; to be thus associated with twenty-three men who forget more every day than I ever knew. Yet there was nothing embarrassing about it, because loaded men and empty ones look about alike, and I knew that to that multitude there I was a professor. It required but little art to catch the ways and attitude of those men and imitate them, and I had no difficulty in looking as much like a professor as anybody there.

We arrived early; so early that only Professors Virchow and Helmholtz and a dozen guests of the special tables were ahead of us, and 300 or 400 students. But people were arriving in floods, now, and within fifteen minutes all but the special tables were occupied and the great house was crammed, the aisles included. It was said that there were 4,000 men present. It was a most animated scene, there is no doubt about that; it was a stupendous beehive. At each end of each table stood a corps student in the uniform of his corps. These quaint costumes are of brilliant colored silks and velvets, with sometimes a high plumed hat, sometimes a broad Scotch cap, with a great plume wound about it, sometimes—oftenest—a little shallow silk cap on the tip of the crown, like an inverted saucer; sometimes the pantaloons are snow-white, sometimes of other colors; the boots in all cases come up well above the knee; and in all cases also white gauntlets are worn; the sword is a rapier with a bowl-shaped guard for the hand, painted in several colors. Each corps has a uniform of its own, and all are of rich material, brilliant in color, and exceedingly picturesque; for they are survivals of the vanished costumes of the Middle Ages, and they reproduce for us the time when men were beautiful to look at. The student who stood guard at our end of the table was of grave countenance and great frame and grace of form, and he was doubtless an accurate reproduction, clothes and all, of some ancestor of his of two or three centuries ago—a reproduction as far as the outside, the animal man, goes, I mean.

As I say, the place was now crowded. The nearest aisle was packed with students standing up, and they made a fence which shut off the rest of the house from view. As far down this fence as you could see all these wholesome young faces were turned in one direction, all these intent and worshiping eyes were centered upon one spot—the place where Virchow and Helmholtz sat. The boys seemed lost to everything, unconscious of their own existence; they devoured these two intellectual giants with their eyes, they feasted upon them, and the worship that was in their hearts shone in their faces. It seemed to me that I would rather be flooded with a glory like that, instinct with sincerity, innocent of self-seeking than win a hundred battles and break a million hearts.

There was a big mug of beer in front of each of us, and more to come when wanted. There was also a quarto pamphlet containing the words of the songs to be sung. After the names of the officers of the feast were these words in large type:

"Während des Kommerses herrscht allgemeiner Burgfriede."

I was not able to translate this to my satisfaction, but a professor helped me out. This was his explanation: The students in uniform belong to different college corps; not all students belong to corps; none join the corps except those who enjoy fighting. The corps students fight duels with swords every week, one corps challenging another corps to furnish a certain number of duelists for the occasion, and it is only on this battlefield that students of different corps exchange courtesies. In common life they do not drink with each other or speak. The above line now translates itself: there is truce during the Commers, war is laid aside and fellowship takes its place.

Now the performance began. The concealed band played a piece of martial music; then there was a pause. The students on the platform rose to their feet, the middle one gave a toast to the Emperor, then all the house rose, mugs in hand. At the call "One—two—three!" all glasses were drained and then brought down with a slam on the tables in unison. The result was as good an imitation of thunder as I have ever heard. From now on, during an hour, there was singing, in mighty chorus. During each interval between songs a number of the special guests—the professors—arrived. There seemed to be some signal whereby the students on the platform were made aware that a professor had arrived at the remote door of entrance; for you would see them suddenly rise to their feet, strike an erect military attitude, then draw their swords; the swords of all their brethren standing guard at the innumerable tables would flash from the scabbards and be held aloft—a handsome spectacle! Three clear bugle notes would ring out, then all these swords would come down with a crash, twice repeated, on the tables, and be uplifted and held aloft again; then in the distance you would see the gay uniforms and uplifted swords of a guard of honor clearing the way and conducting the guest down to his place. The songs were stirring, the immense outpour from young life and young lungs, the crash of swords and the thunder of the beer mugs gradually worked a body up to what seemed the last possible summit of excitement. It surely seemed to me that I had reached that summit, that I had reached my limit, and that there was no higher lift desirable for me. When apparently the last eminent guest had long ago taken his place, again those three bugle blasts rang out and once more the swords leaped from their scabbards. Who might this latecomer be? Nobody was interested to inquire. Still, indolent eyes were turned toward the distant entrance, we saw the silken gleam and the lifted swords of a guard of honor plowing through the remote crowds. Then we saw that end of the house rising to its feet; saw it rise abreast the advancing guard all along, like a wave. This supreme honor had been offered to no one before. Then there was an excited whisper at our table—"MOMMSEN!" and the whole house rose. Rose and shouted and stamped and clapped, and banged the beer mugs. Just simply a storm! Then the little man with his long hair and Emersonian face edged his way past us and took his seat. I could have touched him with my hand—Mommsen!—think of it!

This was one of those immense surprises that can happen only a few times in one's life. I was not dreaming of him, he was to me only a giant myth, a world-shadowing specter, not a reality. The surprise of it all can be only comparable to a man's suddenly coming upon Mont Blanc with its awful form towering into the sky, when he didn't suspect he was in its neighborhood. I would have walked a great many miles to get a sight of him, and here he was, without trouble or tramp or cost of any kind. Here he was, clothed in a Titanic deceptive modesty which made him look like other men. Here he was, carrying the Roman world and all the Cæsars in his hospitable skull and doing it as easily as that other luminous vault, the skull of the universe, carries the Milky Way and the constellations.

One of the professors said that once upon a time an American young lady was introduced to Mommsen, and found herself badly scared and speechless. She dreaded to see his mouth unclose, for she was expecting him to choose a subject several miles above her comprehension, and didn't suppose he *could* get down to the world that other people lived in; but when his remark came, her terrors disappeared: "Well how do you do? Have you read Howells's last book? *I* think it's his best."

The active ceremonies of the evening closed with the speeches of welcome delivered by two students and the replies made by Professors Virchow and Helmholtz.

Virchow has long been a member of the city government of Berlin. He works as hard for the city as does any other Berlin alderman, and gets the same pay—nothing. I don't know that we in America could venture to ask our most illustrious citizen to serve in a board of aldermen, and if we might venture it I am not positively sure that we could elect him. But here the municipal system is such that the best men in the city consider it an honor to serve gratis as aldermen, and the people have the good sense to prefer these men and to elect them year after year. As a result, Berlin is a thoroughly well-governed city. It is a free city; its affairs are not meddled with by the State; they are managed by its own citizens, and after methods of their own devising.

A PETITION TO THE QUEEN OF
ENGLAND

HARTFORD, *Nov.* 6, 1887.

MADAM: YOU will remember that last May Mr. Edward Bright, the clerk of the Inland Revenue Office, wrote me about a tax which he said was due from me to the Government on books of mine published in London—that is to say, an income tax on the royalties. I do not know Mr. Bright, and it is embarrassing to me to correspond with strangers; for I was raised in the country and have always lived there, the early part in Marion county Missouri before the war, and this part in Hartford county Connecticut, near Bloomfield and about 8 miles this side of Farmington, though some call it 9, which it is impossible to be, for I have walked it many and many a time in considerably under three hours, and General Hawley says he has done it in two and a quarter, which is not likely; so it has seemed best that I write your Majesty. It is true that I do not know your Majesty personally, but I have met the Lord Mayor, and if the rest of the family are like him, it is but just that it should be named royal; and likewise plain that in a family matter like this, I cannot better forward my case than to frankly carry it to the head of the family itself. I have also met the Prince of Wales once in the fall of 1873, but it was not in any familiar way, but in a quite informal way, being casual, and was of course a surprise to us both. It was in Oxford street, just where you come out of Oxford into Regent Circus, and just as he turned up one side of the circle at the head of a procession, I went down the other side on the top of an omnibus. He will remember me on account of a gray coat with flap pockets that I wore, as I was the only person on the omnibus that had on that kind of a coat; I remember him of course as easy as I would a comet. He looked quite proud and satisfied, but that is not to be wondered at, he has a good situation. And once I called on your Majesty, but you were out.

But that is no matter, it happens with everybody. However, I have wandered a little, away from what I started about. It was this way. Young Bright wrote my London publishers Chatto and Windus—their place is the one on the left as you come down Piccadilly, about a block and a half above where the minstrel show is—he wrote them that he wanted them to pay income tax on the royalties of some foreign authors, namely, "Miss De La Ramé (Ouida), Dr. Oliver Wendell Holmes, Mr. Francis Bret Harte, and Mr. Mark Twain." Well, Mr. Chatto diverted him from the others, and tried to divert him from me, but in this case he failed. So then, young Bright wrote me. And not only that, but he sent me a printed document the size of a newspaper, for me to sign, all over in different places. Well, it was that kind of a document that the more you study it the more it undermines you and makes everything seem uncertain to you; and so, while in that condition, and really not responsible for my acts, I wrote Mr. Chatto to pay the tax and charge to me. Of course my idea was, that it was for only one year, and that the tax would be only about one per cent or along there somewhere, but last night I met Professor Sloane of Princeton—you may not know him, but you have probably seen him every now and then, for he goes to England a good deal, a large man and very handsome and absorbed in thought, and if you have noticed such a man on platforms after the train is gone, that is the one, he generally gets left, like all those specialists and other scholars who know everything but how to apply it—and he said it was a back tax for *three* years, and no one per cent, but two and a half!

That gave what had seemed a little matter, a new aspect. I then began to study the printed document again, to see if I could find anything in it that might modify my case, and I had what seems to be a quite promising success. For instance, it opens thus—polite and courteous, the way those English government documents always are—I do not say that to hear myself talk, it is just the fact, and it is a credit:

"To Mr. Mark Twain: IN PURSUANCE of the Acts of Parliament for granting to Her Majesty Duties and Profits," etc.

I had not noticed that before. My idea had been that it was for the Government, and so I wrote *to* the Government; but now I saw that it was a private matter, a family matter, and that the proceeds went to yourself, not the Government. I would always rather treat with principals, and I am glad I noticed that clause. With a principal, one can always get at a fair and right understanding, whether it is about potatoes, or continents, or any of those things, or something entirely different; for the size or nature of the thing does not affect the fact; whereas, as a rule, a subordinate is more or less troublesome to satisfy. And yet this is not against them, but the other way. They have their duties to do, and must be harnessed to rules, and not allowed any discretion. Why if your Majesty should equip young Bright with discretion—I mean his own discretion—it is an even guess that he would discretion you out of house and home in 2 or 3 years. He would not *mean* to get the family into straits, but that would be the upshot, just the same. Now then, with Bright out of the way, this is not going to be an Irish question; it is going to be settled pleasantly and satisfactorily for all of us, and when it is finished your Majesty is going to stand with the American people just as you have stood for fifty years, and surely no monarch can require better than that of an alien nation. They do not all pay a British income tax, but the most of them will in time, for we have shoals of new authors coming along every year; and of the population of your Canada, upwards of four-fifths are wealthy Americans, and more going there all the time.

Well, another thing which I noticed in the Document, was an item about "Deductions." I will come to that presently, your Majesty. And another thing was this: that Authors are not mentioned in the Document at all. No, we have "Quarries, Mines, Iron Works, Salt Springs, Alum Mines, Water Works, Canals, Docks, Drains, Levels, Fishings, Fairs, Tolls, Bridges, Ferries," and so-forth and so-forth and so-on—well, as much as a yard or a yard and a half of them, I should think—anyway a very large quantity or number. I read along—down, and down, and down the list, further, and further, and further, and as I approached the bottom my hopes began to rise higher and higher, because I saw that everything in England, *that* far, was taxed by name and in detail, except perhaps the family, and maybe Parliament, and yet still no mention of Authors. Apparently they were going to be overlooked. And sure enough, they were! My heart gave a great bound. But I was too soon. There was a footnote, in Mr. Bright's hand, which said: "You are taxed under Schedule D, section 14." I turned to that place, and found these three things: "Trades, Offices, Gas Works."

Of course, after a moment's reflection, hope came up again, and then certainty: Mr. Bright was in error, and clear off the track; for Authorship is not a Trade, it is an inspiration; Authorship does not keep an Office, its habitation is all out under the sky, and everywhere where the winds are blowing and the sun is shining and the creatures of God are free. Now then, since I have no Trade and keep no Office, I am not taxable under Schedule D, section 14. Your Majesty sees that; so I will go on to that other thing that I spoke of, the "deductions"—deductions from my tax which I may get allowed, under conditions. Mr. Bright says all deductions to be claimed by me must be restricted to the provisions made in Paragraph No. 8, entitled "Wear and Tear of Machinery, or Plant." This is curious, and shows how far he has gotten away on his wrong course after once he has got started wrong: for Offices and Trades do not have Plant, they do not have Machinery, such a thing was never heard of; and moreover they do not wear and tear. You see that, your Majesty, and that it is true. Here is the Paragraph No. 8:

> Amount claimed as a deduction for diminished value by reason of Wear and Tear, where the Machinery or Plant belongs to the Person or Company carrying on the Concern, or is let to such Person or Company so that the Lessee is bound to maintain and deliver over the same in good condition:—

> *Amount £————————————————*

There it is—the very words.

I could answer Mr. Bright thus:

It is my pride to say that my Brain is my Plant; and I do not claim any deduction for diminished value by reason of Wear and Tear, for the reason that it does not wear and tear, but stays sound and whole all the time. Yes, I could say to him, my Brain is my Plant, my Skull is my Workshop, my Hand is my Machinery, and I am the Person carrying on the Concern; it is not leased to anybody, and so there is no Lessee bound to maintain and deliver over the same in good condition. There. I do not wish to any way overrate this argument and answer, dashed off just so, and not a word of it altered from the way I first wrote it, your Majesty, but indeed it does seem to pulverize that young fellow, you can see that yourself. But that is all I say; I stop there; I never pursue a person after I have got him down.

Having thus shown your Majesty that I am not taxable, but am the victim of the error of a clerk who mistakes the nature of my commerce, it only remains for me to beg that you will of your justice annul my letter that I spoke of, so that my publisher can keep back that tax-money which, in the confusion and aberration caused by the Document, I ordered him to pay. You will not miss the sum, but this is a hard year for authors; and as for lectures, I do not suppose your Majesty ever saw such a dull season.

With always great, and ever increasing respect, I beg to sign myself your Majesty's servant to command, MARK TWAIN.

HER MAJESTY THE QUEEN, LONDON

A MAJESTIC LITERARY FOSSIL

IF I were required to guess off-hand, and without collusion with higher minds, what is the bottom cause of the amazing material and intellectual advancement of the last fifty years, I should guess that it was the modern-born and previously nonexistent disposition on the part of men to believe that a new idea can have value. With the long roll of the mighty names of history present in our minds, we are not privileged to doubt that for the past twenty or thirty centuries every conspicuous civilization in the world has produced intellects able to invent and create the things which made our day a wonder; perhaps we may be justified in inferring, then, that the reason they did not do it was that the public reverence for old ideas and hostility to new ones always stood in their way, and was a wall they could not break down or climb over. The prevailing tone of old books regarding new ideas is one of suspicion and uneasiness at times, and at other times contempt. By contrast, our day is indifferent to old ideas, and even considers that their age makes their value questionable, but jumps at a new idea with enthusiasm and high hope—a hope which is high because it has not been accustomed to being disappointed. I make no guess as to just when this disposition was born to us, but it certainly is ours, was not possessed by any century before us, is our peculiar mark and badge, and is doubtless the bottom reason why we are a race of lightning-shod Mercuries, and proud of it—instead of being, like our ancestors, a race of plodding crabs, and proud of that.

So recent is this change from a three or four thousand year twilight to the flash and glare of open day that I have walked in both, and yet am not old. Nothing is to-day as it was when I was an urchin; but when I was an urchin, nothing was much different from what it had always been in this world. Take a single detail, for example—medicine. Galen could have come into my sick-room at any time during my first seven years—I mean any day when it wasn't fishing weather, and there wasn't any choice but school or sickness—and he could have sat down there and stood my doctor's watch without asking a question. He would have smelled around among the wilderness of cups and bottles and phials on the table and the shelves, and missed not a stench that used to glad him two thousand years before, nor discovered one that was of a later date. He would have examined me, and run across only one disappointment—I was already salivated; I would have him there; for I was always salivated, calomel was so cheap. He would get out his lancet then; but I would have him again; our family doctor didn't allow blood to accumulate in the system. However, he could take dipper and ladle, and freight me up with old familiar doses that had come down from Adam to his time and mine; and he could go out with a wheelbarrow and gather weeds and offal, and build some more, while those others were getting in their work. And if our reverend doctor came and found him there, he would be dumb with awe, and would get down and worship him. Whereas if Galen should appear among us to-day, he could not stand anybody's watch; he would inspire no awe; he would be told he was a back number, and it would surprise him to see that that fact counted against him, instead of in his favor. He wouldn't know our medicines; he wouldn't know our practice; and the first time he tried to introduce his own, we would hang him.

This introduction brings me to my literary relic. It is a *Dictionary of Medicine*, by Dr. James, of London, assisted by Mr. Boswell's Doctor Samuel Johnson, and is a hundred and fifty years old, it having been published at the time of the rebellion of '45. If it had been sent against the Pretender's troops there probably wouldn't have been a survivor. In 1861 this deadly book was still working the cemeteries—down in Virginia. For three generations and a half it had been going quietly along, enriching the earth with its slain. Up to its last free day it was trusted and believed in, and its devastating advice taken, as was shown by notes inserted between its leaves. But our troops captured it and brought it home, and it has been out of business since. These remarks from its preface are in the true spirit of the olden time, sodden with worship of the old, disdain of the new:

> If we inquire into the Improvements which have been made by the Moderns, we shall be forced to confess that we have so little Reason to value ourselves beyond the Antients, or to be tempted to contemn them, that we cannot give stronger or more convincing Proofs of our own Ignorance, as well as our Pride.
>
> Among all the systematical Writers, I think there are very few who refuse the Preference to *Hieron, Fabricius ab Aquapendente,* as a Person of unquestion'd Learning and Judgment; and yet is he not asham'd to let his Readers know that *Celsus* among the Latins, *Paulus Aegineta* among the Greeks, and *Albucasis* among the Arabians, whom I am unwilling to place among the Moderns, tho' he liv'd but six hundred Years since, are the Triumvirate to whom he principally stands indebted, for the Assistance he had receiv'd from them in composing his excellent Book.
>
> [In a previous paragraph are puffs of Galen, Hippocrates, and other débris of the Old Silurian Period of Medicine.] How many Operations are there now in Use which were unknown to the Antients?

That is true. The surest way for a nation's scientific men to prove that they were proud and ignorant was to claim to have found out something fresh in the course of a thousand years or so. Evidently the peoples of this book's day regarded themselves as children, and their remote ancestors as the only grown-up people that had existed. Consider the contrast: without offence, without over-egotism, our own scientific men may and do regard themselves as grown people and their grandfathers as children. The change here presented is probably the most sweeping that has ever come over mankind in the history of the race. It is the utter reversal, in a couple of generations, of an attitude which had been maintained without challenge or interruption from the earliest antiquity. It amounts to creating man over again on a new plan; he was a canal-boat before, he is an ocean greyhound to-day. The change from reptile to bird was not more tremendous, and it took longer.

It is curious. If you read between the lines what this author says about Brer Albucasis, you detect that in venturing to compliment him he has to whistle a little to keep his courage up, because Albucasis "liv'd but six hundred Years since," and therefore came so uncomfortably near being a "modern" that one couldn't respect him without risk.

Phlebotomy, Venesection—terms to signify bleeding—are not often heard in our day, because we have ceased to believe that the best way to make a bank or a body healthy is to squander its capital; but in our author's time the physician went around with a hatful of lancets on his person all the time, and took a hack at every patient whom he found still alive. He robbed his man of pounds and pounds of blood at a single operation. The details of this sort in this book make terrific reading. Apparently even the healthy did not escape, but were bled twelve times a year, on a particular day of the month, and exhaustively purged besides. Here is a specimen of the vigorous old-time practice; it occurs in our author's adoring biography of a Doctor Aretæus, a licensed assassin of Homer's time, or thereabouts:

> In a Quinsey he used Venesection, and allow'd the Blood to flow till the Patient was ready to faint away.

There is no harm in trying to cure a headache—in our day. You can't do it, but you get more or less entertainment out of trying, and that is something; besides, you live to tell about it, and that is more. A century or so ago you could have had the first of these features in rich variety, but you might fail of the other once—and once would do. I quote:

> As Dissections of Persons who have died of severe Headachs, which have been related by Authors, are too numerous to be inserted in this Place, we shall here abridge some of the most curious and important Observations relating to this Subject, collected by the celebrated *Bonetus*.

The celebrated Bonetus's "Observation No 1" seems to me a sufficient sample, all by itself, of what people used to have to stand any time between the creation of the world and the birth of your father and mine when they had the disastrous luck to get a "Head-ach":

> A certain Merchant, about forty Years of Age, of a Melancholic Habit, and deeply involved in the Cares of the World, was, during the Dog-days, seiz'd with a violent pain of his Head, which some time after oblig'd him to keep his Bed.
>
> I, being call'd, order'd Venesection in the Arms, the Application of Leeches to the Vessels of his Nostrils, Forehead, and Tem-

ples, as also to those behind his Ears; I likewise prescrib'd the
Application of Cupping-glasses, with Scarification, to his Back:
But, notwithstanding these Precautions, he dy'd. If any Surgeon,
skill'd in Arteriotomy, had been present, I should have also order'd
that Operation.

I looked for "Arteriotomy" in this same Dictionary, and found this
definition, "The opening of an Artery with a View of taking away Blood."
Here was a person who was being bled in the arms, forehead, nostrils,
back, temples, and behind the ears, yet the celebrated Bonetus was not
satisfied, but wanted to open an artery, "with a View" to inserting a
pump, probably. "Notwithstanding these Precautions"—he dy'd. No art
of speech could more quaintly convey this butcher's innocent surprise.
Now that we know what the celebrated Bonetus did when he wanted to
relieve a Head-ach, it is no trouble to infer that if he wanted to comfort a
man that had a Stomach-ach he disembowelled him.

I have given one "Observation"—a single Head-ach case; but the celebrated Bonetus follows it with eleven more. Without enlarging upon the
matter, I merely note this coincidence—they all "dy'd." Not one of these
people got well; yet this obtuse hyena sets down every little gory detail of
the several assassinations as complacently as if he imagined he was doing
a useful and meritorious work in perpetuating the methods of his crimes.
"Observations," indeed! They are confessions.

According to this book, "the Ashes of an Ass's hoof mix'd with Woman's milk cures chilblains." Length of time required not stated. Another
item: "The constant Use of Milk is bad for the Teeth, and causes them to
rot, and loosens the Gums." Yet in our day babies use it constantly
without hurtful results. This author thinks you ought to wash out your
mouth with wine before venturing to drink milk. Presently, when we come
to notice what fiendish decoctions those people introduced into their stomachs by way of medicine, we shall wonder that they could have been
afraid of milk.

It appears that they had false teeth in those days. They were made of
ivory sometimes, sometimes of bone, and were thrust into the natural
sockets, and lashed to each other and to the neighboring teeth with wires
or with silk threads. They were not to eat with, nor to laugh with, because
they dropped out when not in repose. You could smile with them, but you
had to practice first, or you would overdo it. They were not for business,
but just decoration. They filled the bill according to their lights.

This author says "the Flesh of Swine nourishes above all other eatables." In another place he mentions a number of things, and says "these
are very easy to be digested; so is Pork." This is probably a lie. But he is
pretty handy in that line; and when he hasn't anything of the sort in stock
himself he gives some other expert an opening. For instance, under the
head of "Attractives" he introduces Paracelsus, who tells of a nameless
"Specific"—quantity of it not set down—which is able to draw a hundred
pounds of flesh to itself—distance not stated—and then proceeds, "It
happen'd in our own Days that an Attractive of this Kind drew a certain
Man's Lungs up into his Mouth by which he had the Misfortune to be
suffocated." This is more than doubtful. In the first place, his Mouth

couldn't accommodate his Lungs—in fact, his Hat couldn't; secondly, his Heart being more eligibly Situated, it would have got the Start of his Lungs, and being a lighter Body, it would have Sail'd in ahead and Occupied the Premises; thirdly, you will Take Notice a Man with his Heart in his Mouth hasn't any Room left for his Lungs—he has got all he can Attend to; and finally, the Man must have had the Attractive in his Hat, and when he saw what was going to Happen he would have Remov'd it and Sat Down on it. Indeed he would; and then how could it Choke him to Death? I don't believe the thing ever happened at all.

Paracelsus adds this effort: "I myself saw a Plaister which attracted as much Water as was sufficient to fill a Cistern; and by these very Attractives Branches may be torn from Trees; and, which is still more surprising, a Cow may be carried up into the Air." Paracelsus is dead now; he was always straining himself that way.

They liked a touch of mystery along with their medicine in the olden time; and the medicine-man of that day, like the medicine-man of our Indian tribes, did what he could to meet the requirement:

> *Arcanum.* A Kind of Remedy whose Manner of Preparation, or singular Efficacy, is industriously concealed, in order to enhance its Value. By the Chymists it is generally defined a thing secret, incorporeal, and immortal, which cannot be Known by Man, unless by Experience; for it is the Virtue of every thing, which operates a thousand times more than the thing itself.

To me the butt end of this explanation is not altogether clear. A little of what they knew about natural history in the early times is exposed here and there in the *Dictionary*.

> *The Spider.* It is more common than welcome in Houses. Both the Spider and its Web are used in Medicine: The Spider is said to avert the Paroxysms of Fevers, if it be apply'd to the Pulse of the Wrist, or the Temples; but it is peculiarly recommended against a Quartan, being enclosed in the Shell of a Hazlenut.
>
> Among approved Remedies, I find that the distill'd Water of Black Spiders is an excellent Cure for Wounds, and that this was one of the choice Secrets of Sir Walter Raleigh.
>
> The Spider which some call the Catcher, or Wolf, being beaten into a Plaister, then sew'd up in Linen, and apply'd to the Forehead or Temples, prevents the Returns of a Tertian.
>
> There is another Kind of Spider, which spins a white, fine, and thick Web. One of this Sort, wrapp'd in Leather, and hung about the Arm, will avert the Fit of a Quartan. Boil'd in Oil of Roses, and instilled into the Ears, it eases Pains in those Parts. *Dioscorides, Lib. 2, Cap. 68.*
>
> Thus we find that Spiders have in all Ages been celebrated for their febrifuge Virtues; and it is worthy of Remark, that a Spider is usually given to Monkeys, and is esteem'd a sovereign Remedy for the Disorders those Animals are principally subject to.

Then follows a long account of how a dying woman, who had suffered nine hours a day with an ague during eight weeks, and who had been bled dry some dozens of times meantime without apparent benefit, was at last forced to swallow several wads of "Spiders-web," whereupon she straightway mended, and promptly got well. So the sage is full of enthusiasm over the spider-webs, and mentions only in the most casual way the discontinuance of the daily bleedings, plainly never suspecting that this had anything to do with the cure.

> As concerning the venomous Nature of Spiders, *Scaliger* takes notice of a certain Species of them (which he had forgotten), whose Poison was of so great Force as to affect one *Vincentinus* thro' the Sole of his Shoe, by only treading on it.

The sage takes that in without a strain, but the following case was a trifle too bulky for him, as his comment reveals:

> In Gascony, observes *Scaliger*, there is a very small Spider, which, running over a Looking-glass, will crack the same by the Force of her Poison.   (*A mere Fable.*)

But he finds no fault with the following facts:

> Remarkable is the Enmity recorded between this Creature and the Serpent, as also the Toad: Of the former it is reported, That, lying (as he thinks securely) under the Shadow of some Tree, the Spider lets herself down by her Thread, and, striking her Proboscis or Sting into the Head, with that Force and Efficacy, injecting likewise her venomous Juice, that, wringing himself about, he immediately grows giddy, and quickly after dies.
>
> When the Toad is bit or stung in Fight with this Creature, the Lizard, Adder, or other that is poisonous, she finds relief from Plantain, to which she resorts. In her Combat with the Toad, the Spider useth the same Stratagem as with the Serpent, hanging by her own Thread from the Bough of some Tree, and striking her Sting into her enemy's Head, upon which the other, enraged, swells up, and sometimes bursts.
>
> To this Effect is the Relation of *Erasmus*, which he saith he had from one of the Spectators, of a Person lying along upon the Floor of his Chamber, in the Summer-time, to sleep in a supine Posture, when a Toad, creeping out of some green Rushes, brought just before in, to adorn the Chimney, gets upon his Face, and with his Feet sits across his Lips. To force off the Toad, says the Historian, would have been accounted sudden Death to the Sleeper; and to leave her there, very cruel and dangerous; so that upon Consultation it was concluded to find out a Spider, which, together with her Web, and the Window she was fasten'd to, was brought carefully, and so contrived as to be held perpendicularly to the Man's Face; which was no sooner done, but the Spider, discovering his Enemy, let himself down, and struck in his Dart, afterwards betak-

ing himself up again to his Web; the Toad swell'd, but as yet kept his Station: The second Wound is given quickly after by the Spider, upon which he swells yet more, but remain'd alive still.—The Spider, coming down again by his Thread, gives the third Blow; and the Toad, taking off his Feet from over the Man's Mouth, fell off dead.

To which the sage appends this grave remark, "And so much for the historical Part." Then he passes on to a consideration of "the Effects and Cure of the Poison."

One of the most interesting things about this tragedy is the double sex of the Toad, and also of the Spider.

Now the sage quotes from one Turner:

I remember, when a very young Practitioner, being sent for to a certain Woman, whose Custom was usually, when she went to the Cellar by Candle-light, to go also a Spider-hunting, setting Fire to their Webs, and burning them with the Flame of the Candle still as she pursued them. It happen'd at length, after this Whimsy had been follow'd a long time, one of them sold his Life much dearer than those Hundreds she had destroy'd; for, lighting upon the melting Tallow of her Candle, near the Flame, and his legs being entangled therein, so that he could not extricate himself, the Flame or Heat coming on, he was made a Sacrifice to his cruel Persecutor, who delighting her Eyes with the Spectacle, still waiting for the Flame to take hold of him, he presently burst with a great Crack, and threw his Liquor, some into her Eyes, but mostly upon her Lips; by means of which, flinging away her Candle, she cry'd out for Help, as fansying herself kill'd already with the Poison. However in the Night her Lips swell'd up excessively, and one of her Eyes was much inflam'd; also her Tongue and Gums were somewhat affected; and, whether from the Nausea excited by the Thoughts of the Liquor getting into her Mouth, or from the poison- ous Impressions communicated by the nervous *Fibrillae* of those Parts to those of the Ventricle, a continual Vomiting attended: To take off which, when I was call'd. I order'd a Glass of mull'd Sack, with a Scruple of Salt of Wormwood, and some hours after a Theriacal Bolus, which she flung up again. I embrocated the Lips with the Oil of Scorpions mix'd with the Oil of Roses; and, in Consideration of the Ophthalmy, tho' I was not certain but the Heat of the Liquor, rais'd by the Flame of the Candle before the Body of the Creature burst, might, as well as the Venom, excite the Disturbance, (altho' Mr. *Boyle's* Case of a Person blinded by this Liquor dropping from the living Spider, makes the latter suf- ficient;) yet observing the great Tumefaction of the Lips, together with the other Symptoms not likely to arise from simple Heat, I was inclin'd to believe a real Poison in the Case; and therefore not daring to let her Blood in the Arm [If a man's throat were cut in those old days, the doctor would come and bleed the other end of him], I did, however, with good Success, set Leeches to her Temples, which took off much of the Inflammation; and her Pain was likewise abated, by instilling into her Eyes a thin Mucilage of the Seeds of Quinces and white Poppies extracted with Rose-water; yet the Swelling on the Lips increased; upon which, in the Night, she wore a Cataplasm prepared by boiling the Leaves of Scordium, Rue, and Elderflowers, and afterwards thicken'd with the Meal of Vetches. In the mean time, her Vomiting having left her, she had given her, between whiles, a little Draught of distill'd Water of Carduus Benedictus and Scordium, with some of the Theriaca dissolved; and upon going off of the Symptoms, an old Woman came luckily in, who, with Assurance suitable to those People, (whose Ignorance and Poverty is their Safety and Protection,) took off the Dressings, promising to cure her in two Days time, altho' she made it as many Weeks, yet had the Reputation of the Cure; applying only Plantain Leaves bruis'd and mixed with Cobwebs, dropping the Juice into her Eye, and giving some Spoonfuls of the same inwardly, two or three times a day.

So ends the wonderful affair. Whereupon the sage gives Mr. Turner the following shot—strengthening it with italics—and passes calmly on:

> *"I must remark upon this History, that the Plantain, as a Cooler, was much more likely to cure this Disorder than warmer Applications and Medicines."*

How strange that narrative sounds to-day, and how grotesque, when one reflects that it was a grave contribution to medical "science" by an old and reputable physician! Here was all this to-do—two weeks of it—over a woman who had scorched her eye and her lips with candle grease. The poor wench is as elaborately dosed, bled, embrocated, and otherwise harried and bedeviled, as if there had been really something the matter with her; and when a sensible old woman comes along at last, and treats the trivial case in a sensible way, the educated ignoramus rails at her ignorance, serenely unconscious of his own. It is pretty suggestive of the former snail-pace of medical progress that the spider retained his terrors during three thousand years, and only lost them within the last thirty or forty.

Observe what imagination can do. "This same young Woman" used to be so affected by the strong (imaginary) smell which emanated from the burning spiders that "the Objects about her seem'd to turn round; she grew faint also with cold Sweats, and sometimes a light Vomiting." There could have been Beer in that cellar as well as Spiders.

Here are some more of the effects of imagination: "*Sennertus* takes Notice of the Signs of the Bite or Sting of this Insect to be a Stupor or Numbness upon the Part, with a sense of Cold, Horror, or Swelling of the Abdomen, Paleness of the Face, involuntary Tears, Trembling, Contractions, a (****), Convulsions, cold Sweats; but these latter chiefly when the Poison has been received inwardly," whereas the modern physician holds that a few spiders taken inwardly, by a bird or a man, will do neither party any harm.

The above "Signs" are not restricted to spider bites—often they merely indicate fright. I have seen a person with a hornet in his pantaloons exhibit them all.

> As to the Cure, not slighting the usual Alexipharmics taken internally, the Place bitten must be immediately washed with Salt Water, or a Sponge dipped in hot Vinegar, or fomented with a Decoction of Mallows, Origanum, and Mother of Thyme; after which a Cataplasm must be laid on of the Leaves of Bay, Rue, Leeks, and the Meal of Barley, boiled with Vinegar, or of Garlick and Onions, contused with Goat's Dung and fat Figs. Mean time the Patient should eat Garlick and drink Wine freely.

As for me, I should prefer the spider bite. Let us close this review with a sample or two of the earthquakes which the old-time doctor used to introduce into his patient when he could find room. Under this head we have "Alexander's Golden Antidote," which is good for—well, pretty much everything. It is probably the old original first patent-medicine. It is built as follows:

> Take of Afarabocca, Henbane, Carpobalsamum, each two Drams and a half; of Cloves, Opium, Myrrh, Cyperus, each two Drams; of Opobalsamum, Indian Leaf, Cinamon, Zedoary, Ginger, Coftus, Coral, Cassia, Euphorbium, Gum Tragacanth, Frankincense, Styrax Calamita, Celtic, Nard, Spignel, Hartwort, Mustard, Saxifrage, Dill, Anise, each one Dram; of Xylaloes, Rheum, Ponticum, Alipta Moschata, Castor, Spikenard, Galangals, Opoponax, Anacardium, Mastich, Brimstone, Peony, Eringo, Pulp of Dates, red and white Hermodactyls, Roses, Thyme, Acorns, Penyroyal, Gentian, the Bark of the Root of Mandrake, Germander, Valerian, Bishops Weed, Bay-Berries, long and white Pepper, Xylobalsamum, Carnabadium, Macodonian, Parsley-seeds, Lovage, the Seeds of Rue, and Sinon, of each a Dram and a half; of pure Gold, pure Silver, Pearls not perforated, the Blatta Byzantina, the Bone of the Stag's Heart, of each the Quantity of fourteen Grains of Wheat; of Sapphire, Emerald, and Jasper Stones, each one Dram; of Haslenut, two Drams; of Pellitory of Spain, Shavings of Ivory, Calamus Odoratus, each the Quantity of twenty-nine Grains of Wheat; of Honey or Sugar a sufficient Quantity.

Serve with a shovel. No; one might expect such an injunction after such formidable preparation; but it is not so. The dose recommended is "the Quantity of an Hasle-nut." Only that; it is because there is so much jewelry in it, no doubt.

> *Aqua Limacum.* Take a great Peck of Garden-snails, and wash them in a great deal of Beer, and make your Chimney very clean, and set a Bushel of Charcoal on Fire; and when they are thoroughly kindled, make a Hole in the Middle of the Fire, and put the Snails in, and scatter more Fire amongst them, and let them roast till

they make a Noise; then take them out, and, with a Knife and coarse Cloth, pick and wipe away all the green Froth: Then break them, Shells and all, in a Stone Mortar. Take also a Quart of Earth-worms, and scour them with Salt, divers times over. Then take two Handfuls of Angelica and lay them in the Bottom of the Still; next lay two Handfuls of Celandine; next a Quart of Rose-mary-flowers; then two Handfuls of Bears-foot and Agrimony; then Fenugreek; then Turmerick; of each one Ounce: Red Dock-root, Bark of Barberry-trees, Wood-sorrel, Betony, of each two Handfuls.—Then lay the Snails and Worms on the Top of the Herbs; and then two Handfuls of Goose-dung, and two Handfuls of Sheep-dung. Then put in three Gallons of Strong Ale, and place the pot where you mean to set Fire under it: Let it stand all Night, or longer; in the Morning put in three Ounces of Cloves well beaten, and a small Quantity of Saffron, dry'd to Powder; then six Ounces of Shavings of Hartshorn, which must be uppermost. Fix on the Head and Refrigeratory, and distil according to Art.

There. The book does not say whether this is all one dose, or whether you have a right to split it and take a second chance at it, in case you live. Also, the book does not seem to specify what ailment it was for; but it is of no consequence, for of course that would come out on the inquest.

Upon looking further, I find that this formidable nostrum is "good for raising Flatulencies in the Stomach"—meaning *from* the stomach, no doubt. So it would appear that when our progenitors chanced to swallow a sigh, they emptied a sewer down their throats to expel it. It is like dislodging skippers from cheese with artillery.

When you reflect that your own father had to take such medicines as the above, and that you would be taking them to-day yourself but for the introduction of homeopathy, which forced the old-school doctor to stir around and learn something of a rational nature about his business, you may honestly feel grateful that homeopathy survived the attempts of the allopathists to destroy it, even though you may never employ any physician but an allopathist while you live.

The American Claimant

AND I AS USURPER—A NAMELESS PAUPER, A TRAMP.

EXPLANATORY

THE COLONEL Mulberry Sellers here re-introduced to the public is the same person who appeared as *Eschol* Sellers in the first edition of the tale entitled "The Gilded Age," years ago, and as *Beriah* Sellers in the subsequent editions of the same book, and finally as *Mulberry* Sellers in the drama played afterward by John T. Raymond.

The name was changed from Eschol to Beriah to accommodate an Eschol Sellers who rose up out of the vasty deeps of uncharted space and preferred his request—backed by threat of a libel suit—then went his way appeased, and came no more. In the play Beriah had to be dropped to satisfy another member of the race, and Mulberry was substituted in the hope that the objectors would be tired by that time and let it pass unchallenged. So far it has occupied the field in peace; therefore we chance it again, feeling reasonably safe, this time, under shelter of the statute of limitations.

MARK TWAIN

Hartford, 1891

THE WEATHER IN THIS BOOK

NO WEATHER will be found in this book. This is an attempt to pull a book through without weather. It being the first attempt of the kind in fictitious literature, it may prove a failure, but it seemed worth the while of some dare-devil person to try it, and the author was in just the mood.

Many a reader who wanted to read a tale through was not able to do it because of delays on account of the weather. Nothing breaks up an author's progress like having to stop every few pages to fuss-up the weather. Thus it is plain that persistent intrusions of weather are bad for both reader and author.

Of course weather is necessary to a narrative of human experience. That is conceded. But it ought to be put where it will not be in the way; where it will not interrupt the flow of the narrative. And it ought to be the ablest weather that can be had, not ignorant, poor-quality, amateur weather. Weather is a literary specialty, and no untrained hand can turn out a good article of it. The present author can do only a few trifling ordinary kinds of weather, and he cannot do those very good. So it has seemed wisest to borrow such weather as is necessary for the book from qualified and recognized experts—giving credit, of course. This weather will be found over in the back part of the book, out of the way. *See Appendix*. The reader is requested to turn over and help himself from time to time as he goes along.

Chapter 1

IT IS a matchless morning in rural England. On a fair hill we see a majestic pile, the ivied walls and towers of Cholmondeley Castle, huge relic and witness of the baronial grandeurs of the Middle Ages. This is one of the seats of the Earl of Rossmore, K. G., G. C. B., K. C. M. G., etc., etc., etc., etc., etc., who possesses twenty-two thousand acres of English land, owns a parish in London with two thousand houses on its lease-roll, and struggles comfortably along on an income of two hundred thousand pounds a year. The father and founder of this proud old line was William the Conqueror his very self; the mother of it was not inventoried in history by name, she being merely a random episode and inconsequential, like the tanner's daughter of Falaise.

In a breakfast room of the castle on this breezy fine morning there are two persons and the cooling remains of a deserted meal. One of these persons is the old lord, tall, erect, square-shouldered, white-haired, stern-browed, a man who shows character in every feature, attitude, and movement, and carries his seventy years as easily as most men carry fifty. The other person is his only son and heir, a dreamy-eyed young fellow, who looks about twenty-six but is nearer thirty. Candor, kindliness, honesty, sincerity, simplicity, modesty—it is easy to see that these are cardinal traits of his character; and so when you have clothed him in the formidable components of his name, you somehow seem to be contemplating a lamb in armor: his name and style being the Honorable Kirkcudbright Llanover Marjoribanks Sellers Viscount Berkeley, of Cholmondeley Castle, Warwickshire. (Pronounced K'koobry Thlanover Marshbanks Sellers Vycount Barkly, of Chumly Castle, Warrikshr.) He is standing by a great window, in an attitude suggestive of respectful attention to what his father is saying and equally respectful dissent from the positions and arguments offered. The father walks the floor as he talks, and his talk shows that his temper is away up toward summer heat.

"Soft-spirited as you are, Berkeley, I am quite aware that when you have once made up your mind to do a thing which your ideas of honor and justice require you to do, argument and reason are (for the time being,) wasted upon you—yes, and ridicule, persuasion, supplication, and command as well. To my mind—"

"Father, if you will look at it without prejudice, without passion, you must concede that I am not doing a rash thing, a thoughtless, wilful thing, with nothing substantial behind it to justify it. *I* did not create the American claimant to the earldom of Rossmore; I did not hunt for him, did not find him, did not obtrude him upon your notice. He found himself, he injected himself into our lives—"

"And has made mine a purgatory for ten years with his tiresome letters, his wordy reasonings, his acres of tedious evidence,—"

"Which you would never read, would never consent to read. Yet in common fairness he was entitled to a hearing. That hearing would either prove he was the rightful earl—in which case our course would be plain—or it would prove that he wasn't—in which case our course would be equally plain. I have read his evidences, my lord. I have conned them well, studied them patiently and thoroughly. The chain seems to be complete, no important link wanting. I believe he is the rightful earl."

"And I a usurper—a nameless pauper, a tramp! Consider what you are saying, sir."

"Father, *if* he is the rightful earl, would you, could you—that fact being established—consent to keep his titles and his properties from him a day, an hour, a minute?"

"You are talking nonsense—nonsense—lurid idiocy! Now, listen to me. I will make a confession—if you wish to call it by that name. I did not read those evidences because I had no occasion to—I was made familiar with them in the time of this claimant's father and of my own father forty years ago. This fellow's predecessors have kept mine more or less familiar with them for close upon a hundred and fifty years. The truth is, the rightful heir did go to America, with the Fairfax heir or about the same time—but disappeared somewhere in the wilds of Virginia, got married, and began to breed savages for the Claimant market; wrote no letters home; was supposed to be dead; his younger brother softly took possession; presently the American did die, and straightway his eldest product put in his claim—by letter—letter still in existence—and died before the uncle in possession found time—or maybe inclination—to answer. The infant son of that eldest product grew up—long interval, you see—and *he* took to writing letters and furnishing evidences. Well, successor after successor has done the same, down to the present idiot. It was a succession of paupers; not one of them was ever able to pay his passage to England or institute suit. The Fairfaxes kept their lordship alive, and so they have never lost it to this day, although they live in Maryland; their friend lost his by his own neglect. You perceive now, that the facts in this case bring us to precisely this result: morally the American tramp *is* rightful earl of Rossmore; legally he has no more right than his dog. There now—are you satisfied?"

There was a pause, then the son glanced at the crest carved in the great oaken mantel and said, with a regretful note in his voice:

"Since the introduction of heraldic symbols, the motto of this house has been *Suum cuique*—to every man his own. By your own intrepidly frank confession, my lord, it is become a sarcasm. If Simon Lathers—"

"Keep that exasperating name to yourself! For ten years it has pestered my eye and tortured my ear; till at last my very footfalls time themselves to the brain-racking rhythm of *Simon Lathers!—Simon Lathers!—Simon Lathers!* And now, to make its presence in my soul eternal, immortal, imperishable, you have resolved to—to—what is it you have resolved to do?''

"To go to Simon Lathers, in America, and change places with him.''

"What? Deliver the reversion of the earldom into his hands?''

"That is my purpose.''

"Make this tremendous surrender without even trying the fantastic case in the Lords?''

"Ye—s—'' with hesitation and some embarrassment.

"By all that is amazing, I believe you are insane, my son. See here— have you been training with that ass again—that radical, if you prefer the term, though the words are synonymous—Lord Tanzy, of Tollmache?''

The son did not reply, and the old lord continued:

"Yes, you confess. That puppy, that shame to his birth and caste, who holds all hereditary lordships and privilege to be usurpation, all nobility a tinsel sham, all aristocratic institutions a fraud, all inequalities in rank a legalized crime and an infamy, and no bread honest bread that a man doesn't earn by his own work—*work,* pah!''—and the old patrician brushed imaginary labor-dirt from his white hands. "You have come to hold just those opinions yourself, I suppose,'' he added with a sneer.

A faint flush in the younger man's cheek told that the shot had hit and hurt, but he answered with dignity—

"I have. I say it without shame—I feel none. And now my reason for resolving to renounce my heirship without resistance is explained. I wish to retire from what to me is a false existence, a false position, and begin my life over again—begin it right—begin it on the level of mere man-hood, unassisted by factitious aids, and succeed or fail by pure merit or the want of it. I will go to America, where all men are equal and all have an equal chance; I will live or die, sink or swim, win or lose as just a man—that alone, and not a single helping gaud or fiction back of it.''

"Hear, hear!'' The two men looked each other steadily in the eye a moment or two, then the elder one added, musingly, "Ab-so-lutely cra-zy—ab-so-lutely!'' After another silence, he said, as one who, long trou-bled by clouds, detects a ray of sunshine, "Well, there will be one satis-faction—Simon Lathers will come here to enter into his own, and I will drown him in the horsepond. That poor devil—always so humble in his letters, so pitiful, so deferential; so steeped in reverence for our great line and lofty station; so anxious to placate us, so prayerful for recognition as a relative, a bearer in his veins of our sacred blood—and withal so poor, so needy, so threadbare and pauper-shod as to raiment, so despised, so laughed at for his silly claimantship by the lewd American scum around him—ach, the vulgar, crawling, insufferable tramp! To read one of his cringing, nauseating letters—well?''

This to a splendid flunkey, all in inflamed plush and buttons and knee-breeches as to his trunk, and a glinting white frost-work of ground-glass paste as to his head, who stood with his heels together and the upper half of him bent forward, a salver in his hands:

"The letters, my lord.''

My lord took them, and the servant disappeared.

"Among the rest, an American letter. From the tramp, of course. Jove, but here's a change! No brown paper envelope this time, filched from a shop and carrying the shop's advertisement in the corner. Oh, no, a proper enough envelope—with a most ostentatiously broad mourning border—for his cat, perhaps, since he was a bachelor—and fastened with red wax—a batch of it as big as a half-crown—and—and—our crest for a seal!—motto and all. And the ignorant, sprawling hand is gone; he sports a secretary, evidently—a secretary with a most confident swing and flourish to his pen. Oh indeed, our fortunes are improving over there—our meek tramp has undergone a metamorphosis."

"Read it, my lord, please."

"Yes, this time I will. For the sake of the cat:

14,042 Sixteenth Street,
Washington, May 2.

MY LORD—

It is my painful duty to announce to you that the head of our illustrious house is no more—The Right Honorable, The Most Noble, The Most Puissant Simon Lathers Lord Rossmore having departed this life ("Gone at last—this is unspeakably precious news, my son,") at his seat in the environs of the hamlet of Duffy's Corners in the grand old State of Arkansas,—and his twin brother with him, both being crushed by a log at a smoke-house-raising, owing to carelessness on the part of all present, referable to over-confidence and gaiety induced by overplus of sour-mash—("Extolled by sour-mash, whatever that may be, eh Berkeley?") five days ago, with no scion of our ancient race present to close his eyes and inter him with the honors due his historic name and lofty rank—in fact, he is on the ice yet, him and his brother—friends took up a collection for it. But I shall take immediate occasion to have their noble remains shipped to you ("Great heavens!") for interment, with due ceremonies and solemnities, in the family vault or mausoleum of our house. Meantime I shall put up a pair of hatchments on my house-front, and you will of course do the same at your several seats.

I have also to remind you that by this sad disaster I as sole heir, inherit and become seized of all the titles, honors, lands, and goods of our lamented relative, and must of necessity, painful as the duty is, shortly require at the bar of the Lords restitution of these dignities and properties, now illegally enjoyed by your titular lordship.

With assurance of my distinguished consideration and warm cousinly regard, I remain

Your titular lordship's
Most obedient servant,
MULBERRY SELLERS EARL ROSSMORE.

"Im-mense! Come, this one's interesting. Why, Berkeley, his breezy impudence is—is—why, it's colossal, it's sublime."

"No, this one doesn't seem to cringe much."

"Cringe—why, he doesn't know the meaning of the word. Hatchments!

To commemorate that sniveling tramp and his fraternal duplicate. And he is going to send me the remains. The late Claimant was a fool, but plainly this new one's a maniac. What a name! *Mulberry* Sellers—there's music for you. Simon Lathers—Mulberry Sellers—Mulberry Sellers—Simon Lathers. Sounds like machinery working and churning. Simon Lathers, Mulberry Sel— Are you going?''

"If I have your leave, father."

The old gentleman stood musing some time, after his son was gone. This was his thought:

"He is a good boy, and lovable. Let him take his own course—as it would profit nothing to oppose him—make things worse, in fact. My arguments and his aunt's persuasions have failed; let us see what America can do for us. Let us see what equality and hardtimes can effect for the mental health of a brain-sick young British lord. Going to renounce his lordship and be a man! Yas!''

Chapter 2

COLONEL MULBERRY Sellers—this was some days before he wrote his letter to Lord Rossmore—was seated in his "library," which was also his "drawing-room" and was also his "picture gallery" and likewise his "work-shop." Sometimes he called it by one of these names, sometimes by another, according to occasion and circumstance. He was constructing what seemed to be some kind of a frail mechanical toy, and was apparently very much interested in his work. He was a white-headed man, now, but otherwise he was as young, alert, buoyant, visionary and enterprising as ever. His loving old wife sat nearby, contentedly knitting and thinking, with a cat asleep in her lap. The room was large, light, and had a comfortable look, in fact a home-like look, though the furniture was of a humble sort and not overabundant, and the knick-knacks and things that go to adorn a living-room not plenty and not costly. But there were natural flowers, and there was an abstract and unclassifiable something about the place which betrayed the presence in the house of somebody with a happy taste and an effective touch.

Even the deadly chromos on the walls were somehow without offence; in fact they seemed to belong there and to add an attraction to the room—a fascination, anyway; for whoever got his eye on one of them was like to gaze and suffer till he died—you have seen that kind of picture. Some of these terrors were landscapes, some libeled the sea, some were ostensible portraits, all were crimes. All the portraits were recognizable as dead Americans of distinction, and yet, through labeling added by a daring hand, they were all doing duty here as "Earls of Rossmore." The newest one had left the works as Andrew Jackson, but was doing its best now, as "Simon Lathers Lord Rossmore, Present Earl." On one wall was a cheap old railroad map of Warwickshire. This had been newly labeled "The Rossmore Estates." On the opposite wall was another map, and this was the most imposing decoration of the establishment and the first to catch a stranger's attention, because of its great size. It had once borne simply

HE WAS CONSTRUCTING WHAT SEEMED TO BE SOME KIND OF
FRAIL MECHANICAL TOY.

the title SIBERIA; but now the word "FUTURE" had been written in
front of that word. There were other additions, in red ink—many cities,
with great populations set down, scattered over the vast country at points
where neither cities nor populations exist to-day. One of these cities, with
population placed at 1,500,000, bore the name "Libertyorloffskoizalin-
ski," and there was a still more populous one, centrally located and
marked "Capital," which bore the name "Freedomolovnaivanovich."

The "mansion"—the Colonel's usual name for the house—was a rick-
ety old two-story frame of considerable size, which had been painted,
some time or other, but had nearly forgotten it. It was away out in the
ragged edge of Washington and had once been somebody's country place.
It had a neglected yard around it, with a paling fence that needed straightening up, in places, and a gate that would stay shut. By the door-post
were several modest tin signs. "Col. Mulberry Sellers, Attorney at Law
and Claim Agent," was the principal one. One learned from the others
that the Colonel was a Materializer, a Hypnotizer, a Mind-Cure dabbler,
and so on. For he was a man who could always find things to do.

A white-headed negro man, with spectacles and damaged white cotton
gloves appeared in the presence, made a stately obeisance and announced—

"Marse Washington Hawkins, suh."

"Great Scott! Show him in, Dan'l, show him in."

The Colonel and his wife were on their feet in a moment, and the next
moment were joyfully wringing the hands of a stoutish, discouraged-
looking man whose general aspect suggested that he was fifty years old,
but whose hair swore to a hundred.

"Well, well, well, Washington, my boy, it *is* good to look at you again.
Sit down, sit down, and make yourself at home. There, now—why, you
look perfectly natural; aging a little, just a little, but you'd have known
him anywhere, wouldn't you, Polly?"

"Oh, yes, Berry, he's *just* like his pa would have looked if he'd lived.
Dear, dear, where have you dropped from? Let me see, how long is it
since—"

"I should say it's all of fifteen years, Mrs. Sellers."

"Well, well, how time does get away with us. Yes, and oh, the changes that—"

There was a sudden catch of her voice and a trembling of the lip, the men waiting reverently for her to get command of herself and go on; but after a little struggle she turned away, with her apron to her eyes, and softly disappeared.

"Seeing you made her think of the children, poor thing—dear, dear, they're all dead but the youngest. But banish care, it's no time for it now—on with the dance, let joy be unconfined is my motto, whether there's any dance to dance, or any joy to unconfine—you'll be the healthier for it every time,—every time, Washington—it's my experience, and I've seen a good deal of this world. Come—where have you disappeared to all these years, and are you from there, now, or where are you from?"

"I don't quite think you would ever guess, Colonel. Cherokee Strip."

"My land!"

"Sure as you live."

"You can't mean it. Actually *living* out there?"

"Well, yes, if a body may call it that; though it's a pretty strong term for 'dobies and jackass rabbits, boiled beans and slapjacks, depression, withered hopes, poverty in all its varieties—"

"Louise out there?"

"Yes, and the children."

"Out there now?"

"Yes, I couldn't afford to bring them with me."

"Oh, I see,—you had to come—claim against the government. Make yourself perfectly easy—I'll take care of that."

"But it isn't a claim against the government."

"No? Want to be postmaster? *That's* all right. Leave it to me. I'll fix it."

"But it isn't postmaster—you're all astray yet."

"Well, good gracious, Washington, why don't you come out and tell me what it is? What do you want to be so reserved and distrustful with an old friend like me, for? Don't you reckon I can keep a se—"

"There's no secret about it—you merely don't give me a chance to—"

"Now look here, old friend, I know the human race; and I know that when a man comes to Washington, I don't care if it's from heaven, let alone Cherokee Strip, it's because he *wants* something. And I know that as a rule he's not going to get it; that he'll stay and try for another thing and won't get that; the same luck with the next and the next and the next; and keeps on till he strikes bottom, and is too poor and ashamed to go back, even to Cherokee Strip; and at last his heart breaks and they take up a collection and bury him. There—don't interrupt me, I know what I'm talking about. Happy and prosperous in the Far West wasn't I? *You* know that. Principal citizen of Hawkeye, looked up to by everybody, kind of an autocrat, actually a kind of an autocrat, Washington. Well, nothing would do but I must go Minister to St. James, the Governor and everybody insisting, you know, and so at last I consented—no getting out of it, *had* to do it, so here I came. *A day too late,* Washington. Think of that—what little things change the world's history—yes, sir, the place had been filled. Well, there I was, you see. I offered to compromise and go to Paris. The President was very sorry and all that, but *that* place, you see, didn't belong to the West, so there I was again. There was no help for it, so I had to stoop a little—we all reach the day some time or other when we've got to do that, Washington, and it's not a bad thing for us, either, take it by and large and all around—I had to stoop a little and offer to take Constantinople. Washington, consider this—for it's perfectly true—within a month I *asked* for China; within another month I *begged* for Japan; one year later I was away down, down, down, supplicating with tears and anguish for the bottom office in the gift of the government of the United States—Flint-Picker in the cellars of the War Department. And by George I didn't get it."

"Flint-Picker?"

"Yes. Office established in the time of the Revolution, last century. The musket-flints for the military posts were supplied from the capitol. They do it yet; for although the flint-arm has gone out and the forts have tumbled down, the decree hasn't been repealed—been overlooked and forgotten, you see—and so the vacancies where old Ticonderoga and others used to stand, still get their six quarts of gun-flints a year just the same."

Washington said musingly after a pause:

"How strange it seems—to start for Minister to England at twenty thousand a year and fail for flint-picker at—"

"Three dollars a week. It's human life, Washington—just an epitome of human ambition, and struggle, and the outcome: you aim for the palace and get drowned in the sewer."

There was another meditative silence. Then Washington said, with earnest compassion in his voice—

"And so, after coming here, against your inclination, to satisfy your sense of patriotic duty and appease a selfish public clamor, you get absolutely nothing for it."

"Nothing?" The Colonel had to get up and stand, to get room for his amazement to expand. "*Nothing,* Washington? I ask you this: to be a Perpetual Member and the *only* Perpetual Member of a Diplomatic Body accredited to the greatest country on earth—do you call that nothing?"

It was Washington's turn to be amazed. He was stricken dumb; but the wide-eyed wonder, the reverent admiration expressed in his face were more eloquent than any words could have been. The Colonel's wounded spirit was healed and he resumed his seat pleased and content. He leaned forward and said impressively:

"What was due to a man who had become forever conspicuous by an experience without precedent in the history of the world?—a man made permanently and diplomatically sacred, so to speak, by having been connected, temporarily, through solicitation, with every single diplomatic post in the roster of this government, from Envoy Extraordinary and Minister Plenipotentiary to the Court of St. James all the way down to Consul to a guano rock in the Straits of Sunda—salary payable in guano—which disappeared by volcanic convulsion the day before they got down to my name in the list of applicants. Certainly something august enough to be answerable to the size of this unique and memorable experience was my due, and I got it. By the common voice of this community, by acclamation of the people, that mighty utterance which brushes aside laws and legislation, and from whose decrees there is no appeal, I was named Perpetual Member of the Diplomatic Body representing the multifarious sovereignties and civilizations of the globe near the republican court of the United States of America. And they brought me home with a torchlight procession."

"It is wonderful, Colonel, simply wonderful."

"It's the loftiest official position in the whole earth."

"I should think so—and the most commanding."

"You have named the word. Think of it. I frown, and there is war; I smile, and contending nations lay down their arms."

"It is awful. The responsibility, I mean."

"It is nothing. Responsibility is no burden to me; I am used to it; have always been used to it."

"And the work—the work! Do you have to attend all the sittings?"

"Who, I? Does the Emperor of Russia attend the conclaves of the governors of the provinces? He sits at home, and indicates his pleasure."

Washington was silent a moment, then a deep sigh escaped him.

"How proud I was an hour ago; how paltry seems my little promotion now! Colonel, the reason I came to Washington is,—I am Congressional Delegate from Cherokee Strip!"

The Colonel sprang to his feet and broke out with prodigious enthusiasm:

"Give me your hand, my boy—this is immense news! I congratulate you with all my heart. My prophecies stand confirmed. I always said it was in you. I always said you were born for high distinction and would achieve it. You ask Polly if I didn't."

Washington was dazed by this most unexpected demonstration.

"Why, Colonel, there's nothing *to* it. That little narrow, desolate, unpeopled, oblong streak of grass and gravel, lost in the remote wastes of the vast continent—why, it's like representing a billiard table—a discarded one."

"Tut-tut, it's a great, it's a staving preferment, and just opulent with influence here."

"Shucks, Colonel, I haven't even a vote."

"That's nothing; you can make speeches."

"No, I can't. The population's only two hundred—"

"That's all right, that's all right—"

"And they hadn't any right to elect me; we're not even a territory, there's no Organic Act, the government hasn't any official knowledge of us whatever."

"Never mind about that; I'll fix that. I'll rush the thing through, I'll get you organized in no time."

"*Will* you, Colonel?—it's *too* good of you; but it's just your old sterling self, the same old ever-faithful friend," and the grateful tears welled up in Washington's eyes.

"It's just as good as done, my boy, just as good as done. Shake hands. We'll hitch teams together, you and I, and we'll make things hum!"

Chapter 3

MRS. SELLERS returned, now, with her composure restored, and began to ask after Hawkins's wife, and about his children, and the number of them, and so on, and her examination of the witness resulted in a circumstantial history of the family's ups and downs and driftings to and fro in the far West during the previous fifteen years. There was a message, now, from out back, and Colonel Sellers went out there in answer to it. Hawkins took this opportunity to ask how the world had been using the Colonel during the past half-generation.

"Oh, it's been using him just the same; it couldn't change its way of using him if it wanted to, for he wouldn't let it."

"I can easily believe that, Mrs. Sellers."

"Yes, you see, he doesn't change, himself—not the least little bit in the world—he's always Mulberry Sellers."

"I can see *that* plain enough."

"Just the same old scheming, generous, good-hearted, moonshiny, hopeful, no-account failure he always was, and still everybody likes him just as well as if he was the shiningest success."

"They always did: and it was natural, because he was so obliging and accommodating, and had something about him that made it kind of easy to ask help of him, or favors—you didn't feel shy, you know, or have that wish-you-didn't-have-to-try feeling that you have with other people."

"It's just so, yet; and a body wonders at it, too, because he's been shamefully treated, many times, by people that had used him for a ladder to climb up by, and then kicked him down when they didn't need him any more. For a time you can see he's hurt, his pride's wounded, because he shrinks away from that thing and don't want to talk about it—and so I used to think *now* he's learned something and he'll be more careful hereafter—but laws! in a couple of weeks he's forgotten all about it, and any selfish tramp out of nobody knows where can come and put up a poor mouth and walk right into his heart with his boots on."

"It must try your patience pretty sharply sometimes."

"Oh, no, I'm used to it; and I'd rather have him so than the other way. When I call him a failure, I mean to the world he's a failure; he isn't to me. I don't know as I want him different—much different, anyway. I have to scold him some, snarl at him, you might even call it, but I reckon I'd do that just the same, if he was different—it's my make. But I'm a good deal less snarly and more contented when he's a failure than I am when he isn't."

"Then he isn't always a failure," said Hawkins, brightening.

"Him? Oh, bless you, no. He makes a strike, as he calls it, from time to time. Then's my time to fret and fuss. For the money just flies—first come first served. Straight off, he loads up the house with cripples and idiots and stray cats and all the different kinds of poor wrecks that other people don't want and he *does,* and then when the poverty comes again I've *got* to clear the most of them out or we'd starve; and that distresses him, and me the same, of course. Here's old Dan'l and old Jinny, that the

IT MUST TRY YOUR PATIENCE PRETTY SHARPLY SOMETIMES.

sheriff sold south one of the times that we got bankrupted before the war—they came wandering back after the peace, worn out and used up on the cotton plantations, helpless, and not another lick of work left in their old hides for the rest of this earthly pilgrimage—and we so pinched, *oh* so pinched for the very crumbs to keep life in us, and he just flung the door wide, and the way he received them you'd have thought they had come straight down from heaven in answer to prayer. I took him one side and said, 'Mulberry we can't have them—we've nothing for ourselves— we can't feed them.' He looked at me kind of hurt, and said, 'Turn them out?—and they've come to me just as confident and trusting as—as— why Polly, I must have *bought* that confidence sometime or other a long time ago, and given my note, so to speak—you don't get such things as a *gift*—and how am I going to go back on a debt like that? And you see, they're so poor, and old, and friendless, and—' But I was ashamed by that time, and shut him off, and somehow felt a new courage in me, and so I said, softly, 'We'll keep them—the Lord will provide.' He was glad, and started to blurt out one of those over-confident speeches of his, but checked himself in time, and said humbly, '*I* will, anyway.' It was years and years and years ago. Well, you see those old wrecks are here yet.''

"But don't they do your housework?''

"Laws! The idea. They would if they could, poor old things, and perhaps they think they *do* do some of it. But it's a superstition. Dan'l waits on the front door, and sometimes goes on an errand; and sometimes you'll see one or both of them letting on to dust around in here—but that's because there's something they want to hear about and mix their gabble into. And they're always around at meals, for the same reason. But the fact is, we have to keep a young negro girl just to take care of *them,* and a negro woman to do the housework and *help* take care of them.''

"Well, they ought to be tolerably happy, I should think.''

"It's no name for it. They quarrel together pretty much all the time— most always about religion, because Dan'l's a Dunker Baptist and Jinny's a shouting Methodist, and Jinny believes in special Providences and Dan'l don't, because he thinks he's a kind of a free-thinker—and they play and sing plantation hymns together, and talk and chatter just eternally and forever, and are sincerely fond of each other and think the world of Mulberry, and he puts up patiently with all their spoiled ways and foolishness, and so—ah, well, they're happy enough if it comes to that. And I don't mind—I've got used to it. I can get used to anything, with Mulberry to help; and the fact is, I don't much care what happens, so long as he's spared to me."

"Well, here's to him, and hoping he'll make another strike soon."

"And rake in the lame, the halt and the blind, and turn the house into a hospital again? It's what he would do. I've seen a plenty of that and more. No, Washington, I want his strikes to be mighty moderate ones the rest of the way down the vale."

"Well, then, big strike or little strike, or no strike at all, here's hoping he'll never lack for friends—and I don't reckon he ever will while there's people around who know enough to—"

"Him lack for friends!" and she tilted her head up with a frank pride— "why, Washington, you can't name a man that's anybody that isn't fond of him. I'll tell you privately, that I've had Satan's own time to keep them from appointing him to some office or other. They knew he'd no business with an office, just as well as I did, but he's the hardest man to refuse anything to, a body ever saw. Mulberry Sellers with an office! laws goodness, you know what that would be like. Why, they'd come from the ends of the earth to see a circus like that. I'd just as lieves be married to Niagara Falls, and done with it." After a reflective pause she added— having wandered back, in the interval, to the remark that had been her text: "Friends?—oh, indeed, no man ever had more; and *such* friends: Grant, Sherman, Sheridan, Johnston, Longstreet, Lee—many's the time they've sat in that chair you're sitting in—" Hawkins was out of it instantly, and contemplating it with a reverential surprise, and with the awed sense of having trodden shod upon holy ground—

"*They!*" he said.

"Oh, indeed, yes, a many and a many a time."

He continued to gaze at the chair fascinated, magnetized; and for once in his life that continental stretch of dry prairie which stood for his imagination was afire, and across it was marching a slanting flame-front that joined its wide horizons together and smothered the skies with smoke. He was experiencing what one or another drowsing, geographically-ignorant alien experiences every day in the year when he turns a dull and indifferent eye out of the car window and it falls upon a certain station-sign which reads "Stratford-on-Avon!" Mrs. Sellers went gossiping comfortably along:

"Oh, they like to hear him talk, especially if their load is getting rather heavy on one shoulder and they want to shift it. He's all air, you know,— breeze, you may say—and he freshens them up; it's a trip to the country, they say. Many a time he's made General Grant laugh—and that's a tidy job, I can tell you, and as for Sheridan, his eye lights up and he listens to Mulberry Sellers the same as if he was artillery. You see, the charm about Mulberry is, he is so catholic and unprejudiced that he fits in anywhere and everywhere. It makes him powerful good company, and as popular as scandal. You go to the White House when the President's holding a general reception—sometime when Mulberry's there. Why, dear me, *you* can't tell which of them it is that's holding that reception.''

"Well he certainly is a remarkable man—and he always was. Is he religious?''

"Clear to his marrow—does more thinking and reading on that subject than any other except Russia and Siberia: thrashes around over the whole field, too; nothing bigoted about him.''

"What is his religion?''

"He—'' She stopped, and was lost for a moment or two in thinking, then she said, with simplicity, "I think he was a Mohammedan or something last week.''

Washington started downtown, now, to bring his trunk, for the hospitable Sellerses would listen to no excuses; their house must be his home during the session. The Colonel returned presently and resumed work upon his plaything. It was finished when Washington got back.

"There it is,'' said the Colonel, "all finished.''

"What is it for, Colonel?''

"Oh, it's just a trifle. Toy to amuse the children.''

Washington examined it.

"It seems to be a puzzle.''

"Yes, that's what it is. I call it Pigs in the Clover. Put them in—see if you can put them in the pen.''

After many failures Washington succeeded, and was as pleased as a child.

"It's wonderfully ingenious, Colonel, it's ever so clever. And interesting—why, I could play with it all day. What are you going to do with it?''

"Oh, nothing. Patent it and throw it aside.''

"Don't you do anything of the kind. There's money in that thing.''

A compassionate look traveled over the Colonel's countenance, and he said:

"Money—yes; pin money: a couple of hundred thousand, perhaps. Not more.''

Washington's eyes blazed.

"A couple of hundred thousand dollars! do you call that pin money?''

The Colonel rose and tip-toed his way across the room, closed a door that was slightly ajar, tip-toed his way to his seat again, and said, under his breath—

"You can keep a secret?''

Washington nodded his affirmative, he was too awed to speak.

"You have heard of materialization—materialization of departed spirits?''

Washington had heard of it.

"And probably didn't believe in it; and quite right, too. The thing as practised by ignorant charlatans is unworthy of attention or respect—where there's a dim light and a dark cabinet, and a parcel of sentimental gulls gathered together, with their faith and their shudders and their tears all ready, and one and the same fatty degeneration of protoplasm and humbug comes out and materializes himself into anybody you want, grandmother, grandchild, brother-in-law, Witch of Endor, John Milton, Siamese twins, Peter the Great, and all such frantic nonsense—no, that is all foolish and pitiful. But when a man that is competent brings the vast powers of *science* to bear, it's a different matter, a totally different matter, you see. The specter that answers *that* call has come to stay. Do you note the commercial value of that detail?''

"Well, I—the—the truth is, that I don't quite know that I do. Do you mean that such, being permanent, not transitory, would give more general satisfaction, and so enhance the price of tickets to the show—''

"Show? Folly—listen to me; and get a good grip on your breath, for you are going to need it. Within three days I shall have completed my method, and then—let the world stand aghast, for it shall see marvels. Washington, within three days—ten at the outside—you shall see me call the dead of any century, and they will arise and walk. Walk?—they shall walk forever, and never die again. Walk with all the muscle and spring of their pristine vigor.''

"Colonel! Indeed it does take one's breath away.''

"*Now* do you see the money that's in it?''

"I'm—well, I'm—not really sure that I do.''

"Great Scott, look here. I shall have a monopoly; they'll all belong to me, won't they? Two thousand policemen in the city of New York. Wages, four dollars a day. I'll replace them with dead ones at half the money.''

"Oh, prodigious! I never thought of that. F-o-u-r thousand dollars a day. Now I do begin to see! But will dead policemen answer?''

"Haven't they—up to this time?''

"Well, if you put it that way—''

"Put it any way you want to. Modify it to suit yourself, and my lads shall still be superior. They won't eat, they won't drink—don't need those things; they won't wink for cash at gambling dens and unlicensed rum-holes, they won't spark the scullery maids; and moreover the bands of toughs that ambuscade them on lonely beats, and cowardly shoot and knife them will only damage the uniforms and not live long enough to get more than a momentary satisfaction out of that.''

"Why, Colonel, if you can furnish policemen, then of course—''

"Certainly—I can furnish any line of goods that's wanted. Take the army, for instance—now twenty-five thousand men; expense, twenty-two millions a year. I will dig up the Romans, I will resurrect the Greeks, I will furnish the government, for ten millions a year, ten thousand veterans drawn from the victorious legions of all the ages—soldiers that will chase Indians year in and year out on materialized horses, and cost never a cent for rations or repairs. The armies of Europe cost two billions a year now—I will replace them all for a billion. I will dig up the trained statesmen of all ages and all climes, and furnish this country with a Congress that knows enough to come in out of the rain—a thing that's never happened yet, since the Declaration of Independence, and never will happen till these practically dead people are replaced with the genuine article. I will re-stock the thrones of Europe with the best brains and the best morals that all the royal sepulchers of all the centuries can furnish—which isn't promising very much—and I'll divide the wages and the civil list, fair and square, merely taking my half and—''

"Colonel, if the half of this is true, there's millions in it—millions.''

"Billions in it—billions; that's what you mean. Why, look here; the thing is so close at hand, so imminent, so absolutely immediate, that if a man were to come to me now and say, Colonel, I am a little short, and if you could lend me a couple of billion dollars for—come in!''

This in answer to a knock. An energetic looking man bustled in with a big pocket-book in his hand, took a paper from it and presented it, with the curt remark—

"Seventeenth and last call—you want to out with that three dollars and forty cents this time without fail, Colonel Mulberry Sellers.''

The Colonel began to slap this pocket and that one, and feel here and there and everywhere, muttering—

"What *have* I done with that wallet?—let me see—um—not here, not there—Oh, I must have left it in the kitchen; I'll just run and—''

"No you won't—you'll stay right where you are. And you're going to disgorge, too—this time.''

Washington innocently offered to go and look. When he was gone the Colonel said—

"The fact is I've got to throw myself on your indulgence just this once more, Suggs; you see the remittances I was expecting—''

"Hang the remittances—it's too stale—it won't answer. Come!''

The Colonel glanced about him in despair. Then his face lighted; he ran to the wall and began to dust off a peculiarly atrocious chromo with his handkerchief. Then he brought it reverently, offered it to the collector, averted his face and said—

"Take it, but don't let me see it go. It's the sole remaining Rembrandt that—''

"Rembrandt be damned, it's a chromo.''

"Oh, don't speak of it so, I beg you. It's the only really great original, the only supreme example of that mighty school of art which—''

"Art! It's the sickest looking thing I—''

The Colonel was already bringing another horror and tenderly dusting it.

"Take this one too—the gem of my collection—the only genuine Fra Angelico that—''

"Illuminated liver-pad, that's what it is. Give it here—good day—people will think I've robbed a nigger barber-shop.''

As he slammed the door behind him the Colonel shouted with an anguished accent—

"Do please cover them up—don't let the damp get at them. The delicate tints in the Angelico—''

But the man was gone.

Washington re-appeared and said he had looked everywhere, and so had Mrs. Sellers and the servants, but in vain; and went on to say he wished he could get his eye on a certain man about this time—no need to hunt up that pocket-book then. The Colonel's interest was awake at once.

"What man?''

"One-armed Pete they call him out there—out in the Cherokee country I mean. Robbed the bank in Tahlequah.''

"Do they have banks in Tahlequah?''

"Yes—*a* bank, anyway. He was suspected of robbing it. Whoever did it got away with more than twenty thousand dollars. They offered a reward of five thousand. I believe I saw that very man, on my way east.''

"No—is that so?"

"I certainly saw a man on the train, the first day I struck the railroad, that answered the description pretty exactly—at least as to clothes and a lacking arm."

"Why didn't you get him arrested and claim the reward?"

"I couldn't. I had to get a requisition, of course. But I meant to stay by him till I got my chance."

"Well?"

"Well, he left the train during the night some time."

"Oh, hang it, that's too bad."

"Not so very bad, either."

"Why?"

"Because he came down to Baltimore in the very train I was in, though I didn't know it in time. As we moved out of the station I saw him going toward the iron gate with a satchel in his hand."

"Good; we'll catch him. Let's lay a plan."

"Send description to the Baltimore police?"

"Why, what are you talking about? No. Do you want them to get the reward?"

"What shall we do, then?"

The Colonel reflected.

"I'll tell you. Put a personal in the Baltimore *Sun*. Word it like this:

> A. DROP ME A LINE, PETE—

—"Hold on. Which arm has he lost?"

"The right."

"Good. Now then—

> A. DROP ME A LINE, PETE, EVEN IF YOU HAVE to write
> with your left hand. Address X. Y. Z., General Postoffice, Wash-
> ington. From YOU KNOW WHO.

"There—that'll fetch him."

"But he *won't* know who—will he?"

"No, but he'll want to know, won't he?"

"Why, certainly—I didn't think of that. What made you think of it?"

"Knowledge of human curiosity. Strong trait, very strong trait."

"Now I'll go to my room and write it out and enclose a dollar and tell them to print it to the worth of that."

Chapter 4

THE DAY wore itself out. After dinner the two friends put in a long and harassing evening trying to decide what to do with the five thousand dollars reward which they were going to get when they should find One-Armed Pete, and catch him, and prove him to be the right person, and

ONE-ARMED PETE.

extradite him, and ship him to Tahlequah in the Indian Territory. But there were so many dazzling openings for ready cash that they found it impossible to make up their minds and keep them made up. Finally, Mrs. Sellers grew very weary of it all, and said:

"What is the sense in cooking a rabbit before it's caught?"

Then the matter was dropped, for the time being, and all went to bed. Next morning, being persuaded by Hawkins, the Colonel made drawings and specifications and went down and applied for a patent for his toy puzzle, and Hawkins took the toy itself and started out to see what chance there might be to do something with it commercially. He did not have to go far. In a small old wooden shanty which had once been occupied as a dwelling by some humble negro family he found a keen-eyed Yankee engaged in repairing cheap chairs and other second-hand furniture. This man examined the toy indifferently; attempted to do the puzzle; found it not so easy as he had expected; grew more interested, and finally emphatically so; achieved a success at last, and asked—

"Is it patented?"

"Patent applied for."

"That will answer. What do you want for it?"

"What will it retail for?"

"Well, twenty-five cents, I should think."

"What will you give for the exclusive right?"

"I couldn't give twenty dollars, if I had to pay cash down; but I'll tell you what I'll do. I'll make it and market it, and pay you five cents royalty on each one."

Washington sighed. Another dream disappeared; no money in the thing. So he said—

"All right, take it at that. Draw me a paper."

He went his way with the paper, and dropped the matter out of his mind—dropped it out to make room for further attempts to think out the most promising way to invest his half of the reward, in case a partnership investment satisfactory to both beneficiaries could not be hit upon.

He had not been very long at home when Sellers arrived sodden with grief and booming with glad excitement—working both these emotions successfully, sometimes separately, sometimes together. He fell on Hawkins's neck sobbing, and said—

"Oh, mourn with me my friend, mourn for my desolate house: death has smitten my last kinsman and I am Earl of Rossmore—congratulate me!"

He turned to his wife, who had entered while this was going on, put his arms about her and said—"You will bear up, for my sake, my lady—it had to happen, it was decreed."

She bore up very well, and said—

"It's no great loss. Simon Lathers was a poor well-meaning useless thing and no account, and his brother never was worth shucks."

The rightful earl continued—

"I am too much prostrated by these conflicting griefs and joys to be able to concentrate my mind upon affairs; I will ask our good friend here to break the news by wire or post to the Lady Gwendolen and instruct her to—"

"*What* Lady Gwendolen?"

"Our poor daughter, who, alas!—"

"Sally Sellers? Mulberry Sellers, are you losing your mind?"

"There—please do not forget who you are, and who I am; remember your own dignity, be considerate also of mine. It were best to cease from using my family name, now, Lady Rossmore."

"Goodness gracious, well, I never! What *am* I to call you then?"

"In private, the ordinary terms of endearment will still be admissible, to some degree; but in public it will be more becoming if your ladyship will speak *to* me as my lord, or your lordship, and *of* me as Rossmore, or the Earl, or his Lordship, and—"

"Oh, scat! I can't ever do it, Berry."

"But indeed you must, my love—we must live up to our altered position and submit with what grace we may to its requirements."

"Well, all right, have it your own way; I've never set my wishes against your commands yet, Mul—my lord, and it's late to begin now, though to my mind it's the rottenest foolishness that ever was."

"Spoken like my own true wife! There, kiss and be friends again."

"But—Gwendolen! I don't know how I am ever going to stand that name. Why, a body wouldn't *know* Sally Sellers in it. It's too large for her; kind of like a cherub in an ulster, and it's a most outlandish sort of a name, anyway, to my mind."

"You'll not hear her find fault with it, my lady."

"That's a true word. She takes to any kind of romantic rubbish like she was born to it. She never got it from me, that's sure. And sending her to that silly college hasn't helped the matter any—just the other way."

"Now hear her, Hawkins! Rowena-Ivanhoe College is the selectest and most aristocratic seat of learning for young ladies in our country. Under no circumstances can a girl get in there unless she is either very rich and fashionable or can prove four generations of what may be called American nobility. Castellated college-buildings—towers and turrets and an imitation moat—and everything about the place named out of Sir Walter Scott's books and redolent of royalty and state and style; and all the richest girls keep phaetons, and coachmen in livery, and riding-horses, with English grooms in plug hats and tight-buttoned coats, and top-boots, and a whip-handle without any whip to it, to ride sixty-three feet behind them—''

"And they don't learn a blessed thing, Washington Hawkins, not a single blessed thing but showy rubbish and unamerican pretentiousness. But send for the Lady Gwendolen—do; for I reckon the peerage regulations require that she must come home and let on to go into seclusion and mourn for those Arkansas blatherskites she's lost.''

"My darling! Blatherskites? Remember—*noblesse oblige*.''

"There, there—talk to me in your own tongue, Ross—you don't know any other, and you only botch it when you try. Oh, don't stare—it was a slip, and no crime; customs of a life-time can't be dropped in a second. Ross*more*—there, now, be appeased, and go along with you and attend to Gwendolen. Are you going to write, Washington?—or telegraph?''

"He will telegraph, dear.''

"I thought as much,'' my lady muttered, as she left the room. "Wants it so the address will have to appear on the envelope. It will just make a fool of that child. She'll get it, of course, for if there are any other Sellerses there they'll not be able to claim it. And just leave her alone to show it around and make the most of it.——Well, maybe she's forgivable for that. She's so poor and they're so rich, of course she's had her share of snubs from the livery-flunkey sort, and I reckon it's only human to want to get even.''

Uncle Dan'l was sent with the telegram; for although a conspicuous object in a corner of the drawingroom was a telephone hanging on a transmitter, Washington found all attempts to raise the central office vain. The Colonel grumbled something about its being *"always* out of order when you've got particular and especial use for it,'' but he didn't explain that one of the reasons for this was that the thing was only a dummy and hadn't any wire attached to it. And yet the Colonel often used it—when visitors were present—and seemed to get messages through it. Mourning paper and a seal were ordered, then the friends took a rest.

Next afternoon, while Hawkins, by request, draped Andrew Jackson's protrait with crape, the rightful earl wrote off the family bereavement to the usurper in England—a letter which we have already read. He also, by letter to the village authorities at Duffy's Corners, Arkansas, gave order that the remains of the late twins be embalmed by some St. Louis expert and shipped at once to the usurper—with bill. Then he drafted out the Rossmore arms and motto on a great sheet of brown paper, and he and Hawkins took it to Hawkins's Yankee furniture-mender and at the end of an hour came back with a couple of stunning hatchments, which they nailed up on the front of the house—attractions calculated to draw, and they did; for it was mainly an idle and shiftless negro neighborhood, with plenty of ragged children and indolent dogs to spare for a point of interest like that, and keep on sparing them for it, days and days together.

The new earl found—without surprise—this society item in the evening paper, and cut it out and scrapbooked it:

By a recent bereavement our esteemed fellow citizen, Colonel Mulberry Sellers, Perpetual Member-at-large of the Diplomatic

Body, succeeds, as rightful lord, to the great earldom of Rossmore, third by order of precedence in the earldoms of Great Britain, and will take early measures, by suit in the House of Lords, to wrest the title and estates from the present usurping holder of them. Until the season of mourning is past, the usual Thursday evening receptions at Rossmore Towers will be discontinued.

Lady Rossmore's comment—to herself:

"Receptions! People who don't rightly know him may think he is commonplace, but to my mind he is one of the most unusual men I ever saw. As for suddenness and capacity in imagining things, his beat don't exist, I reckon. As like as not it wouldn't have occurred to anybody else to name this poor old rat-trap Rossmore Towers, but it just comes natural to him. Well, no doubt it's a blessed thing to have an imagination that can always make you satisfied, no matter how you are fixed. Uncle Dave Hopkins used to always say, 'Turn me into John Calvin, and I want to know which place I'm going to; turn me into Mulberry Sellers and I don't care.' "

The rightful earl's comment—to himself:

"It's a beautiful name, beautiful. Pity I didn't think of it before I wrote the usurper. But I'll be ready for him when he answers."

Chapter 5

NO ANSWER to that telegram; no arriving daughter. Yet nobody showed any uneasiness or seemed surprised; that is, nobody but Washington. After three days of waiting, he asked Lady Rossmore what she supposed the trouble was. She answered, tranquilly;

"Oh, it's some notion of hers, you never can tell. She's a Sellers, all through—at least in some of her ways; and a Sellers can't tell you before-hand what he's going to do, because he don't know himself till he's done it. *She's* all right; no occasion to worry about *her*. When she's ready she'll come or she'll write, and you can't tell which, till it's happened."

It turned out to be a letter. It was handed in at that moment, and was received by the mother without trembling hands or feverish eagerness, or any other of the manifestations common in the case of long delayed answers to imperative telegrams. She polished her glasses with tranquility and thoroughness, pleasantly gossiping along, the while, then opened the letter and began to read aloud:

Kenilworth Keep, Redgauntlet Hall,
Rowena-Ivanhoe College, Thursday.

DEAR PRECIOUS MAMMA ROSSMORE:

Oh, the joy of it!—you can't think. They had always turned up their noses at our pretentions, you know; and I had fought back as well as I could by turning up mine at theirs. They always said it might be something great and fine to be rightful Shadow of an earldom, but to merely be shadow *of* a shadow, and two or three times removed at that—pooh-pooh! And I always retorted that not to be able to show four generations of American-Colonial-Dutch-Peddler-and-Salt-Cod-McAllister-Nobility might be endurable, but to *have* to confess such an origin—pfew-few! Well, the telegram, it was just a cyclone! The messenger came right into the great Rob Roy Hall of Audience, as excited as he could be, singing out, "Dispatch for Lady Gwendolen Sellers!" and you ought to have seen that simpering chattering assemblage of pinchbeck aristocrats turn to stone! I was off in the corner, of course, by myself—it's where Cinderella belongs. I took the telegram and read it, and tried to faint—and I could have done it if I had had any preparation, but it was all so sudden, you know—but no matter, I did the next best thing: I put my handkerchief to my eyes and fled sobbing to my room, dropping the telegram as I started. I released one corner of my eye a moment—just enough to see the herd swarm for the telegram—and then continued my broken-hearted flight just as happy as a bird.

Then the visits of condolence began, and I had to accept the loan of Miss Augusta-Templeton-Ashmore Hamilton's quarters because the press was so great and there isn't room for three and a cat in mine. And I've been holding a Lodge of Sorrow ever since and defending myself against people's attempts to claim kin. And do you know, the very first girl to fetch her tears and sympathy to my market was that foolish Skimperton girl who has always snubbed me so shamefully and claimed lordship and precedence of the whole college because some ancestor of hers, some time or other, was a McAllister. Why it was like the bottom bird in the menagerie putting on airs because its head ancestor was a pterodactyl.

But the ger-reatest triumph of all was—guess. But you'll never. This is it. That little fool and two others have always been fussing and fretting over which was entitled to precedence—by rank, you know. They've nearly starved themselves at it; for each claimed the right to take precedence of all the college in leaving the table, and so neither of them ever finished her dinner, but broke off in the middle and tried to get out ahead of the others. Well, after my first day's grief and seclusion—I was fixing up a mourning dress you see—I appeared at the public table again, and then—what do you think? Those three fluffy goslings sat there contentedly, and squared up the long famine—lapped and lapped, munched and munched, ate and ate, till the gravy appeared in their eyes—humbly waiting for the Lady Gwendolen to take precedence and move out first, you see!

Oh, yes, I've been having a darling good time. And do you know, not one of these collegians has had the cruelty to ask me how I came by my new name. With some, this is due to charity, but with the others it isn't. They refrain, not from native kindness but from educated discretion. I educated them.

Well, as soon as I shall have settled up what's left of the old scores and snuffed up a few more of those pleasantly intoxicating clouds of incense. I shall pack and depart homeward. Tell papa I am as fond of him as I am of my new name. I couldn't put it stronger than that. What an inspiration it was! But inspirations come easy to him.

These, from your loving daughter,
GWENDOLEN.

Hawkins reached for the letter and glanced over it.

"Good hand," he said, "and full of confidence and animation, and goes racing right along. She's bright—that's plain."

"Oh, they're all bright—the Sellerses. Anyway, they would be, if there were any. Even those poor Latherses would have been bright if they had been Sellerses; I mean full blood. Of course they had a Sellers strain in them—a big strain of it, too—but being a Bland dollar don't make it a *dollar* just the same."

The seventh day after the date of the telegram Washington came dreaming down to breakfast and was set wide awake by an electrical spasm of pleasure. Here was the most beautiful young creature he had ever seen in his life. It was Sally Sellers Lady Gwendolen; she had come in the night. And it seemed to him that her clothes were the prettiest and the daintiest he had ever looked upon, and the most exquisitely contrived and fashioned and combined, as to decorative trimmings, and fixings, and melting harmonies of color. It was only a morning dress, and inexpensive, but he confessed to himself, in the English common to Cherokee Strip, that it was a "corker." And now, as he perceived, the reason why the Sellers household poverties and sterilities had been made to blossom like the rose, and charm the eye and satisfy the spirit, stood explained; here was the magician; here in the midst of her works, and furnishing in her own person the proper accent and climaxing finish of the whole.

"My daughter, Major Hawkins—come home to mourn; flown home at the call of affliction to help the authors of her being bear the burden of bereavement. She was very fond of the late earl—idolized him, sir, idolized him—"

"Why, father, I've never seen him."

"True—she's right, I was thinking of another—er—of her mother—"

"*I* idolized that smoked haddock?—that sentimental, spiritless—"

"I was thinking of myself! Poor noble fellow, we were inseparable com—"

"Hear the man! Mulberry Sel—Mul—Rossmore!—hang the troublesome name I can never—if I've heard you say once, I've heard you say a thousand times that if that poor sheep—"

"I was thinking of—of—I don't know who I was thinking of, and it doesn't make any difference anyway; *some*body idolized him, I recollect it as if it were yesterday; and—"

"Father, I am going to shake hands with Major Hawkins, and let the introduction work along and catch up at its leisure. I remember you very well indeed, Major Hawkins, although I was a little child when I saw you last; and I am very, very glad indeed to see you again and have you in our house as one of us''; and beaming in his face she finished her cordial shake with the hope that he had not forgotten her.

He was prodigiously pleased by her outspoken heartiness, and wanted to repay her by assuring her that he remembered her, and not only that but better even than he remembered his own children, but the facts would not quite warrant this; still, he stumbled through a tangled sentence which answered just as well, since the purport of it was an awkward and unintentional confession that her extraordinary beauty had so stupefied him that he hadn't got back to his bearings, yet, and therefore couldn't be certain as to whether he remembered her at all or not. The speech made him her friend; it couldn't well help it.

In truth the beauty of this fair creature was of a rare type, and may well excuse a moment of our time spent in its consideration. It did not consist in the *fact* that she had eyes, nose, mouth, chin, hair, ears, it consisted in their arrangement. In true beauty, more depends upon right location and judicious distribution of feature than upon multiplicity of them. So also as regards color. The very combination of colors which in a volcanic irruption would add beauty to a landscape might detach it from a girl. Such was Gwendolen Sellers.

The family circle being completed by Gwendolen's arrival, it was decreed that the official mourning should now begin; that it should begin at six o'clock every evening, (the dinner hour), and end with the dinner.

"It's a grand old line, major, a sublime old line, and deserves to be mourned for, almost royally; almost imperially, I may say. Er—Lady Gwendolen—but she's gone; never mind; I wanted my Peerage; I'll fetch it myself, presently, and show you a thing or two that will give you a realizing idea of what our house is. I've been glancing through Burke, and I find that of William the Conqueror's sixty-four natural ch—my dear, would you mind getting me that book? It's on the escritoire in our boudoir. Yes, as I was saying, there's only St. Albans, Buccleugh and Grafton ahead of us on the list—all the rest of the British nobility are in procession behind us. Ah, thanks, my lady. Now then, we turn to William, and we find—letter for XYZ? Oh, splendid—when'd you get it?''

FATHER, I AM GOING TO SHAKE HANDS WITH MAJOR HAWKINS.

"Last night; but I was asleep before you came, you were out so late; and when I came to breakfast Miss Gwendolen—well, she knocked everything out of me, you know—"

"Wonderful girl, wonderful; her great origin is detectable in her step, her carriage, her features—but what does he *say?* Come, this is exciting."

"I haven't read it—er—Rossm—Mr. Rossm—er—"

"M'lord! Just cut it short like that. It's the English way. I'll open it. Ah, now let's see."

A. TO YOU KNOW WHO. Think I know you. Wait ten days. Coming to Washington.

The excitement died out of both men's faces. There was a brooding silence for a while, then the younger one said with a sigh:

"Why, *we* can't wait ten days for the money."

"No—the man's unreasonable; we are down to the bed rock, financially speaking."

"If we could explain to him in some way, that we are so situated that time is of the utmost importance to us—"

"Yes-yes, that's it—and so if it would be as convenient for him to come at once it would be a great accommodation to us, and one which we—which we—"

—"which we—wh—"

—"well, which we should sincerely appreciate—"

"That's it—and most gladly reciprocate—"

"Certainly—that'll fetch him. Worded right, if he's a *man*—got any of the *feelings* of a man, *sympathies* and all that, he'll be here inside of twenty-four hours. Pen and paper—come, we'll get right at it."

Between them they framed twenty-two different advertisements, but none was satisfactory. A main fault in all of them was urgency. That feature was very troublesome: if made prominent, it was calculated to excite Pete's suspicion; if modified below the suspicion-point it was flat and meaningless. Finally the Colonel resigned, and said—

"I have noticed, in such literary experiences as I have had, that one of the most taking things to do is to conceal your meaning when you are *trying* to conceal it. Whereas, if you go at literature with a free conscience and nothing to conceal, you can turn out a book, every time, that the very elect can't understand. They all do."

Then Hawkins resigned also, and the two agreed that they must manage to wait the ten days somehow or other. Next, they caught a ray of cheer: since they had something definite to go upon, now, they could probably borrow money on the reward—enough, at any rate, to tide them over till they got it; and meantime the materializing recipe would be perfected, and then good bye to trouble for good and all.

The next day, May the tenth, a couple of things happened—among others. The remains of the noble Arkansas twins left our shores for England, consigned to Lord Rossmore, and Lord Rossmore's son, Kirkcudbright Llanover Marjoribanks Sellers Viscount Berkeley, sailed from Liverpool for America to place the reversion of the earldom in the hands of the rightful peer, Mulberry Sellers, of Rossmore Towers in the District of Columbia, U.S.A.

These two impressive shipments would meet and part in mid-Atlantic, five days later, and give no sign.

Chapter 6

IN THE course of time the twins arrived and were delivered to their great kinsman. To try to describe the rage of that old man would profit nothing, the attempt would fall so far short of the purpose. However when he had worn himself out and got quiet again, he looked the matter over and decided that the twins had some moral rights, although they had no legal ones; they were of his blood, and it could not be decorous to treat them as common clay. So he laid them with their majestic kin in the Cholmondeley church, with imposing state and ceremony, and added the supreme touch by officiating as chief mourner himself. But he drew the line at hatchments.

Our friends in Washington watched the weary days go by, while they waited for Pete and covered his name with reproaches because of his calamitous procrastinations. Meantime, Sally Sellers, who was as practical and democratic as the Lady Gwendolen Sellers was romantic and aristocratic, was leading a life of intense interest and activity and getting the most she could out of her double personality. All day long in the privacy of her work-room, Sally Sellers earned bread for the Sellers family; and all the evening Lady Gwendolen Sellers supported the Rossmore dignity. All day she was American, practically, and proud of the work of her head and hands and its commercial result; all the evening she took holiday and dwelt in a rich shadow-land peopled with titled and coroneted fictions. By day, to her, the place was a plain, unaffected, ramshackle old trap—just that, and nothing more; by night it was Rossmore Towers. At college she had learned a trade without knowing it. The girls had found out that she was the designer of her own gowns. She had no idle moments after that, and wanted none; for the exercise of an extraordinary gift is the supremest pleasure in life, and it was manifest that Sally Sellers possessed a gift of that sort in the matter of costume-designing. Within three days after reaching home she had hunted up some work; before Pete was yet due in Washington, and before the twins were fairly asleep in English soil, she was already nearly swamped with work, and the sacrificing of the family chromos for debt had got an effective check.

"She's a brick," said Rossmore to the Major; "just her father all over: prompt to labor with head or hands, and not ashamed of it; capable, always capable, let the enterprise be what it may; successful by nature—don't know what defeat is; thus, intensely and practically American by inhaled nationalism, and at the same time intensely and aristocratically European by inherited nobility of blood. Just me, exactly: Mulberry Sellers in matter of finance and invention; after office hours, what do you find? The same clothes, yes, but what's in them? Rossmore of the peerage."

The two friends had haunted the general post-office daily. At last they had their reward. Toward evening the 20th of May, they got a letter for

XYZ. It bore the Washington postmark; the note itself was not dated. It said:

> "Ash barrel back of lamp post Black horse Alley. If you are playing square go and set on it to-morrow morning 21st 10:22 not sooner not later wait till I come."

The friends cogitated over the note profoundly. Presently the earl said:

"Don't you reckon he's afraid we are a sheriff with a requisition?"

"Why, m'lord?"

"Because that's no place for a séance. Nothing friendly, nothing sociable about it. And at the same time, a body that wanted to know who was roosting on that ash barrel without exposing himself by going near it, or seeming to be interested in it, could just stand on the street corner and take a glance down the alley and satisfy himself, don't you see?"

"Yes, his idea is plain, now. He seems to be a man that can't *be* candid and straightforward. He acts as if he thought we—shucks, I wish he had come out like a man and told us what hotel he—"

"Now you've struck it! you've struck it sure, Washington; he has told us."

"Has he?"

"Yes, he has; but he didn't mean to. That alley is a lonesome little pocket that runs along one side of the New Gadsby. That's his hotel."

"What makes you think that?"

"Why, I just know it. He's got a room that's just across from that lamp post. He's going to sit there perfectly comfortable behind his shutters at 10:22 to-morrow, and when he sees us sitting on the ash barrel, he'll say to himself, 'I saw *one* of those fellows on the train'—and then he'll pack his satchel in half a minute and ship for the ends of the earth."

Hawkins turned sick with disappointment:

"Oh, dear, it's all up, Colonel—it's exactly what he'll do."

"Indeed he won't!"

"Won't he? Why?"

"Because *you* won't be holding the ash barrel down, it'll be me. You'll be coming in with an officer and a requisition in plain clothes—the officer, I mean—the minute you see him arrive and open up a talk with me."

"Well, what a head you have got, Colonel Sellers! I never should have thought of that in the world."

"Neither would any earl of Rossmore, betwixt William's contribution and Mulberry—*as* earl; but it's office hours, now, you see, and the earl in me sleeps. Come—I'll show you his very room."

They reached the neighborhood of the New Gadsby about nine in the evening, and passed down the alley to the lamp post.

"There you are," said the colonel, triumphantly, with a wave of his hand which took in the whole side of the hotel. "There it is—what did I tell you?"

"Well, but—why, Colonel, it's six stories high. I don't quite make out which window you—"

"All the windows, all of them. Let him have his choice—I'm indifferent, now that I have located him. You go and stand on the corner and wait; I'll prospect the hotel."

The earl drifted here and there through the swarming lobby, and finally took a waiting position in the neighborhood of the elevator. During an hour crowds went up and crowds came down; and all complete as to limbs; but at last the watcher got a glimpse of a figure that was satisfactory—got a glimpse of the back of it, though he had missed his chance at the face through waning alertness. The glimpse revealed a cowboy hat, and below it a plaided sack of rather loud pattern, and an empty sleeve pinned up to the shoulder. Then the elevator snatched the vision aloft and the watcher fled away in joyful excitement, and rejoined the fellow-conspirator.

"We've got him, Major—got him sure! I've seen him—seen him good; and I don't care where or when that man approaches me backwards, I'll recognize him everytime. We're all right. Now for the requisition."

They got it, after the delays usual in such cases. By half past eleven they were at home and happy, and went to bed full of dreams of the morrow's great promise.

Among the elevator load which had the suspect for fellow-passenger was a young kinsman of Mulberry Sellers, but Mulberry was not aware of it and didn't see him. It was Viscount Berkeley.

Chapter 7

ARRIVED IN his room Lord Berkeley made preparations for that first and last and all-the-time duty of the visiting Englishman—the jotting down in his diary of his "impressions" to date. His preparations consisted in ransacking his "box" for a pen. There was a plenty of steel pens on his table with the ink bottle, but he was English. The English people manufacture steel pens for nineteen-twentieths of the globe, but they never use any themselves. They use exclusively the pre-historic quill. My lord not only found a quill pen, but the best one he had seen in several years—and after writing diligently for some time, closed with the following entry:

But in one thing I have made an immense mistake. I ought to have sunk my title and changed my name before I started.

He sat admiring that pen a while, and then went on:

> All attempts to mingle with the common people and become permanently one of them are going to fail, unless I can get rid of it, disappear from it, and re-appear with the solid protection of a new name. I am astonished and pained to see how eager the most of these Americans are to get acquainted with a lord, and how diligent they are in pushing attentions upon him. They lack English servility, it is true—but they could acquire it, with practice. My quality travels ahead of me in the most mysterious way. I write my family name without additions, on the register of this hotel, and imagine that I am going to pass for an obscure and unknown wanderer, but the clerk promptly calls out, "Front! show his lordship to four-eighty-two!" and before I can get to the lift there is a reporter trying to interview me, as they call it. This sort of thing shall cease at once. I will hunt up the American Claimant the first thing in the morning, accomplish my mission, then change my lodging and vanish from scrutiny under a fictitious name.

He left his diary on the table, where it would be handy in case any new "impressions" should wake him up in the night, then he went to bed and presently fell asleep. An hour or two passed, and then he came slowly to consciousness with a confusion of mysterious and augmenting sounds hammering at the gates of his brain for admission; the next moment he was sharply awake, and those sounds burst with the rush and roar and boom of an undammed freshet into his ears. Banging and slamming of shutters; smashing of windows and the ringing clash of falling glass; clatter of flying feet along the halls; shrieks, supplications, dumb moanings of despair, within, hoarse shouts of command outside; cracklings and snappings, and the windy roar of victorious flames!

Bang, bang, bang! on the door, and a cry—

"Turn out—the house is on fire!"

The cry passed on, and the banging. Lord Berkeley sprang out of bed and moved with all possible speed toward the clothes-press in the darkness and the gathering smoke, but fell over a chair and lost his bearings. He groped desperately about on his hands, and presently struck his head against the table and was deeply grateful, for it gave him his bearings again, since it stood close by the door. He seized his most precious possession, his journaled Impressions of America, and darted from the room.

He ran down the deserted hall toward the red lamp which he knew indicated the place of a fire-escape. The door of the room beside it was open. In the room the gas was burning full head; on a chair was a pile of clothing. He ran to the window, could not get it up, but smashed it with a chair, and stepped out on the landing of the fire-escape; below him was a crowd of men, with a sprinkling of women and youth, massed in a ruddy light. Must he go down in his spectral night dress? No—this side of the house was not yet on fire except at the further end; he would snatch on those clothes. Which he did. They fitted well enough, though a trifle loosely, and they were just a shade loud as to pattern. Also as to hat—

MUST HE GO DOWN IN HIS SPECTRAL NIGHT DRESS?

which was of a new breed to him, Buffalo Bill not having been to England
yet. One side of the coat went on, but the other side refused; one of its
sleeves was turned up and stitched to the shoulder. He started down
without waiting to get it loose, made the trip successfully, and was promptly
hustled outside the limit-rope by the police.

The cowboy hat and the coat but half on made him too much of a center
of attraction for comfort, although nothing could be more profoundly
respectful, not to say deferential, than was the manner of the crowd
toward him. In his mind he framed a discouraged remark for early entry
in his diary: "It is of no use; they know a lord through any disguise, and
show awe of him—even something very like fear, indeed."

Presently one of the gaping and adoring half-circle of boys ventured a
timid question. My lord answered it. The boys glanced wonderingly at
each other and from somewhere fell the comment—

"*English* cowboy! Well, if that ain't curious."

Another mental note to be preserved for the diary: "Cowboy. Now what
might a cowboy be? Perhaps—" But the viscount perceived that some
more questions were about to be asked; so he worked his way out of the
crowd, released the sleeve, put on the coat and wandered away to seek a
humble and obscure lodging. He found it and went to bed and was soon
asleep.

In the morning, he examined his clothes. They were rather assertive, it
seemed to him, but they were new and clean, at any rate. There was
considerable property in the pockets. Item, five one-hundred-dollar bills.
Item, near fifty dollars in small bills and silver. Plug of tobacco. Hymn-
book, which refuses to open; found to contain whiskey. Memorandum
book bearing no name. Scattering entries in it, recording in a sprawling,
ignorant hand, appointments, bets, horse-trades, and so on, with people
of strange, hyphenated name—Six-Fingered Jake, Young-Man-afraid-of-
his-Shadow, and the like. No letters, no documents.

The young man muses—maps out his course. His letter of credit is
burned; he will borrow the small bills and the silver in these pockets,
apply part of it to advertising for the owner, and use the rest for sustenance

while he seeks work. He sends out for the morning paper, next, and proceeds to read about the fire. The biggest line in the display-head announces his own death! The body of the account furnishes all the particulars; and tells how, with the inherited heroism of his caste, he went on saving women and children until escape for himself was impossible; then with the eyes of weeping multitudes upon him, he stood with folded arms and sternly awaited the approach of the devouring fiend; "and so standing, amid a tossing sea of flame and on-rushing billows of smoke, the noble young heir of the great house of Rossmore was caught up in a whirlwind of fiery glory, and disappeared forever from the vision of men."

The thing was so fine and generous and knightly that it brought the moisture to his eyes. Presently he said to himself: "What to do is as plain as day, now. My Lord Berkeley is dead—let him stay so. Died creditably, too; that will make the calamity the easier for my father. And I don't have to report to the American Claimant, now. Yes, nothing could be better than the way matters have turned out. I have only to furnish myself with a new name, and take my new start in life totally untrammeled. Now I breathe my first breath of real freedom; and how fresh and breezy and inspiring it is! At last I am a man! a man on equal terms with my neighbor; and by my manhood, and by it alone, I shall rise and be seen of the world, or I shall sink from sight and deserve it. This *is* the gladdest day, and the proudest, that ever poured its sun upon my head!"

Chapter 8

"GOD BLESS my soul, Hawkins!"

The morning paper dropped from the Colonel's nerveless grasp.

"What is it?"

"He's gone!—the bright, the young, the gifted, the noblest of his illustrious race—gone! gone up in flames and unimaginable glory!"

"Who?"

"My precious, precious young kinsman—Kirkcudbright Llanover Marjoribanks Sellers Viscount Berkeley, son and heir of usurping Rossmore."

"No!"

"It's true—too true."

"When?"

"Last night."

"Where?"

"Right here in Washington, where he arrived from England last night, the papers say."

"You don't say!"

"Hotel burned down."

"What hotel?"

"The New Gadsby!"

"Oh, my goodness! And have we lost *both* of them?"

"Both *who*?"

"One-Arm Pete."

"Oh, great guns, I forgot all about him. Oh, I hope not."

"Hope! Well, I should say! Oh, we *can't* spare *him!* We can better afford to lose a million viscounts than our only support and stay."

They searched the paper diligently, and were appalled to find that a one-armed man had been seen flying along one of the halls of the hotel in his underclothing and apparently out of his head with fright, and as he would listen to no one and persisted in making for a stairway which would carry him to certain death, his case was given over as a hopeless one.

"Poor fellow," sighed Hawkins; "and he had friends so near. I wish we hadn't come away from there—maybe we could have saved him."

The earl looked up and said calmly—

"His being dead doesn't matter. he was uncertain before. We've got him sure, this time."

"Got him? How?"

"I will materialize him."

"Rossmore, don't—don't trifle with me. Do you mean that? Can you do it?"

"I can do it, just as sure as you are sitting there. And I will."

"Give me your hand, and let me have the comfort of shaking it. I was perishing, and you have put new life into me. Get at it, oh, get at it right away."

"It will take a little time, Hawkins, but there's no hurry, none in the world—in the circumstances. And of course certain duties have devolved upon me now, which necessarily claim my first attention. This poor young nobleman—"

"Why, yes, I am sorry for my heartlessness, and you smitten with this new family affliction. Of course you must materialize him first—I quite understand that."

"I—I—well, I wasn't meaning just that, but,—why, what am I thinking of! Of course I must materialize him. Oh, Hawkins, selfishness is the bottom trait in human nature; I was only thinking that now, with the usurper's heir out of the way— But you'll forgive that momentary weakness and forget it. Don't ever remember it against me that Mulberry Sellers was once mean enough to think the thought that I was thinking. I'll materialize him—I will, on my honor—and I'd do it were he a thousand heirs jammed into one and stretching in a solid rank from here to the stolen estates of Rossmore, and barring the road forever to the rightful earl!"

"There spoke the real Sellers—the other had a false ring, old friend."

"Hawkins, my boy, it just occurs to me—a thing I keep forgetting to mention—a matter that we've got to be mighty careful about."

"What is that?"

"We must keep absolutely still about these materializations. Mind, not a hint of them must escape—not a hint. To say nothing of how my wife and daughter—high-strung, sensitive organizations—might feel about them, the negroes wouldn't stay on the place a minute."

"That's true, they wouldn't. It's well you spoke, for I'm not naturally discreet with my tongue when I'm not warned."

Sellers reached out and touched a bell-button in the wall; set his eye upon the rear door and waited; touched it again and waited; and just as

Hawkins was remarking admiringly that the Colonel was the most progressive and most alert man he had ever seen, in the matter of impressing
into his service every modern convenience the moment it was invented,
and always keeping breast to breast with the drum major in the great work
of material civilization, he forsook the button (which hadn't any wire
attached to it), rang a vast dinner bell which stood on the table, and
remarked that he had tried that new-fangled dry battery, now, to his entire
satisfaction, and had got enough of it; and added—

"Nothing would do Graham Bell but I must try it; said the mere *fact* of
my trying it would secure public confidence, and get it a chance to show
what it could do. I *told* him that in theory a dry battery was just a curled
darling and no mistake, but when it come to *practice,* sho!—and here's
the result. Was I right? What should *you* say, Washington Hawkins? You've
seen me try that button twice. Was I right?—that's the idea. Did I know
what I was talking about, or didn't I?"

"Well, you know how I feel about you, Colonel Sellers, and always
have felt. It seems to me that you always know everything about *everything*. If that man had known you as I know you he would have taken your
judgment at the start, and dropped his dry battery where it was."

"Did you ring, Marse Sellers?"

"No, Marse Sellers didn't."

"Den it was you, Marse Washington. I's heah, suh."

"No, it wasn't Marse Washington, either."

"De good lan'! who did ring her, den?"

"Lord Rossmore rang it!"

The old negro flung up his hands and exclaimed—

"Blame my skin if I hain't gone en forgit dat name agin! Come heah,
Jinny—run heah, honey."

Jinny arrived.

"You take dish-yer order de lord gwine to give you. I's gwine down
suller and study dat name tell I git it."

"I take de order! Who's yo' nigger las' year? De bell rung for *you*."

"Dat don't make no diffunce. When a bell ring for anybody, en old
marster tell me to—"

"Clear out, and settle it in the kitchen!"

The noise of the quarreling presently sank to a murmur in the distance,
and the earl added: "That's a trouble with old house servants that were
your slaves once and have been your personal friends always."

"Yes, and members of the family."

"Members of the family is just what they become—*the* members of the
family, in fact. And sometimes master and mistress of the household.
These two are mighty good and loving and faithful and honest, but hang
it, they do just about as they please, they chip into a conversation whenever they want to, and the plain fact is, they ought to be killed."

It was a random remark, but it gave him an idea—however, nothing
could happen without that result.

"What I wanted, Hawkins, was to send for the family and break the
news to them."

"O, never mind bothering with the servants, then. I will go and bring
them down."

While he was gone, the earl worked his idea.

"Yes," he said to himself, "when I've got the materializing down to a certainty, I will get Hawkins to kill them, and after that they will be under better control. Without doubt a materialized negro could easily be hypnotized into a state resembling silence. And this could be made permanent— yes, and also modifiable, at will—sometimes *very* silent, sometimes turn on more talk, more action, more emotion, according to what you want. It's a prime good idea. Make it adjustable—with a screw or something."

The two ladies entered, now, with Hawkins, and the two negroes followed, uninvited, and fell to brushing and dusting around, for they perceived that there was matter of interest to the fore, and were willing to find out what it was.

Sellers broke the news with stateliness and ceremony, first warning the ladies, with gentle art, that a pang of peculiar sharpness was about to be inflicted upon their hearts—hearts still sore from a like hurt, still lamenting a like loss—then he took the paper, and with trembling lips and with tears in his voice he gave them that heroic death-picture.

The result was a very genuine outbreak of sorrow and sympathy from all the hearers. The elder lady cried, thinking how proud that great-hearted young hero's mother would be, if she were living, and how unappeasable her grief; and the two old servants cried with her, and spoke out their applauses and their pitying lamentations with the eloquent sincerity and simplicity native to their race. Gwendolen was touched, and the romantic side of her nature was strongly wrought upon. She said that such a nature as that young man's was rarely and truly noble, and nearly perfect; and that with nobility of birth added it was entirely perfect. For such a man she could endure all things, suffer all things, even to the sacrificing of her life. She wished she could have seen him; the slightest, the most momentary, contact with such a spirit would have ennobled her own character and made ignoble thoughts and ignoble acts thereafter impossible to her forever.

"Have they found the body, Rossmore?" asked the wife.

"Yes, that is, they've found several. It must be one of them, but none of them are recognizable."

"What are you going to do?"

"I am going down there and identify one of them and send it home to the stricken father."

"But papa, did you ever see the young man?"

"No, Gwendolen—why?"

"How will you identify it?"

"I—well, you know it says none of them are recognizable. I'll send his father one of them—there's probably no choice."

Gwendolen knew it was not worth while to argue the matter further, since her father's mind was made up and there was a chance for him to appear upon that sad scene down yonder in an authentic and official way. So she said no more—till he asked for a basket.

"A basket, papa? What for?"

"It might be ashes."

Chapter 9

THE EARL and Washington started on the sorrowful errand, talking as they walked.

"And as *usual*!"

"What, Colonel?"

"Seven of them in that hotel. Actresses. And all burnt out, of course."

"Any of them burnt *up*?"

"Oh, no they escaped; they always do; but there's never a one of them that knows enough to fetch out her jewelry with her."

"That's strange."

"Strange—it's the most unaccountable thing in the world. Experience teaches them nothing; they can't seem to learn anything except out of a book. In some cases there's manifestly a fatality about it. For instance, take What's-her-name, that plays those sensational thunder and lightning parts. She's got a perfectly immense reputation—draws like a dog-fight—and it all came from getting burnt out in hotels."

"Why, how could that give her a reputation as an actress?"

"It didn't—it only made her name familiar. People want to see her play because her name is familiar, but they don't know what made it familiar, because they don't remember. First, she was at the bottom of the ladder, and absolutely obscure—wages thirteen dollars a week and find her own pads."

"Pads?"

"Yes—things to fat up her spindles with so as to be plump and attractive. Well, she got burnt out in a hotel and lost $30,000 worth of diamonds—"

"She? Where'd she get them?"

"Goodness knows—given to her, no doubt, by spoony young flats and sappy old bald-heads in the front row. All the papers were full of it. She struck for higher pay and got it. Well, she got burnt out again and lost all her diamonds, and it gave her such a lift that she went starring."

"Well, if hotel fires are all she's got to depend on to keep up her name, it's a pretty precarious kind of a reputation I should think."

"Not with her. No, anything but that. Because she's so lucky; born lucky, I reckon. Every time there's a hotel fire she's in it. She's always there—and if she can't be there herself, her diamonds are. Now you can't make anything out of that but just sheer luck."

"I never heard of such a thing. She must have lost quarts of diamonds."

"Quarts, she's lost bushels of them. It's got so that the hotels are superstitious about her. They won't let her in. They think there will be a fire; and besides, if she's there it cancels the insurance. She's been waning a little lately, but this fire will set her up. She lost $60,000 worth last night."

"I think she's a fool. If I had $60,000 worth of diamonds I wouldn't trust them in a hotel."

"I wouldn't either; but you can't teach an actress that. This one's been burnt out thirty-five times. And yet if there's a hotel fire in San Francisco to-night she's got to bleed again, you mark my words. Perfect ass; they say she's got diamonds in every hotel in the country.''

When they arrived at the scene of the fire the poor old earl took one glimpse at the melancholy morgue and turned away his face overcome by the spectacle. He said:

"It is too true, Hawkins—recognition is impossible, not one of the five could be identified by its nearest friend. You make the selection, I can't bear it.''

"Which one had I better—''

"Oh, take any of them. Pick out the best one.''

However, the officers assured the earl—for they knew him, everybody in Washington knew him—that the position in which these bodies were found made it impossible that any one of them could be that of his noble young kinsman. They pointed out the spot where, if the newspaper account was correct, he must have sunk down to destruction; and at a wide distance from this spot they showed him where the young man must have gone down in case he was suffocated in his room; and they showed him still a third place, quite remote, where he might possibly have found his death if perchance he tried to escape by the side exit toward the rear. The old Colonel brushed away a tear and said to Hawkins—

"As it turns out there was something prophetic in my fears. Yes, it's a matter of ashes. Will you kindly step to a grocery and fetch a couple more baskets?''

Reverently they got a basket of ashes from each of those now hallowed spots, and carried them home to consult as to the best manner of forwarding them to England, and also to give them an opportunity to "lie in state,''—a mark of respect which the Colonel deemed obligatory, considering the high rank of the deceased.

They set the baskets on the table in what was formerly the library, drawingroom and workshop—now the Hall of Audience—and went up stairs to the lumber room to see if they could find a British flag to use as a part of the outfit proper to the lying in state. A moment later, Lady Rossmore came in from the street and caught sight of the baskets just as old Jinny crossed her field of vision. She quite lost her patience and said—

"Well, what will you do next? What in the world possessed you to clutter up the parlor table with these baskets of ashes?''

"Ashes?'' And she came to look. She put up her hands in pathetic astonishment. "Well, I *never* see de like!''

"Didn't you do it?''

"Who, me? Clah to goodness it's de fust time I've sot eyes on 'em, Miss Polly. Dat's Dan'l. Dat ole moke is losin' his mine.''

But it wasn't Dan'l, for he was called, and denied it.

"Dey ain't no way to 'splain dat. Wen hit's one er dese-yer common 'currences, a body kin reckon maybe de cat—''

"Oh!'' and a shudder shook Lady Rossmore to her foundations. "I see it all. Keep away from them—they're *his*.''

"*His*, m'lady?''

"Yes—your young Marse Sellers from England that's burnt up.''

She was alone with the ashes—alone before she could take half a breath. Then she went after Mulberry Sellers, purposing to make short

CLAH TO GOODNESS IT'S DE FUST TIME I'VE SOT EYES ON 'EM.

work with his program, whatever it might be; "for," said she, "when his sentimentals are up, he's a numskull, and there's no knowing what extravagance he'll contrive, if you let him alone." She found him. He had found the flag and was bringing it. When she heard that his idea was to have the remains "lie in state, and invite the government and the public," she broke it up. She said—

"Your intentions are all right—they always are—you want to do honor to the remains, and surely nobody can find any fault with that, for he was your kin; but you are going the wrong way about it, and you will see it yourself if you stop and think. You can't file around a basket of ashes trying to look sorry for it and make a sight that is really solemn, because the solemner it is, the more it isn't—anybody can see that. It would be so with one basket; it would be three times so with three. Well, it stands to reason that if it wouldn't be solemn with one mourner, it wouldn't be with a procession—and there would be five thousand people here. I don't know but it would be pretty near ridiculous; I think it would. No, Mulberry, they can't lie in state—it would be a mistake. Give that up and think of something else."

So he gave it up; and not reluctantly, when he had thought it over and realized how right her instinct was. He concluded to merely sit up with the remains—just himself and Hawkins. Even this seemed a doubtful attention, to his wife, but she offered no objection, for it was plain that he had a quite honest and simple-hearted desire to do the friendly and honorable thing by these forlorn poor relics which could command no hospitality in this far off land of strangers but his. He draped the flag about the baskets, put some crape on the door-knob, and said with satisfaction—

"There—he is as comfortable, now, as we can make him in the circumstances. Except—yes, we must strain a point there—one must do as one would wish to be done by—he must have it."

"Have what, dear?"

"Hatchment."

The wife felt that the house-front was standing about all it could well stand, in that way; the prospect of another stunning decoration of that nature distressed her, and she wished the thing had not occurred to him. She said, hesitatingly—

"But I thought such an honor as that wasn't allowed to any but very *very* near relations, who—"

"Right, you are quite right, my lady, perfectly right; but there aren't any nearer relatives than relatives by usurpation. We cannot avoid it; we are slaves of aristocratic custom and must submit."

The hatchments were unnecessarily generous, each being as large as a blanket, and they were unnecessarily volcanic, too, as to variety and violence of color, but they pleased the earl's barbaric eye, and they satisfied his taste for symmetry and completeness, too, for they left no waste room to speak of on the house-front.

Lady Rossmore and her daughter assisted at the sitting-up till near midnight, and helped the gentlemen to consider what ought to be done next with the remains. Rossmore thought they ought to be sent home— with a committee and resolutions,—at once. But the wife was doubtful. She said:

"Would you send all of the baskets?"

"Oh, yes, all."

"All at once?"

"To his father? Oh, no—by no means. Think of the shock. No—one at a time; break it to him by degrees."

"Would *that* have that effect, father?"

"Yes, my daughter. Remember, you are young and elastic, but he is old. To send him the whole at once might well be more than he could bear. But mitigated—one basket at a time, with restful intervals between, he would be used to it by the time he got all of him. And sending him in three ships is safer anyway. On account of wrecks and storms."

"I don't like the idea, father. If I were his father it would be dreadful to have him coming in that—in that—"

"On the installment plan," suggested Hawkins, gravely, and proud of being able to help.

"Yes—dreadful to have him coming in that incoherent way. There would be the strain of suspense upon me all the time. To have so depressing a thing as a funeral impending, delayed, waiting, unaccomplished—"

"Oh, no, my child," said the earl reassuringly, "there would be nothing of that kind; so old a gentleman could not endure a long-drawn suspense like that. There will be three funerals."

Lady Rossmore looked up surprised, and said—

"How is *that* going to make it easier for him? It's a total mistake, to my mind. He ought to be buried all at once; I'm sure of it."

"I should think so, too," said Hawkins.

"And certainly *I* should," said the daughter.

"You are all wrong," said the earl. "You will see it yourselves, if you think. Only one of these baskets has got him in it."

"Very well, then," said Lady Rossmore, "the thing is perfectly simple—bury *that* one."

"Certainly," said Lady Gwendolen.

"But it is *not* simple," said the earl, "because we do not know which basket he is in. We know he is in *one* of them, but that is all we *do* know. You see now, I reckon, that I was right; it takes three funerals, there is no other way.''

"And three graves and three monuments and three inscriptions?'' asked the daughter.

"Well—yes—to do it right. That is what I should do.''

"It could not be done so, father. Each of the inscriptions would give the same name and the same facts and say he was under each and all of these monuments, and that would not answer at all.''

The earl nestled uncomfortably in his chair.

"No,'' he said, "that *is* an objection. That is a serious objection. I see no way out.''

There was a general silence for a while. Then Hawkins said—

"It seems to me that if we mixed the three ramifications together—''

The earl grasped him by the hand and shook it gratefully.

"It solves the whole problem,'' he said. "One ship, one funeral, one grave, one monument—it is admirably conceived. It does you honor, Major Hawkins, it has relieved me of a most painful embarrassment and distress, and it will save that poor stricken old father much suffering. Yes, he shall go over in one basket.''

"When?'' asked the wife.

"To-morrow—immediately, of course.''

"I would wait, Mulberry.''

"Wait? Why?''

"*You* don't want to break that childless old man's heart.''

"God knows I don't!''

"Then wait till he sends for his son's remains. If you do that, you will never have to give him the last and sharpest pain a parent can know—I mean, the *certainty* that his son is dead. For he will never send.''

"Why won't he?''

"Because to send—and find out the truth—would rob him of the one precious thing left him, the *uncertainty*, the dim hope that maybe, after all, his boy escaped, and he will see him again some day.''

"Why Polly, he'll know by the *papers* that he was burnt up.''

"He won't let himself *believe* the papers; he'll argue against anything and everything that proves his son is dead; and he will keep that up and live on it, and on nothing else till he dies. But if the *remains* should actually come, and be put before that poor old dim-hoping soul—''

"Oh, my God, they never shall! Polly, you've saved me from a crime, and I'll bless you for it always. *Now* we know what to do. We'll place them reverently away, and he shall never know.''

Chapter 10

THE YOUNG Lord Berkeley, with the fresh air of freedom in his nostrils, was feeling invincibly strong for his new career; and yet—and yet—if the fight should prove a very hard one at first, very discouraging, very taxing on untoughened moral sinews, he might in some weak moment want to retreat. Not likely, of course, but possibly that might happen. And so on the whole it might be pardonable caution to burn his bridges behind him. Oh, without doubt. He must not stop with advertising for the owner of that money, but must put it where he could not borrow from it himself, meantime, under stress of circumstances. So he went downtown, and put in his advertisement, then went to a bank and handed in the $500 for deposit.

"What name?"

He hesitated and colored a little; he had forgotten to make a selection. He now brought out the first one that suggested itself—

"Howard Tracy."

When he was gone the clerks, marveling, said—

"The cowboy blushed."

The first step was accomplished. The money was still under his command and at his disposal, but the next step would dispose of that difficulty. He went to another bank and drew upon the first bank for the $500 by check. The money was collected and deposited a second time to the credit of Howard Tracy. He was asked to leave a few samples of his signature, which he did. Then he went away, once more proud and of perfect courage, saying—

"No help for me now, for henceforth I couldn't draw that money without identification, and that is become legally impossible. No resources to fall back on. It is work or starve from now to the end. I am ready—and not afraid!"

Then he sent this cablegram to his father:

> Escaped unhurt from burning hotel. Have taken fictitious name. Goodbye.

During the evening, while he was wandering about in one of the outlying districts of the city, he came across a small brick church, with a bill posted there with these words printed on it: "MECHANICS' CLUB DEBATE. ALL INVITED." He saw people, apparently mainly of the working class, entering the place, and he followed and took his seat. It was a humble little church, quite bare as to ornamentation. It had painted pews without cushions, and no pulpit, properly speaking, but it had a platform. On the platform sat the chairman, and by his side sat a man who held a manuscript in his hand and had the waiting look of one who is going to perform the principal part. The church was soon filled with a quiet and orderly congregation of decently dressed and modest people. This is what the chairman said:

"The essayist for this evening is an old member of our club whom you all know, Mr. Parker, assistant editor of the Daily Democrat. The subject of his essay is the American Press, and he will use as his text a couple of paragraphs taken from Mr. Matthew Arnold's new book. He asks me to read these texts for him. The first is as follows:

> " 'Goethe says somewhere that "the thrill of awe," that is to say, REVERENCE,' is the best thing humanity has."

"Mr. Arnold's other paragraph is as follows:

"'I should say that if one were searching for the best means to efface and kill in a whole nation the discipline of respect, one could not do better than take the American newspapers.'"

Mr. Parker rose and bowed, and was received with warm applause. He then began to read in a good round resonant voice, with clear enunciation and careful attention to his pauses and emphases. His points were received with approval as he went on.

The essayist took the position that the most important function of a public journal in any country was the propagating of national feeling and pride in the national name—the keeping the people "in love with *their* country and *its* institutions and shielded from the allurements of alien and inimical systems." He sketched the manner in which the reverent Turkish or Russian journalist fulfilled this function—the one assisted by the prevalent "discipline of respect" for the bastinado, the other for Siberia. Continuing, he said—

The chief function of an English journal is that of all other journals the world over: it must keep the public eye fixed admiringly upon certain things, and keep it diligently diverted from certain others. For instance, it must keep the public eye fixed admiringly upon the glories of England, a processional splendor stretching its receding line down the hazy vistas of time, with the mellowed lights of a thousand years glinting from its banners; and it must keep it diligently diverted from the fact that all these glories were for the enrichment and aggrandizement of the petted and privileged few, at cost of the blood and sweat and poverty of the unconsidered masses who achieved them but might not enter in and partake of them. It must keep the public eye fixed in loving and awful reverence upon the throne as a sacred thing, and diligently divert it from the fact that no throne was ever set up by the

PARKER, ASSISTANT EDITOR OF THE *DEMOCRAT*.

unhampered vote of a majority of any nation; and that hence no throne exists that has a right to exist, and no symbol of it, flying from any flagstaff, is righteously entitled to wear any device but the skull and crossbones of that kindred industry which differs from royalty only business-wise—merely as retail differs from wholesale. It must keep the citizen's eye fixed in reverent docility upon that curious invention of machine politics, an Established Church, and upon that bald contradiction of common justice, a hereditary nobility; and diligently divert it from the fact that the one damns him if he doesn't wear its collar and robs him under the gentle name of taxation whether he wears it or not, and the other gets all the honors while he does all the work.

The essayist thought that Mr. Arnold, with his trained eye and intelligent observation, ought to have perceived that the very quality which he so regretfully missed from our press—respectfulness, reverence—was exactly the thing which would make our press useless to us if it had it— rob it of the very thing which differentiates it from all other journalism in the world and makes it distinctively and preciously American, its frank and cheerful irreverence being by all odds the most valuable of all its qualities. "For its mission—overlooked by Mr. Arnold—is to stand guard over a nation's liberties, not its humbugs and shams." He thought that if during fifty years the institutions of the old world could be exposed to the fire of a flouting and scoffing press like ours, "monarchy and its attendant crimes would disappear from Christendom." Monarchists might doubt this; then "why not persuade the Czar to give it a trial in Russia?" Concluding, he said—

> Well, the charge is, that our press has but little of that old world quality, reverence. Let us be candidly grateful that it is so. With its limited reverence it at least reveres the things which this nation reveres, as a rule, and that is sufficient: what other people revere is fairly and properly matter of light importance to us. Our press does not reverence kings, it does not reverence so called nobilities, it does not reverence established ecclesiastical slaveries, it does not reverence laws which rob a younger son to fatten an elder one, it does not reverence any fraud or sham or infamy, howsoever old or rotten or holy, which sets one citizen above his neighbor by accident of birth: it does not reverence any law or custom, howsoever old or decayed or sacred, which shuts against the best man in the land the best place in the land and the divine right to prove property and go up and occupy it. In the sense of the poet Goethe— that meek idolator of provincial three carat royalty and nobility— our press is certainly bankrupt in the "thrill of awe"—otherwise reverence; reverence for nickel plate and brummagem. Let us sincerely hope that this fact will remain a fact forever: for to my mind a discriminating irreverence is the creator and protector of human liberty—even as the other thing is the creator, nurse, and steadfast protector of all forms of human slavery, bodily and mental.

Tracy said to himself, almost shouted to himself, "I'm glad I came to this country. I was right. I was right to seek out a land where such healthy principles and theories are in men's hearts and minds. Think of the innumerable slaveries imposed by misplaced reverence! How well he brought that out, and how true it is. There's manifestly prodigious force in reverence. If you can get a man to reverence your ideals, he's your slave. Oh, yes, in all the ages the peoples of Europe have been diligently taught to avoid reasoning about the shams of monarchy and nobility, been taught to avoid examining them, been taught to reverence them; and now, as a natural result, to reverence them is second nature. In order to shock them it is sufficient to inject a thought of the opposite kind into their dull minds. For ages, any expression of so-called irreverence from their lips has been sin and crime. The sham and swindle of all this is apparent the moment one reflects that he is himself the only legitimately qualified judge of what *is* entitled to reverence and what is not. Come, I hadn't thought of that before, but it is true, absolutely true. What right has Goethe, what right has Arnold, what right has any dictionary, to define the word Irreverence for me? What their ideals are is nothing to me. So long as I reverence my own ideals my whole duty is done, and I commit no profanation if I laugh at theirs. I may scoff at other people's ideals as much as I want to. It is my right and my privilege. No man has any right to deny it."

Tracy was expecting to hear the essay debated, but this did not happen. The chairman said, by way of explanation—

"I would say, for the information of the strangers present here, that in accordance with our custom the subject of this meeting will be debated at the next meeting of the club. This is in order to enable our members to prepare what they may wish to say upon the subject with pen and paper, for we are mainly mechanics and unaccustomed to speaking. We are obliged to write down what we desire to say."

Many brief papers were now read, and several offhand speeches made in discussion of the essay read at the last meeting of the club, which had been a laudation, by some visiting professor, of college culture, and the grand results flowing from it to the nation. One of the papers was read by a man approaching middle age, who said he hadn't had a college education, that he had got his education in a printing office, and had graduated from there into the patent office, where he had been a clerk now for a great many years. Then he continued to this effect:

> The essayist contrasted the America of to-day with the America of bygone times, and certainly the result is the exhibition of a mighty progress. But I think he a little overrated the college-culture share in the production of that result. It can no doubt be easily shown that the colleges have contributed the intellectual part of this progress and that that part is vast; but that the material progress has been immeasurably vaster, I think you will concede. Now I have been looking over a list of inventors—the creators of this amazing material development—and I find that they were not college-bred men. Of course there are exceptions—like Professor Henry of Princeton, the inventor of Mr. Morse's system of teleg-

raphy—but these exceptions are few. It is not overstatement to say
that the imagination-stunning material development of this century, the only century worth living in since time itself was invented, is the creation of men not college-bred. We think we see
what these inventors have done: no, we see only the visible vast
frontage of their work; behind it is their far vaster work, and it is
invisible to the careless glance. They have reconstructed this nation—made it over, that is—and metaphorically speaking, have
multiplied its numbers almost beyond the power of figures to express. I will explain what I mean. What constitutes the population
of a land? Merely the numberable packages of meat and bones in
it called by courtesy men and women? Shall a million ounces of
brass and a million ounces of gold be held to be of the same value?
Take a truer standard: the measure of a man's contributing capacity
to his time and his people—the work he can do—and then number
the population of this country to-day, as multiplied by what a man
can now do, more than his grandfather could do. By this standard
of measurement, this nation, two or three generations ago, consisted of mere cripples, paralytics, dead men, as compared with
the men of to-day. In 1840 our population was 17,000,000. By
way of rude but striking illustration, let us consider, for argument's
sake, that four of these millions consisted of aged people, little
children, and other incapables, and that the remaining 13,000,000
were divided and employed as follows:

2,000,000 as ginners of cotton.

6,000,000 (women) as stocking-knitters.

2,000,000 (women) as thread-spinners.

500,000 as screw makers.

400,000 as reapers, binders, etc.

1,000,000 as corn shellers.

40,000 as weavers.

1,000 as stitchers of shoe soles.

Now the deductions which I am going to append to these figures
may sound extravagant, but they are not. I take them from Miscel-
laneous Documents No. 50, second session 45th Congress, and
they are official and trustworthy. To-day, the work of those 2,000,000
cotton-ginners is done by 2,000 men; that of the 6,000,000 stocking-knitters is done by 3,000 boys; that of the 2,000,000 thread-
spinners is done by 1,000 girls; that of the 500,000 screw makers
is done by 500 girls; that of the 400,000 reapers, binders, etc., is
done by 4,000 boys; that of the 1,000,000 corn shellers is done by
7,500 men; that of the 40,000 weavers is done by 1,200 men; and
that of the 1,000 stitchers of shoe soles is done by 6 men. To
bunch the figures, 17,000 persons to-day do the above work, whereas
fifty years ago it would have taken thirteen millions of persons to
do it. Now then, how many of that ignorant race—our fathers and
grandfathers—with their ignorant methods, would it take to do our
work to-day? It would take forty thousand millions—a hundred
times the swarming population of China—twenty times the present
population of the globe. You look around you and you see a nation

of sixty millions—apparently; but secreted in their hands and brains, and invisible to your eyes, is the true population of this Republic, and it numbers forty billions! It is the stupendous creation of those humble unlettered, un-college-bred inventors—all honor to their name.

"How grand that is!" said Tracy, as he wended homeward. "What a civilization it is, and what prodigious results these are! and brought about almost wholly by common men; not by Oxford-trained aristocrats, but men who stand shoulder to shoulder in the humble ranks of life and earn the bread that they eat. Again, I'm glad I came. I have found a country at last where one may start fair, and breast to breast with his fellow man, rise by his own efforts, and be something in the world and be proud of that something; not be something created by an ancestor three hundred years ago."

Chapter 11

DURING THE first few days he kept the fact diligently before his mind that he was in a land where there was "work and bread for all." In fact, for convenience' sake he fitted it to a little tune and hummed it to himself; but as time wore on the fact itself began to take on a doubtful look, and next the tune got fatigued and presently ran down and stopped. His first effort was to get an upper clerkship in one of the departments, where his Oxford education could come into play and do him service. But he stood no chance whatever. There, competency was no recommendation; political backing, without competency, was worth six of it. He was glaringly English, and that was necessarily against him in the political center of a nation where both parties prayed for the Irish cause on the house-top and blasphemed it in the cellar. By his dress he was a cowboy; that won him respect—when his back was not turned—but it couldn't get a clerkship for him. But he had said, in a rash moment, that he would wear those clothes till the owner or the owner's friends caught sight of them and asked for that money, and his conscience would not let him retire from that engagement now.

At the end of a week things were beginning to wear rather a startling look. He had hunted everywhere for work, descending gradually the scale of quality, until apparently he had sued for all the various kinds of work a man without a special calling might hope to be able to do, except ditching and the other coarse manual sorts—and had got neither work nor the promise of it.

He was mechanically turning over the leaves of his diary, meanwhile, and now his eye fell upon the first record made after he was burnt out:

I myself did not doubt my stamina before, nobody could doubt it now, if they could see how I am housed, and realize that I feel absolutely no disgust with these quarters, but am as serenely con-

tent with them as any dog would be in a similar kennel. Terms,
twenty-five dollars a week. I said I would start at the bottom. I
have kept my word.

A shudder went quaking through him, and he exclaimed—
"What have I been thinking of! *This* the bottom! Mooning along a
whole week, and these terrific expenses climbing and climbing all the
time! I must end this folly straightway."

He settled up at once and went forth to find less sumptuous lodgings.
He had to wander far and seek with diligence, but he succeeded. They
made him pay in advance—four dollars and a half; this secured both bed
and food for a week. The good-natured, hard-worked landlady took him
up three flights of narrow, uncarpeted stairs and delivered him into his
room. There were two double-bedsteads in it, and one single one. He
would be allowed to sleep alone in one of the double beds until some new
boarder should come, but he wouldn't be charged extra.

So he would presently be required to sleep with some stranger! The
thought of it made him sick. Mrs. Marsh, the landlady, was very friendly
and hoped he would like her house—they all liked it, she said.

"And they're a very nice set of boys. They carry on a good deal, but
that's their fun. You see, this room opens right into this back one, and
sometimes they're all in one and sometimes in the other; and hot nights
they all sleep on the roof when it don't rain. They get out there the minute
it's hot enough. The season's so early that they've already had a night or
two up there. If you'd like to go up and pick out a place, you can. You'll
find chalk in the side of the chimney where there's a brick wanting. You
just take the chalk and—but of course you've done it before."

"Oh, no, I haven't."

"Why, of course you haven't—what am I thinking of? Plenty of room
on the Plains without chalking, I'll be bound. Well, you just chalk out a
place the size of a blanket anywhere on the tin that ain't already marked
off, you know, and that's your property. You and your bed-mate take turn-
about carrying up the blanket and pillows and fetching them down again;
or one carries it up and the other fetches them down, you fix it the way
you like, you know. You'll like the boys, they're everlasting sociable—
except the printer. He's the one that sleeps in that single bed—the strangest creature; why, I don't believe you could get that man to sleep with
another man, not if the house was afire. Mind you, I'm not just talking, I
know. The boys tried him, to see. They took his bed out one night, and
so when he got home about three in the morning—he was on a morning
paper then, but he's on an evening one now—there wasn't any place for
him but with the iron-molder; and if you'll believe me, he just set up the
rest of the night—he did, honest. They say he's cracked, but it ain't so,
he's English—they're awful particular. You won't mind my saying that.
You—you're English?"

"Yes."

"I thought so. I could tell it by the way you mispronounce the words
that's got *a*'s in them, you know; such as saying loff when you mean
laff—but you'll get over that. He's a right down good fellow, and a little
sociable with the photographer's boy and the caulker ⌐ 1 the blacksmith

that work in the navy yard, but not so much with the others. The fact is, though it's private, and the others don't know it, he's a kind of an aristocrat, his father being a doctor, and *you* know what style *that* is—in England, I mean, because in this country a doctor ain't so *very* much, even if he's *that*. But over there of course it's different. So this chap had a falling out with his father, and was pretty high strung, and just cut for this country, and the first he knew he had to get to work or starve. Well, he'd been to college, you see, and so he judged *he* was all right—did you say anything?"

"No—I only sighed."

"And there's where he was mistaken. Why, he mighty near starved. And I reckon he would have starved sure enough, if some jour' printer or other hadn't took pity on him and got him a place as apprentice. So he learnt the trade, and then he was all right—but it was a close call. Once he thought he had *got* to haul in his pride and holler for his father and— why, you're sighing again. Is anything the matter with you?—does my clatter—"

"Oh, *dear*-no. Pray go on—I like it."

"Yes, you see, he's been over here ten years; he's twenty-eight, now, and he ain't pretty well satisfied in his mind, because he can't get reconciled to being a mechanic and associating with mechanics, he being, as he says to me, a *gentleman*, which is a pretty plain letting-on that the boys ain't, but of course I know enough not to let *that* cat out of the bag."

"Why—would there be any harm in it?"

"Harm in it? They'd lick him, wouldn't they? Wouldn't *you*? Of course you would. Don't you ever let a man say you ain't a gentleman in *this* country. But laws, what am I thinking about? I reckon a body would think twice before he said a cowboy wasn't a gentleman."

A trim, active, slender and very pretty girl of about eighteen walked into the room now, in the most satisfied and unembarrassed way. She was cheaply but smartly and gracefully dressed, and the mother's quick glance at the stranger's face as he rose, was of the kind which inquires what effect has been produced, and expects to find indications of surprise and admiration.

"This is my daughter Hattie—we call her Puss. It's the new boarder, Puss." This without rising.

The young Englishman made the awkward bow common to his nationality and time of life in circumstances of delicacy and difficulty, and these were of that sort; for, being taken by surprise, his natural, lifelong self sprang to the front, and that self of course would not know just how to act when introduced to a chambermaid, or to the heiress of a mechanics' boarding house. His other self—the self which recognized the equality of all men—would have managed the thing better, if it hadn't been caught off guard and robbed of its chance. The young girl paid no attention to the bow, but put out her hand frankly and gave the stranger a friendly shake and said—

"How do you do?"

Then she marched to the one washstand in the room, tilted her head this way and that before the wreck of a cheap mirror that hung above it, dampened her fingers with her tongue, perfected the circle of a little lock

HOW DO YOU DO?

of hair that was pasted against her forehead, then began to busy herself with the slops.

"Well, I must be going—it's getting towards supper time. Make yourself at home, Mr. Tracy, you'll hear the bell when it's ready."

The landlady took her tranquil departure, without commanding either of the young people to vacate the room. The young man wondered a little that a mother who seemed so honest and respectable should be so thoughtless, and was reaching for his hat, intending to disembarrass the girl of his presence; but she said—

"Where are you going?"

"Well—nowhere in particular, but as I am only in the way here—"

"Why, who said you were in the way? Sit down—I'll move you when you are in the way."

She was making the beds, now. He sat down and watched her deft and diligent performance.

"What gave you that notion? Do you reckon I need a whole room just to make up a bed or two in?"

"Well no, it wasn't that, exactly. We are away up here in an empty house, and your mother being gone—"

The girl interrupted him with an amused laugh, and said—

"Nobody to protect me? Bless you, I don't need it. I'm not afraid. I might be if I was alone, because I do hate ghosts, and I don't deny it. Not that I believe in them, for I don't. I'm only just afraid of them."

"How can you be afraid of them if you don't believe in them?"

"Oh, *I* don't know the *how* of it—that's too many for *me*; I only know it's *so*. It's the same with Maggie Lee."

"Who is that?"

"One of the boarders; young lady that works in the factry."

"She works in a factory?"

"Yes. Shoe factry."

"In a shoe factory; and you call her a young lady?"

"Why, she's only twenty-two; what should you call her?"

"I wasn't thinking of her age, I was thinking of the title. The fact is, I came away from England to get away from artificial forms—for artificial forms suit artificial people only—and here you've got them too. I'm sorry. I hoped you had only men and women; everybody equal; no differences in rank.''

The girl stopped with a pillow in her teeth and the case spread open below it, contemplating him from under her brows with a slightly puzzled expression. She released the pillow and said—

"Why, they *are* all equal. Where's any difference in rank?"

"If you call a factory girl a young *lady*, what do you call the President's wife?"

"Call her an *old* one."

"Oh, you make age the only distinction?"

"There ain't any other to make as far as I can see."

"Then *all* women are ladies?"

"Certainly they are. All the respectable ones."

"Well, that puts a better face on it. Certainly there is no harm in a title when it is given to everybody. It is only an offense and a wrong when it is restricted to a favored few. But Miss—er—"

"Hattie."

"Miss Hattie, be frank; confess that that title *isn't* accorded by everybody to everybody. The rich American doesn't call her cook a lady—isn't that so?"

"Yes, it's so. What of it?"

He was surprised and a little disappointed, to see that his admirable shot had produced no perceptible effect.

"What *of* it?" he said. "Why this: equality is *not* conceded here, after all, and the Americans are no better off than the English. In fact there's no difference."

"Now *what* an idea. There's nothing in a title except what is *put* into it—you've said that yourself. Suppose the title is *clean*, instead of lady. You get that?"

"I believe so. Instead of speaking of a woman as a *lady*, you substitute clean and say she's a clean person."

"That's it. In England the swell folks don't speak of the working people as gentlemen and ladies?"

"Oh, no."

"And the working people don't call *themselves* gentlemen and ladies?"

"Certainly not."

"So if you used the other word there wouldn't be any change. The swell people wouldn't call anybody but themselves 'clean,' and those others would drop sort of meekly into their way of talking and *they* wouldn't call themselves clean. We don't do that way here. Everybody calls himself a lady or gentleman, and thinks he *is*, and don't care what anybody else thinks him, so long as he don't say it out loud. You think there's no difference. You *knuckle down* and we *don't*. Ain't that a difference?"

"It is a difference I hadn't thought of; I admit that. Still—*calling* one's self a lady doesn't—er—"

"I wouldn't go on if I were you."

Howard Tracy turned his head to see who it might be that had introduced this remark. It was a short man about forty years old, with sandy hair, no beard, and a pleasant face badly freckled but alive and intelligent, and he wore slop-shop clothing which was neat but showed wear. He had come from the front room beyond the hall, where he had left his hat, and he had a chipped and cracked white wash-bowl in his hand. The girl came and took the bowl.

"I'll get it for you. You go right ahead and *give* it to him, Mr. Barrow. He's the new boarder—Mr. Tracy—and I'd just got to where it was getting too deep for me."

"Much obliged if you will, Hattie. I was coming to borrow of the boys." He sat down at his ease on an old trunk, and said, "I've been listening and got interested; and as I was saying, I wouldn't go on, if I were you. You see where you are coming to, don't you? *Calling* yourself a lady doesn't elect you; that is what you were going to say; and you saw that if you said it you were going to run right up against another difference that you hadn't thought of: to-wit, Whose *right* is it to do the electing? Over there, twenty thousand people in a million elect themselves gentlemen and ladies, and the nine hundred and eighty thousand *accept* that decree and swallow the affront which it puts upon them. Why, if they didn't accept it, it wouldn't *be* an election, it would be a dead letter and have no force at all. Over here the twenty thousand would-be exclusives come up to the polls and vote themselves to be ladies and gentlemen. But the thing doesn't stop there. The nine hundred and eighty thousand come and vote themselves to be ladies and gentlemen *too*, and that elects the whole nation. Since the whole million vote themselves ladies and gentlemen, there is no question about that election. It *does* make absolute equality, and there is no fiction about it; while over yonder the *inequality*, (by decree of the infinitely feeble, and consent of the infinitely strong), is also absolute—as real and absolute as our equality."

Tracy had shrunk promptly into his English shell when this speech began, notwithstanding he had now been in severe training several weeks for contact and intercourse with the common herd on the common herd's terms; but he lost no time in pulling himself out again, and so by the time the speech was finished his valves were open once more, and he was forcing himself to accept without resentment the common herd's frank fashion of dropping sociably into other people's conversations unembarrassed and uninvited. The process was not very difficult this time, for the man's smile and voice and manner were persuasive and winning. Tracy would even have liked him on the spot, but for the fact—fact which he was not really aware of—that the equality of men was not yet a reality to him, it was only a theory; the *mind* perceived, but the *man* failed to feel it. It was Hattie's ghost over again, merely turned around. Theoretically Barrow was his equal, but it was distinctly distasteful to see him exhibit it. He presently said:

"I hope in all sincerity that what you have said is true, as regards the Americans, for doubts have crept into my mind several times. It seemed that the equality must be ungenuine where the sign-names of castes were still in vogue; but those sign-names have certainly lost their offence and are wholly neutralized, nullified and harmless if they are the undisputed property of every individual in the nation. I think I realize that caste does not exist and cannot exist except by common consent of the masses outside of its limits. I thought caste created itself and perpetuated itself; but it seems quite true that it only creates itself, and is perpetuated by the people whom it despises, and who can dissolve it at any time by assuming its mere sign-names themselves.''

"It's what I think. There isn't any power on earth that can prevent England's thirty millions from electing themselves dukes and duchesses to-morrow and calling themselves so. And within six months all the former dukes and duchesses would have retired from the business. I wish they'd try that. Royalty itself couldn't survive such a process. A handful of frowners against thirty million laughers in a state of irruption: Why, it's Herculaneum against Vesuvius; it would take another eighteen centuries to find that Herculaneum after the cataclysm. What's a Colonel in our South? He's a nobody; because they're all colonels down there. No, Tracy'' (shudder from Tracy) ''nobody in England would call you a gentleman and you wouldn't call yourself one; and I tell you it's a state of things that makes a man put himself into most unbecoming attitudes sometimes—the broad and general recognition and acceptance of caste *as* caste does, I mean. Makes him do it unconsciously—being bred in him, you see, and never thought over and reasoned out. You couldn't conceive of the Matter-horn being flattered by the notice of one of your comely little English hills, could you?''

"Why, no.''

"Well, then, let a man in his right mind try to conceive of Darwin feeling flattered by the notice of a princess. It's so grotesque that it— well, it paralyzes the imagination. Yet that Memnon *was* flattered by the notice of that statuette; he *says* so—says so himself. The system that can make a god disown his godship and profane it—oh, well, it's all wrong, it's all wrong and ought to be abolished, I should say.''

The mention of Darwin brought on a literary discussion, and this topic roused such enthusiasm in Barrow that he took off his coat and made himself the more free and comfortable for it, and detained him so long that he was still at it when the noisy proprietors of the room came shouting and skylarking in and began to romp, scuffle, wash, and otherwise enter-tain themselves. He lingered yet a little longer to offer the hospitalities of his room and his book shelf to Tracy and ask him a personal question or two:

"What is your trade?''

"They—well, they call me a cowboy, but that is a fancy; I'm not that. I haven't any trade.''

"What do you work at for your living?''

"Oh, anything—I mean I *would* work at anything I could get to do, but thus far I haven't been able to find an occupation.''

"Maybe I can help you; I'd like to try.''

"I shall be very glad. I've tried, myself, to weariness.''

"Well, of course where a man hasn't a regular trade he's pretty bad off in this world. What you needed, I reckon, was less book learning and more bread-and-butter learning. I don't know what your father could have been thinking of. You ought to have had a trade, you ought to have had a trade, by *all* means. But never mind about that; we'll stir up *something* to do, I guess. And don't you get homesick; that's a bad business. We'll talk the thing over and look around a little. You'll come out all right. Wait for me—I'll go down to supper with you.''

By the time Tracy had achieved a very friendly feeling for Barrow and would have *called* him a friend, maybe, if not taken too suddenly on a straight-out requirement to realize on his theories. He was glad of his society, anyway, and was feeling lighter hearted than before. Also he was pretty curious to know what vocation it might be which had furnished Barrow such a large acquaintanceship with books and allowed him so much time to read.

Chapter 12

PRESENTLY THE supper bell began to ring in the depths of the house, and the sound proceeded steadily upward, growing in intensity all the way up towards the upper floors. The higher it came the more maddening was the noise, until at last what it lacked of being absolutely deafening, was made up of the sudden crash and clatter of an avalanche of boarders down the uncarpeted stairway. The peerage did not go to meals in this fashion; Tracy's training had not fitted him to enjoy this hilarious zoölogical clamor and enthusiasm. He had to confess that there was something about this extraordinary outpouring of animal spirits which he would have to get inured to before he could accept it. No doubt in time he would prefer it; but he wished the process might be modified and made just a little more gradual, and not quite so pronounced and violent. Barrow and Tracy followed the avalanche down through an ever increasing and ever more and more aggressive stench of bygone cabbage and kindred smells; smells which are to be found nowhere but in a cheap private boarding house; smells which once encountered can never be forgotten; smells which encountered generations later are instantly recognizable, but never recognizable with pleasure. To Tracy these odors were suffocating, horrible, almost unendurable; but he held his peace and said nothing. Arrived in the basement, they entered a large dining-room where thirty-five or forty people sat at a long table. They took their places. The feast had already begun and the conversation was going on in the liveliest way from one end of the table to the other. The table cloth was of very coarse material and was liberally spotted with coffee stains and grease. The knives and forks were iron, with bone handles, the spoons appeared to be iron or sheet iron or something of the sort. The tea and coffee cups were of the commonest and heaviest and most durable stone ware. All the furniture of the table was of the commonest and cheapest sort. There was a single large thick slice of bread by each boarder's plate, and it was observable that he economized it as if he were not expecting it to be duplicated. Dishes of butter were distributed along the table within reach of people's arms, if they had long ones, but there were no private butter plates. The butter was perhaps good enough, and was quiet and well behaved; but it had more bouquet than was necessary, though nobody commented upon that fact or seemed in any way disturbed by it. The main feature of the feast was a piping hot Irish stew made of the potatoes and meat left over from a procession of previous meals. Everybody was liberally supplied with this dish. On the table were a couple of great dishes of sliced ham, and there were some other eatables of minor importance—preserves and New Orleans molasses and such things. There was also plenty of tea and coffee of an infernal sort, with brown sugar and condensed milk, but the milk and sugar supply was not left at the discretion of the boarders, but was rationed out at headquarters—one spoonful of sugar and one of condensed milk to each cup and no more. The table was waited upon by two stalwart negro women who raced back and forth from the bases of supplies with splendid dash and clatter and energy. Their labors were supplemented after a fashion by the young girl Puss. She carried coffee and tea back and forth among the boarders, but she made pleasure excursions rather than business ones in this way, to speak strictly. She made jokes with various people. She chaffed the young men pleasantly—and wittily, as she supposed, and as the rest also supposed, apparently, judging by the applause and laughter which she got by her efforts. Manifestly she was a favorite with most of the young fellows and sweetheart of the rest of them. Where she conferred notice she conferred happiness, as was seen by the face of the recipient; and at the same time she conferred unhappiness—one could see it fall and dim the faces of the other young fellows like a shadow. She never "Mistered" these friends of hers, but called them "Billy," "Tom," "John," and they called her "Puss" or "Hattie."

Mr. Marsh sat at the head of the table, his wife sat at the foot. Marsh was a man of sixty, and was an American; but if he had been born a month earlier he would have been a Spaniard. He was plenty good enough Spaniard as it was; his face was very dark, his hair very black, and his eyes were not only exceedingly black but were very intense, and there was something about them that indicated that they could burn with passion upon occasion. He was stoop-shouldered and lean-faced, and the general aspect of him was disagreeable; he was evidently not a very companionable person. If looks went for anything, he was the very opposite of his wife, who was all motherliness and charity, good will and good nature. All the young men and the women called her Aunt Rachael, which was another sign. Tracy's wandering and interested eye presently fell upon one boarder who had been overlooked in the distribution of the stew. He was very pale and looked as if he had but lately come out of a sick bed, and also as if he ought to get back into it again as soon as possible. His face was very melancholy. The waves of laughter and conversation broke upon it without affecting it any more than if it had been a rock in the sea and the words and the laughter veritable waters. He held his head down and looked ashamed. Some of the women cast glances of pity toward him from time to time in a furtive and half afraid way, and some of the youngest of the men plainly had compassion on the young fellow—a compassion exhibited in their faces but not in any more active or compromising way. But the great majority of the people present showed entire indifference to the youth and his sorrows. Marsh sat with his head down, but one could catch the malicious gleam of his eyes through his shaggy brows. He was watching that young fellow with evident relish. He had not neglected him through carelessness, and apparently the table understood that fact. The spectacle was making Mrs. Marsh very uncomfortable. She had the look of one who hopes against hope that the impossible may happen. But as the impossible did not happen, she finally ventured to speak up and remind her husband that Nat Brady hadn't been helped to the Irish stew.

Marsh lifted his head and gasped out with mock courtliness, "Oh, he hasn't, hasn't he? What a pity that is. I don't know how I came to overlook him. Ah, he must pardon me. You must indeed Mr—er—Baxter—Barker, you must pardon me. I—er—my attention was directed to some other matter, I don't know what. The thing that grieves me mainly is, that it happens every meal now. But you must try to overlook these little things, Mr. Bunker, these little neglects on my part. They're always likely to happen with me in any case, and they are especially likely to happen where a person has—er—well, where a person is, say, about three weeks in arrears for his board. You get my meaning?—you get my idea? Here is your Irish stew, and—er—it gives me the greatest pleasure to send it to you, and I hope that you will enjoy the charity as much as I enjoy confer-ring it."

A blush rose in Brady's white cheeks and flowed slowly backward to his ears and upward toward his forehead, but he said nothing and began to eat his food under the embarrassment of a general silence and the sense that all eyes were fastened upon him. Barrow whispered to Tracy:

"The old man's been waiting for that. He wouldn't have missed that chance for anything."

"It's a brutal business," said Tracy. Then he said to himself, purposing to set the thought down in his diary later:

"Well, here in this very house is a republic where all are free and equal, if men are free and equal anywhere in the earth, therefore I have arrived at the place I started to find, and I am a man among men, and on the strictest equality possible to men, no doubt. Yet here on the threshold I find an inequality. There are people at this table who are looked up to for some reason or another, and here is a poor devil of a boy who is looked down upon, treated with indifference, and shamed by humiliations, when he has committed no crime but that common one of being poor. Equality ought to make men noble-minded. In fact I had supposed it did do that."

After supper, Barrow proposed a walk, and they started. Barrow had a purpose. He wanted Tracy to get rid of that cowboy hat. He didn't see his way to finding mechanical or manual employment for a person rigged in that fashion. Barrow presently said—

"As I understand it, you're not a cowboy."

"No, I'm not."

"Well, now if you will not think me too curious, how did you come to mount that hat? Where'd you get it?"

Tracy didn't know quite how to reply to this, but presently said,—

"Well, without going into particulars, I exchanged clothes with a stranger under stress of weather, and I would like to find him and re-exchange."

"Well, why don't you find him? Where is he?"

"I don't know. I supposed the best way to find him would be to continue to wear his clothes, which are conspicuous enough to attract his attention if I should meet him on the street."

"Oh, very well," said Barrow, "the rest of the outfit is well enough, and while it's not too conspicuous, it isn't quite like the clothes that anybody else wears. Suppress the hat. When you meet your man he'll recognize the rest of his suit. That's a mighty embarrassing hat, you know, in a center of civilization like this. I don't believe an angel could get employment in Washington in a halo like that."

Tracy agreed to replace the hat with something of a modester form, and they stepped aboard a crowded car and stood with others on the rear platform. Presently, as the car moved swiftly along the rails, two men crossing the street caught sight of the backs of Barrow and Tracy, and both exclaimed at once, "There he is!" It was Sellers and Hawkins. Both were so paralyzed with joy that before they could pull themselves together and make an effort to stop the car, it was gone too far, and they decided to wait for the next one. They waited a while; then it occurred to Washington that there could be no use in chasing one horse-car with another, and he wanted to hunt up a hack. But the Colonel said:

"When you come to think of it, there's no occasion for that at all. Now that I've got him materialized, I can command his motions. I'll have him at the house by the time we get there."

Then they hurried off home in a state of great and joyful excitement.

The hat exchange accomplished, the two new friends started to walk back leisurely to the boarding house. Barrow's mind was full of curiosity about this young fellow. He said,—

"You've never been to the Rocky Mountains?"

"No."

"You've never been out on the plains?"

"No."

"How long have you been in this country?"

"Only a few days."

"You've never been in America before?"

BOTH WERE SO PARALYZED WITH JOY.

"No."

Then Barrow communed with himself. "Now what odd shapes the notions of romantic people take. Here's a young fellow who's read in England about cowboys and adventures on the plains. He comes here and buys a cowboy's suit. Thinks he can play himself on folks for a cowboy, all inexperienced as he is. Now the minute he's caught in this poor little game, he's ashamed of it and ready to retire from it. It is that exchange that he has put up as an explanation. It's rather thin, too thin altogether. Well, he's young, never been anywhere, knows nothing about the world, sentimental, no doubt. Perhaps it was the natural thing for him to do, but it was a most singular choice, curious freak, altogether."

Both men were busy with their thoughts for a time, then Tracy heaved a sigh and said,—

"Mr. Barrow, the case of that young fellow troubles me."

"You mean Nat Brady?"

"Yes, Brady, or Baxter, or whatever it was. The old landlord called him by several different names."

"Oh, yes, he has been very liberal with names for Brady, since Brady fell into arrears for his board. Well, that's one of his sarcasms—the old man thinks he's great on sarcasm."

"Well, what is Brady's difficulty? What is Brady—who is he?"

"Brady is a tinner. He's a young journeyman tinner who was getting along all right till he fell sick and lost his job. He was very popular before he lost his job; everybody in the house liked Brady. The old man was rather especially fond of him, but you know that when a man loses his job and loses his ability to support himself and to pay his way as he goes, it makes a great difference in the way people look at him and feel about him."

"Is that so! *Is* it so?"

Barrow looked at Tracy in a puzzled way. "Why of course it's so. Wouldn't you know that, naturally. Don't you know that the wounded deer is always attacked and killed by its companions and friends?"

Tracy said to himself, while a chilly and boding discomfort spread itself through his system, "In a republic of deer and men where all are free and equal, misfortune is a crime, and the prosperous gore the unfortunate to death." Then he said aloud, "Here in the boarding house, if one would have friends and be popular instead of having the cold shoulder turned upon him, he must be prosperous."

"Yes," Barrow said, "that is so. It's their human nature. They do turn against Brady, now that he's unfortunate, and they don't like him as well as they did before; but it isn't because of any lack in Brady—he's just as he was before, has the same nature and the same impulses, but they— well, Brady is a thorn in their consciences, you see. They know they ought to help him and they're too stingy to do it, and they're ashamed of themselves for that, and they ought also to hate themselves on that account, but instead of that they hate Brady because he makes them ashamed of themselves. I say that's human nature; that occurs everywhere; this boarding house is merely the world in little, it's the case all over—they're all alike. In prosperity we are popular; popularity comes easy in that case, but when the other thing comes our friends are pretty likely to turn against us.''

Tracy's noble theories and high purposes were beginning to feel pretty damp and clammy. He wondered if by any possibility he had made a mistake in throwing his own prosperity to the winds and taking up the cross of other people's unprosperity. But he wouldn't listen to that sort of thing; he cast it out of his mind and resolved to go ahead resolutely along the course he had mapped out for himself.

Extracts from his diary:

> Have now spent several days in this singular hive. I don't know quite what to make out of these people. They have merits and virtues, but they have some other qualities, and some ways that are hard to get along with. I can't enjoy them. The moment I appeared in a hat of the period, I noticed a change. The respect which had been paid me before, passed suddenly away, and the people became friendly—more than that—they became familiar, and I'm not used to familiarity, and can't take to it right off; I find that out. These people's familiarity amounts to impudence, some-times. I suppose it's all right; no doubt I can get used to it, but it's not a satisfactory process at all. I have accomplished my dearest wish, I am a man among men, on an equal footing with Tom, Dick and Harry, and yet it isn't just exactly what I thought it was going to be. I—I miss home. Am obliged to say I am homesick. Another thing—and this is a confession—a reluctant one, but I will make it: The thing I miss most and most severely, is the respect, the deference, with which I was treated all my life in England, and which seems to be somehow necessary to me. I get along very well without the luxury and the wealth and the sort of society I've been accustomed to, but I do miss the respect and can't seem to get reconciled to the absence of it. There is respect, there is deference here, but it doesn't fall to my share. It is lavished on two men. One of them is a portly man of middle age who is a retired plumber. Everybody is pleased to have that man's notice. He's full of pomp and circumstance and self complacency and bad grammar, and at table he is Sir Oracle and when he opens his mouth not any dog in the kennel barks. The other person is a policeman at the capitol-building. He represents the government. The deference paid to these two men is not so very far short of that which is paid to an earl in England, though the method of it differs. Not so much courtliness, but the deference is all there.
>
> Yes, and there is obsequiousness, too.
>
> It does rather look as if in a republic where all are free and equal, prosperity and position constitute *rank*.

Chapter 13

THE DAYS drifted by, and they grew ever more dreary. For Barrow's efforts to find work for Tracy were unavailing. Always the first question asked was, "What Union do you belong to?"

Tracy was obliged to reply that he didn't belong to any trade-union.

"Very well, then, it's impossible to employ you. My men wouldn't stay with me if I should employ a 'scab,' or 'rat,' " or whatever the phrase was.

Finally, Tracy had a happy thought. He said, "Why the thing for me to do, of course, is to *join* a trade-union."

"Yes," Barrow said, "that is the thing for you to do—if you can."

"If I *can?* Is it difficult?"

"Well, yes," Barrow said, "it's sometimes difficult—in fact, very difficult. But you can try, and of course it will be best to try."

Therefore Tracy tried; but he did not succeed. He was refused admission with a good deal of promptness, and was advised to go back home, where he belonged, not come here taking honest men's bread out of their mouths. Tracy began to realize that the situation was desperate, and the thought made him cold to the marrow. He said to himself, "So there is an aristocracy of position here, and an aristocracy of prosperity, and apparently there is also an aristocracy of the ins as opposed to the outs, and I am with the outs. So the ranks grow daily, here. Plainly there are all kinds of castes here and only one that I belong to, the outcasts." But he couldn't even smile at his small joke, although he was obliged to confess that he had a rather good opinion of it. He was feeling so defeated and miserable by this time that he could no longer look with philosophical complacency on the horseplay of the young fellows in the upper rooms at night. At first it had been pleasant to see them unbend and have a good time after having so well earned it by the labors of the day, but now it all rasped upon his feelings and his dignity. He lost patience with the spectacle. When they were feeling good, they shouted, they scuffled, they sang songs, they romped about the place like cattle, and they generally wound up with a pillow fight, in which they banged each other over the head, and threw the pillows in all directions, and every now and then he got a buffet himself; and they were always inviting him to join in. They called him "Johnny Bull," and invited him with excessive familiarity to take a hand. At first he had endured all this with good nature, but latterly he had shown by his manner that it was distinctly distasteful to him, and very soon he saw a change in the manner of these young people toward him. They were souring on him as they would have expressed it in their language. He had never been what might be called popular. That was hardly the phrase for it; he had merely been liked, but now dislike for him was growing. His case was not helped by the fact that he was out of luck, couldn't get work, didn't belong to a union, and couldn't gain admission to one. He got a good many slights of that small ill-defined sort that you can't quite put your finger on, and it was manifest that there was only one thing which protected him from open insult, and that was his muscle. These young people had seen him exercising, mornings, after his cold sponge bath, and they had perceived by his performance and the build of his body, that he was athletic, and also versed in boxing. He felt pretty naked now, recognizing that he was shorn of all respect except respect for his fists. One night when he entered his room he found about a dozen of the young fellows there carrying on a very lively conversation punctuated with horse-laughter. The talking ceased instantly, and the frank affront of a dead silence followed. He said,

"Good evening gentlemen," and sat down.

There was no response. He flushed to the temples but forced himself to maintain silence. He sat there in this uncomfortable stillness some time, then got up and went out.

The moment he had disappeared he heard a prodigious shout of laughter break forth. He saw that their plain purpose had been to insult him. He ascended to the flat roof, hoping to be able to cool down his spirit there and get back his tranquility. He found the young tinner up there, alone and brooding, and entered into conversation with him. They were pretty fairly matched, now, in popularity and general ill-luck and misery, and they had no trouble in meeting upon this common ground with advantage and something of comfort to both. But Tracy's movements had been watched, and in a few minutes the tormentors came straggling one after another to the roof, where they began to stroll up and down in an apparently purposeless way. But presently they fell to dropping remarks that were evidently aimed at Tracy, and some of them at the tinner. The ringleader of this little mob was a short-haired bully and amateur prize-fighter named Allen, who was accustomed to lording it over the upper floor, and had more than once shown a disposition to make trouble with Tracy. Now there was an occasional cat-call, and hootings, and whistlings, and finally the diversion of an exchange of connected remarks was introduced:

"How many does it take to make a pair?"

"Well, two generally makes a pair, but sometimes there ain't stuff enough in them to make a whole pair." General laugh.

"What were you saying about the English a while ago?"

"Oh, nothing, the English are all right, only—I—"

"What was it you *said* about them?"

"Oh, I only said they swallow well."

"Swallow better than other people?"

"Oh, yes, the English swallow a good deal better than other people."

"What is it they swallow best?"

"Oh, insults." Another general laugh.

"Pretty hard to make 'em fight, ain't it?"

"No, tain't hard to make 'em fight."

"Ain't it, really?"

"No, tain't hard. It's impossible." Another laugh.

"This one's kind of spiritless, that's certain."

"*Couldn't* be the other way—in his case."

"Why?"

"Don't you know the secret of his birth?"

"No! has *he* got a secret of his birth?"

"You bet he has."

"What is it?"

"His father was a wax-figger."

Allen came strolling by where the pair were sitting; stopped, and said to the tinner:

"How are you off for friends, these days?"

"Well enough off."

"Got a good many?"

"Well, as many as I need."

"A friend is valuable, sometimes—as a protector, you know. What do you reckon would happen if I was to snatch your cap off and slap you in the face with it?"

"Please don't trouble me, Mr. Allen, I ain't doing anything to you."

"You answer me! What do you reckon would happen?"

"Well, I don't know."

Tracy spoke up with a good deal of deliberation and said,

"Don't trouble the young fellow, I can tell you what would happen."

"Oh, you can, can you? Boys, Johnny Bull can tell us what would happen if I was to snatch this chump's cap off and slap him in the face with it. Now you'll see."

He snatched the cap and struck the youth in the face, and before he could inquire what was going to happen, it had already happened, and he was warming the tin with the broad of his back. Instantly there was a rush, and shouts of "A ring, a ring, make a ring! Fair play all round! Johnny's grit; give him a chance."

The ring was quickly chalked on the tin, and Tracy found himself as eager to begin as he could have been if his antagonist had been a prince instead of a mechanic. At bottom he was a little surprised at this, because although his theories had been all in that direction for some time, he was not prepared to find himself actually eager to measure strength with quite so common a man as this ruffian. In a moment all the windows in the neighborhood were filled with people, and the roofs also. The men squared off, and the fight began. But Allen stood no chance whatever, against the young Englishman. Neither in muscle nor in science was he his equal. He measured his length on the tin time and again; in fact, as fast as he could

IT HAD ALREADY HAPPENED.

get up he went down again, and the applause was kept up in liberal fashion from all the neighborhood around. Finally, Allen had to be helped up. Then Tracy declined to punish him further and the fight was at an end. Allen was carried off by some of his friends in a very much humbled condition, his face black and blue and bleeding, and Tracy was at once surrounded by the young fellows, who congratulated him, and told him that he had done the whole house a service, and that from this out Mr. Allen would be a little more particular about how he handled slights and insults and maltreatment around amongst the boarders.

Tracy was a hero now, and exceedingly popular. Perhaps nobody had ever been quite so popular on that upper floor before. But if being dis-countenanced by these young fellows had been hard to bear, their lavish commendations and approval and hero-worship was harder still to endure. He felt degraded, but he did not allow himself to analyze the reasons why, too closely. He was content to satisfy himself with the suggestion that he looked upon himself as degraded by the public spectacle which he had made of himself, fighting on a tin roof, for the delectation of everybody a block or two around. But he wasn't entirely satisfied with that explanation of it. Once he went a little too far and wrote in his diary that his case was worse than that of the prodigal son. He said the prodigal son merely fed swine, he didn't have to chum with them. But he struck that out, and said "All men are equal. I will not disown my principles. These men are as good as I am."

Tracy was become popular on the lower floors also. Everybody was grateful for Allen's reduction to the ranks, and for his transformation from a doer of outrages to a mere threatener of them. The young girls, of whom there were half a dozen, showed many attentions to Tracy, particularly that boarding house pet Hattie, the landlady's daughter. She said to him, very sweetly,—

"I think you're ever so nice." And when he said, "I'm glad you think so, Miss Hattie," she said, still more sweetly,—

"Don't call me Miss Hattie—call me Puss."

Ah, here was promotion! He had struck the summit. There were no higher heights to climb in that boarding house. His popularity was complete.

In the presence of people, Tracy showed a tranquil outside, but his heart was being eaten out of him by distress and despair.

In a little while he should be out of money, and then what should he do? He wished, now, that he had borrowed a little more liberally from that stranger's store. He found it impossible to sleep. A single torturing, terri-fying thought went racking round and round in his head, wearing a groove in his brain: What should he do—What was to become of him? And along with it began to intrude a something presently which was very like a wish that he had not joined the great and noble ranks of martyrdom, but had stayed at home and been content to be merely an earl and nothing better, with nothing more to do in this world of a useful sort than an earl finds to do. But he smothered that part of his thought as well as he could; he made every effort to drive it away, and with fair success, but he couldn't keep it from intruding a little now and then, and when it intruded it came suddenly and nipped him like a bite, a sting, a burn. He recognized that thought by the peculiar sharpness of its pang. The others were painful enough, but that one cut to the quick when it came. Night after night he lay tossing to the music of the hideous snoring of the honest bread-winners until two and three o'clock in the morning, then got up and took refuge on the roof, where he sometimes got a nap and sometimes failed entirely. His appetite was leaving him and the zest of life was going along with it. Finally, one day, being near the imminent verge of total discouragement, he said to himself—and took occasion to blush privately when he said it, "If my father knew what my American name is,—he—well, my duty to my father rather requires that I furnish him my name. I have no right to make his days and nights unhappy, I can do enough unhappiness for the family all by myself. Really he ought to know what my American name is." He thought over it a while and framed a cablegram in his mind to this effect:

"My American name is Howard Tracy."

That wouldn't be suggesting anything. His father could understand that as he chose, and doubtless he would understand it as it was meant, as a dutiful and affectionate desire on the part of a son to make his old father happy for a moment. Continuing his train of thought, Tracy said to himself, "Ah, but if he should cable me to come home! I—I—couldn't do that—I *mustn't* do that. I've started out on a mission, and I mustn't turn my back on it in cowardice. No, no, I couldn't go home, at—at—least I shouldn't want to go home." After a reflective pause: "Well, maybe—perhaps—it would be my *duty* to go in the circumstances; he's very old and he does need me by him to stay his footsteps down the long hill that inclines westward toward the sunset of his life. Well, I'll think about that. Yes, of course it wouldn't be right to stay here. I—if I—well, perhaps I could just drop him a line and put it off a little while and satisfy him in that way. It would be—well, it would mar everything to have him require me to come instantly." Another reflective pause—then: "And yet if he should do that I don't know but—oh, dear me—*home!* how good it sounds! and a body is excusable for wanting to see his home again, now and then, anyway."

He went to one of the telegraph offices in the avenue and got the first end of what Barrow called the "usual Washington courtesy," where "they treat you as a tramp until they find out you're a congressman, and then they slobber all over you." There was a boy of seventeen on duty there, tying his shoe. He had his foot on a chair and his back turned towards the wicket. He glanced over his shoulder, took Tracy's measure, turned back, and went on tying his shoe. Tracy finished writing his telegram and waited, still waited, and still waited, for that performance to finish, but there didn't seem to be any finish to it; so finally Tracy said:

"Can't you take my telegram?"

The youth looked over his shoulder and said, by his manner, not his words:

"Don't you think you could wait a minute, if you tried?"

However, he got the shoe tied at last, and came and took the telegram, glanced over it, then looked up surprised, at Tracy. There was something in his look that bordered upon respect, almost reverence, it seemed to Tracy, although he had been so long without anything of this kind he was not sure that he knew the signs of it.

The boy read the address aloud, with pleased expression in face and voice.

"The Earl of Rossmore! Cracky! Do you know him?"

"Yes."

"Is that so! Does he know you?"

"Well—yes."

"Well, I swear! Will he answer you?"

"I think he will."

"Will he though? Where'll you have it sent?"

"Oh, nowhere. I'll call here and get it. When shall I call?"

"Oh, I don't know—I'll send it to you. Where shall I send it? Give me your address; I'll send it to you soon's it comes."

But Tracy didn't propose to do this. He had acquired the boy's admiration and deferential respect, and he wasn't willing to throw these precious things away, a result sure to follow if he should give the address of that boarding house. So he said again that he would call and get the telegram, and went his way.

He idled along, reflecting. He said to himself, "There *is* something pleasant about being respected. I have acquired the respect of Mr. Allen and some of those others, and almost the deference of some of them on pure merit, for having thrashed Allen. While their respect and their deference—if it is deference—is pleasant, a deference based upon a sham, a shadow, does really seem pleasanter still. It's no real merit to be in correspondence with an earl, and yet after all, that boy makes me feel as if there was."

The cablegram was actually gone home! the thought of it gave him an immense uplift. He walked with a lighter tread. His heart was full of happiness. He threw aside all hesitances and confessed to himself that he was glad through and through that he was going to give up this experiment and go back to his home again. His eagerness to get his father's answer began to grow, now, and it grew with marvelous celerity, after it began. He waited an hour, walking about, putting in his time as well as he could, but interested in nothing that came under his eye, and at last he presented himself at the office again and asked if any answer had come yet. The boy said,

"No, no answer yet," then glanced at the clock and added, "I don't think it's likely you'll get one to-day."

"Why not?"

"Well, you see it's getting pretty late. You can't always tell where 'bouts a man is when he's on the other side, and you can't always find him just the minute you want him, and you see it's getting about six o'clock now, and over there it's pretty late at night."

"Why yes," said Tracy, "I hadn't thought of that."

"Yes, pretty late, now, half past ten or eleven. Oh yes, you probably won't get any answer to-night."

Chapter 14

So TRACY went home to supper. The odors in that supper room seemed more strenuous and more horrible than ever before, and he was happy in the thought that he was so soon to be free from them again. When the supper was over he hardly knew whether he had eaten any of it or not, and he certainly hadn't heard any of the conversation. His heart had been dancing all the time, his thoughts had been far away from these things, and in the visions of his mind the sumptuous appointments of his father's castle had risen before him without rebuke. Even the plushed flunkey, that walking symbol of a sham inequality, had not been unpleasant to his dreaming view. After the meal Barrow said,—

"Come with me. I'll give you a jolly evening."

"Very good. Where are you going?"

"To my club."

"What club is that?"

"Mechanics' Debating Club."

Tracy shuddered, slightly. He didn't say anything about having visited that place himself. Somehow he didn't quite relish the memory of that time. The sentiments which had made his former visit there so enjoyable, and filled him with such enthusiasm, had undergone a gradual change, and they had rotted away to such a degree that he couldn't contemplate another visit there with anything strongly resembling delight. In fact he was a little ashamed to go; he didn't want to go there and find out by the rude impact of the thought of those people upon his reorganized condition of mind, how sharp the change had been. He would have preferred to stay away. He expected that now he should hear nothing except sentiments which would be a reproach to him in his changed mental attitude, and he rather wished he might be excused. And yet he didn't quite want to say that, he didn't want to show how he did feel, or show any disinclination to go, and so he forced himself to go along with Barrow, privately purposing to take an early opportunity to get away.

HIS THOUGHTS HAD BEEN FAR AWAY FROM THESE THINGS.

After the essayist of the evening had read his paper, the chairman announced that the debate would now be upon the subject of the previous meeting, "The American Press." It saddened the back-sliding disciple to hear this announcement. It brought up too many reminiscences. He wished he had happened upon some other subject. But the debate began, and he sat still and listened.

In the course of the discussion one of the speakers—a blacksmith named Tompkins—arraigned all monarchs and all lords in the earth for their cold selfishness in retaining their unearned dignities. He said that no monarch and no son of a monarch, no lord and no son of a lord ought to be able to look his fellow man in the face without shame. Shame for consenting to keep his unearned titles, property, and privileges at the expense of other people; shame for consenting to remain, on any terms, in dishonorable possession of these things, which represented bygone robberies and wrongs inflicted upon the general people of the nation. He said, "if there were a lord or the son of a lord here, I would like to reason with him, and try to show him how unfair and how selfish his position is. I would try to persuade him to relinquish it, take his place among men on equal terms, earn the bread he eats, and hold of slight value all deference paid him because of artificial position, all reverence not the just due of his own personal merits."

Tracy seemed to be listening to utterances of his own made in talks with his radical friends in England. It was as if some eavesdropping phonograph had treasured up his words and brought them across the Atlantic to accuse him with them in the hour of his defection and retreat. Every word spoken by this stranger seemed to leave a blister on Tracy's conscience, and by the time the speech was finished he felt that he was all conscience and one blister. This man's deep compassion for the enslaved and oppressed millions in Europe who had to bear with the contempt of that small class above them, throned upon shining heights whose paths were shut against them, was the very thing he had often uttered himself. The pity in this man's voice and words was the very twin of the pity that used to reside in his own heart and come from his own lips when he thought of these oppressed peoples.

The homeward tramp was accomplished in brooding silence. It was a silence most grateful to Tracy's feelings. He wouldn't have broken it for anything; for he was ashamed of himself all the way through to his spine. He kept saying to himself:

"How unanswerable it all is—how absolutely unanswerabe! It *is* basely, degradingly selfish to keep those unearned honors, and—and—oh, hang it, nobody but a cur—"

"What an idiotic damned speech that Tompkins made!"

This outburst was from Barrow. It flooded Tracy's demoralized soul with waters of refreshment. These were the darlingest words the poor vacillating young apostate had ever heard—for they whitewashed his shame for him, and that is a good service to have when you can't get the best of all verdicts, self-acquittal.

"Come up to my room and smoke a pipe, Tracy."

Tracy had been expecting this invitation, and had had his declination all ready: but he was glad enough to accept, now. Was it possible that a reasonable argument could be made against that man's desolating speech? He was burning to hear Barrow try it. He knew how to start him, and keep him going: it was to seem to combat his positions—a process effective with most people.

"What is it you object to in Tompkins's speech, Barrow?"

"Oh, the leaving out of the factor of human nature; requiring another man to do what you wouldn't do yourself."

"Do you mean—"

"Why here's what I mean; it's very simple. Tompkins is a blacksmith; has a family; works for wages; and hard, too—fooling around won't furnish the bread. Suppose it should turn out that by the death of somebody in England he is suddenly an earl—income, half a million dollars a year. What would he do?"

"Well, I—I suppose he would have to decline to—"

"Man, he would grab it in a second!"

"Do you really think he would?"

"Think?—I don't think anything about it, I know it."

"Why?"

"Why? Because he's not a fool."

"So you think that if he were a fool, he—"

"No, I don't. Fool or *no* fool, he would grab it. Anybody would. Anybody that's alive. And I've seen dead people that would get up and go for it. I would myself."

This was balm, this was healing, this was rest and peace and comfort.

"But I thought you were opposed to nobilities."

"Transmissible ones, yes. But that's nothing. I'm opposed to millionaires, but it would be dangerous to offer me the position."

"You'd take it?"

"I would leave the funeral of my dearest enemy to go and assume its burdens and responsibilities."

Tracy thought a while, then said—

"I don't know that I quite get the bearings of your position. You say

FOOL OR *NO* FOOL, HE WOULD GRAB IT.

you are opposed to hereditary nobilities, and yet if you had the chance you would—"

"Take one? In a minute I would. And there isn't a mechanic in that entire club that wouldn't. There isn't a lawyer, doctor, editor, author, tinker, loafer, railroad president, saint—land, there isn't a human *being* in the United States that wouldn't jump at the chance!"

"Except me," said Tracy softly.

"Except you!" Barrow could hardly get the words out, his scorn so choked him. And he couldn't get any further than that form of words; it seemed to dam his flow, utterly. He got up and came and glared upon Tracy in a kind of outraged and unappeasable way, and said again, "Except *you!*" He walked around him—inspecting him from one point of view and then another, and relieving his soul now and then by exploding that formula at him; "Except *you!*" Finally he slumped down into his chair with the air of one who gives it up, and said—

"He's straining his viscera and he's breaking his heart trying to get some low-down job that a good dog wouldn't have, and yet wants to let on that if he had a chance to scoop an earldom he wouldn't do it. Tracy, don't put this kind of a strain on me. Lately I'm not as strong as I was."

"Well, I wasn't meaning to put a strain on you, Barrow, I was only meaning to intimate that if an earldom ever does fall in my way—"

"There—I wouldn't give myself any worry about *that,* if I was you. And besides, I can settle what you would do. Are you any different from me?"

"Well—no."

"Are you any better than me?"

"O,—er—why, certainly not."

"Are you as *good?* Come!"

"Indeed, I—the fact is you take me so suddenly,—"

"Suddenly? What is there sudden about it? It isn't a difficult question is it? Or doubtful? Just measure us on the only fair lines—the lines of merit—and of course you'll admit that a journeyman chair-maker that earns his twenty dollars a week, and has had the good and genuine culture of contact with men, and care, and hardship, and failure, and success, and downs and ups and ups and downs, is just a trifle the superior of a young fellow like you, who doesn't know how to do anything that's valuable, can't earn his living in any secure and steady way, hasn't had any experience of life and its seriousness, hasn't any culture but the artificial culture of books, which adorns but doesn't really educate— come! if *I* wouldn't scorn an earldom, what the devil right have *you* to do it!"

Tracy dissembled his joy, though he wanted to thank the chair-maker for that last remark. Presently a thought struck him, and he spoke up briskly and said:

"But look here, I really can't quite get the hang of your notions—your principles, if they are principles. You are inconsistent. You are opposed to aristocracies, yet you'd take an earldom if you could. Am I to understand that you don't blame an earl for being and remaining an earl?"

"I certainly don't."

"And you wouldn't blame Tompkins, or yourself, or me, or anybody, for accepting an earldom if it was offered?"

"Indeed I wouldn't."

"Well, then, who *would* you blame?"

"The whole nation—any bulk and mass of population anywhere, in any country, that will put up with the infamy, the outrage, the insult of a hereditary aristocracy which *they* can't enter—and on absolutely free and equal terms."

"Come, aren't you beclouding yourself with distinctions that are not differences?"

"Indeed I am not. I am entirely clear-headed about this thing. If I could extirpate an aristocratic system by declining its honors, *then* I should be a rascal to accept them. And if enough of the mass would join me to make the extirpation possible, *then* I should be a rascal to do otherwise than help in the attempt."

"I believe I understand—yes, I think I get the idea. You have no blame for the lucky few who naturally decline to vacate the pleasant nest they were born into, you only despise the all-powerful and stupid mass of the nation for allowing the nest to exist."

"That's it, that's it! You *can* get a simple thing through your head if you work at it long enough."

"Thanks."

"Don't mention it. And I'll give you some sound advice: when you go back, if you find your nation up and ready to abolish that hoary affront, lend a hand; but if that isn't the state of things and you get a chance at an earldom, don't you be a fool—you take it."

Tracy responded with earnestness and enthusiasm—

"As I live, I'll do it!"

Barrow laughed.

"I never saw such a fellow. I begin to think you've got a good deal of imagination. With you, the idlest fancy freezes into a reality at a breath. Why, you looked, then, as if it wouldn't astonish you if you did tumble into an earldom." Tracy blushed. Barrow added: "Earldom! Oh, yes, take it, if it offers; but meantime we'll go on looking around, in a modest way, and if you get a chance to superintend a sausage-stuffer at six or eight dollars a week, you just trade off the earldom for a last year's almanac and stick to the sausage-stuffing."

Chapter 15

TRACY WENT to bed happy once more, at rest in his mind once more. He had started out on a high emprise—that was to his credit, he argued; he had fought the best fight he could, considering the odds against him—that was to his credit; he had been defeated—certainly there was nothing discreditable in that. Being defeated, he had a right to retire with the honors of war and go back without prejudice to the position in the world's society to which he had been born. Why not? even the rabid republican chair-maker would do that. Yes, his conscience was comfortable once more.

He woke refreshed, happy, and eager for his cablegram. He had been born an aristocrat, he had been a democrat for a time, he was now an aristocrat again. He marveled to find that this final change was not merely intellectual, it had invaded his feeling; and he also marveled to note that this feeling seemed a good deal less artificial than any he had entertained in his system for a long time. He could also have noted, if he had thought of it, that his bearing had stiffened, over night, and that his chin had lifted itself a shade. Arrived in the basement, he was about to enter the breakfast room when he saw old Marsh in the dim light of a corner of the hall, beckoning him with his finger to approach. The blood welled slowly up in Tracy's cheek, and he said with a grade of injured dignity almost ducal—

"Is that for me?"

"Yes."

"What is the purpose of it?"

"I want to speak to you—in private."

"This spot is private enough for me."

Marsh was surprised; and not particularly pleased. He approached and said—

"Oh, in public, then, if you prefer. Though it hasn't been my way."

The boarders gathered to the spot, interested.

"Speak out," said Tracy. "What is it you want?"

"Well, haven't you—er—forgot something?"

"I? I'm not aware of it."

"Oh, you're not? Now you stop and think, a minute."

"I refuse to stop and think. It doesn't interest me. If it interests you, speak out."

"Well, then," said Marsh, raising his voice to a slightly angry pitch, "You forgot to pay your board yesterday—if you're *bound* to have it public."

Oh, yes, this heir to an annual million or so had been dreaming and soaring, and had forgotten that pitiful three or four dollars. For penalty he must have it coarsely flung in his face in the presence of these people— people in whose countenances was already beginning to dawn an uncharitable enjoyment of the situation.

"Is *that* all! Take your money and give your terrors a rest."

Tracy's hand went down into his pocket with angry decision. But—it didn't come out. The color began to ebb out of his face. The countenances about him showed a growing interest; and some of them a heightened satisfaction. There was an uncomfortable pause—then he forced out, with difficulty, the words—

"I've—been robbed!"

Old Marsh's eyes flamed up with Spanish fire, and he exclaimed—

"Robbed, is it? *That's* your tune? It's too old—been played in this house too often; everybody plays it that can't get work when he wants it, and won't work when he can get it. Trot out Mr. Allen, somebody, and let *him* take a toot at it. It's *his* turn next, *he* forgot, too, last night. I'm laying for him."

One of the negro women came scrambling down stairs as pale as a sorrel horse with consternation and excitement:

"Misto Marsh, Misto Allen's skipped out!"

"What!"

"Yes-sah, and cleaned out his room *clean;* tuck bofe towels en de soap!"

"You lie, you hussy!"

"It's jes' so, jes' as I tells you—en Misto Sumner's socks is gone, en Misto Naylor's yuther shirt."

Mr. Marsh was at boiling point by this time. He turned upon Tracy—

"Answer up now—when are you going to settle?"

"To-day—since you seem to be in a hurry."

"*To-day* is it? Sunday—and you out of work? I like that. Come—where are you going to get the money?"

Tracy's spirit was rising again. He proposed to impress these people:

"I am expecting a cablegram from home."

Old Marsh was caught out, with the surprise of it. The idea was so immense, so extravagant, that he couldn't get his breath at first. When he did get it, it came rancid with sarcasm.

"A *cablegram*—think of it, ladies and gents, he's expecting a cablegram! *He's* expecting a cablegram—this duffer, this scrub, this bilk! From his father—eh? Yes—without a doubt. A dollar or two a word—oh, that's nothing—*they* don't mind a little thing like that—*this* kind's fathers don't. Now his father is—er—well, I reckon his father—"

"My father is an English earl!"

The crowd fell back aghast—aghast at the sublimity of the young loafer's "cheek." Then they burst into a laugh that made the windows rattle. Tracy was too angry to realize that he had done a foolish thing. He said—

"Stand aside, please. I—"

"Wait a minute, your lordship," said Marsh, bowing low, "where is your lordship going?"

"For the cablegram. Let me pass."

"Excuse me, your lordship, you'll stay right where you are."

"What do you mean by that?"

"I mean that I didn't begin to keep boarding-house yesterday. It means that I am not the kind that can be taken in by every hack-driver's son that comes loafing over here because he can't bum a living at home. It means that you can't skip out on any such—"

Tracy made a step toward the old man, but Mrs. Marsh sprang between, and said—

"Don't, Mr. Tracy, please." She turned to her husband and said, "*Do* bridle your tongue. What has he done to be treated so? Can't you *see* he has lost his mind, with trouble and distress? He's not responsible."

"Thank your kind heart, madam, but I've not lost my mind; and if I can have the mere privilege of stepping to the telegraph office—"

"Well, you can't," cried Marsh.

"—or sending—"

"Sending! That beats everything. If there's anybody that's fool enough to go on such a chuckleheaded errand—"

"Here comes Mr. Barrow—he will go for me. Barrow—"

A brisk fire of exclamations broke out—

"Say, Barrow, he's expecting a cablegram!"

"Cablegram from his father, you know!"

"Yes—cablegram from the wax-figger!"

"And say, Barrow, this fellow's an earl—take off your hat, pull down your vest!"

"Yes, he's come off and forgot his crown, that he wears Sundays. He's cabled over to his pappy to send it."

"You step out and get that cablegram, Barrow; his majesty's a little lame to-day."

"Oh stop," cried Barrow; "give the man a chance." He turned, and said with some severity, "Tracy, what's the matter with you? What kind of foolishness is this you've been talking. You ought to have more sense."

"I've not been talking foolishness; and if you'll go to the telegraph office—"

"Oh, don't talk so. I'm your friend in trouble and out of it, before your face and behind your back, for anything in *reason;* but you've lost your head, you see, and this moonshine about a cablegram—"

"*I'll* go there and ask for it!"

"Thank you from the bottom of my heart, Brady. Here, I'll give you a written order for it. Fly, now, and fetch it. We'll soon see!"

Brady flew. Immediately the sort of quiet began to steal over the crowd which means dawning doubt, misgiving; and might be translated into the words, "Maybe he *is* expecting a cablegram—maybe he *has* got a father somewhere—maybe we've been just a little too fresh, just a shade too 'previous'!" Loud talk ceased; then the mutterings and low murmurings and whisperings died out. The crowd began to crumble apart. By ones and twos the fragments drifted to the breakfast table. Barrow tried to bring Tracy in; but he said—

"Not yet, Barrow—presently."

Mrs. Marsh and Hattie tried, offering gentle and kindly persuasions; but he said;

"I would rather wait—till he comes."

Even old Marsh began to have suspicions that maybe he had been a trifle too "brash," as he called it in the privacy of his soul, and he pulled himself together and started toward Tracy with invitation in his eyes; but Tracy warned him off with a gesture which was quite positive and elo-quent. Then followed the stillest quarter of an hour which had ever been known in that house at that time of day. It was so still, and so solemn withal, that when somebody's cup slipped from his fingers and landed in his plate the shock made people start, and the sharp sound seemed as indecorous there and as out of place as if a coffin and mourners were imminent and being waited for. And at last when Brady's feet came clattering down the stairs the sacrilege seemed unbearable. Everybody rose softly and turned toward the door, where stood Tracy; then with a common impulse, moved a step or two in that direction, and stopped. While they gazed, young Brady arrived, panting, and put into Tracy's hand,—sure enough—an envelope. Tracy fastened a bland victorious eye upon the gazers, and kept it there till one by one they dropped their eyes, vanquished and embarrassed. Then he tore open the telegram and glanced at its message. The yellow paper fell from his fingers and fluttered to the floor, and his face turned white. There was nothing there but one word—

"Thanks."

The humorist of the house, the tall, raw-boned Billy Nash, caulker from the navy yard, was standing in the rear of the crowd. In the midst of the pathetic silence that was now brooding over the place and moving some few hearts there toward compassion, he began to whimper, then he put his handkerchief to his eyes and buried his face in the neck of the bashfulest young fellow in the company, a navy-yard blacksmith, shrieked "Oh, pappy, how *could* you!" and began to bawl like a teething baby, if one may imagine a baby with the energy and the devastating voice of a jackass.

So perfect was the imitation of a child's cry, and so vast the scale of it, and so ridiculous the aspect of the performer, that all gravity was swept from the place as if by hurricane, and almost everybody there joined in the crash of laughter provoked by the exhibition. Then the small mob began to take its revenge—revenge for the discomfort and apprehension it had brought upon itself by its own too rash freshness of a little while before. It guyed its poor victim, baited him, worried him, as dogs do with a cornered cat. The victim answered back with defiances and challenges which included everybody, and which only gave the sport new spirit and variety; but when he changed his tactics and began to single out individuals and invite them by name, the fun lost its funniness and the interest of the show died out, along with the noise.

Finally Marsh was about to take an inning, but Barrow said—

"Never mind, now—leave him alone. You've no account with him but a money account. I'll take care of that myself."

The distressed and worried landlady gave Barrow a fervently grateful look for his championship of the abused stranger; and the pet of the house, a very prism in her cheap but ravishing Sunday rig, blew him a kiss from the tips of her fingers and said, with the darlingest smile and sweet little toss of her head—

"You're the only man here, and I'm going to set my cap for you, you dear old thing!"

"For shame, Puss! How you talk! I *never* saw such a child!"

It took a good deal of argument and persuasion—that is to say, petting, under these disguises—to get Tracy to entertain the idea of breakfast. He at first said he would never eat again in that house; and added that he had enough firmness of character, he trusted, to enable him to starve like a man when the alternative was to eat insult with his bread.

When he had finished his breakfast, Barrow took him to his room, furnished him a pipe, and said cheerily—

"*Now,* old fellow, take in your battle-flag out of the wet, you're not in the hostile camp any more. You're a little upset by your troubles, and that's natural enough, but don't let your mind run on them any more than you can help; drag your thoughts away from your troubles— by the ears, by the heels, or any other way, so you manage it; it's the healthiest thing a body can do; dwelling on troubles is deadly, just deadly—and that's the softest name there is for it. You must keep your mind amused—you must, indeed."

"Oh, miserable me!"

"*Don't!* There's just pure heart-break in that tone. It's just as I say;

you've got to get right down to it and amuse your mind, as if it was salvation.''

"They're easy words to say, Barrow, but how am I going to amuse, entertain, divert a mind that finds itself suddenly assaulted and overwhelmed by disasters of a sort not dreamed of and not provided for? No-no, the bare idea of amusement is repulsive to my feelings. Let us talk of death and funerals.''

"No—not yet. That would be giving up the ship. We'll not give up the ship yet. I'm going to amuse you; I sent Brady out for the wherewithal before you finished breakfast.''

"You did? What is it?''

"Come, this is a good sign—curiosity. Oh, there's hope for you yet.''

Chapter 16

BRADY ARRIVED with a box, and departed, after saying—

"They're finishing one up, but they'll be along as soon as it's done.''

Barrow took a frameless oil portrait a foot square from the box, set it up in a good light, without comment, and reached for another, taking a furtive glance at Tracy, meantime. The stony solemnity in Tracy's face remained as it was, and gave out no sign of interest. Barrow placed the second portrait beside the first, and stole another glance while reaching for a third. The stone image softened, a shade. No. 3 forced the ghost of a smile, No. 4 swept indifference wholly away, and No. 5 started a laugh which was still in good and hearty condition when No. 14 took its place in the row.

"Oh, *you're* all right, yet,'' said Barrow. "You see you're not past amusement.''

The pictures were fearful, as to color, and atrocious as to drawing and expression; but the feature which squelched animosity and made them funny was a feature which could not achieve its full force in a single

NO. 5 STARTED A LAUGH.

picture, but required the wonder-working assistance of repetition. One loudly dressed mechanic in stately attitude, with his hand on a cannon, ashore, and a ship riding at anchor in the offing,—this is merely odd; but when one sees the same cannon and the same ship in fourteen pictures in a row, and a different mechanic standing watch in each, the thing gets to be funny.

"Explain—explain these aberrations," said Tracy.

"Well, they are not the achievement of a single intellect, a single talent—it takes two to do these miracles. They are collaborations; the one artist does the figure, the other the accessories. The figure-artist is a German shoemaker with an untaught passion for art, the other is a simple hearted old Yankee sailor-man whose possibilities are strictly limited to his ship, his cannon and his patch of petrified sea. They work these things up from twenty-five-cent tintypes; they get six dollars apiece for them, and they can grind out a couple a day when they strike what they call a boost—that is, an inspiration."

"People actually pay money for these calumnies?"

"They actually do—and quite willingly, too. And these abortionists could double their trade and work the women in, if Capt. Saltmarsh could whirl a horse in, or a piano, or a guitar, in place of his cannon. The fact is, he fatigues the market with that cannon. Even the male market, I mean. These fourteen in the procession are not all satisfied. One is an old "independent" fireman, and he wants an engine in place of the cannon; another is a mate of a tug, and wants a tug in place of the ship—and so on, and so on. But the captain can't make a tug that is deceptive, and a fire engine is many flights beyond his power."

"That *is* a most extraordinary form of robbery, I never have heard of anything like it. It's interesting."

"Yes, and so are the artists. They are perfectly honest men, and sincere. And the old sailor-man is full of sound religion, and is as devoted a student of the Bible and misquoter of it as you can find anywhere. I don't know a better man or kinder hearted old soul than Saltmarsh, although he does swear a little, sometimes."

"He seems to be perfect. I want to know him, Barrow."

"You'll have the chance. I guess I hear them coming, now. We'll draw them out on their art, if you like."

The artists arrived and shook hands with great heartiness. The German was forty and a little fleshy, with a shiny bald head and a kindly face and deferential manner. Capt. Saltmarsh was sixty, tall, erect, powerfully built, with coal-black hair and whiskers, and he had a well tanned complexion, and a gait and countenance that were full of command, confidence and decision. His horny hands and wrists were covered with tattoo-marks, and when his lips parted, his teeth showed up white and blemishless. His voice was the effortless deep bass of a church organ, and would disturb the tranquility of a gas flame fifty yards away.

"They're wonderful pictures," said Barrow. "We've been examining them."

"It is very bleasant dot you like dem," said Handel, the German, greatly pleased. "Und you, Herr Tracy, you haf peen bleased mit dem too, alretty?"

CAPTAIN SALTMARSH AND BROTHER OF THE BUSH.

"I can honestly say I have never seen anything just like them before."

"Schön!" cried the German, delighted. "You hear, Gaptain? Here is a chentleman, yes, vot abbreciate unser aart."

The captain was charmed, and said:

"Well, sir, we're thankful for a compliment yet, though they're not as scarce now as they used to be before we made a reputation."

"Getting the reputation is the up-hill time in most things, Captain."

"It's so. It ain't enough to know how to reef a gasket, you got to make the mate know you know it. That's reputation. The good word, said at the right time, that's the word that makes us; and evil be to him that evil thinks, as Isaiah says."

"It's very relevant, and hits the point exactly," said Tracy.

"Where did you study art, Captain?"

"I haven't studied; it's a natural gift."

"He is born mit dose cannon in him. He tondt haf to do noding, his chenius do all de vork. Of he is asleep, und take a pencil in his hand, out come a cannon. Py crashus, of he could do a clavier, of he could do a guitar, of he could do a vashtub, it is a fortune, heiliger Yohanniss it is yoost a fortune!"

"Well, it is an immense pity that the business is hindered and limited in this unfortunate way."

The captain grew a trifle excited, himself, now—

"You've said it, Mr. Tracy! Hindered? well, I should say so. Why, look here. This fellow here, No. 11, he's a hackman,—a flourishing hackman, I may say. He wants his hack in this picture. Wants it where the cannon is. I got around that difficulty, by telling him the cannon's our trademark, so to speak—proves that the picture's our work, and I was afraid if we left it out people wouldn't know for certain if it *was* a Saltmarsh-Handel—now you wouldn't yourself—"

"What, Captain? You wrong yourself, indeed you do. Anyone who has once seen a genuine Saltmarsh-Handel is safe from imposture forever. Strip it, flay it, skin it out of every detail but the bare color and expression, and that man will still recognize it, still stop to worship—"

"Oh, how it makes me feel to hear dose oxpressions!—"

—"still say to himself again as he had said a hundred times before, the art of the Saltmarsh-Handel is an art apart, there is nothing in the heavens above or in the earth beneath that resembles it,—"

"Py chiminy, nur hören Sie einmal! In my lifeday haf I never heard so brecious worts."

"So I talked him out of the hack, Mr. Tracy, and he let up on that, and said put in a hearse, then—because he's chief mate of a hearse but don't own it—stands a watch for wages, you know. But I can't do a hearse any more than I can a hack; so here we are—becalmed, you see. And it's the same with women and such. They come and they want a little johnry picture—"

"It's the accessories that make it a *genre?*"

"Yes—cannon, or cat, or any little thing like that, that you heave in to whoop up the effect. We could do a prodigious trade with the women if we could foreground the things they like, but they don't give a damn for artillery. Mine's the lack," continued the captain with a sigh, "Andy's end of the business is all right—I tell you *he's* an artist from wayback!"

"Yoost hear dot old man! He always talk 'poud me like dot," purred the pleased German.

"Look at his work yourself! Fourteen portraits in a row. And no two of them alike."

"Now that you speak of it, it is true; I hadn't noticed it before. It is very remarkable. Unique, I suppose."

"I should say so. That's the very *thing* about Andy—he *discriminates*. Discrimination's the thief of time—forty-ninth Psalm; but that ain't any matter, it's the honest thing, and it pays in the end."

"Yes, he certainly is great in that feature, one is obliged to admit it; but—now mind, I'm not really criticising—don't you think he is just a trifle overstrong in technique?"

The captain's face was knocked expressionless by this remark. It remained quite vacant while he muttered to himself—"Technique—technique—polytechnique—pyro-technique; that's it, likely—fireworks—too much color." Then he spoke up with serenity and confidence, and said—

"Well, yes, he does pile it on pretty loud; but they all like it, you know—fact is, it's the life of the business. Take that No. 9, there, Evans the butcher. He drops into the stoodio as sober-colored as anything you ever see: *now* look at him. You can't tell him from scarlet fever. Well, it pleases that butcher to death. I'm making a study of a sausage-wreath to hang on the cannon, and I don't really reckon I can do it right, but if I can, we can break the butcher."

"Unquestionably your confederate—I mean your—your fellowcraftsman—is a great colorist—"

"Oh, danke schön!—"

—"in fact a quite extraordinary colorist; a colorist, I make bold to say, without imitator here or abroad—and with a most bold and effective touch, a touch like a battering ram; and a manner so peculiar and romantic, and extraneous, and ad libitum, and heart-searching, that—that—he—he is an impressionist, I presume?"

"No," said the captain simply, "he is a Presbyterian."

"It accounts for all—all—there's something divine about his art,—soulful, unsatisfactory, yearning, dim-hearkening on the void horizon, vague-murmuring to the spirit out of ultra-marine distances and far-sounding cataclysms of uncreated space—oh, if he—if he—has he ever tried distemper?"

The captain answered up with energy—

"Not if he knows himself! But his dog has, and—"

"Oh, no, it vas not *my* dog."

"Why, you *said* it was your dog."

"Oh, no, Gaptain, I—"

"It was a white dog, wasn't it, with his tail docked, and one ear gone, and—"

"Dot's him, dot's him!—der fery dog. Wy, py Chorge, dot dog he vould eat baint yoost de same like—"

"Well, never mind that, now—'vast heaving—I never saw such a man. You start him on that dog and he'll dispute a year. Blamed if I haven't *seen* him keep it up a level two hours and a half."

"Why Captain!" said Barrow. "I guess that must be hearsay."

"No, sir, no hearsay about it—he disputed with me."

"I don't see how you stood it."

"Oh, you've got to—if you run with Andy. But it's the only fault he's got."

"Ain't you afraid of acquiring it?"

"Oh, no," said the captain, tranquilly, "no danger of that, I reckon."

The artists presently took their leave. Then Barrow put his hands on Tracy's shoulder and said—

"Look me in the eye, my boy. Steady, steady. There—it's just as I thought—hoped, anyway; *you're* all right, thank goodness. Nothing the matter with your mind. But don't do that again—even for fun. It isn't wise. They wouldn't have believed you if you'd *been* an earl's son. Why, they *couldn't*—don't you know that? What ever possessed you to take such a freak? But never mind about that; let's not talk of it. It was a mistake; you see that yourself."

"Yes—it *was* a mistake."

"Well, just drop it out of your mind; it's no harm; we all make them. Pull your courage together, and don't brood, and don't give up. I'm at your back, and we'll pull through, don't you be afraid."

When he was gone, Barrow walked the floor a good while, uneasy in his mind. He said to himself, "I'm troubled about him. He never would have made a break like that if he hadn't been a little off his balance. But I know what being out of work and no prospect ahead can do for a man. First it knocks the pluck out of him and drags his pride in the dirt; worry does the rest, and his mind gets shaky. I must talk to these people. No—if there's any humanity in them—and there is, at bottom—they'll be easier on him if they think his troubles have disturbed his reason. But I've *got* to find him some work; work's the only medicine for disease. Poor devil! away off here, and not a friend."

Chapter 17

THE MOMENT Tracy was alone his spirits vanished away, and all the misery of his situation was manifest to him. To be moneyless and an object of the chairmaker's charity—this was bad enough, but his folly in proclaiming himself an earl's son to that scoffing and unbelieving crew, and, on top of that, the humiliating result—the recollection of these things was a sharper torture still. He made up his mind that he would never play earl's son again before a doubtful audience.

His father's answer was a blow he could not understand. At times he thought his father imagined he could get work to do in America without any trouble, and was minded to let him try it and cure himself of his radicalism by hard, cold, disenchanting experience. That seemed the most plausible theory, yet he could not content himself with it. A theory that pleased him better was, that this cablegram would be followed by another, of a gentler sort, requiring him to come home. Should he write and strike his flag, and ask for a ticket home? Oh, no, that he couldn't *ever* do. At least, not yet. That cablegram would come, it certainly would. So he went from one telegraph office to another every day for nearly a week, and asked if there was a cablegram for Howard Tracy. No, there wasn't any. So they answered him at first. Later, they said it before he had a chance to ask. Later still they merely shook their heads impatiently as soon as he came in sight. After that he was ashamed to go any more.

He was down in the lowest depth of despair, now; for the harder Barrow tried to find work for him the more hopeless the possibilities seemed to grow. At last he said to Barrow—

"Look here. I want to make a confession. I have got down, now, to where I am not only willing to acknowledge to myself that I am a shabby creature and full of false pride, but am willing to acknowledge it to you. Well, I've been allowing you to wear yourself out hunting for work for me when there's been a chance open to me all the time. Forgive my pride—what was left of it. It is all gone, now, and I've come to confess that if those ghastly artists want another confederate, I'm their man—for at last I am dead to shame."

"No? Really, can you paint?"

"Not as badly as *they*. No, I don't claim that, for I am not a genius; in fact, I am a very indifferent amateur, a slouchy dabster, a mere artistic sarcasm; but drunk or asleep I can beat *those* buccaneers."

"Shake! I want to shout! Oh, I tell you, I am immensely delighted and relieved. Oh, just to work—that is life! No matter what the work is—that's of no consequence. Just work itself is bliss when a man's been starving for it. I've *been* there! Come right along, we'll hunt the old boys up. Don't you feel good? I tell you *I* do."

The freebooters were not at home. But their "works" were,—displayed in profusion all about the little ratty studio. Cannon to the right of them, cannon to the left of them, cannon in front—it was Balaclava come again.

"Here's the uncontented hackman, Tracy. Buckle to—deepen the sea-green to turf, turn the ship into a hearse. Let the boys have a taste of your quality.''

The artists arrived just as the last touch was put on. They stood transfixed with admiration.

"My souls but she's a stunner, that hearse! The hackman will just go all to pieces when he sees that—won't he Andy?''

"Oh, it is sphlennid, sphlennid! Herr Tracy, why haf you not said you vas a so sublime aartist? Lob' Gott, of you had lif'd in Paris you would be a Pree de Rome, dot's vot's de matter!''

The arrangements were soon made. Tracy was taken into full and equal partnership, and he went straight to work, with dash and energy, to reconstructing gems of art whose accessories had failed to satisfy. Under his hand, on that and succeeding days, artillery disappeared and the emblems of peace and commerce took its place—cats, hacks, sausages, tugs, fire engines, pianos, guitars, rocks, gardens, flower-pots, landscapes—whatever was wanted, he flung it in; and the more out of place and absurd the required object was, the more joy he got out of fabricating it. The pirates were delighted, the customers applauded, the sex began to flock in, great was the prosperity of the firm. Tracy was obliged to confess to himself that there was something about work,—even such grotesque and humble work as this—which most pleasantly satisfied a something in his nature which had never been satisfied before, and also gave him a strange new dignity in his own private view of himself.

The Unqualified Member from Cherokee Strip was in a state of deep rejection. For a good while, now, he had been leading a sort of life which was calculated to kill; for it had consisted in regularly alternating days of brilliant hope and black disappointment. The brilliant hopes were created by the magician Sellers, and they always promised that *now* he had got the trick, sure, and would effectively influence that materialized cowboy to call at the Towers before night. The black disappointments consisted in the persistent and monotonous failure of these prophecies.

At the date which this history has now reached, Sellers was appalled to find that the usual remedy was inoperative, and that Hawkins's low spirits refused absolutely to lift. Something must be done, he reflected; it was heart-breaking, this woe, this smileless misery, this dull despair that looked out from his poor friend's face. Yes, he must be cheered up. He mused a while, then he saw his way. He said in his most conspicuously casual vein—

"Er-uh—by the way, Hawkins, we are feeling disappointed about this thing—the way the materializee is acting, I mean—we are disappointed; you concede that?''

"Concede it? Why, yes, if you like the term.''

"Very well; so far, so good. Now for the *basis* of the feeling. It is not that your heart, your affections are concerned; that is to say, it is not that you *want* the materializee *Itself*. You concede that?''

"Yes, I concede that, too—cordially.''

"Very well, again; we are making progress. To sum up: The feeling, it is conceded, is not engendered by the mere conduct of the materializee; it is conceded that it does not arise from any pang which the *personality* of the materializee could assuage. Now then,'' said the earl, with the light of triumph in his eye, ''the inexorable logic of the situation narrows us down to this: our feeling has its source in the *money*-loss involved. Come—isn't that so?''

''Goodness knows I concede that, with all my heart.''

''Very well. When you've found out the source of a disease, you've also found out what remedy is required—just as in this case. In this case money is required. And *only* money.''

The old, old seduction was in that airy, confident tone and those significant words—usually called pregnant words in books. The old answering signs of faith and hope showed up in Hawkins's countenance, and he said—

''*Only* money? Do you mean that you know a way to—''

''Washington, have you the impression that I have no resources but those I allow the public and my intimate friends to know about?''

''Well, I—er—''

''Is it *likely*, do you think, that a man moved by nature and taught by experience to keep his affairs to himself and a cautious and reluctant tongue in his head, wouldn't be thoughtful enough to keep a few resources in reserve for a rainy day, when he's got as many as I have to select from?''

''Oh, you make me feel so much better already, Colonel!''

''Have you ever been in my laboratory?''

''Why, no.''

''That's it. You see you didn't even know that I had one. Come along. I've got a little trick there that I want to show you. I've kept it perfectly quiet, not fifty people know anything about it. But that's my way, always been my way. Wait till you're *ready,* that's the idea; and *when* you're ready, *zzip!*—let her go!''

''Well, Colonel, I've never seen a man that I've had such unbounded confidence in as you. When you say a thing right out, I always feel as if that ends it; as if that is evidence, and proof, and everything else.''

The old earl was profoundly pleased and touched.

''I'm glad *you* believe in me, Washington; not everybody is so just.''

''I always have believed in you; and I always shall as long as I live.''

''Thank you, my boy. You shan't repent it. And you *can't.*'' Arrived in the ''laboratory,'' the earl continued, ''Now, cast your eye around this room—what do you see? *Apparently* a junk-shop; *apparently* a hospital connected with a patent office—in *reality,* the mines of Golconda in disguise! Look at that thing there. Now what would you take that thing to be?''

''I don't believe I could ever imagine.''

''Of course you couldn't. It's my grand adaptation of the phonograph to the marine service. You store up profanity in it for use at sea. You know that sailors don't fly around worth a cent unless you swear at them—so the mate that can do the best job of swearing is the most valuable man. In great emergencies his talent saves the ship. But a ship is a large thing, and he can't be everywhere at once; so there have been times when one mate has lost a ship which could have been saved if they had had a hundred. Prodigious storms, you know. Well, a ship can't afford a hundred mates; but she can afford a hundred Cursing Phonographs, and distribute them all over the vessel—and there, you see, she's armed at every point. Imagine a big storm, and a hundred of my machines all cursing away at once—splendid spectacle, splendid!—you couldn't hear yourself think. Ship goes through that storm perfectly serene—she's just as safe as she'd be on shore.''

"It's a wonderful idea. How do you prepare the thing?"

"Load it—simply load it."

"How?"

"Why you just stand over it and swear into it."

"That loads it, does it?"

"Yes—because every word it collars, it *keeps*—keeps it forever. Never wears out. Any time you turn the crank, out it'll come. In times of great peril, you can reverse it, and it'll swear backwards. *That* makes a sailor hump himself!''

"O, I see. Who loads them!—the mate?"

"Yes, if he chooses. Or I'll furnish them already loaded. I can hire an expert for $75 a month who will load a hundred and fifty phonographs in 150 hours, and do it *easy*. And an expert can furnish a stronger article, of course, than the mere average uncultivated mate could. Then you see, all the ships of the world will buy them ready loaded—for I shall have them loaded in any language a customer wants. Hawkins, it will work the grandest moral reform of the 19th century. Five years from now, *all* the swearing will be done by machinery—you won't ever hear a profane word come from human lips on a ship. Millions of dollars have been spent by the churches, in the effort to abolish profanity in the commercial marine. Think of it—my name will live forever in the affections of good men as the man, who, solitary and alone, accomplished this noble and elevating reform.''

"O, it *is* grand and beneficent and beautiful. How *did* you ever come to think of it? You have a wonderful mind. How did you say you loaded the machine?"

"O, it's no trouble—perfectly simple. If you want to load it up loud and strong, you stand right over it and shout. But if you leave it open and all set, it'll *eavesdrop*, so to speak—that is to say, it will load itself up with any sounds that are made within six feet of it. Now I'll show you how it works. I had an expert come and load this one up yesterday. Hello, it's been left open—it's too bad—still I reckon it hasn't had much chance to collect irrelevant stuff. All you do is to press this button in the floor—so.''

The phonograph began to sing in a plaintive voice:

> There is a boarding-house, far far away,
> Where they have ham and eggs, 3 times a day.

"Hang it, *that* ain't it. Somebody's been singing around here."

The plaintive song began again, mingled with a low, gradually rising wail of cats slowly warming up toward a fight;

O, *how* the boarders yell,
When they hear that dinner bell—
They give that landlord—

(momentary outburst of terrific catfight which drowns out one word.)

Three times a day.

(Renewal of furious catfight for a moment. The plaintive voice on a high fierce key, "*Scat,* you devils''—and a racket as of flying missiles.)

"Well, never mind—let it go. I've got some sailor-profanity down in there somewhere, if I could get to it. But it isn't any matter; you see how the machine works."

Hawkins responded with enthusiasm—

"O, it works admirably! I know there's a hundred fortunes in it."

"And mind, the Hawkins family get their share, Washington."

"O, thanks, thanks; you are just as generous as ever. Ah, it's the grandest invention of the age!"

"Ah, well, we live in wonderful times. The elements are crowded *full* of beneficent forces—always *have* been—and ours is the first generation to turn them to account and make them work for us. Why Hawkins, *everything* is useful—*nothing* ought ever to be wasted. Now look at sewer-gas, for instance. Sewer-gas has always been wasted, heretofore; nobody tried to save up sewer-gas—you can't name me a man. Ain't that so? *you* know perfectly well it's so."

"Yes it is so—but I never—er—I don't quite see why a body—"

"Should *want* to save it up? Well, I'll tell you. Do you see this little invention here?—it's a decomposer—I call it a decomposer. I give you my word of honor that if you show me a house that produces a given quantity of sewer-gas in a day, I'll engage to set up my decomposer there and make that house produce a hundred times that quantity of sewer-gas in less than half an hour."

"Dear me, but why should you want to?"

"*Want* to? Listen, and you'll see. My boy, for illuminating purposes and economy combined, there's nothing in the world that begins with sewer-gas. And really, it don't cost a cent. You put in a good inferior article of plumbing,—such as you find everywhere—and add my decomposer, and there you are. Just use the ordinary gas pipes—and there your expense ends. Think of it. Why, Major, in five years from now you won't see a house lighted with anything but sewer-gas. Every physician I talk to, recommends it; and every plumber."

"But isn't it dangerous?"

"O, yes, more or less, but everything is—coal gas, candles, electricity—there isn't anything that ain't."

"It lights up well, does it?"

"O, magnificently."

"Have you given it a good trial?"

"Well, no, not a first rate one. Polly's prejudiced, and she won't let me put it in here; but I'm playing my cards to get it adopted in the President's house, and *then* it'll go—don't you doubt it. I shall not need this one for the present, Washington; you may take it down to some boarding-house and give it a trial if you like.''

Chapter 18

WASHINGTON SHUDDERED slightly at the suggestion, then his face took on a dreamy look and he dropped into a trance of thought. After a little, Sellers asked him what he was grinding in his mental mill.

"Well, this. Have you got some secret project in your head which requires a Bank of England back of it to make it succeed?''

The Colonel showed lively astonishment, and said—

"Why, Hawkins, are you a mind-reader?''

"I? I never thought of such a thing.''

"Well, then how did you happen to drop onto that idea in this curious fashion? It's just mind-reading,—that's what it is, though you may not know it. Because I *have* got a private project that requires a Bank of England at its back. How could you divine that? What was the process? This is interesting.''

"There wasn't any process. A thought like this happened to slip through my head by accident: How much would make you or me comfortable? A hundred thousand. Yet you are expecting two or three of these inventions of yours to turn out some billions of money—and you are *wanting* them to do that. If you wanted ten millions, I could understand that—it's inside the human limits. But billions! That's clear outside the limits. There must be a definite project back of that somewhere.''

The earl's interest and surprise augmented with every word, and when Hawkins finished, he said with strong admiration—

"It's wonderfully reasoned out, Washington, it certainly is. It shows what I think is quite extraordinary penetration. For you've hit it; you've driven the center, you've plugged the bulls-eye of my dream. Now I'll tell you the whole thing, and you'll understand it. I don't need to ask you to keep it to yourself, because you'll see that the project will prosper all the better for being kept in the background till the right time. Have you noticed how many pamphlets and books I've got lying around relating to Russia?''

"Yes, I think most anybody would notice that—anybody who wasn't dead.''

"Well, I've been posting myself a good while. That's a great and splendid nation, and deserves to be set free.'' He paused, then added in a quite matter-of-fact way, "When I get this money I'm going to set it free.''

"Great guns!''

"Why, what makes you jump like that?''

"Dear me, when you are going to drop a remark under a man's chair that is likely to blow him out through the roof, why don't you put some expression, some force, some noise into it that will prepare him? You shouldn't flip out such a gigantic thing as this in that colorless kind of a way. You do jolt a person up, so. Go on, now, I'm all right again. Tell me all about it. I'm all interest—yes, and sympathy, too."

"Well, I've looked the ground over, and concluded that the methods of the Russian patriots, while good enough considering the way the boys are hampered, are not the best; at least not the quickest. They are trying to revolutionize Russia from *within;* that's pretty slow, you know, and liable to interruption all the time, and is full of perils for the workers. Do you know how Peter the Great started his army? He didn't start it on the family premises under the noses of the Strelitzes; no, he started it away off yonder, privately,—only just one regiment, you know, and he built to *that.* The first thing the Strelitzes knew, the regiment was an *army,* their position was turned, and they had to take a walk. Just that little idea *made* the biggest and worst of all the despotisms the world has seen. The same idea can *un*make it. I'm going to prove it. I'm going to get out to one side and work my scheme the way Peter did."

"This is mighty interesting, Rossmore. What is it you are going to do?"

"I am going to buy Siberia and start a republic."

"There,—bang you go again, without giving any notice! Going to *buy* it?"

"Yes, as soon as I get the money. I don't care what the price is, I shall take it. I can afford it, and I will. Now then, consider this—and you've never thought of it, I'll warrant. Where is the place where there is twenty-five times more manhood, pluck, true heroism, unselfishness, devotion to high and noble ideals, adoration of liberty, wide education, and *brains,* per thousand of population, than any other domain in the whole world can show?"

"Siberia!"

"Right."

"It is true; it certainly is true, but I never thought of it before."

"Nobody ever thinks of it. But it's so, just the same. In those mines and prisons are gathered together the very finest and noblest and capablest multitude of human beings that God is able to create. Now if you had that kind of a population to sell, would you offer it to a despotism? No, the despotism has no use for it; you would lose money. A despotism has no use for anything but human cattle. But suppose you want to start a republic?"

"Yes, I see. It's just the material for it."

"Well, I should say so! There's Siberia with just the very finest and choicest material on the globe for a republic, and more coming—more coming all the time, don't you see! It is being daily, weekly, monthly recruited by the most perfectly devised system that has ever been invented, perhaps. By this system the whole of the hundred millions of Russia are being constantly and patiently sifted, sifted, sifted, by myriads of trained experts, spies appointed by the Emperor personally; and whenever they catch a man, woman or child that has got any brains or education or character, they ship that person straight to Siberia. It is admirable, it is wonderful. It is so searching and so effective that it keeps the general level of Russian intellect and education down to that of the Czar."

"Come, that sounds like exaggeration."

"Well, it's what they say anyway. But I think, myself, it's a lie. And it doesn't seem right to slander a whole nation that way, anyhow. Now, then, you see what the material is, there in Siberia, for a republic." He paused, and his breast began to heave and his eye to burn, under the impulse of strong emotion. Then his words began to stream forth, with constantly increasing energy and fire, and he rose to his feet as if to give himself larger freedom. "The minute I organize that republic, the light of liberty, intelligence, justice, humanity, bursting from it, flooding from it, flaming from it, will concentrate the gaze of the whole astonished world as upon the miracle of a new sun; Russia's countless multitudes of slaves will rise up and march, march!—eastward, with that great light transfiguring their faces as they come, and far back of them you will see—what will you see?—a vacant throne in an empty land! It can be done, and by God I will do it!"

He stood a moment bereft of earthy consciousness by his exaltation; then consciousness returned, bringing him a slight shock, and he said, with grave earnestness—

"I must ask you to pardon me, Major Hawkins. I have never used that expression before, and I beg you will forgive it this time."

Hawkins was quite willing.

"You see, Washington, it is an error which I am by nature not liable to. Only excitable people, impulsive people, are exposed to it. But the circumstances of the present case—I being a democrat by birth and preference, and an aristocrat by inheritance and relish—"

The earl stopped suddenly, his frame stiffened, and he began to stare speechless through the curtainless window. Then he pointed, and gasped out a single rapturous word—

"Look!"

"What *is* it, Colonel?"

"*It!*"

"No!"

EASTWARD WITH THAT GREAT LIGHT TRANSFIGURING THEIR FACES.

"Sure as you're born. Keep perfectly still. I'll apply the influence—I'll turn on all my force. I've brought It thus far—I'll fetch It right into the house. You'll see."

He was making all sorts of passes in the air with his hands.

"There! Look at that. I've made It smile! See?"

Quite true. Tracy, out for an afternoon stroll, had come unexpectantly upon his family arms displayed upon this shabby house-front. The hatchments made him smile; which was nothing, they had made the neighborhood cats do that.

"Look, Hawkins, look! I'm drawing It over!"

"You're drawing it sure, Rossmore. If I ever had any doubts about materialization, they're gone, now, and gone for good. Oh, this is a joyful day!"

Tracy was sauntering over to read the door-plate. Before he was half way over he was saying to himself, "Why, manifestly these are the American Claimant's quarters."

"It's coming—coming right along. I'll slide down and pull It in. You follow after me."

Sellers, pale and a good deal agitated, opened the door and confronted Tracy. The old man could not at once get his voice: then he pumped out a scattering and hardly coherent salutation, and followed it with—

"Walk in, walk right in, Mr.—er—"

"Tracy—Howard Tracy."

—"Tracy—thanks—walk right in, you're expected."

Tracy entered, considerably puzzled, and said—

"Expected? I think there must be some mistake."

"Oh, I judge not," said Sellers, who noticing that Hawkins had arrived, gave him a sidewise glance intended to call his close attention to a dramatic effect which he was proposing to produce by his next remark. Then he said, slowly and impressively—"I am—*You Know Who.*"

To the astonishment of both conspirators the remark produced no dramatic effect at all; for the new comer responded with a quite innocent and unembarrassed air—

"No, pardon me. I don't *know* who you are. I only suppose—but no doubt correctly—that you are the gentleman whose title is on the doorplate."

"Right, quite right—sit down, pray sit down." The earl was rattled, thrown off his bearings, his head was in a whirl. Then he noticed Hawkins standing apart and staring idiotically at what to him was the apparition of a defunct man, and a new idea was born to him. He said to Tracy briskly—

"But a thousand pardons, dear sir, I am forgetting courtesies due to a guest and stranger. Let me introduce my friend General Hawkins—General Hawkins, our new Senator—Senator from the latest and grandest addition to the radiant galaxy of sovereign States, Cherokee Strip"—(to himself, "that name will shrivel him up!"—but it didn't, in the least, and the Colonel resumed the introduction piteously disheartened and amazed),—"Senator Hawkins, Mr. Howard Tracy, of—er—"

"England."

"England!—Why that's im—"

"England, yes, native of England."

"Recently from there?"

"Yes, quite recently."

Said the Colonel to himself, "This phantom lies like an expert. Purifying this kind by fire don't work. I'll sound him a little further, give him another chance or two to work his gift." Then aloud—with deep irony—

"Visiting our great country for recreation and amusement, no doubt. I suppose you find that traveling in the majestic expanses of our Far West is—"

"I haven't been West, and haven't been devoting myself to amusement with any sort of exclusiveness, I assure you. In fact, to merely live, an artist has got to work, not play."

"Artist!" said Hawkins to himself, thinking of the rifled bank; "that *is* a name for it!"

"Are *you* an artist?" asked the Colonel; and added to himself, "*now* I'm going to catch him."

"In a humble way, yes."

"What line?" pursued the sly veteran.

"Oils."

"I've got him!" said Sellers to himself. Then aloud, "This is fortunate. Could I engage you to restore some of my paintings that need that attention?"

"I shall be very glad. Pray let me see them."

No shuffling, no evasion, no embarrassment, even under this crucial test. The Colonel was nonplussed. He led Tracy to a chromo which had suffered damage in a former owner's hands through being used as a lamp mat, and said, with a flourish of his hand toward the picture—

"This del Sarto—"

"Is *that* a del Sarto?"

The Colonel bent a look of reproach upon Tracy, allowed it to sink home, then resumed as if there had been no interruption—

"This del Sarto is perhaps the only original of that sublime master in our country. You see, yourself, that the work is of such exceeding delicacy that the risk—could—er—would you mind giving me a little example of what you can do before we—"

"Cheerfully, cheerfully. I will copy one of these marvels."

Water-color materials—relics of Miss Sally's college life—were brought. Tracy said he was better in oils, but would take a chance with these. So he was left alone. He began his work, but the attractions of the place were too strong for him, and he got up and went drifting about, fascinated; also amazed.

Chapter 19

MEANTIME THE earl and Hawkins were holding a troubled and anxious private consultation. The earl said—

"The mystery that bothers me, is, where did It get its other arm?"

"Yes—it worries me, too. And another thing troubles me—that apparition is English. How do you account for that, Colonel?''

"Honestly, I don't know, Hawkins, I don't really know. It is very confusing and awful.''

"Don't you think maybe we've waked up the wrong one?''

"The wrong one? How do you account for the clothes?''

"The clothes *are* right, there's no getting around it. What are we going to do? We can't collect, as I see. The reward is for a one-armed American. This is a two-armed Englishman.''

"Well, it may be that that is not objectionable. You see it isn't *less* than is called for, it is *more,* and so,—''

But he saw that this argument was weak, and dropped it. The friends sat brooding over their perplexities some time in silence. Finally the earl's face began to glow with an inspiration, and he said, impressively:

"Hawkins, this materialization is a grander and nobler science than we have dreamed of. We have little imagined what a solemn and stupendous thing we have done. The whole secret is perfectly clear to me, now, clear as day. *Every man is made up of heredities,* long-descended atoms and particles of his ancestors. This present materialization is incomplete. We have only brought it down to perhaps the beginning of this century.''

"What do you mean, Colonel!'' cried Hawkins, filled with vague alarms by the old man's awe-compelling words and manner.

"This. We've materialized this burglar's ancestor!''

"Oh, don't—don't say that. It's hideous.''

"But it's true, Hawkins, I *know* it. Look at the facts. This apparition is distinctly English—note that. It uses good grammar—note that. It is an Artist—note that. It has the manners and carriage of a gentleman—note that. Where's your cow-boy? Answer me that.''

"Rossmore, this is dreadful—it's too dreadful to think of!''

"Never resurrected a rag of that burglar but the clothes, not a solitary rag of him but the clothes.''

"Colonel, do you really mean—''

The Colonel brought his fist down with emphasis and said—

"I mean exactly this. The materialization was immature, the burglar has evaded us, this is nothing but a damned ancestor!''

He rose and walked the floor in great excitement. Hawkins said plaintively—

"It's a bitter disappointment—bitter.''

"I know it. I know it, Senator; I feel it as deeply as anybody could. But we've got to submit—on moral grounds. I need money, but God knows I am not poor enough or shabby enough to be an accessory to the punishing of a man's ancestor for crimes committed by that ancestor's posterity.''

"But Colonel!'' implored Hawkins; "stop and think; don't be rash; you know it's the *only* chance we've got to get the money; and besides, the Bible itself says posterity to the fourth generation shall be punished for the sins and crimes committed by ancestors four generations back that hadn't anything to do with them; and so it's only fair to turn the rule around and make it work both ways.''

The Colonel was struck with the strong logic of this position. He strode up and down, and thought it painfully over. Finally he said:

"There's reason in it; yes, there's reason in it. And so, although it

seems a piteous thing to sweat this poor ancient devil for a burglary he
hadn't the least hand in, still if duty commands I suppose we must give
him up to the authorities."

"*I* would," said Hawkins, cheered and relieved, "I'd give him up if he
was a thousand ancestors compacted into one."

"Lord bless me, that's just what he is," said Sellers, with something
like a groan, "it's exactly what he is; there's a contribution in him from
every ancestor he ever had. In him there's atoms of priests, soldiers,
crusaders, poets, and sweet and gracious women—all kinds and conditions of folk who trod this earth in old, old centuries, and vanished out of
it ages ago, and now by act of ours they are summoned from their holy
peace to answer for gutting a one-horse bank away out on the borders of
Cherokee Strip, and it's just a howling outrage!"

"Oh, don't talk like that, Colonel; it takes the heart all out of me, and
makes me ashamed of the part I am proposing to—"

"Wait—I've got it!"

"A saving hope? Shout it out, I am perishing."

"It's perfectly simple; a child would have thought of it. He is all right,
not a flaw in him, as far as I have carried the work. If I've been able to
bring him as far as the beginning of this century, what's to stop me now?
I'll go on and materialize him down to date."

"Land, I never thought of that!" said Hawkins all ablaze with joy
again. "It's the very thing. What a brain you have got! And will he shed
the superfluous arm?"

"He will."

"And lose his English accent?"

"It will wholly disappear. He will speak Cherokee Strip—and other
forms of profanity."

"Colonel, maybe he'll confess!"

"Confess? Merely that bank robbery?"

"Merely? Yes, but why 'merely'?"

The Colonel said in his most impressive manner:

"Hawkins, he will be wholly under my command. I will make him
confess every crime he ever committed. There must be a thousand. Do
you get the idea?"

"Well—not quite."

"The rewards will come to us."

"Prodigious conception! I *never* saw such a head for seeing with a
lightning glance all the outlying ramifications and possibilities of a central
idea."

"It is nothing; it comes natural to me. When his time is out in one jail
he goes to the next and the next, and we shall have nothing to do but
collect the rewards as he goes along. It is a perfectly steady income as
long as we live, Hawkins. And much better than other kinds of invest-
ments, because he is indestructible."

"It looks—it really does look the way you say; it does indeed."

"Look?—why it *is*. It will not be denied that I have had a pretty wide
and comprehensive financial experience, and I do not hesitate to say that
I consider this one of the most valuable properties I have ever controlled."

"Do you really think so?"

"I do, indeed."

"O, Colonel, the wasting grind and grief of poverty! If we could realize immediately. I don't mean sell it all, but sell part—enough, you know, to—"

"See how you tremble with excitement. That comes of lack of experience. My boy, when you have been familiar with vast operations as long as I have, you'll be different. Look at me; is my eye dilated? do you notice a quiver anywhere? Feel my pulse: plunk—plunk—plunk—same as if I were asleep. And yet, what is passing through my calm cold mind? A procession of figures which would make a financial novice drunk—just the sight of them. Now it is by keeping cool, and looking at a thing all around, that a man sees what's really in it, and saves himself from the novice's unfailing mistake—the one you've just suggested—eagerness to *realize*. Listen to me. Your idea is to sell a part of him for ready cash. Now mine is—guess."

"I haven't an idea. What is it?"

"Stock him—of course."

"Well, I should never have thought of that."

"Because you are not a financier. Say he has committed a thousand crimes. Certainly that's a low estimate. By the look of him, even in his unfinished condition, he has committed all of a million. But call it only a thousand to be perfectly safe; five thousand reward, multiplied by a thousand, gives us a dead sure cash basis of—what? Five million dollars!"

"Wait—let me get my breath."

"And the property indestructible. Perpetually fruitful—perpetually; for a property with his disposition will go on committing crimes and winning rewards."

"You daze me, you make my head whirl!"

"Let it whirl, it won't do it any harm. Now that matter is all fixed—leave it alone. I'll get up the company and issue the stock, all in good time. Just leave it in my hands. I judge you don't doubt my ability to work it up for all it is worth."

"Indeed I don't. I can say that with truth."

"All right, then. That's disposed of. Everything in its turn. We old operators go by order and system—no helter-skelter business with us. What's the next thing on the docket? The carrying on of the materialization—the bringing it down to date. I will begin on that at once. I think—"

"Look here, Rossmore. You didn't lock It in. A hundred to one it has escaped!"

"Calm yourself, as to that; don't give yourself any uneasiness."

"But why shouldn't it escape?"

"Let it, if it wants to? What of it?"

"Well, *I* should consider it a pretty serious calamity."

"Why, my dear boy, once in my power, always in my power. It may go and come freely. I can produce it here whenever I want it, just by the exercise of my will."

"Well, I am truly glad to hear that, I do assure you."

"Yes, I shall give it all the painting it wants to do, and we and the family will make it as comfortable and contented as we can. No occasion to restrain its movements. I hope to persuade it to remain pretty quiet, though, because a materialization which is in a state of arrested development must of necessity be pretty soft and flabby and substanceless, and—er—by the way, I wonder where It comes from?''

"How? What do you mean?''

The earl pointed significantly—and interrogatively—toward the sky. Hawkins started; then settled into deep reflection; finally shook his head sorrowfully and pointed downwards.

"What makes you think so, Washington?''

"Well, I hardly know, but really you can see, yourself, that he doesn't seem to be pining for his last place.''

"It's well thought! Soundly deduced. We've done that Thing a favor. But I believe I will pump it a little, in a quiet way, and find out if we are right.''

"How long is it going to take to finish him off and fetch him down to date, Colonel?''

"I wish I knew, but I don't. I am clear knocked out by this new detail—this unforeseen necessity of working a subject down gradually from his condition of ancestor to his ultimate result as posterity. But I'll make him hump himself, anyway.''

"Rossmore!''

"Yes, dear. We're in the laboratory. Come—Hawkins is here. Mind, now Hawkins—he's a sound, living, *human being* to all the family—*don't* forget that. Here she comes.''

"Keep your seats, I'm not coming in. I just wanted to ask, who is it that's painting down there?''

"That? Oh, that's a young artist; young Englishman, named Tracy; very promising—favorite pupil of Hans Christian Andersen or one of the other old masters—Andersen I'm pretty sure it is; he's going to half-sole some of our old Italian masterpieces. Been talking to him?''

"Well, only a word. I stumbled right in on him without expecting anybody was there. I tried to be polite to him; offered him a snack''—(Sellers delivered a large wink to Hawkins from behind his hand), "but he declined, and said he wasn't hungry'' (another sarcastic wink); "so I brought some apples'' (double wink), "and he ate a couple of—''

"What!'' and the Colonel sprang some yards toward the ceiling and came down quaking with astonishment.

Lady Rossmore was smitten dumb with amazement. She gazed at the sheepish relic of Cherokee Strip, then at her husband, and then at the guest again. Finally she said—

"What is the matter with you, Mulberry?''

He did not answer immediately. His back was turned; he was bending over his chair, feeling the seat of it. But he answered next moment, and said—

"Ah, there it is; it was a tack.''

The lady contemplated him doubtfully a moment, then said, pretty snappishly—

"All that for a tack! Praise goodness it wasn't a shingle nail, it would have landed you in the Milky Way. I do hate to have my nerves shook up so.'' And she turned on her heel and went her way.

As soon as she was safely out, the Colonel said, in a suppressed voice—
"Come—we must see for ourselves. It *must* be a mistake."

They hurried softly down and peeped in. Sellers whispered, in a sort of despair—

"It *is* eating! What a grisly spectacle! Hawkins it's horrible! Take me away—I can't stand it."

They tottered back to the laboratory.

Chapter 20

TRACY MADE slow progress with his work, for his mind wandered a good deal. Many things were puzzling him. Finally a light burst upon him all of a sudden—seemed to, at any rate—and he said to himself, "I've got the clew at last—this man's mind is off its balance; I don't know how much, but it's off a point or two, sure; off enough to explain this mess of perplexities, anyway. These dreadful chromos—which he takes for old masters; these villainous portraits—which to his frantic mind represent Rossmores; the hatchments; the pompous name of this ramshackle old crib—Rossmore Towers; and that odd assertion of his, that I was expected. How could I be expected? that is, Lord Berkeley. He knows by the papers that that person was burned up in the New Gadsby. Why, hang it, he really doesn't know *who* he was expecting; for his talk showed that he was not expecting an Englishman, or yet an artist, yet I answer his requirements notwithstanding. He seems sufficiently satisfied with me. Yes, he is a little off; in fact I am afraid he is a good deal off, poor old gentleman. But he's interesting—all people in about his condition are, I suppose. I hope he'll like my work; I would like to come every day and study him. And when I write my father—ah, that hurts! I mustn't get on that subject; it isn't good for my spirits. Somebody coming—I must get to work. It's the old gentleman again. He looks bothered. Maybe my clothes are suspicious; and they are—for an artist. If my conscience would allow me to make a change,—but that is out of the question. I wonder what he's making those passes in the air for, with his hands. I seem to be the object of them. Can he be trying to mesmerize me? I don't quite like it. There's something uncanny about it."

The Colonel muttered to himself, "It has an effect on him, I can see it myself. That's enough for one time, I reckon. He's not very solid, yet, I suppose, and I might disintegrate him. I'll just put a sly question or two at him, now, and see if I can find out what his condition is, and where he's from."

He approached and said affably—

"Don't let me disturb you, Mr. Tracy; I only want to take a little glimpse of your work. Ah, that's fine—that's very fine indeed. You are doing it elegantly. My daughter will be charmed with this. May I sit down by you?"

"Oh, do; I shall be glad."

"It won't disturb you? I mean, won't dissipate your inspirations?"

Tracy laughed and said they were not ethereal enough to be very easily discommoded.

The Colonel asked a number of cautious and well-considered questions—questions which seemed pretty odd and flighty to Tracy—but the answers conveyed the information desired, apparently, for the Colonel said to himself, with mixed pride and gratification—

"It's a good job as far as I've got with it. He's solid. Solid and going to last; solid as the real thing. It's wonderful—wonderful. I believe I could petrify him."

After a little he asked, warily:

"Do you prefer being here, or—or there?"

"There? Where?"

"Why—er—where you've been?"

Tracy's thought flew to his boarding-house, and he answered with decision—

"Oh, *here,* much!"

The Colonel was startled, and said to himself, "There's no uncertain ring about that. It indicates where *he's* been to, poor fellow. Well, I am satisfied, now. I'm glad I got him out."

He sat thinking, and thinking, and watching the brush go. At length he said to himself, "Yes, it certainly seems to account for the failure of my endeavors in poor Berkeley's case. *He* went in the other direction. Well, it's all right. He's better off."

Sally Sellers entered from the street, now, looking her divinest, and the artist was introduced to her. It was a violent case of mutual love at first sight, though neither party was entirely aware of the fact, perhaps. The Englishman made this irrelevant remark to himself, "Perhaps he is not insane, after all." Sally sat down, and showed an interest in Tracy's work which greatly pleased him, and a benevolent forgiveness of it which convinced him that the girl's nature was cast in a large mold. Sellers was anxious to report his discoveries to Hawkins; so he took his leave, saying that if the two "young devotees of the colored Muse" thought they could manage without him, he would go and look after his affairs. The artist

IT WAS A VIOLENT CASE OF MUTUAL LOVE AT FIRST SIGHT.

said to himself, "I think he *is* a little eccentric, perhaps, but that is all."
He reproached himself for having injuriously judged a man without giving
him any fair chance to show what he really was.

Of course the stranger was very soon at his ease and chatting along
comfortably. The average American girl possesses the valuable qualities
of naturalness, honesty, and inoffensive straightforwardness; she is nearly
barren of troublesome conventions and artificialities, consequently her
presence and her ways are unembarrassing, and one is acquainted with
her and on the pleasantest terms with her before he knows how it came
about. This new acquaintanceship—friendship, indeed—progressed swiftly;
and the unusual swiftness of it, and the thoroughness of it are sufficiently
evidenced and established by one noteworthy fact—that within the first
half hour both parties had ceased to be conscious of Tracy's clothes. Later
this consciousness was re-awakened; it was then apparent to Gwendolen
that she was almost reconciled to them, and it was apparent to Tracy that
he wasn't. The re-awakening was brought about by Gwendolen's inviting
the artist to stay to dinner. He had to decline, because he wanted to live,
now—that is, now that there was something to live for—and he could not
survive in those clothes at a gentleman's table. He thought he knew that.
But he went away happy, for he saw that Gwendolen was disappointed.

And whither did he go? He went straight to a slopshop and bought as
neat and reasonably well-fitting a suit of clothes as an Englishman could
be persuaded to wear. He said—*to* himself, but *at* his conscience—"I
know it's wrong; but it would be wrong *not* to do it; and two wrongs do
not make a right."

This satisfied him, and made his heart light. Perhaps it will also satisfy
the reader—if he can make out what it means.

The old people were troubled about Gwendolen at dinner, because she
was so distraught and silent. If they had noticed, they would have found
that she was sufficiently alert and interested whenever the talk stumbled
upon the artist and his work; but they didn't notice, and so the chat would
swap around to some other subject, and then somebody would presently
be privately worrying about Gwendolen again, and wondering if she were
not well, of if something had gone wrong in the millinery line. Her mother
offered her various reputable patent medicines, and tonics with iron and
other hardware in them, and her father even proposed to send out for
wine, relentless prohibitionist and head of the order in the District of
Columbia as he was, but these kindnesses were all declined—thankfully,
but with decision. At bedtime, when the family were breaking up for the
night, she privately looted one of the brushes, saying to herself, "It's the
one he has used the most."

The next morning Tracy went forth wearing his new suit, and equipped
with a pink in his button-hole—a daily attention from Puss. His whole
soul was full of Gwendolen Sellers, and this condition was an inspiration,
art-wise. All the morning his brush pawed nimbly away at the canvases,
almost without his awarity—awarity, in this sense being the sense of being
aware, though disputed by some authorities—turning out marvel upon
marvel, in the way of decorative accessories to the portraits, with a felicity
and celerity which amazed the veterans of the firm and fetched out of
them continuous explosions of applause.

Meantime Gwendolen was losing her morning, and many dollars. She supposed Tracy was coming in the forenoon—a conclusion which she had jumped to without outside help. So she tripped downstairs every little while from her work-parlor to arrange the brushes and things over again, and see if he had arrived. And when she was in her work-parlor it was not profitable, but just the other way—as she found out to her sorrow. She had put in her idle moments during the last little while back, in designing a particularly rare and capable gown for herself, and this morning she set about making it up; but she was absent minded, and made an irremediable botch of it. When she saw what she had done, she knew the reason of it and the meaning of it; and she put her work away from her and said she would accept the sign. And from that time forth she came no more away from the Audience Chamber, but remained there and waited. After luncheon she waited again. A whole hour. Then a great joy welled up in her heart, for she saw him coming. So she flew back upstairs thankful, and could hardly wait for him to miss the principal brush, which she had mislaid down there, but knew where she had mislaid it. However, all in good time the others were called in and couldn't find the brush, and then she was sent for, and she couldn't find it herself for some little time; but then she found it when the others had gone away to hunt in the kitchen and down cellar and in the woodshed, and all those other places where people look for things whose ways they are not familiar with. So she gave him the brush, and remarked that she ought to have seen that everything was ready for him, but it hadn't seemed necessary, because it was so early that she wasn't expecting—but she stopped there, surprised at herself for what she was saying; and he felt caught and ashamed, and said to himself, "I knew my impatience would drag me here before I was expected, and betray me, and that is just what it has done; she sees straight through me—and is laughing at me, inside, of course."

Gwendolen was very much pleased, on one account, and a little the other way in another; pleased with the new clothes and the improvement which they had achieved; less pleased by the pink in the buttonhole. Yesterday's pink had hardly interested her; this one was just like it, but somehow it had got her immediate attention, and kept it. She wished she could think of some way of getting at its history in a properly colorless and indifferent way. Presently she made a venture. She said—

"Whatever a man's age may be, he can reduce it several years by putting a bright-colored flower in his button-hole. I have often noticed that. Is that your sex's reason for wearing a boutonnière?"

"I fancy not, but certainly that reason would be a sufficient one. I've never heard of the idea before."

"You seem to prefer pinks. Is it on account of the color, or the form?"

"Oh no," he said, simply, "they are given to me. I don't think I have any preference."

"They are given to him," she said to herself, and she felt a coldness toward that pink. "I wonder who it is, and what she is like." The flower began to take up a good deal of room; it obtruded itself everywhere, it intercepted all views, and marred them; it was becoming exceedingly annoying and conspicuous for a little thing. "I wonder if he cares for her." That thought gave her a quite definite pain.

Chapter 21

SHE HAD made everything comfortable for the artist; there was no further pretext for staying. So she said she would go, now, and asked him to summon the servants in case he should need anything. She went away unhappy; and she left unhappiness behind her; for she carried away all the sunshine. The time dragged heavily for both, now. He couldn't paint for thinking of her; she couldn't design or millinerize with any heart, for thinking of him. Never before had painting seemed so empty to him, never before had millinerizing seemed so void of interest to her. She had gone without repeating that dinner-invitation—an almost unendurable disappointment to him. On her part—well, she was suffering, too; for she had found she *couldn't* invite him. It was not hard yesterday, but it was impossible to-day. A thousand innocent privileges seemed to have been filched from her unawares in the past twenty-four hours. To-day she felt strangely hampered, restrained of her liberty. To-day she couldn't propose to herself to do anything or say anything concerning this young man without being instantly paralyzed into non-action by the fear that he might "suspect." Invite him to dinner *to-day?* It made her shiver to think of it.

And so her afternoon was one long fret. Broken at intervals. Three times she had to go downstairs on errands—that is, she thought she had to go downstairs on errands. Thus, going and coming, she had six glimpses of him, in the aggregate, without seeming to look in his direction; and she tried to endure these electric ecstasies without showing any sign, but they fluttered her up a good deal, and she felt that the naturalness she was putting on was overdone and quite too frantically sober and hysterically calm to deceive.

The painter had his share of the rapture; he had his six glimpses, and they smote him with waves of pleasure that assaulted him, beat upon him, washed over him deliciously, and drowned out all consciousness of what he was doing with his brush. So there were six places in his canvas which had to be done over again.

TIME DRAGGED HEAVILY FOR BOTH NOW.

At last Gwendolen got some peace of mind by sending word to the Thompsons, in the neighborhood, that she was coming there to dinner. She wouldn't be reminded, at *that* table, that there was an absentee who ought to be a presentee—a word which she meant to look out in the dictionary at a calmer time.

About this time the old earl dropped in for a chat with the artist, and invited him to stay to dinner. Tracy cramped down his joy and gratitude by a sudden and powerful exercise of all his forces; and he felt that now that he was going to be close to Gwendolen, and hear her voice and watch her face during several precious hours, earth had nothing valuable to add to his life for the present.

The earl said to himself, "This specter can eat apples, apparently. We shall find out, now, if that is a specialty. I think, myself, it's a specialty. Apples, without doubt, constitute the spectral limit. It was the case with our first parents. No, I am wrong—at least only partly right. The line *was* drawn at apples, just as in the present case, but it was from the other direction." The new clothes gave him a thrill of pleasure and pride. He said to himself, "I've got part of him down to date, anyway."

Sellers said he was pleased with Tracy's work; and he went on and engaged him to restore his old masters, and said he should also want him to paint his portrait and his wife's and possibly his daughter's. The tide of the artist's happiness was at flood, now. The chat flowed pleasantly along while Tracy painted and Sellers carefully unpacked a picture which he had brought with him. It was a chromo; a new one, just out. It was the smirking, self-satisfied portrait of a man who was inundating the Union with advertisements inviting everybody to buy his specialty, which was a three-dollar shoe or a dress-suit or something of that kind. The old gentleman rested the chromo flat upon his lap and gazed down tenderly upon it, and became silent and meditative. Presently Tracy noticed that he was dripping tears on it. This touched the young fellow's sympathetic nature, and at the same time gave him the painful sense of being an intruder upon a sacred privacy, an observer of emotions which a stranger ought not to witness. But his pity rose superior to other considerations, and compelled him to try to comfort the old mourner with kindly words and a show of friendly interest. He said—

"I am very sorry—is it a friend whom—"

"Ah, more than that, far more than that—a relative, the dearest I had on earth, although I was never permitted to see him. Yes, it is young Lord Berkeley, who perished so heroically in the awful confla—why, what is the matter?"

"Oh, nothing, nothing. It was a little startling to be so suddenly brought face to face, so to speak, with a person one has heard so much talk about. Is it a good likeness?"

"Without doubt, yes. I never saw him, but you can easily see the resemblance to his father," said Sellers, holding up the chromo and glancing from it to the chromo misrepresenting the Usurping Earl and back again with an approving eye.

"Well, no—I am not sure that I make out the likeness. It is plain that the Usurping Earl there has a great deal of character and a long face like a horse's, whereas his heir here is smirky, moon-faced and characterless."

"We are all that way in the beginning—all the line," said Sellers, undisturbed. "We all start as moon-faced fools, then later we tadpole along into horse-faced marvels of intellect and character. It is by that sign and by that fact that I detect the resemblance here and know this portrait to be genuine and perfect. Yes, all our family are fools at first."

"This young man seems to meet the hereditary requirement, certainly."

"Yes, yes, he was a fool, without any doubt. Examine the face, the shape of the head, the expression. It's all fool, fool, fool, straight through."

"Thanks," said Tracy, involuntarily.

"Thanks?"

"I mean for explaining it to me. Go on, please."

"As I was saying, fool is printed all over the face. A body can even read the *de*tails."

"What do they say?"

"Well, added up, he is a wobbler."

"A which?"

"Wobbler. A person that's always taking a firm stand about something or other—kind of a Gibraltar stand, *he* thinks, for unshakable fidelity and everlastingness—and then, inside of a little while, he begins to wobble; no more Gibraltar there; no, sir, a mighty ordinary commonplace weakling wobbling around on stilts. That's Lord Berkeley to a dot, you can *see* it— *look* at that sheep! But,—why are you blushing like sunset! Dear sir, have I unwittingly offended in some way?"

"Oh, no indeed, no indeed. Far from it. But it always makes me blush to hear a man revile his own blood." He said to himself, "How strangely his vagrant and unguided fancies have hit upon the truth. By accident, he has described me. I am that contemptible thing. When I left England I thought I knew myself; I thought I was a very Frederick the Great for resolution and staying capacity; whereas in truth I am just a Wobbler, simply a Wobbler. Well—after all, it is at least creditable to *have* high ideals and give birth to lofty resolutions; I will allow myself that comfort." Then he said, aloud, "Could this sheep, as you call him, breed a great and self-sacrificing idea in his head, do you think? Could he meditate such a thing, for instance, as the renunciation of the earldom and its wealth and its glories, and voluntary retirement to the ranks of the commonalty, there to rise by his own merit or remain forever poor and obscure?"

"*Could* he? Why, look at him—look at this simpering self-righteous mug! There is your answer. It's the very thing he would think of. And he would start in to do it, too."

"And then?"

"He'd wobble."

"And back down?"

"Every time."

"Is that to happen with *all* my—I mean would that happen to *all* his high resolutions?"

"Oh certainly—certainly. It's the Rossmore of it."

"Then this creature was fortunate to die! Suppose, for argument's sake, that I was a Rossmore, and—"

"It can't be done."

"Why?"

"Because it's not a supposable case. To be a Rossmore at your age, you'd have to be a fool, and you're not a fool. And you'd have to be a Wobbler, whereas anybody that is an expert in reading character can see at a glance that when you set your foot down once, it's there to stay; an earthquake can't wobble it." He added to himself, "That's enough to say to him, but it isn't half strong enough for the facts. The more I observe him, now, the more remarkable I find him. It is the strongest face I have ever examined. There is almost superhuman firmness here, immovable purpose, iron steadfastness of will. A most extraordinary young man."

He presently said, aloud—

"Some time I want to ask your advice about a little matter, Mr. Tracy. You see, I've got that young lord's remains—my goodness, how you jump!"

"Oh, it's nothing, pray go on. You've got his remains?"

"Yes."

"Are you sure they are his, and not somebody else's?"

"Oh, perfectly sure. Samples, I mean. Not all of him."

"Samples?"

"Yes—in baskets. Some time you will be going home; and if you wouldn't mind taking them along—"

"Who? I?"

"Yes—certainly. I don't mean *now;* but after a while; after—but look here, would you like to see them?"

"No! Most certainly not. I don't want to see them."

"O, very well. I only thought—heyo, where are you going, dear?"

"Out to dinner, papa."

Tracy was aghast. The Colonel said, in a disappointed voice—

"Well, I'm sorry. Sho, I didn't know she was going out, Mr. Tracy." Gwendolen's face began to take on a sort of apprehensive What-have-I-done expression. "Three old people to one young one—well, it *isn't* a good team, that's a fact." Gwendolen's face betrayed a dawning hopefulness and she said—with a tone of reluctance which hadn't the hall-mark on it—

"If you prefer, I will send word to the Thompsons that I—"

"Oh, is it the Thompsons? That simplifies it—sets everything right. We can fix it without spoiling your arrangements, my child. You've got your heart set on—"

"But, papa, I'd *just* as soon go there some other—"

"No—I won't have it. You are a good hard-working darling child, and your father is not the man to disappoint you when you—"

"But papa, I—"

"Go along, I won't hear a word. We'll get along, dear."

Gwendolen was ready to cry with vexation. But there was nothing to do but start; which she was about to do when her father hit upon an idea which filled him with delight because it so deftly covered all the difficulties of the situation and made things smooth and satisfactory:

"I've got it, my love, so that you won't be robbed of your holiday and at the same time we'll be pretty satisfactorily fixed for a good time here. You send Belle Thompson here—perfectly beautiful creature, Tracy, perfectly beautiful; I want you to see that girl; why, you'll just go mad; you'll go mad inside of a minute; yes, you send her right along, Gwendolen, and tell her—why, she's gone!" He turned—she was already passing out at the gate. He muttered, "I wonder what's the matter; I don't know what her mouth's doing, but I think her shoulders are swearing. Well," said Sellers blithely to Tracy, "I shall miss her—parents always miss the children as soon as they're out of sight, it's only a natural and wisely ordained partiality—but you'll be all right, because Miss Belle will supply the youthful element for you and to your entire content; and we old people will do our best, too. We shall have a good enough time. And you'll have a chance to get better acquainted with Admiral Hawkins. That's a rare character, Mr. Tracy—one of the rarest and most engaging characters the world has produced. You'll find him worth studying. I've studied him ever since he was a child and have always found him developing. I really consider that one of the main things that has enabled me to master the difficult science of character-reading was the livid interest I always felt in that boy and the baffling inscrutabilities of his ways and inspirations."

Tracy was not hearing a word. His spirits were gone, he was desolate.

"Yes, a most wonderful character. Concealment—that's the basis of it. Always the first thing you want to do is to find the keystone a man's character is built on—then you've got it. No misleading and apparently inconsistent peculiarities can fool you then. What do you read on the Senator's surface? Simplicity; a kind of rank and protuberant simplicity; whereas, in fact, that's one of the deepest minds in the world. A perfectly honest man—an absolutely honest and honorable man—and yet without doubt the profoundest master of dissimulation the world has ever seen."

"O, it's devilish!" This was wrung from the unlistening Tracy by the anguished thought of what might have been if only the dinner arrangements hadn't got mixed.

"No, I shouldn't call it that," said Sellers, who was now placidly walking up and down the room with his hands under his coat-tails and listening to himself talk. "One could quite properly call it devilish in another man, but not in the Senator. Your *term* is right—perfectly right— I grant that—but the application is wrong. It makes a great difference. Yes, he is a marvelous character. I do not suppose that any other statesman ever had such a colossal sense of humor, combined with the ability to totally conceal it. I may except George Washington and Cromwell, and perhaps Robespierre, but I draw the line there. A person not an expert might be in Judge Hawkins's company a lifetime and never find out he had any more sense of humor than a cemetery."

A deep-drawn yard-long sigh from the distraught and dreaming artist, followed by a murmured "Miserable, oh, miserable!"

"Well, no, I shouldn't say *that* about it, quite. On the contrary, I admire his ability to conceal his humor even more if possible than I admire the gift itself, stupendous as it is. Another thing—General Hawkins is a thinker; a keen, logical, exhaustive, analytical thinker—perhaps the ablest of modern times. That is, of course, upon themes suited to his size, like the glacial period, and the correlation of forces, and the evolution of the Christian from the caterpillar—any of those things; give him a subject according to his size, and just stand back and watch him think! Why you can see the place rock! Ah, yes, you must know him; you must get on the inside of him. Perhaps the most extraordinary mind since Aristotle."

Dinner was kept waiting for a while for Miss Thompson, but as Gwendolen had not delivered the invitation to her the waiting did no good, and the household presently went to the meal without her. Poor old Sellers tried everything his hospitable soul could devise to make the occasion an enjoyable one for the guest, and the guest tried his honest best to be cheery and chatty and happy for the old gentleman's sake; in fact all hands worked hard in the interest of a mutual good time, but the thing was a failure from the start; Tracy's heart was lead in his bosom, there seemed to be only one prominent feature in the landscape and that was a vacant chair, he couldn't drag his mind away from Gwendolen and his hard luck; consequently his distractions allowed deadly pauses to slip in every now and then when it was his turn to say something, and of course this disease spread to the rest of the conversation—wherefore, instead of having a breezy sail in sunny waters, as anticipated, everybody was bailing out and praying for land. What *could* the matter be? Tracy alone could have told, the others couldn't even invent a theory.

Meanwhile they were having a similarly dismal time at the Thompson house; in fact a twin experience. Gwendolen was ashamed of herself for allowing her disappointment to so depress her spirits and make her so strangely and profoundly miserable; but feeling ashamed of herself didn't improve the matter any; it only seemed to aggravate the suffering. She explained that she was not feeling very well, and everybody could see that this was true; so she got sincere sympathy and commiseration; but that didn't help the case. Nothing helps that kind of a case. It is best to just stand off and let it fester. The moment the dinner was over the girl excused herself, and she hurried home feeling unspeakably grateful to get away from that house and that intolerable captivity and suffering.

Will he be gone? The thought arose in her brain, but took effect in her heels. She slipped into the house, threw off her things and made straight for the dining room. She stopped and listened. Her father's voice—with no life in it; presently her mother's—no life in that; a considerable vacancy, then a sterile remark from Washington Hawkins. Another silence; then, not Tracy's but her father's voice again.

"He's gone," she said to herself despairingly, and listlessly opened the door and stepped within.

"Why, my child," cried the mother, "how white you are! Are you—has anything—"

"White?" exclaimed Sellers. "It's gone like a flash; 'twasn't serious. Already she's as red as the soul of a watermelon! Sit down, dear, sit down—goodness knows you're welcome. Did you have a good time? We've had great times here—immense. Why didn't Miss Belle come? Mr. Tracy is not feeling well, and she'd have made him forget it."

She was content now; and out from her happy eyes there went a light that told a secret to another pair of eyes there and got a secret in return. In just that infinitely small fraction of a second those two great confessions were made, received, and perfectly understood. All anxiety, apprehension, uncertainty, vanished out of these young people's hearts and left them filled with a great peace.

Sellers had had the most confident faith that with the new reinforcement victory would be at this last moment snatched from the jaws of defeat, but it was an error. The talk was as stubbornly disjointed as ever. He was proud of Gwendolen, and liked to show her off, even against Miss Belle Thompson, and here had been a great opportunity, and what had she made of it? He felt a good deal put out. It vexed him to think that this Englishman, with the traveling Briton's everlasting disposition to generalize whole mountain ranges from single sample-grains of sand, would jump to the conclusion that American girls were as dumb as himself—generalizing the whole tribe from this single sample and she at her poorest, there being nothing at that table to inspire her, give her a start, keep her from going to sleep. He made up his mind that for the honor of the country he would bring these two together again over the social board before long. There would be a different result another time, he judged. He said to himself, with a deep sense of injury, "He'll put in his diary—they all keep diaries—he'll put in his diary that she was miraculously uninteresting—dear, dear, but *wasn't* she!—I never saw the like—and yet looking as beautiful as Satan, too—and couldn't seem to do anything but paw bread crumbs, and pick flowers to pieces, and look fidgety. And it isn't any better here in the Hall of Audience. I've had enough; I'll haul down my flag; the others may fight it out if they want to."

He shook hands all around and went off to do some work which he said was pressing. The idolators were the width of the room apart, and apparently unconscious of each other's presence. The distance got shortened a little, now. Very soon the mother withdrew. The distance narrowed again. Tracy stood before a chromo of some Ohio politician which had been retouched and chain-mailed for a crusading Rossmore, and Gwendolen was sitting on the sofa not far from his elbow artificially absorbed in examining a photograph album that hadn't any photographs in it.

The "Senator" still lingered. He was sorry for the young people; it had been a dull evening for them. In the goodness of his heart he tried to make it pleasant for them now; tried to remove the ill impression necessarily left by the general defeat; tried to be chatty, even tried to be gay. But the responses were sickly, there was no starting any enthusiasm; he would give it up and quit—it was a day specially picked out and consecrated to failures.

But when Gwendolen rose up promptly and smiled a glad smile and said with thankfulness and blessing—"*Must* you go?" it seemed cruel to desert, and he sat down again.

He was about to begin a remark when—when he didn't. We have all been there. He didn't know how he knew his concluding to stay longer had been a mistake, he merely knew it; and knew it for dead certain, too. And so he bade goodnight, and went mooning out, wondering what he could have done that changed the atmosphere that way. As the door closed behind him those two were standing side by side, looking at that door— looking at it in a waiting, second-counting, but deeply grateful kind of way. And the instant it closed they flung their arms about each other's necks, and there, heart to heart and lip to lip—

"Oh, my God, she's kissing it!"

Nobody heard this remark, because Hawkins, who bred it, only thought it, he didn't utter it. He had turned, the moment he had closed the door, and had pushed it open a little, intending to re-enter and ask what ill-

OH, MY GOD, SHE'S KISSING IT!

advised thing he had done or said, and apologize for it. But he didn't re-enter; he staggered off stunned, terrified, distressed.

Chapter 22

FIVE MINUTES later he was sitting in his room, with his head bowed within the circle of his arms, on the table—final attitude of grief and despair. His tears were flowing fast, and now and then a sob broke upon the stillness. Presently he said—

"I knew her when she was a little child and used to climb about my knees; I love her as I love my own, and now—oh, poor thing, poor thing, I cannot bear it!—she's gone and lost her heart to this mangy materiali-zee! Why *didn't* we see that that might happen? But how could we? Nobody could; nobody could ever have dreamed of such a thing. You couldn't expect a person would fall in love with a wax-work. And this one doesn't even amount to that."

He went on grieving to himself, and now and then giving voice to his lamentations.

"It's done, oh, it's done, and there's no help for it, no undoing the miserable business. If I had the nerve, I would kill it. But that wouldn't do any good. *She* loves it; she thinks it's genuine and authentic. If she lost it she would grieve for it just as she would for a real person. And who's to break it to the family! Not I—I'll die first. Sellers is the best human being I ever knew and I wouldn't any more think of—oh, dear, why it'll break his heart when he finds it out. And Polly's too. *This* comes of meddling with such infernal matters! But for this, the creature would still be roasting in Sheol where it belongs. How is it that these people don't smell the brimstone? Sometimes I can't come into the same room with him without nearly suffocating."

After a while he broke out again:

"Well, there's *one* thing, sure. The materializing has got to stop right where it is. If she's got to marry a specter, let her marry a decent one out of the Middle Ages, like this one—not a cowboy and a thief such as the protoplasmic tadpole's going to turn into if Sellers keeps on fussing at it. It costs five thousand dollars cash and shuts down on the incorporated company to stop the works at this point, but Sally Sellers's happiness is worth more than that."

He heard Sellers coming, and got himself to rights. Sellers took a seat, and said—

"Well, I've got to confess I'm a good deal puzzled. It did certainly eat, there's no getting around it. Not eat, exactly, either, but it nibbled; nibbled in an appetiteless way, but still it nibbled; and that's just a marvel. Now the question is, what does it do with those nibblings? That's it—what does it do with them? My idea is that we don't begin to know all there is to this stupendous discovery yet. But time will show—time and science—give us a chance, and don't get impatient."

But he couldn't get Hawkins interested; couldn't make him talk to amount to anything; couldn't drag him out of his depression. But at last he took a turn that arrested Hawkins's attention.

"I'm coming to like him, Hawkins. He is a person of stupendous character—absolutely gigantic. Under that placid exterior is concealed the most dare-devil spirit that was ever put into a man—he's just a Clive over again. Yes, I'm all admiration for him, on account of his character, and liking naturally follows admiration, you know. I'm coming to like him immensely. Do you know, I haven't the heart to degrade such a character as that down to the burglar estate for money or for anything else; and I've come to ask if you are willing to let the reward go, and leave this poor fellow—"

"Where he is?"

"Yes—not bring him down to date."

"Oh, there's my hand; and my heart's in it, too!"

"I'll never forget you for this, Hawkins," said the old gentleman in a voice which he found it hard to control. "You are making a great sacrifice for me, and one which you can ill afford, but I'll never forget your generosity, and if I live you shall not suffer for it, be sure of that."

Sally Sellers immediately and vividly realized that she was become a new being; a being of a far higher and worthier sort than she had been such a little while before; an earnest being, in place of a dreamer; and supplied with a reason for her presence in the world, where merely a wistful and troubled curiosity about it had existed before. So great and so comprehensive was the change which had been wrought, that she seemed to herself to be a real person who had lately been a shadow; a something which had lately been a nothing; a purpose, which had lately been a fancy; a finished temple, with the altar-fires lit and the voice of worship ascending, where before had been but an architect's confusion of arid working plans, unintelligible to the passing eye and prophesying nothing.

"Lady" Gwendolen! The pleasantness of that sound was all gone; it was an offense to her ear now. She said—

"There—that sham belongs to the past; I will not be called by it any more."

"I may call you simply Gwendolen? You will allow me to drop the formalities straightway and name you by your dear first name without additions?"

She was dethroning the pink and replacing it with a rosebud.

"There—that is better. I hate pinks—some pinks. Indeed yes, you are to call me by my first name without additions—that is,—well, I don't mean without additions *entirely*, but—"

It was as far as she could get. There was a pause; his intellect was struggling to comprehend; presently it did manage to catch the idea in time to save embarrassment all around, and he said gratefully—

"*Dear* Gwendolen! I may say that?"

"Yes—part of it. But—don't kiss me when I am talking, it makes me forget what I was going to say. You can call me by part of that form, but not the last part. Gwendolen is not my name."

"Not your name?" This in a tone of wonder and surprise.

The girl's soul was suddenly invaded by a creepy apprehension, a quite definite sense of suspicion and alarm. She put his arms away from her, looked him searchingly in the eye, and said—

"Answer me truly, on your honor. You are not seeking to marry me on account of my *rank?*"

The shot almost knocked him through the wall, he was so little prepared for it. There was something so finely grotesque about the question and its parent suspicion, that he stopped to wonder and admire, and thus was he saved from laughing. Then, without wasting precious time, he set about the task of convincing her that he had been lured by herself alone, and had fallen in love with her only, not her title and position; that he loved her with all his heart, and could not love her more if she were a duchess, or less if she were without home, name or family. She watched his face wistfully, eagerly, hopefully, translating his words by its expression; and when he had finished there was gladness in her heart—a tumultuous gladness, indeed, though outwardly she was calm, tranquil, even judicially austere. She prepared a surprise for him, now, calculated to put a heavy strain upon those disinterested protestations of his; and thus she delivered it, burning it away word by word as the fuse burns down to a bombshell, and watching to see how far the explosion would lift him:

"Listen—and do not doubt me, for I shall speak the exact truth. Howard Tracy, I am no more an earl's child than you are!"

To her joy—and secret surprise, also—it never phased him. He was ready, this time, and saw his chance. He cried out with enthusiasm, "Thank heaven for that!" and gathered her to his arms.

To express her happiness was almost beyond her gift of speech.

"You make me the proudest girl in all the earth," she said, with her head pillowed on his shoulder. "I thought it only natural that you should be dazzled by the title—maybe even unconsciously, you being English— and that you might be deceiving yourself in thinking you loved only me, and find you didn't love me when the deception was swept away; so it makes me proud that the revelation stands for nothing and that you *do* love just me, only me—oh, prouder than any words can tell!"

"It is only you, sweetheart, I never gave one envying glance toward your father's earldom. That is utterly true, dear Gwendolen."

"There—you mustn't call me that. I hate that false name. I told you it wasn't mine. My name is Sally Sellers—or Sarah, if you like. From this time I banish dreams, visions, imaginings, and will no more of them. I am going to be myself—my genuine self, my honest self, my natural self, clear and clean of sham and folly and fraud, and worthy of you. There is no grain of social inequality between us; I, like you, am poor; I, like you, am without position or distinction; you are a struggling artist, I am that, too, in my humbler way. Our bread is honest bread, we work for our living. Hand in hand we will walk hence to the grave, helping each other in all ways, living for each other, being and remaining one in heart and purpose, one in hope and aspiration, inseparable to the end. And though our place is low, judged by the world's eye, we will make it as high as the highest in the great essentials of honest work for what we eat and wear, and conduct above reproach. We live in a land, let us be thankful, where this is all-sufficient, and no man is better than his neighbor by the grace of God, but only by his own merit."

Tracy tried to break in, but she stopped him and kept the floor herself.

"I am not through, yet. I am going to purge myself of the last vestiges of artificiality and pretence, and then start fair on your own honest level and be worthy mate to you thenceforth. My father honestly thinks he is an earl. Well, leave him his dream, it pleases him and does no one any harm. It was the dream of his ancestors before him. It has made fools of the house of Sellers for generations, and it made something of a fool of me, but took no deep root. I am done with it now, and for good. Forty-eight hours ago I was privately proud of being the daughter of a pinchbeck earl, and thought the proper mate for me must be a man of like degree; but to-day—oh, how grateful I am for your love which has healed my sick brain and restored my sanity!—I could make oath that no earl's son in all the world—"

"Oh,—well, but—but—"

"Why, you look like a person in a panic. What is it! What is the matter?"

"Matter? Oh, nothing—nothing. I was only going to say"—but in his flurry nothing occurred to him to say, for a moment; then by a lucky inspiration he thought of something entirely sufficient for the occasion, and brought it out with eloquent force: "Oh, how beautiful you are! You take my breath away when you look like that."

It was well conceived, well timed, and cordially delivered—and it got its reward.

"Let me see. Where was I? Yes, my father's earldom is pure moonshine. Look at those dreadful things on the wall. You have of course supposed them to be portraits of his ancestors, earls of Rossmore. Well, they are not. They are chromos of distinguished Americans—all moderns; but he has carried them back a thousand years by re-labeling them. Andrew Jackson there, is doing what he can to be the late American earl; and the newest treasure in the collection is supposed to be the young English heir—I mean the idiot with the crape; but in truth it's a shoemaker, and not Lord Berkeley at all."

"Are you sure?"

"Why of course I am. He wouldn't look like that."

"Why?"

"Because his conduct in his last moments, when the fire was sweeping around him shows that he was a man. It shows that he was a fine, high-souled young creature."

Tracy was strongly moved by these compliments, and it seemed to him that the girl's lovely lips took on a new loveliness when they were delivering them. He said, softly—

"It is a pity he could not know what a gracious impression his behavior was going to leave with the dearest and sweetest stranger in the land of—"

"Oh, I almost loved him! Why, I think of him every day. He is always floating about in my mind."

Tracy felt that this was a little more than was necessary. He was conscious of the sting of jealousy. He said—

"It is quite right to think of him—at least now and then—that is, at intervals—in perhaps an admiring way—but it seems to me that—"

"Howard Tracy, are you jealous of that dead man?"

He was ashamed—and at the same time not ashamed. He was jealous—and at the same time he was not jealous. In a sense the dead man was himself; in that case compliments and affection lavished upon that corpse went into his own till and were clear profit. But in another sense the dead man was not himself; and in that case all compliments and affection lavished there were wasted, and a sufficient basis for jealousy. A tiff was the result of the dispute between the two. Then they made it up, and were more loving than ever. As an affectionate clincher of the reconciliation, Sally declared that she had now banished Lord Berkeley from her mind; and added, "And in order to make sure that he shall never make trouble between us again, I will teach myself to detest that name and all that have ever borne it or ever shall bear it."

This inflicted another pang, and Tracy was minded to ask her to modify that a little—just on general principles, and as practice in not overdoing a good thing—perhaps he might better leave things as they were and not risk bringing on another tiff. He got away from that particular, and sought less tender ground for conversation.

"I suppose you disapprove wholly of aristocracies and nobilities, now that you have renounced your title and your father's earldom."

"*Real* ones? Oh, dear no—but I've thrown aside our sham one for good."

This answer fell just at the right time and just in the right place, to save the poor unstable young man from changing his political complexion once more. He had been on the point of beginning to totter again, but this prop shored him up and kept him from foundering back into democracy and re-renouncing aristocracy. So he went home glad that he had asked the fortunate question. The girl would accept a little thing like a genuine earldom, she was merely prejudiced against the brummagem article. Yes, he could have his girl and have his earldom, too: that question was a fortunate stroke.

Sally went to bed happy, too; and remained happy, deliriously happy, for nearly two hours; but at last, just as she was sinking into a contented and luxurious unconsciousness, the shady devil who lives and lurks and hides and watches inside of human beings and is always waiting for a chance to do the proprietor a malicious damage, whispered to her soul and said, "That question had a harmless look, but what was *back* of it?— what was the secret motive of it?—what suggested it?"

The shady devil had knifed her, and could retire, now, and take a rest; the wound would attend to business for him. And it did.

Why should Howard Tracy ask that question? If he was not trying to marry her for the sake of her rank, what should suggest that question to him? Didn't he plainly look gratified when she said her objections to aristocracy had their limitations? Ah, he is after that earldom, that gilded sham—it isn't poor me he wants.

So she argued, in anguish and tears. Then she argued the opposite theory, but made a weak, poor business of it, and lost the case. She kept the arguing up, one side and then the other, the rest of the night, and at last fell asleep at dawn; fell in the fire at dawn, one may say; for that kind of sleep resembles fire, and one comes out of it with his brain baked and his physical forces fried out of him.

Chapter 23

TRACY WROTE his father before he sought his bed. He wrote a letter which he believed would get better treatment than his cablegram received, for it contained what ought to be welcome news; namely, that he had tried equality and working for a living; had made a fight which he could find no reason to be ashamed of, and in the matter of earning a living had proved that he was able to do it; but that on the whole he had arrived at the conclusion that he could not reform the world single-handed, and was willing to retire from the conflict with the fair degree of honor which he had gained, and was also willing to return home and resume his position

THE SHADY DEVIL HAD KNIFED HER.

and be content with it and thankful for it for the future, leaving further experiment of a missionary sort to other young people needing the chastening and quelling persuasions of experience, the only logic sure to convince a diseased imagination and restore it to rugged health. Then he approached the subject of marriage with the daughter of the American Claimant with a good deal of caution and much painstaking art. He said praiseful and appreciative things about the girl, but didn't dwell upon that detail or make it prominent. The thing which he made prominent was the opportunity now so happily afforded, to reconcile York and Lancaster, graft the warring roses upon one stem, and end forever a crying injustice which had already lasted far too long. One could infer that he had thought this thing all out and chosen this way of making all things fair and right because it was sufficiently fair and considerably wiser than the renunciation-scheme which he had brought with him from England. One could infer that, but he didn't say it. In fact the more he read his letter over, the more he got to inferring it himself.

When the old earl received that letter, the first part of it filled him with a grim and snarly satisfaction; but the rest of it brought a snort or two out of him that could be translated differently. He wasted no ink in this emergency, either in cablegrams or letters; he promptly took ship for America to look into the matter himself. He had staunchly held his grip all this long time, and given no sign of the hunger at his heart to see his son; hoping for the cure of his insane dream, and resolute that the process should go through all the necessary stages without assuaging telegrams or other nonsense from home, and here was victory at last. Victory, but stupidly marred by this idiotic marriage project. Yes, he would step over and take a hand in this matter himself.

During the first ten days following the mailing of the letter Tracy's spirits had no idle time; they were always climbing up into the clouds or sliding down into the earth as deep as the law of gravitation reached. He was intensely happy or intensely miserable by turns, according to Miss Sally's moods. He never could tell when the mood was going to change, and when it changed he couldn't tell what it was that had changed it. Sometimes she was so in love with him that her love was tropical, torrid, and she could find no language fervent enough for its expression; then suddenly, and without warning or any apparent reason, the weather would change, and the victim would find himself adrift among the icebergs and feeling as lonesome and friendless as the north pole. It sometimes seemed to him that a man might better be dead than exposed to these devastating varieties of climate.

The case was simple. Sally *wanted* to believe that Tracy's preference was disinterested; so she was always applying little tests of one sort or another, hoping and expecting that they would bring out evidence which would confirm or fortify her belief. Poor Tracy did not know that these experiments were being made upon him, consequently he walked promptly into all the traps the girl set for him. These traps consisted in apparently casual references to social distinction, aristocratic title and privilege, and such things. Often Tracy responded to these references heedlessly and not much caring what he said provided it kept the talk going and prolonged the séance. He didn't suspect that the girl was watching his face and listening for his words as one who watches the judge's face and listens for the words which will restore him to home and friends and freedom or shut him away from the sun and human companionship forever. He didn't suspect that his careless words were being weighed, and so he often delivered sentence of death when it would have been just as handy and all the same to him to pronounce acquittal. Daily he broke the girl's heart, nightly he sent her to the rack for sleep. He couldn't understand it.

Some people would have put this and that together and perceived that the weather never changed until one particular subject was introduced, and that then it *always* changed. And they would have looked further, and perceived that that subject was always introduced by the one party, never the other. They would have argued, then, that this was done for a purpose. If they could not find out what that purpose was in any simpler or easier way, they would *ask*.

But Tracy was not deep enough or suspicious enough to think of these things. He noticed only one particular; that the weather was always sunny when a visit *began*. No matter how much it might cloud up later, it always began with a clear sky. He couldn't explain this curious fact to himself, he merely knew it to be a fact. The truth of the matter was, that by the time Tracy had been out of Sally's sight six hours she was so famishing for a sight of him that her doubts and suspicions were all consumed away in the fire of that longing, and so always she came into his presence as surprisingly radiant and joyous as she wasn't when she went out of it.

In circumstances like these a growing portrait runs a good many risks. The portrait of Sellers, by Tracy, was fighting along, day by day, through this mixed weather, and daily adding to itself ineradicable signs of the checkered life it was leading. It was the happiest portrait, in spots, that was ever seen; but in other spots a damned soul looked out from it; a soul that was suffering all the different kinds of distress there are, from stomach ache to rabies. But Sellers liked it. He said it was just himself all over—a portrait that sweated moods from every pore, and no two moods alike. He said he had as many different kinds of emotions in him as a jug.

It was a kind of a deadly work of art, maybe, but it was a starchy picture for show; for it was life size, full length, and represented the American earl in a peer's scarlet robe, with the three ermine bars indicative of an earl's rank, and on the gray head an earl's coronet, tilted just a wee bit to one side in a most gallus and winsome way. When Sally's weather was sunny the portrait made Tracy chuckle, but when her weather was overcast it disordered his mind and stopped the circulation of his blood.

Late one night when the sweethearts had been having a flawless visit together, Sally's interior devil began to work his specialty, and soon the conversation was drifting toward the customary rock. Presently, in the midst of Tracy's serene flow of talk, he felt a shudder which he knew was not his shudder, but exterior to his breast although immediately against it. After the shudder came sobs; Sally was crying.

"Oh, my darling, what have I done—what have I said? It has happened again! What *have* I done to wound you?"

She disengaged herself from his arms and gave him a look of deep reproach.

"What have you done? I will tell you what you have done. You have unwittingly revealed—oh, for the twentieth time, though I *could* not believe it, *would* not believe it!—that it is not me you love, but that foolish sham my father's imitation earldom; and you have broken my heart!"

"Oh, my child, what are you saying! I never dreamed of such a thing."

"Oh, Howard, Howard, the things you have uttered when you were forgetting to guard your tongue, have betrayed you."

"Things I have uttered when I was *forgetting* to guard my tongue? These are hard words. When have I *remembered* to guard it? Never in one instance. It has no office but to speak the truth. It needs no guarding for that."

"Howard, I have noted your words and weighed them, when you were not thinking of their significance—and they have told me more than you meant they should."

"Do you mean to say you have answered the trust I had in you by using it as an ambuscade from which you could set snares for my unsuspecting tongue and be safe from detection while you did it? You have not done this—surely you have not done this thing. Oh, one's enemy could not do it."

This was an aspect of the girl's conduct which she had not clearly perceived before. Was it treachery? Had she abused a trust? The thought crimsoned her cheeks with shame and remorse.

"Oh, forgive me," she said, "I did not know what I was doing. I have been so tortured—you *will* forgive me, you *must;* I have suffered so much, and I am so sorry and so humble; you *do* forgive me, *don't* you?—don't turn away, don't refuse me; it is only my love that is at fault, and you *know* I love you, love you with all my heart; I couldn't bear to—oh, dear, dear, I am so miserable, and I *never* meant any harm, and I didn't see where this insanity was carrying me, and how it was wronging and abusing the dearest heart in all the world to me—and—and—oh, take me in your arms again, I have no other refuge, no other home and hope!"

There was reconciliation again—immediate, perfect, all-embracing—and with it utter happiness. This would have been a good time to adjourn. But no, now that the cloud-breeder was revealed at last; now that it was manifest that all the sour weather had come from this girl's dread that Tracy was lured by her rank and not herself, he resolved to lay that ghost immediately and permanently by furnishing the best possible proof that he *couldn't* have had back of him at any time the suspected motive. So he said—

"Let me whisper a little secret in your ear—a secret which I have kept shut up in my breast all this time. Your rank *couldn't* ever have been an enticement. I am son and heir to an English earl!"

The girl stared at him—one, two, three moments, maybe a dozen—then her lips parted—

"You?" she said, and moved away from him, still gazing at him in a kind of blank amazement.

"Why—why, certainly I am. Why do you act like this? What have I done *now?*"

"What have you done? You have certainly made a most strange statement. You must see that yourself."

"Well," with a timid little laugh, "it may be a strange enough statement; but of what consequence is that, if it is true?"

"*If* it is true. You are already retiring from it."

"Oh, not for a moment! You should not say that. I have not deserved
it. I have spoken the truth; why do you doubt it?"

Her reply was prompt.

"Simply because you didn't speak it earlier!"

"Oh!" It wasn't a groan, exactly, but it was an intelligible enough
expression of the fact that he saw the point and recognized that there was
reason in it.

"You have seemed to conceal nothing from me that I ought to know
concerning yourself, and you were not privileged to keep back such a
thing as this from me a moment after—after—well, after you had determined to pay your court to me."

"It's true, it's true, I know it! But there were circumstances—in—in
the way—circumstances which—"

She waved the circumstances aside.

"Well, you see," he said, pleadingly, "you seemed so bent on our
traveling the proud path of honest labor and honorable poverty, that I was
terrified—that is, I was afraid—of—of—well, *you* know how you talked."

"Yes, I know how I talked. And I also know that before the talk was
finished you inquired how I stood as regards aristocracies, and my answer
was calculated to relieve your fears."

He was silent a while. Then he said, in a discouraged way—

"I don't see any way out of it. It was a mistake. That is in truth all it
was, just a mistake. No harm was meant, no harm in the world. I didn't
see how it might some time look. It is my way. I don't seem to see far."

The girl was almost disarmed, for a moment. Then she flared up again.

"An Earl's son! Do earls' sons go about working in lowly callings for
their bread and butter?"

"God knows they don't! I have wished they did."

"Do earls' sons sink their degree in a country like this, and come sober
and decent to sue for the hand of a born child of poverty when they can
go drunk, profane, and steeped in dishonorable debt and buy the pick and
choice of the millionaires' daughters of America? *You* an earl's son! Show
me the signs."

"I thank God I am not able—if those are the signs. But yet I am an
earl's son and heir. It is all I can say. I wish you would believe me, but
you will not. I know no way to persuade you."

She was about to soften again, but his closing remark made her bring
her foot down with smart vexation, and she cried out—

"Oh, you drive all patience out of me! Would you have one believe that
you haven't your proofs at hand, and yet are what you say you are? You
do not put your hand in your pocket *now*—for you have nothing there.
You make a claim like this, and then venture to travel without credentials.
These are simply incredibilities. Don't you see that, yourself?"

He cast about in his mind for a defence of some kind or other—
hesitated a little, and then said, with difficulty and diffidence—

"I will tell you just the truth, foolish as it will seem to you—to anybody, I suppose—but it *is* the truth. I had an ideal—call it a dream, a

folly, if you will—but I wanted to renounce the privileges and unfair advantages enjoyed by the nobility and wrung from the nation by force and fraud, and purge myself of my share of those crimes against right and reason, by thenceforth comrading with the poor and humble on equal terms, earning with my own hands the bread I ate, and rising by my own merit if I rose at all.''

The young girl scanned his face narrowly while he spoke; and there was something about his simplicity of manner and statement which touched her—touched her almost to the danger point; but she set her grip on the yielding spirit and choked it to quiescence; it could not be wise to surrender to compassion or any kind of sentiment, yet; she must ask one or two more questions. Tracy was reading her face; and what he read there lifted his drooping hopes a little.

"An earl's son to do that! Why, he were a man! A man to love!—oh, more, a man to worship!''

"Why, I—''

"But he never lived! He is not born, he will not be born. The self-abnegation that could do that—even in utter folly, and hopeless of conveying benefit to any, beyond the mere example—could be mistaken for greatness; why, it would *be* greatness in this cold age of sordid ideals! A moment—wait—let me finish; I have one question more. Your father is earl of what?''

"Rossmore—and I am Viscount Berkeley!''

The fat was in the fire again. The girl felt so outraged that it was difficult for her to speak.

"How *can* you venture such a brazen thing! You know that he is dead, and you know that I know it. Oh, to rob the living of name and honors for a selfish and temporary advantage is crime enough, but to rob the defenceless dead—why it is more than crime, it *degrades* crime!''

"Oh, listen to me—just a word—don't turn away like that. Don't go—don't leave me, so—stay one moment. On my honor—''

"Oh, on your honor!''

"On my honor I am what I say! And I will prove it, and you will believe, I know you will. I will bring you a message—a cablegram—''

"When?''

"To-morrow—next day—''

"Signed 'Rossmore'?''

"Yes—signed Rossmore.''

"What will that prove?''

"What will it prove? What *should* it prove?''

"If you force me to say it—possibly the presence of a confederate somewhere.''

This was a hard blow, and staggered him. He said, dejectedly—

"It is true. I did not think of it. Oh, my God, I do not know any way to do; I do everything wrong. You are going?—and you won't say even good-night—or good-bye? Ah, we have not parted like this before.''

"Oh, I *want* to run and—no, go, now.'' A pause—then she said, "You may bring the message when it comes.''

"Oh, may I? God bless you.''

He was gone; and none too soon; her lips were already quivering, and now she broke down. Through her sobbings her words broke from time to time.

"Oh, he is gone. I have lost him, I shall never see him any more. And he didn't kiss me good-bye; never even offered to force a kiss from me, and he *knowing* it was the very, very last, and I expecting he would, and never *dreaming* he would treat me so after all we have been to each other. Oh, oh, oh, oh, what shall I do, what *shall* I do! He is a dear, poor, miserable, good-hearted, transparent liar and humbug, but oh, I *do* love him so!" After a little she broke into speech again. "How dear he is! and I shall miss him so, I shall miss him so! Why *won't* he ever think to *forge* a message and fetch it?—but no, he never will, he never thinks of any-thing; he's so honest and simple it wouldn't ever occur to him. Oh, what *did* possess him to think he could succeed as a fraud—and he hasn't the first requisite except duplicity that I can see. Oh, dear, I'll go to bed and give it all up. Oh, I *wish* I had told him to come and tell me whenever he didn't get any telegram—and now it's all my own fault if I never see him again. How my eyes must look!"

Chapter 24

NEXT DAY, sure enough, the cablegram didn't come. This was an im-mense disaster; for Tracy couldn't go into the presence without that ticket, although it wasn't going to possess any value as evidence. But if the failure of the cablegram on that first day may be called an immense disaster, where is the dictionary that can turn out a phrase sizeable enough to describe the tenth day's failure? Of course every day that the cablegram didn't come made Tracy all of twenty-four hours' more ashamed of him-self than he was the day before, and made Sally fully twenty-four hours more certain than ever that he not only hadn't any father anywhere, but hadn't even a confederate—and so it followed that he was a double-dyed humbug and couldn't be otherwise.

These were hard days for Barrow and the art firm. All these had their hands full, trying to comfort Tracy. Barrow's task was particularly hard, because he was made a confidant in full, and therefore had to humor Tracy's delusion that he had a father, and that the father was an earl, and that he was going to send a cablegram. Barrow early gave up the idea of trying to convince Tracy that he hadn't any father, because this had such a bad effect on the patient, and worked up his temper to such an alarming degree. He had tried, as an experiment, letting Tracy think he had a father; the result was so good that he went further, with proper caution, and tried letting him think his father was an earl; this wrought so well, that he grew bold, and tried letting him think he had two fathers, if he wanted to, but he didn't want to, so Barrow withdrew one of them and substituted letting him think he was going to get a cablegram—which Barrow judged he wouldn't, and was right; but Barrow worked the cablegram daily for all it was worth, and it was the one thing that kept Tracy alive; that was Bar-row's opinion.

And these were bitter hard days for poor Sally, and mainly delivered up to private crying. She kept her furniture pretty damp, and so caught cold, and the dampness and the cold and the sorrow together undermined her appetite, and she was a pitiful enough object, poor thing. Her state was bad enough, as per statement of it above quoted; but all the forces of nature and circumstance seemed conspiring to make it worse—and succeeding. For instance, the morning after her dismissal of Tracy, Hawkins and Sellers read in the associated press dispatches that a toy puzzle called Pigs in the Clover, had come into sudden favor within the past few weeks, and that from the Atlantic to the Pacific all the populations of all the States had knocked off work to play with it, and that the business of the country had now come to a standstill by consequence; that judges, lawyers, burglars, parsons, thieves, merchants, mechanics, murderers, women, children, babies—everybody, indeed, could be seen from morning till midnight, absorbed in one deep project and purpose, and only one—to pen those pigs, work out that puzzle successfully; that all gayety, all cheerfulness had departed from the nation, and in its place care, preoccupation and anxiety sat upon every countenance, and all faces were drawn, distressed, and furrowed with the signs of age and trouble, and marked with the still sadder signs of mental decay and incipient madness; that factories were at work night and day in eight cities, and yet to supply the demand for the puzzle was thus far impossible. Hawkins was wild with joy, but Sellers was calm. Small matters could not disturb his serenity. He said—

"That's just the way things go. A man invents a thing which could revolutionize the arts, produce mountains of money, and bless the earth, and who will bother with it or show any interest in it?—and so you are just as poor as you were before. But you invent some worthless thing to amuse yourself with, and would throw it away if let alone, and all of a sudden the whole world makes a snatch for it and out crops a fortune. Hunt up that Yankee and collect, Hawkins—half is yours, you know. Leave me to potter at my lecture."

This was a temperance lecture. Sellers was head chief in the Temperance camp, and had lectured, now and then in that interest, but had been dissatisfied with his efforts; wherefore he was now about to try a new plan. After much thought he had concluded that a main reason why his lectures lacked fire or something, was, that they were too transparently amateurish; that is to say, it was probably too plainly perceptible that the lecturer was trying to tell people about the horrid effects of liquor when he didn't really know anything about those effects except from hearsay, since he had hardly ever tasted an intoxicant in his life. His scheme, now, was to prepare himself to speak from bitter experience. Hawkins was to stand by with the bottle, calculate the doses, watch the effects, make notes of results, and otherwise assist in the preparation. Time was short, for the ladies would be along about noon—that is to say, the temperance organization called the Daughters of Siloam—and Sellers must be ready to head the procession.

The time kept slipping along—Hawkins did not return—Sellers could not venture to wait longer; so he attacked the bottle himself, and proceeded to note the effects. Hawkins got back at last; took one comprehensive glance at the lecturer, and went down and headed off the procession.

The ladies were grieved to hear that the champion had been taken suddenly ill and violently so, but glad to hear that it was hoped he would be out again in a few days.

As it turned out, the old gentleman didn't turn over or show any signs of life worth speaking of for twenty-four hours. Then he asked after the procession, and learned what had happened about it. He was sorry; said he had been "fixed" for it. He remained abed several days, and his wife and daughter took turns in sitting with him and ministering to his wants. Often he patted Sally's head and tried to comfort her.

"Don't cry, my child, don't cry so; *you* know your old father did it by mistake and didn't mean a bit of harm; you know he wouldn't intention-ally do anything to make you ashamed for the world; you know he was trying to do good and only made the mistake through ignorance, not knowing the right doses and Washington not there to help. Don't cry so, dear, it breaks my old heart to see you, and think I've brought this humil-iation on you and you so dear to me and so good. I won't ever do it again, indeed I won't; now be comforted, honey, that's a good child."

But when she wasn't on duty at the bedside the crying went on just the same; then the mother would try to comfort her, and say—

"Don't cry, dear, *he* never meant any harm; it was all one of those happens that you can't guard against when you are trying experiments, that way. You see *I* don't cry. It's because I know him so well. I could never look anybody in the face again if he had got into such an amazing condition as that a-purpose; but bless you his intention was pure and high, and that makes the *act* pure, though it was higher than was necessary. We're not humiliated, dear, he did it under a noble impulse and we don't need to be ashamed. There, don't cry any more, honey."

Thus, the old gentleman was useful to Sally, during several days, as an explanation of her tearfulness. She felt thankful to him for the shelter he was affording her, but often said to herself, "It's a shame to let him see in my cryings a reproach—as if he could ever do anything that could make me reproach him! But I can't confess; I've got to go on using him for a pretext, he's the only one I've got in the world, and I do need one so much."

As soon as Sellers was out again, and found that stacks of money had been placed in bank for him and Hawkins by the Yankee, he said, "*Now* we'll soon see who's the Claimant and who's the Authentic. I'll just go over there and warm up that House of Lords." During the next few days he and his wife were so busy with preparations for the voyage that Sally had all the privacy she needed, and all the chance to cry that was good for her. Then the old pair left for New York—and England.

Sally had also had a chance to do another thing. That was, to make up her mind that life was not worth living upon the present terms. If she *must* give up her impostor and die, doubtless she must submit; but might she not lay her whole case before some disinterested person, first, and see if there wasn't perhaps some saving way out of the matter? She turned this idea over in her mind a good deal. In her first visit with Hawkins after her parents were gone, the talk fell upon Tracy, and she was impelled to set her case before the statesman and take his counsel. So she poured out her heart, and he listened with painful solicitude. She concluded, pleadingly, with—

"*Don't* tell me he is an impostor. I suppose he is, but doesn't it look to you as if he isn't? You are cool, you know, and outside; and so, maybe it can look to you as if he isn't one, when it can't to me. *Doesn't* it look to you as if he isn't? Couldn't you—*can't* it look to you that way—for—for my sake?"

The poor man was troubled, but he felt obliged to keep in the neighborhood of the truth. He fought around the present detail a little while, then gave it up and said he couldn't really see his way to clearing Tracy.

"No," he said, "the truth is, he's an impostor."

"That is, you—you feel a little certain, but not entirely—oh, not *entirely*, Mr. Hawkins!"

"It's a pity to have to say it—I do hate to say it,—but I don't think anything about it, I *know* he's an impostor."

"Oh, now, Mr. Hawkins, you *can't* go that far. A body *can't* really know it, you know. It isn't *proved* that he's not what he says he is."

Should he come out and make a clean breast of the whole wretched business? Yes—at least the most of it—it ought to be done. So he set his teeth and went at the matter with determination, but purposing to spare the girl one pain—that of knowing that Tracy was a criminal.

"Now I am going to tell you a plain tale; one not pleasant for me to tell or for you to hear, but we've got to stand it. I know all about that fellow; and I *know* he is no earl's son."

The girl's eyes flashed, and she said:

"I don't care a snap for that—go on!"

This was so wholly unexpected that it at once obstructed the narrative; Hawkins was not even sure that he had heard aright. He said—

"I don't know that I quite understand. Do you mean to say that if he was all right and proper otherwise you'd be indifferent about the earl part of the business?"

"Absolutely."

"You'd be entirely satisfied with him and wouldn't *care* for his not being an earl's son,—that *being* an earl's son wouldn't add any value to him?"

"Not the least value that I would care for. Why, Mr. Hawkins, I've gotten over all that day-dreaming about earldoms and aristocracies and all such nonsense and am become just a plain ordinary nobody and content with it; and it is to *him* I owe my cure. And as to anything being able to add a value to him, nothing can do that. He is the whole world to me, just as he is; he comprehends *all* the values there are—then how can you *add* one?"

"She's pretty far gone." He said that to himself. He continued, still to himself, "I must change my plan again; I can't seem to strike one that will stand the requirements of this most variegated emergency five minutes on a stretch. Without making this fellow a criminal, I believe I will invent a name and a character for him calculated to disenchant her. If it fails to do it, then I'll know that the next rightest thing to do will be to help her to her fate, poor thing, not hinder her." Then he said aloud:

"Well, Gwendolen—"

"I want to be called Sally."

"I'm glad of it; I like it bettter, myself. Well, then, I'll tell you about this man Snodgrass."

"Snodgrass! Is *that* his name?"

"Yes—Snodgrass. The other's his nom de plume."

"It's hideous!"

"I know it is, but we can't help our names."

"And that is truly his real name—and not Howard Tracy?"

Hawkins answered, regretfully—

"Yes, it seems a pity."

The girl sampled the name musingly, once or twice—

"Snodgrass. Snodgrass. No, I could not endure that. I could not get used to it. No, I should call him by his first name. What is his first name?"

"His—er—his initials are S. M."

"His initials? I don't care anything about his initials. I can't call him by his initials. What do they *stand* for?"

"Well, you see, his father was a physician, and he—he—well he was an idolater of his profession, and he—well, he was a very eccentric man, and—"

"What do they *stand* for! What are you shuffling about?"

"They—well they stand for Spinal Meningitis. His father being a phy—"

"I never heard such an infamous name! Nobody can ever call a person *that*—a person they love. I wouldn't call an enemy by such a name. It sounds like an epithet." After a moment, she added with a kind of consternation, "Why, it would be *my* name! Letters would come with it on."

"Yes—Mrs. Spinal Meningitis Snodgrass."

"Don't repeat it—don't; I can't bear it. Was the father a lunatic?"

"No, that is not charged."

"I am glad of that, because that is transmissible. What do you think *was* the matter with him, then?"

"Well, I don't really know. The family used to run a good deal to idiots, and so, maybe—"

"Oh, there isn't any maybe about it. This one was an idiot."

"Well, yes—he could have been. He was suspected."

"Suspected!" said Sally, with irritation. "Would one *suspect* there was going to be a dark time if he saw the constellations fall out of the sky? But that is enough about the idiot, I don't take any interest in idiots; tell me about the son."

"Very well, then, this one was the eldest, but not the favorite. His brother, Zylobalsamum—"

"Wait—give me a chance to realize that. It is perfectly stupefying. Zylo—what did you call it?"

"Zylobalsamum."

"I never heard such a name. It sounds like a disease. Is it a disease?"

"No, I don't think it's a disease. It's either Scriptural or—"

"Well, it's not Scriptural."

"Then it's anatomical. I knew it was one or the other. Yes, I remember, now, it *is* anatomical. It's a ganglion—a nerve center—it is what is called the zylobalsamum process.''

"Well, go on; and if you come to any more of them, omit the names; they make one feel so uncomfortable.''

"Very well, then. As I said, this one was not a favorite in the family, and so he was neglected in every way, never sent to school, always allowed to associate with the worst and coarsest characters, and so of course he has grown up a rude, vulgar, ignorant, dissipated ruffian, and—''

"He? It's no such thing! You ought to be more generous than to make such a statement as that about a poor young stranger who—who—why, he is the very opposite of that! He is considerate, courteous, obliging, modest, gentle, refined, cultivated—*oh,* for shame! how can you say such things about him?''

"I don't blame you, Sally—indeed I haven't a word of blame for you for being blinded by your affection—blinded to these minor defects which are so manifest to others who—''

"Minor defects? Do you call these minor defects? What are murder and arson, pray?''

"It is a difficult question to answer straight off—and of course estimates of such things vary with environment. With us, out our way, they would not necessarily attract as much attention as with you, yet they are often regarded with disapproval—''

"Murder and arson are regarded with disapproval?''

"Oh, frequently.''

"With disapproval. Who *are* those Puritans you are talking about? But wait—how did you come to know so much about this family? Where did you get all this hearsay evidence?''

"Sally, it isn't hearsay evidence. That is the serious part of it. I *knew* that family—personally.''

This was a surprise.

"You? You actually knew them?''

"Knew Zylo, as we used to call him, and knew his father, Dr. Snodgrass. I didn't know your own Snodgrass, but have had glimpses of him from time to time, and I heard about him all the time. He was the common talk, you see, on account of his—''

"On account of his not being a house-burner or an assassin, I suppose. That would have made him commonplace. Where did you know these people?''

"In Cherokee Strip.''

"Oh, how preposterous! There are not enough people in Cherokee Strip to *give* anybody a reputation, good or bad. There isn't a quorum. Why the whole population consists of a couple of wagon loads of horse thieves.''

Hawkins answered placidly—

"Our friend was one of those wagon loads.''

Sally's eyes burned and her breath came quick and fast, but she kept a fairly good grip on her anger and did not let it get the advantage of her tongue. The statesman sat still and waited for developments. He was content with his work. It was as handsome a piece of diplomatic art as he had ever turned out, he thought; and now, let the girl make her own choice.

He judged she would let her specter go; he hadn't a doubt of it in fact; but anyway, let the choice be made, and he was ready to ratify it and offer no further hindrance.

Meantime Sally had thought her case out and made up her mind. To the major's disappointment the verdict was against him. Sally said:

"He has no friend but me, and I will not desert him now. I will not marry him if his moral character is bad; but if he can prove that it isn't, I will—and he shall have the chance. To me he seems utterly good and dear; I've never seen anything about him that looked otherwise—except, of course, his calling himself an earl's son. Maybe that is only vanity, and no real harm, when you get to the bottom of it. I do *not* believe he is any such person as you have painted him. I want to see him. I want you to find him and send him to me. I will implore him to be honest with me, and tell me the whole truth, and not be afraid."

"Very well; if that is your decision I will do it. But Sally, you know, he's poor, and—"

"Oh, *I* don't care anything about that. That's neither here nor there. Will you bring him to me?"

"I'll do it. When?"

"Oh, dear, it's getting toward dark, now, and so you'll have to put it off till morning. But you *will* find him in the morning, *won't* you? Promise."

"I'll have him here by daylight."

"Oh, *now* you're your own old self again—and lovelier than ever?"

"I couldn't ask fairer than that. Good-bye, dear."

Sally mused a moment alone, then said earnestly, "I love him in *spite* of his name!" and went about her affairs with a light heart.

Chapter 25

HAWKINS WENT straight to the telegraph office and disburdened his conscience. He said to himself, "She's not going to give this galvanized cadaver up, that's plain. Wild horses can't pull her away from him. I've done my share; it's for Sellers to take an inning, now." So he sent this message to New York:

"*Come back. Hire special train. She's going to marry the materializee.*"

Meantime a note came to Rossmore Towers to say that the Earl of Rossmore had just arrived from England, and would do himself the pleasure of calling in the evening. Sally said to herself, "It is a pity he didn't stop in New York; but it's no matter; he can go up to-morrow and see my father. He has come over here to tomahawk papa, very likely—or buy out his claim. This thing would have excited me, a while back; but it has only one interest for me now, and only one value. I can say to—to—Spine, Spiny, Spinal—I don't like any *form* of that name!—I can say to him to-morrow, '*Don't* try to keep it up any more, or I shall have to tell you whom I have been talking with last night, and then you will be embarrassed.' "

Tracy couldn't know he was to be invited for the morrow, or he might have waited. As it was, he was too miserable to wait any longer; for his last hope—a letter—had failed him. It was fully due to-day; it had not come. Had his father really flung him away? It looked so. It was not like his father, but it surely looked so. His father was a rather tough nut, in truth, but had never been so with his son—still, this implacable silence had a calamitous look. Anyway, Tracy would go to the Towers and—then what? He didn't know; his head was tired out with thinking—he wouldn't think about what he must do or say—let it all take care of itself. So that he saw Sally once more, he would be satisfied, happen what might; he wouldn't care.

He hardly knew how he got to the Towers, or when. He knew and cared for only one thing—he was alone with Sally. She was kind, she was gentle, there was moisture in her eyes, and a yearning something in her face and manner which she could not wholly hide—but she kept her distance. They talked. Bye and bye she said—watching his downcast countenance out of the corner of her eye—

"It's so lonesome—with papa and mamma gone. I try to read, but I can't seem to get interested in any book. I try the newspapers, but they do put such rubbish in them. You take up a paper and start to read something you think's interesting, and it goes on and on and on about how somebody—well, Dr. Snodgrass, for instance—"

Not a movement from Tracy, not the quiver of a muscle. Sally was amazed—what command of himself he must have! Being disconcerted, she paused so long that Tracy presently looked up wearily and said—

"Well?"

"Oh, I thought you were not listening. Yes, it goes on and on about this Doctor Snodgrass, till you are *so* tired, and then about his younger son—*the favorite son*—Zylobalsamum Snodgrass—"

Not a sign from Tracy, whose head was drooping again. What supernatural self-possession! Sally fixed her eye on him and began again, resolved to blast him out of his serenity this time if she knew how to apply the dynamite that is concealed in certain forms of words when those words are properly loaded with unexpected meanings.

"And next it goes on and on and on about the eldest son—*not* the favorite, this one—and how he is neglected in his poor barren boyhood, and allowed to grow up unschooled, ignorant, coarse, vulgar, the comrade of the community's scum, and become in his completed manhood a rude, profane, dissipated ruffian—"

That head still drooped! Sally rose, moved softly and solemnly a step or two, and stood before Tracy—his head came slowly up, his meek eyes met her intense ones—then she finished with deep impressiveness—

"—named Spinal Meningitis Snodgrass!"

Tracy merely exhibited signs of increased fatigue. The girl was outraged by this iron indifference and callousness, and cried out—

"What *are* you made of?"

"I? Why?"

"Haven't you *any* sensitiveness? Don't these things touch any poor *remnant* of delicate feeling in you?"

"N-no," he said wonderingly, "they don't seem to. Why should they?"

"O, dear me, *how* can you look so innocent, and foolish, and good, and empty, and gentle, and all that, right in the hearing of such things as those! Look me in the eye—straight in the eye. There, now then, answer me without a flinch. Isn't Doctor Snodgrass your father, and isn't Zylobalsamum your brother," [here Hawkins was about to enter the room, but changed his mind upon hearing these words, and elected for a walk down town, and so glided swiftly away], "and isn't your name Spinal Meningitis, and isn't your father a doctor and an idiot, like all the family for generations, and doesn't he name all his children after poisons and pestilences and abnormal anatomical eccentricities of the human body? Answer me, some way or somehow—and quick. *Why* do you sit there looking like an envelope without any address on it and see me going mad before your face with suspense!"

"Oh, I wish I could do—do—I wish I could do something, *anything* that would give you peace again and make you happy; but I know of nothing—I know of no way. I have never heard of these awful people before."

"What? Say it again!"

"I have never—never in my life till now."

"Oh, you *do* look so honest when you say that! It *must* be true—surely you *couldn't* look that way, you *wouldn't* look that way if it were not true—*would* you?"

"I couldn't and wouldn't. It *is* true. Oh, let us end this suffering—take me back into your heart and confidence—"

"Wait—one more thing. Tell me you told that falsehood out of mere vanity and are sorry for it; that you're *not* expecting to ever wear the coronet of an earl—"

"Truly I am cured—cured this very day—I am *not* expecting it!"

"O, now you *are* mine! I've got you back in the beauty and glory of your unsmirched poverty and your honorable obscurity, and nobody shall ever take you from me again but the grave! And if—"

"De earl of Rossmore, fum Englan'!"

"My father!" The young man released the girl and hung his head.

The old gentleman stood surveying the couple—the one with a strongly

MY FATHER!

complimentary right eye, the other with a mixed expression done with the left. This is difficult, and not often resorted to. Presently his face relaxed into a kind of constructive gentleness, and he said to his son—

"Don't you think you could embrace me, too?"

The young man did it with alacrity.

"Then you *are* the son of an earl, after all," said Sally, reproachfully.

"Yes, I—"

"Then I won't have you!"

"O, but you know—"

"No, I will not. You've told me another fib."

"She's right. Go away and leave us. I want to talk with her."

Berkeley was obliged to go. But he did not go far. He remained on the premises. At midnight the conference between the old gentleman and the young girl was still going blithely on, but it presently drew to a close, and the former said—

"I came all the way over here to inspect you, my dear, with the general idea of breaking off this match if there were *two* fools of you, but as there's only one, you can have him if you'll take him."

"Indeed I will, then! May I kiss you?"

"You may. Thank you. Now you shall have that privilege whenever you are good."

Meantime Hawkins had long ago returned and slipped up into the laboratory. He was rather disconcerted to find his late invention, Snodgrass, there. The news was told him: that the English Rossmore was come, "and I'm his son, Viscount Berkeley, not Howard Tracy any more."

Hawkins was aghast. He said—

"Good gracious, then you're dead!"

"Dead?"

"Yes, you are—we've got your ashes."

"Hang those ashes, I'm tired of them; I'll give them to my father."

Slowly and painfully the statesman worked the truth into his head that this was really a flesh and blood young man, and not the insubstantial resurrection he and Sellers had so long supposed him to be. Then he said with feeling—

"I'm so glad; so glad on Sally's account, poor thing. We took you for a departed materialized bank thief from Tahlequah. This will be a heavy blow to Sellers." Then he explained the whole matter to Berkeley, who said—

"Well, the Claimant must manage to stand the blow, severe as it is. But he'll get over the disappointment."

"Who—the Colonel? He'll get over it the minute he invents a new miracle to take its place. And he's already at it by this time. But look here—what do you suppose became of the man you've been *representing* all this time?"

"I don't know. I saved his clothes—it was all I could do. I am afraid he lost his life."

"Well, you must have found twenty or thirty thousand dollars in those clothes, in money or certificates of deposit."

"No, I found only five hundred and a trifle. I borrowed the trifle and banked the five hundred."

"What'll we do about it?"

"Return it to the owner."

"It's easy said, but not easy to manage. Let's leave it alone till we get Sellers's advice. And that reminds me. I've got to run and meet Sellers and explain who you are *not* and who you *are,* or he'll come thundering in here to stop his daughter from marrying a phantom. But—suppose your father came over here to break off the match?"

"Well, isn't he downstairs getting acquainted with Sally? That's all safe."

So Hawkins departed to meet and prepare the Sellerses.

Rossmore Towers saw great times and late hours during the succeeding week. The two earls were such opposites in nature that they fraternized at once. Sellers said privately that Rossmore was the most extraordinary character he had ever met—a man just made out of the condensed milk of human kindness, yet with the ability to totally hide the fact from any but the most practiced character-reader; a man whose whole being was sweetness, patience and charity, yet with a cunning so profound, an ability so marvelous in the acting of a double part, that many a person of considerable intelligence might live with him for centuries and never suspect the presence in him of these characteristics.

Finally there was a quiet wedding at the Towers, instead of a big one at the British embassy, with the militia and the fire brigades and the temperance organizations on hand in torchlight procession, as at first proposed by one of the earls. The art-firm and Barrow were present at the wedding, and the tinner and Puss had been invited, but the tinner was ill and Puss was nursing him—for they were engaged.

The Sellerses were to go to England with their new allies for a brief visit, but when it was time to take the train from Washington, the Colonel was missing. Hawkins was going as far as New York with the party, and said he would explain the matter on the road. The explanation was in a letter left by the Colonel in Hawkins's hands. In it he promised to join Mrs. Sellers later, in England, and then went on to say:

> The truth is, my dear Hawkins, a mighty idea has been born to
> me within the hour, and I must not even stop to say goodbye to

FINALLY THERE WAS A QUIET WEDDING AT THE TOWERS.

my dear ones. A man's highest duty takes precedence of all minor ones, and must be attended to with his best promptness and energy, at whatsoever cost to his affections or his convenience. And first of all a man's duties is his duty to his own honor—he must keep that spotless. Mine is threatened. When I was feeling sure of my imminent future solidity, I forwarded to the Czar of Russia— perhaps prematurely—an offer for the purchase of Siberia, naming a vast sum. Since then an episode has warned me that the method by which I was expecting to acquire this money—materialization upon a scale of limitless magnitude—is marred by a taint of temporary uncertainty. His imperial majesty may accept my offer at any moment. If this should occur now, I should find myself painfully embarrassed, in fact financially inadequate. I could not take Siberia. This would become known, and my credit would suffer.

Recently my private hours have been dark indeed, but the sun shines again, now; I see my way; I shall be able to meet my obligation, and without having to ask an extension of the stipulated time, I think. This grand new idea of mine—the sublimest I have ever conceived, will save me whole, I am sure. I am leaving for San Francisco this moment, to test it, by the help of the great Lick telescope. Like all of my more notable discoveries and inventions, it is based upon hard, practical scientific laws; all other bases are unsound and hence untrustworthy.

In brief, then, I have conceived the stupendous idea of reorganizing the climates of the earth according to the desire of the populations interested. That is to say, I will furnish climates to order for cash or negotiable paper, taking the old climates in part payment, of course, at a fair discount, where they are in condition to be repaired at small cost and let out for hire to poor and remote communities not able to afford a good climate and not caring for an expensive one for mere display. My studies have convinced me that the regulation of climates and the breeding of new varieties at will from the old stock is a feasible thing. Indeed I am convinced that it has been done before; done in prehistoric times by now forgotten and unrecorded civilizations. Everywhere I find hoary evidences of artificial manipulation of climates in bygone times. Take the glacial period. Was that produced by accident? Not at all; it was done for money. I have a thousand proofs of it, and will some day reveal them.

I will confide to you an outline of my idea. It is to utilize the spots on the sun—get control of them, you understand, and apply the stupendous energies which they wield to beneficent purposes in the reorganizing of our climates. At present they merely make trouble and do harm in the evoking of cyclones and other kinds of electric storms; but once under humane and intelligent control this will cease and they will become a boon to man.

I have my plan all mapped out, whereby I hope and expect to acquire complete and perfect control of the sun-spots, also details of the method whereby I shall employ the same commercially; but I will not venture to go into particulars before the patents shall have been issued. I shall hope and expect to sell shop-rights to the minor countries at a reasonable figure and supply a good business article of climate to the great empires at special rates, together with fancy brands for coronations, battles and other great and particular occasions. There are billions of money in this enterprise, no expensive plant is required, and I shall begin to realize in a few days—in a few weeks at furthest. I shall stand ready to pay cash for Siberia the moment it is delivered, and thus save my honor and my credit. I am confident of this.

I would like you to provide a proper outfit and start north as soon as I telegraph you, be it night or be it day. I wish you to take up all the country stretching away from the north pole on all sides for many degrees south, and buy Greenland and Iceland at the best figure you can get now while they are cheap. It is my intention to move one of the tropics up there and transfer the frigid zone to the equator. I will have the entire Arctic Circle in the market as a summer resort next year, and will use the surplusage of the old climate, over and above what can be utilized on the equator, to reduce the temperature of opposition resorts. But I have said enough to give you an idea of the prodigious nature of my scheme and the feasible and enormously profitable character of it. I shall join all you happy people in England as soon as I shall have sold out some of my principal climates and arranged with the Czar about Siberia.

Meantime, watch for a sign from me. Eight days from now, we shall be wide asunder; for I shall be on the border of the Pacific, and you far out on the Atlantic, approaching England. That day, if I am alive and my sublime discovery is proved and established, I will send you greeting, and my messenger shall deliver it where you are, in the solitudes of the sea; for I will waft a vast sun-spot across the disk like drifting smoke, and you will know it for my love-sign, and will say "Mulberry Sellers throws us a kiss across the universe."

APPENDIX

Weather for use in this Book

Selected from the Best Authorities

A brief though violent thunderstorm which had raged over the city was passing away; but still, though the rain had ceased more than an hour before, wild piles of dark and coppery clouds, in which a fierce and rayless glow was laboring, gigantically overhung the grotesque and huddled vista of dwarf houses, while in the distance, sheeting high over the low, misty confusion of gables and chimneys, spread a pall of dead, leprous blue, suffused with blotches of dull, glistening yellow, and with black plague-spots of vapor floating and faint lightnings crinkling on its surface. Thunder, still muttering in the close and sultry air, kept the scared dwellers in the street within, behind their closed shutters; and all deserted, cowed, dejected, squalid, like poor, stupid, top-heavy things that had felt the wrath of the summer tempest, stood the drenched structures on either side of the narrow and crooked way, ghastly and picturesque under the giant canopy. Rain dripped wretchedly in slow drops of melancholy sound from their projecting eaves upon the broken flagging, lay there in pools or trickled into the swollen drains, where the fallen torrent sullenly gurgled on its way to the river.—*"The Brazen Android."*—*W. D. O'Connor.*

> The fiery mid-March sun a moment hung
> Above the bleak Judean wilderness;
> Then darkness swept upon us, and 't was night.
> *"Easter-Eve at Kerak-Moab."*—*Clinton Scollard.*

The quick-coming winter twilight was already at hand. Snow was again falling, sifting delicately down, incidentally as it were.
"Felicia." —*Fanny N. D. Murfree.*

Merciful heavens! The whole west, from right to left, blazes up with a fierce light, and next instant the earth reels and quivers with the awful shock of ten thousand batteries of artillery. It is the signal for the Fury to spring—for a thousand demons to scream and shriek—for innumerable serpents of fire to writhe and light up the blackness.

Now the rain falls—now the wind is let loose with a terrible shriek—now the lightning is so constant that the eyes burn, and the thunder-claps merge into an awful roar, as did the 800 cannon at Gettysburg. Crash! Crash! Crash! It is the cottonwood trees falling to earth. Shriek! Shriek! Shriek! It is the Demon racing along the plain and uprooting even the blades of grass. Shock! Shock! Shock! It is the Fury flinging his fiery bolts into the bosom of the earth.—*"The Demon and the Fury."*—*M. Quad.*

Away up the gorge all diurnal fancies trooped into the wide liberties of endless luminous vistas of azure sunlit mountains beneath the shining azure heavens. The sky, looking down in deep blue placidities, only here and there smote the water to azure emulations of its tint.—*"In the Stranger's Country."*—*Charles Egbert Craddock.*

There was every indication of a dust-storm, though the sun still shone brilliantly. The hot wind had become wild and rampant. It was whipping up the sandy coating of the plain in every direction. High in the air were seen whirling spires and cones of sand—a curious effect against the deep-blue sky. Below, puffs of sand were breaking out of the plain in every direction, as though the plain were alive with invisible horsemen. These sandy cloudlets were instantly dissipated by the wind; it was the larger clouds that were lifted whole into the air, and the larger clouds of sand were becoming more and more the rule.

Alfred's eye, quickly scanning the horizon, descried the roof of the boundary-rider's hut still gleaming in the sunlight. He remembered the hut well. It could not be farther than four miles, if as much as that, from this point of the track. He also knew these dust-storms of old; Bindarra was notorious for them. Without thinking twice, Alfred put spurs to his horse and headed for the hut. Before he had ridden half the distance the detached clouds of sand banded together in one dense whirlwind, and it was only owing to his horse's instinct that he did not ride wide of the hut altogether; for during the last half-mile he never saw the hut, until its outline loomed suddenly over his horse's ears; and by then the sun was invisible.—*"A Bride from the Bush."*

It rained forty days and forty nights.—*Genesis.*

Editorial Wild Oats

I FANCIED HE WAS DISPLEASED.

MY FIRST LITERARY VENTURE

I WAS a very smart child at the age of thirteen—an unusually smart child, I thought at the time. It was then that I did my first newspaper scribbling, and most unexpectedly to me it stirred up a fine sensation in the community. It did, indeed, and I was very proud of it, too. I was a printer's "devil," and a progressive and aspiring one. My uncle had me on his paper (the *Weekly Hannibal Journal*, two dollars a year, in advance—five hundred subscribers, and they paid in cord-wood, cabbages, and unmarketable turnips), and on a lucky summer's day he left town to be gone a week, and asked me if I thought I could edit one issue of the paper judiciously. Ah! didn't I want to try! Higgins was the editor on the rival paper. He had lately been jilted, and one night a friend found an open note on the poor fellow's bed, in which he stated that he could no longer endure life and had drowned himself in Bear Creek. The friend ran down there and discovered Higgins wading back to shore. He had concluded he wouldn't. The village was full of it for several days, but Higgins did not suspect it. I thought this was a fine opportunity. I wrote an elaborately wretched account of the whole matter, and then illustrated it with villainous cuts engraved on the bottoms of wooden type with a jack-knife—one of them a picture of Higgins wading out into the creek in his shirt, with a

HE HAD CONCLUDED HE WOULDN'T.

515

lantern, sounding the depth of the water with a walking-stick. I thought it was desperately funny, and was densely unconscious that there was any moral obliquity about such a publication. Being satisfied with this effort, I looked around for other worlds to conquer, and it struck me that it would make good, interesting matter to charge the editor of a neighboring country paper with a piece of gratuitous rascality and "see him squirm."

I did it, putting the article into the form of a parody on the "Burial of Sir John Moore"—and a pretty crude parody it was, too.

Then I lampooned two prominent citizens outrageously—not because they had done anything to deserve it, but merely because I thought it was my duty to make the paper lively.

Next I gently touched up the newest stranger—the lion of the day, the gorgeous journeyman tailor from Quincy. He was a simpering coxcomb of the first water, and the "loudest" dressed man in the State. He was an inveterate woman-killer. Every week he wrote lushy "poetry" for the *Journal*, about his newest conquest. His rhymes for my week were headed, "TO MARY IN H—L," meaning to Mary in Hannibal, of course. But while setting up the piece I was suddenly riven from head to heel by what I regarded as a perfect thunderbolt of humor, and I compressed it into a snappy footnote at the bottom—thus:

> We will let this thing pass, just this once; but we wish Mr. J. Gordon Runnels to understand distinctly that we have a character to sustain, and from this time forth when he wants to commune with his friends in h—l, he must select some other medium than the columns of this journal!

The paper came out, and I never knew any little thing attract so much attention as those playful trifles of mine.

For once the *Hannibal Journal* was in demand—a novelty it had not experienced before. The whole town was stirred. Higgins dropped in with a double-barrelled shot-gun early in the forenoon. When he found that it was an infant (as he called me) that had done him the damage, he simply pulled my ears and went away; but he threw up his situation that night and left town for good. The tailor came with his goose and a pair of shears; but he despised me, too, and departed for the South that night. The two lampooned citizens came with threats of libel, and went away incensed at my insignificance. The country editor pranced in with a warwhoop next day, suffering for blood to drink; but he ended by forgiving me cordially and inviting me down to the drug-store to wash away all animosity in a friendly bumper of "Fahnestock's Vermifuge." It was his little joke. My uncle was very angry when he got back—unreasonably so, I thought, considering what an impetus I had given the paper, and considering also that gratitude for his preservation ought to have been uppermost in his mind, inasmuch as by his delay he had so wonderfully escaped dissection, tomahawking, libel, and getting his head shot off. But he softened when he looked at the accounts and saw that I had actually booked the unparalled number of thirty-three new subscribers, and had the vegetables to show for it—cord-wood, cabbage, beans, and unsalable turnips enough to run the family for two years!

JOURNALISM IN TENNESSEE

The editor of the Memphis *Avalanche* swoops thus mildly down upon a correspondent who posted him as a Radical: "While he was writing the first word, the middle, dotting his i's, crossing his t's, and punching his period, he knew he was concocting a sentence that was saturated with infamy and reeking with falsehood."—*Exchange*.

I WAS told by the physician that a Southern climate would improve my health, and so I went down to Tennessee and got a berth on the *Morning-Glory and Johnson County Warwhoop* as associate editor. When I went on duty I found the chief editor sitting tilted back in a three-legged chair with his feet on a pine table. There was another pine table in the room and another afflicted chair, and both were half buried under newspapers and scraps and sheets of manuscript. There was a wooden box of sand, sprinkled with cigar-stubs and "old soldiers," and a stove with a door hanging by its upper hinge. The chief editor had a long-tailed black cloth frockcoat on, and white linen pants. His boots were small and neatly blacked. He wore a ruffled shirt, a large seal ring, a standing collar of obsolete pattern, and a checkered neckerchief with the ends hanging down. Date of costume about 1848. He was smoking a cigar, and trying to think of a word, and in pawing his hair he had rumpled his locks a good deal. He was scowling fearfully, and I judged that he was concocting a particularly knotty editorial. He told me to take the exchanges and skim through them and write up the "Spirit of the Tennessee Press," condensing into the article all of their contents that seemed of interest.

I wrote as follows:

SPIRIT OF THE TENNESSEE PRESS

The editors of the *Semi-Weekly Earthquake* evidently labor under a misapprehension with regard to the Ballyhack railroad. It is not the object of the company to leave Buzzardville off to one side. On the contrary, they consider it one of the most important points along the line, and consequently can have no desire to slight it. The gentlemen of the *Earthquake* will, of course, take pleasure in making the correction.

John W. Blossom, Esq., the able editor of the Higginsville *Thunderbolt and Battle-Cry of Freedom*, arrived in the city yesterday. He is stopping at the Van Buren House.

We observe that our contemporary of the Mud Springs *Morning Howl* has fallen into the error of supposing that the election of Van Werter is not an established fact, but he will have discovered his mistake before this reminder reaches him, no doubt. He was doubtless misled by incomplete election returns.

It is pleasant to note that the city of Blathersville is endeavoring to contract with some New York gentlemen to pave its wellnigh impassable streets with the Nicholson pavement. The *Daily Hurrah* urges the measure with ability, and seems confident of ultimate success.

I passed my manuscript over to the chief editor for acceptance, alteration, or destruction. He glanced at it and his face clouded. He ran his eye down the pages, and his countenance grew portentous. It was easy to see that something was wrong. Presently he sprang up and said:

"Thunder and lightning! Do you suppose I am going to speak of those cattle that way? Do you suppose my subscribers are going to stand such gruel as that? Give me the pen!"

I never saw a pen scrape and scratch its way so viciously, or plough through another man's verbs and adjectives so relentlessly. While he was in the midst of his work, somebody shot at him through the open window, and marred the symmetry of my ear.

"Ah," said he, "that is that scoundrel Smith, of the *Moral Volcano*— he was due yesterday." And he snatched a navy revolver from his belt and fired. Smith dropped, shot in the thigh. The shot spoiled Smith's aim, who was just taking a second chance, and he crippled a stranger. It was me. Merely a finger shot off.

Then the chief editor went on with his erasures and interlineations. Just as he finished them a hand-grenade came down the stove-pipe, and the explosion shivered the stove into a thousand fragments. However, it did no further damage, except that a vagrant piece knocked a couple of my teeth out.

"That stove is utterly ruined," said the chief editor.

I said I believed it was.

"Well, no matter—don't want it this kind of weather. I know the man that did it. I'll get him. Now, *here* is the way this stuff ought to be written."

I took the manuscript. It was scarred with erasures and interlineations till its mother wouldn't have known it if it had had one. It now read as follows:

SPIRIT OF THE TENNESSEE PRESS

The inveterate liars of the *Semi-Weekly Earthquake* are evidently endeavoring to palm off upon a noble and chivalrous people another of their vile and brutal falsehoods with regard to that most glorious conception of the nineteenth century, the Ballyhack railroad. The idea that Buzzardville was to be left off at one side originated in their own fulsome brains—or rather in the settlings which *they* regard as brains. They had better swallow this lie if they want to save their abandoned reptile carcasses the cowhiding they so richly deserve.

That ass, Blossom, of the Higginsville *Thunderbolt and Battle-Cry of Freedom*, is down here again sponging at the Van Buren.

We observe that the besotted blackguard of the Mud Springs *Morning Howl* is giving out, with his usual propensity for lying, that Van Werter is not elected. The heaven-born mission of jour-

nalism is to disseminate truth; to eradicate error; to educate, re-
fine, and elevate the tone of public morals and manners, and make
all men more gentle, more virtuous, more charitable, and in all
ways better, and holier, and happier; and yet this black-hearted
scoundrel degrades his great office persistently to the dissemina-
tion of falsehood, calumny, vituperation, and vulgarity.

Blathersville wants a Nicholson pavement—it wants a jail and a
poorhouse more. The idea of a pavement in a one-horse town
composed of two gin-mills, a blacksmith-shop, and that mustard-
plaster of a newspaper, the *Daily Hurrah!* The crawling insect,
Buckner, who edits the *Hurrah*, is braying about this business with
his customary imbecility, and imagining that he is talking sense.

"Now *that* is the way to write—peppery and to the point. Mush-and-
milk journalism gives me the fan-tods."

About this time a brick came through the window with a splintering
crash, and gave me a considerable of a jolt in the back. I moved out of
range—I began to feel in the way.

The chief said: "That was the Colonel, likely. I've been expecting him
for two days. He will be up now right away."

He was correct. The Colonel appeared in the door a moment afterwards
with a dragoon revolver in his hand.

He said: "Sir, have I the honor of addressing the poltroon who edits this
mangy sheet?"

"You have. Be seated, sir. Be careful of the chair, one of its legs is
gone. I believe I have the honor of addressing the putrid liar, Colonel
Blatherskite Tecumseh?"

"Right, sir. I have a little account to settle with you. If you are at leisure
we will begin."

"I have an article on the 'Encouraging Progress of Moral and Intellectual Development in America' to finish, but there is no hurry. Begin."

Both pistols rang out their fierce clamor at the same instant. The chief
lost a lock of his hair, and the Colonel's bullet ended its career in the
fleshy part of my thigh. The Colonel's left shoulder was clipped a little.
They fired again. Both missed their men this time, but I got my share, a
shot in the arm. At the third fire both gentlemen were wounded slightly,
and I had a knuckle chipped. I then said I believed I would go out and
take a walk, as this was a private matter, and I had a delicacy about
participating in it further. But both gentlemen begged me to keep my seat,
and assured me that I was not in the way.

They then talked about the elections and the crops while they reloaded,
and I fell to tying up my wounds. But presently they opened fire again
with animation, and every shot took effect—but it is proper to remark that
five out of the six fell to my share. The sixth one mortally wounded the
Colonel, who remarked, with fine humor, that he would have to say good-
morning now, as he had business up-town. He then inquired the way to
the undertaker's and left.

The chief turned to me and said: "I am expecting company to dinner,
and shall have to get ready. It will be a favor to me if you will read proof
and attend to the customers."

I winced a little at the idea of attending to the customers, but I was too bewildered by the fusillade that was still ringing in my ears to think of anything to say.

He continued: "Jones will be here at three—cowhide him. Gillespie will call earlier, perhaps—throw him out of the window. Ferguson will be along about four—kill him. That is all for to-day, I believe. If you have any odd time, you may write a blistering article on the police—give the chief inspector rats. The cowhides are under the table; weapons in the drawer—ammunition there in the corner—lint and bandages up there in the pigeon-holes. In case of accident, go to Lancet, the surgeon, downstairs. He advertises—we take it out in trade."

He was gone. I shuddered. At the end of the next three hours I had been through perils so awful that all peace of mind and all cheerfulness were gone from me. Gillespie had called and thrown *me* out of the window. Jones arrived promptly, and when I got ready to do the cowhiding he took the job off my hands. In an encounter with a stranger, not in the bill of fare, I had lost my scalp. Another stranger, by the name of Thompson, left me a mere wreck and ruin of chaotic rags. And at last, at bay in the corner, and beset by an infuriated mob of editors, blacklegs, politicians, and desperadoes, who raved and swore and flourished their weapons about my head till the air shimmered with glancing flashes of steel, I was in the act of resigning my berth on the paper when the chief arrived, and with him a rabble of charmed and enthusiastic friends. Then ensued a scene of riot and carnage such as no human pen, or steel one either, could describe. People were shot, probed, dismembered, blown up, thrown out of the window. There was a brief tornado of murky blasphemy, with a confused and frantic war-dance glimmering through it, and then all was over. In five minutes there was silence, and the gory chief and I sat alone and surveyed the sanguinary ruin that strewed the floor around us.

He said: "You'll like this place when you get used to it."

I said: "I'll have to get you to excuse me; I think maybe I might write to suit you after a while; as soon as I had had some practice and learned the language I am confident I could. But, to speak the plain truth, that

GILLESPIE HAD CALLED.

sort of energy of expression has its inconveniences, and a man is liable to interruption. You see that yourself. Vigorous writing is calculated to elevate the public, no doubt, but then I do not like to attract so much attention as it calls forth. I can't write with comfort when I am interrupted so much as I have been to-day. I like this berth well enough, but I don't like to be left here to wait on the customers. The experiences are novel, I grant you, and entertaining, too, after a fashion, but they are not judiciously distributed. A gentleman shoots at you through the window and cripples *me;* a bomb-shell comes down the stove-pipe for your gratification and sends the stove-door down *my* throat; a friend drops in to swap compliments with you, and freckles *me* with bullet-holes till my skin won't hold my principles; you go to dinner, and Jones comes with his cowhide, Gillespie throws me out of the window, Thompson tears all my clothes off, and an entire stranger takes my scalp with the easy freedom of an old acquaintance; and in less than five minutes all the blackguards in the country arrive in their war-paint, and proceed to scare the rest of me to death with their tomahawks. Take it altogether, I never had such a spirited time in all my life as I have had to-day. No; I like you, and I like your calm, unruffled way of explaining things to the customers, but you see I am not used to it. The Southern heart is too impulsive; Southern hospitality is too lavish with the stranger. The paragraphs which I have written to-day, and into whose cold sentences your masterly hand has infused the fervent spirit of Tennessean journalism, will wake up another nest of hornets. All that mob of editors will come—and they will come hungry, too, and want somebody for breakfast. I shall have to bid you adieu. I decline to be present at these festivities. I came South for my health; I will go back on the same errand, and suddenly. Tennesseean journalism is too stirring for me."

After which we parted with mutual regret, and I took apartments at the hospital.

NICODEMUS DODGE—PRINTER

WHEN I was a boy in a printing-office in Missouri, a loose-jointed, long-legged, tow-headed, jeans-clad, countrified cub of about sixteen lounged in one day, and without removing his hands from the depths of his trousers pockets or taking off his faded ruin of a slouch hat, whose broken rim hung limp and ragged about his eyes and ears like a bug-eaten cabbage-leaf, stared indifferently around, then leaned his hip against the editors' table, crossed his mighty brogans, aimed at a distant fly from a crevice in his upper teeth, laid him low, and said, with composure:

"Whar's the boss?"

"I am the boss," said the editor, following this curious bit of architecture wonderingly along up to its clock-face with his eye.

"Don't want anybody fur to learn the business, 'tain't likely?"

"Well, I don't know. Would you like to learn it?"

"Pap's so po' he cain't run me no mo', so I want to git a show somers if I kin, 'tain't no diffunce what—I'm strong and hearty, and I don't turn my back on no kind of work, hard nur soft.''

"Do you think you would like to learn the printing business?''

"Well, I don't re'ly k'yer a durn what I *do* learn, so's I git a chance fur to make my way. I'd jist as soon learn print'n' 's anything.''

"Can you read?''

"Yes—middlin'.''

"Write?''

"Well, I've seed people could lay over me thar.''

"Cipher?''

"Not good enough to keep store, I don't reckon, but up as fur as twelve-times-twelve I ain't no slouch. 'Tother side of that is what gits me.''

"Where is your home?''

"I'm f'm old Shelby.''

"What's your father's religious denomination?''

"Him? Oh, he's a blacksmith.''

"No, no—I don't mean his trade. What's his *religious* denomination?''

"*Oh*—I didn't understand you befo'. He's a Freemason.''

"No, no; you don't get my meaning yet. What I mean is, does he belong to any *church?*''

"*Now* you're talkin'! Couldn't make out what you was a-tryin' to git through yo' head no way. B'long to a *church!* Why, boss, he's be'n the pizenest kind of a Free-will Babtis' for forty year. They ain't no pizener ones 'n' what *he* is. Mighty good man, pap is. Everybody says that. If they said any diffrunt they wouldn't say it whar *I* wuz—not *much* they wouldn't.''

"What is your own religion?''

"Well, boss, you've kind o' got me thar—and yit you hain't got me so mighty much, nuther. I think 't if a feller he'ps another feller when he's in trouble, and don't cuss, and don't do no mean things, nur noth'n' he ain' no business to do, and don't spell the Savior's name with a little g, he ain't runnin' no resks—he's about as saift as if he b'longed to a church.''

"But suppose he did spell it with a little g—what then?''

"Well, if he done it a-purpose, I reckon he wouldn't stand no chance,—he *oughtn't* to have no chance, anyway, I'm most rotten certain 'bout that.''

"What is your name?''

"Nicodemus Dodge.''

"I think maybe you'll do, Nicodemus. We'll give you a trial, anyway.''

"All right.''

"When would you like to begin?''

"Now.''

So, within ten minutes after we had first glimpsed this nondescript he was one of us, and with his coat off and hard at it.

Beyond that end of our establishment which was farthest from the street was a deserted garden, pathless, and thickly grown with the bloomy and villainous "jimpson" weed and its common friend the stately sunflower. In the midst of this mournful spot was a decayed and aged little "frame" house with but one room, one window, and no ceiling—it had been a smoke-house a generation before. Nicodemus was given this lonely and ghostly den as a bedchamber.

The village smarties recognized a treasure in Nicodemus right away— a butt to play jokes on. It was easy to see that he was inconceivably green and confiding. George Jones had the glory of perpetrating the first joke on him; he gave him a cigar with a fire-cracker in it and winked to the crowd to come; the thing exploded presently and swept away the bulk of Nicodemus's eyebrows and eyelashes. He simply said:

"I consider them kind of seeg'yars dangersome"—and seemed to suspect nothing. The next evening Nicodemus waylaid George and poured a bucket of ice-water over him.

One day, while Nicodemus was in swimming, Tom McElroy "tied" his clothes. Nicodemus made a bonfire of Tom's by way of retaliation.

A third joke was played upon Nicodemus a day or two later—he walked up the middle aisle of the village church, Sunday night, with a staring hand-bill pinned between his shoulders. The joker spent the remainder of the night, after church, in the cellar of a deserted house, and Nicodemus sat on the cellar door till towards breakfast-time to make sure that the prisoner remembered that if any noise was made some rough treatment would be the consequence. The cellar had two feet of stagnant water in it, and was bottomed with six inches of soft mud.

But I wander from the point. It was the subject of skeletons that brought this boy back to my recollection. Before a very long time had elapsed, the village smarties began to feel an uncomfortable consciousness of not having made a very shining success out of their attempts on the simpleton from "old Shelby." Experimenters grew scarce and chary. Now the young doctor came to the rescue. There was delight and applause when he proposed to scare Nicodemus to death, and explained how he was going to do it. He had a noble new skeleton—the skeleton of the late and only local celebrity, Jimmy Finn, the village drunkard—a grisly piece of property which he had bought of Jimmy Finn himself, at auction, for fifty dollars, under great competition, when Jimmy lay very sick in the tanyard a fortnight before his death. The fifty dollars had gone promptly for whiskey and had considerably hurried up the change of ownership in the skeleton. The doctor would put Jimmy Finn's skeleton in Nicodemus's bed!

This was done—about half-past ten in the evening. About Nicodemus's usual bedtime—midnight—the village jokers came creeping stealthily through the jimpson weeds and sunflowers towards the lonely frame den. They reached the window and peeped in. There sat the long-legged pauper, on his bed, in a very short shirt, and nothing more; he was dangling his legs contentedly back and forth, and wheezing the music of "Camptown Races" out of a paper-overlaid comb which he was pressing against his mouth; by him lay a new jews-harp, a new top, a solid india-rubber ball, a handful of painted marbles, five pounds of "store" candy, and a well-knawed slab of gingerbread as big and as thick as a volume of sheet music. He had sold the skeleton to a travelling quack for three dollars and was enjoying the result!

WHEEZING THE MUSIC OF "CAMPTOWN RACES."

MR. BLOKE'S ITEM

OUR ESTEEMED friend, Mr. John William Bloke, of Virginia City, walked into the office where we are sub-editor at a late hour last night, with an expression of profound and heartfelt suffering upon his countenance, and, sighing heavily, laid the following item reverently upon the desk, and walked slowly out again. He paused a moment at the door, and seemed struggling to command his feelings sufficiently to enable him to speak, and then, nodding his head towards his manuscript, ejaculated in a broken voice, "Friend of mine—oh! how sad!" and burst into tears. We were so moved at his distress that we did not think to call him back and endeavor to comfort him until he was gone, and it was too late. The paper had already gone to press, but knowing that our friend would consider the publication of this item important, and cherishing the hope that to print it would afford a melancholy satisfaction to his sorrowing heart, we stopped the press at once and inserted it in our columns:

DISTRESSING ACCIDENT.—Last evening, about six o'clock, as Mr. William Schuyler, an old and respectable citizen of South Park, was leaving his residence to go down-town, as has been his usual custom for many years with the exception only of a short interval in the spring of 1850, during which he was confined to his bed by injuries received in attempting to stop a runaway horse by thoughtlessly placing himself directly in its wake and throwing up his hands and shouting, which, if he had done so even a single moment sooner, must inevitably have frightened the animal still more instead of checking its speed, although disastrous enough to himself as it was, and rendered more melancholy and distressing by reason of the presence of his wife's mother, who was there and saw the sad occurrence, notwithstanding it is at least likely, though not necessarily so, that she should be reconnoitring in another direction when incidents occur, not being vivacious and on the

lookout, as a general thing, but even the reverse, as her own
mother is said to have stated, who is no more, but died in the full
hope of a glorious resurrection, upward of three years ago, aged
eighty-six, being a Christian woman and without guile, as it were,
or property, in consequence of the fire of 1849, which destroyed
every single thing she had in the world. But such is life. Let us all
take warning by this solemn occurrence, and let us endeavor so to
conduct ourselves that when we come to die we can do it. Let us
place our hands upon our heart, and say with earnestness and
sincerity that from this day forth we will beware of the intoxicating
bowl.—*First edition of the Californian*.

The head editor has been in here raising the mischief, and tearing his
hair and kicking the furniture about, and abusing me like a pickpocket.
He says that every time he leaves me in charge of the paper for half an
hour, I get imposed upon by the first infant or the first idiot that comes
along. And he says that that distressing item of Mr. Bloke's is nothing but
a lot of distressing bosh, and has no point to it, and no sense in it, and no
information in it, and that there was no sort of necessity for stopping the
press to publish it.

Now all this comes of being good-hearted. If I had been as unaccom-
modating and unsympathetic as some people, I would have told Mr. Bloke
that I wouldn't receive his communication at such a late hour; but no, his
snuffling distress touched my heart, and I jumped at the chance of doing
something to modify his misery. I never read his item to see whether there
was anything wrong about it, but hastily wrote the few lines which preceded it, and sent it to the printers. And what has my kindness done for
me? It has done nothing but bring down upon me a storm of abuse and
ornamental blasphemy.

Now I will read that item myself, and see if there is any foundation for
all this fuss. And if there is, the author of it shall hear from me.

I have read it, and I am bound to admit that it seems a little mixed at a
first glance. However, I will peruse it once more.

I have read it again, and it does really seem a good deal more mixed
than ever.

I have read it over five times, but if I can get at the meaning of it, I
wish I may get my just deserts. It won't bear analysis. There are things
about it which I cannot understand at all. It don't say what ever became
of William Schuyler. It just says enough about him to get one interested
in his career, and then drops him. Who is William Schuyler, anyhow, and
what part of South Park did he live in, and if he started down-town at six
o'clock, did he ever get there, and if he did, did anything happen to him?
Is *he* the individual that met with the "distressing accident"? Considering
the elaborate circumstantiality of detail observable in the item, it seems to

me that it ought to contain more information than it does. On the contrary, it is obscure—and not only obscure, but utterly incomprehensible. Was the breaking of Mr. Schuyler's leg, fifteen years ago, the "distressing accident" that plunged Mr. Bloke into unspeakable grief, and caused him to come up here at dead of night and stop our press to acquaint the world with the circumstance? Or did the "distressing accident" consist in the destruction of Schuyler's mother-in-law's property in early times? Or did it consist in the death of that person herself three years ago (albeit it does not appear that she died by accident)? In a word, what *did* that "distressing accident" consist in? What did that drivelling ass of a Schuyler stand *in the wake* of a runaway horse for, with his shouting and gesticulating, if he wanted to stop him? And how the mischief could he get run over by a horse that had already passed beyond him? And what are we to take "warning" by? And how is this extraordinary chapter of incomprehensibilities going to be a "lesson" to us? And, above all, what has the intoxicating "bowl" got to do with it, anyhow? It is not stated that Schuyler drank, or that his wife drank, or that his mother-in-law drank, or that the horse drank—wherefore, then, the reference to the intoxicating bowl? It does seem to me that if Mr. Bloke had let the intoxicating bowl alone himself, he never would have got into so much trouble about this exasperating imaginary accident. I have read this absurd item over and over again, with all its insinuating plausibility, until my head swims, but I can make neither head nor tail of it. There certainly seems to have been an accident of some kind or other, but it is impossible to determine what the nature of it was, or who was the sufferer by it. I do not like to do it, but I feel compelled to request that the next time anything happens to one of Mr. Bloke's friends, he will append such explanatory notes to his account of it as will enable me to find out what sort of an accident it was and whom it happened to. I had rather all his friends should die than that I should be driven to the verge of lunacy again in trying to cipher out the meaning of another such production as the above.

I HAVE READ THIS ABSURD ITEM OVER.

HOW I EDITED AN AGRICULTURAL PAPER

I DID not take temporary editorship of an agricultural paper without misgivings. Neither would a landsman take command of a ship without misgivings. But I was in circumstances that made the salary an object. The regular editor of the paper was going off for a holiday, and I accepted the terms he offered, and took his place.

The sensation of being at work again was luxurious, and I wrought all the week with unflagging pleasure. We went to press, and I waited a day with some solicitude to see whether my effort was going to attract any notice. As I left the office, towards sundown, a group of men and boys at the foot of the stairs dispersed with one impulse, and gave me passageway, and I heard one or two of them say, "That's him!" I was naturally pleased by this incident. The next morning I found a similar group at the foot of the stairs, and scattering couples and individuals standing here and there in the street, and over the way, watching me with interest. The group separated and fell back as I approached, and I heard a man say, "Look at his eye!" I pretended not to observe the notice I was attracting, but secretly I was pleased with it, and was purposing to write an account of it to my aunt. I went up the short flight of stairs, and heard cheery voices and a ringing laugh as I drew near the door, which I opened, and caught a glimpse of two young rural-looking men, whose faces blanched and lengthened when they saw me, and then they both plunged through the window with a great crash. I was surprised.

In about half an hour an old gentleman, with a flowing beard and a fine but rather austere face, entered, and sat down at my invitation. He seemed to have something on his mind. He took off his hat and set it on the floor, and got out of it a red silk handkerchief and a copy of our paper.

He put the paper on his lap, and while he polished his spectacles with his handkerchief, he said, "Are you the new editor?"

I said I was.

"Have you ever edited an agricultural paper before?"

"No," I said; "this is my first attempt."

"Very likely. Have you had any experience in agriculture practically?"

"No; I believe I have not."

"Some instinct told me so," said the old gentleman, putting on his spectacles, and looking over them at me with asperity, while he folded his paper into a convenient shape. "I wish to read you what must have made me have that instinct. It was this editorial. Listen, and see if it was you that wrote it:

> "Turnips should never be pulled, it injures them. It is much
> better to send a boy up and let him shake the tree."

"Now, what do you think of that—for I really suppose you wrote it?"

"Think of it? Why, I think it is good. I think it is sense. I have no doubt that every year millions and millions of bushels of turnips are spoiled in this township alone by being pulled in a half-ripe condition, when, if they had sent a boy up to shake the tree—"

"Shake your grandmother! Turnips don't grow on trees!"

"Oh, they don't, don't they! Well, who said they did! The language was intended to be figurative, wholly figurative. Anybody that knows anything will know that I meant that the boy should shake the vine."

Then this old person got up and tore his paper all into small shreds, and stamped on them, and broke several things with his cane, and said I did not know as much as a cow; and then went out and banged the door after him, and, in short, acted in such a way that I fancied he was displeased about something. But not knowing what the trouble was, I could not be any help to him.

Pretty soon after this a long cadaverous creature, with lanky locks hanging down to his shoulders, and a week's stubble bristling from the hills and valleys of his face, darted within the door, and halted, motionless, with finger on lip, and head and body bent in listening attitude. No sound was heard. Still he listened. No sound. Then he turned the key in the door, and came elaborately tiptoeing towards me till he was within long reaching distance of me, when he stopped and, after scanning my face with intense interest for a while, drew a folded copy of our paper from his bosom, and said:

"There, you wrote that. Read it to me—quick! Relieve me. I suffer."

I read as follows; and as the sentences fell from my lips I could see the relief come, I could see the drawn muscles relax, and the anxiety go out of the face, and rest and peace steal over the features like the merciful moonlight over a desolate landscape:

> "The guano is a fine bird, but great care is necessary in rearing it. It should not be imported earlier than June or later than September. In the winter it should be kept in a warm place, where it can hatch out its young.
>
> "It is evident that we are to have a backward season for grain. Therefore it will be well for the farmer to begin setting out

A LONG CADAVEROUS CREATURE.

his corn-stalks and planting his buckwheat-cakes in July instead of August.

"Concerning the pumpkin.—This berry is a favorite with the natives of the interior of New England, who prefer it to the gooseberry for the making of fruit-cake, and who likewise give it the preference over the raspberry for feeding cows, as being more filling and fully as satisfying. The pumpkin is the only esculent of the orange family that will thrive in the North, except the gourd and one or two varieties of the squash. But the custom of planting it in the front yard with the shrubbery is fast going out of vogue, for it is now generally conceded that the pumpkin as a shade tree is a failure.

"Now, as the warm weather approaches, and the ganders begin to spawn"—

The excited listener sprang towards me to shake hands, and said:

"There, there—that will do. I know I am all right now, because you have read it just as I did, word for word. But, stranger, when I first read it this morning, I said to myself, I never, never believed it before, notwithstanding my friends kept me under watch so strict, but now I believe I *am* crazy; and with that I fetched a howl that you might have heard two miles, and started out to kill somebody—because, you know, I knew it would come to that sooner or later, and so I might as well begin. I read one of them paragraphs over again, so as to be certain, and then I burned my house down and started. I have crippled several people, and have got one fellow up a tree, where I can get him if I want him. But I thought I would call in here as I passed along and make the thing perfectly certain; and now it *is* certain, and I tell you it is lucky for the chap that is in the tree. I should have killed him sure, as I went back. Good-bye, sir, good-bye; you have taken a great load off my mind. My reason has stood the strain of one of your agricultural articles, and I know that nothing can ever unseat it now. *Good*-bye, sir."

I felt a little uncomfortable about the cripplings and arsons this person had been entertaining himself with, for I could not help feeling remotely accessory to them. But these thoughts were quickly banished, for the regular editor walked in! [I thought to myself, Now if you had gone to Egypt, as I recommended you to, I might have had a chance to get my hand in; but you wouldn't do it, and here you are. I sort of expected you.]

The editor was looking sad and perplexed and dejected.

He surveyed the wreck which that old rioter and these two young farmers had made, and then said: "This is a sad business—a very sad business. There is the mucilage-bottle broken, and six panes of glass, and a spittoon, and two candlesticks. But that is not the worst. The reputation of the paper is injured—and permanently, I fear. True, there never was such a call for the paper before, and it never sold such a large edition or soared to such celebrity; but does one want to be famous for lunacy, and prosper upon the infirmities of his mind? My friend, as I am an honest man, the street out here is full of people, and others are roosting on the fences, waiting to get a glimpse of you, because they think you are crazy. And well they might after reading your editorials. They are a disgrace to journalism. Why, what put it into your head that you could edit a paper of this nature? You do not seem to know the first rudiments of agriculture. You speak of a furrow and a harrow as being the same thing; you talk of the molting season for cows; and you recommend the domestication of the polecat on account of its playfulness and its excellence as a ratter! Your remark that clams will lie quiet if music be played to them was superfluous—entirely superfluous. Nothing disturbs clams. Clams *always* lie quiet. Clams care nothing whatever about music. Ah, heavens and earth, friend! if you had made the acquiring of ignorance the study of your life, you could not have graduated with higher honor than you could to-day. I never saw anything like it. Your observation that the horse-chestnut as an article of commerce is steadily gaining in favor, is simply calculated to destroy this journal. I want you to throw up your situation and go. I want no more holiday—I could not enjoy it if I had it. Certainly not with you in my chair. I would always stand in dread of what you might be going to recommend next. It makes me lose all patience every time I think of your discussing oyster-beds under the head of 'Landscape Gardening.' I want you to go. Nothing on earth could persuade me to take another holiday. Oh! why didn't you *tell* me you didn't know anything about agriculture?''

"*Tell* you, you cornstalk, you cabbage, you son of a cauliflower? It's the first time I ever heard such an unfeeling remark. I tell you I have been in the editorial business going on fourteen years, and it is the first time I ever heard of a man's having to know anything in order to edit a newspaper. You turnip! Who write the dramatic critiques for the second-rate papers? Why, a parcel of promoted shoemakers and apprentice apothecaries, who know just as much about good acting as I do about good farming and no more. Who review the books? People who never wrote one. Who do up the heavy leaders on finance? Parties who have had the largest opportunities for knowing nothing about it. Who criticise the Indian campaigns? Gentlemen who do not know a warwhoop from a wigwam, and who never have had to run a foot-race with a tomahawk, or pluck arrows out of the several members of their families to build the evening campfire with. Who write the temperance appeals, and clamor about the flowing bowl? Folks who will never draw another sober breath till they do it in the grave. Who edit the agricultural papers, you—yam? Men, as a general thing, who fail in the poetry line, yellow-colored novel line, sensation-drama line, city-editor line, and finally fall back on agriculture as a temporary reprieve from the poor-house. *You* try to tell *me* anything about the newspaper business! Sir, I have been through it from Alpha to Omaha, and I tell you that the less a man knows the bigger the noise he makes and the higher the salary he commands. Heaven knows if I had but been ignorant instead of cultivated, and impudent instead of diffident, I could have made a name for myself in this cold selfish world. I take my leave, sir. Since I have been treated as you have treated me, I am perfectly willing to go. But I have done my duty. I have fulfilled my contract as far as I was permitted to do it. I said I could make your paper of interest to all classes—and I have. I said I could run your circulation up to twenty thousand copies, and if I had had two more weeks I'd have done it. And I'd have given you the best class of readers that ever an agricultural paper had—not a farmer in it, nor a solitary individual who could tell a watermelon-tree from a peach-vine to save his life. *You* are the loser by this rupture, not me, Pie-plant. Adios.''

I then left.

THE KILLING OF JULIUS CAESAR "LOCALIZED"

Being the only true and reliable account ever published; taken from the "Roman Daily Evening Fasces," of the date of that tremendous occurrence.

NOTHING IN the world affords a newspaper reporter so much satisfaction as gathering up the details of a bloody and mysterious murder, and writing them up with aggravating circumstantiality. He takes a living delight in this labor of love—for such it is to him, especially if he knows that all the other papers have gone to press, and his will be the only one that will contain the dreadful intelligence. A feeling of regret has often come over me that I was not reporting in Rome when Caesar was killed—reporting on an evening paper, and the only one in the city, and getting at least twelve hours ahead of the morning-paper boys with this most magnificent "item" that ever fell to the lot of the craft. Other events have happened as startling as this, but none that possessed so peculiarly all the characteristics of the favorite "item" of the present day, magnified into grandeur and sublimity by the high rank, fame, and social and political standing of the actors in it.

However, as I was not permitted to report Caesar's assassination in the regular way, it has at least afforded me rare satisfaction to translate the following able account of it from the original Latin of the *Roman Daily Evening Fasces* of that date—second edition.

> Our usually quiet city of Rome was thrown into a state of wild excitement yesterday by the occurrence of one of those bloody affrays which sicken the heart and fill the soul with fear, while they inspire all thinking men with forebodings for the future of a city where human life is held so cheaply, and the gravest laws are so openly set at defiance. As the result of that affray, it is our painful duty, as public journalists, to record the death of one of our most esteemed citizens—a man whose name is known wherever this paper circulates, and whose fame it has been our pleasure and our privilege to extend, and also to protect from the tongue of slander and falsehood, to the best of our poor ability. We refer to Mr. J. Caesar, the Emperor-elect.
>
> The facts of the case, as nearly as our reporter could determine them from the conflicting statements of eyewitnesses, were about as follows:—The affair was an election row, of course. Nine-tenths of the ghastly butcheries that disgrace the city nowadays

grow out of the bickerings and jealousies and animosities engendered by these accursed elections. Rome would be the gainer by it
if her very constables were elected to serve a century; for in our
experience we have never even been able to choose a dog-pelter
without celebrating the event with a dozen knockdowns and a
general cramming of the station-house with drunken vagabonds
overnight. It is said that when the immense majority for Caesar at
the polls in the market was declared the other day, and the crown
was offered to that gentleman, even his amazing unselfishness in
refusing it three times was not sufficient to save him from the
whispered insults of such men as Casca, of the Tenth Ward, and
other hirelings of the disappointed candidate, hailing mostly from
the Eleventh and Thirteenth and other outside districts, who were
overheard speaking ironically and contemptuously of Mr. Caesar's
conduct upon that occasion.

We are further informed that there are many among us who
think they are justified in believing that the assassination of Julius
Caesar was a put-up thing—a cut-and-dried arrangement, hatched
by Marcus Brutus and a lot of his hired roughs, and carried out
only too faithfully according to the programme. Whether there be
good grounds for this suspicion or not, we leave to the people to
judge for themselves, only asking that they will read the following
account of the sad occurrence carefully and dispassionately before
they render that judgment.

The Senate was already in session, and Caesar was coming
down the street towards the Capitol, conversing with some personal friends, and followed, as usual, by a large number of citizens. Just as he was passing in front of Demosthenes & Thucyd-
ides' drug-store, he was observing casually to a gentleman, who,
our informant thinks, is a forture-teller, that the Ides of March
were come. The reply was, "Yes, they are come, but not gone
yet." At this moment Artemidorus stepped up and passed the time
of day, and asked Caesar to read a schedule or a tract or something
of the kind, which he had brought for his perusal. Mr. Decius
Brutus also said something about an "humble suit" which *he*
wanted read. Artemidorus begged that attention might be paid to
his first, because it was of personal consequence to Caesar. The
latter replied that what concerned himself should be read last, or
words to that effect. Artemidorus begged and beseeched him to
read the paper instantly.* However, Caesar shook him off, and
refused to read any petition in the street. He then entered the
Capitol, and the crowd followed him.

About this time the following conversation was overheard, and
we consider that, taken in connection with the events which succeeded it, it bears an appalling significance: Mr. Papilius Lena
remarked to George W. Cassius (commonly known as the 'Nobby

---

*Mark that: It is hinted by William Shakespeare, who saw the beginning and the end of the
unfortunate affray, that this "schedule" was simply a note discovering to Caesar that a plot was
brewing to take his life.

Boy of the Third Ward'), a bruiser in the pay of the Opposition, that he hoped his enterprise to-day might thrive; and when Cassius asked, "What enterprise?" he only closed his left eye temporarily and said with simulated indifference, "Fare you well," and sauntered towards Caesar. Marcus Brutus, who is suspected of being the ringleader of the band that killed Caesar, asked what it was that Lena had said. Cassius told him, and added, in a low tone, *"I fear our purpose is discovered."*

Brutus told his wretched accomplice to keep an eye on Lena, and a moment after Cassius urged that lean and hungry vagrant, Casca, whose reputation here is none of the best, to be sudden for *he feared prevention*. He then turned to Brutus, apparently much excited, and asked what should be done, and swore that either he or Caesar *should never turn back*—he would kill himself first. At this time Caesar was talking to some of the back-country members about the approaching fall elections, and was paying little attention to what was going on around him. Billy Trebonius got into conversation with the people's friend and Caesar's—Mark Antony—and under some pretence or other got him away, and Brutus, Decius, Casca, Cinna, Metellus Cimber, and others of the gang of infamous desperadoes that infest Rome at present, closed around the doomed Caesar. Then Metellus Cimber knelt down and begged that his brother might be recalled from banishment, but Caesar rebuked him for his fawning conduct, and refused to grant his petition. Immediately, at Cimber's request, first Brutus and then Cassius begged for the return of the banished Publius; but Caesar still refused. He said he could not be moved; that he was as fixed as the North Star, and proceeded to speak in the most complimentary terms of the firmness of that star and its steady character. Then he said he was like it, and he believed he was the only man in the country that was; therefore, since he was "constant" that Cimber should be banished, he was also "constant" that he should stay banished, and he'd be hanged if he didn't keep him so!

Instantly seizing upon this shallow pretext for a fight, Casca sprang at Caesar and struck him with a dirk, Caesar grabbing him by the arm with his right hand, and launching a blow straight from the shoulder with his left that sent the reptile bleeding to the earth. He then backed up against Pompey's statue, and squared himself to receive his assailants. Cassius and Cimber and Cinna rushed upon him with their daggers drawn, and the former succeeded in inflicting a wound upon his body; but before he could strike again, and before either of the others could strike at all, Caesar stretched the three miscreants at his feet with as many blows of his powerful fist. By this time the Senate was in an indescribable uproar; the throng of citizens in the lobbies had blockaded the doors in their frantic efforts to escape from the building, the sergeant-at-arms and his assistants were struggling with the assassins, venerable senators had cast aside their encumbering robes, and were leaping over benches and flying down the aisles in wild confusion towards the shelter of the committee-rooms, and a thousand voices were shouting "Po-lice! Po-lice!" in discordant tones that rose above the frightful din like shrieking winds above the roaring of a tempest. And amid it all, great Caesar stood with his back against the statue, like a lion at bay, and fought his assailants weaponless and hand to hand, with the defiant bearing and the unwavering courage which he had shown before on many a bloody field. Billy Trebonius and Caius Legarius struck him with their daggers and fell, as their brother-conspirators before them had fallen. But at last, when Caesar saw his old friend Brutus step forward armed with a murderous knife, it is said he seemed utterly overpowered with grief and amazement, and dropping his invincible left arm by his side, he hid his face in the folds of his mantle and received the treacherous blow without an effort to stay the hand that gave it. He only said, *"Et tu, Brute?"* and fell lifeless on the marble pavement.

We learn that the coat deceased had on when he was killed was the same one he wore in his tent on the afternoon of the day he overcame the Nervii, and that when it was removed from the corpse it was found to be cut and gashed in no less than seven different places. There was nothing in the pockets. It will be exhibited at the coroner's inquest, and will be damning proof of the fact of the killing. These latter facts may be relied on, as we get them from Mark Antony, whose position enables him to learn every item of news connected with the one subject of absorbing interest of to-day.

LATER.—While the coroner was summoning a jury, Mark Antony and other friends of the late Caesar got hold of the body, and lugged it off to the Forum, and at last accounts Antony and Brutus were making speeches over it and raising such a row among the people that, as we go to press, the chief of police is satisfied there is going to be a riot, and is taking measures accordingly.

THERE WAS NOTHING IN THE POCKETS.

Fenimore Cooper's Literary Offenses

FENIMORE COOPER'S LITERARY
OFFENSES

The Pathfinder and *The Deerslayer* stand at the head of Cooper's novels as artistic creations. There are others of his works which contain parts as perfect as are to be found in these, and scenes even more thrilling. Not one can be compared with either of them as a finished whole.

The defects in both of these tales are comparatively slight. They were pure works of art.—*Prof. Lounsbury.*

The five tales reveal an extraordinary fullness of invention. . . . One of the very greatest characters in fiction, Natty Bumppo. . . .

The craft of the woodsman, the tricks of the trapper, all the delicate art of the forest, were familiar to Cooper from his youth up.—*Prof. Brander Matthews.*

Cooper is the greatest artist in the domain of romantic fiction yet produced by America.—*Wilkie Collins.*

IT SEEMS to me that it was far from right for the Professor of English Literature in Yale, the Professor of English Literature in Columbia, and Wilkie Collins to deliver opinions on Cooper's literature without having read some of it. It would have been much more decorous to keep silent and let persons talk who have read Cooper.

Cooper's art has some defects. In one place in *Deerslayer,* and in the restricted space of two-thirds of a page, Cooper has scored 114 offenses against literary art out of a possible 115. It breaks the record.

There are nineteen rules governing literary art in the domain of romantic fiction—some say twenty-two. In *Deerslayer* Cooper violated eighteen of them. These eighteen require:

1. That a tale shall accomplish something and arrive somewhere. But the *Deerslayer* tale accomplishes nothing and arrives in the air.

2. They require that the episodes of a tale shall be necessary parts of the tale and shall help to develop it. But as the *Deerslayer* tale is not a tale and accomplishes nothing and arrives nowhere, the episodes have no rightful place in the work, since there was nothing for them to develop.

3. They require that the personages in a tale shall be alive, except in

the case of corpses, and that always the reader shall be able to tell the corpses from the others. But this detail has often been overlooked in the *Deerslayer* tale.

4. They require that the personages in a tale, both dead and alive, shall exhibit a sufficient excuse for being there. But this detail also has been overlooked in the *Deerslayer* tale.

5. They require that when the personages of a tale deal in conversation, the talk shall sound like human talk, and be talk such as human beings would be likely to talk in the given circumstances, and have a discoverable meaning, also a discoverable purpose and a show of relevancy, and remain in the neighborhood of the subject in hand, and be interesting to the reader, and help out the tale, and stop when the people cannot think of anything more to say. But this requirement has been ignored from the beginning of the *Deerslayer* tale to the end of it.

6. They require that when the author describes the character of a personage in his tale, the conduct and conversation of that personage shall justify said description. But this law gets little or no attention in the *Deerslayer* tale, as Natty Bumppo's case will amply prove.

7. They require that when a personage talks like an illustrated, gilt-edged, tree-calf, hand-tooled, seven-dollar Friendship's Offering in the beginning of a paragraph, he shall not talk like a Negro minstrel in the end of it. But this rule is flung down and danced upon in the *Deerslayer* tale.

8. They require that crass stupidities shall not be played upon the reader as "the craft of the woodsman, the delicate art of the forest," by either the author or the people in the tale. But this rule is persistently violated in the *Deerslayer* tale.

9. They require that the personages of a tale shall confine themselves to possibilities and let miracles alone; or, if they venture a miracle, the author must so plausibly set it forth as to make it look possible and reasonable. But these rules are not respected in the *Deerslayer* tale.

10. They require that the author shall make the reader feel a deep interest in the personages of his tale and in their fate, and that he shall make the reader love the good people in the tale and hate the bad ones. But the reader of the *Deerslayer* tale dislikes the good people in it, is indifferent to the others, and wishes they would all get drowned together.

11. They require that the characters in a tale shall be so clearly defined that the reader can tell beforehand what each will do in a given emergency. But in the *Deerslayer* tale this rule is vacated.

In addition to these large rules there are some little ones. These require that the author shall

12. *Say* what he is proposing to say, not merely come near it.

13. Use the right word, not its second cousin.

14. Eschew surplusage.

15. Not omit necessary details.

16. Avoid slovenliness of form.

17. Use good grammar.

18. Employ a simple and straightforward style.

Even these seven are coldly and persistently violated in the *Deerslayer* tale.

Cooper's gift in the way of invention was not a rich endowment but such as it was he liked to work it, he was pleased with the effects, and indeed he did some quite sweet things with it. In his little box of stage-properties he kept six or eight cunning devices, tricks, artifices for his savages and woodsmen to deceive and circumvent each other with, and he was never so happy as when he was working these innocent things and seeing them go. A favorite one was to make a moccasined person tread in the tracks of the moccasined enemy, and thus hide his own trail. Cooper wore out barrels and barrels of moccasins in working that trick. Another stage-property that he pulled out of his box pretty frequently was his broken twig. He prized his broken twig above all the rest of his effects, and worked it the hardest. It is a restful chapter in any book of his when somebody doesn't step on a dry twig and alarm all the reds and whites for two hundred yards around. Every time a Cooper person is in peril and absolute silence is worth four dollars a minute, he is sure to step on a dry twig. There may be a hundred handier things to step on but that wouldn't satisfy Cooper. Cooper requires him to turn out and find a dry twig, and if he can't do it, go and borrow one. In fact, the Leatherstocking Series ought to have been called the Broken Twig Series.

I am sorry there is not room to put in a few dozen instances of the delicate art of the forest, as practised by Natty Bumppo and some of the other Cooperian experts. Perhaps we may venture two or three samples. Cooper was a sailor, a naval officer; yet he gravely tells us how a vessel, driving toward a lee shore in a gale, is steered for a particular spot by her skipper because he knows of an *undertow* there which will hold her back against the gale and save her. For just pure woodcraft, or sailorcraft, or whatever it is, isn't that neat? For several years Cooper was daily in the society of artillery and he ought to have noticed that when a cannon-ball strikes the ground it either buries itself or skips a hundred feet or so, skips again a hundred feet or so, and so on till finally it gets tired and rolls. Now in one place he loses some "females"—as he always calls women— in the edge of a wood near a plain at night in a fog, on purpose to give Bumppo a chance to show off the delicate art of the forest before the reader. These mislaid people are hunting for a fort. They hear a cannon-blast, and a cannon-ball presently comes rolling into the wood and stops at their feet. To the females this suggests nothing. The case is very different with the admirable Bumppo. I wish I may never know peace again if he doesn't strike out promptly and *follow the track* of that cannon-ball across the plain through the dense fog and find the fort. Isn't it a daisy? If Cooper had any real knowledge of Nature's ways of doing things, he had a most delicate art in concealing the fact. For instance: one of his acute Indian experts, Chingachgook (pronounced Chicago, I think), has lost the trail of a person he is tracking through the forest. Apparently that trail is hopelessly lost. Neither you nor I could ever have guessed out the way to find it. It was very different with Chicago. Chicago was not stumped for long. He turned a running stream out of its course and there, in the slush in its old bed, were that person's moccasin tracks. The current did not wash them away, as it would have done in all other like cases— no, even the eternal laws of Nature have to vacate when Cooper wants to put up a delicate job of woodcraft on the reader.

We must be a litttle wary when Brander Matthews tells us that Cooper's books "reveal an extraordinary fullness of invention." As a rule, I am quite willing to accept Brander Matthews's literary judgments and applaud his lucid and graceful phrasing of them, but that particular statement needs to be taken with a few tons of salt. Bless your heart, Cooper hadn't any more invention than a horse, and I don't mean a high-class horse, either, I mean a clothes-horse. It would be very difficult to find a really clever "situation" in Cooper's books, and still more difficult to find one of any kind which he has failed to render absurd by his handling of it. Look at the episodes of "the caves"; and at the celebrated scuffle between Maqua and those others on the table-land a few days later; and at Hurry Harry's queer watertransit from the castle to the ark; and at Deerslayer's half-hour with his first corpse; and at the quarrel between Hurry Harry and Deer-slayer later; and at— But choose for yourself, you can't go amiss.

If Cooper had been an observer his inventive faculty would have worked better: not more interestingly but more rationally, more plausibly. Coo-per's proudest creations in the way of "situations" suffer noticeably from the absence of the observer's protecting gift. Cooper's eye was splendidly inaccurate. Cooper seldom saw anything correctly. He saw nearly all things as through a glass eye, darkly. Of course a man who cannot see the commonest little every-day matters accurately is working at a disadvan-tage when he is constructing a "situation." In the *Deerslayer* tale Cooper has a stream which is fifty feet wide where it flows out of a lake; it presently narrows to twenty as it meanders along for no given reason, and yet when a stream acts like that it ought to be required to explain itself. Fourteen pages later the width of the brook's outlet from the lake has suddenly shrunk thirty feet and become "the narrowest part of the stream." This shrinkage is not accounted for. The stream has bends in it, a sure indication that it has alluvial banks and cuts them, yet these bends are only thirty and fifty feet long. If Cooper had been a nice and punctilious observer he would have noticed that the bends were oftener nine hundred feet long than short of it.

Cooper made the exit of that stream fifty feet wide in the first place for no particular reason; in the second place, he narrowed it to less than twenty to accommodate some Indians. He bends a "sapling" to the form of an arch over this narrow passage and conceals six Indians in its foliage. They are "laying" for a settler's scow or ark which is coming up the stream on its way to the lake; it is being hauled against the stiff current by a rope whose stationary end is anchored in the lake; its rate of progress cannot be more than a mile an hour. Cooper describes the ark, but pretty obscurely. In the matter of dimensions "it was little more than a modern canalboat" Let us guess, then, that it was about one hundred and forty feet long. It was of "greater breadth than common." Let us guess, then, that it was about sixteen feet wide. This leviathan had been prowling down bends which were but a third as long as itself and scraping between banks where it had only two feet of space to spare on each side. We cannot too much admire this miracle. A low-roofed log dwelling occupies "two-thirds of the ark's length"—a dwelling ninety feet long and sixteen feet wide, let us say, a kind of vestibule train. The dwelling has two rooms, each forty-five feet long and sixteen feet wide, let us guess. One of them is the bedroom of the Hutter girls, Judith and Hetty; the other is the parlor in the daytime, at night it is papa's bed-chamber. The ark is arriving at the stream's exit now, whose width has been reduced to less than twenty feet to accommodate the Indians—say to eighteen. There is a foot to spare on each side of the boat. Did the Indians notice that there was going to be a tight squeeze there? Did they notice that they could make money by climbing down out of that arched sapling and just stepping aboard when the ark scraped by? No, other Indians would have noticed these things but Cooper's Indians never notice anything. Cooper thinks they are marvelous creatures for noticing but he was almost always in error about his Indians. There was seldom a sane one among them.

The ark is one hundred and forty feet long; the dwelling is ninety feet long. The idea of the Indians is to drop softly and secretly from the arched sapling to the dwelling as the ark creeps along under it at the rate of a mile an hour, and butcher the family. It will take the ark a minute and a half to pass under. It will take the ninety-foot dwelling a minute to pass under. Now, then, what did the six Indians do? It would take you thirty years to guess and even then you would have to give up, I believe. Therefore, I will tell you what the Indians did. Their chief, a person of quite extraordinary intellect for a Cooper Indian, warily watched the canal-boat as it squeezed along under him and when he had got his calculations fined down to exactly the right shade, as he judged, he let go and dropped. And *missed the house!* That is actually what he did. He missed the house and landed in the stern of the scow. It was not much of a fall, yet it knocked him silly. He lay there unconscious. If the house had been ninety-seven feet long he would have made the trip. The fault was Cooper's, not his. The error lay in the construction of the house. Cooper was no architect.

There still remained in the roost five Indians. The boat has passed under and is now out of their reach. Let me explain what the five did— you would not be able to reason it out for yourself. No. 1 jumped for the boat but fell in the water astern of it. Then No. 2 jumped for the boat but fell in the water still farther astern of it. Then No. 3 jumped for the boat and fell a good way astern of it. Then No. 4 jumped for the boat and fell in the water *away* astern. Then even No. 5 made a jump for the boat—for he was a Cooper Indian. In the matter of intellect, the difference between a Cooper Indian and the Indian that stands in front of the cigarshop is not spacious. The scow episode is really a sublime burst of invention but it does not thrill, because the inaccuracy of the details throws a sort of air of fictitiousness and general improbability over it. This comes of Cooper's inadequacy as an observer.

The reader will find some examples of Cooper's high talent for inaccurate observation in the account of the shooting-match in *The Pathfinder*.

> A common wrought nail was driven lightly into the target, its
> head having been first touched with paint.

The color of the paint is not stated—an important omission, but Cooper deals freely in important omissions. No, after all, it was not an important omission, for this nail-head is *a hundred yards from* the marksmen and could not be seen by them at that distance, no matter what its color might be. How far can the best eyes see a common house-fly? A hundred yards? It is quite impossible. Very well, eyes that cannot see a house-fly that is a hundred yards away cannot see an ordinary nail-head at that distance, for the size of the two objects is the same. It takes a keen eye to see a fly or a nail-head at fifty yards—one hundred and fifty feet. Can the reader do it?

The nail was lightly driven, its head painted, and game called. Then the Cooper miracles began. The bullet of the first marksman chipped an edge of the nail-head; the next man's bullet drove the nail a little way into the target—and removed all the paint. Haven't the miracles gone far enough now? Not to suit Cooper, for the purpose of this whole scheme is to show off his prodigy, Deerslayer-Hawkeye-Long-Rifle-Leatherstocking-Pathfinder-Bumppo before the ladies.

> "Be all ready to clench it, boys!" cried out Pathfinder, stepping into his friend's tracks the instant they were vacant. "Never mind a new nail; I can see that, though the paint is gone, and what I can see I can hit at a hundred yards, though it were only a mosquito's eye. Be ready to clench!"
>
> The rifle cracked, the bullet sped its way, and the head of the nail was buried in the wood, covered by the piece of flattened lead.

There, you see, is a man who could hunt flies with a rifle, and command a ducal salary in a Wild West show today if we had him back with us.

The recorded feat is certainly surprising just as it stands, but it is not surprising enough for Cooper. Cooper adds a touch. He has made Pathfinder do this miracle with another man's rifle; and not only that, but Pathfinder did not have even the advantage of loading it himself. He had everything against him, and yet he made that impossible shot, and not only made it but did it with absolute confidence, saying, "Be ready to clench." Now a person like that would have undertaken the same feat with a brickbat, and with Cooper to help he would have achieved it, too.

Pathfinder showed off handsomely that day before the ladies. His very first feat was a thing which no Wild West show can touch. He was standing with the group of marksmen, observing—a hundred yards from the target, mind; one Jasper raised his rifle and drove the center of the bull's-eye. Then the Quartermaster fired. The target exhibited no result this time. There was a laugh. "It's a dead miss," said Major Lundie. Pathfinder waited an impressive moment or two, then said in that calm, indifferent, know-it-all way of his, "No, Major, he has covered Jasper's bullet, as will be seen if anyone will take the trouble to examine the target."

Wasn't it remarkable! How *could* he see that little pellet fly through the air and enter that distant bullet-hole? Yet that is what he did, for nothing is impossible to a Cooper person. Did any of those people have any deep-seated doubts about this thing? No; for that would imply sanity and these were all Cooper people.

> The respect for Pathfinder's skill and for his *quickness and accuracy of sight* [the italics are mine] was so profound and gen-

eral, that the instant he made this declaration the spectators began to distrust their own opinions, and a dozen rushed to the target in order to ascertain the fact. There, sure enough, it was found that the Quartermaster's bullet had gone through the hole made by Jasper's, and that, too, so accurately as to require a minute examination to be certain of the circumstance, which, however, was soon clearly established by discovering one bullet over the other in the stump against which the target was placed.

They made a "minute" examination; but never mind, how could they know that there were two bullets in that hole without digging the latest one out? for neither probe nor eyesight could prove the presence of any more than one bullet. Did they dig? No; as we shall see. It is the Pathfinder's turn now; he steps out before the ladies, takes aim, and fires.

But, alas! here is a disappointment, an incredible, an unimaginable disappointment—for the target's aspect is unchanged; there is nothing there but that same old bullet-hole!

"If one dared to hint at such a thing," cried Major Duncan, "I should say that the Pathfinder has also missed the target!"

As nobody had missed it yet, the "also" was not necessary, but never mind about that for the Pathfinder is going to speak.

"No, no, Major," said he, confidently, "that *would* be a risky declaration. I didn't load the piece, and can't say what was in it; but if it was lead, you will find the bullet driving down those of the Quartermaster and Jasper, else is not my name Pathfinder."

A shout from the target announced the truth of this assertion.

Is the miracle sufficient as it stands? Not for Cooper. The Pathfinder speaks again, as he "now slowly advances toward the stage occupied by the females":

"That's not all, boys, that's not all; if you find the target touched at all, I'll own to a miss. The Quartermaster cut the wood, but you'll find no wood cut by that last messenger."

The miracle is at last complete. He knew—doubtless *saw*—at the distance of a hundred yards—that his bullet had passed into the hole *without fraying the edges*. There were now three bullets in that one hole, three bullets embedded processionally in the body of the stump back of the target. Everybody knew this, somehow or other, and yet nobody had dug any of them out to make sure. Cooper is not a close observer but he is interesting. He is certainly always that, no matter what happens. And he is more interesting when he is not noticing what he is about than when he is. This is a considerable merit.

The conversations in the Cooper books have a curious sound in our modern ears. To believe that such talk really ever came out of people's mouths would be to believe that there was a time when time was of no value to a person who thought he had something to say, when it was the custom to spread a two-minute remark out to ten, when a man's mouth was a rolling-mill and busied itself all day long in turning four-foot pigs of thought into thirty-foot bars of conversational railroad iron by attenuation, when subjects were seldom faithfully stuck to but the talk wandered all around and arrived nowhere, when conversations consisted mainly of irrelevancies with here and there a relevancy, a relevancy with an embarrassed look, as not being able to explain how it got there.

Cooper was certainly not a master in the construction of dialogue. Inaccurate observation defeated him here as it defeated him in so many other enterprises of his. He even failed to notice that the man who talks corrupt English six days in the week must and will talk it on the seventh, and can't help himself. In the *Deerslayer* story he lets Deerslayer talk the showiest kind of book-talk sometimes, and at other times the basest of base dialects. For instance, when some one asks him if he has a sweetheart, and if so where she abides, this is his majestic answer:

> "She's in the forest—hanging from the boughs of the trees, in a soft rain—in the dew on the open grass—the clouds that float about in the blue heavens—the birds that sing in the woods—the sweet springs where I slake my thirst—and in all the other glorious gifts that come from God's Providence!"

And he preceded that, a little before, with this:

> "It consarns me as all things that touches a fri'nd consarns a fri'nd."

And this is another of his remarks:

> "If I was Injin born, now, I might tell of this, or carry in the scalp and boast of the expl'ite afore the whole tribe; or if my inimy had only been a bear"—[and so on].

We cannot imagine such a thing as a veteran Scotch Commander-in-Chief comporting himself in the field like a windy melodramatic actor, but Cooper could. On one occasion Alice and Cora were being chased by the French through a fog in the neighborhood of their father's fort:

> *"Point de quartier aux coquins!"* cried an eager pursuer, who seemed to direct the operations of the enemy.
>
> "Stand firm and be ready, my gallant 60ths!" suddenly exclaimed a voice above them; "wait to see the enemy; fire low, and sweep the glacis."
>
> "Father! father," exclaimed a piercing cry from out the mist; "it is I! Alice! thy own Elsie! spare, O! save your daughters!"
>
> "Hold!" shouted the former speaker, in the awful tones of parental agony, the sound reaching even to the woods, and rolling back in solemn echo. " 'Tis she! God has restored me my children! Throw open the sally-port; to the field, 60ths, to the field!

pull not a trigger, lest ye kill my lambs! Drive off these dogs of
France with your steel!''

Cooper's word-sense was singularly dull. When a person has a poor
ear for music he will flat and sharp right along without knowing it. He
keeps near the tune, but it is *not* the tune. When a person has a poor ear
for words, the result is a literary flatting and sharping; you perceive what
he is intending to say but you also perceive that he doesn't *say* it. This is
Cooper. He was not a word-musician. His ear was satisfied with the
approximate word. I will furnish some circumstantial evidence in support
of this charge. My instances are gathered from half a dozen pages of the
tale called *Deerslayer*. He uses ''verbal'' for ''oral''; ''precision'' for
''facility''; ''phenomena'' for ''marvels''; ''necessary'' for ''predeter-
mined''; ''unsophisticated'' for ''primitive''; ''preparation'' for ''expectancy''; ''rebuked'' for ''subdued''; ''dependent on'' for ''resulting from'';
''fact'' for ''condition''; ''fact'' for ''conjecture''; ''precaution'' for ''caution''; ''explain'' for ''determine''; ''mortified'' for ''disappointed'';
''meretricious'' for ''factitious''; ''materially'' for ''considerably''; ''decreasing'' for ''deepening''; ''increasing'' for ''disappearing''; ''embedded'' for ''inclosed''; ''treacherous'' for ''hostile''; ''stood'' for ''stooped'';
''softened'' for ''replaced''; ''rejoined'' for ''remarked''; ''situation'' for
''condition''; ''different'' for ''differing''; ''insensible'' for ''unsentient'';
''brevity'' for ''celerity''; ''distrusted'' for ''suspicious''; ''mental imbecility'' for ''imbecility''; ''eyes'' for ''sight''; ''counteracting'' for ''op-
posing''; ''funeral obsequies'' for ''obsequies.''

There have been daring people in the world who claimed that Cooper
could write English but they are all dead now—all dead but Lounsbury. I
don't remember that Lounsbury makes the claim in so many words, still
he makes it for he says that *Deerslayer* is a ''pure work of art.'' Pure, in
that connection, means faultless—faultless in all details—and language is
a detail. If Mr. Lounsbury had only compared Cooper's English with the
English which he writes himself—but it is plain that he didn't, and so it
is likely that he imagines until this day that Cooper's is as clean and
compact as his own. Now I feel sure, deep down in my heart, that Cooper
wrote about the poorest English that exists in our language and that the
English of *Deerslayer* is the very worst that even Cooper ever wrote.

I may be mistaken, but it does seem to me that *Deerslayer* is not a work
of art in any sense; it does seem to me that it is destitute of every detail
that goes to the making of a work of art; in truth, it seems to me that
Deerslayer is just simply a literary *delirium tremens*.

A work of art? It has no invention; it has no order, system, sequence,
or result; it has no lifelikeness, no thrill, no stir, no seeming of reality; its
characters are confusedly drawn and by their acts and words they prove
that they are not the sort of people the author claims that they are; its
humor is pathetic; its pathos is funny; its conversations are—oh! indescribable; its lovescenes odious; its English a crime against the language.

Counting these out, what is left is Art. I think we must all admit that.

Extracts from Adam's Diary

WRITING IN HIS DIARY.

[NOTE.—I translated a portion of this diary some years ago, and a friend of mine printed a few copies in an incomplete form, but the public never got them. Since then I have deciphered some more of Adam's hieroglyphics, and think he has now become sufficiently important as a public character to justify this publication.—M. T.]

Monday

THIS NEW creature with the long hair is a good deal in the way. It is always hanging around and following me about. I don't like this; I am not used to company. I wish it would stay with the other animals. . . . Cloudy today, wind in the east; think we shall have rain. . . . *We?* Where did I get that word? . . . I remember now—the new creature uses it.

Tuesday

BEEN EXAMINING the great waterfall. It is the finest thing on the estate, I think. The new creature calls it Niagara Falls—why, I am sure I do not know. Says it *looks* like Niagara Falls. That is not a reason; it is mere waywardness and imbecility. I get no chance to name anything myself. The new creature names everything that comes along, before I can get in a protest. And always that same pretext is offered—it *looks* like the thing. There is the dodo, for instance. Says the moment one looks at it one sees at a glance that it "looks like a dodo." It will have to keep that name, no doubt. It wearies me to fret about it, and it does no good, anyway. Dodo! It looks no more like a dodo than I do.

Wednesday

BUILT ME a shelter against the rain, but could not have it to myself in peace. The new creature intruded. When I tried to put it out it shed water out of the holes it looks with, and wiped it away with the back of its paws, and made a noise such as some of the other animals make when they are in distress. I wish it would not talk; it is always talking. That sounds like a cheap fling at the poor creature, a slur; but I do not mean it so. I have never heard the human voice before, and any new and strange sound intruding itself here upon the solemn hush of these dreaming solitudes offends my ear and seems a false note. And this new sound is so close to me; it is right at my shoulder, right at my ear, first on one side and then on the other, and I am used only to sounds that are more or less distant from me.

Friday

THE NAMING goes recklessly on, in spite of anything I can do. I had a very good name for the estate, and it was musical and pretty—GARDEN-OF-EDEN. Privately, I continue to call it that, but not any longer publicly. The new creature says it is all woods and rocks and scenery, and therefore has no resemblance to a garden. Says it *looks* like a park, and does not look like anything *but* a park. Consequently, without consulting me, it has been new-named—NIAGARA FALLS PARK. This is sufficiently high-handed, it seems to me. And already there is a sign up:

> KEEP OFF
> THE GRASS

My life is not as happy as it was.

Saturday

THE NEW creature eats too much fruit. We are going to run short, most likely. "We" again—that is *its* word; mine too, now, from hearing it so much. Good deal of fog this morning. I do not go out in the fog myself. The new creature does. It goes out in all weathers, and stumps right in with its muddy feet. And talks. It used to be so pleasant and quiet here.

Sunday

PULLED THROUGH. This day is getting to be more and more trying. It was selected and set apart last November as a day of rest. I already had six of them per week, before. This morning found the new creature trying to clod apples out of that forbidden tree.

Monday

THE NEW creature says its name is Eve. That is all right, I have no objections. Says it is to call it by when I want it to come. I said it was superfluous, then. The word evidently raised me in its respect; and indeed it is a large, good word, and will bear repetition. It says it is not an It, it is a She. This is probably doubtful; yet it is all one to me; what she is were nothing to me if she would but go by herself and not talk.

Tuesday

SHE HAS littered the whole estate with execrable names and offensive signs:

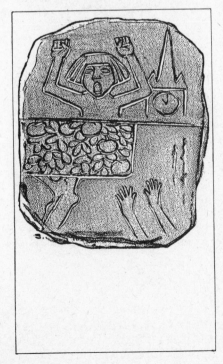

☞ THIS WAY TO THE WHIRLPOOL.

☞ THIS WAY TO GOAT ISLAND.

☞ CAVE OF THE WINDS THIS WAY.

She says this park would make a tidy summer resort, if there was any custom for it. Summer resort—another invention of hers—just words, without any meaning. What is a summer resort? But it is best not to ask her, she has such a rage for explaining.

Friday

SHE HAS taken to beseeching me to stop going over the Falls. What harm does it do? Says it makes her shudder. I wonder why. I have always done it—always liked the plunge, and the excitement, and the coolness. I supposed it was what the Falls were for. They have no other use that I can see, and they must have been made for something. She says they were only made for scenery—like the rhinoceros and the mastodon.

I went over the Falls in a barrel—not satisfactory to her. Went over in a tub—still not satisfactory. Swam the Whirlpool and the Rapids in a fig-leaf suit. It got much damaged. Hence, tedious complaints about my extravagance. I am too much hampered here. What I need is change of scene.

Saturday

I ESCAPED last Tuesday night, and travelled two days, and built me another shelter, in a secluded place, and obliterated my tracks as well as I could, but she hunted me out by means of a beast which she has tamed and calls a wolf, and came making that pitiful noise again, and shedding that water out of the places she looks with. I was obliged to return with her, but will presently emigrate again, when occasion offers. She engages herself in many foolish things: among others, trying to study out why the animals called lions and tigers live on grass and flowers, when, as she says, the sort of teeth they wear would indicate that they were intended to eat each other. This is foolish, because to do that would be to kill each other, and that would introduce what, as I understand it, is called "death"; and death, as I have been told, has not yet entered the Park. Which is a pity, on some accounts.

Sunday

PULLED THROUGH.

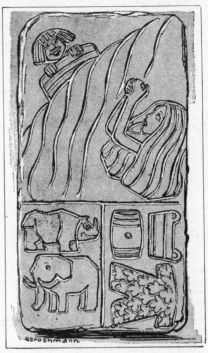

Monday

I BELIEVE I see what the week is for: it is to give time to rest up from the weariness of Sunday. It seems a good idea. . . . She has been climbing that tree again. Clodded her out of it. She said nobody was looking. Seems to consider that a sufficient justification for chancing any dangerous thing. Told her that. The word justification moved her admiration—and envy too, I thought. It is a good word.

Thursday

SHE TOLD me she was made out of a rib taken from my body. This is at least doubtful, if not more than that. I have not missed any rib. . . . She is in much trouble about the buzzard; says grass does not agree with it; is afraid she can't raise it; thinks it was intended to live on decayed flesh. The buzzard must get along the best it can with what is provided. We cannot overturn the whole scheme to accommodate the buzzard.

Saturday

SHE FELL in the pond yesterday, when she was looking at herself in it, which she is always doing. She nearly strangled, and said it was most uncomfortable. This made her sorry for the creatures which live in there, which she calls fish, for she continues to fasten names on to things that don't need them and don't come when they are called by them, which is a matter of no consequence to her, as she is such a numskull anyway; so she got a lot of them out and brought them in last night and put them in my bed to keep warm, but I have noticed them now and then all day, and I don't see that they are any happier there than they were before, only quieter. When night comes I shall throw them out-doors. I will not sleep with them again, for I find them clammy and unpleasant to lie among when a person hasn't anything on.

Sunday

PULLED THROUGH.

Tuesday

SHE HAS taken up with a snake now. The other animals are glad, for she was always experimenting with them and bothering them; and I am glad, because the snake talks, and this enables me to get a rest.

Friday

SHE SAYS the snake advises her to try the fruit of that tree, and says the result will be a great and fine and noble education. I told her there would

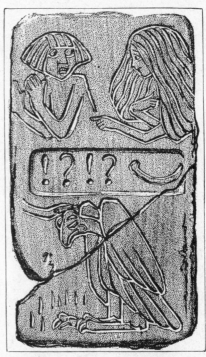

be another result, too—it would introduce death into the world. That was a mistake—it had been better to keep the remark to myself; it only gave her an idea—she could save the sick buzzard, and furnish fresh meat to the despondent lions and tigers. I advised her to keep away from the tree. She said she wouldn't. I foresee trouble. Will emigrate.

Wednesday

I HAVE had a variegated time. I escaped that night, and rode a horse all night as fast as he could go, hoping to get clear out of the Park and hide in some other country before the trouble should begin; but it was not to be. About an hour after sunup, as I was riding through a flowery plain where thousands of animals were grazing, slumbering, or playing with each other, according to their wont, all of a sudden they broke into a tempest of frightful noises, and in one moment the plain was in a frantic commotion and every beast was destroying its neighbor. I knew what it meant—Eve had eaten that fruit, and death was come into the world. . . . The tigers ate my horse, paying no attention when I ordered them to desist, and they would even have eaten me if I had stayed—which I didn't, but went away in much haste. . . . I found this place, outside the Park, and was fairly comfortable for a few days, but she has found me out. Found me out, and has named the place Tonawanda—says it *looks* like that. In fact, I was not sorry she came, for there are but meager pickings here, and she brought some of those apples. I was obliged to eat them, I was so hungry. It was against my principles, but I find that principles have no real force except when one is well fed. . . . She came curtained in boughs and bunches of leaves, and when I asked her what she meant by such nonsense, and snatched them away and threw them down, she tittered and blushed. I had never seen a person titter and blush before, and to me it seemed unbecoming and idiotic. She said I would soon know how it was myself. This was correct. Hungry as I was, I laid down the apple half eaten—certainly the best one I ever saw, considering the lateness of the season—and arrayed myself in the discarded boughs and branches, and then spoke to her with some severity and ordered her to go and get some more and not make such a spectacle of herself. She did it, and after this we crept down to where the wild-beast battle had been, and collected some skins, and I made her patch together a couple of suits proper for public occasions. They are uncomfortable, it is true, but stylish, and that is the main point about clothes. . . . I find she is a good deal of a companion. I see I should be lonesome and depressed without her, now that I have lost my property. Another thing, she says it is ordered that we work for our living hereafter. She will be useful. I will superintend.

Ten Days Later

SHE ACCUSES *me* of being the cause of our disaster! She says, with apparent sincerity and truth, that the Serpent assured her that the forbidden fruit was not apples, it was chestnuts. I said I was innocent, then, for I

had not eaten any chestnuts. She said the Serpent informed her that "chestnut" was a figurative term meaning an aged and moldy joke. I turned pale at that, for I have made many jokes to pass the weary time, and some of them could have been of that sort, though I had honestly supposed that they were new when I made them. She asked me if I had made one just at the time of the catastrophe. I was obliged to admit that I had made one to myself, though not aloud. It was this.

Ten Days Later

I WAS thinking about the Falls, and I said to myself, "How wonderful it is to see that vast body of water tumble down there!" Then in an instant a bright thought flashed into my head, and I let it fly, saying, "It would be a deal more wonderful to see it tumble *up* there!"—and I was just about to kill myself with laughing at it when all nature broke loose in war and death, and I had to flee for my life. "There," she said, with triumph, "that is just it; the Serpent mentioned that very jest, and called it the First Chestnut, and said it was coeval with the creation." Alas, I am indeed to blame. Would that I were not witty; oh, would that I had never had that radiant thought!

Next Year

WE HAVE named it Cain. She caught it while I was up country trapping on the North Shore of the Erie; caught it in the timber a couple of miles from our dug-out—or it might have been four, she isn't certain which. It resembles us in some ways, and may be a relation. That is what she thinks, but this is an error, in my judgment. The difference in size warrants the conclusion that it is a different and new kind of animal—a fish, perhaps, though when I put it in the water to see, it sank, and she plunged in and snatched it out before there was opportunity for the experiment to determine the matter. I still think it is a fish, but she is indifferent about what it is, and will not let me have it to try. I do not understand this. The coming of the creature seems to have changed her whole nature and made her unreasonable about experiments. She thinks more of it than she does of any of the other animals, but is not able to explain why. Her mind is disordered—everything shows it. Sometimes she carries the fish in her arms half the night when it complains and wants to get to the water. At such times the water comes out of the places in her face that she looks out of, and she pats the fish on the back and makes soft sounds with her mouth to soothe it, and betrays sorrow and solicitude in a hundred ways. I have never seen her do like this with any other fish, and it troubles me greatly. She used to carry the young tigers around so, and play with them, before we lost our property; but it was only play; she never took on about them like this when their dinner disagreed with them.

Sunday

SHE DOESN'T work Sundays, but lies around all tired out, and likes to have the fish wallow over her; and she makes fool noises to amuse it, and

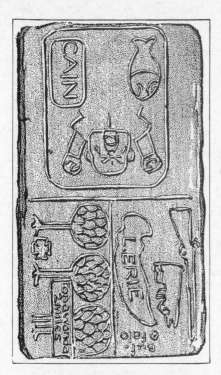

pretends to chew its paws, and that makes it laugh. I have not seen a fish before that could laugh. This makes me doubt. . . . I have come to like Sunday myself. Superintending all the week tires a body so. There ought to be more Sundays. In the old days they were tough, but now they come handy.

Wednesday

IT ISN'T a fish. I cannot quite make out what it is. It makes curious, devilish noises when not satisfied, and says "goo-goo" when it is. It is not one of us, for it doesn't walk; it is not a bird, for it doesn't fly; it is not a frog, for it doesn't hop; it is not a snake, for it doesn't crawl; I feel sure it is not a fish, though I cannot get a chance to find out whether it can swim or not. It merely lies around, and mostly on its back, with its feet up. I have not seen any other animal do that before. I said I believed it was an enigma, but she only admired the word without understanding it. In my judgment it is either an enigma or some kind of a bug. If it dies, I will take it apart and see what its arrangements are, I never had a thing perplex me so.

Three Months Later

THE PERPLEXITY augments instead of diminishing. I sleep but little. It has ceased from lying around, and goes about on its four legs now. Yet it differs from the other four-legged animals in that its front legs are unusually short, consequently this causes the main part of its person to stick up uncomfortably high in the air, and this is not attractive. It is built much as we are, but its method of travelling shows that it is not of our breed. The short front legs and long hind ones indicate that it is of the kangaroo family, but it is a marked variation of the species, since the true kangaroo hops, whereas this one never does. Still, it is a curious and interesting variety, and has not been catalogued before. As I discovered it, I have felt justified in securing the credit of the discovery by attaching my name to it, and hence have called it *Kangaroorum Adamiensis*. . . . It must have been a young one when it came, for it has grown exceedingly since. It must be five times as big, now, as it was then, and when discontented is able to make from twenty-two to thirty-eight times the noise it made at first. Coercion does not modify this, but has the contrary effect. For this reason I discontinued the system. She reconciles it by persuasion, and by giving it things which she had previously told it she wouldn't give it. As already observed, I was not at home when it first came, and she told me she found it in the woods. It seems odd that it should be the only one, yet it must be so, for I have worn myself out these many weeks trying to find another one to add to my collection, and for this one to play with; for surely then it would be quieter, and we could tame it more easily. But I find none, nor any vestige of any; and strangest of all, no tracks. It has to live on the ground, it cannot help itself; therefore, how does it get about without leaving a track? I have set a dozen traps, but they do no good. I

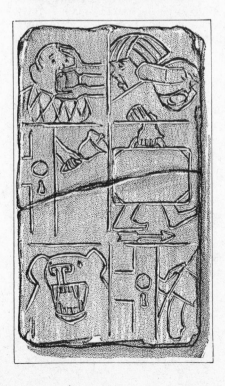

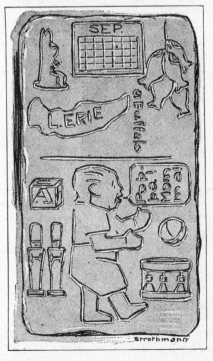

catch all small animals except that one; animals that merely go into the trap out of curiosity, I think, to see what the milk is there for. They never drink it.

The kangaroo still continues to grow, which is very strange and perplexing. I never knew one to be so long getting its growth. It has fur on its head now; not like kangaroo fur, but exactly like our hair, except that it is much finer and softer, and instead of being black is red. I am like to lose my mind over the capricious and harassing developments of this unclassifiable zoological freak. If I could catch another one—but that is hopeless; it is a new variety, and the only sample; this is plain. But I caught a true kangaroo and brought it in, thinking that this one, being lonesome, would rather have that for company than have no kin at all, or any animal it could feel a nearness to or get sympathy from in its forlorn condition here among strangers who do not know its ways or habits, or what to do to make it feel that it is among friends; but it was a mistake— it went into such fits at the sight of the kangaroo that I was convinced it had never seen one before. I pity the poor noisy little animal, but there is nothing I can do to make it happy. If I could tame it—but that is out of the question; the more I try, the worse I seem to make it. It grieves me to the heart to see it in its little storms of sorrow and passion. I wanted to let it go, but she wouldn't hear of it. That seemed cruel and not like her; and yet she may be right. It might be lonelier than ever; for since I cannot find another one, how could *it?*

Five Months Later

IT IS not a kangaroo. No, for it supports itself by holding to her finger, and thus goes a few steps on its hind legs, and then falls down. It is probably some kind of a bear; and yet it has no tail—as yet—and no fur, except on its head. It still keeps on growing—that is a curious circumstance, for bears get their growth earlier than this. Bears are dangerous— since our catastrophe—and I shall not be satisfied to have this one prowling about the place much longer without a muzzle on. I have offered to get her a kangaroo if she would let this one go, but it did no good—she is determined to run us into all sorts of foolish risks, I think. She was not like this before she lost her mind.

A Fortnight Later

I EXAMINED its mouth. There is no danger yet; it has only one tooth. It has no tail yet. It makes more noise now than it ever did before—and mainly at night. I have moved out. But I shall go over, mornings, to breakfast, and to see if it has more teeth. If it gets a mouthful of teeth, it will be time for it to go, tail or no tail, for a bear does not need a tail in order to be dangerous.

Four Months Later

I HAVE been off hunting and fishing a month, up in the region that she calls Buffalo; I don't know why, unless it is because there are not any

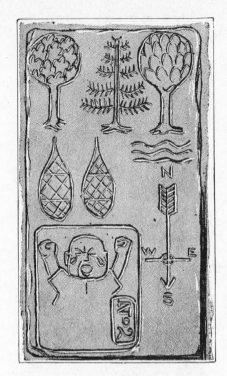

buffaloes there. Meantime the bear has learned to paddle around all by itself on its hind legs, and says "poppa" and "momma." It is certainly a new species. This resemblance to words may be purely accidental, of course, and may have no purpose or meaning; but even in that case it is still extraordinary, and is a thing which no other bear can do. This imitation of speech, taken together with general absence of fur and entire absence of tail, sufficiently indicates that this is a new kind of bear. The further study of it will be exceedingly interesting. Meantime I will go off on a far expedition among the forests of the North and make an exhaustive search. There must certainly be another one somewhere, and this one will be less dangerous when it has company of its own species. I will go straightway; but I will muzzle this one first.

Three Months Later

IT HAS been a weary, weary hunt, yet I have had no success. In the mean time, without stirring from the home estate, she has caught another one! I never saw such luck. I might have hunted these woods a hundred years, I never should have run across that thing.

Next Day

I HAVE been comparing the new one with the old one, and it is perfectly plain that they are the same breed. I was going to stuff one of them for my collection, but she is prejudiced against it for some reason or other; so I have relinquished the idea, though I think it is a mistake. It would be an irreparable loss to science if they should get away. The old one is tamer than it was, and can laugh and talk like the parrot, having learned this, no doubt, from being with the parrot so much, and having the imitative faculty in a highly developed degree. I shall be astonished if it turns out to be a new kind of parrot; and yet I ought not to be astonished, for it has already been everything else it could think of, since those first days when it was a fish. The new one is as ugly now as the old one was at first; has the same sulphur-and-raw-meat complexion and the same singular head without any fur on it. She calls it Abel.

Ten Years Later

THEY ARE boys; we found it out long ago. It was their coming in that small, immature shape that puzzled us; we were not used to it. There are some girls now. Abel is a good boy, but if Cain had stayed a bear it would have improved him. After all these years, I see that I was mistaken about Eve in the beginning; it is better to live outside the Garden with her than inside it without her. At first I thought she talked too much; but now I should be sorry to have that voice fall silent and pass out of my life. Blessed be the chestnut that brought us near together and taught me to know the goodness of her heart and the sweetness of her spirit!

Eve's Diary

Saturday

I AM almost a whole day old, now. I arrived yesterday. That is as it seems to me. And it must be so, for if there was a day-before-yesterday I was not there when it happened, or I should remember it. It could be, of course, that it did happen, and that I was not noticing. Very well; I will be very watchful, now, and if any day-before-yesterdays happen I will make a note of it. It will be best to start right and not let the record get confused, for some instinct tells me that these details are going to be important to the historian some day. For I feel like an experiment, I feel exactly like an experiment; it would be impossible for a person to feel more like an experiment than I do, and so I am coming to feel convinced that that is what I *am*—an experiment; just an experiment, and nothing more.

Then if I am an experiment, am I the whole of it? No, I think not; I think the rest of it is part of it. I am the main part of it, but I think the rest of it has its share in the matter. Is my position assured, or do I have to watch it and take care of it? The latter, perhaps. Some instinct tells me that eternal vigilance is the price of supremacy. [That is a good phrase, I think, for one so young.]

Everything looks better to-day than it did yesterday. In the rush of finishing up yesterday, the mountains were left in a ragged condition, and some of the plains were so cluttered with rubbish and remnants that the aspects were quite distressing. Noble and beautiful works of art should not be subjected to haste; and this majestic new world is indeed a most noble and beautiful work. And certainly marvellously near to being perfect, notwithstanding the shortness of the time. There are too many stars in some places and not enough in others, but that can be remedied presently, no doubt. The moon got loose last night, and slid down and fell out of the scheme—a very great loss; it breaks my heart to think of it. There isn't another thing among the ornaments and decorations that is comparable to it for beauty and finish. It should have been fastened better. If we can only get it back again—

But of course there is no telling where it went to. And besides, whoever gets it will hide it; I know it because I would do it myself. I believe I can be honest in all other matters, but I already begin to realize that the core and center of my nature is love of the beautiful, a passion for the beautiful, and that it would not be safe to trust me with a moon that belonged to another person and that person didn't know I had it. I could give up a

567

moon that I found in the daytime, because I should be afraid some one was looking; but if I found it in the dark, I am sure I should find some kind of an excuse for not saying anything about it. For I do love moons, they are so pretty and so romantic. I wish we had five or six; I would never go to bed; I should never get tired lying on the mossbank and looking up at them.

Stars are good, too. I wish I could get some to put in my hair. But I suppose I never can. You would be surprised to find how far off they are, for they do not look it. When they first showed, last night, I tried to knock some down with a pole, but it didn't reach, which astonished me; then I tried clods till I was all tired out, but I never got one. It was because I am left-handed and cannot throw good. Even when I aimed at the one I wasn't after I couldn't hit the other one, though I did make some close shots, for I saw the black blot of the clod sail right into the midst of the golden clusters forty or fifty times, just barely missing them, and if I could have held out a little longer maybe I could have got one.

So I cried a little, which was natural, I suppose, for one of my age, and after I was rested I got a basket and started for a place on the extreme rim of the circle, where the stars were close to the ground and I could get them with my hands, which would be better, anyway, because I could gather them tenderly then, and not break them. But it was farther than I thought, and at last I had to give it up; I was so tired I couldn't drag my feet another step; and besides, they were sore and hurt me very much.

I couldn't get back home; it was too far, and turning cold; but I found some tigers, and nestled in among them and was most adorably comfortable, and their breath was sweet and pleasant, because they live on strawberries. I had never seen a tiger before, but I knew them in a minute by the stripes. If I could have one of those skins, it would make a lovely gown.

To-day I am getting better ideas about distances. I was so eager to get hold of every pretty thing that I giddily grabbed for it, sometimes when it was too far off, and sometimes when it was but six inches away but seemed a foot—alas, with thorns between! I learned a lesson; also I made an axiom, all out of my own head—my very first one: *The scratched Experiment shuns the thorn.* I think it is a very good one for one so young.

I followed the other Experiment around, yesterday afternoon, at a distance, to see what it might be for, if I could. But I was not able to make out. I think it is a man. I had never seen a man, but it looked like one, and I feel sure that that is what it is. I realize that I feel more curiosity about it than about any of the other reptiles. If it is a reptile, and I suppose it is, for it has frowsy hair and blue eyes, and looks like a reptile. It has no hips; it tapers like a carrot; when it stands, it spreads itself apart like a derrick; so I think it is a reptile, though it may be architecture.

I was afraid of it at first, and started to run every time it turned around, for I thought it was going to chase me; but by-and-by I found it was only trying to get away, so after that I was not timid any more, but tracked it along, several hours, about twenty yards behind, which made it nervous and unhappy, and climbed a tree. I waited a good while, then gave it up and went home.

To-day the same thing over. I've got it up the tree again.

Sunday

IT IS up there yet. Resting, apparently. But that is a subterfuge: Sunday isn't the day of rest; Saturday is appointed for that. It looks to me like a creature that is more interested in resting than in anything else. It would tire me to rest so much. It tires me just to sit around and watch the tree. I do wonder what it is for; I never see it do anything.

They returned the moon last night, and I was *so* happy! I think it is very honest of them. It slid down and fell off again, but I was not distressed; there is no need to worry when one has that kind of neighbors; they will fetch it back. I wish I could do something to show my appreciation. I would like to send them some stars, for we have more than we can use. I mean I, not we, for I can see that the reptile cares nothing for such things.

It has low tastes, and is not kind. When I went there yesterday evening in the gloaming it had crept down and was trying to catch the little speckled fishes that play in the pool, and I had to clod it to make it go up the tree again and let them alone. I wonder if *that* is what it is for? Hasn't it any heart? Hasn't it any compassion for those little creatures? Can it be that it was designed and manufactured for such ungentle work? It has the look of it. One of the clods took it back of the ear, and it used language. It gave me a thrill, for it was the first time I had ever heard speech, except my own. I did not understand the words, but they seemed expressive.

When I found it could talk, I felt a new interest in it, for I love to talk; I talk all day, and in my sleep, too, and I am very interesting, but if I had another to talk to I could be twice as interesting, and would never stop, if desired.

If this reptile is a man, it isn't an *it,* is it? That wouldn't be grammatical, would it? I think it would be *he.* I think so. In that case one would parse it thus: nominative, *he;* dative, *him;* possessive, *his'n.* Well, I will consider it a man and call it he until it turns out to be something else. This will be handier than having so many uncertainties.

Next week Sunday

ALL THE week I tagged around after him and tried to get acquainted. I had to do the talking, because he was shy, but I didn't mind it. He seemed pleased to have me around, and I used the sociable "we" a good deal, because it seemed to flatter him to be included.

Wednesday

WE ARE getting along very well indeed, now, and getting better and better acquainted. He does not try to avoid me any more, which is a good sign, and shows that he likes to have me with him. That pleases me, and I study to be useful to him in every way I can, so as to increase his regard. During the last day or two I have taken all the work of naming things off his

hands, and this has been a great relief to him, for he has no gift in that line, and is evidently very grateful. He can't think of a rational name to save him, but I do not let him see that I am aware of his defect. Whenever a new creature comes along, I name it before he has time to expose himself by an awkward silence. In this way I have saved him many embarrassments. I have no defect like his. The minute I set eyes on an animal I know what it is. I don't have to reflect a moment; the right name comes out instantly, just as if it were an inspiration, as no doubt it is, for I am sure it wasn't in me half a minute before. I seem to know just by the shape of the creature and the way it acts what animal it is.

When the dodo came along he thought it was a wildcat—I saw it in his eye. But I saved him. And I was careful not to do it in a way that could hurt his pride. I just spoke up in a quite natural way of pleased surprise, and not as if I was dreaming of conveying information, and said, "Well, I do declare if there isn't the dodo!" I explained—without seeming to be explaining—how I knew it for a dodo, and although I thought maybe he was a little piqued that I knew the creature when he didn't, it was quite evident that he admired me. That was very agreeable, and I thought of it more than once with gratification before I slept. How little a thing can make us happy when we feel that we have earned it.

Thursday

MY FIRST sorrow. Yesterday he avoided me and seemed to wish I would not talk to him. I could not believe it, and thought there was some mistake, for I loved to be with him, and loved to hear him talk, and so how could it be that he could feel unkind towards me when I had not done anything? But at last it seemed true, so I went away and sat lonely in the place where I first saw him the morning that we were made and I did not know what he was and was indifferent about him; but now it was a mournful place, and every little thing spoke of him, and my heart was very sore. I did not know why very clearly, for it was a new feeling; I had not experienced it before, and it was all a mystery, and I could not make it out.

But when night came I could not bear the lonesomeness, and went to the new shelter which he has built, to ask him what I had done that was wrong and how I could mend it and get back his kindness again; but he put me out in the rain, and it was my first sorrow.

Sunday

IT IS pleasant again, now, and I am happy; but those were heavy days; I do not think of them when I can help it.

I tried to get him some of those apples, but I cannot learn to throw straight. I failed, but I think the good intention pleased him. They are forbidden, and he says I shall come to harm; but so I come to harm through pleasing him, why shall I care for that harm?

Monday

THIS MORNING I told him my name, hoping it would interest him. But he did not care for it. It is strange. If he should tell me his name, I would care. I think it would be pleasanter in my ears than any other sound.

He talks very little. Perhaps it is because he is not bright, and is sensitive about it and wishes to conceal it. It is such a pity that he should feel so, for brightness is nothing; it is in the heart that the values lie. I wish I could make him understand that a loving good heart is riches, and riches enough, and that without it intellect is poverty.

Although he talks so little he has quite a considerable vocabulary. This morning he used a surprisingly good word. He evidently recognized, himself, that it was a good one, for he worked it in twice afterwards, casually. It was not good casual art, still it showed that he possesses a certain quality of perception. Without a doubt that seed can be made to grow, if cultivated.

Where did he get that word? I do not think I have ever used it.

No, he took no interest in my name. I tried to hide my disappointment, but I suppose I did not succeed. I went away and sat on the moss-bank with my feet in the water. It is where I go when I hunger for companionship, some one to look at, some one to talk to. It is not enough—that lovely white body painted there in the pool—but it is something, and something is better than utter loneliness. It talks when I talk; it is sad when I am sad; it comforts me with its sympathy; it says, "Do not be downhearted, you poor friendless girl; I will be your friend." It *is* a good friend to me, and my only one; it is my sister.

That first time that she forsook me! ah, I shall never forget that—never, never. My heart was lead in my body! I said, "She was all I had, and now she is gone!" In my despair I said, "Break, my heart; I cannot bear my life any more!" and hid my face in my hands, and there was no solace for me. And when I took them away, after a little, there she was again, white and shining and beautiful, and I sprang into her arms!

That was perfect happiness; I had known happiness before, but it was not like this, which was ecstasy. I never doubted her afterwards. Sometimes she stayed away—maybe an hour, maybe almost the whole day, but I waited and did not doubt; I said, "She is busy, or she is gone a journey, but she will come." And it was so: she always did. At night she would not come if it was dark, for she was a timid little thing; but if there was a moon she would come. I am not afraid of the dark, but she is younger than I am; she was born after I was. Many and many are the visits I have paid her; she is my comfort and my refuge when my life is hard—and it is mainly that.

Tuesday

ALL THE morning I was at work improving the estate; and I purposely kept away from him in the hope that he would get lonely and come. But he did not.

At noon I stopped for the day and took my recreation by flitting all about with the bees and the butterflies and revelling in the flowers, those beautiful creatures that catch the smile of God out of the sky and preserve it! I gathered them, and made them into wreaths and garlands and clothed myself in them while I ate my luncheon—apples, of course; then I sat in the shade and wished and waited. But he did not come.

But no matter. Nothing would have come of it, for he does not care for flowers. He calls them rubbish and cannot tell one from another, and thinks it is superior to feel like that. He does not care for me, he does not care for flowers, he does not care for the painted sky at eventide—is there anything he does care for, except building shacks to coop himself up in from the good clean rain, and thumping the melons, and sampling the grapes, and fingering the fruit on the trees, to see how those properties are coming along?

I laid a dry stick on the ground and tried to bore a hole in it with another one, in order to carry out a scheme that I had, and soon I got an awful fright. A thin, transparent, bluish film rose out of the hole, and I dropped everything and ran! I thought it was a spirit, and I *was* so frightened! But I looked back, and it was not coming; so I leaned against a rock and rested and panted, and let my limbs go on trembling until they got steady again; then I crept warily back, alert, watching, and ready to fly if there was occasion; and when I was come near, I parted the branches of a rose-bush and peeped through—wishing the man was about, I was looking so cunning and pretty—but the sprite was gone. I went there, and there was a pinch of delicate pink dust in the hole. I put my finger in, to feel it, and said *ouch!* and took it out again. It was a cruel pain. I put my finger in my mouth; and by standing first on one foot and then the other, and grunting, I presently eased my misery; then I was full of interest, and began to examine.

I was curious to know what the pink dust was. Suddenly the name of it occurred to me, though I had never heard of it before. It was *fire!* I was as certain of it as a person could be of anything in the world. So without hesitation I named it that—fire.

I had created something that didn't exist before; I had added a new thing to the world's uncountable properties; I realized this, and was proud of my achievement, and was going to run and find him and tell him about it, thinking to raise myself in his esteem—but I reflected, and did not do it. No—he would not care for it. He would ask what it was good for, and what could I answer? For if it was not *good* for something, but only beautiful, merely beautiful—

So I sighed, and did not go. For it wasn't good for anything; it could not build a shack, it could not improve melons, it could not hurry a fruit crop; it was useless, it was a foolishness and a vanity; he would despise it and say cutting words. But to me it was not despicable; I said, "Oh, you fire, I love you, you dainty pink creature, for you are *beautiful*—and that is enough!" and was going to gather it to my breast. But refrained. Then I made another maxim out of my own head, though it was so nearly like the first one that I was afraid it was only a plagiarism: *"The burnt Experiment shuns the fire."*

I wrought again; and when I had made a good deal of fire-dust I emptied

it into a handful of dry brown grass, intending to carry it home and keep it always and play with it; but the wind struck it and it sprayed up and spat out at me fiercely, and I dropped it and ran. When I looked back the blue spirit was towering up and stretching and rolling away like a cloud, and instantly I thought of the name of it—*smoke!*—though, upon my word, I had never heard of smoke before.

Soon, brilliant yellow-and-red flares shot up through the smoke, and I named them in an instant—*flames!*—and I was right, too, though these were the very first flames that had ever been in the world. They climbed the trees, they flashed splendidly in and out of the vast and increasing volume of tumbling smoke, and I had to clap my hands and laugh and dance in my rapture, it was so new and strange and so wonderful and so beautiful!

He came running, and stopped and gazed, and said not a word for many minutes. Then he asked what it was. Ah, it was too bad that he should ask such a direct question. I had to answer it, of course, and I did. I said it was fire. If it annoyed him that I should know and he must ask, that was not my fault; I had no desire to annoy him. After a pause he asked:

"How did it come?"

Another direct question, and it also had to have a direct answer.

"I made it."

The fire was travelling farther and farther off. He went to the edge of the burned place and stood looking down, and said:

"What are these?"

"Fire-coals."

He picked up one to examine it, but changed his mind and put it down again. Then he went away. *Nothing* interests him.

But I was interested. There were ashes, gray and soft and delicate and pretty—I knew what they were at once. And the embers; I knew the embers, too. I found my apples, and raked them out, and was glad; for I am very young and my appetite is active. But I was disappointed; they were all burst open and spoiled. Spoiled apparently; but it was not so; they were better than raw ones. Fire is beautiful; some day it will be useful, I think.

Friday

I saw him again, for a moment, last Monday at nightfall, but only for a moment. I was hoping he would praise me for trying to improve the estate, for I had meant well and had worked hard. But he was not pleased, and turned away and left me. He was also displeased on another account: I tried once more to persuade him to stop going over the Falls. That was because the fire had revealed to me a new passion—quite new, and distinctly different from love, grief, and those others which I had already discovered—*fear*. And it is horrible!—I wish I had never discovered it; it gives me dark moments, it spoils my happiness, it makes me shiver and tremble and shudder. But I could not persuade him, for he has not discovered fear yet, and so he could not understand me.

EXTRACT FROM ADAM'S DIARY

Perhaps I ought to remember that she is very young, a mere girl, and make allowances. She is all interest, eagerness, vivacity, the world is to her a charm, a wonder, a mystery, a joy; she can't speak for delight when she finds a new flower, she must pet it and caress it and smell it and talk to it, and pour out endearing names upon it. And she is color-mad: brown rocks, yellow sand, gray moss, green foliage, blue sky; the pearl of the dawn, the purple shadows on the mountains, the golden islands floating in crimson seas at sunset, the pallid moon sailing through the shredded cloud-rack, the star-jewels glittering in the wastes of space—none of them is of any practical value, so far as I can see, but because they have color and majesty, that is enough for her, and she loses her mind over them. If she could quiet down and keep still a couple of minutes at a time, it would be a reposeful spectacle. In that case I think I could enjoy looking at her; indeed I am sure I could, for I am coming to realize that she is a quite remarkably comely creature—lithe, slender, trim, rounded, shapely, nimble, graceful; and once when she was standing marble-white and sun-drenched on a boulder, with her young head tilted back and her hand shading her eyes, watching the flight of a bird in the sky, I recognized that she was beautiful.

Monday noon.—If there is anything on the planet that she is not interested in it is not in my list. There are animals that I am indifferent to, but it is not so with her. She has no discrimination, she takes to all of them, she thinks they are all treasures, every new one is welcome.

When the mighty brontosaurus came striding into camp, she regarded it as an acquisition, I considered it a calamity; that is a good sample of the lack of harmony that prevails in our views of things. She wanted to domesticate it, I wanted to make it a present of the homestead and move out. She believed it could be tamed by kind treatment and would be a good pet; I said a pet twenty-one feet high and eighty-four feet long would be no proper thing to have about the place, because, even with the best intentions and without meaning any harm, it could sit down on the house and mash it, for any one could see by the look of its eye that it was absent-minded.

Still, her heart was set upon having that monster, and she couldn't give it up. She thought we could start a dairy with it, and wanted me to help her milk it; but I wouldn't; it was too risky. The sex wasn't right, and we hadn't any ladder anyway. Then she wanted to ride it, and look at the scenery. Thirty or forty feet of its tail was lying on the ground, like a fallen tree, and she thought she could climb it, but she was mistaken; when she got to the steep place it was too slick and down she came, and would have hurt herself but for me.

Was she satisfied now? No. Nothing ever satisfies her but demonstration; untested theories are not in her line, and she won't

have them. It is the right spirit, I concede it; it attracts me; I feel the influence of it; if I were with her more I think I should take it up myself. Well, she had one theory remaining about this colossus: she thought that if we could tame him and make him friendly we could stand him in the river and use him for a bridge. It turned out that he was already plenty tame enough—at least as far as she was concerned—so she tried her theory, but it failed; every time she got him properly placed in the river and went ashore to cross over on him, he came out and followed her around like a pet mountain. Like the other animals. They all do that.

Tuesday—Wednesday—Thursday—and to-day: all without seeing him. It is a long time to be alone; still, it is better to be alone than unwelcome.

I *had* to have company—I was made for it, I think—so I made friends with the animals. They are just charming, and they have the kindest disposition and the politest ways; they never look sour, they never let you feel that you are intruding, they smile at you and wag their tail, if they've got one, and they are always ready for a romp or an excursion or anything you want to propose. I think they are perfect gentlemen. All these days we have had such good times, and it hasn't been lonesome for me, ever. Lonesome! No, I should say not. Why, there's always a swarm of them around—sometimes as much as four or five acres—you can't count them; and when you stand on a rock in the midst and look out over the furry expanse, it is so mottled and splashed and gay with color and frisking sheen and sun-flash, and so rippled with stripes, that you might think it was a lake, only you know it isn't; and there's storms of sociable birds, and hurricanes of whirring wings; and when the sun strikes all that feathery commotion, you have a blazing up of all the colors you can think of, enough to put your eyes out.

We have made long excursions, and I have seen a great deal of the world—almost all of it, I think; and so I am the first traveler, and the only one. When we are on the march, it is an imposing sight—there's nothing like it anywhere. For comfort I ride a tiger or a leopard, because it is soft and has a round back that fits me, and because they are such pretty animals; but for long distance or for scenery I ride the elephant. He hoists me up with his trunk, but I can get off myself; when we are ready to camp, he sits and I slide down the back way.

The birds and animals are all friendly to each other, and there are no disputes about anything. They all talk, and they all talk to me, but it must be a foreign language, for I cannot make out a word they say; yet they often understand me when I talk back, particularly the dog and the elephant. It makes me ashamed. It shows that they are brighter than I am, and are therefore my superiors. It annoys me, for I want to be the principal Experiment myself—and I intend to be, too.

I have learned a number of things, and am educated, now, but I wasn't at first. I was ignorant at first. At first it used to vex me because, with all my watching, I was never smart enough to be around when the water was running up-hill; but now I do not mind it. I have experimented and experimented until now I know it never does run up-hill, except in the dark. I know it does in the dark, because the pool never goes dry; which

it would, of course, if the water didn't come back in the night. It is best to prove things by actual experiment; then you *know;* whereas if you depend on guessing and supposing and conjecturing, you will never get educated.

Some things you *can't* find out; but you will never know you can't by guessing and supposing: no, you have to be patient and go on experimenting until you find out that you can't find out. And it is delightful to have it that way, it makes the world so interesting. If there wasn't anything to find out, it would be dull. Even trying to find out and not finding out is just as interesting as trying to find out and finding out, and I don't know but more so. The secret of the water was a treasure until I *got* it; then the excitement all went away, and I recognized a sense of loss.

By experiment I know that wood swims, and dry leaves, and feathers, and plenty of other things; therefore by all that cumulative evidence you know that a rock will swim; but you have to put up with simply knowing it, for there isn't any way to prove it—up to now. But I shall find a way— then *that* excitement will go. Such things make me sad; because by-and-by when I have found out everything there won't be any more excitements, and I do love excitements so! The other night I couldn't sleep for thinking about it.

At first I couldn't make out what I was made for, but now I think it was to search out the secrets of this wonderful world and be happy and thank the Giver of it all for devising it. I think there are many things to learn yet—I hope so; and by economizing and not hurrying too fast I think they will last weeks and weeks. I hope so. When you cast up a feather it sails away on the air and goes out of sight; then you throw up a clod and it doesn't. It comes down, every time. I have tried it and tried it, and it is always so. I wonder why it is? Of course it *doesn't* come down, but why should it *seem* to? I suppose it is an optical illusion. I mean, one of them is. I don't know which one. It may be the feather, it may be the clod; I can't prove which it is, I can only demonstrate that one or the other is a fake, and let a person take his choice.

By watching, I know that the stars are not going to last. I have seen some of the best ones melt and run down the sky. Since one can melt, they can all melt; since they can all melt, they can all melt the same night. That sorrow will come—I know it. I mean to sit up every night and look at them as long as I can keep awake; and I will impress those sparkling fields on my memory, so that by-and-by when they are taken away I can by my fancy restore those lovely myriads to the black sky and make them sparkle again, and double them by the blur of my tears.

After the Fall

WHEN I look back, the Garden is a dream to me. It was beautiful, sur-passingly beautiful, enchantingly beautiful; and now it is lost, and I shall not see it any more.

The Garden is lost, but I have found *him,* and am content. He loves me as well as he can; I love him with all the strength of my passionate nature, and this, I think, is proper to my youth and sex. If I ask myself why I love

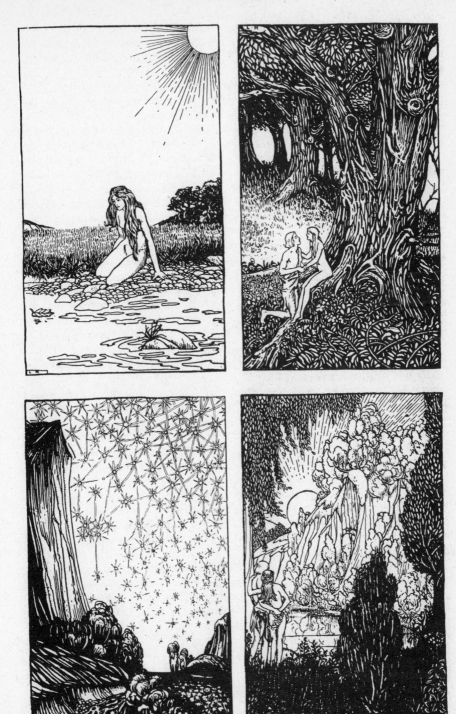

him, I find I do not know, and do not really much care to know; so I
suppose that this kind of love is not a product of reasoning and statistics,
like one's love for other reptiles and animals. I think that this must be so.
I love certain birds because of their song; but I do not love Adam on
account of his singing—no, it is not that; the more he sings the more I do
not get reconciled to it. Yet I ask him to sing, because I wish to learn to
like everything he is interested in. I am sure I can learn, because at first I
could not stand it, but now I can. It sours the milk, but it doesn't matter;
I can get used to that kind of milk.

It is not on account of his brightness that I love him—no, it is not that.
He is not to blame for his brightness, such as it is, for he did not make it
himself; he is as God made him, and that is sufficient. There was a wise
purpose in it; *that* I know. In time it will develop, though I think it will
not be sudden; and, besides, there is no hurry; he is well enough just as
he is.

It is not on account of his gracious and considerate ways and his delicacy that I love him. No, he has lacks in these regards, but he is well
enough just so, and is improving.

It is not on account of his industry that I love him—no, it is not that. I
think he has it in him, and I do not know why he conceals it from me. It
is my only pain. Otherwise he is frank and open with me, now. I am sure
he keeps nothing from me but this. It grieves me that he should have a
secret from me, and sometimes it spoils my sleep, thinking of it, but I
will put it out of my mind; it shall not trouble my happiness, which is
otherwise full to overflowing.

It is not on account of his education that I love him—no, it is not that.
He is self-educated, and does really know a multitude of things, but they
are not so.

It is not on account of his chivalry that I love him—no, it is not that.
He told on me, but I do not blame him; it is a peculiarity of sex, I think,
and he did not make his sex. Of course I would not have told on him, I
would have perished first; but that is a peculiarity of sex, too, and I do
not take credit for it, for I did not make my sex.

Then why is it that I love him? *Merely because he is masculine,* I think.

At bottom he is good, and I love him for that, but I could love him
without it. If he should beat me and abuse me, I should go on loving him.
I know it. It is a matter of sex, I think.

He is strong and handsome, and I love him for that, and I admire him
and am proud of him, but I could love him without those qualities. If he
were plain, I should love him; if he were a wreck, I should love him; and
I would work for him, and slave over him, and pray for him, and watch
by his bedside until I died.

Yes, I think I love him merely because he is *mine* and is *masculine.*
There is no other reason, I suppose. And so I think it is as I first said: that
this kind of love is not a product of reasonings and statistics. It just
comes—none knows whence—and cannot explain itself. And doesn't
need to.

It is what I think. But I am only a girl, and the first that has examined
this matter, and it may turn out that in my ignorance and inexperience I
have not got it right.

Forty Years Later

IT IS my prayer, it is my longing, that we may pass from this life together—a longing which shall never perish from the earth, but shall have
place in the heart of every wife that loves, until the end of time; and it
shall be called by my name.

But if one of us must go first, it is my prayer that it shall be I; for he is
strong, I am weak, I am not so necessary to him as he is to me—life
without him would not be life; how could I endure it? This prayer is also
immortal, and will not cease from being offered up while my race continues. I am the first wife; and in the last wife I shall be repeated.

At Eve's Grave

ADAM: WHERESOEVER she was, *there* was Eden.

'1601'
A Tudor Fireside Conversation

'1601' A TUDOR FIRESIDE CONVERSATION

Mem:—The following is supposed to be an extract from the diary of the Pepys of that day, the same being cup-bearer to Queen Elizabeth. It is supposed that he is of ancient and noble lineage; that he despises those canaille; that his soul consumes with wrath to see the Queen stooping to talk to such; and that the old man feels his nobility defiled by contact with Shakespeare, etc., and yet he has got to stay there till Her Majesty chooses to dismiss him.

YESTERNIGHT TOOK Her Majestie, ye Queene, a fantasie such as she sometimes hath, and hadde to her closet certain that do write playes, bookes and such like—these being by Lord Bacon, his worship, Sir Walter Raleigh, Mr. Ben Jonson, & ye childe Francis Beaumont, which being but sixteen hath yet turned his hande to ye doing of ye Latin masters into our English tongue with great discretion and much applause. Also came with those ye famous Shaxpur. A right strange mingling of mightie blood with meane, ye more in especial since ye Queene's Grace was present, as likewise these following to wit: Ye Duchesse of Bilgewater, twenty-two years of age; ye Countess of Granby, thirty-six; her doter, ye Lady Helen; as also ye two maides of honor to wit: Ye Lady Margery Bothby, sixty-five; ye Lady Alice Dilbur, turned seventy, she being two years ye Queene's Graces elder.

I, being Her Majestie's cup-bearer, had no choice but to remain & behold rank forgot, & ye high hold converse with ye low as upon equal termes, & a great scandal did ye world heare thereof. In ye heate of ye talke, it befel that one did breake wynde, yielding an exceeding mightie and distressful stinke, whereat all did laffe full sore, and then:

Ye Queene:

Verily, in mine eight and sixty years have I not hearde ye fellow to this fartte. Meseemth by ye greate sound and clamour of it, it was male, yet ye bellie it did lurke behind should now falle lene and flat against ye spine of him that hath been delivered of so stately & so vaste a bulke, whereas ye guts of them that doe quiff-splitters beare, stand comely, stille & rounde. Prithee, let ye author confess ye offspring. Will my Lady Alice testify?

Lady Alice:

Goode, your Grace, an' I hadde roome for such a thundergust within mine ancient bowels, 'tis not in reason I could discharge the same and live to thank God for that he did chuse handmayd so humble to show his power. Nay, 'tis not I that have brought forth this rych o'ermastering fog, this fragrant gloom, so pray seek ye further.

Ye Queene:

Mayhap ye Lady Margery hath done ye companie this favour?

Lady Margery:

So please you, Madame, my limbs are feeble with ye weighte and drouthe of five and sixty winters, & it behooveth that I be tender with them. In ye good providence of God, an' hadde I contained this wonder forsooth would I have given ye whole evening of my sinking life to ye dribbling of it forthe with trembling and uneasy soul, not launched it sudden in its matchless might, taking my own life with violence, rending my weake frame like rotten rags. It was not I, Your Majestie.

Ye Queene:

In God's name who hath favoured us? Hath it come to pass that a fartte shall fartte itself? Not such a one as this I trow. Young Master Beaumont? But no, 'twould have wafted him to Heaven like down of goose's bodie. 'Twas not ye little Lady Helen,—nay, ne'er blush, my childe, thou'lt tickle thy tender maiden-hedde with many a mousie squeak before thou learn'st to blow a hurricant. Wasn't you, my learned and ingenius Jonson?

Jonson:

So felle a blaste hath ne'er mine ears saluted, nor yet a stenche so all-pervading & immortal. 'Twas not a novice did it, good Your Majestie, but one of veteran experience—else had he failed of confidence. In sooth it was not I.

Ye Queene:

My Lord Bacon?

Lord Bacon:

Not from my lene entrailes hath this prodigie burst forth, so please Your Grace. Nau't doth so befit ye greate as greate performance; and haply shall ye find that 'tis not from mediocrity this miracle hath issued.

Tho ye subject bee but a fartte, yet will this tedious sink of learning ponderously philosophize. Meantime did ye foul & deadly stinke pervade all places to that degree, that never smelt I ye like, yet dared I not leave ye Presence, albeit I was like to suffocate.

Ye Queene:

What saith your worshipful Master Shaxpur?

Shaxpur:

In ye greate hande of God, I stande & so proclaim my innocence. Tho' ye sinlesse hostess of Heaven hadde fortold ye coming of this most deso-lating breathe, proclaiming it a worke of uninspired man; its quaking thunders, its firmament-clogging rottenness his own achievement in due course of nature, yet hadde I not believed it; but hadde said, "ye Pit itself hath furnished forth ye stinke and Heaven's artillery hath shook ye globe in admiration of it."

Then there was a silence, & each did turne him toward ye worshipful Sir Walter Raleigh, that browned, embattled, bloudy swashbuckler, who rousing up did smile and simpering say:

Sir Walter:

Most gracious Majestie, 'Twas I that did it; but, indeed, it was so poor and fragile a note compared with such as I am wont to furnish, that in sooth I was ashamed to call ye weakling mine in so august a Presence. It was nothing—less than nothing—Madame. I did it but to clear my nether throat; but hadde I come prepared then hadde I delivered something wor-thie. Beare with me, please your Grace, till I can make amends.

Then delivered he himself of such a god-lesse & rock-shivering blaste, that all were fain to stop their ears, and following it did come so dense and foul a stinke, that that which went before did seem a poor and trifling thing beside it. Then saith he, feigning that he blushed and was confused, '*I perceive that I am weake today & cannot justice doe unto my powers,*' and sat him down as who should say,—There, it is not much, yet he that

hath an arse to spare, let him follow that, an' he think he can. By God, and I were ye Queene, I would e'en tip this swaggering braggart out o' ye court, & let him air his grandeurs & breake his intolerable wynd before ye deaf & such as suffocation pleaseth.

Then fell they to talk about ye manners and customs of many peoples, and master Shaxpur spake of ye booke of Sir Michael Montaine, wherein was mention of ye custom of widows of Perigord, to wear upon ye head-dress, in sign of widowhood, a jewel in ye similitude of a man's member wilted and limber, whereat ye Queene did laffe and say, widows in England do wear prickers too, but 'twixt ye thyghs and not wilted either, till coition hath done that office for them. Master Shaxpur did also observe that the Sieur de Montaine hath also spoken of a certain emperor of such mightie prowess that he did take ten maiden-heddes in ye compass of a single night, and while his empress did entertain two & twenty lusty knights atween her sheets & yet was not satisfied; whereat ye merrie Countess Granby saith, a ram is yet ye Emperor's superior, since he will top above a hundred ewes 'twixt sun & sun, & after, if he can have none more to shag, will masturbate until he hath enryched whole acres with hys seed.

Then spake ye dammed wynd-mill, Sir Walter, of a people in ye utter-most parts of America, that copulate not until they be five and thirty yeares of age, ye women being eight and twenty, and do it then but once in seven yeares.

Ye Queene:

How doth that like my little Lady Helen? Shall we send thee thither and preserve thy belly?

Lady Helen:

Please your Highness' Grace, mine olde nurse hath told me there bee more ways of serve God than by locking the thyghs together; yet I am ready to serve him in that way too, since your Highness' Grace hath set ye example.

Ye Queene:

God's woundes, a good answer, childe.

Lady Alice:

Mayhap 'twill weaken when ye hair sprouts below ye naval.

Lady Helen:

Nay, it sprouted two years since; I can scurce more than cover it with my hand now.

Ye Queene:

Heare ye that, my little Beaumont? Have you not a small birdie about ye that stirs at hearing of so sweet a neste?

Beaumont:

'Tis not insensible, moste illustrious Madame; but mousing owls and bats of low degree may not aspire to bliss so overwhelming and ecstatic as is found in the downy nestes of birdes of Paradise.

Ye Queene:

By ye gullet of God, 'tis a neat turned compliment. With such a tongue as thyne, lad, thou'lt spread the ivorie thyghs of many a willing maide in thy goode time, an' thy cod-piece be as handy as thy speech.

Then spake ye Queene of how she met old Rabelais when she was turned of fifteen, & hee did tell her of a man his father knew that hadde a double pair of bollocks, whereon a controversy followed as concerning ye most just way to spell ye word, ye controversy running high 'twixt ye learned Bacon and ye ingenious Jonson, until at last ye olde Lady Margery, wearing of it, saith,

GENTLES, WHAT MATTERETH IT HOW YE SPELL YE WORD? I WARRANT YE WHEN YE USE YOUR BOLLOCKS YE SHALL NOT THINK OF IT; AND MY LADY GRANBY, BEE YE CONTENT, LET YE SPELLING BE; YE SHALL ENJOY YE BEATING OF THEM ON YOUR BUTTOCKS JUST YE SAME I TROW. BEFORE I HAD GAINED MY FOURTEENTH YEARE, I HADDE LEARNED THAT THEM THAT WOULD EXPLORE A CUNT, STOPP'D NOT TO CONSIDER YE SPELLIN O'T.

Sir Walter:

In sooth, when a shift's turned uppe, delay is meete for naught but dalliance. Bocaccio hath a story of a priest that did beguile a mayd into his cell, then knelt him in a corner to pray for grace that he bee rightly thankful for this tender maiden-hedde the Lorde hadde sent him, but the abbot spying through ye keyhole did see a tuft of brownish hair with fair